The new scientific revolution p. 592

science

HUGH GRAYSON-SMITH

Professor Emeritus of Physics
University of Alberta

PRENTICE-HALL, INC., Englewood Cliffs, New Jersey

the changing concepts of science

Hugh Grayson-Smith

Current printing (last digit):

10 9 8 7 6 5 4 3 2 1

Library of Congress Catalog Card Number 67-10746
Printed in the United States of America

PRENTICE-HALL INTERNATIONAL, INC., *London*
PRENTICE-HALL OF AUSTRALIA, PTY. LTD., *Sydney*
PRENTICE-HALL OF CANADA, LTD., *Toronto*
PRENTICE-HALL OF INDIA (PRIVATE) LTD., *New Delhi*
PRENTICE-HALL OF JAPAN, INC., *Tokyo*

preface

This book grew out of a course of lectures on physical science given annually at the University of Alberta over a period of several years. The course was designed for students majoring in the humanities and social sciences, and for students in education. I believe that in our modern scientific and technological age a general university education should include some understanding of science—at a more sophisticated level than students usually encounter in high school. I believe too that for the non-specialist an understanding of the way scientists think and work, and of the philosophical and social implications of science, is more important than knowledge of a lot of factual detail. In my experience the historical approach, showing how science has developed over the years, is particularly suitable for this purpose, and is appreciated by the type of student for whom the course was designed.

But science is factual, and any book on science must contain a great deal of descriptive, factual material. The way nature behaves is summarized in the so-called scientific laws, and students must become familiar with the most important of these laws. Science aims at being precise and logical, and this requires careful definition in a logical sequence of the concepts used. Throughout the book careful attention has been paid to definitions, not only to the logical sequence of basic concepts, but also to definitions of technical terms that are likely to be unfamiliar to nonscience students. In order to help students to understand the language, technical terms are collected in glossaries at the end of each chapter.

Physical science is essentially quantitative and mathematical. In modern science the argument that leads logically from a hypothesis to a conclusion is almost always expressed in the language of mathematical symbols, and carried out by means of mathematical techniques. A physicist or a chemist today has to be a competent mathematician—even if he spends most of his working hours in the laboratory—and he uses mathematical language in communicating his findings to his colleagues. However, this does not mean that a knowledge of mathematical techniques is necessary in order to understand what the scientist is trying to do. Neither should scientific information be denied to a student who is not equipped to follow the steps of a scientific argument. Frequently students who are not mathematically inclined or scientifically equipped attain later to positions of influence in society. It is important that they should know something about the findings and the trends of modern science. The hypothesis and the conclusion of an argument can be expressed in language that any student can understand, and it can be assumed that the mathematician who connected them together has carried out his task correctly. In this book mathematics has been kept to a minimum. Mathematical symbols have been used wherever necessary, but only a very few mathematical developments have been given in detail, in order to demonstrate to students the role mathematics plays in science. The only mathematical technique required of the student is that of simple algebra.

Science is a living discipline. It is continually developing and expanding, new discoveries are made every day, and scientific knowledge grows at an ever increasing rate. The total accumulation of knowledge has probably doubled in the last quarter of a century, and it is said that 90 per cent of all the scientists who ever lived are still alive and working today. As new facts are discovered, old laws and concepts have to be modified—hence the title of the book. Here again I believe that the best approach to understanding is a historical treatment, culminating in the revolutionary modern discoveries that have taken place in my own lifetime, and leading to a revolution in scientific thinking that is only now beginning to percolate through to the educated layman.

Science is a unity. Its laws are the same everywhere, and the conventional division of physical science into physics, chemistry, astronomy, geology, has arisen mainly as a matter of convenience based upon subject matter and method, as has the division of physics into mechanics, optics, electricity, etc. Discoveries in one field often lead to a better understanding of a quite different field. One cannot even make a clear-cut distinction between the physical science of inanimate nature and the biological science of living beings. The conventional divisions have not been followed here. Instead, the seven parts into which the book is divided have been centered around seven major scientific developments, each of which has in its turn profoundly affected the course of science, from Newton's law of gravitation to Heisenberg's uncertainty principle. Other writers might choose different developments in order to mark the great scientific advances; others might put them in a different order. However, I believe that this type of division—to which the historical treatment readily lends itself—is more significant than the division by discipline.

I wish to acknowledge with gratitude all those who helped in one way and another in the preparation of the manuscript. My especial thanks go to two colleagues who read some of the chapters that deal with topics outside my own field, and who made valuable suggestions. Professor R. E. Folinsbee advised me on the geology, and Professor H. B. Collier on the organic chemistry and biochemistry. I wish to thank also all those individuals and organizations who contributed photographs; their assistance is acknowledged in the captions to the illustrations. I owe much to the reviewers who read my original manuscript, and whose corrections and suggestions were incorporated into the final revision. For the appearance of the book, much of the credit goes to the artist who converted my rough pencil sketches into handsome drawings. It is impossible to document all the statements in a book of this kind, or to acknowledge the sources of the information; most of it is common scientific knowledge. Hence no attempt has been made to give detailed references. A number of general reference books are included in the appendix of recommended supplementary reading, and I have, of course, made use of these when necessary.

H. Grayson-Smith

Victoria, B.C.

contents

CHAPTER 1 **physical law and scientific method, 1**

1-1. Natural Science, 1.   1-2. Physical Laws, 2.   1-3. The Real and
Orderly World, 3.   1-4. Scientific Method, 4.

UNIVERSAL GRAVITATION **part one**

CHAPTER 2 **astronomy—the first real science, 11**

2-1. The Beginnings of Astronomy, 11.   2-2. Greek Astronomy, 14.
2-3. Aristarchus and Eratosthenes, 14.   2-4. The Ptolemaic System, 16.
2-5. Copernicus, 21.   2-6. Galileo, 22.   2-7. Heliocentric vs. Geocentric, 23.   2-8. The Phases of Venus, 24.   2-9. Parallax, 24.

CHAPTER 3 **the solar system, 28**

3-1. Some Statistics, 28.   3-2. Nature of the Sun, 28.   3-3. The Rest-
less Sun, 30.   3-4. The Planets, 32.   3-5. Earthlike Bodies, 33.

ix

3-6. The Great Planets, 34.   3-7. The Moon, 36.   3-8. Satellites of the Other Planets, 38.   3-9. The Asteroids, 38.   3-10. Comets, 39. 3-11. Meteors and Meteorites, 40.   3-12. Kepler's Laws of Planetary Motion, 41.   3-13. Determination of the Distance of the Moon, 43. 3-14. Distance of the Sun, 44.

CHAPTER 4   the laws of motion, 48

4-1. Galileo and the Falling Stone, 48.   4-2. Velocity and Acceleration, 50.   4-3. Uniform Acceleration, 51.   4-4. Newton's Laws of Motion, 52.   4-5. The First Law and the Concept of Force, 53.   4-6. Weight and Mass, Newton's Second Law, 54.   4-7. Units of Mass and Force, 56. 4-8. Newton's Third Law, Action and Reaction, 58.

CHAPTER 5   measurement, 63

5-1. The Importance of Measurement, 63.   5-2. Measurement of Length, 64.   5-3. Measurement of Time, 66.   5-4. Measurement of Mass, 67. 5-5. Systems of Units, 68.   5-6. Revision of the Units, 69.   5-7. Precision of Measurement, 70.

CHAPTER 6   gravitation and the earth, sun, and moon, 73

6-1. Universal Gravitation, 73.   6-2. The Moon and the Apple, 74. 6-3. Gravitation and Kepler's Laws, 75.   6-4. The Constant of Gravitation and the Mass of the Earth, 76.   6-5. Masses of the Sun and Planets, 78.   6-6. The Ocean Tides and the Mass of the Moon, 79. 6-7. Artificial Satellites, 82.   6-8. Eclipses of the Sun and the Moon, 84. 6-9. Corrections to Kepler's and Newton's Laws, 87.   6-10. The Role of Mathematics, 87.

THE ENERGY PRINCIPLE   part two

CHAPTER 7   work, energy, and power, 95

7-1. A Further Sequence of Definitions, 95.   7-2. Three Ways of Doing Work, 96.   7-3. Potential and Kinetic Energy, 98.   7-4. Heat and Temperature, 99.   7-5. The Thermometer, 102.   7-6. The Mechanical Equivalent of Heat, 105.

CHAPTER 8   the conservation of energy and the energy supply, 109

8-1. Different Forms of Energy, 109.   8-2. The Principle of Conservation of Energy, 111.   8-3. Conversion of Energy, 112.   8-4. Conservation of Mass and Mass-Energy, 113.   8-5. Momentum and Angular Momentum, 115.   8-6. The Energy of the Sun, 116.   8-7. Fossil Fuels, 118.   8-8. Civilization and the Use of Energy, 119.   8-9. Three Revolutionary Inventions, 121.   8-10. The World Energy Problem, 123.

ATOMS AND MOLECULES **part three**

CHAPTER 9 **the fundamental laws of chemistry, 131**

9-1. Ancient Chemistry, 131.   9-2. The Alchemists, 132.   9-3. Oxidation and Reduction, 134.   9-4. The Discovery of Oxygen and the Law of Conservation of Mass, 136.   9-5. Elements and Compounds, 137. 9-6. More Fundamental Laws, 139.   9-7. Chemical Symbols, Atomic and Molecular Weights, 140.   9-8. Chemical Equations, 142.   9-9. Dissociation, Ions, 143.   9-10. Acids, Bases, and Salts, 144.   9-11. The Periodic Table, 145.

CHAPTER 10 **gases, liquids, and solids, 153**

10-1. Pressure in Liquids and Gases, 153.   10-2. Atmospheric Pressure and the Barometer, 155.   10-3. Boyle's Law of Gas Pressure, 157. 10-4. Variation with Temperature; the General Gas Law, 158.   10-5. Change of State: Solid to Liquid, 159.   10-6. Change of State: Liquid to Gas, 161.   10-7. Latent Heat, 164.

CHAPTER 11 **atoms and molecules, 167**

11-1. Democritus and the Concept of Discontinuity in Nature, 167. 11-2. Dalton's Atomic Hypothesis, 168.   11-3. Avogadro's Law, 170. 11-4. The Kinetic Theory of Gases, 171.   11-5. Corrections to the Simple Theory, 173.   11-6. Brownian Movement, 174.   11-7. A Hypothesis Becomes an Accepted Fact of Nature, 176.

CHAPTER 12 **the earth's atmosphere, 179**

12-1. Sources of Information about the Atmosphere, 179.   12-2. Composition of the Atmosphere, 181.   12-3. Humidity, 182.   12-4. Structure of the Atmosphere, 183.   12-5. The World Circulation of Wind, 184.   12-6. The Polar Front: Highs and Lows, 188.   12-7. Clouds and Rain, 191.

CHAPTER 13 **the chemistry of living things, 198**

13-1. Homopolar and Covalent Bonding, 198.   13-2. The Peculiar Properties of Carbon, 200.   13-3. Organic Chemistry, 202.   13-4. Photosynthesis and the Oxygen and Carbon Cycles, 203.   13-5. Proteins, 205.   13-6. Enzymes and Hormones, 206.   13-7. The Mechanism of Heredity, 207.

ELECTRICITY, LIGHT AND WAVE MOTION **part four**

CHAPTER 14 **what is electricity? 217**

14-1. Electric Charge, 217.   14-2. Properties of Electrostatic Charge, 218.   14-3. The Electric Fluid, 221.   14-4. Coulomb's Law, 223.

14-5. The Voltaic Cell, 224.   14-6. The Electric Circuit, 226.   14-7. Potential and Electromotive Force, 227.   14-8. Ohm's Law, 229. 14-9. The System of Electrical Units, 230.

CHAPTER **15**   **magnetism, 236**

15-1. Magnets and the Compass Needle, 236.   15-2. Comparison of Magnetism and Electrostatics, 237.   15-3. The Process of Magnetization, 238.   15-4. Magnetic Fields, 240.   15-5. Reality and the Non-delineable, 243.   15-6. The Magnetic Field of the Earth, 243.   15-7. Magnetic Field of an Electric Current, 245.   15-8. Magnetic Flux, 248.

CHAPTER **16**   **induced currents, 252**

16-1. Electromagnetic Induction, 252.   16-2. The Law of Induction, 254.   16-3. The Principle of the Electric Generator, 255.   16-4. The Direct-Current Generator, 256.   16-5. Development of the Alternating-Current Generator, 257.   16-6. Current-Voltage Relations in Alternating Current, 259.   16-7. The Transformer and Electrical Power Systems, 260.   16-8. Electric Motors, 262.   16-9. A New Way of Life, 263.

CHAPTER **17**   **the empirical laws of light, 267**

17-1. Radiant Energy, 267.   17-2. Light Intensity and Illumination, 269. 17-3. The Law of Reflection, Optical Images, 270.   17-4. Diffuse Reflection: Scattering and Absorption, 273.   17-5. Refraction, 274.   17-6. Lenses, 277.   17-7. The Velocity of Light, 280.

CHAPTER **18**   **waves, 286**

18-1. Transfer of Energy by Wave Motion, 286.   18-2. Transverse and Longitudinal Waves, 288.   18-3. Frequency, Wavelength, and Velocity, 289.   18-4. Sound Waves, 289.   18-5. Resonance, 290.   18-6. Reflection and Refraction of Waves, 292.   18-7. Interference and Diffraction of Waves, 294.   18-8. Wave Properties of Light, 297.

CHAPTER **19**   **the spectrum and what it shows, 303**

19-1. The Spectrum and the Prism Spectrograph, 303.   19-2. The Diffraction Grating, 305.   19-3. Line Spectra, 306.   19-4. The Continuous Spectrum of Heat Radiation, 307.   19-5. Band Spectra of Molecules, 309.   19-6. Absorption Spectra, 309.   19-7. Spectrum of the Sun, 310.   19-8. Spectra of the Stars, 312.   19-9. The Doppler Effect, 313.

CHAPTER **20**   **electromagnetic radiation, 317**

20-1. Polarization of Light Waves, 317.   20-2. Maxwell and the Electromagnetic Theory of Light, 319.   20-3. The Mysterious Ether, 320.

20-4. Waves From an Oscillating Electric Circuit, 321.   20-5. The
Complete Electromagnetic Spectrum, 324.   20-6. Infrared Radiation,
326.   20-7. Ultraviolet "Light," 328.   20-8. Fluorescence, 329.
20-9. X Rays, 329.

ELECTRONS AND PROTONS part five

CHAPTER 21 the electron, 339

21-1. Electrolysis and the Discontinuity of Electric Charge, 339.   21-2.
Cathode Rays, 340.   21-3. Thomson's Experiment on Cathode Rays and
the Identification of the Electron, 342.   21-4. The Thermionic Effect,
344.   21-5. Millikan and the Electronic Charge, 346.   21-6. Four
Manifestations of the Electron, 348.   21-7. Diode and Triode Tubes,
349.   21-8. Science and Technology, 350.

CHAPTER 22 inside the atom, 354

22-1. The Discovery of Radioactivity, 354.   22-2. The Three Kinds of
Rays, 355.   22-3. Identification of the Three Rays, 356.   22-4. Detection of Single Particles, 357.   22-5. Tracks of High-Speed Particles,
359.   22-6. Rutherford and the Nuclear Atom, 361.   22-7. The
Physical Basis of Chemical Combination, 364.   22-8. Electron Structure
of Covalent Bonds, 366.   22-9. Isotopes, 368.   22-10. Preparation of
Pure Samples of an Isotope, 369.

CHAPTER 23 nuclear chemistry, 373

23-1. Radioactive Disintegration, 373.   23-2. Energy of Nuclear Reactions, 375.   23-3. The Law of Radioactive Decay, 376.   23-4. Induced
Nuclear Reactions, 378.   23-5. "Atom Smashers," 380.   23-6. Neutrons, 382.   23-7. Nuclear Structure, 384.   23-8. "Artificial" Radioactive Isotopes, 386.   23-9. Positrons, 387.   23-10. Neutrinos, 388.

CHAPTER 24 nuclear atomic energy, 393

24-1. Nuclear Fission, 393.   24-2. Chain Reactions and Nuclear Explosions, 395.   24-3. The Nuclear Atomic Pile, 397.   24-4. Fusion Reactions, 400.   24-5. The Production of Nuclear Power, 402.   24-6.
Problems of Radioactive Contamination, 404.

THE CHANGING COSMOS part six

CHAPTER 25 writing the earth's history, 413

25-1. The Principle of Uniform Evolution, 413.   25-2. The Role of
Deduction in Modern Science, 415.   25-3. Evidence of Change in the
Earth's Crust, 416.   25-4. Types of Rock, 419.   25-5. Sediments and
Their Origin, 419.   25-6. Igneous and Metamorphic Rocks, 421.
25-7. Compiling the Geological Record, 422.

CHAPTER 26 the story of evolution written in the rocks, 427

26-1. Geological Eras and Revolutions, 427.   26-2. Dating the Geological Record, 429.   26-3. The Age of the Earth, 432.   26-4. Precambrian Times, 433.   26-5. How Did Life Begin? 435.   26-6. The
Paleozoic Era, 437.   26-7. The Invasion of the Land, 440.   26-8. The
Age of Reptiles, 442.   26-9. Mammals and Man, 448.

CHAPTER 27 the not-so-solid earth, 455

27-1. Inside the Earth, 455.   27-2. Earthquakes, 456.   27-3. Propa-
gation and Detection of Earthquake Waves, 459.   27-4. Location of the
Earthquake Focus, 462.   27-5. Structure of the Earth, 463.   27-6.
The Isostasy Principle, 466.   27-7. Origin of the Earth's Magnetism,
Fossil Magnetism, 467.   27-8. Drifting Continents, 468.

CHAPTER 28 mountains, rivers, and ice, 474

28-1. Mountain Building, 474.   28-2. Age of a Mountain Range, 476.
28-3. Rivers, Young and Old, 478.   28-4. Mountain Glaciers, 480.
28-5. The Great Ice Age, 481.   28-6. Theories of the Ice Ages, 484.

CHAPTER 29 evolution on other worlds, 489

29-1. The Nebular Theory of the Birth of the Solar System, 489.   29-2.
Modern Theories of the Solar System, 490.   29-3. Growth of a Planet,
491.   29-4. Atmospheres of the Planets, 492.   29-5. Evolution of the
Earth's Atmosphere, 495.   29-6. Life on Other Worlds, 496.   29-7.
Mars and Venus, 499.

CHAPTER 30 the detective story of the stars, 502

30-1. Classification of the Stars According to Magnitude, 502.   30-2.
Distances and Proper Motions of the Stars, 503.   30-3. Absolute Magni-
tude, 505.   30-4. Temperatures and Sizes of the Stars, 506.   30-5. The
Dwarf Companion of Sirius, 507.   30-6. Double Stars and Stellar
Masses, 509.   30-7. Star Groups and the Extension of the Distance Scale,
511.   30-8. The Milky Way, 514.   30-9. Other Galaxies, the Visible
Cosmos, 517.

CHAPTER 31 evolution in the cosmos, 522

31-1. Inside the Stars, 522.   31-2. Energy of the Sun and Stars, 523.
31-3. Lifetime of a Star, 525.   31-4. Novae and Supernovae, 525.
31-5. Life and Death of a Star, 528.   31-6. Quasars, 530.   31-7. The
Expanding Cosmos, 531.   31-8. Creation—Catastrophic or Continuous?
533.

DISCONTINUITY AND UNCERTAINTY part seven

CHAPTER 32 the failure of classical physics, 543

32-1. "Modern Physics," 543.   32-2. Mechanistic Laws, 544.   32-3.
Mechanistic Atomic Physics, 545.   32-4. The Emission of Light, 546.
32-5. Photoelectricity, 548.   32-6. The Photoelectric Cell, 549.

CHAPTER 33 quantum theory and relativity, 551

33-1. The First Quantum Principle, 551.   33-2. Energy Levels in
Atoms, 553.   33-3. The Second Quantum Principle—for Atoms, 555.
33-4. Quantum Emission of Radiation, 557.   33-5. Quantum Numbers,
558.   33-6. Photons and the Compton Effect, 560.   33-7. Matter
Waves, 562.   33-8. Masers and Lasers, 563.   33-9. The Relativity
Principle, 566.   33-10. The Special Theory of Relativity, 568.   33-11.
Some Deductions From the Special Theory, 569.   33-12. The General
Theory, 570.

CHAPTER 34 mysterious rays, strange particles, and antimatter, 574

34-1. Cosmic Rays, 574.   34-2. Mesons, 576.   34-3. Particles and
Antiparticles, 579.   34-4. Hyperons, 581.   34-5. Four Categories of
Interaction Between Particles, 582.   34-6. Systematics and Conservation
Rules, 584.   34-7. Symmetry Groups of Particles, 586.   34-8. Ques-
tions, 588.

CHAPTER 35 the new scientific revolution, 592

35-1. The Danger of Extrapolation, 592.   35-2. Science Abandons the
Mechanistic Model, 593.   35-3. Quantum Mechanics, 594.   35-4.
Probability and Predictability, 595.   35-5. The Uncertainty Principle,
597.   35-6. The Duality of Wave and Particle, 599.   35-7. What of
the Future? 599.

appendices, 603

A. Some Numerical Values, 603.   B. Bibliography of Supplementary
Reading, 605.

index, 610

physical law and scientific method

Nowadays, when we speak of science we usually mean natural science, the study of the material world around us. This, of course, includes our own bodies, insofar as they are material, as well as the bodies of other animals and plants. When we speak of physical science we usually limit the discussion to inanimate nature, although this distinction cannot be strictly maintained, because living things cannot violate fundamental laws which are true everywhere, both for the nonliving and for the living.

This is a scientific age, and the impact of scientific discovery on modern living has been so great that most people today possess a smattering of scientific fact. However, it is often difficult for the nonspecialist to keep abreast of the subject and to understand the ideas of the contemporary scientist. This is largely a question of language, for scientists have frequently had to invent new technical terms to describe their work, but a difficulty in understanding also sometimes arises through a manner of thinking which is unfamiliar to the general public. Within our own twentieth century the total of scientific knowledge has multiplied more than

1

tenfold. New discoveries, reaching out into the vastness of the universe of stars and galaxies, and delving into the innermost secrets of the atom, have required new concepts and new theories about the workings of nature. These in turn have led to a revolution in scientific thinking, which is only now being appreciated by the scientist and the philosopher who have the time and inclination to look at the broad picture, but which eventually will permeate the thinking of the whole of society.

In what follows we shall try to show what has led up to the twentieth century change in thinking, and to explain it in a form intelligible to a reader who has only an elementary knowledge of modern science, and whose main interest is in other fields. To do this we must go back to the first great scientific revolution, that of the sixteenth and seventeenth centuries, when such men as Galileo and Isaac Newton laid the first of the foundations upon which our present-day technological society has been built.

*1-2 **Physical Laws***

The ultimate aim of all natural science is to find out how the material world functions. The results are expressed in a series of generalized statements, and it is to these statements that we refer when we speak of "scientific laws." Among these, the laws of physics, which describe the behavior of inanimate nature, are in the background of all other laws, and the specialized branches of physical science—astronomy, chemistry, geology—are built upon physics.

The use of the word "law" in this sense has a time-honored tradition, but it is to some extent a misnomer, for to most people the word implies something exact and rigorous, or something legalistic. In a survey of the kind we are about to make it must be remembered that science knows no absolutes, and that most scientific laws are true only within certain limitations, or perhaps are only approximately true. The term "law" has been applied to generalizations having all degrees of exactitude, from the law of conservation of angular momentum (Sec. 8-5) which has no known exceptions, to statements like the so-called laws of friction that are quoted in many physics textbooks, but that are little more than rough rules for estimating the amount of friction involved in a particular case. If we know the limitations or the degree of approximation, the law will probably be useful for making practical calculations. However, throughout the history of science many statements which were thought to be useful laws have had to be abandoned or modified, or have been superseded by better laws. We always have to keep an open mind and look at the laws of nature with a certain amount of healthy skepticism, for we can never be sure that scientists fifty years from now will be using the same laws that we use today.

Finally, we must remember that scientific laws are not legislation, but discoveries that have always been waiting for man to find. Man cannot change the *laws* of nature, but when he has found them—and understands them—he can use them in many ways to modify his immediate surroundings and to improve his way of life. Scientific laws are *descriptions* of what happens in the material world; man-made, legislative laws are *prescriptions* of what men ought to do.

There have been many attempts to legislate nature—from the Egyptian Pharaoh who declared that in his kingdom the ratio of the circumference of a circle to its diameter (the quantity 3.14159 . . . which we usually denote as π) would be simply 3, to the Nazi ruling that newly discovered laws of the atom must not be used because they had been discovered by non-Aryans, the Communist statements about the inheritance of acquired characteristics, or the official attitude in some quarters toward the theory of biological evolution. Obviously, legislation of this kind cannot change the facts. All it can do is to command an erroneous use of the facts, or to prescribe what shall or shall not be taught in the schools.

1-3   *The Real and Orderly World*

In order to make any progress in scientific discovery, we must make two very fundamental assumptions, first, that *the material world we observe through our senses is real*, and that it will continue to exist and to function in the same way as we have observed in the past whether or not there is anybody there to observe it. Secondly, we must assume that *nature is essentially orderly*, and behaves according to laws which are there for man to discover through his ingenuity and his reason.

It may seem trivial to discuss these two assumptions, because modern man, quite properly, takes them for granted, just as the scientist has to take them for granted before he can commence his work. However, it is worthwhile to think of them briefly before we start our scientific survey, because actually neither statement can be proved, and their tacit acceptance, which makes them appear as trivialities, is a result of the fact that the thinking of modern man is conditioned by the success of the first scientific revolution, and by his technological society.

It is a commonplace of philosophical argument that there is no way in which I, by myself, can prove the existence of anything outside my own mind, and it is no use appealing to what other people have told me, because how am I to be sure that their voices also are not just in my imagination. Some writers have therefore suggested that thought and ideas are the only true reality. To stretch the argument to its limit, and conclude that the material world is merely an illusion, is just nonsense to a modern mind. However, philosophical systems and religious beliefs have been based on such a conclusion, and it is well to remember that all scientific thinking is based upon an unproved and unprovable metaphysical hypothesis, that has to be accepted a priori (that is, before we start).

The second assumption, that of the orderliness of nature, requires more emphasis. In ancient and medieval times the ordinary man had no conception of an orderly world, behaving according to laws that could be discovered. True, the sun always rose and the stars followed their regular courses, a stone always fell, a stream always ran downhill. But the wind and the rain, earthquake, storm and flood seemed to be capricious. Growth is very variable, and seasons of scarcity followed years of plenty, for no reason that men could understand. Astronomers charted the stars and described the regular motions of the heavenly bodies with accuracy. Philosophers argued about the causes that made the stone fall. However, ordinary men were more interested in the weather and the seasons that affected their well-being; they saw the irregularities and missed the underlying order. Most people believed that the material world was controlled in all its details, if not by God himself, at least by spirits and demons who could be cajoled by the appropriate ceremonies. Even yet, and even in civilized countries, many people are not fully convinced that the material world is basically orderly. They may understand fairly well the workings of a machine such as an electric motor, but when it comes to a natural phenomenon like the weather, for example, they are liable to give way to superstitious beliefs. They do not see that the regularity involved in the worldwide movements of the atmosphere are more fundamental than the accidental fluctuations that give rise to the day-to-day variations in the weather.

We have to admit that the assumption of orderly nature, like that of the reality of the physical world, is one that cannot be rigorously proved. Belief in it rests upon the fact that calculations based upon scientific laws have given results in agreement with experience, within the limits of accuracy of the laws. The use of scientific laws has worked in the past, and we are confident that it will continue to work in the future, although it is always conceivable that exceptions could occur.

1-4 Scientific Method

Ever since science began to evolve into its modern form, in the sixteenth and seventeenth centuries, most scientific discoveries have followed a pattern that has come to be known as the *scientific method.*° Different writers

° Sir Francis Bacon (1561–1626) discussed scientific method at length in several publications (1605–1620). He also proposed that governments and universities should set up institutes in which teams of scientists could undertake systematic studies of nature, something which has finally come about in our own time, 300 years later.

have given somewhat different descriptions of the pattern, but it is usually held to involve four steps, which we shall call:

1. Observation
2. Generalization
3. Confirmation
4. Application

Study of any phenomenon, in the inanimate natural world, in the realm of living things, or in the sphere of human affairs, must start with *observation*, the collection and systematic arrangement of the facts. But we can never observe all the facts, all the occurrences of a particular phenomenon, and obviously we want to draw a conclusion now without waiting for future occurrences. We must therefore assume that the observed facts are a fair sample, and we make a *generalized* statement about them, in the form of a tentative scientific law, as yet unproved.

If the generalization is a useful one, likely to become a useful scientific law, it will have a wider field of application than that covered by the original observations. The tentative law can be used as a basis from which to deduce, by logical argument, the expected occurrences in this wider field. The newly deduced consequences must then be tested to find out whether they are in fact correct, and we enter upon the third step of the method, the step we have called *confirmation*. If the confirmations agree with the predictions, the law becomes more and more firmly established. This, remember, does not mean that it is universally valid or that it is absolute truth, but only that it is valid and useful over a wide range of phenomena, within certain limits of approximation. When this stage is reached, the hypothesis and the theory can be used to predict with confidence future results, and we enter upon the final step of scientific method, that of *application*.

Wherever possible the steps of observation and confirmation involve carefully planned experiments. In any natural phenomenon the observed occurrences may be the result of a number of different causative factors, and we have to select from all the possible factors those that are relevant and those that are not. One method of making the selection is by means of carefully designed experiments, in which factors which seem to be irrelevant are eliminated by good experimental technique, and factors which seem to be relevant are varied one by one and the results of the variation noted.

Thus experimentation has often paralleled the search for the general law; a tentative hypothesis suggests new experiments, these in turn may suggest a modification of the hypothesis, until a satisfactory theory emerges. Finally, more experiments will probably be performed in order to test the theory, and confirm it or otherwise. It follows that progress toward the solution of a problem is likely to be much more rapid when experimentation is feasible than when we have to depend on the mere observation of natural occurrences—this is one reason why physics and chemistry have developed so much further than the life sciences, and these in turn so much further than the social sciences. One science which has made great progress in spite of the fact that experimentation is impossible is astronomy. This is because the secondary factors which affect, for example, the motion of a planet turn out to be insignificant, and the selection of the important factor—the motion around the sun—could be made.

Just as scientific laws may be approximations that are useful only under certain limitations, and are never to be considered as absolute, rigorous truth, so the scientific method has limitations, and the description of the process is only an approximation. The concept is a useful generalization that can help in designing an experiment or a program of observations, but the procedure should not be considered as a magic formula capable of solving all possible problems, including the difficult social problems that the human race has to face. The four steps are seldom as clearly separated as the description suggests; the observer usually has at least a tentative hypothesis in mind before he starts work, and this may color his observations. Again, the solution of a scientific problem has often been a slow process, and it is doubtful if one can find a single example where the whole procedure has been carried out systematically by one individual, or even by one research group or institution. Always it has been a gradual growth, to which many workers have contributed. In some of the classical examples, such as motion and gravitation (Chapter 6), centuries have elapsed from the first systematic observations to the expression of the laws in their present form. Today, with the rapid communication between scientists, a new problem may be attacked by hundreds of workers in many different places, and a few years may suffice to find a solution.

GLOSSARY

A priori assumption An assumption or hypothesis, which has to be assumed to hold before we commence our arguments, in order that we may make any progress whatever.

Hypothesis A statement, not yet proved, which forms the basis, or starting point, of a theoretical argument.

Scientific law A generalized statement of the way in which the material world acts under specified circumstances; the law may be precise and hold without exception, or it may have known limitations.

1. State the two a priori assumptions upon which all science is based.

2. "The material world is real." Why is this statement unprovable? State briefly reasons for believing it nevertheless.

3. "Nature behaves according to law." At what period in history was this concept first accepted generally? Give examples of human behavior which indicate that even in civilized countries it is not yet fully accepted.

4. Give examples of attempts by man to legislate scientific law.

5. What are the four steps that are usually regarded as constituting "scientific method"?

6. Why are carefully designed experiments so important in science? Give four examples of natural sciences in which experimentation is almost or quite impossible; give reasons for your choice.

UNIVERSAL GRAVITATION

part one

*Every particle in the cosmos attracts every
other particle with a force which is proportional
to the product of their masses, and inversely
proportional to the square of the distance
between them.*

—ISAAC NEWTON

astronomy—the first real science

Men have always been curious about the world around them, and, among all the wonders of nature, nothing has inspired awe to the same extent as the contemplation of the vault of heaven. From the dimmest beginnings of history men have recognized the sun as the source of life-giving warmth. Among the inconstancies of nature, the vagaries of wind and storm and flood, the one dependable constant that the ancients recognized was the heaven above. When the clouds cleared away, there were the sun and moon and stars in their appointed places.

Science begins with systematic observation, and the first observations that have any claim to be labeled scientific seem to have been those of the heavenly bodies. From the very beginnings of civilization careful records of the motions of the sun and moon must have been kept, for these motions were the means for determining the calendar and the times of religious feasts. Some of the earliest written records from China and India show that men knew the details of the motions. The Mayas of

11

Mexico must have studied them centuries before the time of Columbus, for the accurate calendar they devised has been found by archeologists. In Europe there are several circles of great stone monuments, including the famous one at Stonehenge, England, which was built by the prehistoric Britons about 1500 B.C.° It has long been recognized that such monuments were used to mark the seasons, but recently careful measurements of Stonehenge have been compared with calculations, made on an electronic computer, of the positions of the sun and moon in 1500 B.C. The comparison has shown that the ancient British priests had an excellent knowledge of the movements of the heavenly bodies. Moreover, they were willing to expend a tremendous amount of labor in erecting the stone pillars so that sighting across pairs of stones would mark the positions of the sun and moon on important dates. For example, two prominent sighting lines marked the summer solstice, when the sun is highest in the sky, and the position of sunrise on midsummer day. Another pair of stones marked the most northerly position of the moon, which occurs about every 9 years.

However, our most complete information about early astronomical

° The date is now known from radiocarbon analysis.

FIG. 2-1

Part of the ancient British monument at Stonehenge, a combination of temple and astronomical observatory; the great pair of stones in the center of the picture provides one of the important sighting marks. (Photograph courtesy of British Travel Association, London and Toronto.)

observations comes from Babylonia° and Egypt, for written records from these two civilizations have survived. These records give numerical measurements, especially of angles, which were surprisingly accurate. We still have an inheritance from them, in our circle of 360° and hour of 60 minutes, both of which can be traced to the Babylonian system of counting, by sixties instead of by hundreds.

The ancients knew seven planets, wanderers among the "fixed" stars: Sun, Moon, Mercury, Venus, Mars, Jupiter, Saturn. They divided the stars into groups, or constellations, like the Great Bear (Ursa ·Major) or the Dipper, Orion, Andromeda, and many of their groupings have come down to us with very little change except in name. They traced the annual path of the sun among the stars, the great circle that we call the *ecliptic,* and they knew perfectly well which constellation would be behind the sun on any given day, even though the light of the stars was obliterated by the superior brilliance of the sun. They plotted the paths of the planets with reference to the ecliptic, and were able to use their plots to predict the future position of a planet quite accurately. They also understood eclipses of the sun and moon, although the claim that they predicted eclipses of the sun is hard to believe (see Sec. 6-8). Thus by 600 B.C. the scientific study of our solar system was well along in its first stage, that of observation, although it would be many centuries before significant progress was made on the second stage, that of generalized law.

Astronomy in Egypt and Babylonia had its practical side. The motions of the sun and moon fixed the calendar, as the sun does today. The equinoxes, when the sun crosses the equator in spring and fall, the solstices, when it reaches its highest point in summer and its lowest in winter, were occasions of feasts in many of the ancient civilizations, and precise measurements were needed to fix the feast times. In Egypt, land surveying with the help of astronomical observations was well developed.

Throughout the ancient world, and for centuries afterward, the motions of the planets were associated with astrological predictions. Astrology is an excellent example, by no means the only one, of a "science" gone wrong, because it was based on an erroneous a priori hypothesis, namely, the *assumption* that the positions in the sky of Venus or Mars could influence the affairs of men. However, the ancient astrologers should not be ignored, because they needed, or thought they needed, precise knowledge of the motions of the planets, and the observations they made contributed materially to the early knowledge of astronomy.

° Babylonia is here used in a broad sense for the region centered on the Tigris and Euphrates rivers. Astronomical observations from that area long antedate the city of Babylon and the historical Babylonian Empire.

2-2 Greek Astronomy

The ancients accepted the world as they saw it. In their eyes the earth was a flat disk, stationary in the center of the universe. The stars were attached to a great crystal sphere which revolved around the earth once a day. Between the earth and the sphere of the stars, other spheres, each revolving at its own rate, carried the sun and the moon and the five known planets, so that each of these appeared to trace out its own path against the background of the "fixed" stars. There was, of course, no conception of the vast distances involved, and the heavenly spheres were placed somewhere not far beyond the geographical limits of the known world. The early astronomers must sometimes have asked "why?" But it was a sufficient answer to ascribe the motions of the heavenly bodies to the gods. It was so ordained, and so it was.

Many centuries passed before, in the heyday of Greek civilization, a few men began to wonder if things were in fact just the way they looked, and if there might not be a logical explanation for the "appearances," to use a word which became popular with later philosophers. There was very little progress in astronomy during the Athenian period of Greek history, although other sciences developed significantly, but after the death of Alexander the Great (323 B.C.), and the decay of Greece proper, the center of Greek culture moved to Alexandria in Egypt, and the great Alexandrian school, which flourished for many centuries, was responsible for the first germs of our modern ideas.

2-3 Aristarchus and Eratosthenes

About 280 or 270 B.C. Aristarchus realized that, because the apparent position of the sun among the stars is the same no matter from where it is observed, it must be at a far greater distance from the earth than anybody so far had conceived, and the sphere of the stars must be far beyond the sun. It follows that the sun, instead of being a fiery ball suspended in the heavens 1000 miles or so above the ground, must actually be far larger than the earth. It did not seem logical to him that the big sun should revolve around the smaller earth, and still less so that the vast sphere of the stars should rotate while the earth remained stationary. He therefore taught that the sun was fixed at the center of the cosmos,° with the earth revolving around it, while the apparent daily motion of the stars, and the alternation of day and

---

° In this book the technical term "cosmos" will be used to denote the totality of all material things. "Universe," in the sense of everything that is, may, and probably does, have wider implications, although an out-and-out materialist would maintain that the words are synonymous.

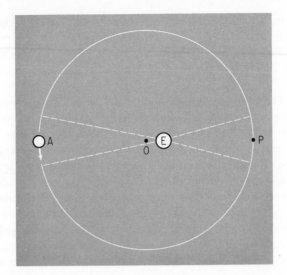

FIG. 2-5

Eccentric circular orbit of the moon, as assumed by Ptolemy; the angles in the diagram represent the apparent motion in two days.

To explain the apparent motions of the other planets, he supposed the planet, P (Fig. 2-6), to describe an eccentric circle, known as the "epicycle," around the point, C, while C in turn describes another eccentric circle, the "deferent," around the earth. The result is a series of loops, as shown in the right-hand half of the figure.

FIG. 2-6

Deferent and epicycle of a planet, as conceived by Ptolemy; the resulting motion is the series of loops shown on the right.

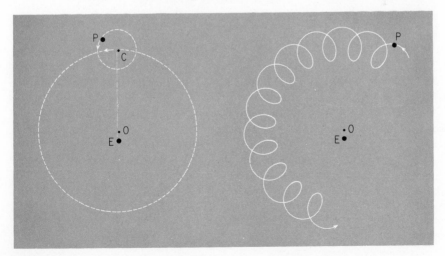

The final result is shown, not to scale, in Fig. 2-7. The relative sizes of the circles and the eccentric displacements of their centers were, of course, adjusted to give the best possible agreement with observation. Beyond all the planets lay the sphere of the fixed stars, rotating around the earth once a day.

The Ptolemaic system remained the basis for astronomical calculations for many centuries, while great political upheavals were taking place throughout the known world. The Western Roman Empire collapsed and Europe passed through its medieval period, when, for a time, the scientific tradition almost disappeared. The Arabs conquered and overran North Africa and even invaded parts of Europe. They, fortunately, absorbed the Greek-based cultural traditions of the Eastern Mediterranean rather than destroying them, and among other sciences, astronomy and its dubious sister, astrology, continued to flourish with the principal center at Baghdad. Gradually, the Ptolemaic system began to show discrepancies between prediction and observation, but the Arabs never abandoned Ptolemy's

FIG. 2-7

Ptolemaic conception of the solar system, not to scale.

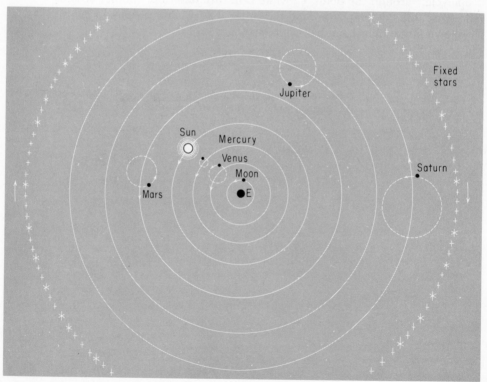

basic principles. Instead, they merely corrected and modified his system by adding more and more epicycles until finally no less than 80 circles were required to describe the motions of the seven planets. However, it is not fair to belittle the work of Ptolemy and his Arab successors. The fact that they could use this complicated system to make accurate predictions argues both mathematical and observational skill of a very high order. The specific observations which finally upset the Ptolemaic system were simply not available, since they had to await the invention of the telescope.

2-5   Copernicus

Up to the fifteenth century such Greek learning as was known in Europe was based on a few Latin translations, made in the time of the Roman Empire, and on a few ideas which had filtered in by way of the Arabs. In matters scientific, Aristotle was the principal authority—astronomy was based entirely on Ptolemy. The great theologian, St. Thomas Aquinas, had accepted the ideas of Aristotle and Ptolemy, and his authority was undisputed. Gradually, however, after several centuries during which authority was rarely questioned, European scholars began once more to think for themselves.

Among the new thinkers was the Polish physician and astronomer, Nicolaus Copernicus (1473–1543). He realized that if he placed the sun at the center, with the earth revolving around it in 365¼ days, many of Ptolemy's circles would be unnecessary. Furthermore, day and night could be much more simply explained by assuming the earth to rotate on its axis than by imagining a rotation of the vast sphere of the fixed stars.

Copernicus therefore set out to construct a heliocentric (sun-centered) system to describe the apparent motions of the sun, moon, and planets, putting them in the same relative positions as we place them today. He still used circles, but he succeeded in reducing the 80 circles of the later Ptolemaic system to 34, without any loss of accuracy. A modest man, Copernicus was reluctant to go against authority or to publish his revolutionary ideas until they had been proved beyond all doubt. It was not until shortly before his death, several years after he made his principal calculations, that friends persuaded him to let them publish his famous work, *De revolutionibus orbium coelestium*, which, of course, was written in Latin, the international scholarly language of his time. As finally produced, the work included a preface, probably written by his friend, Osiander, who edited it for the press, disclaiming the heliocentric system as factual truth, and stating that it was devised only to "save the appearances," that is, to provide a method of computing the apparent motions which would be simpler and more workable than the Ptolemaic method.

At first Copernicus' work aroused only moderate controversy, and it was not until some 50 years after it was published that arguments over the position of the earth in space became almost violent. Galileo Galilei (1564–1642) has a good claim to being considered the first physicist and astronomer in the modern tradition, and his name will appear in other connections besides his involvement in the earth-sun controversy.

Galileo was a man of a very different temperament from Copernicus, and when he became convinced that the Copernican heliocentric system was objective fact and not merely a convenient way of making computations, he said so, unequivocally. Due to the influence of the traditionalists upon the Church authorities, he was arrested and brought before the Inquisition.

At first he was merely forbidden to teach the Copernican system. However, he could not keep quiet for long, and in 1632 he published his ideas in a justly famous book, *Dialogue Concerning the Two Principal Systems of the World.* This took the form of a series of conversations among three principal characters, Salviati, a pupil of Galileo, Sagredo, an intelligent and open-minded critic, and Simplicio, who clearly represented the traditional scholastic philosophy based mainly on the writings of Aquinas. Throughout the dialogues the other two characters make sly fun of Simplicio, especially when the latter refused to look through the telescope for fear of seeing something contradictory to what he had been taught. It was this, even more than Galileo's advocacy of the Copernican system, that aroused the ire of the traditionalists. Galileo was arrested again, and this time he was convicted of heresy. He was persuaded to make a formal recantation, and so he did not suffer the usual penalty of burning at the stake, as did his contemporary Copernican advocate, Giordano Bruno, whose heresies were, indeed, religious as well as scientific. Galileo was placed under house arrest for the remainder of his life, which did not prevent him from writing another dialogue, setting out his ideas on mechanics.

Among Galileo's reputed accomplishments is the invention of the telescope. There is a good deal of doubt whether he was the first to use a combination of two lenses in order to make distant objects appear closer and larger. However, he certainly built himself a telescope, and he was probably the first to use it to make qualitative observations of the heavenly bodies. With it he observed mountains and craters on the moon and spots on the sun, another heretical notion for his time, since it contradicts Aristotle's principle of perfection of the heavenly bodies. By watching sunspots, he determined that the sun is rotating on its axis, making the rotation of the earth more plausible by analogy. He discovered the four principal moons of Jupiter, showing that the earth-moon combination is not unique. Of course, his telescope showed hosts of stars which are not visible to the naked eye, and this must have given him some glimmering of the immensity of the universe. All these new observations helped to convince him of the correctness of the heliocentric system, but one further observation that he made was crucial, that of the phases of Venus, which will be discussed more fully in Sec. 2-8.

2-7 *Heliocentric vs. Geocentric*

It will be worthwhile to examine objectively, leaving aside all religious and philosophical preconceptions, the controversy between those who believed that the sun revolves around the earth (geocentric system) and the advocates of the Copernican system with the sun at the center (heliocentric). It is often through the resolution of arguments of this kind that science makes progress.

In the first place, it is quite impossible to distinguish between the two systems if we observe only the earth and the sun; we must look at other bodies in order to come to a decision. Imagine two trains standing on parallel tracks, and that you are sitting in one of them, waiting to start your journey. You see the windows of the other train begin to slide by, and at first you are not sure whether it is your train or the other one that has started to move. You have to look out the other side of the train at the landscape in order to decide. The protagonists in the sixteenth-century controversy realized this, but they missed the deeper implications, and actually they were asking a meaningless question to which there is no answer, when they argued whether the earth or the sun is "at rest" or in the "center of the cosmos." All motion is relative, and it is meaningless to say that a body A is at rest, or is moving, unless we state (or imply) that it is moving relative to some other body B.

It is not actually a question of which system is *correct;* but only which is appropriate and convenient for a description of the motions of the planets, a heliocentric system based upon the sun, or a geocentric system based upon the earth. Osiander was unconsciously approaching the modern point of view when he made the concession to authority of saying that the Copernican system was designed only to "save the appearances," and not as objective fact. On the other hand, the traditionalists, in placing the earth at the center, largely on religious grounds, were making a completely unjustified claim. Actually, there is more reason than mere convenience to prefer a heliocentric system of astronomy, and we are quite justified in saying that the sun, which is by far the largest body in the solar system, is the center of *that* system. However, that does not mean that the sun is at rest, or that it is at the center of the cosmos. The center of the cosmos has never been identified, and it is possible (though not proved) that the

cosmos is infinite in extent, in which case "center" is a completely meaningless term.

Having discussed the real implications of the controversy, we may now
examine the seventeenth-century arguments for and against the heliocentric system, remembering that we are dealing *only* with the solar system,
the sun and its family of planets, and that we are comparing two competing theories of planetary motion, those of Ptolemy and Copernicus, respectively, and that they differ in more respects than the mere location of the
center. The superficial evidence clearly favors Ptolemy, for in our daily
living we are quite unconscious of the earth's motion. On the other hand,
Copernicus' system is simpler,° and this is a valid scientific argument, for
experience has often shown that of two competing theories the simpler is
more likely to be correct.

2-8   The Phases of Venus

As in the case of the parallel trains, we have to look beyond the sun-earth
combination for the evidence. There are then two important early observations which can be considered decisive. The first concerns the phases of
Venus, and was one of Galileo's own arguments when he observed the
effect with his telescope. To the naked eye, Venus, although the brightest
object in the sky after the moon, appears only as a point of light, and so
the ancients were never able to determine its apparent shape, which is, of
course, a sphere with the half facing the sun illuminated. If Ptolemy is
right, Venus is always closer than the sun and we can never see more than
a fraction of the illuminated half, so that it should always look like more or
less of a crescent moon. If Copernicus is right, Venus is beyond the sun at
"superior conjunction" ($E_1 V_1$, Fig. 2-8), and near this position it should
appear as an almost full moon. Near "inferior conjunction" ($E_3 V_3$), it
should show only a thin crescent, and somewhere in between ($E_2 V_2$),
it should show a semicircle. What Galileo saw through his telescope was
unmistakable; Venus goes through the full series of phases, just as the moon.

2-9   Parallax

The second decisive effect is that of the so-called annual parallax of the
stars (Fig. 2-9). If the earth revolves around the sun, as seen from the
frame of reference of another star, then there ought to be an apparent
displacement of this star, when it is seen from different points in the

---

° Today we actually use Kepler's system (Sec. 3-12), which is simpler still. This is also heliocentric, and so the present arguments apply equally well to Kepler as to Copernicus.

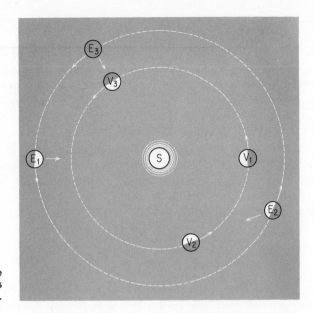

FIG. 2-8

Orbits of Venus and the earth, showing how Venus exhibits moonlike phases.

earth's orbit, at different times of the year. If you look through a window at a tree, say, with one eye at a time, alternating the two eyes, the uprights of the window appear to shift with respect to the tree. This is the optical effect known technically as "parallax," an apparent change in the scene when viewed from slightly different points. It is really a lack

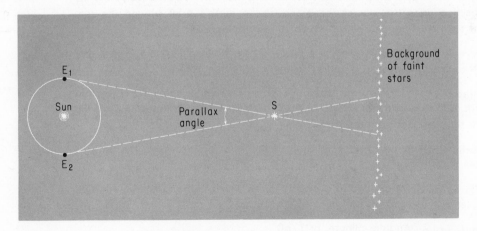

FIG. 2-9

Parallax of a relatively close star (S) as seen from two points in the earth's orbit (E_1, E_2) 6 months apart.

of parallelism in the light rays drawn from the nearer object to the two points of observation.

In the case of the stars, one of the strongest arguments of the traditionalists was that the parallax effect was *not* observed. Copernicus and Galileo replied, quite correctly as it turned out, that this must mean that the stars are so far beyond the sun that the parallax is too small to measure by the methods then available. The effect does exist but was not observed until 1838, by Bessel. It cannot be detected by direct measurement of the angular position of a star, but only by comparing relatively close stars with the background of faint telescopic stars, which are presumably much farther away. Parallax is a routine astronomical observation today and all computations of distance—within the solar system as well as of the distant stars—are based upon measurements of parallax (Secs. 3-13 and 30-2).

GLOSSARY

Conjunction In astronomy, the condition when two heavenly bodies appear to be in line, as seen from the earth. The term is most frequently used of a planet in line with the sun. The conjunction is "superior" if the planet is beyond the sun, "inferior" if the planet is between the earth and the sun.

Cosmos The totality of all material things.

Deferent In the Ptolemaic description of the solar system, the principal circular orbit that a planet describes around a point at or near the earth.

Ecliptic The apparent path of the sun among the stars. Alternatively, it is the projection upon the sky of the plane of the earth's orbit around the sun. (This term must not be confused with ellipse or elliptical.)

Epicycle The secondary orbit of a planet in the Ptolemaic system. The center of the epicycle moves at a uniform speed around the deferent.

Equinox Strictly, the instant when the sun crosses the equator, from south to north in March, and from north to south in September. At these times of the year day and night are approximately equal.

Geocentric Applied to a description of the solar system when the earth is taken to be the center.

Heliocentric Term applied to a description in which the sun is assumed to be the center.

Minute of arc Angular minute, or $1/60°$.

Parallax The apparent displacement or the difference in apparent direction of an object when it is viewed first from one point, then from another.

Specifically, the difference in direction of a celestial body as measured from two points on earth. When two bodies are seen nearly in line and the point of observation changes, the nearer body appears to be displaced with respect to the one farther away. Annual parallax is the effect when stars are seen from different points in the earth's orbit around the sun.

Revolution The description of a closed path around a center, as the earth around the sun.

Rotation The turning upon an axis, as the earth rotates around its north-south axis, producing day and night.

Solstice The times when the sun is highest in the sky, in June, and lowest, in December. These are also the times of the longest and shortest days.

EXERCISES

1. What evidence have we that the science of astronomy was well advanced before the beginning of recorded history?

2. What is the origin of our 60-minute hour, and our 360° circle?

3. "Astrology is a 'science' gone wrong." Explain this statement.

4. To what was Shakespeare referring when he talked about the "music of the spheres"?

5. What is the oldest known reference to a heliocentric system of the cosmos? Who advanced this theory, and where and when did he live? What led him to make this radical departure from the accepted ideas of his contemporaries?

6. What is the average circumference of the earth in miles? If two points are 500 miles apart on a north-south line, what is the difference in latitude, to the nearest minute of arc?

7. Who first realized that the earth is a sphere and also estimated its size? Describe the principle of his method. Briefly, how is this type of measurement made today?

8. Apart from the fact that it was geocentric, what were the principal features of the Ptolemaic description of the cosmos?

9. Why is the Arab civilization important to the history of science?

10. What led Copernicus to develop a heliocentric description?

11. Give two decisive arguments in favor of a heliocentric description of the solar system.

12. Considering all the arguments which took place in the sixteenth and seventeenth centuries, where is the center of the cosmos?

13. Outline Galileo's work in astronomy. Apart from his advocacy of the Copernican heliocentric system, what observations did he make that were inconsistent with the traditional Aristotelian ideas?

14. At what times does Venus look like a crescent moon? a nearly full moon?

the solar system

3-1   Some Statistics

The first half of this chapter will be mainly descriptive of the solar system as we now know it. Then as the work proceeds, in this and later chapters, we shall discuss some of the further history, subsequent to Galileo, and the methods by which some of the details have been determined. Table 3-1 gives up-to-date statistics of the sun, the moon, and the nine major planets.*

3-2   Nature of the Sun

As is well known, our sun is a typical star, similar in nature to millions of other stars, and is the only self-luminous body in the solar system; the planets, and all other bodies of the system, are visible because they are illuminated by sunlight. As a star, the sun is a fairly good specimen. Among the estimated 100 billion stars in the Milky Way, there are billions larger and brighter

* Numerical values, here and elsewhere, are from Danby, *Celestial Mechanics* (New York: The Macmillan Company, 1962).

TABLE 3-1   STATISTICS OF THE SOLAR SYSTEM

Sun

Mean diameter	864,900 miles
Times earth	109.30
Mass, times earth	333,420
Mean density (water = 1)	1.41
Rotation period	25 to 33 days
Escape velocity	39.2 miles per second

Moon

Mean distance from earth	238,857 miles
Period of revolution	27.32158 days
Diameter	2159.9 miles
Times earth	0.27179
Mass, times earth	1/81.31
Mean density, times water	3.342
Escape velocity	1.5 miles per second

	Mercury	Venus	Earth	Mars
Mean distance from sun, millions of miles	35.98	67.24	92.96	141.62
Orbital period, days	87.969	224.701	365.256	686.980
Mean diameter, miles	3007	7700	7917.78	4270
Times earth	0.382	0.972	1	0.539
Mass, times earth	1/18.9	0.81485	1	0.107
Density, times water	5.3	4.95	5.52	3.95
Rotation period	88 days	uncertain	23.9345 hours	24.623 hours
Escape velocity, miles per second	2.4	6.5	7.1	3.2

	Jupiter	Saturn	Uranus	Neptune	Pluto
Mean distance from sun, millions of miles	483.6	887.1	1784	2795	3670
Orbital period, years	11.86223	29.45774	84.018	164.78	248.4
Mean diameter, miles	86,840	71,500	29,100	27,700	9000 (?)
Times earth	10.968	9.03	3.68	3.50	1.1 (?)
Mass, times earth	318.0	95.22	14.55	17.23	0.9 (?)
Density, times water	1.330	0.687	1.56	2.27	4 (?)
Rotation period, hours	9.84	10.23	10.81	15.7	16
Escape velocity, miles per second	38	23.0	14.0	15	2.2

than the sun, but there are probably 100 times as many that are fainter.

The average surface temperature of the sun is 5740°K (Sec. 30-4), and its internal temperature must be far higher, or else it would collapse; it is estimated to be 14,000,000°K at the center. Under conditions prevailing on the sun every known material is gaseous, and even though the mean density is 1.41 times that of water, the sun behaves throughout as a great sphere of gas. There is therefore no sharp boundary between the main body of the sun, the *photosphere* which is the source of its light and heat, and the slightly cooler atmosphere. The sun's atmosphere contains about 86 per cent hydrogen, 13 per cent helium, and 1 per cent heavier elements, including all the common elements found on earth, but all in the vaporized form. The atmosphere extends far out from the body of the sun and merges gradually into the *corona,* the faint halo of greenish light which becomes visible at the time of a total eclipse, when the bright photosphere is obscured by the moon (Fig. 3-1). Here the temperature rises again, to some 100,000°K. However, the gases of the corona are so diffuse that their high temperature contributes very little to the total output of light and heat. The visible streamers of the corona extend at times to a distance comparable with the sun's own radius, but there is really no distinct boundary between the outer corona and the very diffuse gas which constitutes the "solar wind," the stream that is continually being ejected from the sun, to distances far beyond the earth's orbit.

3-3   The Restless Sun

As might be expected at such high temperatures, the gases of the photosphere, atmosphere, and corona are in a continual state of turbulence,

FIG. 3-1

The solar corona, photographed at the time of a total eclipse. (Photograph from Mt. Wilson Observatory.)

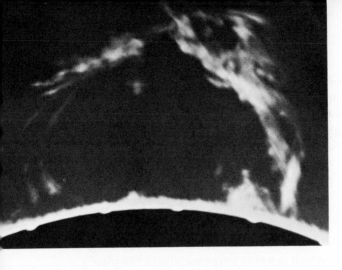

FIG. 3-2

A conspicuous solar prominence. (Photograph from Mt. Wilson Observatory.)

rising and falling back again. At times there are great eruptions of relatively cool gas which appear as dark streaks against the brighter disk. When the sun's rotation brings one of these to the edge of the disk, it can be seen to be a great stream of gas arching out of the sun, sometimes to a height of 100,000 miles or more, and falling back again (Fig. 3-2). They are consequently known as *prominences*. At other times there are eruptions of very hot gas, described as *flares*. In this case gas is ejected with such a high velocity that it escapes from the sun altogether, and some of it may reach the earth a day or two later. Here the high-velocity gas entering the earth's atmosphere can cause a brilliant display of aurora, and at the same time interrupt radio communications through a so-called "magnetic storm."

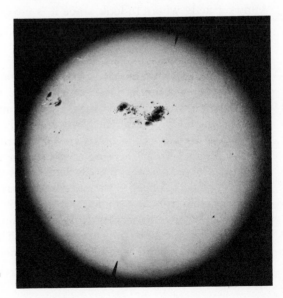

FIG. 3-3

A group of large sunspots. (Photograph from Mt. Wilson Observatory.)

Finally, there are the *sunspots*, which were first observed by Galileo, and which led him to reject once and for all Aristotle's idea that the heavenly bodies should be perfect and should be made of a finer kind of matter than the earth. Although there is still some uncertainty about the mechanism of the spots, they seem to be associated with whirling vortices, sometimes several thousand miles across and extending deep into the sun's interior. They appear dark because they are cooler than the surrounding, undisturbed solar surface.

Sunspots and other irregularities are temporary features, but they commonly persist for several days, or even, in the case of a large spot, for 2 or 3 months. They then appear to move across the face of the sun, showing that it is rotating around an axis which is nearly perpendicular to the plane of the earth's orbit. Since the sun is not a solid body, different latitude zones rotate at different speeds, the rotation period varying from 24.6 days at the sun's equator to 34 days near the poles.

3-4   The Planets

Of the nine principal planets the ancients knew only five: Mercury, Venus, Mars, Jupiter, and Saturn. Naturally, they did not include Earth in the list, but on the other hand they added Sun, which we now recognize as the massive center around which all the others are revolving, and Moon, which we know as a satellite of Earth. The five true planets of the ancient list are easily visible to the naked eye, although Mercury is hard to find unless one knows exactly where to look, since it is never far from the sun, and it is visible only for a few weeks at a time, either just after sunset or just before sunrise.

Venus is unmistakable, and is seen as the brilliant "evening star" in the western sky for 6 months or so, then reappearing in the east in the early morning a few months later. It is greatly to the credit of the early Babylonian astronomers that they knew the morning and evening star to be the same body in different positions relative to the sun. Mars, Jupiter, and Saturn, because their orbits are outside that of the earth, can appear at any distance from the sun, anywhere in the Zodiac.° They are all prominent objects, and can easily be located with the aid of an almanac. All these planets appear to the naked eye merely as points of light, hardly distinguishable from any bright star, but even with a moderate-sized telescope they show measurable disks, with more or less phase effect, as described previously in the case of Venus. Their diameters in miles can therefore be calculated as soon as their distances are known.

° The Zodiac is the zone of the sky that contains the 12 constellations of stars that the sun appears to traverse during the year.

The four inner planets, Mercury to Mars, are fundamentally much alike— compact, solid bodies with densities similar to that of the earth. However, some differences are worth noting. Mercury has little, if any, atmosphere, and shows a rugged, mountainous surface. Its rotation can therefore be observed, and it can be seen that it always keeps the same face toward the sun°; its rotational period and its orbital period are the same. It must be intensely hot on the side which is continually exposed to the sun, and far below zero in temperature on the dark side.

Venus is superficially quite different. It has an atmosphere about the same density as that of the earth, but the atmosphere is continually filled with clouds, so that the solid surface has never been seen. The upper surface of the clouds appears to us as a brilliant, uniform white, with no recognizable features, so that it has been very difficult to determine whether the planet is rotating or not, and only recently has rotation been detected. However, the period of rotation is still uncertain; the latest measurements indicate that the planet is rotating slowly in the opposite direction to its revolution around the sun. The surface temperature of Venus is another important property about which there is still uncertainty. In 1963 the American space probe, Mariner II, passed within 20,000 miles of the planet, and took observations that were automatically transmitted back to earth by radio. Certain of these observations indicated temperatures as high as 500°C, much higher than had previously been suspected, but it has been suggested that these readings were spurious, caused by the effect upon the instruments of thunderstorms in the dense Venusian atmosphere; we are certain only that underneath the cloud layer Venus is much too hot for comfortable living.

Mars has an atmosphere with a density that has been variously estimated as 1 to 10 per cent of that on earth. It has no high mountains, but the close-up pictures that were taken by Mariner IV in 1965 showed many small craters similar to those on the moon, still showing their circular form because there is very little erosion in the thin Martian atmosphere. There are several recognizable permanent markings that can be used to make accurate measurements of the rotation period. In this respect Mars is very like the earth; its day and night are about the same length as those on earth, and, because its axis is inclined to its orbit like that of the earth, it must have summer and winter seasons. The seasons are accompanied by changes in the coloring. The white spots around the poles of the planet (Fig. 3-4) increase in size in winter and recede in summer, strongly suggesting a snow-covered area, for this phenomenon is what a Martian observer would

° This conclusion has been questioned; some recent radar observations seem to indicate a very slow rotation of Mercury.

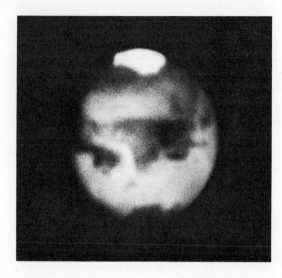

FIG. 3-4

Mars, showing the polar cap.
(Photograph from Mt. Wilson
Observatory.)

see when looking toward earth. There are large areas which are normally reddish-brown and which give the planet its ruddy color. In the Martian spring these areas take on a greenish tinge, suggesting the possibility of vegetation, and so of some form of life, but this is only conjecture, and we may not know for certain until an astronaut goes to Mars and brings back an eyewitness report.

Martian features which have given rise to a great deal of speculation are the so-called "canals." In 1877 the Italian astronomer, Schiaparelli, drew pictures of Mars showing the surface crossed by a number of nearly straight lines. Later, Lowell also observed these markings, and mapped them in great detail. Photographs have never shown the markings as clearly as Schiaparelli and Lowell drew them, but at certain seasons there are visible streaks which extend toward the equator from smooth, dark areas that might be taken for seas, but that are probably only level plains. The curious result of Schiaparelli's pictures came partly from a too literal translation of the Italian word *canali*, which he used in describing the markings he had seen. Writers combined their imaginations with the mistranslation and assumed them to be artificial irrigation canals, or rather belts of vegetation along the sides of the canals, and so to be evidence of an advanced civilization on the planet. Actually we are still not sure what the markings mean; possibly they are linear groupings of small craterlike features, but some astronomers have dismissed them as an optical illusion.

3-6   The Great Planets

Between Mars and Jupiter there is a wide gap populated by the asteroids (Sec. 3-9). Then follow the four great planets, Jupiter, Saturn, Uranus, and

FIG. 3-5

Saturn and its rings.
(Photograph from Mt.
Wilson Observatory.)

Neptune, very different from the inner group of earthlike planets, both in size and structure. Jupiter is the giant, containing more than twice the material of all the other planets and their moons put together, but still only 1/1000 of the sun. The outer planets all have a much lower average density than the earth, Saturn in particular being lighter than water, so they cannot be composed of solid rock. Saturn is uniquely distinguished by its system of rings (Fig. 3-5), which have turned out to be swarms of small solid particles, possibly largely ice, revolving around the planet in its equatorial plane. The rings extend to a distance of 68,000 miles from the surface of the planet, but are nowhere more than about 12 miles thick, and their total mass would only make the equivalent of a small moon.

The large planets must have extended atmospheres containing very large quantities of hydrogen. Probably we never see the solid planets, but only the outer limits of a dense, and possibly cloud-filled atmosphere. The low mean densities would then be accounted for by the fact that the measured diameters far exceed those of the solid planets. On the other hand, there are recognizable features, like the great red spot on Jupiter (Fig. 3-6), from which the rotation periods can be determined. If there is a large excess of hydrogen, as is almost certain, other fairly common elements such as oxygen, nitrogen, and carbon would have combined with hydrogen to form water, ammonia, and hydrocarbons. At the low temperatures that must exist so far away from the sun, water, ammonia, and the heavier hydrocar-

FIG. 3-6

Jupiter, showing the great red spot, and one of its satellites. The dark spot on the upper left is the shadow of the satellite. (Photograph from Mt. Palomar Observatory.)

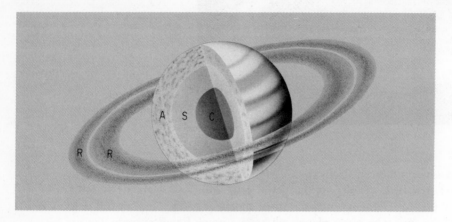

FIG. 3-7

Conjectured structure of Saturn. C, core of rocklike materials
and iron; S, shell largely of ice and solid ammonia; A, atmosphere, mainly hydrogen and methane, with dense clouds of
solid particles; R, rings of small solid particles.

bons would be solid. It has been conjectured, admittedly on rather slim
evidence, that these planets may have shells, thousands of miles thick,
composed largely of ice and solid ammonia (Fig. 3-7). This would help to
account for the low average densities.

3-7   The Moon

Some statistics for our own moon are given in Table 3-1, and Fig. 3-8 is a
photograph taken near half-moon so that the mountains and the circular
craters stand out near the edge of the illuminated portion. The heights of
the mountains and crater walls can be estimated by measuring the shadows
they cast when they are near the illuminated boundary, and some of them
are found to be higher than the highest mountains on earth. As is well
known, the moon keeps the same face turned toward the earth at all times;
its period of rotation relative to the sun or stars is the same as its period of
revolution around the earth. However, because the orbit is elliptical, and
because there is a slight wobble (known as libration) in the moon's motion,
we do at times see a little beyond the diametral plane, and lunar geographers
have been able to map 58 per cent of the moon's surface.

A prominent and well-known feature of the lunar landscape is the
multitude of nearly circular craters. Those that have been seen with
telescopes and that appear on lunar maps vary in size from 150 miles to
about 500 feet, many of the smaller ones lying inside the larger. However,

FIG. 3-8

Photograph of a portion of the moon. (Photograph from Mt. Wilson Observatory.)

in July, 1964, an American space probe carrying a television camera landed on the moon and viewed the surface as the vehicle approached it, the last view being taken from a distance of only 1000 feet. An area that appears smooth on earth-based photographs was found to be pockmarked with tiny craters, some of them only 3 feet in diameter. Since many of these small craters form a cluster around a nearby large one, it is likely that they were formed by fragments from the explosion that produced the large crater. Most astronomers believe that the craters and pits are the result of meteorites falling into the moon. There are a few similar features on the earth, almost certainly caused by meteorites, the Meteor Crater in Arizona and the great Chubb Crater in northern Quebec, for example, and in historical times a large meteorite fell in Siberia leaving a small crater and devastating the forest for many miles around. On earth such features are worn away by the rain or buried under sediment in a few thousand years; on the airless and rainless moon there is nothing to wear them down, and they must be nearly as rugged today as when they were first formed. The large craters are not just the result of splashes. If a rock 100 feet in diameter hit the moon with the speed of a meteorite, the heat produced would cause an explosion powerful enough to blast out a crater several miles wide and to hurl fragments over a wide area. In the early days of the moon's history there were probably a great many such rocks flying about.

As far as it has been possible to learn, the moon is an airless° and lifeless mass of rock, but there is probably some erosion of the crater rims and the mountains nevertheless. The surface is exposed to the full intensity of the sun's rays for 14 days at a time, and then to the blackness of empty space for another 14 days. In the sun the temperature probably rises well above the boiling point of water, and in the dark it falls to the point where our air would liquefy. With these extreme changes of temperature, expansion and contraction of the rock would cause flakes to chip off, a process which is known to occur in arid areas on earth. Hence lunar explorers will probably find dust and chips of rock lying on the floors of the craters. However, in 1966 an American space probe landed successfully without damaging its equipment, and it was found that the amount of debris is much less than some lunar students had expected.

3-8   Satellites of the Other Planets

All the planets except Mercury, Venus, and Pluto have natural satellites revolving around them, although the Earth-Moon combination is the only case where the satellite is comparable in size to its parent. Mars has two tiny moons, Phobos and Deimos, respectively 10 and 5 miles in diameter. They are quite close to the planet, and Phobos' period of revolution is only 7.65 hours, so that it describes its orbit three times in a Martian day. It would rise in the west, and set in the east.

Jupiter has no less than 12 moons, of which the 4 largest are the ones discovered by Galileo. These four have diameters of 1970 to 3240 miles, comparable with our own moon, but far smaller than Jupiter itself. The other eight are all less than 100 miles. Saturn has nine known moons, of which the largest, Titan, is somewhat larger than ours. Uranus has five moons, and Neptune two.

3-9   The Asteroids

Space between the nine planets of the solar system is far from empty, although the total mass of the matter which is not consolidated into planets is probably less than that of the earth. The particles of material range in size all the way from single gas molecules to the so-called minor planets, or *asteroids*. It had long been thought that there ought to be a planet in the gap between Mars and Jupiter, and in 1801 a small body was discovered in this region and was given the name Ceres. Very soon 3 more were

° The moon may not be completely devoid of atmosphere. Russian astronomers have reported sudden changes in the lunar landscape, which look like volcanic eruptions, and recently something similar has been seen by other observers. If this conclusion is correct, there is probably a bit of heavy gas in the bottoms of some of the craters (see also Sec. 30-5).

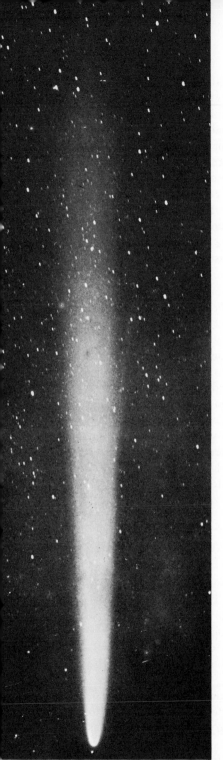

found, and later, when systematic photographic surveys began to be made, new discoveries came thick and fast, until today there are estimated to be about 30,000 sufficiently bright to be photographed with a large telescope. Of these only about 2000 have been followed carefully enough to determine their orbits. Astronomers have given up trying to find names for them, and most are known only by a letter and the date of discovery.

Ceres, the first to be found, is also the largest, about 500 miles in diameter. Most of them range from 5 to 50 miles, and the entire 30,000 would make up less than 1 per cent of the bulk of the earth. The smaller ones seem to be irregular chunks of rock. A particularly interesting one, Eros, of which more later, has been estimated to measure $22 \times 10 \times 5$ miles, and has been described as a "flying brick." It rotates around its shortest dimension as axis, with a period of 5¼ hours.

3-10   Comets

Every few years a comet passes quite close to the earth in its journey from the outer fringes of the solar system to its perihelion* near the sun, and then there

---

* "Perihelion" of an elliptical orbit is the point closest to the sun, from the Greek words *peri* (near) and *helios* (sun). "Aphelion," from *apo* (away), is the most distant point in the orbit. Similarly, "perigee" and "apogee" are the closest and farthest points in the orbit of a satellite around the earth.

FIG. 3-9

Halley's comet when near the sun. (Photograph from Mt. Wilson Observatory.)

is a spectacular view of its bright, hazy head and its long glowing tail (Fig. 3-9). The superstitious awe with which bright comets used to be received has never quite died out, and many people still think that they must be harbingers of some important event, probably a disaster. The excitement caused by a comet is out of all proportion to its real importance in the scheme of the solar system. The hazy head turns out to be a cluster of small solid particles immersed in a diffuse globe of gas. The tail, which is present only when the comet is close to the sun, consists of gas and dust forced out of the head by the pressure of sunlight. It is so diffuse that the earth has been known to pass right through the tail of a comet without any appreciable effects. Even though the head of a large comet may be 100,000 miles in diameter, the mass is only that of a small asteroid, and the density is comparable with that of the gas in a good "vacuum."

Another special characteristic of comets is the very long elliptical orbit, usually extending from far beyond Neptune to perihelion as close to the sun as Mercury. Even with a telescope, the comet can only be seen and followed when it is fairly close to the sun. A few comets have periodic orbits, and have been seen several times. The most famous of these is Halley's comet, which has a period of about 75 years, and which has been traveling nearly the same orbit since its first recorded appearance in 240 B.C. It passed perihelion in 1910 and should be seen again in 1986.

The origin of comets is quite mysterious. They are almost certainly part of the sun's family, spending most of their time moving slowly around the distant outer portions of their orbits. Astronomers therefore talk of a reservoir of comets in the outer limits of the solar system, far beyond Neptune. From this reservoir a few each year enter the inner regions of the system to make their passage near the sun.

3-11   Meteors and Meteorites

Meteors are small solid fragments which may consist of either stony or metallic material, in the latter case largely iron. They vary in size from fine grains of sand to a ton or more, although those weighing more than a pound are rare. Like all other bodies in the solar system they travel in elliptical orbits around the sun except when they come close to a planet. They are everywhere, and the earth collects about a ton of meteoritic material every day.

Their average velocity relative to the earth is about 40 miles per second, and when they enter the atmosphere with this speed they are heated to the boiling point by friction. The hot gases from a meteor weighing as much as an ounce are enough to make it visible as a "shooting star" if it enters the atmosphere after dark. An average of five or six per hour can be recorded by an experienced watcher on any night, and many more can be photographed with special cameras. The smaller ones are completely vaporized, and only the largest survive atmospheric friction long enough to strike the ground, as *meteorites*.

Although some meteors can be seen every night, there are several well-recognized swarms clustered around identifiable elliptic orbits. When the earth crosses one of these paths, an abundant display of shooting stars can be expected, such as that which occurs between August 11 and 14 every year. At least one of these swarms is known to be the remains of a periodic comet which must have lost its gas and finer dust, and others are in nearly the same orbits as known comets. When Biela's comet was expected to return in 1865, a profuse meteor shower turned up in its place.

There is now ample evidence that comets and meteors have a common origin. The history in a particular case is probably as follows. A comet from the reservoir beyond Neptune enters the inner regions of the solar system and accidentally passes near Saturn or Jupiter so that it is captured into a closer orbit with a period of less than 100 years. Every time it passes its perihelion the sun drives away some of the gas and dust, and perturbations by the planets further separate particles from the loosely bound head. Finally, the particles which formerly composed the head are spread all around the orbit as a swarm of meteors, and the comet can no longer be identified as such.

3-12 *Kepler's Laws of Planetary Motion*

The most famous practical astronomer of the sixteenth century was the Dane, Tycho Brahe (1546–1601). He was a most skillful and meticulous observer, and he spent a large part of his life tabulating the angular positions of the planets from night to night, with an accuracy far superior to anything that had gone before. These were still naked eye observations, mostly made by means of a large quadrant. This consisted of a pair of fine slits mounted on a long arm, which rotated on a scale of degrees some 10 feet in radius, so that the elevation of a planet above the horizon could be measured to within 10 seconds of arc.° Accurate clocks were also available to give the precise time of transit of the planet across the southern meridian. With a little computation these two measurements gave the position of the planet, night after night.

Brahe was not a mathematician, but fortunately during the latter years of his life he had Johannes Kepler (1571–1630) to assist him in making calculations. Kepler tried to fit Brahe's observed angular positions into a modification of the geocentric Ptolemaic system, but it did not work. He

° Ten seconds of arc represents a width of 1 foot seen from a distance of about 4 miles.

tried the Copernican system; this was better, but there were still discrepancies, amounting at times to several minutes, between the calculated and observed positions of Mars. The ancient solution would have been to add another epicycle, but Kepler had a better idea. When calculation and observation do not agree we may have to make a fresh start, and in this case we may have to abandon the preconceived idea that heavenly motions are always circular and try some other geometrical curve. Kepler tried ellipses, and by a proper adjustment of their dimensions he was able not only to make the motion of Mars fit the observations, but also to get rid of all the other epicycles and eccentrics that cluttered the Copernican system.

In 1609, therefore, he enunciated the first two of his *laws of planetary motion:*

1. **The planets move in elliptical orbits around the sun, with the latter at one focus of the ellipse.**

2. **The line joining the planet to the sun sweeps out equal areas in equal intervals of time, as the planet describes its orbit (Fig. 3-10).**

A little later (1619) he added his third law, comparing the orbits of the different planets:

3. **The (period of revolution)^2 varies as the (mean distance)^3.**

Apart from small "perturbations," due mainly to the effect of one planet on another, these laws have stood the test of time and are still the basis for calculations of the positions of the planets.

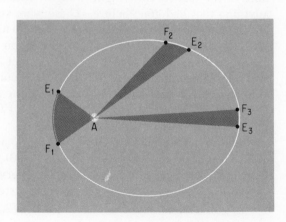

FIG. **3-10**

Illustrating Kepler's second law. If F_1E_1, F_2E_2, F_3E_3 are the distances the planet travels in a given time, then the shaded areas are equal.

3-13   *Determination of the Distance of the Moon*

The distance of the moon, the closest body of the solar system, is quite easily determined by means of the parallax principle, by making observations from two different points on the earth's surface (Fig. 3-11). It is necessary to know the base line, $d = AB$, which is the distance between the two points of observation, measured in a direction perpendicular to the line to the moon. The parallax angle, $\theta = \angle AMB$, is then measured by making astronomical observations from A and B. Since the angle is only about one degree, the straight line AB is very nearly the same as the arc of a circle with center at M. Then the base line is to the circumference of this circle as the angle θ is to 360°, or,

$$\frac{d}{2\pi D} = \frac{\theta \text{ (degrees)}}{360},$$

and so the required distance D can be determined.

The astronomical observations of Tycho Brahe and Kepler were precise enough to make a fairly good determination of the parallax angle of the moon, and it was known in Kepler's time that its distance is about 60 times the radius of the earth. Therefore, knowing its apparent angular width, it follows that it is a little over a quarter of the size of the earth.

With photography taking the place of visual observations with a quadrant, and with almost instantaneous communication between the two observing points (by telegraph or radio), the accuracy has been greatly increased. The modern method is to take simultaneous photographs of the moon against the background of stars, from the two observatories, preferably at crescent moon, and preferably when a fairly bright star (S) is near the dark edge. The parallax angle is then easily found by comparing the

FIG. **3-11**

Determination of the distance of the moon by the parallax method.

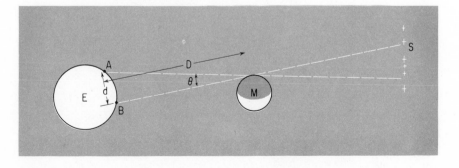

two photographs and measuring the apparent displacement of the star relative to the edge of the moon.

The modern value of the average parallax, reduced to the radius of the earth as base line, is 57 minutes, 2.7 seconds, which means that the average distance of the moon is 60.263 times the earth's radius, or 238,857 miles.

3-14   Distance of the Sun

It is quite a different matter when we try to determine the distance of the sun, and it turns out that it is quite impractical to do this directly. In the first place, it is very difficult to make direct observations of the edge of the brilliant sun, and in the second place, the parallax angle which has to be measured is very much smaller than that of the moon. The angle is, in fact, just about the limit which could be detected by methods such as those used by Tycho Brahe, and the early astronomers were never able to make more than very rough estimates of the sun's distance.

Modern determinations of the parallax and distance of the sun have all been made indirectly. Using the long series of observations of the apparent angular positions of the sun and the planets, it is possible to draw a plan of the solar system with all the angles, the shapes of the orbits, and the relative sizes of the orbits correct, but without any scale of distances. This, in effect, is what Kepler had to do to arrive at his famous three laws. It is now as if we had a map of a piece of country with all the angles, and the shapes of the lakes and rivers correct, but without a scale of miles attached to the map. If we could measure any one distance on the map we would have our scale of miles and could scale off all the other distances. Figure 3-12 is a portion of such a map of the solar system, showing the orbits of Earth, Mars, and the minor planet Eros (R). The lines E_1R_1, etc., join simultaneous positions of Earth and Eros, at different times. If any one of these distances is measured, using the parallax method as described above

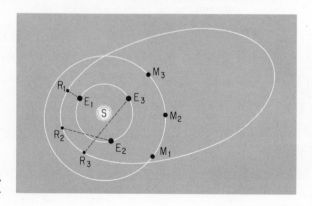

FIG. 3-12

Orbits of Earth, Mars, and Eros, not to scale.

for the moon, the scale factor is known. In practice, of course, many measurements are made, on different nights, and the "best" value is taken to be the average of all the separate determinations.

The first reliable determination of the scale factor, or the *astronomical unit*, the average distance of the earth from the sun, was made in 1862 by observations of Mars when it was near its closest approach to the earth, about 35 million miles away. When Eros was discovered in 1897, and it was found that it is describing a highly elliptical orbit which brings it within 15 million miles of the earth at the most favorable times, astronomers realized that it would be the best planet of all to use in determining the scale factor of the whole solar system, both on account of the lesser distance, and because it is easier to make accurate settings on a smaller object. Astronomers all over the world cooperated in making careful observations of Eros in order to establish its orbit as precisely as possible and to determine its distance at the times of closest approach, in 1901 and again in 1931.

The average of the best determinations to date for the mean distance of the sun is 92,960,000 miles, with a possible error of $\pm 10,000$. On account of the eccentricity of the earth's orbit, the distance varies from 91,410,000 miles at perihelion, which occurs in January, to 94,510,000 miles at aphelion in July.

GLOSSARY

Aphelion The point farthest away from the sun in the orbit of a planet or comet.

Apogee The point farthest from the earth in the orbit of the moon or of an artificial satellite.

Asteroids   The several thousand small planetlike bodies of the solar system, all of which are describing orbits around the sun; most of them lie in the gap between Mars and Jupiter.

Astronomical unit The average distance from the earth to the sun, used as a unit of distance in astronomical measurements.

Corona The very diffuse gas that extends beyond the sun's atmosphere to a distance comparable with the sun's radius; it can be seen as a faint greenish light at the time of a total eclipse.

Eccentricity As applied to an ellipse, a quantity that measures the extent of the deviation from a circle.

Ellipse The geometrical figure traced out by a point moving in such a way that the sum of its distances from two fixed points (the foci) is a constant.

Escape velocity The speed that a rocket or other body must attain in order to escape from the gravitational attraction of a planet and fly off into space.

Flares Streams of very hot gas that are ejected from the sun at intervals; they are seen as brilliant white patches against the yellower background of the photosphere.

Libration A perturbation of the moon's orbit that causes the axis of the satellite to "wobble" slightly.

Magnetic storm Large, irregular fluctuations in the earth's magnetic field, usually caused by a stream of ionized gas from the sun.

Meteor Term applied to the small bodies that are continually flying around in the solar system; when a meteor enters the earth's atmosphere it is seen as a "shooting star."

Meteorite A meteor that is large enough to survive the passage through the atmosphere and reach the surface of the earth.

Perigee The point closest to the earth in the orbit of the moon or an artificial satellite.

Perihelion The point closest to the sun in the orbit of a planet or a comet.

Perturbation In astronomy, a small deviation from the proper elliptical orbit, usually caused by the attraction of some other planet.

Photosphere The main body of the sun, the source of its light and heat.

Prominences Great streamers of gas erupting from the sun, usually falling back to form an arch; during an eclipse they look like reddish flames.

Satellite In astronomy, a body that is revolving around one of the planets, rather than around the sun.

Solar wind The steady stream of gas flowing away from the sun and reaching the earth; when a solar flare erupts in the direction of the earth, the intensity of the solar wind is markedly increased.

Zodiac The 12 constellations of stars—well known to the ancients—which form a belt around the sky on either side of the ecliptic; the sun, moon, and principal planets always appear somewhere within the zodiac.

EXERCISES

1. Outline the evidence that the sun is a great sphere of gas, and that it is in a highly turbulent state.

2. Describe the transient features of the sun: sunspots, prominences, flares, the corona.

3. From the data in Table 3-1 compute: (a) the radius of the sun in meters; (b) its volume in cubic miles; (c) the mean density of the moon in grams per cubic centimeter; (d) the average speed of the earth in its orbit around the sun in miles per second; (e) the speed with which a point on the earth's equator travels, due to the earth's rotation; (f) the orbital speed and the equatorial rotation speed for the planet Jupiter.

4. Why is the earth's period of rotation not given as 24 hours?

5. There is an old rule, known as Bode's law, which states that the distances of the planets from the sun should be in the ratio of the numbers: 4; $4 + 3$; $4 + 2 \times 3$; $4 + 4 \times 3$; $4 + 8 \times 3$; etc. Test the accuracy of this law.

6. Why was the discovery of the first asteroid, Ceres, no surprise to astronomers?

7. Why has it been so difficult to determine the rotation period of Venus? Why are the temperatures of Venus determined by the space probe, Mariner, suspect?

8. Mercury, as seen in a telescope, shows a rugged, mountainous surface, whereas Mars appears comparatively flat. Why should this be?

9. How did the curious story arise about the highly civilized Martians who built great canals to irrigate the desert areas of their planet?

10. The great outer planets all have average densities much less than that of the earth; give a reasonable explanation for this observation.

11. What are the rings of Saturn composed of?

12. When the Russian satellite, Lunik I, sent back a photograph of the far side of the moon it was reported that the far side is much less rugged than the side we see. Assuming that the craters of the moon are due to the impacts of meteorites, try to think of a reasonable explanation for the Russian observation.

13. What could produce dust and loose debris on the floors of the craters on the moon?

14. Why do astronomers think that comets, meteors, and meteorites have a common origin?

15. Make brief notes about the lives and work of Tycho Brahe and Johannes Kepler.

16. Remembering the definition of the ellipse, as given in the glossary, try drawing one with a loop of string and two thumbtacks, and explain how this method works.

17. State Kepler's three laws of planetary motion; explain what the second law means.

18. Test Kepler's third law by computing (period of revolution)^2/(mean distance)^3 for the five planets which were known to Brahe and Kepler.

19. Describe how the distance of the moon has been determined.

20. Find the apparent difference, in minutes of arc, in the positions of the moon as seen from two observatories 1000 miles apart.

21. The average value of the apparent angular diameter of the moon is 32.55 minutes of arc; compute its diameter in miles.

22. Why is it impractical to measure the distance of the sun by the same method as that used for the moon? Describe in detail how the distance has been determined.

the laws of motion

To understand more about the solar system we must turn to a more general study of physics, and in particular to mechanics, the branch of physics that deals with moving bodies. In doing so, we make another fundamental metaphysical assumption, which, like those discussed in Sec. 1-3, may appear trivial and may be something that everyone takes for granted. Because we do take these things for granted nowadays it is important to pause and examine just what assumptions we are making. The assumption here is that the basic laws of physics are the same everywhere in the cosmos—on the earth, on the sun, and in the farthest galaxies.

Aristotle and his followers believed that the heavenly bodies were made of some finer, more "perfect" material than gross earth and stone. They believed that a stone falls to the ground because it has a desire to head for its natural location—as close as possible to the center of the earth which contains all the other gross material. They noticed how a stone falls vertically, whereas a leaf flutters to the ground, taking much longer than the stone. Misled by this observation as well as by philosophical arguments about the causes of fall, they made an erroneous generalization and concluded that the rate at which a body falls must increase with the weight.

It was Galileo who finally saw the fallacy in the traditional Aristotelian arguments and who realized that it is the resistance of the air that causes a leaf to flutter, or a block of wood to take a fraction of a second longer than a stone of the same size to fall from a given height. There is a story that has been repeated many times in history books to the effect that Galileo proved his point by dropping stones and cannonballs from the Leaning Tower of Pisa. Modern historical research has shown that the story is almost certainly mythical and that the demonstration was attributed to Galileo after his death by some of his admirers. However, in his arguments about falling bodies he followed the correct scientific procedure of eliminating—in imagination—the air as an irrelevant factor. There then follows the first law of falling bodies, which reads, in a modernized form:

In the absence of the air, all bodies would fall with the same speed at the same place on the earth's surface.

In Galileo's time "absence of the air" was an idealization of the circumstances surrounding the phenomenon, quite unattainable in practice. Nowadays it is possible to verify this part of the law, by removing most of the air from a long vertical tube with a vacuum pump, and showing that in a vacuum even a coin and a feather fall together (Fig. 4-1).

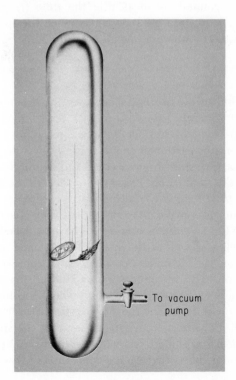

To vacuum pump

FIG. 4-1

The coin and feather experiment, to demonstrate that bodies of very different weights fall with the same speed in vacuum.

Galileo's observations with the telescope, his arguments about falling bodies, and his experiments on acceleration (Sec. 4-3) give him a strong claim to be considered the first great physicist of the modern tradition. He was one of the first to see that the first two steps of scientific method, observation and generalization, must be supplemented by the third step, confirmation, and that carefully planned experiments are a very important part of both observation and confirmation.

4-2   Velocity and Acceleration

In Galileo's time we see also the beginnings of another essential procedure of modern science. Physical experiments almost always involve measurement, and measurement involves careful definition of the thing to be measured (Sec. 5-1). At this point, therefore, we must begin to construct a logical sequence of definitions of the quantities encountered in a study of mechanics.

After the intuitive concepts of length (or distance) and time, the first concept to be encountered is that of *speed*. The definition is more or less implied when we define the units of measurement and say that speed will be stated in meters per second or miles per hour. Fundamentally, the speed (v) is determined by measuring the time (t) required for the body to traverse a measured distance (s), as when the speedometer of an automobile is tested by timing it over a measured mile. Then

$$v = \frac{s}{t}.$$

Strictly, this is the average speed over the time or the distance concerned, and we frequently have to deal with bodies moving with varying speeds. We then have to consider what we mean by the speed at a particular instant or at a particular point in the body's path. To do so, we have to imagine a very short time interval, and define the speed at a particular instant as the *ratio of the distance traveled to the time elapsed, in the limit when both of these are very small.*

We must also make a distinction between speed and velocity, and when we state the *velocity* of a body we have to specify the direction in which it is moving as well as the speed, for 60 miles per hour south is not the same thing as 60 miles per hour east, since one arrives at a different destination. This introduces a new kind of quantity, one which possesses direction as well as magnitude, and which is called a *vector*, in contrast to a *scalar* quantity, which has no direction, or for which the direction is irrelevant. For example, when we say that the speed limit is 60 miles per hour, this has nothing to do with direction, so "speed" is the correct word to use and it shows that we are concerned only with the scalar aspect.

We can generalize the idea of a very small change in a very small interval and define the limit of the ratio of change to interval as the *rate of change.*° For example, velocity can be considered as the rate of change of position. Then *acceleration is defined as rate of change of velocity*, where again we have to think of a very small change divided by the time interval during which the change takes place. The change of velocity may be in magnitude, or in direction, or in both, and so acceleration is, strictly speaking, always a vector quantity, possessing direction as well as amount. The correct metric unit of acceleration is (meters per second) per second, that is, change of velocity in meters per second divided by time in seconds. This is often written meters per second², indicating that we have divided by time twice. The popular unit, used mainly in discussing performance of automobiles, is (miles per hour) per second, which, however, is not the proper scientific unit since it involves arbitrary conversion factors.

4-3   Uniform Acceleration

Galileo seems to have been the first to use the concept of acceleration, although not in quite as explicit a form as we do today. In particular, he discussed the problem of motion with a constant acceleration and proved that the distance a body travels, starting from rest, is proportional to the (time)². Expressed in mathematical language the proof is quite simple, for the only mathematical technique required is that of elementary algebra.

Suppose a body starts from rest and travels for a time t seconds with a constant acceleration of a meters per second². In that time it will acquire a velocity of v meters per second (in the same direction as the acceleration) where

$$v = at.$$

Since the velocity is increasing at a uniform rate, the average velocity will be just ½v. Then the distance the body travels is s meters, where

$$s = \tfrac{1}{2}v \times t = \tfrac{1}{2}at^2.$$

Galileo believed that this should apply to a freely falling object, but a stone falling vertically moves much too fast for him to test his conclusion with the means at his disposal. Instead he experimented with balls rolling down inclined troughs and compared the time required to travel different distances on a given slope, as well as the time required on different slopes. His experiments confirmed his idea of constant acceleration, and so his final conclusion can be put in the form of a law expressing the second of his important contributions to the science of mechanics:

° Students who are familiar with calculus notation will recognize this as the derivative with respect to the time.

A body falling freely, or rolling down a uniform incline, moves with constant acceleration, and therefore the distance traveled is proportional° to the (time)^2.

Combining Galileo's two laws we can see that the acceleration of free fall is a definite quantity, although we know now that it varies slightly from place to place on the earth, depending on geographical latitude, on height above sea level, and to some extent on local topography. It is denoted conventionally by the symbol, g, for *acceleration due to gravity*, or briefly "gravity." The standard value is taken to be that at sea level in latitude 45°, where it is 9.80621 meters per second^2.

4-4   Newton's Laws of Motion

Galileo's laws of falling bodies and Kepler's laws of planetary motion are *empirical laws*. That is, they are generalized statements of observed facts, either of natural phenomena or of a set of experiments, without any attempt at explanation and without any statement concerning the cause of the phenomena. Furthermore, there is no apparent connection between the two sets of facts. The usefulness of empirical laws is strictly limited, and it is one of the general aims of science to reduce the number of independent laws to a minimum by expressing them as the logical consequences of a few fundamental principles. When we do so we may think that we have discovered the cause of the phenomena involved, or have "explained" them. In a way this is true, but we should remember that we have really only pushed the sequence of cause and effect a bit further back, and that we may still be a long way from the first cause or the ultimate explanation.

It was one of the greatest advances in the whole history of science when Sir Isaac Newton (1642–1727), with the inspiration of genius, saw that the fall of a stone and the motion of a planet around the sun had a common cause in *gravitational attraction*. However, before he could discuss gravitation, Newton had to put the science of mechanics on a firmer, better organized basis. This is summed up in his *Philosophiae naturalis principia mathematica†* in the *three laws of motion*. Along with a discussion of these laws must go definitions of the concepts of force, mass, and weight, and of the units of these quantities, none of which were fully understood until Newton clarified the whole subject.

° "Proportional" here, and elsewhere in statements of scientific laws, is used in its strict mathematical sense. "X proportional to Y" means that the ratio X/Y is constant.

† *Mathematical Principles of Natural Philosophy*. It was written in Latin, the international scholarly language of the time.

4-5   The First Law and the Concept of Force

Newton's first law can be stated as follows:

A body continues in its state of rest, or of uniform motion in a straight line, unless it is acted on by some external force.

This was implied in some of Galileo's statements, and is a flat contradiction of Aristotle's theories of causation. When a planet describes an orbit around the sun, the direction of its velocity is changing, and so it must be acted on by a force, which we shall shortly identify with the gravitational attraction exerted by the sun. If for some unimaginable reason this attraction should suddenly disappear, the planet must travel off into space with a constant velocity in a straight line. A man standing on the ground is actually traveling a thousand or so miles an hour in a circle around the axis of the earth, kept in orbit by the attraction of the earth. If the antigravity shield imagined by some fiction writers should ever come into existence, the man using it would fly off at a tangent, never to return, instead of executing the feats attributed to him in the story.

As already mentioned in connection with the heliocentric argument, motion is relative, and in discussion of the laws of motion the frame of reference must be stated or implied; in the case of a planet the motion is relative to the sun; in the other case cited it is relative to the center of the earth. It should be noted, also, that the first law is a drastic idealization—there never has been and never can be a real body which is actually moving in a straight line, or which does not have forces of some kind acting upon it.

Newton's first law leads directly to a definition of *force*. When this concept is first used it can be identified with the semi-intuitive idea of muscular effort—of a push, or a pull, or a lift. However, this is too vague for a satisfactory scientific definition, and it must now be clarified by saying:

Force is that which changes, or tends to change the state of motion of a body.

The qualification "tends to change" is important. Everyone is familiar with muscular efforts, that is, forces, which do not cause changes in the state of motion of any body. We can push against the wall of a building, or we can hold a rock in our hands, and we are conscious that we are exerting effort, but nothing happens. Force is a vector quantity, possessing direction as well as magnitude, and there are many cases where two or more forces acting in different directions on the same body combine so

Lift

Weight

FIG. 4-2

The weight of the rock and the lift exerted by the man are in equilibrium.

that the *resultant* (or net) force is zero. The forces are then said to be *in equilibrium.* The simplest case of equilibrium is that of two equal and opposite forces. The rock we are holding is subject to equal and opposite forces, the muscular lift acting upward, of which we are conscious, and the gravitational attraction of the earth acting downward. Similarly, a book resting on a table is in equilibrium under two equal and opposite forces, the downward gravitational attraction and an upward pressure exerted by the table top. That these are forces consistent with the definition is evident if we let go of the rock. It immediately starts to fall, accelerated by the gravitational attraction, which is now unbalanced—the state of motion of the rock is altered.

4-6   *Weight and Mass, Newton's Second Law*

Weight and mass are two quantities that are very often confused, partly because in popular usage the same name is used for the units of both—a pound can sometimes mean weight and sometimes mean mass.

Firstly, *the weight of a body is the gravitational attraction exerted upon it by the earth.*° Weight is therefore a force—the force that causes a body to fall to the ground, equal to the force required to support it, or the force that is just sufficient to lift it slowly. The weight of a body is not a constant quantity, since the force of attraction varies slightly from place to place upon the earth, and would be quite different on the moon or on another planet.

A body tends to resist changes in its state of motion, or to resist being set in motion (relative to the ground). Think of pushing a child on a tri-

° More generally, the attraction exerted by the planet on which the body is located.

cycle, and then think of pushing an automobile to start it rolling, or think of kicking a football and then of kicking a stone of about the same size. In the case of the heavier body a very much greater effort is required in order to produce the same motion. The heavier body is said to have more *inertia*, where inertia is defined as *that property of a body that causes it to resist changes in its state of motion. Mass* can than be defined as *synonymous with inertia.* Mass can also be identified with *quantity of matter,* matter being defined as *that which possesses mass or inertia.*°

It will help to clarify the distinction between mass and weight if you think of buying a 10-pound bag of sugar. When you pay for the sugar you are interested in the amount you are getting for your money, and so you are paying for mass. But when you carry the bag home you are conscious of the effort involved, and so you are interested in the weight. Or suppose you took the bag of sugar to the moon; you would still have 10 pounds-mass because you would still have the same amount of sugar and it would still possess the same inertia. However, you would only have to lift 1.66 pounds-weight because the gravitational attraction on the moon is only about ⅙ of that on earth. Again, think of rolling a 10-pound ball down a lunar bowling alley. You would only have to exert 1.66 pounds-force to pick the ball up, but the effort of throwing it would be the same as on earth, because you still have to overcome an inertia of 10 pounds-mass.

We are now ready for *Newton's second law of motion.* In its original form it states:

° In old textbooks mass was usually *defined* as quantity of matter, implying that we know intuitively what matter is. However, we cannot trust our intuition here, for it should be clear that the material does not necessarily make up the whole of human existence and reality, and so we may need a criterion to distinguish the material from the nonmaterial. There is also a technical objection to the old definition, in that the attracting mass that appears in the law of universal gravitation (Sec. 6-1) is not necessarily the same as the inertia that appears in the second law of motion. Very careful experiments have indicated that they are in fact identical, but this could not be assumed.

FIG. 4-3

You pay for mass but you lift weight.

The resultant force acting on a body is proportional to the rate of change of momentum, where momentum is defined as the product of the mass times the velocity.

In the case of a definite body with a constant mass, the momentum can only change through changes in the velocity, and the rate of change of velocity is the acceleration. For most practical purposes, therefore, the second law can be put in the form:

The force is proportional to the product of the mass times the acceleration.

However, in the case of a rocket or a similar object that propels itself by expelling matter, both the mass and the velocity are changing, and the law has to be used in its original, more rigorous form.

4-7   Units of Mass and Force

By international agreement scientists everywhere use the metric units of measurement, and for mechanical quantities they generally use a systematic set of units based upon the meter of length, the kilogram of mass, and the second of time, and therefore known as MKS units.° In developing the MKS mechanical units one starts with mass and defines the *kilogram* (1000 grams) as the *mass of a certain cylinder of platinum-iridium alloy known as the International kilogram,* which is preserved at the International Bureau of Weights and Measures at Sèvres, near Paris.

Newton's second law then permits the definition of an MKS unit of force. For a definite body the law states that force (F) is proportional to mass (m) times acceleration (a), or in symbols:

$$F \propto ma.$$

In this equation the mass is measured in kilograms and the acceleration in meters per second^2, but the units of the force have not yet been assigned. Following a logical procedure that will be frequently encountered in defining units, the unit of force is chosen in such a way that the constant of proportionality in the algebraic expression of the law is equal to unity, so that the sign of proportionality can be replaced by a sign of equality. The unit of force defined in this way is called a *newton,*† and the law can now

---

° There is also a CGS system of units, based on the centimeter, gram, and second, which was in general use for scientific purposes for many years, and is still often encountered. The CGS unit of force is the *dyne,* defined in a manner analogous to the newton.

† Many of the mechanical (and electrical) units of the MKS system are named after famous scientists or inventors whose work is in some way associated with the use of the unit. When used as a unit the name is written with a small letter.

be written

$$F \text{ (newtons)} = m \text{ (kilograms)} \times a \text{ (meters per second}^2\text{)}.$$

In this equation if m is put equal to 1 kilogram and a equal to 1 meter per second^2, then F is equal to 1 newton, and so the newton can be defined formally as *the force that will impart to a mass of 1 kilogram an acceleration of 1 meter per second^2.* The unit of force defined in this way is an absolute derived unit—absolute because it is the same everywhere, independent of local variations in the weight of the body—derived because it is defined in terms of other previously defined units, without the use of any arbitrary numerical factors.

Suppose a body of mass m kilograms is allowed to fall to the ground. Neglecting air resistance, its acceleration is the quantity we have denoted by g, the acceleration due to gravity (Sec. 4-3), approximately 9.8 meters per second^2. The force causing this acceleration is the weight (w) of the body, and so in MKS units weight is measured in newtons where

$$w \text{ (newtons)} = m \text{ (kilograms)} \times g \text{ (meters per second}^2\text{)}.$$

At any given location the acceleration g is the same for all bodies, and so weight and mass are proportional. A mass can therefore be *compared* with a standard by comparing the weights, and this is precisely what is done when a mass (that is, a quantity of matter) is measured by "weighing" it on a chemical balance (Fig. 4-4) or a grocer's scales.

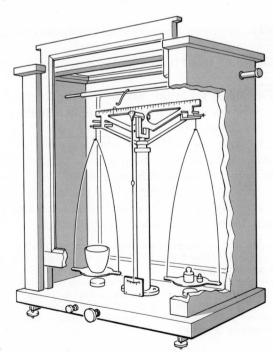

FIG. 4-4

A chemical balance.

In the everyday units used for commercial purposes in English-speaking countries—the FPS units based upon the foot, the pound, and the second—the units of force and mass are still somewhat confused because "pound" is commonly used for both. The Committee on Units and Nomenclature of the American Institute of Physics recommends the following procedure in order to avoid this confusion:

The *pound* is to be considered as a *unit of force* (or weight), and is *the weight of the standard pound* at sea level in latitude 45°, where the acceleration g has its standard value of 32.1725 feet per second². ° Then Newton's second law permits the definition of an absolute derived unit of mass, called a *slug*, and defined as *the mass in which a force of* 1 *pound will cause an acceleration of* 1 *foot per second².*† Again consider a body falling freely. The force acting on it is its own weight, say, w pounds, and Newton's law takes the form

w (pounds-force) $=$ m (slugs) $\times$ g (feet per second²).

Therefore the mass associated with a weight of w pounds is given by

m (slugs) $=$ w (pounds) $\div$ g (feet per second²).

4-8   Newton's Third Law, Action and Reaction

The *third law of motion* is usually stated in the simple form:

To every action there is an equal and opposite reaction.

In this statement the word "action" usually implies force—if one body exerts a force upon another there must be an opposite force of reaction on the first body. There are examples everywhere. When a gun is fired the bullet exerts a reaction on the gun, which recoils. The earth exerts a force of attraction on the moon to keep it in its proper orbit; the moon must attract the earth with an equal force, and this force causes the earth to deviate from a true elliptical orbit around the sun, by swinging about 3000 miles to either side of the ellipse each month, an amount which is easily detectable in modern astronomical observations.

° It follows that the true weight of the piece of metal that is labeled "1 pound," and that is used for *comparing* weights or masses on a balance, varies slightly from place to place, depending on the local value of gravity.

† The name "slug" for a unit of mass has not come into general use among those who use FPS mechanical units in their business, the engineers in English-speaking countries. However, most of them produce the same result by putting the inertia equal to w/g whenever it enters into their calculations. The slug has never been used as a commercial unit of quantity of matter—one still buys sugar by the pound.

If you pull on one end of a rope, the rope pulls back on you, and if the other end happened to be attached to a moving automobile, the rope would probably win, and it would be your own body whose state of motion was changed, in conformity with Newton's second law. A car propels itself by exerting a force on the road through its driving wheels. Normally the road is attached to a much more massive body—the earth—and the reaction force drives the car forward. If the road is not firmly attached—if it is soft sand, or slippery mud or snow—the road is driven backward and the car hardly moves.

"Action" in the statement of the third law can also imply change of momentum, and this point of view is useful in discussing collisions between different bodies, for example, the collision between two billiard balls, *A* and *B*. In this case a large force (described as an impulsive force) acts during the very short time that the balls are in contact. It is impossible to measure the force; instead the collision is characterized by measuring the total change of momentum, which is called the *impulse*. At every instant during the collision the reaction force of the struck ball *B* on the cue ball *A* is equal and opposite to the primary force exerted by *A* on *B*, and so the total changes of momentum are equal and opposite. When *A* imparts a certain impulse, or change of momentum, to *B*, *A* experiences an exactly equal impulse in the opposite direction—the net change of momentum of the pair of balls is zero.

As a final example of the application of the third law of motion, consider the launching of a spaceship by means of a rocket. The rocket propels itself by ejecting a stream of gas or smokelike particles with a very high velocity. A large force is exerted in accelerating the ejected material, and

FIG. 4-5

Launching of a Tiros weather satellite from Cape Kennedy, Florida. (Photograph courtesy of U.S. Weather Bureau.)

the reaction force accelerates the rocket in the opposite direction.° The forward momentum acquired by the rocket must be equal to the total backward momentum of the ejected particles. When the spaceship is in orbit it can navigate by firing small rockets in different directions to make slight changes in the orbit, that is, in the state of motion. Similarly, when an astronaut leaves his spaceship to take a "walk" in space, he can maneuver by ejecting short bursts from a cylinder of compressed gas.

GLOSSARY

Acceleration Rate of change of velocity, in speed, in direction, or in both.

Empirical law A generalized statement of observed facts, capable of being verified, but without any attempt at explanation.

Equilibrium The state such that two or more forces acting in different directions upon a body are balanced so that there is no tendency to motion.

Impulse Total change of momentum; the term is especially used when a very large force acts for a very short time.

Inertia The property of a body that causes it to resist being set in motion; equal to the mass.

Meters per second^2 Abbreviation for (meters per second) per second, the MKS unit of acceleration.

MKS units The consistent system of units derived from the meter of length, the kilogram of mass, and the second of time.

Momentum The product of mass times velocity.

Newton The unit of force in the MKS system.

Resultant The sum, or combined effect of two or more vector quantities when their direction is taken into account as well as their magnitude.

Scalar quantity A quantity which has no direction, or for which the direction is irrelevant.

Slug Unit of mass in the absolute foot-pound-second system.

Vector quantity A quantity that possesses direction as well as magnitude.

Velocity Speed in a specified direction.

° The question frequently heard: "How can a rocket propel itself in empty space, where there is nothing for the expelled gas to push against?" reveals a complete misunderstanding of the rocket principle. Actually, a rocket is more efficient in empty space, where there is no opposing friction.

EXERCISES

1. Galileo, Kepler, and Newton were able to make the progress they did because they made a third a priori assumption, in addition to those discussed in Chapter 1. What was this assumption, and how did it run counter to the ideas of Galileo's traditionalist contemporaries?

2. State Galileo's first law of falling bodies. Explain why this law is an idealization as well as a generalization.

3. Define "speed" and "velocity," and distinguish between the two terms. Explain what is meant by the velocity at a given instant, or at a given point of a body's path.

4. Define "acceleration." Give examples of motions that are accelerated by (a) change of speed only, (b) change of direction only.

5. State Galileo's second law. What quantity is constant under the conditions where this law applies? How did Galileo test the law?

6. Neglecting the effect of the air, how far would a stone fall in 5 seconds? (Take $g = 32$ feet per second^2).

7. The Leaning Tower of Pisa is 54 meters high. How long would it take a stone to fall this distance? (Take $g = 9.8$ meters per second^2). Supposing there were no wind, do you think the same answer would apply to a man's body? to a block of wood? to a small grain of sand? to a raindrop? to a leaf? If you think the answer would be different, give your reason.

8. State Newton's first law of motion. What is defined with the aid of this law? To what extent is the law an idealization?

9. Give two forms of Newton's second law, expressing them both in words and in mathematical symbols. Why is the form that has the simpler mathematical expression sometimes limited in its application?

10. Define "mass" and "weight," and distinguish clearly between the two terms. Mass is often defined as "quantity of matter"; why is this definition unsatisfactory?

11. Find the force in newtons required to give a car of mass 1500 kilograms an acceleration of 1.2 meters per second^2. What will be the velocity after 10 seconds, and how far will the car have traveled in this time?

12. Find the force in pounds-weight required to accelerate 3200 pounds-mass to a velocity of 44 feet per second (30 miles per hour) in 6 seconds. (Take $g = 32$ feet per second^2).

13. What is the velocity acquired if a force of 80 newtons acts on a mass of 25 kilograms for 4 seconds?

14. State Newton's third law; give three simple examples.

15. According to Newton's third law there must be a reaction to the force that accelerates an automobile; where is this reaction?

16. Where is the reaction of the earth's attraction for the moon? What effect does this cause, if any?

17. Comparing different planets, the acceleration due to gravity is proportional to the mass divided by the (radius)^2. Find the acceleration on the moon and on Mars.

18. The members of an expedition to the moon decide to have a game of baseball. (a) How much does the ball weigh? (A standard baseball weighs 5 ounces.) (b) The batter finds the ordinary bat so light that he does not think he is hitting anything with it, and so he gets one that weighs about five times as much. Can he hit the ball any harder with this bat than he could with the ordinary one, supposing that he exerts all his strength in both cases? (c) Suppose that on earth he is capable of driving the ball 300 feet, and that he gives it an equal blow in the course of the game on the moon. How far will the ball travel?

measurement

5-1 The Importance of Measurement

Physics is an exact science; most of its laws express quantitative relations between two or more measurable quantities, such as the relation between force, mass, and acceleration in Newton's second law of motion (Sec. 4-6), or the law which gives the force of repulsion between two electric charges (Sec. 14-4). Other important laws state that the total amount of a measurable quantity, for example the total mass of the reacting materials in a chemical reaction (Sec. 9-4), remains constant throughout the action. It is precisely because the laws of physical science are quantitative that such tremendous progress has been possible during our scientific age.

In order to establish a quantitative law, or to make use of the law, the quantities involved have to be measured. The development and improvement of methods of measurement have therefore played a large part in the progress of physical science. Before starting a series of measurements, we must decide just what it is that we wish to measure, and this is not always as simple as it sounds. It involves giving precise definitions of such terms as mass, acceleration, energy, and the dozens of others that are encountered in the course of a study of physical science. Once the quantity to be measured has been properly defined, it is necessary to select a standard, that is, a unit. Finally, we must devise a method of comparing the quantity to be measured with the standard, so as to determine the number of units contained in it. Some simple examples to be given in this chapter will illustrate the procedure; other examples will occur as the study proceeds.

5-2   Measurement of Length

Not all measurable quantities are capable of, or require, precise definition. In building up a sequence of definitions we have to begin somewhere, and so we have to assume that certain basic quantities have a meaning which is known intuitively through common sense. Two such intuitive concepts are length and the lapse of time. For these it is necessary only to define units and to devise methods of comparison.

At the time of the French Revolution the new government wanted to break with all old royalist traditions. One sensible and lasting break they made was to discard all the complicated and nonuniform weights and measures and coinage which had prevailed, not only in France, but throughout Europe. A committee of scientists was appointed to revise the weights and measures, and in 1799 this committee recommended the adoption of a decimal system based on a suggestion that had been made a few years earlier by a group of scientists. The committee expanded the original suggestion into what we now know as the *metric system,* and a government decree made this the legal system in France. Use of the new units was resisted at first, but gradually the simplicity and convenience of a consistent international system became recognized, and by the end of the nineteenth century metric units had been adopted throughout continental Europe. Today they are the internationally accepted basic standards; they are the units in day-to-day use in most foreign countries, and are used in all scientific work.

The original metric system was based on the unit of length, the *meter,* which was intended to be 1/10,000,000 of the distance from the equator to the North Pole, but for convenience a platinum bar was made, as nearly as possible equal to the required length. Later, after the International Bureau of Weights and Measures was organized, a new bar was made from platinum-iridium alloy (Fig. 5-1), and this is now preserved at the Bureau's establishment at Sèvres, near Paris. It was also found that there was a small error in the survey of the earth's circumference on which the original meter had been based, and rather than change everything the platinum alloy bar was made the legal standard.

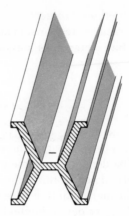

FIG. 5-1

The standard meter.

Until recently, therefore, the meter was defined by international agreement as the distance between two marks on the bar at Sèvres, when it is packed in melting ice. This is still the practical standard, but the International Committee has never been entirely happy about basing all measurements, all over the world, on a single physical object, and in 1959 the definition was changed to read: 1,650,763.73 times the wavelength of the orange line in the spectrum of krypton 86.

Similarly, there is a physical standard *yard*, in the form of a certain metal bar preserved in London, England. However, in the United States the yard has long been *defined* for legal purposes as a certain fraction, $3600/3937$, of a meter,° and the same practice is now followed in all countries where the yard, foot, and inch are still used as the popular measures of commerce. The standard metal bars of the meter and the yard are not subdivided into centimeters† or inches; this is done only on copies that are used for day-to-day practical measurements.

We shall not attempt to describe the many ingenious methods that have been devised for measuring very large or very small lengths, where it is not feasible simply to lay a meterstick beside the unknown length. However, we must notice how the comparison with the international standard is carried out step by step, by the use of substandards. The meter bar itself is handled infrequently. Copies of it have been made, as exact as possible, and these have been distributed to all the governments that support the International Bureau by their contributions, along with a statement of the minute error in each copy. These national copies again are rarely handled,

° It follows from this definition of the yard that a meter is precisely 39.37 inches.

† Readers should remember the most common of the prefixes that are used throughout the metric system to denote fractions and multiples of any of the units: centi- means 1/100; milli-, 1/1000; micro-, 1/1,000,000; nano-, 1/1,000,000,000; kilo-, 1000; mega-, 1,000,000; giga-, 1,000,000,000.

and are used only in central government laboratories to certify standards (of stainless steel or similar material) for distribution to companies that manufacture metersticks, surveyor's tapes, and other measuring instruments.

Another measurable quantity, the concept of which can be considered intuitive, is time, meaning here lapse of time, the time required for something to be done, or for some change to take place, rather than time of day or calendar date. In this sense we are all conscious of the passage of time, and no further definition is necessary, but we have to choose a standard, and we have to devise methods of comparison.

For lapse of time there is a rather obvious natural unit, the day. But the length of the day from noon to noon (when the sun is directly south) varies during the course of the year. It is longer than average at the summer and winter solstices and when the earth is closest to the sun in January; it is less than average at the spring and fall equinoxes. Therefore, until quite recently, the basic unit of time was the *mean solar day*, the average time from noon to noon. A great many measurements in science and engineering are of quite short time intervals, and so the commonly used unit, in both metric and British systems, is the *second*, which was defined as $\frac{1}{86,400}$ of a mean solar day. The time of day, conveniently described as "clock time," is then the elapsed time since some definite moment.

Almost all practical time measurements—comparisons with the unit—depend on the observation of some periodic motion, something that is repeated at regular intervals. The day itself depends on the rotation of the earth on its axis, and the year on the earth's orbital motion around the sun. Galileo is credited with the discovery that the regular period of swing of a pendulum is independent of the extent of the swing. Ever since his time most good clocks have been controlled by a swinging pendulum. Similarly, a watch is controlled by the oscillations of the balance wheel and hairspring.

Along with the development of electricity, a number of devices have been invented for controlling the oscillations of an alternating electric current. The alternating current can then be used to operate the hands of a clock, to make regular time marks on a moving strip of paper, or on a photographic film, and in many other ways. For example, the familiar household electric clock keeps accurate time because the generators at the central powerhouse are kept rotating at a constant speed under the control of a master clock. The electrical output from the powerhouse then alternates very accurately at (usually) 60 cycles per second. The result is that in most parts of the country a standard time interval of $\frac{1}{60}$ second is available by plugging into any electrical outlet.

Just as in the matter of the standardization of length measurements, there has to be a step-by-step comparison with the basic standard. Central astronomical observatories in Washington, in Greenwich, England, in Ottawa, and in many other national capitals, have very precisely built standard clocks, and these are compared with the apparent motion of the stars every clear night. In this case the basic timekeeper is really the rotation of the earth on its axis, but, since the difference between the earth's period of rotation and the average solar day is very accurately known, the reduction of the star observations to time in terms of mean solar days of 86,400 seconds is easily made. The standard clock is never adjusted by moving its hands; if it runs a little fast or slow it is corrected by making a small adjustment of movable weights on the pendulum bob. The standard observatory clock, itself adjusted by comparison with the stars, is used to control the electric circuit that sends out the well-known time signals over the radio, at noon each day. The radio time signal can be used to adjust other clocks, all over the country.

5-4   Measurement of Mass

In the metric system of units the third basic quantity is *mass,* which was discussed in Sec. 4-6, and the standard unit is the international kilogram at Sèvres. The gram was originally intended to be the mass of a cubic centimeter of water at its temperature of maximum density (4°C), but, as happened in establishing the meter, a slight error was made in reproducing the standard, and the international standard is the actual platinum-iridium cylinder.*

The commercial unit of mass, in the sense of quantity of material, in English-speaking countries is the pound, which was originally the mass of a certain block of gold preserved in London, but which is now defined as

1 pound-mass = 0.45359243 kilogram.

Except for very large and very small quantities, most practical measurements of mass are direct comparisons with a standard, using various modifications of the familiar chemical balance. As in the case of length, there are national copies of the international kilogram, secondary standards, and legalized substandards, so that there is a step-by-step chain of comparisons from the platinum cylinder at Sèvres down to the swinging mass in the scale at the grocery store.

---

* The volume occupied by a kilogram of pure water at 4°C is a *liter,* which is the unit used for selling gasoline or wine in European countries. It is equal to 1000.027 cubic centimeters, but it does not concern us here because it is not the properly derived MKS unit of volume, which is the cubic meter.

The units of length, time, and mass are arbitrary. This is obvious when we consider the meter and the kilogram, which are based on particular objects. It is not quite so obvious in the case of the second, but one has only to realize that this is based upon an arbitrary choice of a quantity that occurs in nature. It is desirable to keep the number of arbitrary units in use to the absolute minimum, and, as far as possible, to define the units of other quantities in terms of those already defined, without introducing any arbitrary numerical factors.

For example, area can be measured in square meters or square feet, volume in cubic meters or cubic feet, speed in meters per second or feet per second. On the other hand, mile per hour as a unit of speed is not a proper derived unit, because it involves the arbitrary factors:

1 mile = 5280 feet,
1 hour = 3600 seconds,

with the result:

1 mile per hour = 5280/3600 = 22/15 feet per second.

No more than three arbitrary units are needed in order to define units of all the quantities which have to be discussed in the science of mechanics, that branch of physics which deals with forces and motion. The three units might be selected in a number of different ways, but, for scientific purposes, convention has now settled upon the meter of length, the kilogram of mass, and the second of time. The selected arbitrary units are referred to as *fundamental units*. Based upon them, the complete MKS system of logically derived units is constructed, and these suffice for the measurement of all mechanical quantities. An additional arbitrary definition has to be used for the degree of temperature, and an arbitrary numerical factor has to be introduced in order to extend the system to include measurements in electricity and magnetism. Effectively, therefore, five fundamental units are needed in all.

The great advantage of using a consistent system of derived units is that an elaborate numerical computation, or an algebraic manipulation, can be carried through without introducing any numerical conversion factors (such as the number of feet in a mile), and the result will automatically be expressed in the appropriate unit of the system. A disadvantage, and one reason why other metric units survive, even in scientific circles, is that the proper MKS unit may not be a convenient size for a particular measurement. Consistent use of the system frequently introduces very small or very large numbers,° and it does sound a little absurd to state the thickness of a fine wire in meters, or the mass of the sun in kilograms.

5-6 *Revision of the Units*

From time to time improvements in methods of measurement make it necessary to reconsider the definitions of some of the units, both fundamental and derived, and this is one of the functions of the International Bureau of Weights and Measures, when they hold their full meetings every four years. It would not seriously affect the average citizen, or even the ordinary scientist in his laboratory, if the original standard meter or kilogram should be damaged or destroyed. However, it could lead to legal complications, and those concerned with standardization have decided that it is not satisfactory to base all our measurements on two completely arbitrary pieces of metal. This is why the meter has now been redefined as a certain number of wavelengths of the light emitted by a krypton atom. This can be reproduced as accurately as necessary at any time, and the question of damage or loss will not arise. †

Much more serious is the case of the second, which is basically derived from the period of rotation of the earth on its axis. It has long been suspected that the earth's rotation might be slowing down, and recently this suspicion has been confirmed by comparing astronomical time with the time kept by some of the supremely precise clocks now available. The ocean tides, flowing toward and away from the continental coasts twice a day, cause friction, and since it is the earth's rotation which causes the tide to appear to flow around the earth each half day, the friction must react to retard the speed of rotation. The amount is extremely small; the length of the day is increasing by about ⅟₁₀₀₀ second in 100 years. But the effect is cumulative. The earth has been spinning on its axis, and the tides have been washing the shores of the oceans for over 4 billion years. Assuming that the estimated rate of slowing down has been constant, the accumulated amount would be 40,000 seconds, or about 11 hours. This is probably too low, since the moon was closer to the earth in early days, and the tides would have been greater. The conclusion is that when the earth first formed oceans it had a "day" only 9 or 10 hours long.

Here is a case where improved techniques have made the method of

---

° The scientist deals with very large and very small quantities by means of the power-of-10 notation, which will be frequently encountered in this book. 10^n means a unit followed by n zeros; for example, $10^9 = 1,000,000,000 =$ one billion. 10^{-n} means $1/10^n$; for example, $10^{-6} = 1/1,000,000 = 0.000001 =$ one millionth. In this notation a quantity like 7,360,000,000 is written 7.36×10^9; 0.00000736 is written 7.36×10^{-6}.

† A satisfactory way of redefining the kilogram has not yet been agreed upon.

comparison more precise than the basic standard, so that fluctuations in the standard have been discovered. There are other similar examples in the history of measurement, and when it happens, the standard has to be redefined, even though the amount involved is so small as to seem of no practical importance. The International Bureau has therefore recommended that the second be defined as 1/31,556,925.9747 of the year 1900. In terms of this unit, the mean solar day in 1965 was 86,400.0007 seconds.

5-7   *Precision of Measurement*

No measurement can ever be absolutely exact. In all measurements, and in all statements of numerical quantities, the limits of the possible (or probable) error have to be considered. For example, suppose we measure the length of a rod with a meterstick which has a scale divided in millimeters. Probably we note the millimeter marks closest to the ends of the rod, and state the result as, say, 736 millimeters, or 0.736 meter. Clearly, this statement could be in error by as much as half a millimeter, but very likely there is no need to be more precise, or in fact the thing we are trying to measure does not justify closer precision. Possibly the ends of the rod are not quite square, or are scarred with marks of the saw, so that its "length" is somewhat indefinite. Possibly the meterstick is not quite true. Even if we have tested it and know it is reliable, the millimeter marks have a certain width.

Where a single definite measurement, such as a length, is made carefully, using an instrument known to be reliable, a good working rule for the precision, or limit of error, is that it is one-half of the smallest division on the scale. The measurement used as an example above is said to have three *significant figures*, or to be a three-figure measurement, and this is the case whether it is given as 736 millimeters, 0.736 meter, or even as 0.000736 kilometer.

Again, the quantity to be measured, or the method of measurement may be of such a nature that successive measurements differ among themselves by more than the smallest division on the scale. For example, we might want the effective diameter of a rod which is not quite circular and not quite uniform along its length. In this instance we would make a number of measurements in different places and in different directions at each place, and take the average. The precision of the result is then very often indicated by giving the "probable error." This quantity is calculated statistically, and is defined in such a way that there is a 50 per cent chance that the measured average differs from the "true" value by less than the probable error.

Finally, it must be noted that a computed result which involves measurements of several different quantities cannot be more accurate than the least precise of the factors involved.

Arbitrary units Units whose definitions depend upon a specified physical object or natural phenomenon, or which involve an arbitrary numerical factor.

Derived units Units whose definitions depend only upon other units that have already been defined—therefore eventually upon the set of fundamental units —without the introduction of any numerical factors.

Fundamental units Those particular arbitrary units from which a consistent system of units is built up.

Probable error Deviation from a measured or computed numerical figure such that there is a 50 per cent chance that the true value differs from the measured value by less than the probable error.

Significant figures Those digits in the numerical expression of a measurement which the experimenter looked for and which he recorded, or, in the case of a computed quantity, those digits of whose accuracy he is confident (see Sec. 5-7). The number of figures that are significant is an indication of the precision of the measurement.

1. (a) Find examples of laws that state that one quantity (X) is proportional to another quantity (Y). (b) Find examples of laws that state that the total amount of a certain quantity is constant.

2. What are the three steps involved in the preparation for any measurement? As an example, discuss these steps in the case of velocity.

3. How and when did the metric system of units come into being?

4. Give three definitions of the meter: (a) that of the original committee; (b) that in use for many years; (c) that which is legal today.

5. An approximate rule for converting metric measurements to feet and inches is 1 meter = 40 inches. How much error is made in using this rule? Express the error as a percentage of the measurement.

6. Use the rule in Exercise 5 to find the approximate number of centimeters in a foot.

7. Check the accuracy of the approximate rules, 1 kilometer = ⅝ mile, 1 kilogram = 2.2 pounds.

8. A liter was originally intended to be 1000 cubic centimeters. Why is this no longer quite correct?

9. Who decides upon the proper definitions of the units of measurement? Who is ultimately responsible for seeing that measuring instruments in daily use are properly graduated?

10. Trace the steps which lead (a) from the basic definition of the meter to the inch marks on a carpenter's rule; (b) from the basic kilogram to the graduations on a grocery store balance; (c) from the definition of the second to the second hand on an electric wall clock.

11. Why has it recently been necessary to change the definition of the second?

12. Convert 60 miles per hour to meters per second, correct to three figures; convert 20 meters per second to miles per hour.

13. Express the following quantities in the appropriate MKS units, using the power-of-10 notation: 174,000,000 meters; 149,500,000 kilometers; 1/2,000,000 milligram; 56 nanoseconds; 10,000 days.

14. Write out the following quantities in ordinary decimal notation, using MKS units: 5.975×10^{24} kilograms; 6.37×10^{6} meters; 1.673×10^{-24} gram; 1.08×10^{-8} centimeter.

15. Express 4.55 billion years in seconds, using the power-of-10 notation and giving the result to the appropriate number of significant figures.

gravitation and the earth, sun, and moon

In this chapter we shall explain how Newton brought together the terrestrial mechanics of bodies moving about on the surface of the earth, or falling to the ground, and the celestial mechanics of planets revolving around the sun, and showed how both follow from one fundamental principle. On the one hand we have Galileo's ideas about falling bodies and about acceleration, as clarified and organized in Newton's own three laws of motion; on the other hand we have Kepler's empirical laws of planetary motion. Then the unifying principle is Newton's *law of universal gravitation:*

Every particle in the cosmos attracts every other particle with a force which is proportional to the product of their masses, and inversely proportional to the square of the distance between them.

In symbols, the force between two particles of masses (m_1 and m_2) separated by a distance (d) is given by

73

$$F = \frac{Gm_1m_2}{d^2},$$

where G is a "universal constant," one of the fundamental quantities of nature—the same everywhere in the cosmos. Its numerical value depends on the system of units used, but its amount must be connected with the intrinsic properties of space itself, in a way we still do not understand.

6-2   *The Moon and the Apple*

Newton devised a simple numerical test of the law of gravitation by comparing the force exerted by the earth on the moon with that exerted on an apple falling from a tree.[°] Let E be the mass of the earth, and R be its mean radius. Then, by the law of gravitation, the force of attraction on an apple of mass, m, is equal to its weight, and we have

$$mg = \frac{GEm}{R^2}.$$

Canceling m, the acceleration of free fall should be given by

$$g = \frac{GE}{R^2},$$

which depends only on the mass of the *attracting* body, here the earth.

Now consider the moon, and for purposes of this approximate numerical comparison, treat it as traveling in a circular orbit of radius (D meters) equal to its mean distance from the earth, with a period (P seconds). If a body is moving with constant speed in a circle, its velocity is continually changing in direction (Fig. 6-1); therefore it has an acceleration which is always directed toward the center of the circle. This is the so-called *centripetal acceleration,* and the corresponding force is the centripetal force which has to be exerted in order to keep the body in its circle instead of letting it continue in a straight line.

We shall omit the proof of the theorem involved, and simply state that the centripetal acceleration is given by

$$a = \frac{v^2}{r},$$

[°] Mention of an apple in this connection refers, of course, to the oft-repeated story about Isaac Newton. He is supposed to have been lying on his back in his orchard, pondering the causes of motion, when an apple fell from the tree above and hit him on the head, whereupon he was struck with the solution of his problem, and he then proceeded to work it out in detail. It is a nice story, and quite in keeping with Newton's character, but is probably mythical.

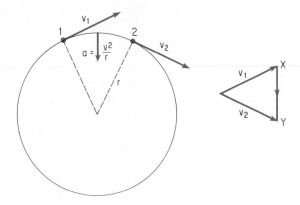

FIG. 6-1

A body moving uniformly in a circle. The instantaneous velocity at the points 1 and 2 is represented by the arrows marked v_1 and v_2. The change in velocity is proportional to the length XY and is directed toward the center of the circle.

where v is the speed and r is the radius of the circle. In the case of the moon $v = 2\pi D/P$, and so we have

$$a = \frac{4\pi^2 D}{P^2} = \frac{GE}{D^2}$$

by Newton's law of gravitation.

If we divide the equation for the moon into the equation for free fall, on both sides, the still unknown factors, G and E, cancel out, and we are left with

$$\frac{g}{a} = \frac{gP^2}{4\pi^2 D} = \frac{D^2}{R^2}.$$

In this we can substitute the known numerical values: $g = 9.806$ meters per second^2, $P = 27.32 \times 86{,}400$ seconds, $D = 3.844 \times 10^8$ meters, and the result is

$$3600.3 = (60.263)^2 = 3631.6.$$

The difference is less than 1 per cent, which can be considered satisfactory agreement when we remember that we have neglected several factors, and have used an approximation for the moon's orbit.

6-3   Gravitation and Kepler's Laws

It remains to show that Kepler's laws of planetary motion (Sec. 3-12) are a consequence of Newton's law of gravitation. The arguments are necessarily mathematical, and we shall not give them in detail, but merely state the results of the three important theorems involved.

The first of these theorems states that for any body moving in a *central orbit,* that is, in such a way that the acceleration (and therefore the force) is always directed toward a fixed center, the rate of description of area must be constant. Kepler's second law therefore follows from the fact that the principal force acting on a planet is the attraction of the sun, and all other forces are negligible in comparison. Similarly, the motion of the moon around the earth and of the satellites of the other planets is determined primarily by the force of attraction of the parent planet.

The second theorem relates the shape of the central orbit to the way in which the attracting force varies with distance from the fixed center. If the force varies inversely as (distance)^2, as stated by Newton's law, the orbit must be either a hyperbola, a parabola, or an ellipse, with focus at the attracting center. Hyperbolic and parabolic orbits, which are open-ended, may sometimes occur for stray comets which make one passage around the sun and then fly off into space, never to return.[*] The only possible closed, periodic orbit is the ellipse, and so Kepler's first law follows from the fact that the force of attraction is proportional to $1/d^2$.

Finally, if there are several comparatively small satellites or planets revolving in circular orbits around the same very much larger central body of mass (M), the algebra of Sec. 6-2 shows that

$$\frac{4\pi^2 D}{P^2} = \frac{GM}{D^2},$$

or

$$\frac{P^2}{D^3} = \frac{4\pi^2}{GM},$$

and Newton's more complete mathematics showed that this also holds for elliptical orbits if D is the mean distance. The right-hand side of this equation involves only the central body, and therefore Kepler's third law,

$$\textbf{(period)}^2 \propto \textbf{(mean distance)}^3,$$

must hold when we compare the different planets of the solar system, the different satellites of a particular planet, or an artificial earth satellite with the moon.

6-4   The Constant of Gravitation and the Mass of the Earth

In Sec. 6-2 it was shown that the acceleration of a falling body is given by

$$g = \frac{GE}{R^2},$$

---

[*] When the Mariner space probes passed near Venus and Mars the portions of their paths close to the planets approximated hyperbolic orbits.

where E and R are the mass and radius of the earth, respectively, and G is the constant of universal gravitation. Similarly, the product (GE) appears in the expression for the acceleration of the moon toward the earth, and it turns out that whenever the earth is one of the two masses involved in Newton's law of gravitation, E is bound to appear only as a factor in this product. Therefore, in order to determine the mass of the earth, by itself, in kilograms or tons, we need an additional piece of information.

The necessary information can be obtained by means of an experiment to determine the constant (G) by measuring the force of attraction between two masses, both of which are known. As G is one of the basic universal constants of nature, it is important to know its numerical value as accurately as possible, and a number of different experimental methods of determining it have been devised. One of the simplest experiments of the kind, although neither the earliest nor the most accurate, was that carried out by von Jolly at Munich in 1881.

The experiment is illustrated in Fig. 6-2. A sphere (M_1) of about 5 kilograms-mass was suspended by a long wire from one pan of a very precise chemical balance, and the weights required to balance it as accurately as possible were placed in the other pan. A large lead sphere (M_2), weighing about 5800 kilograms, was then wheeled under M_1, so that the distance (d) from center to center was about 0.6 meter. The lead sphere exerted an attraction on M_1, according to Newton's law, but the weights in the

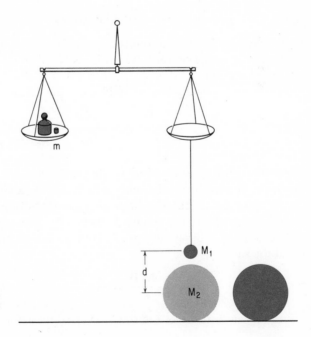

FIG. 6-2

Von Jolly's method of determining the constant of universal gravitation.

other pan were far enough away for the attraction upon them to be negligible. The balance was therefore disturbed, and a small mass (m) had to be added to the other pan to restore it. The weight of m must be equal to the gravitational attraction between the two spheres, or

$$mg = \frac{GM_1M_2}{d^2}.$$

In this equation the distance and all the masses are known, and so the constant G can be calculated.

Simple in conception, and simple to describe, the experiment was nevertheless by no means easy to carry out, because the added mass (m) was only 0.6 milligram in a total of 5 kilograms, and it was very difficult to measure it accurately. There are several better methods, all of them dependent on measuring—in various ingenious ways—the force of attraction between two spheres of known mass. The result quoted in the latest tables of physical constants is an average of the most precise modern measurements, and is

$$G = 6.668 \times 10^{-11} \text{ MKS units.}$$

This means that the attraction between two spheres, each of 1 kilogram, 1 meter apart, would be 6.668×10^{-11} newton.

We can substitute this value into the expression given above for the acceleration of free fall and obtain a value for the mass of the earth,

$$E = 5.977 \times 10^{24} \text{ kilograms.}$$

When we come to discuss the internal structure of the earth we shall need to know the average density, which is obtained simply by dividing the above figure for the total mass by the volume, $\frac{4}{3}\pi R^3$. The result is 5522 kilograms per cubic meter, or 5.522 times the density of water.

6-5 Masses of the Sun and Planets

Having determined the constant of universal gravitation, we can now calculate the mass of any heavenly body which has a satellite revolving around it. The problem is the same in principle as that of the acceleration of the moon in its orbit around the earth (Sec. 6-2). Thus, using average values and treating the orbit as very nearly circular, the acceleration of the earth toward the sun is

$$a_{\text{earth}} = \frac{4\pi^2 D}{P^2} = \frac{GM_{\text{sun}}}{D^2},$$

where D is the mean distance of the sun, expressed in meters, and P is the length of the year, in seconds. This gives

$$M_{sun} = 1.991 \times 10^{30} \text{ kilograms,}$$

or 333,420 times the mass of the earth. This in turn gives a mean density
for the sun of 1.410 times the density of water.

Since Mars, Jupiter, Saturn, Uranus, and Neptune all have satellites
revolving around them in well-determined orbits, the masses of these
planets have been accurately known for many years (see Table 3-1). Venus
has no known natural satellite, but it exerts an attraction on the innermost
planet, Mercury, and this causes a perturbation in the orbit of Mercury,
making it deviate appreciably from the proper ellipse. This, and the similar
but smaller effect of Venus on the earth's orbit, were until recently the
only source of information for an estimate of the mass of Venus. However,
when the space probe, Mariner II, described a partial orbit around Venus,
it was watched very carefully and it became possible to compute the
mass of the planet as accurately as those of any of the others.

If Venus exerts a force on Mercury, the latter must react on Venus and
cause a similar type of perturbation in the orbit. However, because Mercury is smaller than Venus the effect of the reaction is less, and because
the orbit of Venus is very nearly circular the perturbation is difficult
to measure accurately. As a result it has been possible to make only a rough
estimate of the mass of Mercury. Similarly, the mass of Pluto has been
roughly estimated from the very small perturbation that its attraction
causes in the orbit of Neptune.

6-6   The Ocean Tides and the Mass of the Moon

It is a commonplace that the ocean tides are caused mainly by the attraction
of the moon, but why are there two tides daily, with a high tide on the
side of the earth remote from the moon at the same time as on the
side near the moon? The force exerted by the moon, of mass M, on each
kilogram of the solid earth is GM/D^2 newtons per kilogram (Fig. 6-3). The

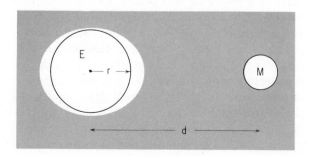

FIG. 6-3

The tide-raising force of
the moon.

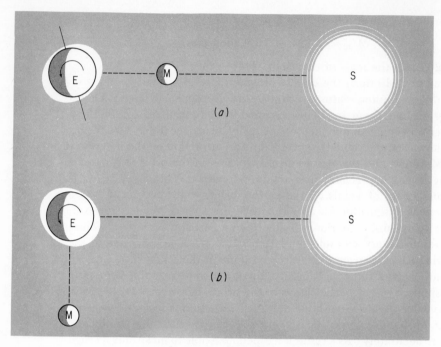

FIG. 6-4

The lunar and solar tides: (a) spring tide; (b) neap tide.

force on the water on the side near the moon is $GM/(D - R)^2$ newtons per kilogram, which is somewhat greater, and the water is, so to speak, pulled away from the earth. On the far side, the attraction per kilogram of water is $GM/(D + R)^2$, which is less than that on the solid earth; the earth is pulled away from the water. The result is that the water rises in a bulge on both sides of the earth, as shown, greatly exaggerated, in the diagram.

Figure 6-3 depicts the situation that would arise if the moon alone were responsible for the tides, and if the earth were at rest relative to the moon, or rather if it kept the same face turned always toward the moon, as the moon does toward the earth. Actually, the sun also exerts a tide-raising force, and the earth is rotating, so that the real situation is that shown in Fig. 6-4. The earth's rotation drags the tidal bulge with it, so that the highest ocean level is somewhat in advance of the line to the moon. The bulge maintains this position relative to the moon and sun as the earth rotates, and so, relative to the solid earth, there appear to be two long, shallow waves in the ocean, traveling around the earth once a day. On account of the moon's orbital motion, the earth's rotation period relative to the moon is 24 hours 49 minutes, and so the average interval between successive high tides is 12 hours 25 minutes. Because the north-south axis of rotation of the earth is inclined to the moon's orbit, the two high tides are not of equal height, and the intervals between successive highs are not equal in length.

In the open ocean, far from any extensive land mass, the wave of the tides, the "bulge" shown in the diagrams, is only 2 to 4 feet high. As the wave approaches the coast of a continent, the water tends to pile up, so that the rise and fall of the tide on the continental shore can be very much greater, and strong currents of ebb and flow can be set up. The highest tides in the world occur in the Bay of Fundy on the Atlantic coast of America (Fig. 6-5), where the difference between the extreme high and extreme low tide is over 60 feet at the head of the bay. The tidal current sweeps up the East coast of the continent, and a large volume of water has to funnel into the bay, to pile up at its head. There are rivers flowing into the Bay of Fundy which at low tide are mere trickles of water in a muddy trough, but at high tide are brim full of seawater, so that quite large ships can sail up the river and dock at a town several miles from the open sea.

FIG.   6-5

Funneling of the tide into the Bay of Fundy.

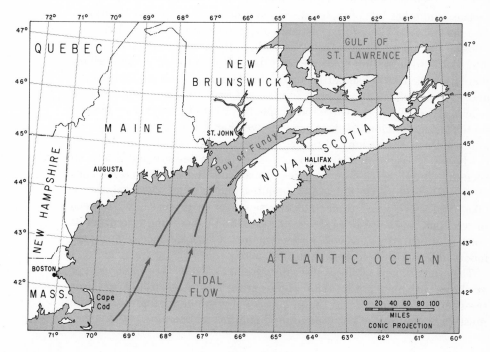

At new moon the tide-raising forces of the moon and the sun are in the same direction [Fig. 6-4(a)], and we have a maximum difference between high and low tide, the so-called spring tide. The same occurs at full moon, when the sun and moon are in line on opposite sides of the earth. When the moon is in first or third quarter [Fig. 6-4(b)] the tide-raising force of the sun opposes that of the moon, and we have a minimum difference or a neap tide. By comparing the average height of the spring tides with that of the neap tides it is possible to calculate the ratio of the moon's tide-raising force to that of the sun, the moon's effect being greater than that of the sun because it is so much closer. From this we can calculate the mass of the moon, and we find it to be 7.38×10^{22} kilograms, or $1/81.3$ of the mass of the earth.

6-7   ***Artificial Satellites***

On October 4, 1957, the U.S.S.R. put their first artificial satellite, Sputnik I, into an orbit around the earth. Since then the launching of satellites and space vehicles has become routine procedure in both the United States and Russia (although still very expensive). According to an estimate made in 1965 there were some 500 man-made objects circling the earth; satellites still active, satellites whose radio transmitters had ceased to function, spent rockets, and other bits of material. Space probes have explored Venus and Mars by means of recording instruments, and, having fulfilled their missions, are now in orbit around the sun where they will probably remain as long as the solar system continues to exist. Most of the artificial satellites were put into orbit for scientific and technological purposes—to study the highest layers of the atmosphere and the diffuse material that exists in the solar system beyond the earth's atmosphere—to study weather conditions by televising the cloud pattern from above (Fig. 6-6)—to relay telephone and television signals long distances over the ocean. Manned space flight has been a dream of fiction writers for more than a century and is now an accomplished fact, for both American astronauts and Russian cosmonauts have orbited the earth in manned satellites, and have left their vehicles to take "walks in space" protected only by their space suits. It has been proved that it is feasible to navigate a satellite in space and to correct its course—preparations are well under way for the first manned flight to the moon, and trips to Venus and Mars will surely follow.

The orbit of a new satellite must satisfy Kepler's first two laws, and must be an ellipse with focus at the center of the earth. The mean distance (d) from the center of the earth and the period (P) of revolution around the earth must be related to the corresponding quantities for the moon by Kepler's

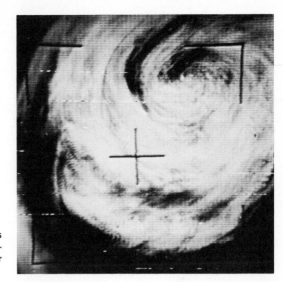

FIG. 6-6

Pattern of clouds in a cyclonic storm, as seen from above by a Tiros weather satellite. (Photograph courtesy of U.S. Weather Bureau.)

third law: (period)² varies as (distance)³. Suppose that a news report says that a satellite has been successfully put into orbit at a height varying from 200 to 1000 miles. Since the mean radius of the earth is 3959 miles, this really means that the satellite's distance from the center varies from 4159 to 4959 miles, with an average of 4559 miles. Then by Kepler's third law

$$\left(\frac{\textbf{period of the satellite}}{\textbf{period of the moon}}\right)^2 = \left(\frac{\textbf{4559}}{\textbf{mean distance of the moon}}\right)^3,$$

which gives 103.7 minutes for the period of the satellite.

If the rocket that launches the satellite is fired in a nearly vertical direction from the point A (Fig. 6-7), the first part of the path will be a long narrow ellipse which must strike the earth again at B. In order to achieve an orbit ($CSPQ$) that circles the earth, a second-stage rocket must be fired at C, to divert the satellite in the direction of the arrow. If the speed and direction at this point are properly adjusted, the satellite will continue in the desired orbit without further attention until the friction of the very rare atmosphere through which it is traveling gradually slows it down, and it eventually falls back to earth, probably burning up in the denser lower layers of the atmosphere, like a meteor. A manned satellite must have a small additional rocket to divert it into an orbit that will hit the earth at the desired spot when the astronaut wants to land. The descent through the lower atmosphere must be very gradual, and reverse rockets may have to be used to slow it down, to prevent the space vehicle from burning up.

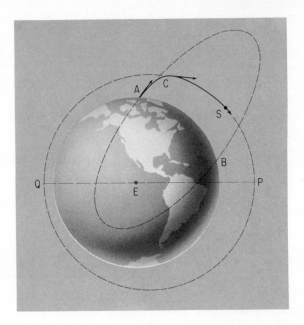

FIG. 6-7

Putting an artificial satellite in orbit.

6-8   *Eclipses of the Sun and Moon*

One of the most spectacular of all natural phenomena is a total eclipse of the sun, when the moon passes in front of it, and for a few minutes the direct light is cut off. This is the one time when the great flames of the prominences, and the pale green streamers of the corona (Sec. 3-3) become visible. As the time for the eclipse approaches, the dark new moon, invisible in the bright sunshine, starts to cross the face of the sun, and appears to cut out a lune-shaped section. There is little apparent change in the brightness of the daylight until the time comes when all that is left of the sun's visible disk is a thin crescent, and then the light rapidly fails. Totality is attained the instant the sun's disk is completely covered. The prominences and the corona suddenly appear, surrounding the black disk of the moon. Darkness falls over the landscape, and the brighter stars can be seen. The darkness is not complete, because the atmosphere scatters a certain amount of light from outside the shadow zone; rather it is comparable to evening dusk. Totality usually lasts 2 or 3 minutes, although it can be as much as 7 minutes. Then the disk of the sun begins to reappear as a bright crescent behind the advancing moon, and the special features of totality vanish. Gradually the moon moves away, and the full sun is visible once more.

Obviously, solar eclipses can only occur at new moon; their spectacular features are the result of the moon's average apparent diameter being nearly equal to that of the sun. Other conditions, relating to the size and position of the shadow cast by the moon (Fig. 6-8), have to be satisfied before an eclipse can be seen. Because the sun is actually very much larger than the moon, the shadow proper, the shaded area in the diagram (known technically as the *umbra*) is a narrow cone, of average length 234,000 miles. A total eclipse can only be observed from somewhere within this cone. From a point (*P*) within the lightly shaded area (the *penumbra*) the moon appears to cover only a portion of the sun's disk, as it does before and after a total eclipse. There is then a partial eclipse.

The first condition for a total eclipse is that the sun, moon, and earth should be nearly enough in line for the moon's shadow cone to strike the earth. The moon's orbit is inclined to the ecliptic (the plane of the earth's orbit around the sun) at an angle of 5°9′, and the moon has to be within about 1° of the ecliptic for an eclipse to occur. On the average, the first condition is satisfied at about one new moon in five; there have to be at least two solar eclipses each year, and there can be as many as five, since it often happens that the moon is in a suitable position at both of a pair of successive new moons, one above the ecliptic and one below.

The second condition for a total eclipse is that the distance of the moon from the earth's surface should be less than the length of the shadow. The distance varies from 221,700 miles to 249,000, with average a little greater than the average length of the umbra, and so only a few less than half of all solar eclipses are total. If an eclipse should occur when the moon is at its closest possible distance, the width of the shadow where it intersects the surface of the earth would be 168 miles. A shadow width approaching the theoretical maximum is a very rare occurrence; usually it is some 50 to 100 miles. As the moon moves across the sun, and as the earth rotates, the shadow travels over the ground at a speed of over 1000 miles per hour, and sweeps out a path 50 or 100 miles wide and several thousand miles long. In order to see the eclipse as total, the observer must be located within this path, and so, although a total eclipse occurs somewhere on earth nearly

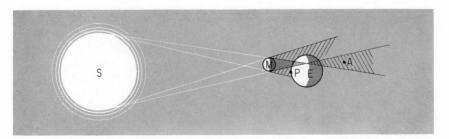

FIG. 6-8

Formation of an eclipse of the sun.

every year, it is only once in 360 years on the average that one will be seen at any given place. The fictional situation where the hero's savage enemies are thrown into confusion at the opportune moment by an eclipse of the sun, predicted of course by the hero, goes back to Herodotus and has been used by many adventure writers, but it is really a little absurd.

For over a century elaborate expeditions have been sent out to make astronomical observations along the path of totality at every feasible total eclipse. At first the main interest was in the study of the prominences and corona, and in a search for the hypothetical planet, Vulcan, which many astronomers thought should exist inside the orbit of Mercury. Nowadays, the corona can be photographed at any time, by using an artificial obscuring disk in the focal plane of the telescope, and no Vulcan has ever been found. More recently there has been a great interest in photographing the pattern of stars very close to the sun, looking for the shift in apparent position caused by the effect of the massive sun on light rays passing close to it as they come from a distant star (Sec. 33-12). This effect is well established today, and, although expeditions continue to be sent out, no startling new discoveries seem likely. Of continuing interest is the determination of the exact instant when totality commences and of the exact edge of the shadow. This information is always useful in improving our knowledge of the moon's orbit and for detecting slow changes in the orbit.

Eclipses of the moon occur when it is full, as it passes through the shadow of the earth (Fig. 6-9). The first condition is more stringent, because the moon is farther away from the sun at the full than at the new, and on the average there is an eclipse at one full moon in nine. The second condition is always fulfilled, since the length of the earth's shadow is much greater than the distance of the moon. Moreover, the eclipse can be seen from any point on the night side of the earth, and so the chances of seeing a lunar eclipse from any given location are much better than for a solar eclipse. However, there are no spectacular effects other than the passage of the shadow over the moon.

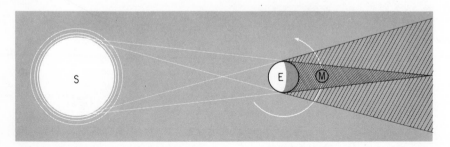

FIG. 6-9

Formation of an eclipse of the moon.

6-9   Corrections to Kepler's and Newton's Laws

Newton's law of gravitation, as applied to the solar system, not only leads to Kepler's empirical laws as the first approximation, but it shows also that these laws are only a very good approximation. All the planetary orbits show "perturbations," usually expressed in the form of slow changes in the shapes and orientations of the elliptic orbits. Almost all these perturbations are caused by the attractions of the planets for one another or by the planets not being perfect spheres. If Newton's law is universal, as it purports to be, these perturbing forces should exist, but should be very small compared with the central attraction of the sun, as is indeed found to be the case.

Nevertheless, we know now that Newton's laws of motion and of gravitation are not the last word, and Einstein has shown how further considerations have to be taken into account when the velocities involved are very large, or when we are close to a very large mass.°

The history of increasing accuracy and increasing comprehension can be summed up as follows:

First, we have Kepler's empirical laws of the planets (1609–1618) and Galileo's mechanics (1638).

Second, Isaac Newton (1687) brings these together and gives us a means of making much more accurate calculations, covering an even wider range of phenomena.

Third, Einstein (1905–1915) provides a basis even more fundamental than that of Newton and shows that Newton's mechanics are indeed a very close approximation, but not ultimate truth.

Is this final? At present we have no clue to anything more fundamental than Einstein's principle of general relativity, and so far calculations based on his theories have been in complete agreement with the facts, but we have no right to claim absolute finality for any theory, no matter how satisfactory it may appear to be.

6-10   The Role of Mathematics

The mathematical formulae, the simple algebraic deductions, and the references to various mathematical theorems contained in the last three chapters have served their purpose if they have given the reader some idea of the essential role that mathematics plays as one of the most important

---

° The only place in the solar system where the corrections required by Einstein's theory of relativity become important is in the orbit of Mercury, where proximity to the large mass of the sun causes a small perturbation in the elliptical orbit (Sec. 33-12). The observed perturbation is in agreement with computations based on Einstein's theory. The theory also predicts that light rays passing close to the sun as they come from a distant star will be slightly deviated. The effect is observed as predicted, at the time of a solar eclipse (Sec. 6-8).

tools of modern science. As soon as we attempt—with Newton in mechanics, and with some of his contemporaries and close followers in other fields— to formulate basic principles, such as the law of gravitation, which are not the immediate consequences of observation, we have to demonstrate that the observed facts follow logically as results of the laws. Only in the very simplest cases can this demonstration be made by a logical argument in words; almost always the argument has to take the form of a mathematical derivation, using the language of mathematical symbols. We have to express the fundamental principle as a mathematical equation (as, for example, the law of gravitation in Sec. 6-1) and use this equation as the hypothesis, or starting point, for a series of mathematical theorems. The conclusions of these theorems can be compared with the observations, or can be tested by new experiments. Finally, they can be used in the computations necessary in designing practical, technological applications, and again mathematics is an essential tool.

Isaac Newton ranks as the first great theoretical physicist—the first to develop a systematic sequence of mathematical arguments, linking a fundamental hypothesis to a whole series of observed and experimental facts. Actually, he was a highly competent experimentalist as well, as exemplified by the work in optics which occupied a great part of his later years. Finally, he ranks also among the truly great in pure mathematics. When he commenced his work the mathematical techniques available to him were not adequate for the treatment of some of the problems presented by the complete theory of gravitation. He had to devise a new mathematical method that is essentially the same as that of the differential calculus. Newton therefore shares with the mathematician, Leibnitz, the credit for the invention of the calculus. It is well to remember how the early scientists were so often restricted in their work by the lack of mathematical and experimental techniques that are commonplace today.

GLOSSARY

Central orbit Motion such that the acceleration is always directed toward a fixed center.

Centrifugal force Reaction of the centripetal force upon the central attracting body or central support.

Centripetal acceleration The acceleration toward the center of curvature of a body that is describing a curved path, due to the change in direction of the velocity.

Centripetal force The force that must act upon the body in order to change the direction of motion.

Constant of gravitation The constant of proportionality in Newton's law of universal gravitation.

Lune Figure formed by the area that is common to a pair of intersecting circles.

Neap tide Tide of minimum range between high and low, occurring when the sun and moon are at right angles so that their tidal effects oppose each other.

Spring tide Tide of maximum range, occurring when the earth, moon, and sun are in line, so that the tidal effects of the sun and moon combine.

Umbra The shadows cast by an extended source of light, such as the sun, are long, narrow cones; the shadow proper, the cone within which the source cannot be seen, is known as the umbra. The zone of partial shadow surrounding the umbra, where a portion of the source can be seen, is known as the penumbra.

Universal constant One of a small number of quantities which are the same everywhere in the cosmos, and which evidently express some fundamental property of space or of matter. The *numerical expression* of the quantity depends upon the units used.

EXERCISES

1. State the law of universal gravitation, in words and in symbols.

2. Calculate the average acceleration of the moon toward the earth, in meters per second^2.

3. Describe how Kepler's first two laws follow from Newton's law of gravitation.

4. Why does a calculation based upon the orbit of a planet around the sun, or upon the orbit of a satellite around its planet, give the mass of the central attracting body, and not that of the body which is describing the orbit?

5. Why is an experiment that is designed to measure the constant G in Newton's law of gravitation often referred to as "weighing the earth"? Why is this indirect method necessary? Describe one method of carrying out the experiment.

6. Calculate the force of attraction, in newtons and in grams-weight, between the two spheres in von Jolly's experiment. Take the masses to be 5800 kilograms and 5.00 kilograms, respectively, and the distance between their centers to be 0.600 meter.

7. Calculate the force of attraction of the sun upon the earth, in newtons.

8. If the ocean tides are caused by the attraction of the moon and sun for the water surrounding the earth, why are there *two* high tides daily?

9. In which direction around the earth does the wave of the tides travel?

10. What is the phenomenon commonly known as a "tidal wave," and sometimes reported in the newspapers? Has it anything to do with the wave referred to in Exercise 9?

11. Where are the highest tides in the world? Look at a globe, and suggest other places where you might expect to find very high tides.

12. In putting an artificial satellite into orbit, why is it necessary to fire a second rocket when the satellite has nearly reached the desired height?

13. At what height can a satellite appear to hang in space, above a fixed point on the earth's equator? (*Hint:* The satellite is actually describing an orbit with a period exactly equal to the earth's period of rotation, 23 hours 56 minutes.)

14. Is a rocket engine more efficient or less so in empty space than it is in the earth's atmosphere? Explain.

15. State the conditions that have to be fulfilled so that a total eclipse of the sun can be seen at a given point on the earth.

16. Whenever an eclipse of the sun is expected to be visible from some reasonably accessible spot, scientific expeditions are sent out to study it. What new scientific information has been expected from these expeditions at different times of their history? in the late nineteenth century? in the 1920's? in the most recent expeditions?

REVIEW EXERCISES FOR CHAPTERS 1 THROUGH 6

1. Define in logical order: speed at an instant, velocity, acceleration, force, mass, weight, momentum.

2. Name the MKS units of the following quantities, and define the units in logical order: distance, time, velocity, acceleration, mass, volume, density, force, weight.

3. Outline Galileo's discoveries in mechanics, and those of Kepler in astronomy, and explain how the two streams of thought were brought together by Isaac Newton.

4. Show how the steps of the so-called scientific method have been approximately followed through the history of the astronomy of the solar system. Give as well as you can the dates when the important advances were made.

5. Summarize from the same point of view the history of knowledge concerning the mechanics of moving bodies.

6. What were the features of Aristotle's philosophy that held up progress in physics and astronomy for many centuries? How were his erroneous preconceptions finally refuted?

THE ENERGY PRINCIPLE

part two

The total energy of a closed system is constant.

—LAW OF CONSERVATION OF ENERGY

work, energy, and power

Several common English words are used in physics as technical terms with rigorously defined meanings, much more restrictive than their everyday usage. One of these, force, has already been encountered; three more are now to be defined. At first, the use of common words in a technical sense is confusing to the student, and it might have been better to have invented new words, as, indeed, has been suggested by certain semanticists and pedagogues. However, the terms have become so firmly entrenched in all scientific literature that an attempt to change them now would compound the confusion. Scientists are not always as consistent and logical as one would like to think.

Work, in mechanics, is defined as follows: *The work done in any action is equal to the force acting multiplied by the distance the body moves in the direction of the force.*

The MKS unit of work is the *joule**, which is the *work done when a force*

---

* After James Prescott Joule (1818–1889), a wealthy English brewer who made scientific experiments his hobby. It was he who firmly established the relation between heat and work (Sec. 7-6).

of 1 *newton moves a body a distance of* 1 *meter.* The British FPS unit is the foot-pound, with a rather obvious meaning, namely the work done when a force of 1 pound moves a body a distance of 1 foot.

Energy is defined as *the capacity to do work.* That is, any physical system is said to possess energy if its condition is such that it might do work. The amount of energy is equal to the amount of work that might be done and is measured in the same units, joules or foot-pounds. This formal definition is very close to the meaning implied in the common use of the word, but we must remember that the work involved is the strictly defined mechanical work.

Power, in the technical sense, is defined as *the rate of doing work, or the rate of supply of energy.* A power of 1 watt° supplies energy at the rate of 1 joule per second. One horsepower supplies 550 foot-pounds per second. Since it involves an arbitrary numerical factor, it is not the properly derived FPS unit, although it is the unit commonly used in calculations on the FPS system†.

Watt is very often used with the metric prefixes, for example, kilowatt for a power of 1000 watts. This leads to the common commercial unit of energy, the kilowatt-hour (KWH), which represents the supplying of energy at the rate of 1 kilowatt for a period of 1 hour. Therefore

1 kilowatt-hour = 1000 watts × 3600 seconds = 3,600,000 joules.

To those who are familiar with electric light bills, this will be a reminder that energy is a salable commodity. Electric service is charged to the customer according to the number of kilowatt-hours of energy supplied, and at 2 or 3 cents per kilowatt-hour, this type of energy is a very cheap commodity indeed.

7-2 Three Ways of Doing Work

There are three principal ways in which forces can do mechanical work, and these are nicely illustrated if we think of an automobile starting from

---

° After James Watt (1736–1819) of steam engine fame.

† There is a story about the assignment of the horsepower. When James Watt was selling steam engines he wanted to advertise them as the equal of a certain number of horses, and to arrive at a figure he measured the work done by an actual horse pulling a barge along a canal, by putting a spring balance in the tow rope. The horse walked at 2½ miles per hour (220 feet per minute), and exerted a steady pull of 100 pounds. It was therefore doing 22,000 foot-pounds of work per minute. According to the story, Watt added 50 per cent to allow for friction and other sources of inaccuracy, and used the figure of 33,000 foot-pounds per minute in order to calculate the horse-equivalent of his engines. It is a very good horse that can produce a horsepower continuously.

For comparison of MKS and FPS units, a joule is 0.738 foot-pound, and a kilowatt is 1.341 horsepower. A kilowatt-hour is 2,655,000 foot-pounds, which means that it would provide enough work to hoist a 5-ton truck 265 feet.

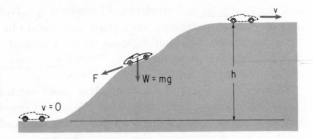

FIG. 7-1

Three ways of doing work
on a car: to lift it through
a height (h), to accelerate
it to a speed (v), and to
overcome the friction force
(F).

rest at the bottom of a hill, and accelerating as it climbs (Fig. 7-1). The
work done by the engine can be divided into three parts.° The first contribution is the work required to climb the hill. The lifting force is equal
and opposite to the weight ($W = mg$), which acts vertically downward.
The displacement in the direction of the force is simply the vertical height
(h) from the bottom to the top of the hill, regardless of the slope and of
the contours of the road. More generally, the work done when a body of
mass (m) is lifted through a height (h) is

(Work to lift) $= mgh$**.**

The second contribution is the work required to accelerate the car,
which is traveling with a speed (v) when it reaches the top of the hill. If
we apply Newton's second law of motion we can prove by a little mathematical manipulation that

(Work to accelerate) $= \frac{1}{2}\,mv^2$**.**

It depends only on the final speed, regardless of the direction, and regardless of the way in which the accelerating force might vary during the journey.

The third contribution to the work is that required to overcome friction.
Friction can always be treated as a force opposing motion. In the case of
the car it comprises (1) the friction of the tires rolling on the road,
the amount of friction depending on the state of the tires and on the road
surface; and (2) wind resistance, which increases rapidly with the speed
and becomes the most important factor at high speeds. When the average
friction force has to be measured in a specific instance, this can be done
by finding how far the car would roll on a level road, with the engine cut
off. Since the friction force is always in the opposite direction to the motion,

(Work against friction) $=$ **(average friction force)** $\times$ **(distance traveled).**

The first two of these contributions to the work depend only on the initial
and final states, regardless of the way in which the final state is attained.
This is characteristic of a great many problems concerning work, not only

° If consistent MKS units are used for the data all the results will be in joules.

those where gravitational and mechanical forces are involved, and makes the concept of work an extremely important and useful one. In the case of work against friction, the result depends on the total distance traveled, regardless of possible changes in direction. Work therefore does not involve direction, and is a scalar quantity.

Before we leave the subject of work one other point needs to be emphasized. The definition means precisely what it says, no more and no less, and so there is no work unless there is a force acting, and unless there is a displacement *in the direction of that force.* Suppose you carry a 100-pound sack of grain on your shoulder. There is some work done when you hoist it onto your back, but there is no more work in carrying it as far as you like on a level road, because the force is vertical and the displacement is horizontal. As I write this, the only work I do is the little bit required to punch the typewriter keys. In spite of what the student may think, studying is not work, in the technical sense. This is, of course, what makes the use of the word "work" for a technical scientific concept so confusing to the novice and the layman.

7-3   *Potential and Kinetic Energy*

When the automobile (Fig. 7-1) is at the top of the hill, with the engine shut off, it possesses energy, because it might roll down, gaining speed as it does so, and doing work against friction. Similarly, a weight hanging on a rope which passes over a pulley possesses energy, because it could be used to hoist something attached to the other end of the rope. Generally, any body which is in a position where it might fall, or descend a slope, possesses energy, because we can always think of some way of rigging it so that it will do work as it descends.

This is *gravitational potential energy,* where the word "potential," as used here and in other connections in physics, has a significance very close to its everyday meaning: something which could happen, but does not necessarily do so. The amount of potential energy is equal to the work the body might do in falling, or to the work which would have to be done on the body to lift it. Therefore the potential energy of a body of mass (m) is

$$\text{P.E.} = mgh,$$

where h is the vertical height above the lowest accessible point.

This is somewhat arbitrary, since we have to decide upon the "lowest accessible point." In a laboratory experiment, h might be the height above the floor, but this may be many meters above the ground outside, and that again might be on a hill. An important practical case of potential energy is that possessed by the water stored in an artificial lake behind a dam, for this water is about to do work in driving the turbines in the power plant below the dam. For purposes of calculation of the performance of the plant, h would be the vertical height from the downstream water outlet to the water level in the lake. But the water leaving the plant still has potential energy, because it is going to flow down the river, and it may pass through more power plants before it reaches the sea. "Lowest accessible point" in the definition is really an arbitrarily selected "zero level," where convenience is the principal consideration in the choice, and h is the height above zero.

A body in motion possesses energy by virtue of its speed, referred to as *kinetic energy*. If it is rolling along the road, like the car in Sec. 7-2, or if it is sliding over a smooth surface, it is going to do work against friction as it gradually comes to a stop. Generally, we can always conceive of some device for connecting the moving body to a machine, and making it do some useful work as it slows down. Again, the rotating flywheel of an engine possesses kinetic energy, and some of this energy is used to keep the engine turning over in between the impulses it receives from the pistons. The kinetic energy of a body of mass (m) moving with a speed (v) is equal to the work done when it is brought to rest, and is given by

$$\textbf{K.E.} = \tfrac{1}{2}\ \textbf{\textit{mv}}^2,$$

the same as the work done in accelerating it from rest to the given speed.

If the only forces involved are gravitational, in particular if there is no friction, the sum of potential energy plus kinetic energy is constant. If a stone falls freely through a height (h) it loses potential energy but at the same time it is accelerated and gains an equal amount of kinetic energy. If the stone is thrown vertically upward it will come to rest and start to fall again when all its kinetic energy is converted into potential energy. In the case of a planet revolving in its orbit around the sun there is no friction, and the sum of potential and kinetic energy is rigorously constant, although the expression for the potential energy is less simple than that for a suspended weight because the force varies with distance from the center. As the planet approaches perihelion and gains speed in conformity with Kepler's second law, it gains kinetic energy at the expense of the potential energy caused by its attraction by the sun, and vice versa (Fig. 7-2).

7-4   *Heat and Temperature*

The problem of the nature of heat has been an important one in the history of science. We know today that heat is a form of energy, for it

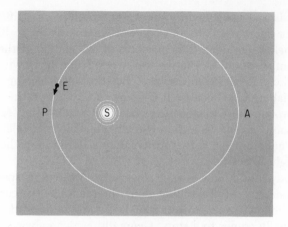

FIG. 7-2

A planet (E) describing an elliptical orbit around the sun; at perihelion (P) the planet has its greatest speed and the kinetic energy is a maximum; at aphelion (A) the speed is least and the potential energy is a maximum.

satisfies the definition, "capacity to do work." We know, moreover, that it can be associated with the energy of the molecules of a material. For example, when water is converted into steam by the application of heat, work is done in separating the molecules against the forces that hold them together in the liquid state; the steam can then do work in a steam engine. However, the equivalence of heat with work or energy was not realized and established by experiment until the middle of the nineteenth century. The older idea was that heat was a substance, sometimes given the name "caloric," and this view was generally accepted until very careful experiments failed to show any increase in mass when a body is heated. When the Greek philosophers talked of "fire" as one of the four elements of which the earth is composed, implying that it was a material substance, they were actually thinking of something very similar to what we call heat.

Although heat is a form of energy rather than a substance, the unit devised many years ago for the measurement of quantity of heat is still useful: *A calorie is the amount of heat required to raise the temperature of 1 gram of pure water by 1 degree on the Celsius scale.*

The proper MKS unit is the kilocalorie, referring to 1 kilogram of water. This has also been called simply "calorie" by some writers, or "large calorie," thus causing some confusion. For example, the calorie used in measuring food values is really the kilocalorie; it represents the heat energy produced when the foodstuff is burned.

Before discussing heat energy any further we must define what we mean by *temperature*, and discuss methods of measuring it. Everybody has a fair idea of what we mean when we say that a thing is hot or cold, and realizes that the figure on the thermometer indicates how hot or how cold. However, when we come to study the matter we find that it is not easy to give a clear definition of the concept of temperature, or to devise a satisfactory method of putting the numbers on the thermometer. This is because temperature is a quality, not a quantity. When we say that a stove is hot, we use the adjective, and we do not think of the stove as possessing or containing a certain amount of hotness. If the latter phrase did mean anything, it would refer to the content of heat energy, and we would be confusing the two quite different concepts of temperature and of heat. The layman quite often does just this, using the word heat when he really means temperature, and vice versa. A discussion of temperature therefore provides an excellent example of a type of measurement that is more sophisticated than any we have encountered so far. Strictly speaking, we are not measuring an entity, but are expressing the qualitative ideas of hot or cold on a numerical scale. With temperature and with a few other qualities, such as brightness or loudness, this can be done unequivocally. With others it is difficult; for example, color has to be expressed by means of a three-figure code, rather than by a numerical measurement. With some qualities it is obviously impossible—someone has yet to devise a numerical scale of beauty or pleasure.

At first we can only define a *difference of temperature: If, when two bodies, A and B are placed in contact, heat energy flows from A to B, then A is said to be at a higher temperature than B.*

Two corollaries follow immediately from this definition: If there is no exchange of heat energy, the two bodies must be at the same temperature; if there is no other source of energy, two bodies placed in contact will eventually come to the same temperature.

In order to devise a numerical scale of temperature, we have first to choose two standard temperatures. These must be easily reproducible. That is, we must choose some simple phenomenon which always occurs at the same temperature, according to the definition. Experience has shown that the phenomena of melting and boiling of pure materials fulfill the necessary conditions admirably. The standard temperatures universally used are therefore defined as follows: The *ice point* is the temperature of melting pure ice at standard atmospheric pressure. This is arbitrarily assigned the number 0 on the Celsius scale (0°C), or 32 on the Fahrenheit scale (32°F), the scale in common use in North America° (Fig. 7-3).

The ice point cannot be taken to be the temperature at which water freezes, for water can often be "supercooled" well below 0°C before freezing actually starts. Neither can it be the temperature of a mixture of ice and water, for water has a maximum density at 4°C, and ice floats on water,

° Fahrenheit, a German physician, made the first reliable mercury thermometers in 1724. He took 0° to be the temperature of a mixture of ice and ammonium chloride, the lowest temperature he could produce in his laboratory. Since he was interested in using his thermometers for diagnosing fever, he took his upper temperature to be the normal temperature of the human body, and at first he called this 24°, using the duodecimal division that was very common in old systems of measurement. Later he decided that this made the degree divisions too long, and he changed the 24 to 96. Neither the freezing mixture nor the human body give accurately reproducible temperatures, and it was soon found that they are not satisfactory standards.

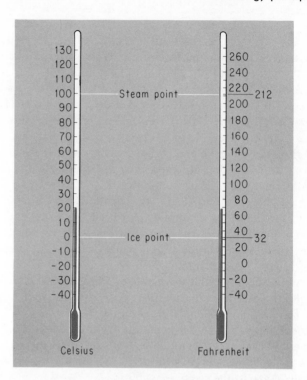

FIG. 7-3

The Celsius and Fahrenheit scales of temperature.

with the result that in a vessel containing ice floating in water the temperature at the bottom is usually somewhere between 0° and 4°. A simple way of reproducing the proper standard ice point is to put some finely chopped ice into a funnel so that the water can drain away as the ice melts (Fig. 7-4), and insert the thermometer to be tested in the ice.

The *steam point* is the temperature of the steam rising from pure boiling water when the surrounding pressure is standard atmospheric. This is arbitrarily fixed at 100°C, or 212°F.

Again, it is the temperature of the steam (Fig. 7-5) which is taken as standard, not that of the boiling water, for the latter may have to be a little higher than 100°C before the bubbles will form and rise, consequently its temperature is not accurately reproducible.

7-5   *The Thermometer*

Having assigned numbers to the two standard temperatures, we have to select a temperature indicator in order to extend the scale. The indicator has to be a substance that possesses an easily measurable, quantitative

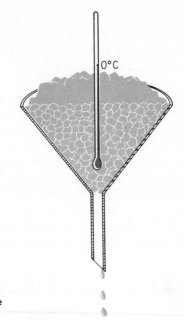

FIG. 7-4

A simple method of reproducing the standard ice point.

property that varies with temperature, and yet always has the same value at any given temperature. In Fahrenheit's earliest thermometers, as in the commonly used mercury thermometer of today, the indicator is the volume

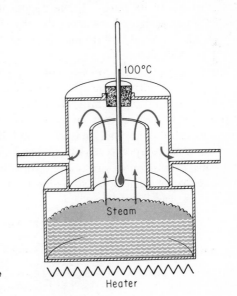

FIG. 7-5

An apparatus for the determination of the steam point.

of a quantity of mercury enclosed in a glass bulb, connected to a long tube of carefully selected uniform bore. When this tube is to be inscribed with a Celsius scale, it is placed in melting ice and in steam, and the 0° and 100° marks are put on it. The stem in between is then divided into 100 parts of equal length to give intermediate temperatures. Degree intervals of the same length are extended below 0° and above 100° in order to measure lower and higher temperatures.

The mercury thermometer is obviously limited in that it cannot be used below the freezing point of mercury, $-39°$C. It can be used for temperatures somewhat higher than the boiling point ($357°$C) up to the point where the glass begins to soften and the bulb will no longer keep its shape, the practical upper limit being about $500°$C. The range can be extended by employing various other liquids, particularly alcohol, which is used in weather thermometers in climates where extreme cold is liable to be encountered. However, no liquid provides an entirely satisfactory indicator, useful throughout the entire range of possible temperatures, and the accepted standard is now the pressure exerted by an *ideal gas,* when confined to a constant volume, an ideal gas being defined as *one which would obey Boyle's law of gas pressure (pressure $\times$ volume = constant) at all temperatures and pressures* (Sec. 10-3). This is obviously impossible in practice, since all gases can be liquefied, but the ideal gas is approximated by gases such as hydrogen and helium that have very low liquefaction temperatures, and the departure from the ideal can be calculated. Compared with the ideal gas as standard, mercury does not expand at a uniform rate throughout its range. If the degree marks on a mercury thermometer are evenly spaced, as is usually the case, and if it is correct at $0°$C and $100°$C, it will be slightly inaccurate at $50°$C, and may be in error by a degree or more above $200°$C.

Calculation shows that the pressure of an ideal gas would become zero at $-273.16°$C, and other considerations lead to the conclusion that no body can be cooled to a temperature lower than this. In fact, at this temperature the kinetic energy of molecular motions would be at an irreducible minimum, and all matter would be solid,° in its simplest possible state. This temperature is therefore known as *absolute zero,* and it is often convenient to measure temperatures from absolute zero instead of from the ice point. The scale so defined is known as the Kelvin scale, and we have

$$T°K = t°C + 273.16.$$

True to prediction, it becomes increasingly difficult to reduce the tempera-

° With one exception; helium is still liquid at absolute zero, and can only be solidified under pressure.

ture further as absolute zero is approached, and it has never actually been attained. It is possible to cool to a little below 1°K by means of liquid helium, which boils at 4.2°K. Other methods can be used to push the temperature still lower, and the present record is about 0.00005°K.

7-6   The Mechanical Equivalent of Heat

The first to question seriously the caloric theory of heat was Benjamin Thompson, Count Rumford,° in 1798. He was impressed by the tremendous quantities of heat produced in the operation of a lathe while observing the process of boring out bronze cannon for the army. Naturally, the generation of heat by friction was well known; even the primitive savage knew how to light a fire by rubbing two sticks together. According to the theory current in Rumford's time, latent caloric was thought to be in some way entangled in the solid material, and some of this caloric was supposed to be released when chips were cut from the metal in the lathe. Rumford made two observations which convinced him that this could not be the correct explanation: First, if the boring tool is blunt the boring operation is less efficient and there are not as many chips, but there is actually more heat than there is with a freshly sharpened tool. Second, there is apparently no limit to the amount of heat which can be generated by prolonged operation on the one piece of metal. From this he came to the conclusion that heat is not a measurable substance but must be related in some way to motion, or as we put it today, to kinetic energy.

Rumford tried to measure the amount of heat produced in some of his experiments, but his quantitative results were inconclusive, and for this reason his ideas did not receive much attention when he reported them. The man who deserves most of the credit for proving the connection between heat and energy is James Joule, about 1840. The most significant of his experiments—and there were many—was that in which a falling weight was made to rotate a paddle and so to stir the water in a specially designed vessel (Fig. 7-6). The rise of temperature of the water was measured with a sensitive thermometer, and Joule was able to show that the heat produced, measured in calories, was proportional to the work done by the falling weight, and to determine the constant of proportionality. This is the quantity known as the *mechanical equivalent of heat,* and is one of the important general physical constants. Its modern value is

1 calorie = 4.186 joules.

° An American by birth, Thompson was created a Bavarian count in recognition of his services to the Bavarian army during the Napoleonic Wars. It was while he was employed as an engineer by the king of Bavaria that he carried out his experiments on heat.

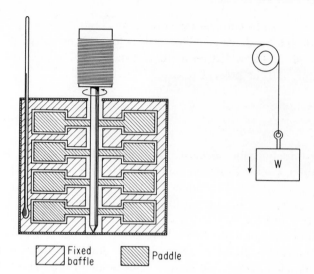

FIG. 7-6

Joule's experiment on heating water by stirring.

[hatched box] Fixed baffle   [cross-hatched box] Paddle

GLOSSARY

Absolute temperature Temperature measured from absolute zero; synonymous with the Kelvin scale.

Absolute zero Temperature at which the pressure of an ideal gas would vanish, and therefore the lowest possible temperature; it is computed to be $-273.16°C$.

Caloric An imaginary material which, before the true nature of heat was understood, was supposed to be produced in a fire or other source of heat.

Calorie Unit of heat energy. (The calorie of the diet lists is really a kilocalorie, causing some confusion in the literature.)

Celsius scale The scale of temperature that takes the ice point as $0°$ and the steam point as $100°$; used along with MKS units, and in general use almost everywhere except in the U.S.A. and Canada. (The Celsius scale was formerly known as "centigrade.")

Fahrenheit scale The scale of temperature that takes the ice point as $32°$ and the steam point as $212°$; the scale with which most of us are familiar.

Foot-pound Unit of work or energy in the FPS system.

Friction Measured by the force opposing the motion of a body.

Horsepower Rate of doing work of 550 foot-pounds per second.

Ice point The temperature of melting pure ice at standard atmospheric pressure.

Ideal gas A gas which would obey Boyle's law of gas pressure (Sec. 10-3) at *all* temperatures and pressures.

joule Unit of work or energy in the MKS system.

Kelvin scale Temperature measured in Celsius degrees from absolute zero; same as the absolute temperature.

Kilowatt-hour (KWH) Energy provided by a power of 1000 watts running for 1 hour.

Kinetic energy Energy due to motion.

Mechanical equivalent of heat The number of units of mechanical energy in a unit of heat; the MKS value is 4.186 joules per calorie.

Potential energy Energy due to the position or state of a body.

Steam point The temperature of the steam rising from pure boiling water when the surrounding pressure is standard atmospheric.

Supercooled Most liquids can be cooled well below their normal freezing points before freezing actually starts; they are then said to be supercooled.

watt Unit of power or rate of supply of energy in the MKS system.

EXERCISES

(In the following exercises take $g = 9.8$ meters per second^2 wherever necessary.)

1. Define the terms work, energy, and power, as used in mechanics. Name and define the MKS units of these quantities.

2. Find examples from your own major discipline of common English words that are used in a technical sense.

3. How much energy does a 60-watt electric light supply in running for 20 minutes? How much heat is this, in calories?

4. At 2 cents per kilowatt-hour, how many times would a dollar's worth of energy take your body up a flight of stairs? (Assume a mass of 75 kilograms and a height of 3 meters.)

5. What are the three most important ways of doing mechanical work?

6. A car weighing 1500 kilograms starts from rest at the bottom of a hill 40 meters high and 600 meters long (measured along the road); when the car reaches the top of the hill it is traveling 20 meters per second; the friction force is 150 kilograms-weight. Compute the total work done.

7. If the acceleration were uniform, the car in Exercise 6 would take 60 seconds to climb the hill; what is the average power exerted by the engine?

8. Exercises 6 and 7 are not very realistic. If the acceleration were uniform, the power could not be constant and, conversely, if the engine exerted a constant power, the acceleration would not be uniform. Why is this? Further, the friction force cannot be constant (regardless of the state of the road). Why is this?

9. A pile driver makes use of a weight of 200 kilograms, which at each stroke is hoisted to a height of 19.6 meters and then dropped on the head of the pile. What is the potential energy of the weight at the top of the stroke? How long does it take to fall? What is its velocity just as it hits the pile at the bottom? What is its kinetic energy at this point? How much work does it do upon the pile at each stroke?

10. Discuss the definition of temperature; why is it rather difficult to give a logical definition of this concept? how is it defined?

11. Define each of the three commonly used scales of temperature: Fahrenheit, Celsius, and Kelvin.

12. Express 72°F on the Celsius scale and on the Kelvin scale; express 500°K on the Celsius and Fahrenheit scales; express −183°C on the Fahrenheit scale.

13. Over what range of temperature can a mercury thermometer be used? an alcohol thermometer of the type usually sold for mounting on the back porch?

14. Mercury thermometers are usually made with the degree marks of equal length all along the stem; they are then liable to be considerably in error at temperatures above about 200°C. By what standard do we judge the accuracy of the mercury thermometer?

15. Who was Count Rumford? Explain the two observations he made that convinced him that the "caloric" theory of heat could not be correct.

16. Who finally proved that heat is a form of energy? and when? Describe briefly the principle of his experiment.

17. An electric kettle has an element which takes 1100 watts of electrical power; the kettle is filled with 3 kilograms of water, initially at 10°C. If all the heat goes into the water, how long should it take for the water to boil?

18. Estimate the rise of temperature when the water flowing over Niagara Falls hits the bottom; take the height to be 57 meters.

19. There is a serious source of error that is very hard to eliminate in attempts to measure a quantity of heat energy. Can you see what this is? Suggest ways of minimizing the error.

the conservation of energy and the energy supply

It is obvious that many things besides the falling weight or the steam engine are able to do work, and involve energy according to the definition. In fact, in our modern age, examples which immediately come to mind of machines that do work are the gasoline engine and the electric motor. Energy can therefore take many different forms besides those already discussed.

That *light* is a form of energy can be demonstrated by the device known as the Crookes radiometer (Fig. 8-1). This contrivance is in a partial vacuum and has vanes that are blackened on one side to absorb the light and polished on the other side to reflect it. When the light is turned on, they start to rotate and are kept in rotation against the friction of the bearings. The amount of work done is very small, but the definition of energy says nothing about quantity, and it is certainly the light that causes the rotation of the vanes; therefore the light beam contains energy.

Similarly, *sound* possesses energy, although the amounts usually involved

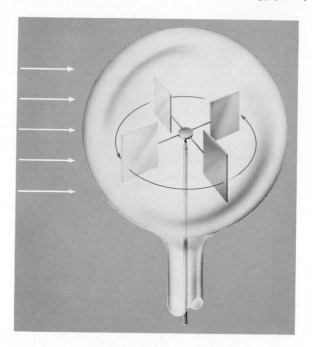

FIG. 8-1

The Crookes radiometer
demonstrates that a beam
of light can do work.

are even smaller than in the case of light. The power received by an ear, in listening to a normal conversation, is about 10^{-9} watt.

A stretched spring or elastic band, or a wound clock spring, possesses *elastic potential energy.* Closely allied to this is the potential energy of a *gas under pressure.* That either of these can do work is obvious.

Better known, and more generally useful, is *electrical energy,* which can be used either to produce heat and light or to run machinery.

Chemical potential energy is most familiar in the burning of fuel, but all chemical reactions involve the release or absorption of energy, usually in the form of heat. Since reactions that produce heat are indirectly capable of doing work, we can think of the energy as a potential residing in the chemicals that are about to react. For example, a quantity of fuel plus the oxygen of the air possesses chemical potential energy, which can be converted into heat as soon as the fuel is ignited. Commonly we forget that the oxygen is involved, and think of this energy as residing in the fuel, rating the quality of different fuels according to the amount of energy they can produce when a kilogram is burned.

Muscular energy of the body, human or animal, is best considered as a special form of chemical energy, for it is the chemical reaction of foodstuffs and oxygen that provides both body heat and the energy to move the muscles, and so to do a certain amount of work, in the technical sense.

This list is far from exhaustive, but we shall mention only one more, which will be important later: *nuclear atomic energy*—the tremendous amount of potential energy that can be released when changes take place in the nuclei of atoms, as in the case of a so-called atomic explosion.

8-2   The Principle of Conservation of Energy

One of the most fundamental laws of nature, ranking with Newton's law of universal gravitation, and so far having no proved exceptions, is the *law of conservation of energy*. Unlike Newton's law, its discovery cannot be credited to the inspired genius of any one man, although Joule's experiments (Sec. 7-6) had a great deal to do with it. Rather, the truth and the importance of the principle gradually dawned on the minds of many scientists, until it came to be clearly enunciated in its modern form:

Energy cannot be created or destroyed, but can only be converted from one form to another. Therefore, in any action the total energy of the bodies involved is a constant.

We have already had an inkling of this principle in the conversion of energy from potential to kinetic as it relates to the falling apple or the orbiting planet. We now recognize that it is universal, applying to all forms of energy, and that everything that happens in the material cosmos involves the conversion of energy from one form to another. However, even the scientist often speaks loosely of the "consumption" of energy—an error in the choice of words. The energy is not consumed, instead it is converted from a useful, readily available form, such as electrical energy or the chemical energy of a fuel, to a less accessible form, and so it may be lost for practical purposes.

The great energy sink is heat, commonly the heat content of the earth and the atmosphere, for heat is the least accessible form. In fact, unless the source of heat is at a higher temperature than its surroundings, the heat energy cannot be made to do work. Thus the vast amount of heat energy stored in the earth and oceans is available only under very special circumstances.° The great waster of energy is friction, for whenever work is done against friction, energy is converted into heat, and this is usually dissipated in the heat sink of the earth, where it causes an infinitesimal rise of temperature, so that the energy is no longer available.

° Even though the interior of the earth is at a high temperature, the only place where it has been possible to make any practical use of this source of energy is where steam from volcanoes or hot springs is available. However, a difference of temperature between different regions of the atmosphere is the primary cause of wind, so that wind represents the conversion of a small portion of the atmospheric heat energy into kinetic energy. To cool a body below the temperature of its surroundings, external work has to be done upon it, as in the household refrigerator. The heat has to be pumped out, so to speak.

8-3   *Conversion of Energy*

It is interesting to trace the energy involved in any action through its various forms. A comparatively simple case, which is easily demonstrated, is that of a weight hanging on a spring and bouncing up and down (Fig. 8-2). When the weight is raised by muscular energy and the spring is released, the system is given gravitational potential energy. When it passes through its normal position (b) the potential energy is converted into kinetic. It is carried below its normal position, and at (c) it has elastic potential energy, which is converted again into kinetic at (d). Then the action repeats periodically as the weight oscillates. The amplitude of the oscillations gradually decreases due to friction until finally the weight comes to rest. This friction is caused partly by air resistance, but predominantly by the internal motion of the molecules in the metal of the spring. As usual, the friction causes conversion of the energy of the oscillations into heat, which produces a slight increase in the temperature of the spring itself.

A more practical example is the internal-combustion engine. The energy is supplied in the form of chemical potential energy of the fuel plus the oxygen of the air, when the fuel-air mixture is drawn into the cylinder of the engine. The fuel is ignited by the spark, and burns to produce heat at a high temperature; consequently the system has available heat energy. Some of the heat is used to raise the pressure of the combustion products and of the nitrogen in the air in the cylinder, so that there is now potential energy of gas pressure. The gas pressure drives the piston of the engine,

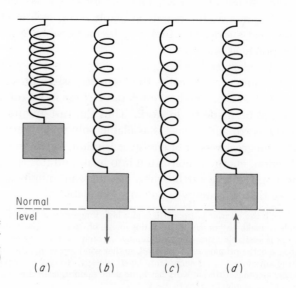

FIG. 8-2

A weight hanging on a spring; at (a) the energy is gravitational potential, at (b) kinetic, at (c) elastic potential, at (d) again kinetic.

Normal level

(*a*)   (*b*)   (*c*)   (*d*)

and we have useful work to move the car or to run machinery. Once again the end result is dissipation of the energy through friction in the machinery, into the heat sink of the earth and atmosphere.

A large proportion of the heat energy produced by the burning fuel, perhaps 75 per cent, remains unconverted and has to be removed by the cooling water, or is carried away in the hot gases which issue from the engine exhaust. Only the remaining 25 per cent of the energy supplied can be used to do work, and so the process is said to have an efficiency of 25 per cent. A major aim of engine designers is to increase the efficiency figure and make more of the total energy available. One way of doing this is to increase the pressure of the fuel-air mixture just before combustion takes place; hence the modern high-compression engines. However, it is not likely that the 30 per cent efficiency of the best diesel engines can be greatly increased.

It would be an interesting exercise for the student to think of additional devices or natural processes by which any of the forms of energy listed in Sec. 8-1 can be converted into any other.

8-4   Conservation of Mass and Mass-Energy

There are a few other laws of physics which are expressed in the form that the total of some measurable entity must be constant, like the law of conservation of energy. These are known generally as the *conservation laws*, and all of them appear to be of fundamental importance. Because they are reliable to the highest degree some theoretical physicists are inclined to think—with or without justification—that they have hit upon the crux of the matter when they are able to generalize a group of phenomena into a conservation law.

The first law of this type to be clearly recognized was that of the *conservation of mass* in chemical reactions. This was largely due to the work of Lavoisier (1743–1794), through his investigations of combustion and of oxidation of metals, although all those chemists who, about the same time, started making precise weighings in the course of their work, contributed to the subject. The law can be stated as follows:

Mass cannot be created or destroyed; in any chemical reaction the total mass of the products is equal to the total mass of the reacting substances.

If there is no chemical reaction involved in a process, the law holds *a fortiori,* and so it implies that the total mass of the cosmos should be constant.

We now have two laws, each of them of the utmost importance within its own field of phenomena, and each of them apparently valid without any proven exception: the conservation of energy, and the conservation of mass. Once again, two laws which apparently refer to quite separate things are brought together into a still more fundamental principle, for it has developed during our own century that the two conservation laws are not independent. One of the predictions of Einstein's theory of relativity (Sec. 33-11) is that if a body is moving with a very high velocity there will be an apparent increase in its inertia, or mass. The kinetic energy and the increase of mass $(m - m_0)$ are connected by Einstein's famous mass-energy relation

$$\text{K.E.} = (m - m_0)c^2,$$

where c is the velocity of light.°

This prediction has been abundantly confirmed by experiment and has turned out to be even more general than the theory implies, for the relation apparently applies to all kinds of energy, not only to kinetic energy of motion. For example, in a heat-producing chemical reaction we now recognize that there must be a loss of mass. However, the amount is very small. One of the most energetic chemical reactions is the burning of hydrogen to produce water vapor, where 1 kilogram of hydrogen combines with 8 kilograms of oxygen to produce 9 kilograms of water, producing 123,000 joules of heat energy in the process. By the Einstein relation, this amount of heat energy corresponds to a loss of mass of only 1.4×10^{-12} kilogram, an amount that is far too small to measure in comparison with the total of 9 kilograms.

It is quite different in the case of a reaction that involves the nuclei of the atoms (Sec. 23-2), such as that of a so-called atomic explosion, for in this case the mass-equivalent of the energy produced is measurable, and experiments on nuclear reactions confirm the mass-energy relation. It follows that we should not consider the conservation of mass and the conservation of energy as separate laws, but we should speak of the *conservation of mass-energy,* and our combined law is that the quantity,

$$E + mc^2 \text{ is a constant,}$$

where E represents all kinds of energy other than mechanical kinetic energy. The latter is included in the term mc^2, through the increase of mass at high velocities.

° If the masses are in kilograms and the velocity of light is given as 3×10^8 meters per second (very nearly), the result will be in joules.

8-5   *Momentum and Angular Momentum*

Two more conservation laws need to be mentioned here. As discussed in Sec. 4-8, Newton's third law of motion, the law of action and reaction, means that whenever two bodies interact, the changes of momentum are equal and opposite, so that the net change is zero. More generally, for any system consisting of any number of interacting bodies the resultant of all the changes of momentum is zero. Newton's third law is therefore equivalent to the *law of conservation of momentum:*

The resultant momentum of a closed system is constant, direction as well as magnitude being taken into account in computing the total.

Similar to the case of momentum, representing the motion of a body in a specified direction, is *angular momentum* of a mass rotating on an axis or revolving in an orbit around a center. If a mass (m) is moving with a speed (v) at a distance (r) from a selected axis (Fig. 8-3), the angular momentum is defined to be the product mvr. In general, this quantity has to be calculated for each particle of mass and then summed over all the particles of a body.° Then the law states:

The total angular momentum of all the bodies in a closed system, taken around any axis, is constant.

In rigorous mathematical logic the two laws are not independent, for the law of linear momentum can be derived from that of angular momentum for the special case where all the motions are in straight lines relative

° The calculation usually involves the methods of the integral calculus.

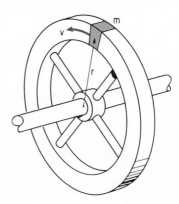

FIG. 8-3

Angular momentum.

to the axis. However, the laws find application in different types of problems—the former for collisions, for the firing of rockets, and for similar problems—the latter for rotations and revolutions. For example, Kepler's second law of planetary motion, that the rate of description of area is constant (Sec. 3-12), is a special case of the conservation of angular momentum, for the angular momentum of a planet around its center of attraction is equal to the mass multiplied by twice the rate of description of area. There is an application of the constancy of angular momentum in rotation when a figure skater performs a spin. The skater starts to turn with her arms spread out wide; then she lowers her arms to her sides, and goes into a rapid spin; to stop the spin she spreads her arms again. When she lowers her arms, part of her mass is brought closer to her axis, and her speed of rotation has to increase to compensate.

8-6   *The Energy of the Sun*

With a few trivial exceptions, all the energy used on earth and on all the other planets of the solar system can ultimately be traced back to the sun, for it is the only energy-producing body in the system. The average amount of light and heat energy received at the earth from the sun, per unit area of receiving surface, per unit time, is known as the *solar constant*. It is rather difficult to determine this accurately, since allowance has to be made

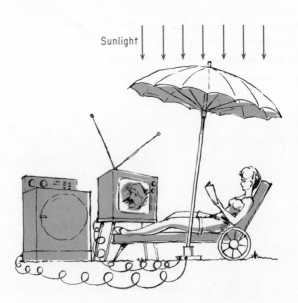

Sunlight

FIG. 8-4

If the energy of sunlight could be converted into electrical energy with 100 per cent efficiency.

for the absorption in the atmosphere, which varies considerably, depending on cloud and other conditions. The value usually accepted is 1350 watts per square meter, and this is approximately the amount that would be received on a beach umbrella on a sunny day. If it could all be converted into electrical energy, it would run a washing machine and a television set.

To find the whole amount of energy received by the earth, we must multiply the solar constant by the area of a disk of radius equal to the mean radius of the earth, and we find the apparently enormous amount of 2.31×10^{14} horsepower, which is the earth's regular power supply. To get the total power produced by the sun, we must multiply the solar constant by the area of a sphere whose radius is equal to the mean distance of the earth from the sun. The result is 3.80×10^{26} watts, or 5.10×10^{23} horsepower.

The sun has been radiating energy at this rate for at least 4½ billion years (Sec. 26-3), and so must have in its interior an energy source which, in terms of human history, is practically unlimited. The only source which can possibly supply the amount required is the conversion of mass into energy according to the Einstein relation (Sec. 8-4). This was recognized early in the present century, long before any mechanism through which it might take place had been discovered. Such a mechanism is now well known in the series of nuclear reactions which synthesize four atoms of hydrogen into one atom of helium, with a loss of mass of 0.716 per cent (Sec. 31-2). We have to conclude that the sun is losing mass by this process at the rate of 4.22×10^9 kilograms per second, or 1.47×10^{14} tons per year. However, this is only a very small fraction of the total mass of the sun, and astronomers estimate that it can continue to pour out energy at the present rate for another 10 billion years.

Most of the heat received by the earth from the sun is used to maintain the earth at its proper temperature. However, it is sunlight that makes the plants grow, through the process of photosynthesis (Sec. 13-4), and some of the sun's energy is used in this way. Since the woody fibers of a plant will burn and produce heat when combined with oxygen, plant growth represents the storage of solar energy in the form of chemical potential energy. Then all animals derive the energy necessary for their growth and movement from the plants, either directly or indirectly.

Again, it is the heat of the sun which evaporates water from the oceans and carries it up into the atmosphere to form clouds. It is the sun's heat which causes the wind to blow and distribute the clouds over the land, so that there is rain to keep the lakes and mountain reservoirs filled. Once again, solar energy is stored as the potential energy of the water behind a dam, and part of this can be converted into electrical energy to aid in running our complex modern civilization.

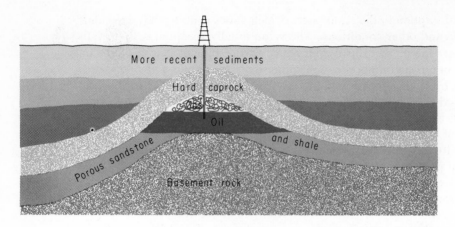

FIG. **8-5**

Fossil fuel; one way in which oil and gas can be trapped underground.

8-7   Fossil Fuels

Wind power and waterpower, the energy of men and animals, wood fuel, are all part of the earth's current energy supply. They represent a portion of the solar energy which is stored for short periods in other forms, but which is continually being replenished. However, the chemical energy that is stored in living bodies, either plant or animal, need not be used at once. When plants die their woody parts may take years to rot away. If the plant growth has been luxuriant, the dead material forms a matted layer that may be several feet thick. In the course of time the mat may be covered by layers of sand or silt, and may eventually be subjected to a pressure of many tons per square inch, decomposition going on slowly all the while. After millions of years the layer of vegetable matter may be compressed into a seam of coal.

As the woody parts of plants can form coal, so the soft parts of both plants and animals can form oil and natural gas. If such material is buried before it has a chance to decay completely, the oil and gas can collect in the surrounding sand and silt, which is in the process of being compressed into rock. Probably most of the oil and gas escapes in the course of time, but under the proper conditions it may be trapped in a porous layer of rock, to be discovered and used millions of years later.

Thus the coal and oil on which so much of our modern civilization is based are the result of the conversion of solar energy into the chemical energy of living things, millions of years ago. The energy has lain stored in the rocks of the earth's crust ever since, and, because the living organisms that produced it were contemporary with those whose remains are found as fossils in the rocks, we refer to coal and oil as *fossil fuels*. When we use them so liberally we should sometimes stop to consider that it took thousands of years for life processes to produce a mat of decaying vegetation thick enough for a useful coal bed, or to accumulate enough animal matter that the hydrocarbons resulting from its decay could collect in a significant pool of oil and gas. Millions more years were needed for slow chemical processes gradually to convert the decomposing materials into the fossil fuels we know today.

8-8   Civilization and the Use of Energy

When primitive man began building fires—for warmth in bad weather, to cook his food, or to frighten away wild animals—he was beginning in a small way the use of energy for purposes other than mere existence. When he began domesticating animals to act as beasts of burden, he was employing their muscular energy instead of his own. The utilization by man of various sources of available energy therefore long precedes what we speak of as civilization. As agriculture developed, more and more energy became available, for plants useful to man were grown in place of the natural flora. At the same time the total amount of solar energy trapped was increased, for improved methods of husbandry, and especially irrigation—a very early development—must have resulted in additional plant growth in those areas where men began to settle down into permanent communities. Agriculture was the basis for a much larger, settled population. Slowly a civilization developed in which energy was used not only for the support of life, but also to embellish a culture. However, the pyramids of Egypt, the temples of Babylon and Athens, and the great engineering and archi-

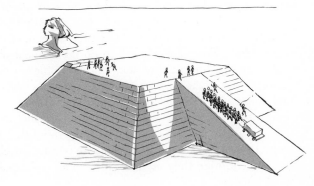

FIG. 8-6

The source of energy to build the pyramids of Egypt.

tectural works of Rome were built entirely by slave labor and beasts of burden. Thus the energy required was muscular energy, of men or of animals. Fuel was still almost exclusively wood, and was used mainly for warmth and cooking, with a little for light.

In the later Roman Empire, and again in populous areas of Europe in the seventeenth and eighteenth centuries, wood fuel was becoming scarce, and the demand for energy, in this case simply for warmth, was beginning to exceed the easily available current supply. We do not know who first discovered that certain soft black rocks would burn. Coal was certainly known to the Romans, although it seems to have been considered mainly as a curiosity, even when firewood had to be transported large distances. However, by the beginning of the eighteenth century, coal was being regularly mined in England and in some parts of Europe, and began to contribute to the fuel supply. Coal was also mined and used for fuel in China at a very early date.

Crude petroleum oil, from natural seepages, seems to have been known in ancient Babylon and to have been used to some extent in lamps. However, for many centuries artificial light was provided by torches dipped in pitch from pine trees, by lamps fueled with vegetable oils and later with whale oil, or by tallow or beeswax candles. Actually, in the Roman Empire and medieval Europe artificial light was largely a luxury for the more prosperous classes, and even they made do with a single candle or a feeble oil lamp, and would have been astounded by the brilliance of the electric light in the poorest American home today. The great bulk of the population could not read or write anyway, and only needed enough light to find their way around; for the most part they went to bed at dark. Mineral oil did not come into extensive use for lighting until it was discovered in the eastern United States in the eighteenth century. When plentiful supplies were found its use spread rapidly, as a cheaper and more efficient substitute for vegetable and animal oils.

To sum up the historical situation: civilization cannot flourish without a supply of surplus energy, above that required for mere maintenance of life. Fuel is needed for warmth, to enable men to live in settled communities in climates that have a more or less severe winter. It is needed again for cooking, and for light. Energy is needed to do mechanical work, in the construction of buildings, for grinding grain and pumping water, for many types of manufacture, for the transportation of goods as trade develops. However, until about A.D. 1700 the civilized world got along quite well by tapping the current supply of solar energy, through wood fuel and muscular energy, with some use of wind- and waterpower. About that time, fossil fuels, coal and oil, began to be used and became regular articles of commerce, but the contribution they made to the world's energy supply was still only a small fraction.

The present use of energy and the demand for fuel to run our industrialized civilization rests largely on three inventions in the field of *prime movers,*° each of which in turn has played a large part in revolutionizing world economy. The first of these inventions was the *steam engine.* The first useful steam engine was built by Thomas Newcomen in England, in 1711, but the man who deserves most of the credit for making the engine practical is James Watt, who started building them about 1770, and the modern reciprocating steam engine—still used on many ocean-going ships—differs only in detail from the Watt engine (Fig. 8-7).†

Newcomen's engines were designed specifically to pump water out of the coal mines that were beginning to dot the landscape in England and in parts of Europe. In these steam pumps the reciprocating motion of the engine piston was simply connected to the piston of the pump, either directly or through a lever. Watt's engines were also used at first to drive pumps, but one of the improvements had been the addition of a crank to convert the reciprocating motion of the piston into the rotary motion of a shaft and flywheel. This made the engines more versatile and more useful, and before long, Watt engines were being used to run machines in the factories that were replacing cottage industry in what is known to historians as the Industrial Revolution. The steam locomotive and the steamship followed; railways began to be built all over Europe and North America;

° The engineer uses the term "prime mover" for a machine that converts the heat energy of burning fuel, or the energy of a flowing river, into useful mechanical work, or into the more versatile electrical energy.

† The reciprocating steam engine, with cylinder and piston, has been replaced by the steam turbine in most places where steam is still used. Similarly, gas turbines are replacing stationary gasoline and diesel engines in some places, and jet engines are replacing the more conventional engines in high-speed aircraft. However, these inventions have not brought about revolutions in world economy in the way that the inventions discussed in this chapter have done.

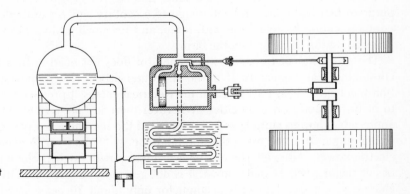

FIG. 8-7

An early Watt steam engine.

FIG. 8-8

Hydroelectric power installation of the Idaho Power Company at Brownlee Dam on the Snake River. Completed in 1959, using electric generators built by the Westinghouse Electric Corporation, and producing 450,000 kilowatts of power, it was at the time of construction the largest investor-owned power plant in the U.S.A. (Photograph courtesy of the Idaho Power Company.)

ocean commerce began to be carried by steam instead of sail. A hundred years after Watt built his first engine the machine that had started as an adjunct to the mining of coal had become the greatest user of coal, and energy derived from fossil fuel greatly exceeded that of muscle power in all those countries where the industrial revolution had flourished.

The second revolutionary invention to be mentioned is the *electric generator* (Chapter 16), which was developed into a practical machine in the late nineteenth century, for the use of electricity has multiplied by a large factor the demand for energy that started with the steam engine. In factories electric motors attached to each machine have replaced the cumbersome shafts and belts that brought the power from a central steam engine. Individual motors are much more efficient, in the sense that far less energy is wasted, but with modern industrialization the total number of machines in use has multiplied many times. Our homes, offices, and factories can now be lighted as brilliantly as we care to make them, and the amount of energy used for lighting alone in a city like New York is many times that used for all purposes in the whole Roman Empire. Availability always creates new demands, and electricity is used today for purposes that had not even been imagined a century ago, for example, for communication by telephone and radio, and for small motors to relieve drudgery in the home and on the farm.

The prime mover for an electric generator does not need to be a fuel-consuming heat engine. In 1885 the first water-driven electric power station was built at Niagara Falls, and the electrical energy it produced began to be distributed to nearby cities. Wherever there is a large river with an appreciable drop in altitude as it flows toward the sea, there is a possibility of building a dam and using the potential energy of the river to generate electric power. Although the existence of great power projects along most of our major rivers is well known, it is not generally realized that hydroelectric power developments account for only about 10 per cent of the electricity generated in North America. The major part of the remaining 90 per cent is generated by steam power, from burning coal or oil. A certain amount, mainly in small local plants, is produced by natural gas, or by oil in diesel engines.

The third revolutionary invention in the power field was the *internal-combustion engine,* in which a liquid or gaseous fuel is ignited inside the engine cylinder, to produce heat and gas pressure to drive the engine. The first practical engine of this type, using liquid fuel, was built by Nicholas Otto in Germany in 1876. Otto's engine was clumsy, and the fuel had to be ignited by a red-hot iron rod inside the cylinder (the original "hot-rod") but improvements quickly followed, leading to the modern gasoline engine, in which the fuel is ignited by an electric spark. A slightly different series of improvements led to the diesel engine, in which the fuel is ignited when the air in the cylinder is rapidly compressed during the compression stroke, and is thereby heated to a high temperature. The internal-combustion engine proved to be the most useful type of prime mover wherever a small portable source of power was needed, and so Otto's engine led to the automobile. The airplane soon followed, for it was the high ratio of power output to weight in the gasoline engine that made possible the first flights.

There is no need to elaborate on the way in which the use of automobiles has spread in only a little over 60 years, or how the airplane has developed in a still shorter period from a novelty (and an implement of war) to the commonplace means of long-distance travel. What concerns us here is the tremendous increase in the demand for liquid fuels, not only to meet these new needs, but also as a replacement for the more cumbersome and less convenient coal, for railway locomotives and ships, and finally for house heating.

8-10   The World Energy Problem

It should be obvious that we cannot continue to base our way of life on the use of fossil fuels at the present extravagant rate of consumption. It is difficult to predict how long the coal and oil buried in the earth's crust will last, and different writers have given very different figures. If we consider only the reserves of oil and gas in the *known* oil fields, and if we assume that the rate of consumption will continue to increase as it has increased since World War II, then the world will begin to run out of oil before the end of the present century. But new oil fields will be discovered, and in addition we know that there are vast quantities of oil bound up in oil-bearing shales and tar sands.° This cannot be exploited by means of the conven-

---

° There are known to be vast deposits of tar-saturated sand in northern Canada, enough to supply the world with oil for 100 years at the present rate of consumption. These deposits are beginning to be exploited on an experimental scale.

tional drilled wells, but it can be mined and the oil extracted. Taking all factors into account, it is more likely that civilization could continue to run on oil for 500, perhaps even 1000 years.

Coal is unpopular as a source of energy at the present time because it is less convenient than oil. However, unless there is some drastic change in the energy picture, it will have to be used again, probably by building large electrical power plants at coal mine sites. Reserves of coal would most likely last another 1000 years, making the total estimate for fossil fuels about 2000 years.

This may seem like a long time, but it is only a small fraction of the time since primitive man built the first fire, and that again is only a small fraction of the history of life on earth. Alarmists may say that civilization is destined to destroy itself in the cataclysm of thermonuclear warfare. Others express concern over the way in which the population of the world is multiplying. These are problems, and very serious problems, and it is well that people should begin to think about them. However, the problems can be solved, and civilization can continue, to exceed by far the time span of its past brief history. Therefore the problem of the energy supply must also be solved.

There are just two alternatives, and fortunately there is hope in both directions. Either the world must learn to live on its current energy resources, that is, on the continual flow of energy from the sun, or else some new source of energy must be developed. The promising new source is, of course, nuclear energy, and its use has already been successful for the practical supply of power, in large ships in the navies of both the U.S.A. and the U.S.S.R., as well as in electrical power plants in a number of places in the world. So far, peaceful uses of nuclear energy have required uranium in one form or another as the basic fuel, and the world supply of uranium is limited. The hope for the distant future is that the reactions involved in the thermonuclear (or hydrogen) bomb explosion can be brought under control and exploited for peaceful purposes. When this is accomplished the hydrogen in the sea will provide enough energy to last civilization for many millions of years.*

As for the current energy supply, the amount received from the sun is theoretically ample to supply all needs, and methods of utilizing it must be exploited to the full. At present the most important of these is waterpower, and there are a number of great rivers whose potential energy is not being fully used, especially in Africa and Asia and in the Far North. However, waterpower cannot meet the whole demand, and methods of utilizing solar energy directly will also have to be exploited. One possibility is the

---

* The principles involved in the release of nuclear energy and the problems involved in exploiting it will be discussed in Chapter 24.

direct conversion of the sun's heat into electrical energy, by means of large thermoelectric cells (Sec. 14-7), a method that is already being used on a small scale to provide power for the instruments in artificial satellites. Another suggested possibility is the cultivation of green algae on a world-wide scale in great ponds, for there are known species of these microscopic plants that grow and multiply 100 times faster than a tree.

GLOSSARY

Amplitude (of an oscillation) The extent of the swing on either side of center.

Angular momentum Quantity that measures the amount of a rotation or revolution; defined as the product of the momentum (mv) and the distance (r) from the axis or center; this has to be computed for each particle (m) of a rotating body, and then summed over the whole body.

Available energy That part of the energy of a system that can be used to do work; the term is used especially of heat energy, only part of which can be used.

Chemical potential energy Energy possessed by a system by virtue of the fact that some of its constituents might combine chemically, and produce heat in doing so.

Conservation laws Those scientific laws that are expressed in the form that the total amount of a certain quantity remains constant when changes in the system take place.

Efficiency (of an engine or similar device) Ratio of the useful work done to the energy supplied, usually expressed as a percentage.

Elastic potential energy Energy possessed by a body when it is under tension or compression; for example, the energy of a stretched spring.

Fossil fuels Coal, oil, and natural gas, which have been formed in the earth's crust by the slow decomposition of the bodies of plants and animals.

Heat sink, or energy sink Reservoir (usually the earth itself) in which heat energy accumulates under conditions such that it is no longer available.

Nuclear atomic energy Energy released when part of the mass of atomic nuclei is converted into kinetic energy and heat.

Photosynthesis The process by which green plants absorb light energy, and then are able to manufacture sugars and starches out of carbon dioxide and water, releasing oxygen gas.

Prime mover Machine (such as a steam engine or a gasoline engine) that converts the energy of a burning fuel either into mechanical work or into electrical energy.

Radiometer In general, a device for detecting and measuring radiation.

Reciprocating motion Back and forth motion in a straight line, applied particularly to the motion of the piston in the cylinder of a piston-type steam engine or of a gasoline engine.

Solar constant The energy received by the earth from the sun in the form of light and heat, expressed in power units per unit area.

Thermoelectric cell Device for producing electric current by the direct conversion of heat energy, by maintaining a difference of temperature across a circuit that contains two different metals.

Thermonuclear reaction A reaction affecting the nuclei of the atoms, initiated by subjecting them to a very high temperature; particularly the synthesis of hydrogen and other light elements into heavier elements in the stars or in a hydrogen bomb explosion.

EXERCISES

1. For each of the forms of energy listed in Sec. 8-1 name a natural phenomenon, a machine, or other device in which this type of energy does mechanical work.

2. Name a natural phenomenon, a device, or a machine in which each of the following energy conversions takes place: (a) light into electrical; (b) light into chemical; (c) sound into electrical; (d) elastic potential into mechanical kinetic; (e) mechanical into electrical and vice versa; (f) heat into electrical, directly as well as indirectly; (g) energy of a compressed gas into sound; (h) elastic energy into sound; (i) chemical into electrical; (j) muscular into mechanical potential.

3. The law of conservation of energy says that energy cannot be created or destroyed, and yet we buy energy from the power company and "consume" it in an electric light or a motor. In what sense is energy "consumed" in each of these cases?

4. What is the necessary condition for heat energy to be available? Is there any condition under which *all* the heat content of a body is available?

5. How does a portion of the heat content of the atmosphere become available? Is it ever possible to use a portion of the heat content of the oceans?

6. Trace the energy conversions in the type of pile driver in which a weight is raised to the top of a derrick by an electric motor, and then is allowed to drop on the head of the pile.

7. How much energy is produced when 1 kilogram of mass is lost in a nuclear reaction?

8. What is the loss of mass when 1 kilogram of gasoline is burned, producing 11,500 kilocalories of heat?

9. Show by simple logical arguments that the law of conservation of momentum follows from Newton's law of action and reaction, and conversely, that the equality of action and reaction follows from the conservation of momentum. Therefore the two laws are alternative statements of the same principle. (If your argument can be expressed by means of a few steps of algebra, so much the better.)

10. What conservation law is equivalent to Kepler's second law of planetary motion? Give other examples of this law.

11. Show how the sun is the ultimate source of almost all the energy used for heating and for the production of electrical power.

12. Name and explain briefly three sources of energy which do *not* derive from the sun, and which are now being exploited or could be exploited.

13. What is the solar constant? Why has it been difficult to determine this important quantity accurately?

14. In some places where fuel is scarce, attempts are being made to use the sun's energy directly for cooking, by using mirrors to focus sunlight on a kettle. Suppose we had a parabolic mirror 5 meters in diameter to concentrate the sunlight on a kettle at the focus of the mirror; how many calories per minute would we get? If the device could be made 40 per cent efficient, how long would it take to raise a kilogram of water from 30°C to the boiling point?

15. Suggest ways in which the sun's current energy supply could be exploited on a much larger scale, and much more efficiently, than is being done at present.

16. Trace the steps of energy conversion from the sun to the ocean, thence to a rain cloud, and finally to the electric generator behind a dam in a major river.

17. When and how did fossil fuels become an important factor in world economy?

18. What sources of energy were used, and for what purposes, up to about A.D. 1700?

19. Describe briefly how the steam engine, the electric generator, and the internal-combustion engine, each in its turn, revolutionized world economy and increased by a large factor the need for fuel.

ATOMS AND MOLECULES

part three

*All matter is made up of indivisible atoms.
Each chemical element has its characteristic
atom, with a definite atomic weight. Compounds are made up of molecules, consisting
of two or more atoms in combination.*

—DALTON'S HYPOTHESIS (1803)

the fundamental laws of chemistry

In a way, chemistry is almost as old a science as astronomy. The discovery that certain ores could be smelted to produce copper or tin is lost in the mist of prehistory, but it is certain that by 3000 B.C. the production of copper implements was a flourishing industry in the civilizations of both Mesopotamia and Egypt. It was well known that alloying the copper with a little tin would make the much harder and more useful bronze, and the discovery of rich deposits of tin in Britain was an important factor in the expansion of maritime commerce outside the confines of the Mediterranean Sea. Iron came later, but probably only because iron ores are not found in quantity in the Mediterranean countries. The use of iron seems to have originated in northern Europe and to have contributed to the development of the Mediterranean civilization coinciding with the migration into that area—in the second millennium B.C.—of the tribes who became the ancestors of the Greeks. The corrosive action of certain materials on the valuable metals was observed in very early times, leading to the very ancient idea that gold is a "noble" metal because of its resistance to corrosion, an idea which colored the thinking of those who practiced the chemical arts for hundreds of years.

In certain other fields of chemistry practical discoveries also go back to very ancient times. Long before the use of metals, Stone Age peoples of the neolithic cultures were familiar with fermentation and distillation; alcoholic drinks were common, as they are in many primitive tribes today. Salt was extracted from seawater and was probably purified of its less desirable constituents in a rather crude manner, to become a very important article of commerce. Dyes were made from animal and vegetable sources and were used almost as soon as the arts of spinning thread and weaving cloth were developed. Cosmetics and perfumes were used by the wealthier citizens in Egypt in the time of the Pharaohs; these must have required a certain knowledge of refining and purification.

All these factors of the ancient civilizations argue an extensive practical knowledge of chemical processes which are still, in improved form, the basis of great and flourishing industries. However, this knowledge was largely empirical, and it was well into modern times before there was any real understanding of what goes on when, for example, iron ore is reduced to produce metallic iron. The smelting of metals and the production of alcoholic drinks and dyestuffs were technical arts rather than the application of scientific knowledge. As such they did not greatly excite the curiosity of the philosophers who concerned themselves with the movements of the heavenly bodies and the origin of the cosmos. There was some speculation on the nature of matter, which will be discussed briefly later, but it had very little relation to the details of chemical technology.

Finally, lest we get the impression that early empirical science was a monopoly of the Mediterranean area, Mesopotamia, and western Europe, it is well to remember that similar discoveries were made independently and more or less simultaneously in other parts of the world, particularly in China and in India. However, there is a direct connection and a continuous thread of history between copper smelting in ancient Mesopotamia and the formulation of the basic laws of chemistry in Europe in the eighteenth and nineteenth centuries. This thread we must proceed to trace.

9-2   The Alchemists

Among the later Alexandrian Greeks, among the Arabs, and in Europe in the Middle Ages, empirical chemistry developed into what came to be known as *alchemy*. The word implies to most people a degraded, and not quite nice, pseudoscience, although it is only a variation of the Arabic for "infusion." When we speak of a medieval alchemist we are liable to picture a bearded and cloaked individual wearing a conical cap inscribed with astrological symbols, working in semidarkness in a secret laboratory, hunting for the magic formula that will turn base metals into gold, or the elixir that will give him eternal life. This is very misleading. An alchemist was simply one who practiced the chemical arts, and he might be anything from a perfectly respectable artisan engaged in refining metals to a philosopher sincerely seeking for the meaning of matter and of life. The grain of truth in the popular picture arises from the facts that many alchemists worked in secret to prevent others from learning their processes—there were no patent laws in medieval times—and that two continuing ambitions were the transmutation of metals and the elixir of life. As a result, in both Muslim and Christian countries, there were times when the alchemists were thought to be in league with the Devil, and their activities were proscribed by the religious authorities.

In ancient times chemical processes, such as smelting, were always somewhat uncertain. They had to be accompanied by the proper magical formula, or the results might be unsatisfactory. Ancient chemical recipes, many of which have been found, often contain not only the practical directions but also the proper words to be recited in order to make the process work. When some of the later Alexandrian philosophers, and still later the rather mystically minded Arabs, became interested in the subject, there grew out of the ancient chemical arts a pseudoscience which was a curious mixture of practical technology, black magic, and mystical religious ideas.

For example, the obsession of some of the alchemists with the transmutation of metals into gold arose from arguments which are quite reasonable if you accept the premise, and which go somewhat as follows. Gold, because it resists corrosion and apparently lasts forever, is the most noble of all the metals, and constitutes the "soul" of all things metallic in the

FIG. 9-1

The popular image of an alchemist.

sense that it is the pure essence of "metalness." In this the mystical alchemists saw an analogy with the immortal soul of man, which could become refined into pure spirit after death. In their eyes it followed that, just as man's soul will eventually be redeemed from the imperfections of sin, so it ought to be possible to dissolve away the gross imperfections that characterize an ignoble metal like lead, leaving behind the pure gold. Naturally, when the philosophical alchemists produced arguments of this kind, others tried to develop the transmutation process for their own profit. There were even some who claimed to have succeeded, when all they had done was to give base metal a yellowish color, by some chemical treatment.

The alchemists never turned lead into gold, but in trying to do so they learned a great deal about the chemistry of metals and made many improvements in methods of metal refining. They never found the magic formula of eternal life, but, since many of them were also physicians, they developed new drugs and new and useful methods for treating diseases.° When the chemists of the late eighteenth century began to discuss chemical processes in purely scientific terms, devoid of mystical preconceptions, they had a fund of empirical material to work with. One important thing the alchemists lacked: it apparently never occurred to any of them to weigh accurately all the materials involved in a chemical process, and this was necessary before the fundamental laws of chemical reaction could be formulated.

9-3   Oxidation and Reduction

Space will not permit a discussion of the many different types of chemical processes that can take place, and a few examples must suffice. One such example is the relation between a metal and its oxide.† If iron is exposed to the air in the presence of moisture, or if it is left under water in a sea or lake, it will rust. We know now that the iron combines with the oxygen of the air, or with oxygen dissolved in the water, to form one of the several different oxides of iron, in a process of slow *oxidation*. The presence of water is necessary for oxygen to combine with iron at ordinary temperatures, and rust will not form if the air is perfectly dry. On the other hand, it is the oxygen and not the water that produces the rust, for iron will stay clean and bright if it is immersed in water that contains no dissolved oxygen.

° Paracelsus (1493–1541), the most famous of the later alchemists, is typical of their thinking. His writings combine mystical philosophical ideas about metals with very practical ideas about the chemistry of the human body, derived from his experience as a medical practitioner.

† Oxides are compounds of an element with oxygen. Binary compounds, those which contain just two elements, are generally indicated by the suffix "-ide." For a discussion of standard chemical nomenclature students should refer to a textbook of elementary chemistry.

All metals can form oxides under the appropriate circumstances, but the rate varies greatly with different metals and under different conditions. Potassium and rubidium oxidize so rapidly that they are liable to catch fire spontaneously when exposed to the air. Some other metals will burn if ignited, and a piece of iron wool will burn vigorously in oxygen gas. Aluminum oxidizes quite rapidly when it is first exposed to the air, but the oxide forms a hard protective coating which prevents any further action. Gold and platinum will not oxidize at all under simple exposure, but the oxides do form under the proper chemical treatment.

The formation of oxides is usually accompanied by the evolution of heat —a conversion of chemical potential energy into heat energy. Ordinary combustion, of wood or oil, is another oxidation process, and it is important here that a "trigger" action is involved. That is, a certain rise of temperature is necessary in order to overcome a *potential energy barrier*, so that the reaction can begin. Once the oil starts to burn, the heat produced keeps the temperature high enough to ignite the next portion of oil. A small flame can be blown out, or an oil well fire can be extinguished by setting off a charge of dynamite in the well mouth, because the blast carries off the hot gases before they have a chance to heat the remaining fuel to the ignition point.

In the fact that the oil has to be ignited before it will burn and release its chemical potential energy there is an analogy with the situation of an automobile that faces a slight rise in the road before starting down a long hill. The car possesses potential energy because it is at a higher level than the lowest point of the road. However, to release this energy, a certain amount of work has to be done by the engine to carry the car over the initial rise (the potential energy barrier), after which it can roll down the hill without any further use of the engine, and can do work in the process.

FIG. 9-2

Trigger action to overcome a potential barrier and start combustion.

The reverse process to oxidation is *reduction*, which is the basic chemical reaction involved in the smelting of many metallic ores, including that of iron. The commonest iron ores are oxides, and the oxygen has to be removed in order to leave behind the metallic iron. This is commonly accomplished by heating the iron ore in the presence of some material that combines with oxygen more readily than does iron. In the primitive smelting operations, the *reducing agent*—the material that combines with the oxygen—was carbon in the form of charcoal. Although this process is still used extensively—generally with coke derived from coal in place of wood charcoal—for some purposes other reducing agents are used, for example, hydrogen gas.

9-4   The Discovery of Oxygen and the Law of Conservation of Mass

The processes of formation of metallic oxides and recovery of the metal from the oxide are important in the history of science because they gave rise in the eighteenth century to a famous scientific controversy, and the elucidation of the problem was one of the most important factors in the development of the basic laws of chemistry. Remember that in the early eighteenth century oxygen gas was unknown, the principle of conservation of energy had yet to be developed, and heat was generally considered to be a material substance, known as "caloric." The controversy arose over the relation between a metal and its "calx"—the material that we now know as the oxide of the metal. The calx could be formed from the metal by heating in air, a process that was evidently closely related to combustion of flammable materials. The metal could be recovered from the calx by heating with charcoal, as in primitive smelting operations. The problem was to decide which is the more fundamental material (what we would now call the chemical element), the metal or the calx. It was also evident that in combustion something rose upward from the fire, and this was probably what led to the idea of a mysterious substance known as "phlogiston," which was supposed to be released along with "caloric" when anything was burned or when a metal was converted into the calx by heating. Following up this idea, most chemists thought that the calx was the more fundamental, and that the metal was a combination of calx with phlogiston.

In the late 1700's a number of the common gases—hydrogen, carbon dioxide, and others—were isolated and their properties studied, refuting the ancient idea that air is an elemental substance. Most important, in 1777 Priestley in England and Scheele in Sweden independently isolated oxygen, demonstrated that its presence is essential for the support of combustion and of animal life, and showed that air is a mixture, consisting mainly of nitrogen and oxygen in the proportion of about 4 to 1.

About the same time Lavoisier* demonstrated conclusively that when a metal is heated in air, the calx produced weighs more than the metal. He then performed the important experiment of calcining tin with air in a sealed vessel and was able to prove that the weight of the vessel was precisely the same after calcination as before. At the same time he showed that the difference in weight between the calx and the metal was equal to the weight of the oxygen which disappeared in the process of calcination. It followed that the metal, not the calx, was the more elemental, and that the latter was a compound of the metal with oxygen.

This and similar experiments led chemists to the realization of the first basic law of chemistry, the *law of conservation of mass:*

In any chemical reaction the total mass remains constant; the combined mass of the products is always equal to the combined mass of the materials entering into the reaction.†

9-5   *Elements and Compounds*

The idea that all materials are made up of a small number of basic substances, the *elements*, is a very ancient one. Never explicitly defined in early writings—and probably not clearly understood until the time of Lavoisier— the idea implied has nearly always been that expressed in the definition:

An element is a pure substance that cannot be analyzed, or separated, into simpler substances.

Nowadays we should add to this definition, "by chemical methods," although it is not always easy to distinguish a chemical method from other processes. In general, if a process starts with one or more pure substances in bulk, and different pure substances having different properties are produced, a chemical change must have taken place.‡ In this and in the

* Antoine Lavoisier (1743–1794) was a French government official whose duties allowed him to spend time on chemical experiments. He can be considered as the father of modern chemistry, and his *Elements of Chemistry* (1789) is a landmark in that subject, comparable to Newton's *Principia* in mechanics.

† Nowadays we have to recognize that there is a minute change of mass when a chemical reaction takes place, due to the conversion of mass into energy or vice versa (Sec. 8-4).

‡ The classical chemical definitions are complicated by two twentieth-century discoveries. (1) Most elements are mixtures of several *isotopes*—substances having almost identical chemical and physical properties, but having different atomic weights and densities (Sec. 22-9). For elements found in nature, the proportion of different isotopes in the mixture is very nearly constant and is only very slightly affected by chemical reaction. Therefore the classical definition of element, as given here, applies with good approximation to materials in bulk. (2) The discovery that one element can be transmuted into another in a nuclear reactor (Sec. 23-4) by a physical process complicates the definition of chemical change. Students must be prepared to encounter exceptions to both the definitions and the simple chemical laws.

definition of element the term "pure substance" has been used, and this needs clarification. Thinking always of materials in bulk, a substance can be considered pure if it satisfies two criteria: (1) all its parts have the same properties; (2) it cannot be separated into two or more different substances with different properties except by a chemical process. This is clearer if we think of substances that are not pure—materials that are *mixtures* of two or more things. In many cases, the fact that a quantity of material is a mixture is obvious, for example, a handful of earth. However, there are many mixtures in which the fact is not obvious, for example, a *solution*, say, of common salt in water. The solution satisfies criterion (1); any portion of it has the same properties of color, taste, density, boiling point, etc. But it does not satisfy criterion (2); by simple heating the water can be driven off, leaving the solid salt.

Most of the Greek philosophers talked of four elements, earth, water, air, and fire. It was usually implied that these were material, although Aristotle and many of his followers thought of them as qualities rather than as actual substances: earth, for example, being the essence which gave things the property of solidity. Gradually, as the concept of the material elements became somewhat more definite, and as more facts concerning chemical processes were discovered, it became evident that things are not as simple as the Greek philosophers believed. To the later alchemists water, air, and fire were still elemental, but earth came to be recognized as a mixture of many things, although most alchemists made the mistake of considering the calxes rather than the metals as the elements.

From the eighteenth-century studies of the chemistry of gases it became evident that air could no longer be considered as an element, and a number of different gases became known, some of them elemental like oxygen, nitrogen, and hydrogen, and some of them compound like the gaseous oxides of carbon. It then became possible for Lavoisier to clarify the whole subject, enabling him to use the terms "element" and "compound" as we use them in modern chemistry: *a compound being a pure substance which consists of two or more elements in combination.*

Lavoisier seems to have been reluctant for a long time to give up the idea that water is one of the material elements, but he finally accepted the experimental evidence of the gas chemists that it is the oxide of hydrogen, and therefore a compound, just as the calxes were proved to be compound oxides of the elemental metals. In his *Elements of Chemistry* he described correctly 23 material elements, and he seems to have realized that many more were still not discovered.

Recent lists contain 103 elements, of which 88 are found in the earth's crust, either free or in combination. The 13 most abundant elements (Table 9-1) account for over 98 per cent of the natural material that

TABLE 9-1   RELATIVE ABUNDANCE ON EARTH OF THE
13 COMMONEST ELEMENTS[1]

Element	Percentage by Mass	Element	Percentage by Mass
Oxygen	49.52	Magnesium	1.94
Silicon	25.75	Chlorine	1.88
Aluminum	7.51	Hydrogen	0.88
Iron	4.70	Titanium	0.58
Calcium	3.39	Phosphorus	0.120
Sodium	2.64	Carbon	0.087
Potassium	2.40		

[1] From Quagliano, Chemistry, 2nd ed. (Englewood Cliffs, N.J.: Prentice-Hall, Inc., 1963).

is available for analysis—the earth's crust, the sea, and the atmosphere.° Seven of the remaining 75 are radioactive and are slowly disappearing by spontaneous disintegration (Sec. 23-1). The 15 known elements that have not been found naturally have been produced artificially in particle accelerators or nuclear reactors (Sec. 23-4)—they are unstable, and if some of them are occasionally produced by natural processes they soon disintegrate. As will be shown later (Sec. 9-11) the list given in Tables 9-3 and 9-4 is complete up to number 103—any new elements that may be identified must be heavier than lawrencium and are almost certain to be highly radioactive.

9-6   More Fundamental Laws

Following Lavoisier, further progress in the science of chemistry was rapid —it soon became possible to formulate two more empirical laws of fundamental importance. In 1797 Proust, a Frenchman who was at the time professor of chemistry at the University of Madrid, stated the *law of constant combining weights:*

A particular chemical compound always contains the same proportions by mass of its constituent elements.

For example, water, at least as it occurs naturally in rivers and seas, always contains 2.0160 parts by mass of hydrogen to 16 parts of oxygen. Similarly, carbon dioxide, the "fixed air" of the early chemists, always contains

° In the cosmos as a whole hydrogen is by far the most abundant element and exceeds all the rest combined. Helium is second and exceeds the total of the heavier elements listed in Table 9-1.

6.005 parts of carbon to 16 parts of oxygen. It follows that 2.0160 parts of hydrogen ought to combine with 6.005 parts of carbon. This in fact produces the gas, methane, the principal constituent of natural well gas, although this is only one of many known hydrocarbons, or compounds of carbon and hydrogen.

In 1804 Dalton, the founder of the modern atomic theory, stated the *law of multiple proportions:*

If a pair of elements, A and B, can combine in different ways to make two or more distinct compounds, the different amounts of B which combine with a fixed amount of A are in simple integral proportion.

For example, carbon and oxygen form two different gaseous compounds, with distinct properties. Carbon dioxide contains 12.010 parts of carbon to 32 parts of oxygen. It is a heavy, inert gas which will neither burn nor support combustion. It condenses into the solid known as "dry ice" at $-78°C$. It is a normal constituent of the atmosphere, and is harmless in small quantities. In larger quantities it will put out a wood fire by smothering it, and will kill animals by suffocation, although it is essential to plant life. Carbon monoxide is a light gas which condenses to a liquid at $-190°C$. It burns when ignited. It is highly poisonous, and, when inhaled in the exhaust fumes from an automobile, may cause death. In agreement with the law of multiple proportions, carbon monoxide contains 12.010 parts of carbon to 16 parts of oxygen. That is, compared with carbon dioxide it contains exactly half as much oxygen for a given amount of carbon, or just twice as much carbon for a given quantity of oxygen, whichever way you like to put it.

9-7   Chemical Symbols, Atomic and Molecular Weights

The law of constant combining weights and the law of multiple proportions make it possible to assign to each element a definite figure, known as its *atomic weight,* such that *in any compound the proportion by mass of the constituent elements is equal to the ratio of the atomic weights, or to the ratio of simple multiples of the atomic weights.* The sum of the multiples of the atomic weights is then the *molecular weight* of the compound.

We are indebted to Dalton for giving us the first systematic table of atomic weights and for the idea of representing the different elements by simple symbols. Dalton's symbols were pictorial, derived in many instances from symbols which had been used by the alchemists to write secret recipes. More convenient, and the basis of the modern system, are the letter symbols introduced a little later by Berzelius. Usually these are one- or two-letter abbreviations of the internationally accepted names of the elements. Thus H stands for hydrogen, O for oxygen, Ca for calcium, Mg for magnesium, etc.—a complete modern list is included in Table 9-3. The symbols for elements known in classical times are often derived from the Latin names, such as Fe (from *ferrum*) for iron.

The *symbol* for an element can represent either one atom of the element or a number of mass units equal to the atomic weight. Thus H represents either an atom of hydrogen or 1.0080 grams of hydrogen; it is also somewhat loosely used merely as an abbreviation for the name "hydrogen"— the context makes it clear which use is intended. The *formula* for a compound is derived by writing the symbols for the constituent elements in succession, with numerical subscripts to represent the number of atoms of each element. Thus H_2O for water normally indicates that water contains two atoms of hydrogen to one atom of oxygen; it can also represent the fact that the proportion by mass of hydrogen to oxygen is (2×1.0080) to 16.

In setting up a table of atomic weights it is necessary to choose one element as standard, and to assign to it an arbitrary value. Dalton and other early writers took the lightest known element, hydrogen, as standard, and assigned to it the atomic weight 1. Later it turned out to be more convenient to take oxygen $= 16.000 \ldots$ as the arbitrary basis, and this was used as the standard for many years. It is now known, however, that oxygen, along with most other elements, is a mixture of several isotopes (Sec. 23-6), and that the proportion in the mixture varies slightly according to the source of the material. A natural element is therefore not a completely satisfactory standard, and in 1961 the international standard was changed to the pure isotope known as carbon 12, $C^{12} = 12.000 \ldots$. There is very little difference between atomic weights based on 16 for average oxygen mixture and those based on 12 for carbon isotope, and older tables based on the oxygen standard are still satisfactory for most purposes.[*]

If, in assigning atomic weights, only two elements and their compounds are taken into account, a certain amount of ambiguity exists. For example, by chemical analysis water contains hydrogen and oxygen in the approximate ratio of $1:8$. If we assign the value 16 to oxygen, it is uncertain whether to take hydrogen as approximately 1, and write the formula H_2O, or to take $H = 2$ and write it HO. To arrive at a consistent scheme it is necessary to intercompare the compounds of several different elements. Take, for example, the four elements, oxygen, hydrogen, nitrogen, and carbon. The simple binary compounds of these are listed in Table 9-2, with the formulae finally arrived at and the proportional ratios, which are consistent with the assignment: $O = 16$, $H = 1$, $N = 14$ and $C = 12$. It

---

[*] The atomic weight of oxygen is 15.9994 on the carbon 12 scale. Hydrogen is 1.0080 on the oxygen scale, 1.00797 on the carbon 12 scale.

TABLE 9-2   SIMPLE BINARY COMPOUNDS OF FOUR ELEMENTS

Compound	Formula	Approximate Ratio by Weight	Approximate Molecular Weight
Water	H_2O	1:8	18
Carbon monoxide	CO	3:4	28
Carbon dioxide	CO_2	3:8	40
Methane	CH_4	3:1	16
Nitrogen monoxide	N_2O	7:4	44
Nitrous oxide	NO	7:8	30
Nitrogen trioxide	N_2O_3	7:12	76
Nitric oxide	NO_2	7:16	46
Nitrogen pentoxide	N_2O_5	7:20	108
Ammonia	NH_3	14:3	17
Cyanogen	CN	6:7	26

now becomes evident that we could not take H = 2, because then ammonia would contain 1½ units of hydrogen, which is not permitted. It might still be possible to take H = 0.5, but then all hydrogen compounds would turn out to contain even numbers of units of the element, so this is clearly wrong, and H = 1 becomes unambiguous.

9-8   *Chemical Equations*

The chemical symbols and molecular formulae provide a very simple way of describing the various possible chemical reactions and processes, easily read and understood once the method is explained. For example, the complete combustion of methane, to produce carbon dioxide and water, would be expressed by the equation,°

$$CH_4 + 2O_2 \longrightarrow CO_2 + 2H_2O.$$

The arrow indicates that the reaction proceeds spontaneously in the direction shown, usually with the release of energy, and possibly after having been ignited. However, it is considered as an equation because, when it is properly written, there must be the same number of atoms of each element on both sides. Since the chemical symbols imply definite amounts of the elements concerned, the information given by the equation includes the relative masses of the materials entering into the reaction.

A double-headed arrow indicates that the materials can coexist in equilibrium, and that the reaction may proceed in either direction. For

° The reason for writing oxygen and other gaseous elements as O_2 in this and other equations will be evident later (Sec. 11-3).

example, if hydrogen and chlorine gases are mixed, a certain amount of hydrogen chloride will form, the amount depending on the temperature, but the reaction will not normally go to completion. This is expressed by the equilibrium equation

$$H_2 + Cl_2 \longleftrightarrow 2HCl.$$

9-9   Dissociation, Ions

A great many substances that are soluble in water *dissociate* when they are dissolved. That is, some or all of the material separates into *ions*, atoms or groups of atoms that carry an electric charge, positive or negative. For example, when common table salt (sodium chloride, NaCl) is dissolved in water it dissociates almost completely into positively charged sodium ions and negatively charged chlorine ions, as indicated by the equation

$$NaCl \text{ (in water)} \longrightarrow Na^+ + Cl^-.$$

Since the sodium chloride was electrically neutral to begin with, the electric charges on the ions must be equal and opposite and there must be equal numbers of each produced. The resulting solution is a conductor of electricity and, if positive and negative electric terminals are immersed in the solution, the sodium ions drift toward the negative terminal and the chlorine ions toward the positive, in the process known as *electrolysis* (Sec. 21-1).

Another example is ammonium nitrate (NH_4NO_3) which dissociates into *polyatomic ions*—positive and negative molecular groups—rather than into individual charged atoms:

$$NH_4NO_3 \longrightarrow NH_4^+ + NO_3^-.$$

Groups such as these, which enter into chemical combination as units and which form polyatomic ions by dissociation, but which do not normally exist as pure substances with stable molecules, are known as *radicals*. Thus ammonium radical (NH_4) occurs only in combination with other atoms or radicals, or as the ammonium ion (NH_4^+). The most closely associated pure compound is ammonia gas, which is NH_3.

There are also many substances that form ions carrying two, or even three units of electric charge. Examples of dissociation producing doubly charged ions are:

$$\text{Calcium chloride, } CaCl_2 \longrightarrow Ca^{++} + 2Cl^-,$$
$$\text{Potassium sulfate, } K_2SO_4 \longrightarrow 2K^+ + SO_4^=,$$
$$\text{Calcium sulfate, } CaSO_4 \longrightarrow Ca^{++} + SO_4^=.$$

Two common trebly charged ions are aluminum, Al^{+++}, and phosphate, $PO_4^{\equiv}$.

The reason why water is so important in chemistry, why it is almost unique as a solvent, and why many chemical reactions will only take place in water solution, is that water greatly facilitates the dissociation into ions. Ions do form without water, for example, in molten materials and in solutions in other liquids. However, dissociation in other solvents is rarely as complete as it is in water, and this, it turns out, is due to the peculiar electrical properties of water. The forces of attraction between positive and negative electric charges are greatly reduced if the charged bodies are immersed in water; therefore, ions in a water solution are freer to move around than they are in other liquids.

9-10   *Acids, Bases, and Salts*

A great many important chemical processes depend upon the relations between three common types of chemical compound, acids, bases, and salts. *Acids* are usually encountered dissolved in water, and then possess the following characteristics: they have a sour taste; they turn litmus dye from blue to red; they react violently with sodium or calcium, less violently with aluminum, zinc, iron, and a number of other metals, to produce metallic oxides and hydrogen gas. However, the most important property, and the characteristic most often used to distinguish acids from other compounds, is that the solution in water contains hydrogen ions (H^+).° With a very few exceptions, therefore, an acid contains an easily detached hydrogen atom, and dissociates in solution as indicated in the following examples:

> **Hydrochloric acid, HCl** $\longrightarrow$ **H^+ + Cl^-,**
> **Nitric acid, HNO_3** $\longrightarrow$ **H^+ + NO_3^-,**
> **Sulfuric acid, H_2SO_4** $\longrightarrow$ **$2H^+$ + $SO_4^=$,**
> **Acetic acid, $HC_2H_3O_2$** $\longrightarrow$ **H^+ + $C_2H_3O_2^-$.**

An acid that has two or more detachable hydrogens can usually form ions in which only one is removed; for example, carbonic acid (H_2CO_3) forms both doubly charged $CO_3^=$ ions and singly charged HCO_3^- ions.

A *base* is essentially a compound that will neutralize an acid and remove the characteristic properties when added to an acid solution. Characteristically the solution of a base has a soapy feeling and a bitter taste often described as "alkaline," because the materials known to the medieval chemists as alkalies are strong bases. A sensitive test is that a basic solution turns litmus dye from red to blue. However, the essential property is that the solution contains hydroxyl ions (OH^-), and so most strong bases contain detachable hydroxyl radicals, like caustic soda (NaOH).

The neutralizing reaction between an inorganic acid and a base produces a compound of the large class of compounds known as *salts*. For example,

° The H^+ ion does not normally exist by itself in solution but is attached to a water molecule.

when solutions of sodium hydroxide and hydrochloric acid are prepared and mixed in the proper proportions we have the following sequence of reactions:

$$NaOH \longrightarrow Na^+ + OH^-,$$
$$HCl \longrightarrow H^+ + Cl^-,$$
$$Na^+ + OH^- + H^+ + Cl^- \longrightarrow H_2O + Na^+ + Cl^-.$$

The water can then be boiled away to leave solid sodium chloride, which is, of course, common salt and which gave the generic name to the whole class of compounds.

Typical salts are compounds of a metal (or a radical such as NH_4, which forms positive ions in solution and can behave like a metal in chemical reactions) with an acid radical. They dissociate to a greater or lesser extent when dissolved in water, forming positive ions of the metal and negative ions of the acid radical, and so the solutions are electrical conductors like those of acids and bases. However, they usually have a stable form and can be obtained as pure compounds by evaporating the water of the solution, whereas many acids and bases exist only as solutions and cannot be obtained pure. In the pure state most salts are crystalline solids at ordinary temperatures, and most of them will melt without decomposing.

Salts and many of the other compounds discussed in this chapter are classed as *ionic compounds* because they not only form ions in solution, but the metallic ion and the acid radical retain their ionic nature in the pure compound, which is held together mainly by electrical attraction.° The stable salt must be electrically neutral, and so singly charged positive and negative ions combine one to one; a doubly charged positive ion combines with one doubly charged negative ion or with two singly charged negative ions, and vice versa. *Oxides* are not classed as salts because they do not contain an acid radical, but most metallic oxides are ionic compounds in which the oxygen atom behaves as a doubly charged negative ion, combining with two singly charged positive ions (as in Na_2O), one to one with doubly charged ions (as in CaO), or three to two with trebly charged ions (as in Al_2O_3).

9-11   The Periodic Table

As soon as a fair number of elements had been identified and their properties studied, it became evident that they could be classified into several *families*—groups of elements with similar chemical properties, but with very different atomic weights and densities. A very distinctive family is that of the "alkali metals": lithium, sodium, potassium, rubidium, and cesium. These all occur in nature only combined as salts, and all the salts

° Hydrogen is an exception; although it forms positive ions its compounds are usually covalent (Sec. 13-1) rather than ionic.

form singly charged positive ions of the element in solution. In the metallic form the elements are all very active, oxidizing rapidly when exposed to the air, and reacting more or less violently with water to form strong bases. Less active, but still producing strong bases are the "alkaline earth metals": beryllium, magnesium, calcium, strontium, barium, and radium, all of which form doubly charged positive ions in solution. Contrasted with these "electropositive," metallic elements are the strongly "electronegative," nonmetallic "halogens": fluorine, chlorine, bromine, and iodine, which form singly charged negative ions in solution and produce strong acids, such as HCl, by direct combination with hydrogen. Another important nonmetallic family is that comprising oxygen, sulfur, selenium, and tellurium. These are also electronegative, behaving as doubly charged negative ions in simple compounds with the metals, but they do not ionize as readily as the halogens and do not form strong acids with hydrogen.°

In 1869 the Russian chemist, Dimitri Mendeleev† (1834–1907), observed that if the known elements were arranged in order of their atomic weights, those belonging to the important families appeared at regular intervals in the list. In order to exhibit this, he drew up a table in which elements of the same family appear in the same vertical column (as shown in Table 9-3), and this device has been very useful in systematic chemistry ever since. Mendeleev used seven columns, numbered I for the singly electropositive alkali metals to VII for the singly electronegative halogens, with an extra column marked VIII for the ironlike and platinumlike metals, which did not fit into any definite family. After the rare atmospheric gases—neon, argon, and others—were discovered in 1898, and appeared to be completely inert and to form no stable chemical compounds, an extra "O" column was added, and it was found that this fitted nicely into place without disturbing the order of the atomic weights.

The arrangement in eight columns only fits naturally the first 20 elements; starting with element number 21 two distinct families alternate in each column, and so elements 19 to 36 should all be considered as belonging in one row. For example, column I of the original form of the table contained primarily the alkali metals, but in the lower half the same column contained also the "noble metals," copper, silver, and gold, which also form singly charged positive ions,‡ but which are much less active than the alkalies and have quite different additional properties. The alkali metals were therefore placed in a group IA and the noble metals in group IB. Nowadays most chemists prefer to use a table with 18 columns, separating the A and B groups, and this is the form shown in Table 9-3. Table 9-3 gives only the

° Hydrogen sulfide (H$_2$S) produces a weak acid.

† There are several different spellings of the transliteration of this Russian name and there seems to be no consensus as to which is correct.

‡ Copper also forms doubly charged positive ions and enters as such into a great many of its compounds.

TABLE 9-3   PERIODIC CLASSIFICATION OF THE ELEMENTS

IA	IIA	IIIB	IVB	VB	VIB	VIIB	VIII	VIII	VIII	IB	IIB	IIIA	IVA	VA	VIA	VIIA	O
1 H																	2 He
3 Li	4 Be											5 B	6 C	7 N	8 O	9 F	10 Ne
11 Na	12 Mg											13 Al	14 Si	15 P	16 S	17 Cl	18 Ar
19 K	20 Ca	21 Sc	22 Ti	23 V	24 Cr	25 Mn	26 Fe	27 Co	28 Ni	29 Cu	30 Zn	31 Ga	32 Ge	33 As	34 Se	35 Br	36 Kr
37 Rb	38 Sr	39 Y	40 Zr	41 Nb	42 Mo	43 (Tc)	44 Ru	45 Rh	46 Pd	47 Ag	48 Cd	49 In	50 Sn	51 Sb	52 Te	53 I	54 Xe
55 Cs	56 Ba	57–71 Lanthanides	72 Hf	73 Ta	74 W	75 Re	76 Os	77 Ir	78 Pt	79 Au	80 Hg	81 Tl	82 Pb	83 Bi	84 Po*	85 (At)	86 Rn*
87 (Fr)	88 Ra*	89–103 Actinides															

Metals

Nonmetals

TABLE 9-4   THE ELEMENTS IN ORDER OF ATOMIC NUMBER

Atomic Number	Symbol	Name	Atomic Weight	Atomic Number	Symbol	Name	Atomic Weight
1	H	Hydrogen	1.00797	53	I	Iodine	126.9044
2	He	Helium	4.0026	54	Xe	Xenon	131.30
3	Li	Lithium	6.939	55	Cs	Cesium	132.905
4	Be	Beryllium	9.0122	56	Ba	Barium	137.34
5	B	Boron	10.811	57	La	Lanthanum	138.91
6	C	Carbon	12.01115	58	Ce	Cerium	140.12
7	N	Nitrogen	14.0067	59	Pr	Praseodymium	140.907
8	O	Oxygen	15.9994	60	Nd	Neodymium	144.24
9	F	Fluorine	18.9984	61	(Pm	Promethium	147)
10	Ne	Neon	20.183	62	Sm	Samarium	150.35
11	Na	Sodium	22.9898	63	Eu	Europium	151.96
12	Mg	Magnesium	24.312	64	Gd	Gadolinium	157.25
13	Al	Aluminum	26.9815	65	Tb	Terbium	158.924
14	Si	Silicon	28.086	66	Dy	Dysprosium	162.50
15	P	Phosphorus	30.9738	67	Ho	Holmium	164.930
16	S	Sulfur	32.064	68	Er	Erbium	167.26
17	Cl	Chlorine	35.453	69	Tm	Thulium	168.934
18	Ar	Argon	39.948	70	Yb	Ytterbium	173.04
19	K	Potassium	39.102	71	Lu	Lutetium	174.97
20	Ca	Calcium	40.08	72	Hf	Hafnium	178.49
21	Sc	Scandium	44.956	73	Ta	Tantalum	180.948
22	Ti	Titanium	47.90	74	W	Tungsten	183.85
23	V	Vanadium	50.942	75	Re	Rhenium	186.2
24	Cr	Chromium	51.996	76	Os	Osmium	190.2
25	Mn	Manganese	54.9380	77	Ir	Iridium	192.2
26	Fe	Iron	55.847	78	Pt	Platinum	195.2
27	Co	Cobalt	58.9332	79	Au	Gold	196.967
28	Ni	Nickel	58.71	80	Hg	Mercury	200.59
29	Cu	Copper	63.54	81	Tl	Thallium	204.37
30	Zn	Zinc	65.37	82	Pb	Lead	207.19
31	Ga	Gallium	69.72	83	Bi	Bismuth	208.980
32	Ge	Germanium	72.59	84	Po	Polonium*	210
33	As	Arsenic	74.9216	85	(At	Astatine	210)
34	Se	Selenium	78.96	86	Rn	Radon*	222
35	Br	Bromine	79.909	87	(Fr	Francium	223)
36	Kr	Krypton	83.80	88	Ra	Radium*	226.1
37	Rb	Rubidium	85.47	89	Ac	Actinium*	227
38	Sr	Strontium	87.62	90	Th	Thorium*	232.038
39	Y	Yttrium	88.905	91	Pa	Protactinium*	231
40	Zr	Zirconium	91.22	92	U	Uranium*	238.03
41	Nb	Niobium	92.906	93	(Np	Neptunium	239)
42	Mo	Molybdenum	95.94	94	(Pu	Plutonium	239)
43	(Tc	Technetium	99)	95	(Am	Americium	243)
44	Ru	Ruthenium	101.07	96	(Cm	Curium	247)
45	Rh	Rhodium	102.905	97	(Bk	Berkelium	249)
46	Pd	Palladium	106.4	98	(Cf	Californium	251)
47	Ag	Silver	107.870	99	(Es	Einsteinium	254)
48	Cd	Cadmium	112.40	100	(Fm	Fermium	253)
49	In	Indium	114.82	101	(Md	Mendelevium	256)
50	Sn	Tin	118.69	102	(No	Nobelium	254)
51	Sb	Antimony	121.75	103	(Lw	Lawrencium	257)
52	Te	Tellurium	127.60				

symbols for the elements and their order numbers, for the purpose of showing the family relationships; the names of the elements and their atomic weights (on the carbon 12 scale) are given in Table 9-4.

An important feature of the periodic table is that it shows just what elements should exist. Mendeleev realized that his original table had a number of gaps. They enabled him to predict the existence, the approximate weights, and the physical properties of a number of elements that have since been discovered. All the gaps have now been filled, and the modern table is complete. No new elements remain to be discovered, except possibly additional short-lived, unstable ones beyond lawrencium, number 103.

There are a few features of the periodic table that require comment. Hydrogen is unique in its properties, but is placed in group I with the alkali metals because it produces active, singly charged positive ions. There are a few places where the order of atomic weights is reversed, but the elements have to be assigned as shown on account of their properties. A whole group of metals, numbers 57 to 71, known as the rare earths, have almost identical properties, and all have to be put together in one place in column IIIB; they are not shown in Table 9-3, but are included in the list in Table 9-4. A similar group starts with number 89 and includes the recently discovered heavy, unstable elements; the group is just complete with number 103. In both tables the naturally occurring radioactive elements are marked with an asterisk; those that are known only as artificially produced, unstable elements are shown in brackets.

GLOSSARY

Acid Normally, a hydrogen-containing compound that produces hydrogen ions when dissolved in water.

Alchemy Derived from the Arabic word for infusion; nowadays the term is applied to the pseudoscience of the Middle Ages, which was a mixture of practical chemistry, sympathetic magic, and mystical philosophy.

Atom The smallest particle of a chemical element that retains the characteristic chemical properties.

Atomic weight The mass of the atoms of an element, as compared with those of a standard element (nowadays carbon 12 isotope); alternatively, the mass of the element that enters into combination with atomic weights of other elements.

Base Normally, a compound that produces negatively charged hydroxyl ions (OH^-) when dissolved in water.

Calcining Anciently, the formation of the oxide of a metal; the term is still used for the process of heating with oxygen in order to effect oxidation.

Calx Term used in early chemical literature, before the discovery of oxygen, for the substances we now recognize as the oxides of the metals.

Charge number The number of units of electric charge, positive or negative, carried by an ion.

Chemical equation Conventional method of indicating the changes that take place in a chemical reaction, using the chemical symbols.

Chemical formula Conventional method of indicating the composition of a substance, using chemical symbols.

Chemical symbols One- or two-letter abbreviations for the names of the chemical elements; in most contexts the symbol stands for a single atom of the element.

Compound A pure substance that contains two or more elements in chemical combination.

Dissociation The process by which an atom or molecule breaks up into ions carrying electric charges of opposite sign.

Electrolysis Separation of the positive and negative ions in a solution or a molten material by passing an electric current through the liquid.

Element A substance that cannot be separated into simpler substances by chemical processes, or made by chemical union.

Hydrocarbons The large number of compounds of hydrogen and carbon.

Ion An electrically charged atom, molecule, or chemical radical.

Ionic compound One in which the elements or radicals enter as ions; held together in the solid state by electrical attractions between ions of opposite sign.

Isotopes Atoms of an element that have different atomic weights, but almost identical chemical properties, having nuclei with equal electric charges but different masses.

Molecular weight The unit of mass of a compound; equal to the sum of the atomic weights of the constituent elements, each multiplied by the appropriate integral factor that indicates the number of atoms of the element in a molecule of the compound.

Molecule The smallest particle of a compound; in the case of a gas or a liquid the term is applied to the smallest quantity that exists as an individual particle whenever this contains two or more atoms, even though the atoms may be of the same element.

Oxidation Process of the formation of oxides, either slowly (as in the formation of rust by exposure of iron to the air) or by combustion.

Oxide Compound of an element or radical with oxygen.

Periodic table Table of the elements, with a few exceptions in the order of their atomic weights, arranged so as to show the relationships between different elements that have similar chemical properties.

Phlogiston Imaginary substance which, according to early theories of combustion, was supposed to be released in the flame when anything was burned.

Potential energy barrier Many processes that involve the conversion of potential energy into other forms will not start until a small amount of energy has been added in a "trigger" action (as fuel will not burn until it is ignited). The process is then said to be held inactive by a barrier; the amount of energy that has to be added gives the height of the barrier.

Radical A group of two or more atoms that enters into chemical combination as a unit, but which exists by itself only as a charged ion in solution, never as a free molecule.

Radioactivity Spontaneous conversion of one element into a different element, accompanied by the emission of radiation.

Reducing agent An element, such as hydrogen or carbon, which combines readily with oxygen, and so can be used to remove the oxygen from the oxides of other elements.

Reduction Usually, the removal of oxygen from an oxide in order to recover the pure element; technically, the term is also applied to certain other chemical processes that show analogous characteristics.

Salts Class of ionic compounds that can be formed by the reaction of an acid with a base.

EXERCISES

1. What were some of the earliest chemical processes to be used for practical purposes, some of them before the beginnings of recorded history?

2. How do you account for the fact that the classical philosophers were engrossed in the subject of astronomy, but paid very little attention to chemistry?

3. In modern terms, to what did the four classical elements, earth, water, air, and fire, actually correspond?

4. What led the medieval alchemists to think that they should be able to find a chemical process that would turn lead into gold?

5. What is an oxide? Give three different ways in which oxides can be formed.

6. Why was the isolation of oxygen gas such an important step in the history of chemistry? Who made the discovery, and when?

7. Explain how Lavoisier, by a study of the processes of oxidation and reduction, arrived at the law of conservation of mass.

8. What is a potential barrier? Explain this concept by reference to combustion as an example.

9. Explain the terms "pure substance," "element," and "compound," as used in chemistry.

10. State the two basic laws of chemical combination. Who formulated these laws, and when?

11. Define "atomic weight" and "molecular weight." Although "weight" is firmly entrenched in the terminology of chemistry, is it the correct word to use?

12. How much of each element is contained in a kilogram of dehydrated magnesium sulfate? a kilogram of aluminum nitrate? (These are both "saturated" compounds, in which the simple rules of ionic combination are satisfied.)

13. Interpret the following chemical equations:

(a) $2Fe_2O_3 + 3C \longrightarrow 4Fe + 3CO_2;$
(b) $2C_2H_6 + 7O_2 \longrightarrow 4CO_2 + 6H_2O;$
(c) $2Na + 2H_2O \longrightarrow 2NaOH + H_2;$
(d) $H_2SO_4 + 2KOH \longrightarrow K_2SO_4 + 2H_2O.$

Besides giving the formal interpretation, state in a few words what process is described in each case. Of the compounds mentioned, which are bases, which are acids, and which are salts?

14. How much lime (calcium hydroxide) would be required to neutralize 300 grams of concentrated nitric acid?

15. Why is the presence of water necessary for a great many chemical reactions?

16. Who devised the idea of the periodic table of the elements, and when?

17. With the help of the periodic table, list the elements belonging to each of the following families: alkali metals, alkaline earths, noble metals, halogens, inert gases. What is the normal ionic charge number in each family? Give some of the other chemical and physical properties that characterize each family.

18. On what facts do we base our assertion that there are no more undiscovered stable elements?

gases, liquids, and solids

Before going into the subject of atoms and molecules in detail, we must know something about the mechanical properties of matter, particularly the laws of gases. These, in turn, are unintelligible without a clear understanding of the meaning of pressure. Pressure is another of those terms which, like force, work, and energy, has a precisely defined scientific meaning, but is used rather loosely in common speech.

Whenever a force is distributed over a surface of appreciable area, rather than applied at a definite point, *the pressure on the surface is equal to the force divided by the area.*

The proper unit of pressure in the MKS system is a newton per square meter, but other units are in common use. In the FPS system, pressure is usually measured in pounds per square inch.

The concept of pressure is most important in dealing with the mechanics of fluids, that is, liquids and gases. The definitive property of a *liquid* is that it *has a fixed volume, but no definite shape;* it spreads out to fill any container in which it is placed, up to a definite height which depends on the volume of liquid present.* The weight of the liquid exerts forces all over the bottom and sides of the container, but the top is free. The forces are therefore most conveniently expressed in terms of pressure, force per unit area.

Two simple *laws* of the so-called *hydrostatic pressure* in a liquid will impart a better understanding of the meaning of pressure in general. The first law is that *the pressure at a given point is the same in all directions.* Suppose we take a small funnel with a tube attached and tie a piece of thin sheet rubber over the open end. Immerse this in water to a depth of a foot or so, leaving the end of the tube in the open air; the pressure of the water will bow the rubber diaphragm inward (Fig. 10-1). Now turn the funnel in any direction, even pointing downward, and the amount of bowing of the diaphragm will be the same. This really means that pressure is a scalar quantity, with no direction. The *forces* are everywhere directed at right angles to the surface on which the pressure acts.

The second law of hydrostatics is that *the pressure in a liquid depends only on the vertical depth below the free surface, and is therefore the same at all points on the same level.* This leads to the famous "hydrostatic paradox," which, in the sixteenth and seventeenth centuries, was another stumbling block to those who followed blindly the philosophical ideas of Aristotle. Suppose we have a number of vessels of different shapes (Fig. 10-2), but all with the same area of base, and let them be filled with water to the same level in each. The weight of water in the different vessels is

---

* This property is obvious when, for example, the liquid is water. It is less obvious in the case of a very "viscous" liquid like a thick tar, but tar will spread and fill its container if it is left long enough, and therefore has to be classed as a liquid.

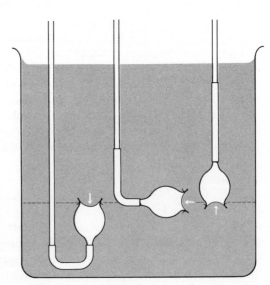

FIG. 10-1

Pressure is the same in all directions at a given depth.

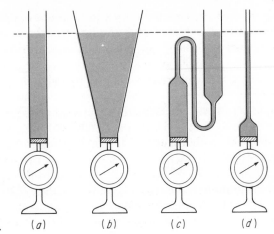

FIG. 10-2

The hydrostatic paradox.   (a)   (b)   (c)   (d)

very different. Yet, because the force on the base is equal to the pressure multiplied by the area of the base, and the pressure is the same at all points at the same depth below the surface, the forces are the same in all four vessels. In vessel (a), with straight vertical sides, the force is simply equal to the weight of the water, but in (b) it is less than the weight of water, and in (d) the force is several times the weight of water.°

The law that the pressure in a liquid depends only on the depth provides the simplest and commonest method of measuring pressure, by balancing it against a column of liquid in a glass tube that has been marked off in inches or centimeters. So extensively is this method used that pressures are very often stated as so many inches of water, or inches or centimeters of mercury. In the more logical weight units, the pressure is then simply equal to the weight of a uniform liquid column having unit area of cross section. Since a cubic inch of water weighs 0.036 pound, the pressure in pounds per square inch corresponding to a height of H inches of water is given by

$$P \text{ (pounds per inch}^2) = 0.036\, H \text{ (inches of water)};$$

or if mercury is used

$$P \text{ (pounds per inch}^2) = 0.491\, H \text{ (inches of mercury)}.$$

10-2   Atmospheric Pressure and the Barometer

We live at the bottom of the great sea of the atmosphere, and the weight of air above us exerts a uniform pressure on everything exposed to it,

° The force exerted by the solid base upon the water in case (d) must be balanced by an equal and opposite force. It is left as an exercise to the student to locate this opposing force.

including our bodies. One of the first to understand this clearly was Torricelli, who assisted Galileo during the last months of the latter's life, and then succeeded to Galileo's professorship in Florence. In 1643 Torricelli discovered the principle of the barometer; an instrument in which the pressure of the atmosphere is measured by balancing it against a column of mercury.

A simple barometer can be made by taking a glass tube about 3 feet long, closed at one end, and filling it completely with mercury, being careful to get rid of all the air bubbles which tend to cling to the glass. The tube is now carefully inverted with its open end below the surface of mercury in an open dish (Fig. 10-3). The mercury level in the tube then settles to some 29 or 30 inches above the level in the dish (*BB*), and, because the pressure due to the mercury column at *A* must be the same as the atmospheric pressure at *BB*, the height of the mercury column is a measure of the atmospheric pressure.

The space above the mercury in the closed tube is an almost perfect vacuum, and, as Torricelli argued, the fact that a vacuum can be produced in this way refutes the ancient dictum that "nature abhors a vacuum." It is not abhorrence of a vacuum that draws the mercury up the tube, or draws water from a well into the cylinder of a pump. It is the pressure of the atmosphere on the free surface that forces it up, and it can only force it to a height where the pressure of the mercury or the water is equal to that of the atmosphere.

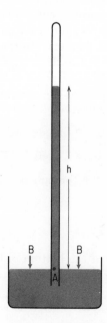

FIG. 10-3

A simple mercury barometer.

The atmospheric pressure varies from place to place over the earth, and varies from day to day at any one place. The pressure distribution is intimately connected with the distribution of wind and weather, and so pressure measurements are one of the most important data in the series of observations taken at all meteorological stations. The pressure also decreases with increasing height in an airplane or balloon flight, or with height above sea level in ground observations, and so the altimeter in an aircraft is really a special type of barometer, with scale reading in feet or meters instead of in pressure units.

Since the pressure of the atmosphere varies, it is necessary to define a *standard atmosphere*, which is taken to be the pressure of a column of 76 centimeters of mercury, measured when the mercury (not the air) is under standard conditions, at 0°C temperature and with its weight measured at sea level in latitude 45°. The standard atmosphere, which is actually a little greater than the average atmospheric pressure, is often used as a unit of pressure, especially for high pressures. It is equal to 101,330 newtons per meter^2, or 14.696 pounds per inch^2.

10-3   Boyle's Law of Gas Pressure

The definitive property of *a gas* is that it *has neither definite shape nor definite volume.* Unless the quantity of gas is large enough that gravitational forces influence its expansion—as in the atmosphere—the gas will expand to fill completely any container in which it is placed. The gas then exerts a uniform pressure on all sides of the container, including the top, and this pressure depends upon the density, and therefore upon the volume which a given quantity of gas occupies.

The relation between the pressure and volume of a gas was discovered by Robert Boyle in England in 1660, using apparatus similar to that illustrated in Fig. 10-4. At first [(a) in the diagram] the tap on the short arm of the U-tube is left open to allow the mercury to come to the same level in both arms. Now the tap is closed, confining a certain quantity of air, initially at atmospheric pressure. Then mercury is added to the long open tube [as in (b)] until the difference of height in the two tubes is equal to the barometer reading, h. The pressure on the confined gas is now 2 atmospheres, and it is found that the volume is reduced to one-half. More generally, the pressure on the confined gas in V is given by the barometer reading plus or minus the difference of the mercury levels. This and similar experiments, carried out with air or with any of the common gases, establish the validity of *Boyle's law:*

For a given mass of any gas, at constant temperature, the volume (V) is inversely proportional to the pressure (P).

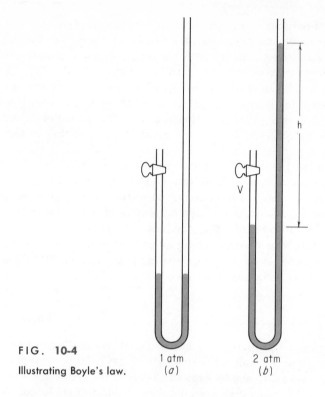

FIG. 10-4

Illustrating Boyle's law.

1 atm
(a)

2 atm
(b)

Or in symbols

PV = constant (at constant temperature).

10-4   *Variation with Temperature; the General Gas Law*

The law relating the volume and pressure of a gas to the temperature was discovered independently by two Frenchmen, Charles and Gay-Lussac, and was published by the latter in 1802.° As stated nowadays it is usually given in two parts:

At constant pressure the volume of a given quantity of gas increases by $\frac{1}{273}$ of the volume at 0°C for each Celsius degree increase in temperature;

If the volume is kept constant, the pressure increases by $\frac{1}{273}$ of its value at 0°C for each degree rise in temperature.

° Students of history of science have never been able to decide to which of the two men this discovery should be credited, with the result that some writers refer to it as Charles' law and others as Gay-Lussac's law. Charles seems to have a good claim to the prior discovery, but Gay-Lussac was certainly the first to announce it publicly.

It follows from the second part of the law that the pressure would vanish at $-273\,°C$ (more precisely, $-273.16\,°$), and so it is this law which leads to the definition of the absolute zero of temperature (Sec. 7-5). It is then often convenient to express the gas laws in terms of absolute temperature ($T\,°K$):

$V \propto T$ (**pressure constant**),

$P \propto T$ (**volume constant**).

These can be combined with Boyle's law into one simple equation,

$$PV = RT,$$

where R is a constant that depends on the mass of gas present.

Obviously, this simple gas law cannot be expected to be universally valid, and must be more or less of an idealized approximation. We therefore define an *ideal gas* as one which *obeys Boyle's law at all temperatures and pressures.* No such gas exists, not only because all real gases become liquid at a sufficiently low temperature, but also because at very high pressures the molecules are forced almost into contact, and further increase of pressure causes only a small change of volume. Gases like oxygen, nitrogen, hydrogen, and helium are a long way from their liquefaction points at ordinary laboratory temperatures, and they obey the general gas law quite accurately except at very high pressures. Measurements made on these gases can be used to predict what an ideal gas would do, and to determine the precise values of the constant R in the gas law, and of the absolute zero of temperature. Gases like carbon dioxide or ammonia, which are much more easily condensed, deviate appreciably from the general gas law even under moderate conditions.

10-5   Change of State: Solid to Liquid

All the chemical elements and a great many simple compounds can exist in all three states—solid, liquid, and gas—under different conditions of temperature and pressure. The definitive property of a *solid* is that it *has a definite shape as well as a definite volume.* In more technical terms: it possesses the property of *rigidity*, which means that it will return to its original shape after being slightly distorted.

It is characteristic of solids in general° that the atoms or molecules are arranged in a regular pattern, as shown in a few examples in Fig. 10-5. In some instances the pattern is regularly repeated over a considerable volume, and the solid occurs in large crystals with well-defined, smooth faces and sharp edges. The angles between the external faces of the crystal are

---

° Glass and many of the so-called plastics are exceptions; they display rigidity but they have no regular internal arrangement and do not form crystals. Some materials that normally behave as solids will flow under pressure; ice is an example.

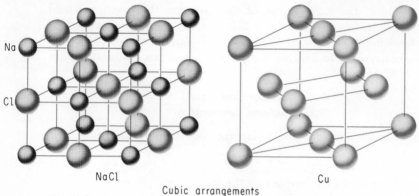

Cubic arrangements

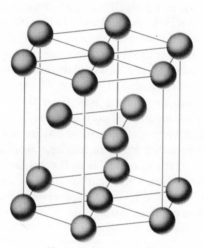

Hexagonal arrangement

FIG. 10-5

Arrangement of the atoms in a few typical solids.

determined by the internal arrangement of the atoms. For example, the beautiful hexagonal patterns of snowflakes are produced by the hexagonal arrangement of the atoms within. Even in a metal like copper, where no crystals are ordinarily visible, the wire or sheet is actually made up of a mosaic of small crystals that can be seen under a microscope.

Simple crystalline solids melt at definite temperatures. In the solid state the heat content is mainly energy of vibration of the atoms around their normal positions. When heat energy is added to raise the temperature, the energy and amplitude of the atomic vibrations increase until the atoms can no longer hold together in their regular positions. The atoms become free to move around and to slide over each other, although they still remain more or less in contact. The material then becomes a liquid, with no definite shape.

While for most solids the melting-point temperature is sharply defined, this temperature does depend somewhat on external conditions, particularly on the pressure. It is a well-known fact that water expands when it freezes. This is actually an unusual behavior, as most materials do just the opposite and expand when they melt. However, consider the case of water and ice. Since the water has the smaller volume, application of pressure to ice which is just on the point of melting tends to promote the change, and the temperature has to be lowered a little to make it freeze again; that is, pressure lowers the melting point. The amount is small, only 0.007°C per atmosphere increase of pressure, but it can be important when we have large masses of ice, as in a mountain glacier. For other materials, which expand on melting, pressure tends to solidify the liquid, and therefore raises the melting point.

10-6   Change of State: Liquid to Gas

The change of state from liquid to gas or vapor takes place quite differently from the change from solid to liquid. As the molecules move around in the liquid there are always a few which have velocities and kinetic energies greater than the average. When a molecule comes to the surface with a sufficiently high velocity it may escape, and if the volume is not confined, or if there is a current of air flowing over the surface of the liquid, the escaping molecules may be carried away. Evaporation therefore occurs at all temperatures. It even takes place to some extent from the solid, and it is well known that even on the coldest day in winter snow will slowly evaporate. On the other hand, if evaporation is taking place into a closed volume (Fig. 10-6), molecules from the vapor will settle on the liquid surface and recondense. Very soon a steady equilibrium state is reached, when the number of molecules recondensing is just equal to the number evaporating. The rate of evaporation depends on the temperature; the rate of recondensation depends on the density, and therefore on the pressure, of the vapor. For this reason there is a direct connection between the temperature of the liquid and the pressure of the vapor.

The equilibrium pressure which the liquid and its vapor reach in a confined volume is referred to as the *saturation pressure*, or the *maximum vapor pressure*. It increases rapidly with increase of temperature, as shown in Fig. 10-7 for the case of water. Boiling into the open air, with the formation of bubbles, takes place when the pressure of the vapor just above the liquid surface is equal to that of the surrounding atmosphere. Figure 10-7 is therefore also a graph of the variation of boiling point with external pressure. The normal boiling point, 100°C for water by definition, is the

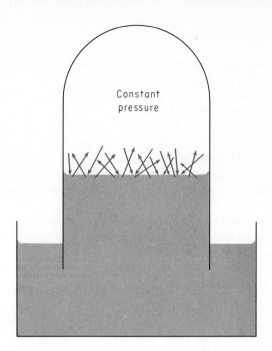

FIG. 10-6

Evaporation of a liquid into a closed volume.

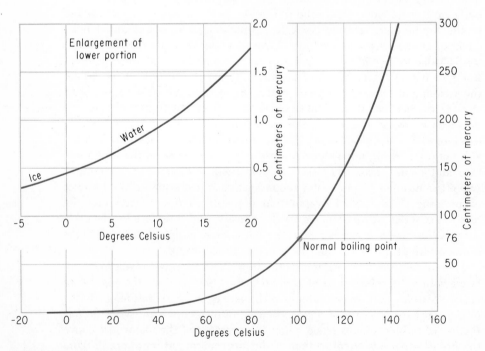

FIG. 10-7

Saturation vapor pressure of water.

temperature at which the vapor pressure is equal to the standard atmosphere, 76 centimeters of mercury.

The temperature of the liquid state cannot be increased indefinitely, even under very high pressures. If the liquid and its vapor are heated in a confined volume to temperatures well above the normal boiling point, with, of course, continually increasing pressure, a point is finally reached where all the remaining liquid is suddenly vaporized. The temperature at which this happens is known as the *critical temperature;* it can be defined as *the temperature above which the material cannot exist in the liquid state.**

Table 10-1 gives melting points, normal boiling points, and critical temperatures for a few materials. Some peculiarities included in the table are worth noting. No melting point is listed for helium. At ordinary pressures helium remains liquid down to the lowest possible temperatures; it is solidified only under pressures of 25 atmospheres or more. For carbon dioxide the melting point is higher than the figure quoted for the boiling point. At normal atmospheric pressure, carbon dioxide passes directly from the solid to the vapor at −78°C, without any intervening liquid phase, a process that is known technically as *sublimation.* Solid carbon dioxide is the material sold commercially as "dry ice," to keep things cold without the untidiness of a melting material. If solid carbon dioxide (that is, dry ice) is heated under a pressure of 5 atmospheres or more, it melts at a temperature of −56°C. The table also covers the complete range of extremes, from helium, the most nearly ideal gas, to graphite, which has the highest melting point of any common material.

* Contrary to what one might expect, this does not apply to solids. Experiments at very high pressures have shown that the common gases can be compressed directly from gas to solid at temperatures well above the critical temperature of the liquid.

TABLE 10-1   MELTING, BOILING, AND CRITICAL TEMPERATURES

Material	Melting Point (°C)	Boiling Point (°C)	Critical Temperature (°C)
Helium	—	−268.9	−267.9
Hydrogen	−259.1	−252.8	−239.9
Nitrogen	−209.9	−195.8	−147.1
Oxygen	−218.4	−183.0	−118.8
Carbon dioxide	−56.2	−78.5	31.1
Ammonia	−77.7	−33.4	132.4
Ethyl alcohol	−117	78.4	243
Water	0	100	374
Mercury	−38.9	357	1550
Lead	327	1620	—
Iron	1535	3000	—
Graphite	3550	4200	—

10-7   Latent Heat

Energy is required to change the state of a material from a low temperature form to that of a higher temperature. In going from the solid to the liquid, work has to be done against the forces which hold the atoms in their regular positions in the crystal. In going from liquid to vapor more work, usually much more, has to be done against the forces of cohesion which hold the molecules together. As a rule, the energy required to do the work of a change of state is supplied in the form of heat. Conversely, when a vapor condenses or a liquid freezes, potential energy of the molecular forces is released and usually appears in the form of heat. In the early days, before the energy principle was properly understood, and heat was thought to be a kind of substance, the heat released on freezing was believed to be concealed in some way in the liquid. It was therefore referred to as *latent heat,* and the name has persisted, so that we still speak of latent heat: the energy required to melt or vaporize a material being stated as so many calories per gram.

GLOSSARY

Altimeter Instrument for measuring height. Most altimeters register changes of atmospheric pressure with altitude.

Barometer Instrument for measuring atmospheric pressure.

Cohesion The property of the molecules of a liquid or a solid to attract each other and to remain close together, whereby the volume is kept approximately constant.

Critical temperature In connection with the change of state from liquid to vapor, the highest temperature at which the liquid can exist.

Hydrostatic paradox The circumstance that the force on the bottom of a vessel containing a liquid can, under some circumstances, be greater than the weight of the liquid.

Hydrostatic pressure Pressure exerted on a body that is immersed in a fluid, usually in a liquid such as water, but it can also be in a gas.

Hydrostatics The branch of physics that deals with fluids at rest.

Latent heat The heat energy required to convert a solid into a liquid, or a liquid into a gas, without any increase in temperature.

Maximum vapor pressure Equilibrium pressure attained by a vapor in contact with its liquid in a confined space; when the number of molecules evaporating is equal to the number recondensing.

Pressure Force per unit area.

Rigidity The type of elasticity a solid body possesses, in virtue of which it returns to its original shape after being distorted.

Saturation State of containing the maximum possible amount of a substance; a vapor is saturated when it is at its maximum vapor pressure.

Sublimation Direct change from the solid state to the vapor without passing through the intervening liquid phase; when a substance behaves in this way it is said to sublime.

Vapor The term "vapor" is often used interchangeably with "gas." Technically, a substance in the gaseous state is referred to as vapor when it is below its critical temperature, and referred to as a true gas when it is above this temperature.

Viscosity The property of all fluids, even gases, to resist change of shape. Technically, the viscosity is a numerical measure of the internal friction when flow takes place; a fluid is said to be viscous when it does not flow readily.

EXERCISES

1. Define pressure, and define the MKS and FPS units of this quantity.

2. What are the definitive distinguishing properties of a solid, a liquid, and a gas? Is it possible for a substance to behave sometimes as a solid and sometimes as a liquid, at the same temperature?

3. State the first two laws of hydrostatics.

4. Is pressure a vector or a scalar quantity? Why?

5. What is the pressure in MKS units, and in pounds per square inch, at a depth of 400 feet in a freshwater lake? Would the pressure be more or would it be less at the same depth in the ocean?

6. Find the force in newtons and in kilograms-weight on the main valve of a water supply system, when the valve is closed. The valve opening has an area of 200 square centimeters, and is located 40 meters below the water level in the tank which controls the pressure in the system.

7. Why is it that the force on the bottom of a vessel can sometimes exceed the weight of the liquid in the vessel? According to Newton's third law there must be a reaction to the excess force; where is this reaction?

8. Convert 65 centimeters of mercury to newtons per square meter. Convert 10^7 newtons per square meter to kilograms-weight per square centimeter, to meters of water, and to atmospheres.

9. Convert 1200 feet of water to pounds per square inch, and to atmospheres.

10. Who was Torricelli, when did he live, and for what is he famous?

11. Describe how to make a simple mercury barometer. What is in the space above the mercury in the barometer tube?

12. In pumping water from a lake into a reservoir tank with a piston-type pump, the pump cannot be located more than about 25 feet above the level of the lake. Why is this? What is the theoretical maximum distance?

13. State Boyle's law of gases. When was this discovered? Did Boyle follow or precede Galileo and Newton?

14. State the Charles–Gay-Lussac law. From this and Boyle's law derive the general law of ideal gases, and state the law both in words and in symbolic form. Derive from these laws also the concept of absolute temperature.

15. Why is it that the general gas law cannot possibly be rigorously correct but must be an idealization?

16. What makes snowflakes always assume a hexagonal pattern?

17. What do you deduce from Fig. 10-5 about the characteristic shape of crystals of common salt?

18. What is happening among the molecules when a solid melts? when a liquid evaporates?

19. Why does an increase of pressure lower the melting point of ice, but raise the melting points of nearly all other solids?

20. What is the maximum vapor pressure of a liquid? Show by a graph of approximately the correct shape how it varies with temperature. What is the relation between the maximum vapor pressure and the boiling point?

21. According to Table 10-1 the boiling point of carbon dioxide is lower than its melting point. What does this mean?

22. Which of the materials listed in Table 10-1 are gaseous under normal laboratory conditions? Which of these could be compressed into liquids without reducing the temperature?

23. The latent heat of fusion of ice is approximately 80 calories per gram, and the latent heat of vaporization of water is 540 calories per gram at its normal boiling point. How much heat would be required to melt half a kilogram of snow, bring it to a boil, and boil it all away?

24. Two saucepans of water are on a stove; one is simmering gently, and the other is boiling violently. Which is the hotter?

atoms and molecules

It is a commonplace today to say that all matter is made up of definite little particles, which we call *atoms*, and actually the idea is a very ancient one, for it was a doctrine of certain schools of Greek philosophy. The first consistent discussion of the atomic concept is usually credited to Democritus, of whom little is known except that he was teaching and writing about 400 B.C. Democritus favored the idea that matter is made up of discrete, indivisible particles because the opposite view, that a piece of material is infinitely divisible, seemed to him to lead to a logical inconsistency. How could one go on and on, cutting something up into smaller and smaller pieces, forever? There must come a time, went the argument, when there is nothing left. The last cut made, just before this, must therefore have left an indivisible particle, that is, an "atom."

Democritus and his followers considered that their atoms were so small as to be invisible and intangible. They believed, as we do today, that a polished table feels hard and smooth because the atoms of the finger cannot intermingle with those of the wood. Atoms of the tenuous elements, air (meaning to us any gas) and fire were thought to be smaller and lighter, and to be quite incapable of detection by the human senses. Out of these ideas they developed a whole cosmology, which included the nature and origin of living things as well as of the earth and the heavenly bodies.

The Greek philosophers who argued against atomism did so largely because they could not stomach the idea of the "void" in which Democritus' atoms were supposed to move. They could not conceive of a space which possessed dimensions and geometrical relations, but which contained —nothing!

The philosophical argument really concerns discontinuity as opposed to continuity, and is closely related to the mathematical concept of continuous quantities. It is still important today because of the several things in nature which do, in fact, turn out to be discontinuous. Consider the mathematical expression of Newton's second law of motion,

$$F = ma,$$

or the expression $\frac{1}{2}mv^2$ for kinetic energy. When these are used it is always implied that the quantities for which the algebraic symbols stand are mathematically continuous. That is, the mass, m, and the velocity, v, can be altered by any quantity we like, however small.* If we accept an atomic view of matter this is not true, but the smallest amount by which the mass can be increased or decreased is the mass of one atom.

This does not mean that the algebraic equations, with their implication of continuity, are no longer useful, as long as we recognize that we may have to restrict them to macroscopic objects. In the case of mass, "macroscopic," or large scale (the opposite of microscopic), means anything which contains a large number of atoms. In practice this can be as small as a dust particle which is visible only under the most powerful microscope, or as large as a star or a complete galaxy. The change of mass which is made by adding or subtracting one atom is too small to detect; it is less than the experimental error which might be made in measuring the mass. Then calculations made with continuous mathematics cannot introduce a detectable error into the computed result.

11-2   Dalton's Atomic Hypothesis

The hypothesis that matter is made up of discrete atoms has been a factor in the thinking of a few philosophers and scientists at all times from Democritus to the eighteenth century. The theory fell into disrepute among the alchemists and the religious philosophers of the Middle Ages, but once again became fairly popular after the work of Isaac Newton sug-

---

* Or, if a quantity is mathematically continuous, any portion of it, no matter how small, can always be divided into still smaller portions.

gested that material phenomena in general might be explained by the laws of mechanics. There are a number of simple natural phenomena which are easily explained qualitatively by the assumption that matter is made of atoms with a certain amount of empty space between them. All materials, even the hardest solids, are more or less compressible; almost all materials expand when heated. Long before it had been conclusively proved that heat is a form of energy, associated mainly with motion of the atoms or molecules, several writers had suggested that the atoms of a solid might be in vibration, and that heat expansion might be due to an increase of the amplitude of vibration. The fact that a gas can expand indefinitely suggests that it consists of atoms which are free to move about.

Another qualitative argument for atomism lies in the phenomenon of *diffusion,* the fact that when two different materials are placed in contact they interpenetrate more or less. Gases diffuse into each other quite rapidly, and two different gases in a container will very soon produce a uniform mixture. Perfume released into a room can soon be detected all over, even if there are no appreciable air currents. Liquids diffuse much less rapidly, but if a little colored dye is carefully introduced into the bottom of a beaker of water, the color will be visible throughout in a matter of a few minutes. Diffusion occurs to some extent even with solids. In some cases gases will very slowly leak through an apparently uniform solid wall. Mercury diffuses quite rapidly into many solid metals, and even two solids will sometimes interdiffuse, for if a piece of lead and a piece of gold are tightly clamped together, then after some months the gold will be found to be contaminated with lead, and the lead with gold.

However, in all this there is no overwhelming necessity to assume the existence of atoms. All these things might be explained in other ways, and there are no simple quantitative relations which might be tested by experiment. Throughout the eighteenth century, therefore, the atomic hypothesis continued to be a philosophical speculation, accepted by some and rejected by others, with no conclusive evidence in either direction.

So matters remained until in 1803 John Dalton, an English schoolteacher, and a Quaker of French Huguenot ancestry, applied the atomic hypothesis to the newly discovered quantitative laws of chemistry, and so became the founder of modern atomic theory. Dalton assumed that:

1. *Every chemical element has its distinctive atom,* those of any particular element being all alike in size and mass.

2. *Atoms are indestructible,* and cannot be divided, created, or destroyed.

3. When two or more elements combine to produce a chemical compound, the atoms attach themselves together to form definite composite particles, which he called *molecules.*

4. Atoms normally combine in simple ratios, so that molecules usually contain only a few atoms of any one element.

It is obvious that these assumptions are consistent with the three basic laws of chemistry, the law of conservation of mass, the law of constant combining weights, and the law of simple proportions. Dalton's atomic theory therefore fulfilled its immediate purpose of explaining the laws of chemical combination.

As in the case of many scientific hypotheses and laws, Dalton's original assumptions have had to be modified in the light of subsequent discoveries. The atoms of an element are not necessarily all alike, but there may be several varieties, the different isotopes. Atoms are not indestructible; they have parts and a structure, they can be split, and atoms of one element can be converted into those of a different element. However, they remain unaltered through any chemical reaction, or in simple physical processes such as melting and evaporation. The ratios are simple, and the numbers of atoms per molecule are small whole numbers, in most inorganic compounds. However, some of the molecules that exist in organic, living matter contain thousands of atoms, and there are some compounds that do not form molecules with a definite composition. These are only modifications of Dalton's theory and they do not affect the important basic principles of the existence of atoms and of their combination to form molecules.

11-3   Avogadro's Law

A hypothesis that is designed to fit in with a certain set of facts assumes much greater significance when it is applied to a different set of facts and is found to be in agreement with these as well. It was therefore a very important advance in atomic theory when in 1811 the Italian physicist, Avogadro, made the first quantitative application of the theory to gases, and stated the further hypothesis which is usually known nowadays as *Avogadro's law:*

Equal volumes of different gases, at the same temperature and pressure, contain equal numbers of molecules.

In Dalton's theory it is implied that the masses of individual atoms and molecules are proportional to their atomic and molecular weights, and therefore that a gram-molecular weight° of any pure substance contains a definite number of molecules. It follows that Avogadro's law can be put in the alternative form:

Gram-molecular weights of different gases occupy the same volume at the same pressure and temperature.

° This means a number of grams equal to the molecular weight; it is commonly called *mole*. The number of moles in a sample of a compound is equal to the mass in grams divided by the molecular weight.

Then the volume occupied by a mole of an ideal gas at $0°C$ and standard atmospheric pressure is an important general physical constant, and is 22,416 cubic centimeters per mole. It follows further that the constant R in the general gas law,

$$PV = RT,$$

has the same numerical value for a mole of any gas.

The number of molecules in a gram-molecular weight of any chemical compound is another important physical constant, and is known as *Avogadro's number*. There was no known way of making even a rough guess at the actual figure in Avogadro's time, and it was 100 years later before an accurate value was determined. The modern accepted value is 6.0234×10^{23} molecules per mole, from which it follows that the mass of a hydrogen atom is 1.6733×10^{-24} gram.°

Avogadro's hypothesis was not generally accepted for many years after he proposed it, because there seemed to be some conspicuous exceptions. For example, equal volumes of hydrogen and chlorine combined to give two volumes of hydrogen chloride, although one might have expected the total number of molecules to be halved. Avogadro got around this apparent difficulty by assuming that the free molecules of hydrogen and chlorine are H_2 and Cl_2, and writing the equation for the reaction,

$$H_2 + Cl_2 \longrightarrow 2\ HCl,$$

with a similar device for a number of other gases, such as O_2 and N_2. Dalton and others refused to accept this because they erroneously supposed that like atoms must repel each other, and therefore that a stable molecule must contain at least two different kinds of atoms. In the course of time further studies of gases proved that Avogadro was right, and that his law is valid, with the same accuracy and limitations as the other laws of gases, Boyle's and Charles' laws. It is on the basis of Avogadro's law that we nowadays assign the correct molecular formulae to many different gases, and that we recognize many of the common gaseous elements to be diatomic.

11-4   The Kinetic Theory of Gases

If a gas consists of discrete molecules flying around in all directions, they must be continually bombarding the walls of any container, and rebounding, as illustrated in Fig. 11-1. Each rebounding molecule must exert a tiny force on the wall during the instant that it is in contact. Individual collisions cannot, in general, be detected, but if the wall is of measurable

° These very large and very small figures are hard to visualize and may appear meaningless. It must be emphasized that they are definite numbers, known with good precision, and are required for many numerical computations.

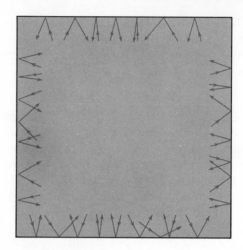

FIG. 11-1

Production of gas pressure by molecular bombardment.

(macroscopic) size there will be billions of collisions per second, and the sum of all these collisions will appear to produce a uniform pressure. The calculation of this pressure in terms of the number of molecules and their average speed forms the first fundamental theorem of the important development which has come to be known as the *kinetic theory of gases* and which provides a quantitative test of the molecular hypothesis.

The first calculation of the gas pressure caused by molecular bombardment was made in 1848 by James Joule, the same man who first measured accurately the mechanical equivalent of heat and proved that heat is a form of energy. Joule was an indifferent mathematician, and his method of performing the calculation leaves much to be desired, although it did lead to the correct result. The first rigorous proof of the theorem—and the development from it of a consistent theory of the molecular properties of gases—is due to the work of Clerk Maxwell in 1866.° The following assumptions have to be made in order to develop the basic theorem:

1. The gas consists of discrete molecules, traveling in all directions. The molecules need not be all alike, and so the theorem applies to mixtures of gases, like ordinary air. They may also be traveling with different velocities.

2. The molecules are continually colliding with each other, and with the walls of the container. The collisions satisfy Newton's laws of mechanics, particularly the third law, which as we have seen, is equivalent to the law of conservation of momentum. The collisions are also perfectly elastic, that is, there is no conversion of kinetic energy into heat.†

° James Clerk Maxwell (1831–1879) was professor of natural philosophy at Cambridge University. He is even more famous for his work in electricity and magnetism (Sec. 20-2), for which he performed the same task of clarification as Newton had performed in mechanics, and Lavoisier in chemistry.

† If this were not true, the wall would become heated at the expense of the molecular energy of the gas, and this happens only if the gas is at a higher temperature than the wall.

3. The molecules exert no forces upon each other, or upon the walls, except at the instant of collision.

4. The molecules are so small that their total volume is negligible in comparison with the volume of the container.

With these assumptions Maxwell computed the average force of molecular bombardment on unit area of the wall, and so derived an expression for the product of pressure, P, and volume, V,

$$PV = \tfrac{2}{3}(\text{total kinetic energy of the molecules}).$$

Boyle's law of gas pressure follows immediately, and the general gas law,

$$PV = RT,$$

follows with the additional very reasonable assumption that the kinetic energy of the molecules is proportional to the absolute temperature, T. This provides an alternative definition of absolute temperature, namely, that it is proportional to the average kinetic energy of gas molecules. This definition is to be preferred to that in terms of the gas pressure, because it gives a meaning to very high temperatures such as those encountered in stars.

Maxwell also proved that, if two gases with molecules of different mass are mixed, collisions between the molecules will very soon produce a condition such that the average kinetic energy per molecule is the same in both gases. Avogadro's law therefore follows, in the form that the constant, R, is the same for gram-molecular weights of all gases. With this, there is complete consistency between the basic theorem of the kinetic theory and the empirical laws of the ideal gas.

11-5   Corrections to the Simple Theory

With the assumptions listed in the preceding section, the simple form of the kinetic theory leads to the properties which have been deduced for the "ideal" gas, the nonexistent gas which would obey Boyle's law at all temperatures and pressures. Even if a theory agrees approximately with the experimental facts, any discrepancy should lead us to reexamine the theory, and particularly the assumptions upon which it is based.

The third and fourth assumptions are clearly only approximations, not strictly in accord with the facts. The molecules do exert forces upon each other, for there must be an attraction between them when they are sufficiently close. Otherwise the gas could not liquefy and eventually solidify, as it does at low temperatures, and the liquid and the solid could not display the property of cohesion which holds them together. The molecules have finite dimensions, even if very small, and they do occupy a certain volume. Maxwell's theory and the general gas law can be modified to take these factors into account, and it turns out that the modified theory predicts liquefaction of the gas. It predicts deviations from Boyle's law when the gas is close to the liquefaction point, so that molecular cohesion becomes important, and again at high pressures when the space occupied by the molecules becomes important. It predicts also the existence of a critical temperature, above which liquefaction cannot occur.

It is a triumph of the kinetic theory that not only does the approximate calculation give the correct form for the ideal gas laws, but corrections to the theory which are obviously necessary predict deviations from the gas laws which do in fact occur. The theory also accounts for other properties of gases, such as conduction of heat, and viscosity, or resistance to flow. Attempts have been made to apply it also to some of the properties of liquids and solids, but very little of a quantitative nature has been accomplished. Melting and vaporization, heat expansion and compressibility are accounted for qualitatively, just as they would be in any form of atomic theory.

11-6   *Brownian Movement*

Nobody has ever seen single molecules of a gas or liquid or traced their individual motions. However, the effects of molecular motion can be made visible with smoke particles suspended in still air, or with tiny solid particles in water, in what is called a *colloidal suspension*. With suitable illumination, these particles can be seen under a microscope to be dancing like the motes in a sunbeam. The effect—referred to as *Brownian movement* —was first observed by an English botanist, Robert Brown, in 1827, when he was examining some tiny plant spores under a powerful microscope. Brown thought at first that the spores he was studying must have the power of independent movement, but later, when others observed the same effect with tiny particles of nonliving matter, they realized that the motion is due to the bombardment of the particles by the molecules of the air or water in which they are suspended.

Brownian movement can be seen very nicely if a little cigarette smoke is introduced into a flat-topped glass cell, where it is protected from air currents. The particles are usually beyond the limits of normal visibility under even the most powerful microscope, but they can be seen as tiny points of light against a dark background if they are strongly illuminated from the side, as shown in Fig. 11-2. Individual particles can be picked out and watched for several seconds until their continual motion causes them to drift out of view. The path of a particle is then seen to be an irregular zigzag (Fig. 11-3).

By careful observation under the microscope the average velocity of the suspended colloidal particles can be estimated, and it turns out to be a few

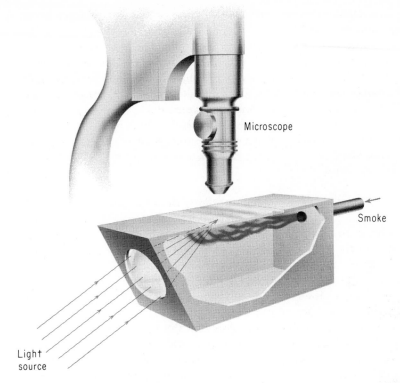

Microscope

Smoke

Light
source

FIG. 11-2

Cell and method of illumination suitable for studying the
Brownian movement of small smoke particles.

millimeters per minute, from which their average kinetic energy can be
determined. The very much smaller molecules of the gas or liquid in
which the particles are suspended are moving with very much higher
velocities, several hundred meters per second, but, according to the kinetic

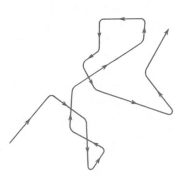

FIG. 11-3

Path of a particle in Brownian movement.

theory, their average energy must be the same as that of the larger particles. We know the total kinetic energy of all the molecules in a mole of gas (of any kind) from the general gas law (Sec. 11-4). If we divide this quantity by the average energy, determined from a study of Brownian movement, we have the number of molecules in a mole, the important physical constant known as Avogadro's number (Sec. 11-3). However, the experimental observations of Brownian movement are subject to large uncertainties, and the value of Avogadro's number derived in this way is only a rough estimate, not to be compared in usefulness with other, more precise determinations.

11-7   A Hypothesis Becomes an Accepted Fact of Nature

It is interesting to note how the theory of atoms has taken on more and more reality in the course of time. Before Dalton, atoms were a speculative concept—which one could believe in or not, according to one's personal inclination; there was simply no definite evidence one way or the other. With Dalton, the existence of atoms and molecules became a concrete hypothesis, the basis of a quantitative theory, formulated to explain the empirical laws of chemical combination. But it was still a hypothesis, requiring a great deal more experimental evidence before it could be considered established beyond any reasonable doubt, and, in fact, many chemists did doubt it. However, it turned out to be a fruitful hypothesis. If it had not, it would have been forgotten, we would not be discussing it in this book, and John Dalton would not have passed into history as a leader in scientific thinking.

The hypothesis became more credible when Avogadro discovered the law which bears his name. When Joule, Maxwell, and others developed the kinetic theory of gases, the concept of atoms and molecules triumphantly passed the first crucial test of any new hypothesis: either it must predict new facts which can be tested by experiment, or else it must form the theoretical basis for an explanation of a new set of facts, other than those for which it was first formulated. The atomic hypothesis has survived this test —in the development of modern atomic physics and in the thousands of new chemical discoveries that have been made since Dalton's time.

Still, no one has ever seen a single atom or molecule, although very large organic molecules, containing many atoms, have been photographed with an electron microscope. There are also several ways of detecting effects produced by single atomic particles, and these methods are used in the study of radioactivity and of nuclear reactions (Sec. 22-4). We have discovered methods of studying the structure of the atom. Atoms have been split into smaller parts, contrary to one item in Dalton's original atomic theory. In sum, the evidence accumulated in the course of time is overwhelming, and no scientist today seriously questions the actual, material existence of the little particle we call an atom.

Avogadro's number The number of atoms or molecules in a gram-molecular weight of any pure substance.

Brownian movement The erratic motion, visible under a microscope, of small particles suspended in a liquid or a gas.

Colloidal suspension A mixture in which particles of submicroscopic size, but still containing many molecules, remain suspended in a fluid without actually dissolving.

Continuous quantity One that can be increased by any amount we like, however small.

Diffusion Spontaneous intermingling of two or more materials, as when an odor permeates a room, or a little dissolved dye spreads throughout a volume of water.

Kinetic theory A theory in physics, largely mathematical in form, which is based on the assumption that all matter is made up of molecules in rapid motion.

Macroscopic Large scale, the antonym of microscopic. In physics, the term usually refers to a unit that contains a large number of atoms.

Mole Term commonly used for gram-molecular weight, which is a mass of an element or compound equal to the molecular weight in grams.

1. Who was the first (as far as we know) to suggest that matter is made up of discrete atoms? What led him to this idea? Is his argument valid?

2. Explain how the existence of atoms and molecules accounts qualitatively for: (a) the fact that all materials are more or less compressible; (b) the fact that most materials expand when they are heated; (c) the diffusion of one material into another; (d) the conduction of heat along a metal bar.

3. List the four assumptions made by Dalton in his atomic theory. Show how these assumptions account quantitatively for the basic laws of chemistry.

4. Which of Dalton's assumptions have had to be modified, and how? How do these modifications affect Dalton's conclusions about the laws of chemistry?

5. Who was Avogadro, and what was his claim to fame?

6. It is implied throughout the work of Dalton and Avogadro that all atoms of the same kind have the same mass. Is it necessary to make this assumption in order to arrive at the correct conclusions?

7. Using the value of Avogadro's number given in Sec. 11-3, calculate to the appropriate number of significant figures the masses of: a sodium atom, a molecule of oxygen gas, a molecule of ammonia.

8. How do we know that many of the common gases, hydrogen, oxygen, etc., have diatomic molecules?

9. State the assumptions made in developing the simple form of the kinetic theory of gases. Which of these assumptions are basic, and which are obviously approximations?

10. What is meant by saying that molecular collisions are "perfectly elastic"? What would happen if the collisions were not perfectly elastic? Does this ever happen?

11. Calculate the total kinetic energy in joules of a mole of gas molecules at $0°C$, and at $1°K$.

12. From the result of Exercise 11 calculate approximately the average speed of hydrogen molecules at $0°C$, and of carbon dioxide molecules at the same temperature.

13. In general, how does the average molecular speed vary with the molecular weight?

14. Explain how the ideal gas laws follow from the basic theorem of the kinetic theory.

15. What are we really saying about the state of matter in the sun when we give its central temperature as $14,000,000°K$?

16. What is Brownian movement? Give, and explain briefly, two ways in which studies of Brownian movement confirm the conclusions of the kinetic theory.

the earth's atmosphere

12-1   Sources of Information about the Atmosphere

Prior to our own twentieth century, scientists knew by direct observation only the very lowermost layers of the cloud of gas which surrounds our planet, and which we know as the atmosphere. A trickle of information from balloon ascents goes back to the brothers Montgolfier, who made the first trip in their hot-air balloon in 1773, but the accumulation of accurate observations coincides roughly with the development of airplane flight. Not that the information comes, in general, from observations made during flights; most of it comes from the use of sounding balloons carrying automatic recording instruments.

Early types of sounding balloons carried light, compact instruments which made permanent records of the pressure and temperature at different heights, and sometimes also of the humidity. They were simply released to fly where they would, in the hope that when the balloon burst, and the instrument fell, somebody would find it and return it to a central office for the sake of a small cash reward. Although it was often months before the instrument was returned and the record analyzed, and many were never

179

found, this was for a good many years the best method of learning something about the structure of the atmosphere, and about 1910 the meteorological services in most of the larger countries started using sounding balloons regularly.

The modern type is a modification called a radiosonde, which carries in addition to the instruments a small radio transmitter. Instead of being merely recorded—to be studied later—the pressure, temperature, and humidity are automatically transmitted to a ground station, so that the information is immediately available. Radiosondes are now sent aloft daily from weather stations all over the world and even from ships at sea.

Direct measurements, using balloons or aircraft, can be made only to a height of 10 to 15 miles. Observations from greater heights have been obtained from rockets, and valuable information about cloud and wind patterns is being supplied by the weather satellites that are now orbiting the earth and sending back television pictures of the upper surface of the clouds at regular intervals. However, much of the information we possess about the state of the atmosphere above 15 miles has been deduced indirectly from study of the various phenomena occurring in the uppermost layers. The principal sources of information are collected in Fig. 12-1.

Study of very low frequency sound waves from large explosions can tell something about the density and temperature between 15 and 50 miles, a region that is particularly difficult to study in other ways. Also, this is the region in which there is a thin layer of ozone, the modification of oxygen

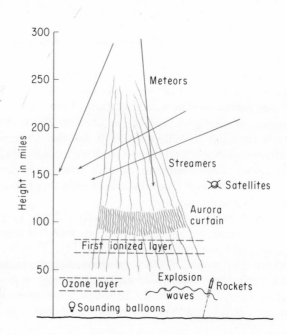

FIG. 12-1

Sources of information about the different layers of the atmosphere.

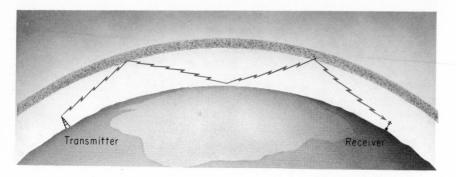

FIG. 12-2

Transmission of a radio wave around the curve of the earth by reflection in the ionized layer.

with molecules, O_3, which absorbs some of the ultraviolet light from the sun and produces a distinctive absorption spectrum.

At 50 to 200 miles the air is strongly ionized and becomes a partial electrical conductor. This layer of ionized gas reflects radio waves, and it is this reflection that permits radio transmission around the curve of the earth, as shown in Fig. 12-2. The intensity of the reflected waves depends on the density of ions and provides another source of information.

The height of the veils, streamers, and arcs of the aurora borealis can be determined by taking simultaneous photographs of a display from two stations a few miles apart. The lower edge of a bright aurora veil is usually between 60 and 80 miles up, sometimes as low as 50 miles; in a brilliant display, streamers may extend upward as much as 400 miles. Study of the spectrum of the aurora therefore yields information about the composition of the outermost layers of the atmosphere.

When meteors enter the atmosphere they are heated by friction and leave bright trails (shooting stars). The brightness along the trail is indicative of the density at great heights. It is difficult to record the spectrum of a meteor trail, but a number of such spectra have now been obtained—using specially designed spectrographs—and have served to supplement the information obtained from spectra of the aurora.

12-2   Composition of the Atmosphere

The percentage, by volume, of the different gases in a sample of dry air is given in Table 12-1. To this must be added a variable amount of water vapor, which, in the tropics, can be as much as 4 per cent on a steaming hot day. In addition there are variable minute traces of methane and other

TABLE 12-1   **COMPOSITION OF THE ATMOSPHERE**

Gas	Percentage by Volume
Nitrogen (N_2)	78.08
Oxygen (O_2)	20.95
Argon (A)	0.93
Carbon dioxide (CO_2)	0.033
Neon (Ne) and other inert gases	0.002

hydrocarbons from natural gas wells, of sulfur and sulfur compounds from volcanoes, of oxides of nitrogen produced in thunderstorms, and the like.

Up to a height of about 20 miles the gases of the atmosphere are kept thoroughly mixed by wind currents and by convection, and except for water vapor, the same basic composition is found all over the world and at all levels. At very high levels there is some variation, due largely to the chemical effects of ultraviolet radiation from the sun. The most important of these effects is the dissociation of ordinary oxygen (O_2) into the atomic form, and the recombination of part of this into ozone (O_3). In this process a great deal of the ultraviolet energy is absorbed, so that we are protected from what could be deleterious effects.

12-3   Humidity

From the point of view of the meteorologist, the varying water vapor content is the most important constituent of the atmosphere, for this is obviously related to the formation of clouds and rain. For his own work in preparing weather forecasts, the meteorologist wants to know the *absolute humidity*, the actual amount of vapor present. This is usually expressed by giving the pressure the vapor would exert if all the other gases were removed. The actual pressure of vapor at any time or place cannot exceed the saturation pressure for the existing temperature (Fig. 10-7), for as soon as this value is reached, condensation will commence and clouds or mist will begin to form.

On the other hand, the general public usually thinks of humidity in terms of what is technically known as *relative humidity*, which is the ratio of the actual pressure of vapor at the time to the saturation pressure at the same temperature. It is the relative humidity which produces the sensation of dampness or dryness in the air, and which gives a very rough indication of whether we can expect cloudy or clear skies. Obviously, the relative humidity depends on the temperature as well as on the vapor content. If the temperature rises without any actual change in the amount of water vapor, the air becomes relatively drier. If the temperature of the air falls, the relative humidity increases; it reaches 100 per cent when the temperature drop is such that the saturation pressure is equal to the actual pressure of vapor. The temperature at which this happens is known as the *dew point*, and it is, of course, the temperature at which dew (or frost if it is below 0°C) will form on an exposed surface.

12-4   Structure of the Atmosphere

Although direct observation of the atmosphere has so far been possible only in the lower layers, and information about the outer regions has had to be obtained indirectly, enough is known to show that the atmosphere is divided into several more or less distinct layers, characterized by the temperature distribution and the state of ionization of the gases. Figure 12-3 shows how the temperature varies with height, on the average.

The lowermost layer, which contains nearly 90 per cent of the total mass, is known technically as the *troposphere*. Most of our weather phenomena take place in this layer, for at higher levels only the very thinnest of hazy clouds can form. The troposphere is characterized by

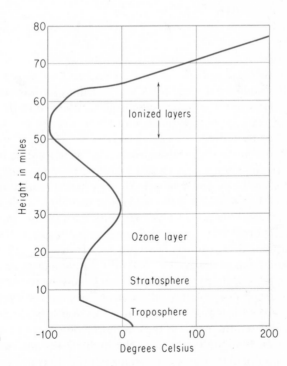

FIG. 12-3

Variation of temperature with height in the atmosphere.

thorough mixing of the air, by a uniform composition, except for water vapor, and by a temperature decreasing with height.

The mixing and the decrease of temperature result from rising and falling convection currents in the air. When air near the ground is warmed in any way, it tends to rise. As it rises it expands due to the decrease of pressure, and in expanding it has to do work. The only source of energy to do this work is the heat content of the air itself, and so the temperature has to decrease. It works out that rising, unsaturated air cools 2.7 Celsius degrees per 1000 feet increase in height, regardless of the condition before the rise begins.

Normally, the troposphere extends only to about 11 miles over the equator, and about 4 miles over the North and South Poles. Above that level is the *stratosphere,* the layer in which the temperature is nearly constant to a considerable height; here long-distance jet aircraft travel most efficiently. At still higher levels, 50 to 100 miles and more, the shortest ultraviolet waves from the sun, as well as high-speed particles—protons and electrons—can penetrate. These particles ionize the air molecules rather than cause chemical reactions, and we find several distinct layers of strongly ionized, electrically conducting gas in the *ionosphere.* Here the temperature increases rapidly with increasing height and is estimated to reach values as high as 1500°C.

12-5   The World Circulation of Wind

It is the heat of the sun, acting upon a rotating earth, that keeps the lower layers of the atmosphere in circulation, and so is the ultimate cause of almost all our wind. The sun's rays fall more or less vertically near the equator, but strike the polar regions at an oblique angle. Therefore the equatorial regions receive much more heat energy per square mile than the poles, and a difference of temperature is produced. Suppose the earth were not rotating on its north-south axis, or were rotating only very slowly. Air near the equator would be heated, would expand, and would rise. Air from more northerly and southerly regions would tend to flow in along the surface to take the place of the equatorial rising air, while the latter would spread out and flow northward and southward in the upper layers of the atmosphere, eventually to descend again near the poles. Thus a worldwide system of convection currents would be set up (Fig. 12-4). The surface winds would almost always be northerly throughout most of the Northern Hemisphere—southerly in the Southern Hemisphere. At higher levels, in the upper troposphere and in the stratosphere, the direction of flow would be reversed, with winds blowing from the south in the Northern Hemisphere, and from the north in the Southern. Since the density in the upper layers is less, the wind velocity in the high return flow would have to be much greater than that near the surface in order to transport the same mass

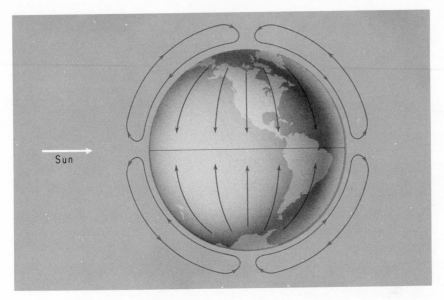

FIG. 12-4

Convection currents due to equatorial heating on a nonrotating earth.

of air and maintain constant atmospheric conditions. Near the equator there would be very little horizontal wind, but the air would be rising; near the poles there would be descending currents.

Now consider the effect of the earth's rotation. Air flowing toward or away from the equator has in addition to its southerly or northerly movement a movement from west to east, imparted to it by the rotation of the earth. The velocity of this easterly motion must be that of the earth's rotation in the latitude from which the air is coming. In accordance with the law of conservation of momentum, this air tends to maintain its easterly velocity when it flows into a different latitude. For air flowing away from the equator, the easterly velocity imparted to it by the rotation is greater than the easterly velocity of the solid surface beneath, and so an outward flowing wind acquires a westerly component (that is, blowing *from* the west). Conversely, a flow toward the equator acquires an easterly component.

By the time the strong outward flowing winds in the upper levels have reached a latitude about 30° north or south of the equator, they are blowing mainly from the west, and the air from the equator tends to descend in this area, rather than flow all the way to the poles in the high levels. Similarly, air flowing away from the poles along the surface is predominantly an easterly wind by the time it reaches a latitude of 60°, and it tends to rise in this area and flow back to the poles at high levels. The rising polar air around latitude 60° and the descending equatorial air around latitude

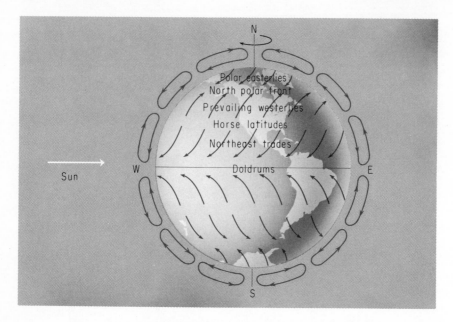

FIG. **12-5**

The actual worldwide circulation on a rotating earth. (Northern spring.)

30° set up a third circulation in between, so that the single circulation in each hemisphere, as shown in Fig. 12-4, is broken up into three main worldwide circulations, as in Fig. 12-5.

Figure 12-5 shows also the principal wind zones of the earth. In latitudes where the circulation is rising or descending there is no prevailing wind direction, and the winds are usually light except when an occasional storm strikes. In latitudes where the surface flow due to the world circulation is strong the wind blows with moderate velocity in a constant direction, for days on end. These facts became well known to sailors in the heyday of the sailing ship—the seventeenth and eighteenth centuries—when long voyages across the open ocean became commonplace, and so the traditional names given to the wind zones reflect the experiences of this past era.

The belt of hot, often nearly windless, rising air which extends about 5° on either side of the equator is known as the *doldrums,* and it was in this area of the Pacific Ocean that the Ancient Mariner in Coleridge's poem was becalmed under a blazing sun:

> *"All in a hot and copper sky, the bloody Sun, at noon,*
> *Right up above the mast did stand, no bigger than the Moon.*
> *Day after day, day after day, we stuck, nor breath nor motion;*
> *As idle as a painted ship upon a painted ocean."*

On either side of the doldrum belt, where surface air is flowing toward the equator, are the zones of the *trade winds;* the northeast trades in the Northern Hemisphere, and the southeast trades in the Southern. These zones derive their traditional name from the extreme regularity of the wind direction over the oceans, so that for purposes of maritime trade the wind could be depended upon almost without fail. Ships sailing from Europe to North America used to make wide detours, far to the south of the direct route, in order to take advantage of the northeast trades for a large part of the voyage.

Where the trade winds peter out there is in each hemisphere a zone of light, uncertain winds, where a ship was in serious danger of being becalmed. These areas are known as the *horse latitudes,* and tradition has it that the name comes from the fact that a ship carrying livestock might have to throw the horses overboard to save drinking water during a long period of calm. From about 35° to 55° the flow is away from the equator, and the prevailing winds are westerly, although they are not as reliable in direction as the trades.° However, a ship returning from North America to Europe would usually have favorable winds on the direct route. Finally, the region above 60° is again an area of equatorward flow and easterly winds. This was not of great importance to navigation in the Northern Hemisphere, but in the ocean around Antarctica strong easterly winds blow almost every day of the year. This continual east wind carries cold air which has passed over the eternal ice of the Antarctic continent. It was this frigid wind that made the passage around Cape Horn, at the southern tip of South America, such a nightmare to sailors on the long voyage from California to Atlantic ports.

The idealized circulation shown in Fig. 12-5 shifts north and south with the seasons of the year. Any reference to the equator in the previous discussion of wind patterns should actually be interpreted to mean the zone of maximum temperature, where the sun's rays are falling more or less perpendicularly upon the earth. In the northern summer the center of the circulation pattern is shifted about 10° to 15° north of the geographical equator, and in northern winter it lies south of the equator. Large and important areas of the earth may lie in a trade-wind zone at one time of the year and in the light winds of the horse latitudes, or even in the westerlies, at another season. Many of these areas experience definite wet and dry seasons, for example the Mediterranean region and southern Europe, where Western civilization first developed, or the monsoon areas of India and Southeast Asia.

The wind zones are also somewhat distorted by the great land masses

° It is in these zones that jet streams develop at high altitudes. As the term implies, the jet stream is a high velocity wind—often reaching 100 miles per hour or more over a narrow front, and flowing from west to east. The movement of frontal lows (Sec. 12-6) is influenced by the jet stream.

of the continents, because a land mass absorbs more heat from the sun than does a wide expanse of ocean. Of greater importance is the influence the continents have in determining the weather within any of the wind zones. The moisture content of the prevailing wind will differ considerably depending on whether it has passed over an ocean or over a wide expanse of dry land. For example, throughout the tropics, where the wind pattern is dominated by the easterly trade winds—even if they do not blow all year —we find the great rain forests of the world toward the east sides of the continents, in areas where the easterly winds approach the land over vast expanses of warm ocean. We find the hot deserts toward the west sides of the continents, where the prevailing winds have passed long distances over the land, and over mountainous areas.

12-6   The Polar Front: Highs and Lows

The northern United States, the populated areas of Canada, the British Isles, and northern Europe lie mostly within the zone of prevailing westerly winds in summer, but in winter the zone where the westerlies and polar easterlies meet lies right across these highly civilized areas. This meeting zone is not characterized by light, indefinite winds like the horse latitudes. Rather there is a sharp boundary, especially in winter, between the prevailing westerlies, with their temperate climate, and the easterlies which bring cold air from the Arctic Ocean. This is the so-called *polar front,* whose behavior is responsible for a great many of the vagaries of the weather with which most of us are familiar.

In winter the well-marked polar front oscillates. At times it is well up in northern Canada, and the United States and much of Canada experience a mild spell. At other times it shifts far to the south, possibly extending a tongue as far as northern Texas, and we have one of our winter cold snaps. The frontal zone is surprisingly narrow. Two places only 100 miles apart, which happen to be on opposite sides of the front for the time being, may have temperatures differing by 30° or more. As the shifting front passes over any location, the temperature may drop 30° or 40° in a few hours.

For a large part of the year the day-to-day variations in our weather are determined by the way in which low-pressure areas develop along the polar front. The development starts from a condition where the westerly winds to the south of the front and the easterly winds to the north flow side by side, in opposite directions, without mixing. This condition is unstable, and a wave begins to form along the front, as shown in Fig. 12-6. Mild, moisture-laden air from the southwest is trying to force its way into the cold zone, and cold, dry air from the northeast is trying to penetrate

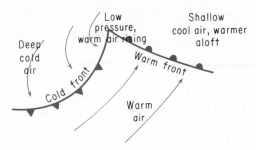

FIG. 12-6

A wave developing in the polar front.

the warmer zone. Still there is very little mixing. Instead, the warm air tends to ride up over the cold air on the easterly side of the wave, and the cold air tends to undercut the warm air on the westerly side. A rising mass of air necessarily causes a lowering of the barometric pressure, and so in its fully developed stage the wave in the front becomes a low-pressure area. This is indicated by the *isobars*, or lines through points of equal pressure, in Fig. 12-7, which shows the fully developed stage of the wave in the polar front. We now have a typical *cyclonic°* *low*, with air from both warm and cold sectors tending to flow in toward the low-pressure center. In conformity with the rule that a northward flow is diverted toward the east by the rotation of the earth (in the Northern Hemisphere), and a southward flow is diverted toward the west, the winds spiral around the

° In meteorological language a *cyclone* is any system of spiraling winds, converging toward a low-pressure center. The term does not imply a destructive storm, which is properly called a hurricane or a tornado.

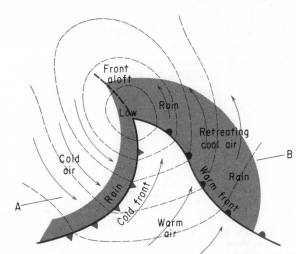

FIG. 12-7

A well-developed frontal low, showing the isobars (----) or lines of equal pressure, and areas of rain (shaded).

low center in a counterclockwise direction. Figure 12-8 is a cross section, with the vertical scale greatly exaggerated, taken along the line *AB* of Fig. 12-7, to show how the warm air is forced aloft. Figure 12-9 shows an actual weather map, with the pressures and the fronts plotted upon it, on a day when there were well-marked low- and high-pressure areas.

When the polar front is clearly marked over a wide area, more or less well developed lows tend to travel along it from west to east at a rate of 500 to 1000 miles a day, and as they pass over they cause much of the variation in the weather, with clouds, and rain or snow. However, very often the polar front is not nearly as clearly defined as has been suggested above. Especially in the northern summer, when the true polar front is usually far to the north, the weather distribution over the United States and Canada may show two or three less conspicuous fronts, marking boundaries between air masses of different origin. These may be "cool Pacific air" from the Gulf of Alaska, "warm Pacific air" from the southwest, "continental air" from the great plains, "maritime air" from the North Atlantic, and so on, each with its own characteristics of temperature and moisture content. Low-pressure weather disturbances can form along these frontal boundaries just as they do along the true polar front, but may be much less typical in their behavior.

High atmospheric pressure develops where the air is settling. Thus there are practically permanent high-pressure areas around the North and South Poles, and the average pressure is higher than normal in the zone of the horse latitudes. More or less isolated high-pressure areas of slowly moving air often develop over the continents, well away from any distinct front, in those zones which are characterized over the oceans by the prevailing westerlies or the polar easterlies. Such areas are known as highs, or *anti-cyclones*, because their light winds arise from a diverging flow, and so spiral clockwise in the Northern Hemisphere, in the opposite direction to that of a typical low.

In North America, in winter, distinctive highs develop well to the north of the polar front and are formed from masses of cold, heavy Arctic air which have settled over the great plains. They sometimes remain nearly motionless for days on end, and bring a prolonged spell of zero weather to

 FIG. 12-8

Cross section through a frontal low, showing warm air aloft and the distribution of cloud and rain.

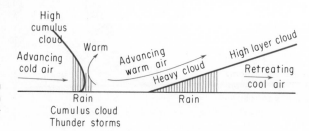

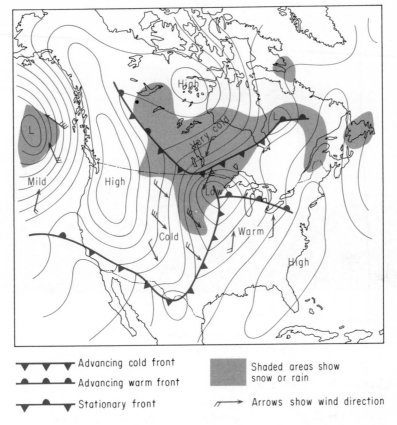

FIG. 12-9

An actual weather map, showing the pressure distribution and fronts on December 7, 1963; typical winter weather in the U.S.A. and Canada.

the northwestern states and the Canadian prairies. Summer highs over the central plains are characterized most of the time by fine, hot weather. However, when a high persists for any length of time it means that the world circulation is ineffective in that area for the time being.

12-7   *Clouds and Rain*

There is no need to discuss separately the causes of clouds and of rain. Rain or snow simply occurs when the water content of a cloud increases to the point where the water droplets become too large to hang suspended so that they fall to the ground. To form clouds, moisture-laden air must be

FIG. 12-10

Cumulus clouds over Mt. Rundle, Banff National Park. (Photograph by author.)

cooled below its dew point. Direct cooling can occur and is often responsible for surface fog, as when warm air flows over cold water, or when a stagnant air mass cools off at night. However, by far the most important cause of ordinary high-level clouds is a rising air current. When a mass of air rises, the pressure is reduced, and the air expands. In expanding it is cooled (Sec. 12-4). If the absolute humidity is high enough and if the vertical uplift extends far enough aloft, the air will be cooled below the dew point. Then condensation must take place and clouds must form. Under given conditions this will happen at a definite level in the atmosphere. For example, this can be noted when the sky is flecked with woolly cumulus clouds; their bases are on almost the same level, although their tops may extend to very different heights (Fig. 12-10).

The simplest cause of uplifted air is wind blowing over a mountain range, and in many parts of the world this produces characteristic "topographic" clouds, often with considerable amounts of rain (Fig. 12-11). An excellent example of topographic clouds and rain occurs along our own West Coast, when moisture-laden winds off the Pacific blow successively across the Coast Ranges, the Sierras, and the Rockies. The rainfall in these ranges is much more abundant on their western slopes—as evidenced by

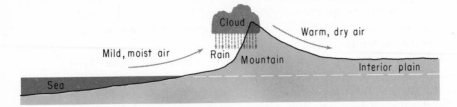

FIG. 12-11

The formation of topographic cloud and rain by a mountain range, and the chinook effect.

the more luxuriant vegetation (Fig. 12-12)—than toward the east. The interior valleys between the ranges are generally arid, or even desert. When the flow over a mountain range descends again on the other side the air is reheated by compression. But it has now lost much of its moisture content, through the rainfall on the western slope, so that when it is reheated it is far below its dew point, and rain seldom occurs in the valley.

This reheating effect reaches an extreme in the famous chinook wind that occurs in Alberta, eastern Montana, and neighboring areas. These

FIG. 12-12

Luxuriant ferns and moss-covered trees in the rain forest of Olympic National Park, Washington. (Photograph by author.)

regions are not desert, as are the interior valleys of California and Oregon, because moisture-laden air often flows into the area from the southeast. But occasionally in winter, when the area has been lying for days under a sub-zero blanket of stagnant polar air, a marked cyclonic low approaching the Pacific Coast sets up a strong westerly wind which may extend far beyond the Rockies into the plains. This air was mild and moist to begin with. By the time it has passed over three mountain ranges, depositing rain on the western slope of each, and then has slid down the eastern slope, or has poured with almost gale force through the mountain passes, it has been heated not only by compression as it descends, but also by the latent heat of condensation, and it is now warm and dry. The results are dramatic. When a strong chinook starts to blow, the temperature can rise 50° or more in 2 or 3 hours. The skies are clear and the warm wind licks up whatever snow may have accumulated on the ground.

Significant as topographic rainfall can be to the economy in some places, it can only occur in limited areas. The most important cause of rising air, resulting in the formation of clouds and rain, is the uplift which occurs along a front. Thus the diagrams (Figs. 12-7 and 12-8) of a typical frontal low show also the distribution of clouds in the uplifted warm air. The details may vary considerably, but a well-developed low usually produces rain or snow in its leading sector, to the east of the center. The rain often slackens as the center itself passes by, and then showers occur again, with a marked drop in temperature, after the center has passed. This is consistent with the common observation that a rapidly falling barometer is an almost sure sign of approaching bad weather, and a rising barometer is an indication that the rain will soon be over.

The third important cause of rising air is convection due to local heating. Usually this produces only the fleecy cumulus clouds which are so common in fine summer weather, but sometimes the convection becomes so strong that the cloud towers thousands of feet into the upper atmosphere, and a sudden thunderstorm results. Occasionally this type of local convection can be the cause of a violent tornado whose intense spiraling winds cover only a small area at any one time, but travel across the country, doing extensive damage.

GLOSSARY

Absolute humidity The actual amount of water vapor present in the atmosphere, usually given by stating the pressure that the vapor exerts.

Anticyclone A system of winds, usually light, that are spiraling outward from a high-pressure area.

Aurora borealis, or northern lights The display of glowing streamers and arcs of light that is often seen in the night sky in northern latitudes. There is also an aurora australis in southern latitudes, and both are commonly known to astronomers and meteorologists simply as aurora.

Chinook Warm dry wind from the west that descends the eastern slopes of the Rocky Mountains at intervals in winter, causing a rapid rise of temperature.

Convection The process whereby gases and liquids are kept in a state of vertical circulation when lower layers are heated, expand, and rise, and upper layers descend to take their place.

Cumulus clouds The white "cotton wool" clouds that sometimes look like castles and sometimes like snow-covered mountains. They are evidence of rising air currents, and when they are very large they may develop into thunder showers.

Cyclone Any system of winds, not necessarily destructive, that is spiraling in toward an area of low pressure.

Dew point Temperature at which the vapor present in the air begins to condense.

Doldrums The zone of hot, nearly stagnant air over the ocean on either side of the equator.

Front A sharp boundary between masses of air of different origins, having different temperatures and moisture content.

Horse latitudes Either of two zones of descending air and light, uncertain winds over the ocean, lying between the trade winds and the prevailing westerlies of higher latitudes.

Ionosphere Outermost of the three principal atmospheric layers, characterized by strong ionization due to the absorption of sunlight.

Isobar Line drawn on a weather map through points of equal atmospheric pressure.

Monsoon A periodic wind that blows at certain seasons of the year over the Indian Ocean and southern Asia; from the southwest in winter and from the northeast in summer.

Polar front The front caused by cold, dry air flowing southward from the north polar regions.

Radiosonde Device used to obtain routine information about the temperature, humidity, and pressure at different heights in the atmosphere. It consists of a small balloon carrying automatic recording instruments, and a radio transmitter that broadcasts the readings to a ground station.

Relative humidity Ratio of the vapor pressure which expresses the absolute humidity to the saturation vapor pressure of water at the existing temperature. (The "humidity" of the published weather reports.)

Stratosphere The second of the three atmospheric layers, characterized by a nearly constant temperature, or by a temperature rising slightly with increasing altitude.

Topographic cloud and rain Technically, any cloud that is produced by the terrain in a particular area; usually caused by wind ascending the slope of a mountain.

Trade winds The winds that blow almost continually toward the equator, from the northeast in the Northern Hemisphere and from the southeast in the Southern Hemisphere, in the subtropical zones on either side of the doldrum belt; so called because sailing ships learned to depend upon them for long ocean voyages.

Troposphere The lowermost of the three principal layers of the atmosphere; the layer which is characterized by convection, and in which most of our familiar weather phenomena take place.

EXERCISES

1. What methods are commonly used to study conditions in the atmosphere?

2. What kind of information can be obtained from the weather satellites that are circling the earth?

3. What are our sources of information for conditions in the atmosphere above the level where direct measurements are possible?

4. What is "ozone," and how is it produced in the atmosphere?

5. What effect does the ionization in the high atmosphere have upon radio reception?

6. What is the third most abundant gas in the atmosphere, after nitrogen and oxygen? What would be the mass of this gas in a cubic meter of air, at $0°C$ and standard atmospheric pressure? What effect does this gas have upon living things?

7. Define "absolute humidity" and "relative humidity."

8. Assuming that the heating system in your house has no provision for controlling humidity, how would you expect the absolute humidity indoors to compare with that outdoors in winter? How would the relative humidity compare?

9. Describe the characteristics of the three principal layers into which the atmosphere is divided.

10. Explain why a flow of air toward the equator is always deflected so as to produce easterly winds.

11. Which way do the winds blow near a low-pressure center in the Northern Hemisphere? near a high-pressure center in the Southern Hemisphere? There is another phenomenon (not having to do with the weather) in which the same causes produce a similar effect; try to find out what this is.

12. Explain how the circulation of air due to heating by the sun in equatorial regions produces several distinct weather zones.

13. What is happening in the zone of indefinite light winds known as the horse latitudes? It is in this zone that tornadoes and other violent storms sometimes develop; what starts them?

14. What is the polar front, and how does it develop?

15. How do low-pressure areas develop along a well-marked front?

16. Draw a simple sketch showing the isobars, the fronts, the distribution of clouds and rain, and the wind directions, in a typical polar front low.

17. Why is the atmospheric pressure nearly always higher than average over the Arctic Ocean? Would you expect to get high barometric readings at the South Pole? What happens there?

18. Give three different causes that can produce rising air currents, resulting in clouds.

19. When there are a number of cumulus clouds in the sky they often have flat bases, all on nearly the same level. Explain why this is so.

20. In the western United States and Canada the vegetation is usually more luxuriant on the western slope of a mountain range than it is on the eastern slope. Give the reason for this.

21. Locate on a globe the principal rain forests and the principal tropical deserts of the world, and try to correlate these with the prevailing wind pattern.

CHAPTER **13**   # the chemistry of living things

13-1   *Homopolar and Covalent Bonding*

The type of chemical combination discussed in Chapter 9 was that known as *ionic bonding;* the forces that hold a compound together in its pure form are mainly electrical attractions between ions of opposite sign, as in sodium chloride (NaCl). The atoms and radicals form ions with definitely positive or definitely negative charges, and with one, two, or three units of charge (Sec. 9-10). The number of negative ions that combine with a given positive ion (or vice versa) is determined by the rule that the total ionic charge must be zero.

In the case of a gas that has simple diatomic molecules, like hydrogen (H_2) or oxygen (O_2), the forces that hold the atoms together must be of a different nature. At ordinary temperatures NaCl is a crystalline solid, with the atomic arrangement shown in Fig. 10-5. Each sodium atom is surrounded by six chlorines, and vice versa, so that we cannot say which sodium and which chlorine belong to the same molecule. H_2 and O_2 are normally gases, with stable molecules, but with only weak attraction between different molecules, so that they liquefy and solidify only at temperatures far below $0°C$. The strong binding forces between atoms are used mainly to hold the atoms together in pairs, and must be of a nature that requires the cooperation of two like atoms. Because the two atoms are indistinguishable and the molecules are symmetrical, this is known as *homopolar* ("like-ended") *bonding.*

A similar type of force can also exist between two unlike atoms in a stable molecule (for example, in H_2O) and so homopolar bonding is a special case of what is known more generally as *covalent bonding.*° In the H_2 molecule each atom can, under other circumstances, form a singly charged positive ion, and the molecule is held together by a *single* covalent bond. Similarly, chlorine atoms form singly charged negative ions in solution, and are held together by a single covalent bond in the gas molecule (Cl_2). When hydrogen and chlorine combine to form stable molecules in hydrogen chloride gas (HCl) there is again a single covalent bond, although as ions one is electropositive and the other electronegative.

Oxygen behaves as a doubly charged negative ion in its ionic compounds (the simple metallic oxides, for example), and the molecules of oxygen gas (O_2) have a *double* covalent bond.† In its stable compound with hydrogen (water, H_2O) the oxygen atom can provide a single bond for each of two hydrogen atoms. An oxygen atom can also make single bonds with each of two chlorine atoms and form molecules with the formula Cl_2O. Nitrogen has a strong tendency to form three covalent bonds; in nitrogen gas the molecules (N_2) have a triple bond; in ammonia gas (NH_3) the nitrogen atom forms three single bonds with hydrogen atoms.

In these and other simple examples elements that form singly charged positive or negative ions (elements from columns I and VII of the periodic table) also have single bonds in covalent compounds; elements from column VI of the table form doubly charged negative ions and have either double covalent bonds or two single bonds; elements from column V have three single covalent bonds available. We note also that covalent bonds are associated mainly with the nonmetallic elements, whereas the metals are more likely to form ionic compounds. Again, most ionic compounds are crystalline solids at ordinary temperatures; most simple covalent compounds are gases or liquids with stable molecules. However, there are many exceptions to all these rules, none of which should be considered general. Also there are a great many compounds in which some of the bonds are ionic and some are covalent.

° The term is derived from the concept of chemical *valence*, the number that was assigned to different atoms and radicals in order to indicate their combining value. For example, in salts the valence of the acid radical is equal to the number of hydrogen atoms in a molecule of the corresponding acid; the valence of the metal is equal to the number of hydrogen atoms it replaces. In these and similar simple cases the valence is equal to the number of units of charge on the ion. In simple covalent compounds the valence is equal to the number of available covalent bonds. Thus an alternative method of discussing the chemical properties of carbon is to relate them to a valence of 4. However, the valence concept is no longer in general use in discussions of chemical combination.

† This has no relation to the strength of the bond; the forces involved in a double bond are not necessarily greater than those of a single bond.

Carbon is element number 6 in the periodic table and falls in column IV. It has four covalent bonds available, and in nearly all its compounds the bonding is of the covalent type. In its simplest hydrogen compound (methane, CH_4) and in carbon tetrachloride (CCl_4) it forms four single bonds with hydrogen or chlorine atoms; in its most stable oxide (carbon dioxide, CO_2) it forms two double bonds with oxygen atoms. The four bonds can be used in many different ways to bond carbon atoms to atoms of other elements. However, what makes carbon almost unique in its chemical properties is the tendency to use one or more of its covalent bonds to combine with other carbon atoms, forming long chains, rings of six, and many other configurations. The many diverse combinations that result make possible an almost unlimited variety of carbon compounds.

For example, carbon and hydrogen form a large number of different binary compounds, known as the *hydrocarbons*. The saturated hydrocarbons, also known as the paraffins, contain the maximum number of hydrogen atoms for a given number of carbon atoms and form a series of which the first few members are methane (CH_4), ethane (C_2H_6), propane (C_3H_8), etc. The densities and boiling points increase progressively with the number of carbon atoms. The lightest members of the series are gases at ordinary temperatures, and together they constitute natural fuel gas. A mixture of somewhat heavier members, from pentane (C_5H_{12}) to decane ($C_{10}H_{22}$), is gasoline. Still heavier members are found in lubricating oil, and the very heaviest, containing up to about 30 carbon atoms, form paraffin wax.

The way in which the carbon atoms link together in the paraffins is shown in the structural formulae for the different molecules, with the first four shown as examples in Fig. 13-1. In these diagrams the single line join-

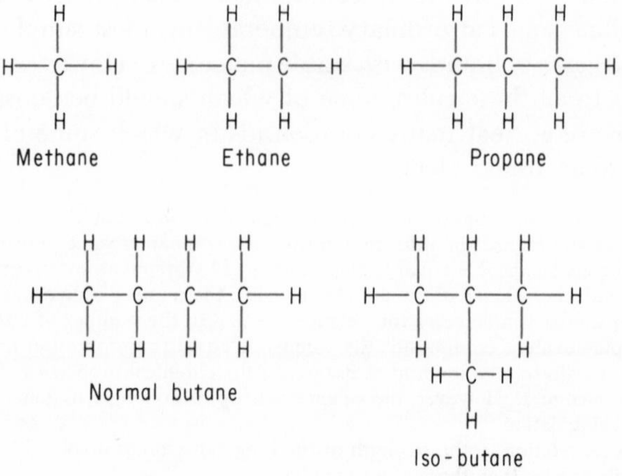

Methane   Ethane   Propane

Normal butane

Iso-butane

FIG. 13-1

Structural formulae for the simplest paraffins.

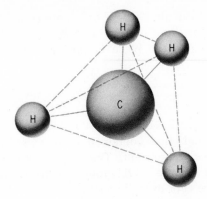

FIG. 13-2

Methane (CH$_4$) molecule. Solid lines are C-H bonds; broken lines are edges of the tetrahedron formed by the four H atoms.

ing neighboring carbon atoms indicates a single covalent bond holding them together. In molecules of this type a chain of n carbon atoms has $2n + 2$ unoccupied bonds by which hydrogen atoms can be attached, and so the generic formula for the paraffins is C_nH_{2n+2}. With four or more carbon atoms there are alternative ways of linking them together, other than the linear chain. For example, Fig. 13-1 shows two different structural formulae for butane (C_4H_{10}); the two forms have slightly different physical properties and are referred to as *isomers.**

The simplest example of a compound in which the carbon atoms form a closed ring is benzene (C_6H_6), which has the structural formula shown in Fig. 13-3. In this case three of the six linkages between neighboring carbon atoms are double covalent bonds. Double bonds can also occur in linear molecules, giving another whole series of possibilities.

In all the hydrocarbons, the hydrogen atoms can be replaced by other atoms or radicals. For example, replacement of the hydrogen in methane by chlorine produces CH_3Cl (methyl chloride), CH_2Cl_2 (dichloromethane), $CHCl_3$ (chloroform), and CCl_4 (carbon tetrachloride). Further, the simple hydrocarbons can produce radicals, such as methyl, $—CH_3$, which is methane with one hydrogen atom missing, so that it has one free bond by

* The structural formulae shown in Figs. 13-1 and 13-3 are not pictures of the molecules, but only schematic diagrams showing the relations between the atoms in the molecules. The actual molecules are three-dimensional, and, for example, CH_4 has the four hydrogens surrounding the central carbon in the form of a tetrahedron (Fig. 13-2). In a long carbon chain the atoms do not lie in a straight line, but are more likely to form a sort of zigzag spiral.

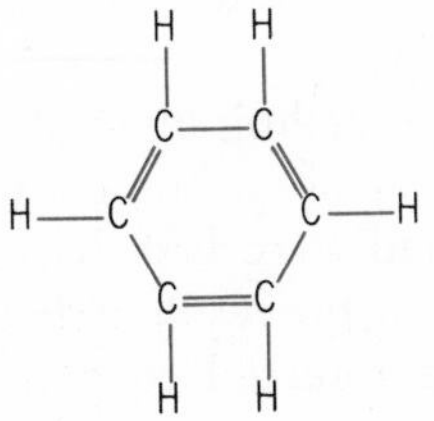

FIG. 13-3

Structural formula for benzene (C_6H_6).

which it can attach itself to a more complicated molecule. Again, isomers occur, for there may be differences in the properties of the compound, according to the place in the base structure where the new radical is attached.

Compounds that contain oxygen along with carbon and hydrogen are particularly important. The simplest of these are the *alcohols*, which contain one or more —OH groups substituted for the hydrogens of the original structure. For example, methyl alcohol is CH_3OH, ethyl alcohol C_2H_5OH. The *carbohydrates* also contain —OH groups, but they have extra oxygen atoms, usually in such a way that the resulting molecule has two hydrogen atoms for each oxygen atom. These include the two common sugars, glucose ($C_6H_{12}O_6$) and sucrose ($C_{12}H_{22}O_{11}$), both of which have several isomeric forms. A number of sugarlike structures can combine into a chain to produce one of the many varieties of starch. Still more complex carbohydrates constitute cellulose, which forms the woody structure of plants, and which exists in thousands of varieties whose molecular structures have never been precisely determined.

Another group that requires special mention is that of the *organic acids*, which contain oxygen combined in a —COOH group. This group can attach itself by means of the carbon to a great variety of base structures, leaving the hydrogen atom on the surface, where it is fairly easily removed in solution as an H^+ ion. Thus, compounds containing this group are weak acids and readily form saltlike compounds. One of the simplest acids of this kind is acetic acid, in which COOH substitutes for one of the hydrogens of methane to produce CH_3COOH. From this, the acetate radical (CH_3CO_2—) can form salts with many metals. Acetic acid can also react with an alcohol to form a compound of the class known as *esters*, in which the acetate radical is attached to a hydrocarbon structure in place of one of the hydrogens. Heavier acids of the same group include those that produce the sour taste in certain foods, like citric acid in many fruits, or acids that develop in stale foods by oxidation, like lactic acid in sour milk. Still heavier members of the group include the fatty acids, whose esters, formed by combination with a hydrocarbon base, are the main constituents of vegetable oils and fats, and whose compounds with sodium or potassium form soaps.

The preceding illustrations should suffice to convey the extraordinary complexity of carbon chemistry. Most of the compounds that have been mentioned were first discovered in material of biological origin, many of them being the result of decay or oxidation of once-living organisms. Hence they are referred to generally as organic compounds, and the highly specialized branch of chemistry that deals with the carbon compounds is known as *organic chemistry*. Because of the painstaking work of hundreds of organic chemists over the years more than a million distinct organic compounds have been recognized and named; most of these can be obtained in a nearly pure state so that their properties can be studied. The ingenuity of these chemists has made it possible to deduce the structural formulae for a great many highly complicated molecules by piecing together many different bits of information derived from the chemical reactions in which the molecules take part. In many cases the actual three-dimensional structure has also been worked out, largely with the help of X-ray analysis.

13-4   *Photosynthesis and the Oxygen and Carbon Cycles*

All living things that we know on earth depend for their metabolism and growth upon chemical reactions involving carbon compounds. All life requires energy, and on earth that energy initially comes from the sun. In the course of time nearly all life on earth has settled down into one or other of two basic forms—plant or animal—both of which derive the energy necessary for growth and movement ultimately through the process know as *photosynthesis*. In this process, carbon dioxide, obtained either from the atmosphere or from carbonate ions dissolved in the sea, is combined with water to produce simple sugars and oxygen in a complicated series of reactions, the final result of which is

$$6\,CO_2 + 6\,H_2O \longrightarrow C_6H_{12}O_6 + 6\,O_2.$$

This reaction requires energy, but the carbon dioxide cannot obtain that energy directly. There has to be a substance present which can absorb light energy from the sun. Although other possibilities are known to play a part in the life cycle, by far the most important agent is chlorophyll, the green pigment found in land plants and in many sea plants. Chlorophyll has a complicated organic molecule in which several different carbon-hydrogen-oxygen combinations are grouped around a central core consisting of a magnesium atom and four nitrogen atoms. This molecule absorbs red and orange light, and reflects or scatters green, whence the green color. The "excited" energy-bearing chlorophyll molecule transfers its energy to the carbon dioxide and water molecules, and so initiates the sequence of synthesis reactions.[*]

Once glucose and other simple sugars are formed, the basis for plant growth is at hand. Starches and cellulose can be formed directly. Ions de-

---

[*] It is an interesting example of nature's economy that in the sea, at depths where the sunlight is dim, whatever plant life exists is mostly brown in color. These "brown algae" contain other pigments besides chlorophyll; the different pigments absorb light energy of different colors and transfer it to the chlorophyll, so that little of the scant sunlight is wasted.

rived from the soil or from the water, particularly nitrates, phosphates, and metallic ions, are added to the organic molecules to make up the host of different materials that enter into the complete plant, including, of course, more chlorophyll.

In the life cycle with which we are familiar, animals live upon plants. Animals take in oxygen by breathing air or, in the case of marine animals, by absorbing oxygen dissolved in water. They use the oxygen to "burn" the organic molecules from the plants, thereby producing the energy necessary for growth and movement. In this process, carbon dioxide is released as a by-product and is used by the plants, thus producing more food for the animals. In all higher animals their metabolism involves the chemical reactions of another complicated and highly specialized organic pigment, hemoglobin, the red coloring matter in the blood. Hemoglobin, which requires iron for the formation of its molecules, absorbs oxygen, and, by means of the blood circulation, distributes it to wherever it is needed for the energy-producing reactions of oxidation.

The plant reactions on the one hand, and the animal reactions on the other hand, keep a large part of the earth's supply of oxygen and carbon circulating continually between the organic materials of living things and the atmosphere or the sea. The two cycles involved can be summarized as shown in Fig. 13-4.

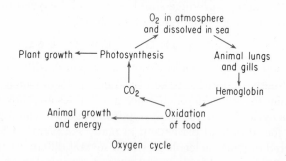

Oxygen cycle

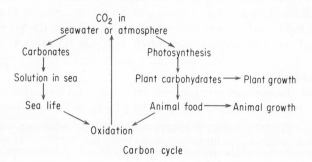

FIG. 13-4

The oxygen and carbon cycles in plant and animal life.

Carbon cycle

All living cells contain *proteins* of many different kinds, all of which contribute in their special ways to the life and growth of the cell. If the single cell is itself a living organism, it still has parts with different functions, the parts containing several different proteins. In the case of a more complicated organism, such as a plant or a complete animal, there are many different kinds of cells, each with its proper function to perform. Another important difference between plants and animals is, usually, in the amount of protein in their structure. In plants, the proteins are found mainly in the fluid contents of the cells, most abundantly in the seeds, the part of the plant which is responsible for reproduction. The hard parts of the cells, and the cell walls, which merge into the woody supporting structure, are composed mainly of cellulose and similar carbohydrates. Animal cells generally contain larger proportions of protein, some of which is in a solid form, in the muscle fibers and even in the skin and hair.

We cannot discuss at length the chemistry of proteins, but to understand what follows we should know in a general way what a protein is, and to understand this we must begin with the *amino acids*. These are organic compounds whose molecules contain a $-COOH$ group and a $-NH_2$ group. They have the special property that the hydrogen from the COOH can transfer to the NH_2, leaving the ends of the molecule electrically charged, COO^- near one end and NH_3^+ near the other end. Because of these charges an amino acid molecule can behave sometimes as a negative ion, and sometimes as a positive ion, but the most important result is that amino acids can join together plus to minus, in long chains known as *peptides*. Peptide chains are then found joined together side by side, with certain additional organic radicals acting as a sort of binder, to form the *proteins*, which therefore consist of giant molecules containing a thousand to a million atoms. Some protein molecules are large enough to be photographed with an electron microscope.

Only 22 distinct amino acids have been found in living cells, although in theory a very large number of such molecules should be possible. These 22 varieties can be linked together in millions of different ways to form peptide chains. Then there are millions of ways in which a given set of peptides could be combined to make a giant protein molecule, so that the number of possible distinct proteins is almost endless. The number cannot be mathematically infinite, but it must exceed by a large factor the total number of living organisms on the earth. Even so, the proteins in a particular organism are specific molecules, having a specific structure and properties and performing specific functions.

13-6   *Enzymes and Hormones*

There are two classes of highly specialized substances which act in various ways to initiate or accelerate chemical reactions involved in metabolism and growth. *Enzymes* are proteinlike molecules which have a specific action in promoting metabolism reactions. A simple example of one of their functions is in connection with digestive processes in animals. Many foodstuffs, particularly proteins and carbohydrates such as fats and cellulose, cannot be utilized directly by the animal, but have to be broken down into simpler molecules before they can be assimilated. This breakdown, along with a certain amount of other chemical action, is the function of the enzymes in the digestive juices. Other enzymes cause the molecular groupings in ingested materials to be shifted around, and make the materials more suitable for use as building blocks in the growth of the plant or animal to which the enzyme is specific.

Hormones have been called the body's messengers because they control activity and growth through highly specific chemical actions and ensure that these functions take place in the proper orderly manner. In animals, most of the hormones are produced in the ductless glands, whence minute quantities are released into the blood stream,° to be transported to where they are needed to initiate the proper activities. Many hormones have been isolated in pure form and their chemical relations studied. In structure they may be anything from a fairly simple organic molecule to a collection of amino acids in a peptide chain or a protein molecule. A few simple examples will illustrate how they function.

Certain hormones which control body growth are produced by the thyroid gland in the neck; if the thyroid is defective in a young animal so that the proper hormones are not produced, a dwarf is liable to result. Insulin, which controls the oxidation of sugars and fats so that they can produce the energy necessary for bodily movement, is secreted by special groups of cells in the pancreas; its absence causes diabetes, when sugar and dangerous acids accumulate in the blood. Insulin is a protein with a molecular weight of about 12,000. It can be prepared in pure crystalline form, and the structure of the molecule has been worked out. Adrenaline, which has quite a simple molecule consisting of radicals attached to a benzene ring, acts to control muscular activity. When unusual activity is needed, for example, when an animal needs to escape from an enemy or to fight, another hormone stimulates the adrenal glands attached to the kidneys and causes them to pour adrenaline into the bloodstream. The heart pumps faster to circulate more blood and produce more energy for increased activity of all the muscles.

° In the case of adrenaline, a solution of 1 part in 3×10^8 parts of water can be detected by its effect on a laboratory animal.

Vitamins are similar to hormones and function in very much the same way, with the distinction that they are produced by plants and by other bodies—or even manufactured synthetically—and ingested, whereas hormones are produced within the organism that requires them. Vitamins may have fairly simple molecules, they may be similar in structure to the chlorophyll-like pigments or they may be complicated organic acids. Many of their structures have been worked out in detail.

13-7   The Mechanism of Heredity

An important breakthrough in the chemistry of life came in the late 1950's, through the elucidation of the structure and functions of the *nucleic acids.* This cannot be ascribed to a definite discovery by a particular individual; rather it was the result of piecing together many bits of evidence, from chemistry, from X-ray analysis, and from studies of cells with the electron microscope.

The nucleic acids are highly specialized substances which are found in the nuclei of all living cells, associated particularly with the *chromosomes,* the little threadlike bodies which have been known for a long time to be the seat of the *genes* which carry the factors of heredity and ensure that an offspring will be similar to its parents in all major features. The nucleic acids have long chain molecules in which sugarlike structures alternate with phosphate radicals; to each sugar is attached one of four highly specific, nitrogen-based organic groups. Two types of chain are found in nature. In ribonucleic acid (familiarly known as RNA) the sugar is ribose ($C_5H_{10}O_5$); in deoxyribonucleic acid (DNA) it is deoxyribose, which has one less oxygen because a simple hydrogen is substituted for one of the —OH groups of the ribose molecule.

We now know that it is DNA in the chromosomes which conveys the inheritable characteristics from parent to offspring in all higher plants and animals and ensures that the offspring will develop in the way that they should. RNA apparently functions in a similar manner in some lower organisms, and possibly in many viruses.

The DNA molecule has two sugar-phosphate chains which coil around each other in a double spiral (Fig. 13-5), with the nitrogenous groups in the middle. This molecule has the extraordinary property that it can make exact copies of itself; it is capable of reproduction! No matter how complicated the molecule may be, the DNA molecules in all the cells of a living body are precisely alike, barring occasional accidents. When a cell divides in the growing body, the chromosomes split down the middle, and each half grows a new half to provide the proper chromosome structure for the two daughter cells. The DNA molecules also split, exposing the groups in

FIG. 13-5

Portion of a DNA molecule, showing the double spiral structure. Dark circles represent atoms of the phosphate-sugar chains; lighter circles represent atoms of the nitrogenous groups that carry the coded information; small white circles are hydrogen atoms (after M. Feughelman et al.).

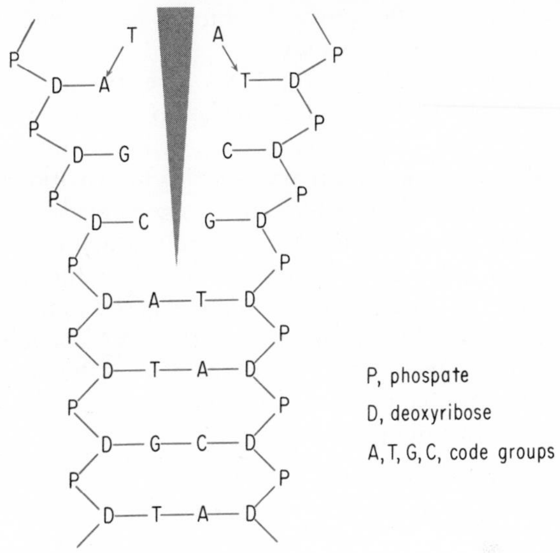

FIG. 13-6

Schematic diagram of a DNA molecule in the process of splitting and reproducing.

P, phospate

D, deoxyribose

A, T, G, C, code groups

the center of the spiral, whereupon each of them attaches to itself a group identical with the partner it had in the original spiral, and the proper sugars and phosphates are filled in to complete two new molecules. Figure 13-6 shows schematically a DNA molecule in the process of splitting and producing a pair of identical offspring.

Among the four nitrogen-based groups which are found in DNA molecules, only two pairs of partners occur in the matching of opposite sides of the spiral; adenine pairs with thymine, and guanine with cytosine, as indicated by the letters A, T, G, C in Fig. 13-6. All the inheritable information which has to be passed from the parents to the offspring,° and then from the original egg cell to all the cells of the fully developed body, is coded by means of the order in which the four groups are arranged in the double spiral. Every cell in the body then bears a copy of this code, and so in a sense carries a complete design of the final body. At first it may seem hard to believe that enough information can be passed on in this way, but a little consideration shows that the code is ample for all needs. In higher animals each cell nucleus contains several chromosomes, and each chromosome contains several DNA molecules. Electron microphotographs have shown the DNA molecules from a cell lying like pieces of thread dropped on the floor, with a total length of nearly a millimeter. The set of molecules would contain at least 100,000 pairs of code-bearing groups, and the number of different ways in which they could be arranged would be

° Obviously, in the case of sexual reproduction the offspring has to get half of its DNA, and so half of its coded information, from each parent. Much of the code will be common to both, for example, that which determines that the body should be a human and not a dog. Details may be slightly different, such as the code for eye color or height.

3 raised to the 100,000th power,° which is many times the total number of atoms in the Milky Way Galaxy.

It remains to suggest how the DNA gives the necessary orders to the proteins and carbohydrates which make up a growing cell. For example, how does the DNA know when to stop making muscle and start making bone or hair, and how does it pass on this information? A theory of the DNA control of growth for which there is good evidence is as follows: The DNA molecule produces an RNA molecule which carries the same code, but which has only one long chain instead of the pair of intertwined chains, so that the code groups are more exposed to the environment than they are in DNA. Different sections of the RNA chain, carrying different items of the code, then gather about themselves the necessary ingredients and synthesize specific proteins, including the enzymes and hormones that control metabolism and growth.

GLOSSARY

Alcohols Compounds in which an —OH group is substituted for one of the hydrogens of a hydrocarbon.

Amino acids Organic compounds whose molecules are characterized by a —COOH group near one end and a —NH_2 group near the other end.

Benzene ring The basic structure of the benzene molecule (C_6H_6). The six carbons form a closed hexagon, with a hydrogen attached to each carbon; various molecular groups can be substituted for any of the hydrogens, so that the ring of carbons forms the basis for a large number of organic compounds.

Carbohydrates Compounds of carbon, hydrogen, and oxygen, usually with two hydrogen atoms to each oxygen; the sugars and the starches are typical.

Cellulose The great variety of complex carbohydrates that make up the fibrous and woody structure of plants.

Chlorophyll The green pigment that is present in most plants and absorbs sunlight to initiate the process of photosynthesis.

Chromosomes Tiny threadlike bodies that can be seen under the microscope in the nuclei of living cells; they contain the nucleic acids.

Covalent bonding The type of chemical combination in which the electrons from two atoms combine to hold the atoms together, without the formation of charged ions; when two atoms of the same element are involved it is also known as homopolar bonding.

° Two like groups cannot follow each other in successive positions; therefore in each position after the first there are three possible choices, 3^n possible variations in the filling of n such positions.

Enzymes Organic compounds, most of them with complex, proteinlike molecules, each of which has a definite role to play in promoting chemical reactions involved in bodily functions; enzymes are primarily associated with the breakdown of foodstuffs to make their parts more readily available for the reactions of metabolism.

Genes The factors that control inherited characteristics by being transmitted from parents to offspring.

Hemoglobin The red pigment present in the blood of all higher animals.

Hormones Specific organic compounds that control specific bodily functions (see *Enzymes*); hormones are normally produced by various organs of the body, and are primarily associated with the synthesis of the molecules needed for growth and bodily activity.

Ionic bonding The type of chemical combination that is primarily due to electrical attraction between ions of opposite sign.

Isomers Compounds having the same composition and molecular weight, but different arrangements of the atoms in the molecule, and hence slightly different physical properties.

Metabolism A general term for the chemical reactions that take place in a living body, from the intake of nourishment to the output in the form of heat and muscular energy, or of bodily growth.

Nucleic acids Two types of extremely complex long-chain molecules (commonly known as DNA and RNA) that are found in the nuclei of all living cells, and that carry the code for all inherited characteristics; they are capable of reproducing themselves, and so of transmitting the control code to all the cells of the body.

Organic acids Compounds whose molecules contain a —COOH group, by virtue of which they form hydrogen ions in solution, and so exhibit acidic properties.

Organic chemistry The branch of chemistry that deals with the great variety of carbon compounds that are found in or derived from living matter.

Paraffins The series of saturated hydrocarbons that have the maximum number of hydrogen atoms for a given number of carbons, and have the generic formula C_nH_{2n+2}.

Peptide chains Long chainlike molecules that consist of a number of amino acids joined together end to end.

Proteins The very complicated molecular structures that make up the bulk of most animal cells, and that occur to a lesser extent in plant cells.

Structural formulae Formulae for chemical compounds written in such a way as to show which atoms are bonded together in the molecules.

Vitamins Specific organic compounds that have controlling functions similar to those of the hormones, but that are not produced in the body and have to be furnished in the diet.

EXERCISES

1. Distinguish between the two principal types of chemical combination, ionic bonding and covalent bonding.

2. Why are ionic compounds likely to be crystalline solids at ordinary temperatures, whereas covalent compounds are likely to be gases or liquids?

3. What is the special property of the carbon atom that makes it so important as the basis for all living things? What other element has a similar property? Is this other element ever used to make compounds similar to the organic compounds of carbon, and, if so, how?

4. What are hydrocarbons? What are the paraffins? How are the simple alcohols related to the paraffins?

5. Construct structural formulae for two isomeric forms of pentane (C_5H_{12}).

6. Write the formulae for methyl chloride, ethyl alcohol, sodium acetate.

7. Quantitative analysis of a certain liquid shows that it contains carbon and hydrogen in the proportion by mass of 12 to 1; measurement of the density of its vapor shows that it has a molecular weight of about 80. What must be its formula? What is its common name?

8. What are carbohydrates, and why are they so important in the chemistry of living things?

9. What is the special characteristic of the organic acids, and why does this make them behave as acids?

10. Is chlorophyll a definite chemical compound? What is the special characteristic of its molecules?

11. Suppose some plants and animals were confined to an area where the soil contained much less than the normal amount of magnesium, and suppose that they managed to survive and to grow after a fashion. What do you think would happen? What might happen if iron were deficient in the soil?

12. What is meant by saying that a molecule is "excited"?

13. Describe in a few words the function of hemoglobin in blood.

14. Outline how the carbon and oxygen cycles function in nature. Where and how are the two cycles connected?

15. Give a brief description of the relation between amino acids, peptide chains, and proteins.

16. What are enzymes and hormones? Give some examples of the way in which they act to control bodily functions.

17. How is a DNA molecule constructed? How does it reproduce itself?

18. If a DNA molecule contains n code groups, the number of different ways in which they could be arranged is 3^n. Explain how we arrive at this statement.

19. The statement is made in Sec. 13-7 that the number of possible ways of arranging the code groups in a typical cell is many times the number of atoms in the Milky Way. Estimate this latter number, knowing the mass of the sun and the approximate number of stars in the Galaxy.

REVIEW EXERCISES FOR CHAPTERS 7 THROUGH 13

1. Define in logical order the following quantities: velocity, acceleration, force, mass, weight, work, energy, power, momentum.

2. Name and define the MKS units of length and time, and hence of the different quantities listed in Review Exercise 1. What is the MKS unit of temperature and how is it defined?

3. How did it gradually become evident to scientists that heat is a form of energy? Describe the work of two men who experimented in this field in the early years of the nineteenth century.

4. List at least 10 different forms of energy, and in each case show that the definition of energy is satisfied.

5. State the four principal conservation laws. Which of these are precise as far as we know, and which of them have known limitations? Explain these limitations.

6. Describe the process known as photosynthesis. Discuss briefly the relation of photosynthesis to the problem of providing fuel to meet the needs of our modern civilization.

7. Outline briefly the contributions of each of the following individuals to the early history of chemistry: Paracelsus, Scheele, Lavoisier, Proust, Dalton, Avogadro, Mendeleev.

8. In each of the following compounds state the type of bonding between adjacent atoms, and state the number of bonds involved in each case: $NaCl$, CaO, NH_4NO_3, CO_2, K_2SO_4, C_2H_6, CH_3Br.

9. Discuss how the concept that the world is made of discrete atoms and molecules, the modern form of which began as an unproved hypothesis of Dalton's theory, gradually became generally accepted fact.

10. Who were James Joule and James Clerk Maxwell, and what were their approximate dates? Each of these men made two important contributions to science; describe these briefly.

11. Describe how clouds and rain are formed in a rising air current. Give and explain three causes of rising air currents. What kinds of weather phenomena would be associated with each of these?

12. Molecules show all stages of complexity from simple atoms to DNA. Choose six types of molecule (for example, diatomic gases, proteins), arrange them in order of increasing complexity, and describe each type.

ELECTRICITY, LIGHT, AND WAVE MOTION

part four

*Like electric charges repel each other, and
unlike charges attract, with forces inversely
proportional to the square of the distance.*
                    —Coulomb (1785)

An electric current produces a magnetic field.
                    —Oersted (1820)

*A varying magnetic field can produce an elec-
tric current.*   *—Faraday (1831)*

*Light consists in undulations of the same medium
which is the seat of electromagnetic phenomena.*
                    —Maxwell (1873)

what is electricity?

Nowadays most people take electrical equipment for granted, and have a good deal of practical knowledge about how it works. They know, for example, that they have to have a closed circuit, usually of metal wires, leading from the battery or from the generator in the power station, through the piece of equipment, and back to the source. They know that the function of the switch by which they turn their equipment on and off is to open and close a gap in the metallic circuit. They may even have a fair understanding of electrical measurements, of voltage and of the function of a transformer in altering the voltage, of amperes and watts. If you were to ask them, "What is electricity?" they might say it is a flow of electrons. Then if you ask further, "What is an electron?" they would have to say it is a little particle with a negative electric charge—and you are back where you started.

To arrive at any kind of an answer to the question, we have to consider the properties of electricity—we have to go far back in the history of the subject and examine the experiments on frictional electricity, or *electro-*

statics, electricity at rest. The Greeks knew that if a piece of amber° were rubbed with fur or wool it would produce little sparks and would attract a light object such as a feather. It is a common experience to walk across a woollen carpet when the atmosphere is dry, and then get a shock when you touch a light switch, or to slide across a plastic-covered seat in a car and cause a spark and feel a shock when you touch the door handle. These are all effects of frictional electricity, and the knowledge of such effects passed from the Greeks to the Arabs and from them to the medieval alchemists, down to the seventeenth century, before any practical use was found for them.

In the seventeenth and eighteenth centuries, when science began to come into its own, electrical phenomena were studied as an interesting curiosity, and parlor tricks, such as electrifying a young lady's hair, became a popular amusement. Gradually information accumulated, and important basic discoveries were made. It was found that there are two kinds of electrification, which are represented in modern laboratory demonstrations by hard rubber (ebonite) rubbed with fur or vinyl plastic rubbed with wool, and by glass rubbed with silk, respectively,† and the rule was discovered:

Like charges repel; unlike charges attract.

We can now give the best available answer to the question, "What is electricity?" by means of an operational definition:

Electric charges exert forces on each other, different in kind from gravitational forces, and of an intensity many times greater; by these forces they can be observed and (in principle) measured.

An *operational definition* is a statement of what a thing does, rather than a description of what it is, or what it looks like. To be technically correct, the definition should describe the experimental operations necessary in order to detect and measure the thing we are trying to define. Alternatively, an operational definition could be a list of the known properties. A definition of this kind is admittedly not very satisfying, but there are a great many things in nature for which it is the only kind of definition possible.

14-2   *Properties of Electrostatic Charge*

In this section we shall summarize the principal properties of electrostatic charge, as they were discovered in early experiments, but we shall illus-

---

° Our term "electric" comes from the Greek word for amber, *elektron.*
† The rubber, the plastic, and the silk become charged negatively; the fur, the wool, and the glass become positively charged.

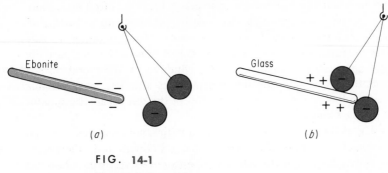

FIG. 14-1

The pith-ball experiment.

trate the properties by descriptions of demonstrations that are still commonly used.

1. *Electric charge can be passed from one body to another by contact.* This can be shown by means of the classic pith-ball experiment, which demonstrates also the rule of like and unlike charges. Two very light spheres, usually made of pith from the inside of a palm tree, are suspended by silk threads from a support, so that they are just touching. When a charged ebonite rod is brought near the pith balls they are at first strongly attracted and cling to the rod. Now let the little balls be detached by giving the rod a quick shake; they now repel each other and hang well separated. If the rod is again brought near, the balls are strongly repelled and get as far away from the rod and from each other as possible [Fig. 14-1(a)]. If a piece of glass that has been rubbed with silk is now brought near, the pith balls are attracted, and cling to it [Fig. 14-1(b)]. They will also be attracted by the fur that was used to charge the ebonite, and cling to the hairs.

2. *Some materials conduct electric charge* from one place to another, and *some do not.* In general, all metals are electrical *conductors.* So are water solutions of salts and acids, and in performing electrostatic experiments all the materials must be kept dry. The human body is a conductor because of the fluids it contains; even the skin usually has a film of moisture although it may appear to be perfectly dry. The ground is a conductor, except in a very dry desert region; on account of its large surface area the earth acts as a sink which can absorb large quantities of electric charge. Ebonite and most types of rubber, most commercial plastics, amber, solid sulfur, glass, most crystalline salts and oxides, and dry vegetable fibers are nonconductors, or *insulators.*

Conduction of electrostatic charge is demonstrated in any of the different experiments that can be performed with the gold-leaf electroscope (Fig. 14-2), an instrument originally designed to detect the presence of electric charge. It consists of a pair of light, flexible metal strips, attached to a metal rod. In the early days the strips were usually made of gold leaf, whence the name of the instrument; nowadays they are often aluminum foil. The metal rod passes through an insulating stopper into a closed container, to protect the leaves from air currents. The container usually incorporates a large area of conducting surface, either a glass jar partially coated with metal foil or a metal box with windows. If the metal surface is connected to the ground the instrument gives steadier, more reliable results, although this is not essential. The top of the rod usually terminates in a metal plate or knob.

The simplest demonstration of conduction with a gold-leaf electroscope is merely to touch the upper plate with a charged ebonite rod. Electricity then passes down the rod of the electroscope to the leaves, which become charged alike, and therefore repel each other and hang at a divergent angle. When the charging rod is removed the leaves remain diverged, showing that the electroscope, along with anything that may be connected to it by a conducting path, has acquired an electric charge.

3. *All materials can be electrified.* Although ebonite, glass, and similar materials are the most suitable and convenient for demonstration experiments, there is nothing unique about their electrical properties. Metals and other conductors cannot be electrified if they are held in the hand, because any charge produced is conducted away by the body, but a piece of metal can be given a very satisfactory charge if it is mounted on an insulating handle and rubbed with wool or fur. In demonstrations of frictional electricity the rubbing is incidental; it is the contact between two different materials that is important, and the rubbing serves only to ensure good contact over a large surface area.

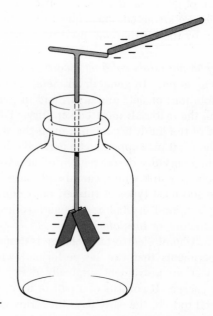

FIG. 14-2

Gold-leaf electroscope charged by contact.

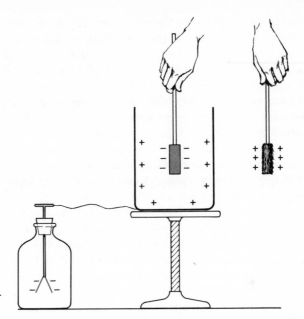

FIG. 14-3

Faraday's ice-pail experiment.

4. *In any charging operation equal amounts of positive and negative electricity are produced.* The classic demonstration of this rule is the so-called ice-pail experiment° (Fig. 14-3). A metal pail is mounted on an insulating stand and connected by a wire to an electroscope. An ebonite rod and a piece of fur wrapped around another insulating rod, used as a handle, are rubbed together inside the pail, being careful not to touch the sides. This has no effect on the electroscope, showing that the total charge on the whole system is zero. The fur-covered rod is now removed, and the electroscope leaves diverge. The negatively charged ebonite has attracted positive charge to the inside surface of the pail, and repelled negative charge to the leaves. The fur is replaced, and the leaves collapse; the ebonite rod is now removed, and the leaves diverge the same amount as before, showing that the charges on the ebonite and on the fur were equal.

14-3   *The Electric Fluid*

It is obvious from the experiments described in the last section that electricity, or electric charge, behaves in some respects like a fluid, and early attempts to develop a qualitative theory of electrical effects were based on the idea of a fluid assumed to exist in all materials. It was held that the

° This demonstration is credited to Michael Faraday (1791–1867), director of the Royal Institution in London. The story behind the name is that when he showed it in a public lecture he used the kind of pail then commonly seen in restaurants, filled with cracked ice to cool a bottle of wine.

fluid could penetrate between the atoms—readily in the case of a conductor, with more or less difficulty in the case of an insulator—and that it could accumulate on the surface of a body, giving it an electric charge.

Some writers believed in the existence of two distinct fluids, normally present in equal amounts in any body, in order to account for the rule of like and unlike charges. Others discussed the phenomena in terms of a single fluid, the other kind of charge representing merely a deficiency in the normal amount of electricity that a body was supposed to contain. The American statesman, philosopher, and scientist, Benjamin Franklin,° was a strong supporter of the single-fluid theory, and we owe to him the useful idea of labeling the charges positive and negative. He applied the plus sign to the electricity on the glass, and the minus sign to that on the ebonite, or on the silk with which the glass had been rubbed. He supposed then that electric fluid was rubbed off the silk onto the glass, and off the ebonite onto the fur, leaving the silk and the ebonite deficient, or "negative."

It makes very little difference whether we think in terms of one fluid or of two in discussing electrostatic phenomena and simple electric circuits on the macroscopic scale; either assumption gives an adequate description of what is happening, and either can be made the basis of a quantitative theory. The one-fluid theory is a little simpler, and is what is implied in most of the language used by the practical electrician, and in putting the plus and minus signs on circuit diagrams. Only when we start to discuss electrical phenomena on the atomic scale, in terms of the ultimate charged particles and of positive and negative ions, is there any difference other than that of convenience. Then we have to recognize that there are in fact two common stable electrically charged particles, the negatively charged electron, and the positively charged proton.† Their charges are numerically equal and opposite, and so the combination of a proton and an electron, which is a normal hydrogen atom, is electrically neutral. In other respects, including size and mass, the electron and the proton are quite different, and so the two-fluid theory is somewhat closer to the facts. The electron is much lighter, and is the one that flows in a metallic conductor, so an ordinary electric current is usually (not always) a flow of negative charge. It would have been more convenient for the present-day student if Benjamin Franklin had put the signs on the other way, but in his time his choice was purely a matter of chance, and he happened to guess wrong. It would cause endless confusion to attempt to change the terminology and all the plus and minus signs on all the circuit diagrams in all the classical textbooks and other works on electricity and electrical engineering—it is simpler to remember that it is usually the negative electrons that flow.

° Franklin's most famous experiment is the one in which he sent a kite aloft during a thunderstorm. He was able to draw sparks—and to charge an electroscope—from the wet kite string. From this he concluded, quite correctly, that the drops in a thundercloud are electrically charged, and that a lightning flash is simply a tremendous electric spark.

† The properties of electrons and protons, and the evidence for their independent existence will be discussed later (Chapters 21 and 22).

14-4   Coulomb's Law

There could be no real progress in the theory of electricity without measurement and quantitative laws. The first law was discovered by a French engineer, Charles Coulomb, in 1785, and concerns the forces between electric charges. Coulomb designed and used a *torsion balance* (Fig. 14-4) to measure these forces, which, although they are very much greater than the gravitational attraction between the same bodies, are usually small compared to the weights of the bodies concerned. In Coulomb's experiments the balance was formed of a light glass rod with small metal spheres attached to the two ends. This was suspended at the center by a fine wire. Then the vertical forces due to the weight of the spheres were balanced, and any horizontal force on either of them produced a twist in the supporting wire. One of the suspended spheres and a nearby fixed sphere were given electric charges, and then the twist in the suspension was proportional to the force of repulsion between the charged spheres, so that the force could be measured. With this apparatus Coulomb established the law which bears his name, *Law I of electricity and magnetism:*

The force between two charges is proportional to the product of the charges, and inversely proportional to the square of the distance between them.

Or in symbols,

$$F = K \cdot \frac{q_1 q_2}{d^2},$$

where q_1 and q_2 are the amounts of charge in any arbitrary unit, say, number of doses from the charging device, d is the distance between them, and K is a numerical constant of proportionality.

It is more than mere coincidence that the mathematical form of Coulomb's law is the same as that of Newton's law of gravitation (Sec. 6-1). Both are expressions of the fact that the gravitational effect of a spherical

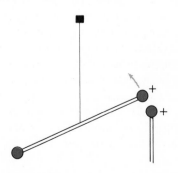

FIG. 14-4

Coulomb's torsion balance.

mass and the electrical effect of a spherical charge (the electric field, Sec. 15-4) spread out uniformly in all directions from the source, and are distributed over a larger area at greater distances. The total influence is distributed over a sphere whose area is proportional to $(distance)^2$; then the intensity of the effect on a given body is proportional to $1/(distance)^2$.

14-5   The Voltaic Cell

As long as electrical knowledge was confined to electrostatics there were hardly any practical uses for it; it remained a scientific curiosity, because electricity at rest cannot *do* anything. There is no work done and no conversion of electrical energy into any other form until the charge moves. When contact is made with a statically charged conductor, the flow of electricity is almost instantaneous; the charges almost immediately disappear or take up their new distribution, and the only external work done is that of the momentary spark at the instant of contact. Practical uses were not developed until methods were discovered for maintaining a continuous flow of charge, that is, a *steady electric current.*

The first method of producing a steady current was the battery, and the basic principle which led to the development of our modern storage batteries and dry cells was discovered by an Italian physicist, Alessandro Volta, in 1799. The story of his discovery is a mixture of accident, misinterpretation, and painstaking research. In 1780 the anatomist, Galvani, was dissecting a frog, and was apparently using two instruments made of different metals while studying the exposed nerve in a recently amputated frog's leg. When the opposite ends of the two instruments accidentally came in contact with each other, the leg jumped, almost as if it were still attached to the live frog (Fig. 14-5). Galvani was interested, among other things, in animal electricity, such as the violent shocks which can be obtained from some species of eel, as well as in the effects of electric shock on living bodies. He thought there might be some connection between the jumping frog's leg and the shock from the electric eel. He followed up his accidental discovery and found that the twitching occurred whenever the nerve formed part of a closed conducting circuit, being most pronounced when the external part of the circuit involved two different metals. He correctly concluded that the effect was due to electricity, but he wrongly attributed it to a special property of the nerve tissue.

Volta became interested in Galvani's discovery, and he found that the electrical effect was not due to any special property of the nerve fiber, but that a current could be produced with any kind of acid solution. After a long series of experiments he was able to announce the rule that is fundamental to all the many varieties of *voltaic cell:*

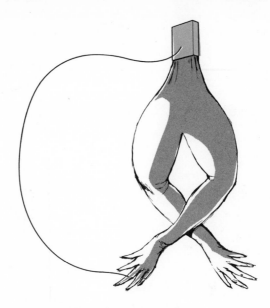

FIG. 14-5

Galvani's observation with a frog's leg.

Whenever two different metals make contact with a solution of an acid or a salt, the metals become electrically charged, one positive and the other negative.

If the opposite ends of the metals are joined in any way, to form a closed conducting circuit, a current will flow.

We shall discuss the action of a voltaic cell in modern terms, using as example one of the simplest practical forms, which consists of zinc and copper in contact with weak sulfuric acid (Fig. 14-6). In solution, the acid dissociates into positively and negatively charged ions:

$$H_2SO_4 \longrightarrow 2\,H^+ + SO_4^=.$$

Zinc has a strong affinity for sulfate ion, to form zinc sulfate, $ZnSO_4$. Some of the sulfate ions are therefore attracted to the zinc, charging it and everything connected to it negatively. At the same time hydrogen ions drift to the copper, and it becomes charged positively. If there is no external connection between the copper and the zinc, the action stops as soon as the two metals have become charged strongly enough to repel more ions of the same sign. When the external circuit is completed by closing the switch, electrons flow through it from the zinc to the copper° tending to neutralize their charges. Then the action of the ions in the solution immediately starts again to maintain the charge, and so a steady cur-

° The conventional diagram shows the current flowing the other way, from + (copper) to − (zinc) through the external circuit, and from − to + inside the cell.

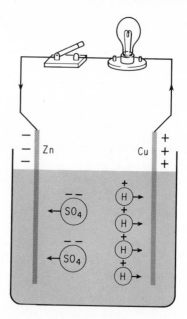

FIG. 14-6

A simple Zn-acid-Cu cell.

rent flows, carried in the external circuit by electrons, and carried in the opposite direction through the electrolyte partly by $SO_4^=$ ions and partly by H^+ ions.

The energy to maintain the current comes from the chemical reaction,

$$\text{Zn} + \text{H}_2\text{SO}_4 \longrightarrow \text{ZnSO}_4 + \text{H}_2.$$

The $ZnSO_4$ is dissolved in the solution, and so the zinc terminal is gradually eaten away; the hydrogen is released as gas at the copper terminal.

Many different types of practical voltaic cell have been devised for different purposes, using all sorts of materials. The common dry cell (which is "dry" only to the extent that the liquid cannot spill) has terminals of zinc and carbon, and the electrolyte is a paste of manganese dioxide and ammonium chloride solution. The energy-producing reaction is

$$\text{Zn} + 2\,\text{NH}_4\text{Cl} + 2\,\text{H}_2\text{O} \longrightarrow \text{ZnCl}_2 + 2\,\text{NH}_4\text{OH} + \text{H}_2.$$

The manganese dioxide absorbs the hydrogen and prevents it from forming an insulating layer around the carbon, as it would otherwise tend to do.

14-6   *The Electric Circuit*

The electric circuit should be considered in terms of its energy relations. Energy is put into the circuit at one place, transported over the wires with very little wastage, and used to do work at some other place, as indicated in Fig. 14-7. The commonest and most useful *sources of energy* are:

The voltaic cell and *storage battery,* which keep the current flowing at the expense of the chemical energy of the reactions which go on within the cell.

The mechanical generator or *dynamo,* in which the current is kept flowing by means of a coil rotating between the poles of a magnet (Chapter 16). The source of energy is mechanical work, provided by a waterfall, a steam engine, or any other kind of prime mover.

The electric current can do work at the other end of the circuit in many different ways, of which the three most important are:

The production of heat and light, in an electric heater or cookstove, in an incandescent lamp, in a gas discharge tube such as is often used for street lighting and in the fluorescent lights in many buildings.

Mechanical work, in electric motors.

Electrolysis, in which the current does work in decomposing various chemical compounds in energy-absorbing reactions, the opposite of the energy-producing reaction in a voltaic cell.

There is always some energy converted into heat in an electric circuit, because it takes work to keep the current flowing and this produces heat, somewhat like the heat produced by friction in any moving machinery. This happens in all parts of the circuit, in the materials of the battery or the wires of the generator, in the connecting wires along the way, and in the wires of an electric motor. This energy is wasted in the sense that it is dissipated where it can do no good, but the amount of waste can be made quite small, and an electric circuit is very efficient in its use of energy.

14-7   *Potential and Electromotive Force*

We must now introduce some definitions and units in order to show how a complicated subject has become systematized, as much by custom (confirmed in the international standardization of the units) as by the work of individuals. In the case of electricity especially, this has proved to be

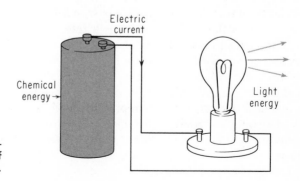

FIG. 14-7

A simple electric circuit, consisting of a battery, a pair of wires, and an electric light.

essential to the full realization of the final step of scientific method, that of application. Without this systematic sequence of laws, definitions, and units, the modern electrical engineer would have great difficulty in developing the host of practical uses for the electric circuit that we see all around us today.

In principle, the forces involved in an electric circuit could be calculated by Coulomb's law of force, but in practice the computation would be extremely intricate in all but the very simplest cases. Fortunately it is not necessary to know the details of the forces in order to introduce quantitative relations; the complicated computation can be avoided entirely by introducing the concept of *electric potential.*

Before any connection is made, the electric charge on the plates of a battery or at the terminals of a wall socket possesses potential energy because it can do work when it flows from one terminal to the other. The amount of work done when a certain quantity of charge flows is independent of the path taken. That is, the work done by a unit of charge is the same whether it passes through a long, complicated circuit, or whether the terminals are short-circuited and the energy is dissipated in a spark. We therefore define:

The electric potential between two points A and B is measured by the work done when unit charge flows from A to B.

A is said to be at a higher potential than *B*, and the potential difference (abbreviated PD) is positive if the natural tendency is for positive charge to flow from *A* to *B* when the circuit is closed. It is a "potential" in the same sense as potential energy because the potential difference already exists between the terminals before the circuit is closed and represents something which *might* be done.

The units we are introducing at this point will be defined systematically in Sec. 14-9. The unit of electric charge is a *coulomb.* In electrostatics a coulomb would actually be a tremendous charge, and nobody has ever accumulated a whole coulomb of static charge at one time. However, in a steady current circuit a coulomb may pass in a fraction of a second. The unit of current is the *ampere,* which is a rate of flow of 1 coulomb per second, although this is not to be taken as the formal definition. The unit of work and energy used in electrical measurements is the *joule,* which has already been defined as a newton-meter. Then the unit of potential, the *volt,* is defined as 1 *joule of work per coulomb of charge* transferred.

The potential difference usually represents work done *by* the current in a *portion* of a circuit, or energy *output.* The *electromotive force* of a battery or generator represents energy *input* to a *complete* circuit, and is defined as follows:

The electromotive force (EMF) is measured by the work done on a circuit when a unit of charge is circulated completely around the circuit.

It is also measured in volts, and so the inclusive term "voltage" can be used for either PD or EMF.°

14-8   Ohm's Law

The quantitative relation between current and potential—*Law II of electricity and magnetism* and the basic law of the electric circuit—was discovered by a German schoolteacher, Georg Ohm, in 1826. Expressed in modern terms, Ohm's law can be stated:

The current flowing through any portion of an electric circuit, temperature and other conditions remaining constant, is proportional to the potential difference across that part of the circuit.

The qualification concerning constant conditions is necessary for two reasons. The constant of proportionality varies with the temperature, and, because passage of a current through a wire always causes some heating, it may be necessary to keep the wire in a constant temperature bath in performing experiments to test the law. In the simple form stated above, the law applies only to portions of a circuit where the energy output is entirely in the form of heat. If mechanical work is done in a motor, so that part of the circuit is in motion, or if chemical work is done in electrolysis, so that there are chemical changes involved, Ohm's law requires modification.

Ohm's law can be written

$$\frac{V}{I} = R,$$

where V is the potential (or voltage) and I is the current. The constant R then measures the *resistance*, which provides a numerical quantity proportional to the friction encountered by the current in passing through the wire. Resistance is measured in *ohms*, where an ohm is defined as 1 volt of potential difference per ampere of current. There are methods of measuring the resistance of a piece of wire with very high precision, and so the

° The use of the word "pressure" for PD and EMF, common in elementary textbooks, is very bad. Volts have nothing whatever to do with force per unit area, and calling voltage "pressure" is at best only a misleading analogy.

resistance, a property of a particular conductor, becomes a very useful quantity, in many different practical calculations.*

We may now sum up a few of the most important circuit relations. The work done in a circuit, or portion of a circuit, is given by

(1) $$W\text{(joules)} = V\text{(volts)} \times Q\text{(coulombs)}.$$

Power (P) is the rate of doing work, and current (I) is the rate of flow of charge, so if we divide both sides of Eq. (1) by the time we have

(2) $$P\text{(watts)} = V\text{(volts)} \times I\text{(amperes)}.$$

Ohm's law can also be expressed

(3) $$V = RI,$$

which of course applies to portions of the circuit where the only output of energy is in the form of heat. If we substitute Eq. (3) into Eq. (2) we have an expression for the heat developed (H),

(4) $$H\text{(joules per second)} = R\text{(ohms)} \times I^2\text{(amperes}^2\text{)}.$$

Equation (4) always gives the heat developed. For example, if there is a motor in the circuit, this equation gives the energy wasted in the form of heat, where R is the resistance of the wire used in winding the coils of the motor.

14-9   The System of Electrical Units

We shall conclude this chapter with a summary of the principal electrical units, with their definitions in logical sequence, in order to show how the consistent system is constructed. The practical electrical units in everyday use are all derived from the MKS system of mechanical units (Sec. 5-5).

Three mechanical units used in electrical measurements should be repeated here, to make the list complete:

Force—a *newton* is the force which gives a kilogram-mass an acceleration of 1 meter per second².

Work and energy—a *joule* is the work done when a force of 1 newton moves a body a distance of 1 meter.

Power—a *watt* is a rate of supply of energy (or of doing work) of 1 joule per second.

There must be one basic connection between the mechanical units and the electrical quantities. It will be shown later (Sec. 15-7) that magnetic

---

* For example, since R depends on the temperature, the resistance of a small coil of wire can be used to measure temperature in a resistance thermometer. This device is useful to measure temperatures beyond the range of an ordinary liquid-filled thermometer—also to measure temperatures in locations not easily accessible, and to make continuous recordings of temperature variations.

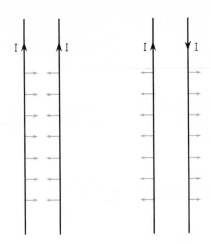

FIG. 14-8

Force between parallel currents.

effects cause an attraction between two parallel wires carrying currents in the same direction. This is used to make the connection, and we define as follows:

Current—an *ampere* is such a current that when two very long parallel wires, 1 meter apart, are each carrying 1 ampere of current they will attract each other with a force of 2×10^{-7} newton per meter length (Fig. 14-8).[*]

Charge—a *coulomb* is the amount of electric charge which passes a point in a circuit when a current of 1 ampere flows for 1 second. With this definition of the unit of charge, the constant K in the expression for Coulomb's law (Sec. 14-4) is 8.9878×10^9, which is equal to $10^{-7}c^2$, where c is the velocity of light,[†] 2.99796×10^8 meters per second.

Potential and EMF—there is a potential difference of 1 *volt* across a section of a circuit when 1 coulomb of charge does 1 joule of work.

Resistance—a section of a circuit has a resistance of 1 *ohm* when a potential difference of 1 volt causes a current of 1 ampere, under conditions such that Ohm's law is valid.

It is not feasible in ordinary day-to-day practice to measure current by a method that depends on the basic definition, and a set of secondary standards and working standards have to be set up by the standardization laboratories in different countries. The secondary standard of the ampere is based on the amount of silver deposited in electrolysis. The current is measured fundamentally by means of a current balance (Fig. 14-9), which consists of two sets of coils on either end of a sensitive balance. The force between the moving and fixed coils is computed according to the definition, and measured by means of the balance. In series with the balance is

[*] This is the definition recommended by the International Bureau of Weights and Measures in 1952. It is now legal in most countries.

[†] It will be seen later (Sec. 20-2) why the velocity of light enters into an electrical equation.

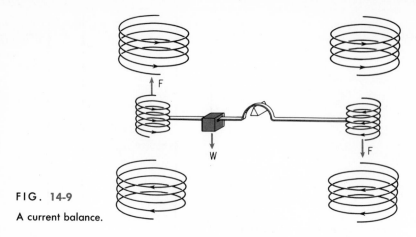

FIG. 14-9

A current balance.

an electrolysis cell, so that the amount of silver deposited by the same current in a given length of time can be determined. According to recent measurements, 1 ampere deposits silver at the rate of 0.00111807 gram per second.

The secondary standard, and the working standard, of the volt depends upon the EMF of the Weston mercury-cadmium cell, which is known to be particularly reliable and constant in its voltage. A known current is passed through a heating coil immersed in a calorimeter, and the amount of heat developed is measured in joules; then the voltage across the coil is compared with that of a Weston cell. In this way the Weston cell has been found to produce 1.0183 volts at 15°C. Other working standards are usually in the form of resistance coils, which can be made and tested to high precision. These are certified by a standardization laboratory, and supplied to other laboratories and to instrument manufacturers.

GLOSSARY

Calorimeter Device for the measurement of a quantity of heat; usually consists of a known mass of water in a vessel, with a thermometer to measure the rise of temperature.

Electric battery Technically, a battery consists of two or more voltaic cells in series.

Electric potential Defined by the work done *by* an electric circuit when unit charge passes through an appliance connected to the circuit (Sec. 14-7).

Electrical resistance Quantity that measures the friction encountered by the current in any part of a circuit; defined as the ratio of voltage to current (Sec. 14-8).

Electrolyte A substance that is dissociated into positive and negative ions when it is dissolved, so that the solution becomes an electrical conductor.

Electromotive force Defined by the work done on a circuit in order to cause unit charge to circulate in the circuit (Sec. 14-7).

Electron The fundamental particle of negative electricity; a constituent of all atoms.

Electrostatics Study of the phenomena associated with electricity at rest.

Gold-leaf electroscope Instrument for the detection of electric charge; it consists of two strips of light metal foil, which repel each other when they are charged.

Operational definition A definition that defines something by stating the experimental operations necessary in order to observe it, or briefly, by saying what the thing does, rather than by attempting to describe it or to state of what it is composed.

Proton Nucleus of a hydrogen atom; fundamental, positively charged particle found in the nuclei of all heavier atoms.

Torsion balance Instrument for measuring small forces by observing the twist produced in a fine wire or in a fiber.

Voltage Comprehensive term that can be used for either electric potential or electromotive force, both of which are measured in volts.

Voltaic cell The prototype of the familiar electric cell; it consists of two dissimilar metals in contact with an electrolyte.

EXERCISES

1. Give several examples, including some natural phenomena, of effects that are due to electrostatic charging.

2. Give an operational definition of electric charge. Why is it necessary to define charge in this way? Why can we not simply say that a negative charge on a body is an accumulation of excess electrons?

3. Which of the definitions that were encountered in the chapters on mechanics are actually operational in character?

4. Describe, with a simple diagram, a typical form of gold-leaf electroscope. How did the instrument get its traditional name?

5. Describe simple experiments (an electroscope may be used) to demonstrate that: (a) there are two kinds of charge, obeying the rule that like charges repel and unlike charges attract; (b) a metal wire is a conductor, whereas a dry nylon thread is not; (c) your own body is a conductor; (d) friction between *any* two different materials produces the two kinds of charge; (e) metals can be electrified.

6. Describe Faraday's ice-pail experiment. What does it prove?

7. Restate the law of equality of positive and negative charge in the form of a conservation law.

8. How did it happen that the charge on an electron is considered negative?

9. Phraseology used by electricians implies the old "one-fluid theory" of electric charge, with the fluid flowing the "wrong" way. Give examples to substantiate this statement.

10. Does the positive electricity ever flow? Give examples.

11. State Coulomb's law of the force between charges. Describe briefly the experiment which Coulomb performed in order to test his law.

12. Calculate the force of attraction between a pair of oppositely charged spheres 10 centimeters apart, each carrying $\frac{1}{1000}$ microcoulomb of charge. Calculate the gravitational attraction between the same spheres if the masses are 20 grams each. (Take the constant in Coulomb's law to be 9×10^9.)

13. How did Galvani and Volta discover the principle of the voltaic cell?

14. Explain the action of the simple cell composed of zinc, sulfuric acid, and copper. What is the source of the energy to maintain the current?

15. What is the source of the energy in a common dry cell? in Galvani's frog?

16. An electric circuit is a means of transporting energy from a source at one place in order to do work at a different place. Explain this statement.

17. What sources of energy can be used for an electric circuit, and what is the form of the energy in each case? What are the three principal ways of using the energy, and into what forms is it converted? What is it that always causes a certain amount of energy to be wasted in the circuit?

18. State Ohm's law. Why is it necessary to specify "constant conditions"?

19. Define in logical order: electric current, electric potential, electromotive force, electrical resistance. Name and define the MKS units of these quantities. Name and define also the MKS unit of electric charge.

20. Although the MKS mechanical units are used in the definitions of the electrical units, one of the latter is not a properly derived unit, and provides the fifth basic unit needed for the complete system. Which of the units is it? In what sense is the definition arbitrary?

21. What is the current through a 100-watt, 120-volt electric light bulb when it is lighted? What is its resistance? Would these be the same when the light is first turned on?

22. What is the current through a 10-ohm resistance connected to a 6-volt battery? How much heat would it produce in 5 minutes, in joules and in calories?

23. A house circuit has a circuit breaker which turns everything off if the current exceeds 15 amperes. How many 120-volt, 60-watt bulbs could be turned on all at once on this circuit?

24. An electric motor draws 9 amperes at 110 volts; what is the power output? Is all this mechanical work? If the efficiency is 90 per cent how much work would it do in

1 hour? Approximately how much would it cost to run it for 1 hour, at 2 cents per kilowatt-hour?

25. A coil of platinum wire connected to a suitable electric circuit forms a useful thermometer. How is this possible? What are some of the advantages of this type of thermometer?

magnetism

15-1   Magnets and the Compass Needle

The magnetic needle—and its use as a compass for navigation—seems to have been first discovered in China, for the oldest known description is in a Chinese document dated A.D. 1094. This document tells how a steel needle can be magnetized by stroking it with a lodestone,° and states that if the needle is placed on a piece of wood floating in a basin of water it will point nearly, but not precisely, to the south. Evidently the phenomenon of declination, the fact that the geographic and magnetic poles do not coincide, was already known. This particular account does not mention the use of the compass in navigation, but other brief references of about the same date indicate that it was being used by Chinese and Arab sailors, both of whom were already making long voyages across the open ocean.

The earliest European references date from a little before 1200, suggesting that it took about 100 years for the knowledge to spread from China

---

° A lodestone, or "leading stone," is a piece of the natural iron ore known as magnetite (Fe_3O_4). Pieces are often found in a magnetized state, having acquired poles by induction from the earth's magnetic field at the time the rock solidified.

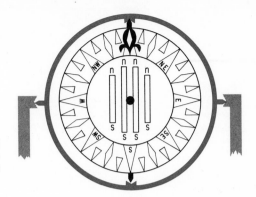

FIG. 15-1

A modern magnetic compass, mounted in gimbals, so that the card, with the magnetized needles attached to the back, is always horizontal.

to Europe, by word of mouth and by example. Then in 1269 one Pierre de Maricourt wrote a letter to a friend describing in detail the construction of a magnetic compass. De Maricourt was aware that a magnetized needle has two poles, and of the rule that like poles repel and unlike poles attract. He also knew that both halves of the broken magnet would still be magnetized, each having the correct pair of poles.

In all early compasses the magnetic needle was prepared by stroking a steel needle with a lodestone or with another magnet (Fig. 15-2). This produces poles by induction, the north pole of the stroking magnet attracting south poles in the needle, and vice versa. Magnets produced in this way could never be very powerful, and would not possess the lifting power which we associate with a modern permanent magnet. It was not until the process of magnetization by means of a coil carrying an electric current was discovered that powerful magnets were possible.

15-2   Comparison of Magnetism and Electrostatics

Magnetism is always a static phenomenon, since there is no such thing as a current of magnetism, analogous to the electric current. However, it will help in understanding if we compare magnetism with electrostatics, for there are some similarities as well as some important differences.

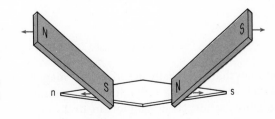

FIG. 15-2

Magnetizing a needle by the ancient process of stroking with a pair of magnets.

FIG. 15-3

Attraction of a magnet for pieces of iron, by the formation of induced poles.

There are two kinds of magnetic poles, analogous to the positive and negative charges in electricity. These are usually designated "north" and "south," meaning the poles which point to the north and south, respectively, when the magnet is suspended. They are sometimes considered to be plus and minus, the north pole being taken as positive. Then the *law of force* is the same as in electrostatics:

Like poles repel, unlike poles attract, with forces inversely proportional to the square of the distance.

However, there is never complete separation of the poles, and a magnet always contains equal quantities of north and south pole. There are magnetic materials, some of which will retain their magnetism so that they can be used for permanent magnets, and some of which will not. Other materials are apparently nonmagnetic, and so at first there seems to be an analogy with electrical conductors and insulators. However, the analogy is not really very close, because there is no actual conduction of magnetism, and the poles never flow through the material. Because poles do not flow, magnetization by contact produces poles of the *opposite* sign, whereas electrification by contact produces charges of the same sign, by conduction of charge.

15-3   The Process of Magnetization

The materials that are usually described as "magnetic" are the three metals, iron, nickel, cobalt, and a few alloys and compounds. Among these the steellike alloys retain their magnetism best, and are the most useful for compass needles and permanent magnets. One of the most suitable is the very hard, brittle steel known under the trade name of Alnico, which consists of about 50 per cent iron, alloyed with lesser amounts of aluminum, nickel, and cobalt. Alnico and similar alloys are used to make the powerful permanent magnets now available for use in electrical measuring instruments, for novelties, and for many other purposes. Pure, "soft" iron is easily magnetized, but loses its magnetism as soon as the inducing magnet is removed. The proper term for materials that can be strongly magnetized is *ferromagnetic* (magnetic like iron). All materials have magnetic properties of a sort, some being very weakly attracted by a magnet, and some being weakly repelled.

The basic difference between magnetism and electricity is that there is nothing in magnetism to correspond to the negatively charged electron or the positively charged proton. Instead, many atoms and molecules are themselves tiny magnets; in fact, the free electron itself has magnetic properties. When a magnet is brought near a material which has magnetic molecules, there is a tendency for these molecules to be pulled into line, and the overall effect is the formation of induced poles and an attraction for the piece of material. If the only source of magnetism in the material consists of magnetic molecules, the effect is quite weak and is easily counterbalanced by the effect of heat vibrations, which tend to prevent the molecules from lining up.

Recent research has shown just how a strongly magnetic material such as iron differs from normal, weakly magnetic materials. In iron, small local regions, known as domains, become spontaneously magnetized when the metal solidifies, and remain magnetized. These domains contain many magnetic atoms, and are large enough to be made visible under a microscope by appropriate techniques. If there were no magnetic influence present at the time the iron solidified, the magnetized domains will be lined up into a balanced pattern (Fig. 15-4). There are no unbalanced poles, and the block of material as a whole shows no magnetization. If a magnet is

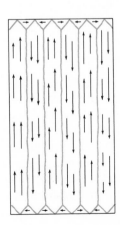

FIG. 15-4

Balanced arrangement of the locally magnetized domains in a piece of unmagnetized iron.

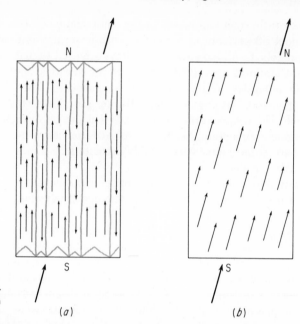

FIG. 15-5

Two stages in the magnet-
ization of a piece of iron
by an inducing magnet.

(a)

(b)

brought near, the first effect is that the magnetized domains which lie most nearly parallel to the inducing magnet grow at the expense of adjacent domains [Fig. 15-5(a)]; the block as a whole now has induced poles of moderate strength. If the strength of the inducing magnetic forces is increased sufficiently, the domains are eventually all pulled nearly into line; the iron approaches its maximum possible magnetization, and is said to be "saturated" [Fig. 15-5(b)]. When the inducing magnet is removed from a piece of soft iron, the local domains quickly return to the balanced arrangement, because this is the condition where the total potential energy is least. In the hard magnetic alloys, when the domains have been pulled more or less into line they remain fixed, and a permanent magnet is the result.

15-4   Magnetic Fields

Because electric charges and magnets could both exert forces on each other over considerable distances, Michael Faraday thought that there must be some actual connection between them by way of the mysterious medium known as the "ether." He therefore talked about "lines of force" joining opposite charges or opposite magnetic poles, and he seems to have thought of them as something like elastic threads which could pull the charges together by a tendency to contract along the length of a line. He considered repulsion between like charges or poles to be due to a tendency of the lines of force to spread out sideways, and, in effect, repel each other laterally. When Clerk Maxwell began, in 1861, to develop a consistent theory of electricity and magnetism and to put the whole subject on a sound mathematical basis, he adopted Faraday's idea and made it quantitative by talking about a system of stresses in the "ether."

Faraday and Maxwell wrote at a time when most scientists thought that everything in nature would eventually prove to have a mechanical explanation, based on Newton's laws, so that their ideas were much too concrete and mechanistic. We no longer believe in a material ether which could carry Maxwell's stresses, nor do we believe in Faraday's elastic threads. However, the concept of lines of force remains extremely useful in the description of electrical and magnetic phenomena; the concept of field, which Maxwell introduced in order to give mathematical expression to the description, is still more useful.

Nowadays, *a field* in physics is simply *a region where forces act.* A magnetic field is the region around a magnet, or a current-carrying circuit, where magnetic forces act. An electric field is the region around a charged body where electrical forces act, a gravitational field is the region around a massive body where gravitational forces act, and so on. The *field strength* at any point is proportional to the force exerted on a unit pole, charge, or mass, and, because the force has a direction, field strength is a vector quantity. The *lines of force* are curves drawn in such a way that the direction of the field at any point is along the tangent to the line of force. As Maxwell proved, the geometrical properties of lines of force, which made it possible for Faraday to use them in the way he did, and which still make them useful as a descriptive device, are a mathematical consequence of Coulomb's law, or force inversely proportional to the square of the distance. It follows from this that the lines of force must either be closed curves, or else they must begin on a north pole (or + charge), and terminate on a south pole (or − charge). Two lines cannot cross, for the field cannot have two different directions at the same point. Where the field is strongest the lines are closely crowded together, where it is weaker they are relatively far apart.

As an example, Fig. 15-6 shows the lines of force in the magnetic field around a bar magnet which has its poles neatly concentrated at the ends of the bar. In this diagram the lines are supposed to have been plotted by exploring the directions of the forces with a little compass needle, as suggested in the figure. Lines of force can be very nicely displayed by the use of fine iron filings, and Fig. 15-7 shows the field of a bar magnet outlined in this way. The pattern is obtained by placing a piece of thin cardboard over the magnet and then sprinkling iron filings upon it. Each iron fragment acquires a pair of poles by induction, and then they line up north to south, north to south, into threads which follow quite closely the lines of force. Where the field is strong, the filings may cling together firmly enough to make the threads self-supporting, so that they may stand out like stiff hairs around the poles of a powerful magnet. Diagrams of lines of

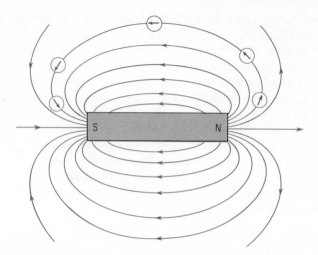

FIG. 15-6

Lines of force around a
bar magnet.

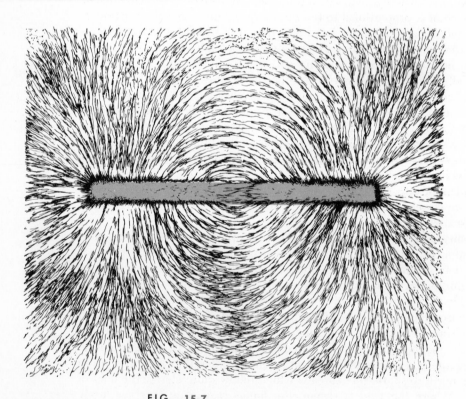

FIG. 15-7

The field around a bar magnet outlined by means of iron
filings.

force and photographs of iron-filing patterns are used so much in elementary physics texts that the student is liable to think of them as pictures of something taking place in the region around the poles. Therefore it must be emphasized that diagrams like Fig. 15-6 are not actual pictures, but rather graphs, designed to display information in a convenient form.

15-5   Reality and the Nondelineable

Is a magnetic field "real" or is it nothing more than a mathematical device for computing results that can be tested by experiment? That is, is there "something" in the region around a magnet *before* the compass needle or the iron filings are put there to detect the forces? This is a matter of semantic philosophy, and depends upon the meaning given to the word "real." If we take an extreme empiricist point of view and restrict reality to things which could conceivably be detected by the senses, or possibly to material objects, then the field has to be considered as a mathematical fiction, and the only reality is the force on the compass needle. If we take a more naïve point of view, and use the word "real" in the slightly vague sense which a person who is not trained in formal philosophy is likely to give to it, then we must say that the field is real.[*]

It is true that it is not material, and that we cannot conceivably see it or feel it without the help of some kind of detecting instrument, like the compass needle, but there certainly seems to be something happening around the magnet, whether or not we take steps to detect it. Then, when we find that a field can become detached from any visible source, travel through space and transport energy, it seems that we must think of it as an actual "something." We shall encounter a number of similar examples of things we cannot see or touch, and it is convenient to refer to them as *nondelineable*, meaning that we cannot draw pictures of them. Nondelineable entities cannot be described in words, because all our descriptive language is based on what we perceive directly, through our human senses. We can only discuss such things operationally, by stating what they do, including the effects which they may have on some kind of detecting device.

15-6   The Magnetic Field of the Earth

Since a compass needle takes up a definite direction relative to the earth, we can say that the earth possesses a magnetic field, which can be displayed graphically by drawing lines of force. Although he did not use the terms "field" and "line of force," the first reasonably complete description of the

[*] P. W. Bridgman, *The Nature of Physical Reality*, has discussed this problem at length. He also would ascribe reality to things like magnetic fields, independent of whether they are in fact observed and measured.

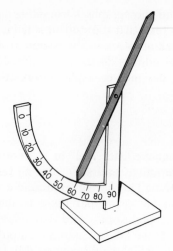

FIG. 15-8

Dip needle, set to show the actual direction of the
earth's magnetic field.

earth's magnetism was given by an English physician, William Gilbert, in
1600. He knew about *declination,* or the deviation of the magnetic compass east or west of the true geographic north, and about *inclination,* or
dip, the fact that a magnetized needle which is free to rotate in a vertical
plane will point downward (in the Northern Hemisphere) at an angle to
the horizontal (Fig. 15-8). Over most of the northern United States the dip
is about 70°, and so the magnetic field is not directed horizontally to the
magnetic north, but toward a point several hundred miles deep inside the
earth (Fig. 15-9). At the magnetic north pole, which is located in the
Arctic islands of Canada, the field is vertically downward.

Gilbert demonstrated his ideas about the earth's magnetism by cutting
spheres of magnetized lodestone and showing that they produced similar
effects of inclination. He therefore suggested that the interior of the earth
must be a huge lodestone. He was wrong in this conjecture; actually, if
the earth contained an interior sphere of permanently magnetized iron or
lodestone the field would be many times stronger than it is. However, the

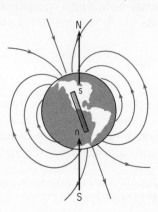

FIG. 15-9

The earth's magnetic field, and the approximately
equivalent bar magnet.

earth's field is roughly equivalent to that of a weakly magnetized bar magnet located as shown in Fig. 15-9, slightly off center, and inclined about 12° to the axis of rotation of the earth. This idealized, approximate field is distorted by the great continental masses, and even more distorted locally by mountains and by deposits of iron ore.

The earth's field is not constant, as it would be if it were due to an actual permanent magnet. There is a slow variation which causes the north magnetic pole to wander, in a somewhat irregular fashion, around the geographic pole, making a complete circuit in 1000 years or so. As a result there is a slow change in the declination of the compass at a given locality, and this has to be taken into account in using a magnetic compass for navigation. There are also small fluctuations from day to day—even from hour to hour—which are apparently due to electric currents in the ionized layers of the atmosphere.

15-7   Magnetic Field of an Electric Current

Influenced by the parallelism between the laws of electrostatics and those of magnetism, many scientists of the late eighteenth century thought there should be some connection between the two phenomena. However, the connection could not be found until Volta's discovery of the cell principle made it possible to produce steady currents in a circuit, for it is a current, electricity in motion, that produces magnetic effects. Finally, the basic discovery which brought electricity and magnetism together for the first time was made by Hans Christian Oersted, professor of physics at Copenhagen, in 1819, when he found that a current in a wire would deflect a compass needle (Fig. 15-10). Oersted realized that the force of the current

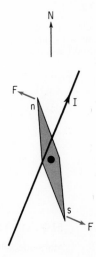

FIG. 15-10

Oersted's basic experiment, demonstrating the forces exerted by a current on the two poles of a magnet.

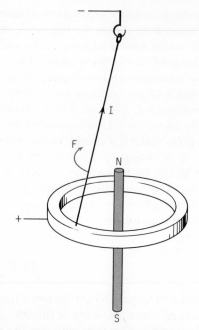

FIG. 15-11

Rotation of a current-carrying wire around a fixed
magnetic pole. Contact to the lower end of the
wire is made by means of mercury in the circular
metal trough.

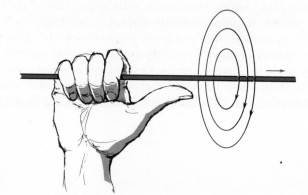

FIG. 15-12

Magnetic field around a
long, straight wire, illustrating the right-hand rule
of direction.

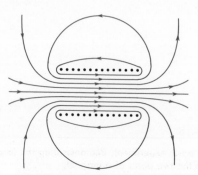

FIG. 15-13

Magnetic field of a solenoid.

on the magnet must have an equal and opposite reaction, and that the magnet must exert a force on the wire. He also succeeded in showing that a current-carrying wire would rotate around a fixed magnetic pole (Fig. 15-11). In both these cases mechanical work is done by the current, and even though these devices are not of much practical use, Oersted's discoveries were the basis upon which subsequent inventors built in developing practical electric motors.

The law of force between a current and a magnet cannot be expressed in simple verbal form, like Coulomb's law. However, not long after Oersted's original discovery, the French mathematician and physicist, André Marie Ampère, gave a mathematical form of the law which could be used to compute the magnetic fields produced by electric circuits of various shapes. We shall not attempt to give Ampère's law (which is *Law III of electricity and magnetism*) in its mathematical form, but only quote two useful rules for the directions of the forces, and show the lines of force of the magnetic field in two simple cases. For a long, straight wire carrying a current the magnetic lines of force are circles around the wire, and the field strength is inversely proportional to the distance from the wire (Fig. 15-12). The direction of the field is given by the *right-hand rule:* Grasp the wire with the right hand, with the thumb in the direction of the current flow; then the fingers encircling the wire give the direction of the magnetic field.

The field of a long coil (a solenoid), whose length is several times its diameter, is almost uniform inside the coil (Fig. 15-13) and is proportional to the number of turns divided by the length. Outside the coil the field resembles that of a bar magnet. The same rule of direction applies if you imagine that you are holding one of the turns of wire as you would hold the handle of a pail, with fingers inside the coil.

The other useful direction rule is the *left-hand rule* for the force exerted by a magnetic field upon a current: Extend the thumb and first two fingers of the left hand so that they are at right angles (Fig. 15-14), with the fore-

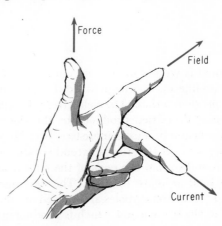

FIG. 15-14

Left-hand rule for the force on a wire in a magnetic field.

finger pointing in the direction of the magnetic field, and the middle finger lying along the wire in the direction of current flow; then the thumb gives the direction of the force on the wire. It is left to the student to demonstrate that combination of the two direction rules leads to the rule that currents flowing in the same direction in a pair of parallel wires attract each other.

15-8   Magnetic Flux

Since there is no such thing as a separate magnetic pole, and since it is hardly ever possible to locate the poles of a magnet at definite points, the concept of magnetic poles is rather unrealistic. If we were asked for a formal definition of magnetic pole, the best we could do is say that it is the region in a piece of magnetized material where the lines of force are most closely concentrated. An electric circuit with no iron nearby has no definite poles, because the lines of force are closed curves, and cannot be considered as having either a beginning or an end.

For quantitative discussion of magnetism a much more useful concept than that of pole is *magnetic flux,* which is defined as follows:

The magnetic flux through any area in a magnetic field is equal to the component of field strength at right angles to the area, multiplied by the area.

For example, the total magnetic flux produced by a solenoid is very nearly equal to the field strength at the center multiplied by the cross-sectional area of the coils. The best measure of the strength of a bar magnet is the total magnetic flux produced. If the bar is uniformly magnetized, so that nearly all the lines of force leave it through the ends, the useful flux is equal to the field strength just outside the ends, multiplied by the area of the end surfaces.

15-9   Iron-Cored Coils

If a solenoid is wound on an iron core the field produced by the electric current can line up the magnetized domains in the iron and cause strong *induced magnetization.* The field strength near the ends of the iron core is then many times that produced by the electric current alone. In other words, the magnetic flux is increased by a large factor by the magnetization of the iron. If the iron is extended beyond the ends of the coil, and curved around so that the ends of the core nearly meet, the lines of magnetic flux tend to follow the iron. The total magnetic flux is increased still further, and very strong poles are formed on the free ends of the core, even though the electric current which is producing the magnetization acts on

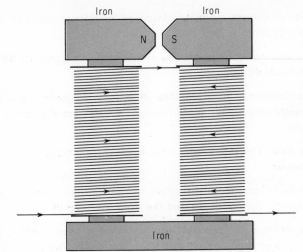

FIG. 15-15

An electromagnet designed to produce a strong magnetic field.

only a portion of the iron. Very strong magnetic fields for experimental purposes can be produced by an electromagnet of the shape shown in Fig. 15-15, where nearly all the external flux is concentrated in the gap between the pole faces of the iron core.

GLOSSARY

Alnico Trade name for a type of hard, brittle steel that is much used to make powerful permanent magnets; it consists of iron alloyed with varying amounts of aluminum, nickel, and cobalt.

Ether Hypothetical material that was supposed by theorists of the eighteenth and nineteenth centuries to fill all space and to be the seat of electrical and magnetic phenomena, including the propagation of light.

Ferromagnetic Having magnetic properties similar to those of iron; the correct technical term for materials that are strongly attracted by a magnet, and that are commonly described as "magnetic."

Field strength Measured by the force exerted upon a unit magnetic pole in a magnetic field, by the force upon a unit charge in an electric field, and by the force on unit mass in a gravitational field.

Induced magnetization The formation of magnetic poles in a piece of material by the influence of a neighboring magnet (or of an electric current).

Line of force A curve drawn in such a way that the tangent to the line of force at a given point shows the direction of the magnetic field at that point; the lines of force provide a convenient way of displaying the magnetic field graphically.

Lodestone A natural magnet, composed mainly of the iron oxide mineral known as magnetite.

Magnetic declination The angular deviation of the compass needle from the true north-south direction.

Magnetic domains Small regions in a ferromagnetic material which are spontaneously magnetized at all times, and which are the source of the strong magnetism.

Magnetic field The region around a magnet (or electric current) where magnetic forces act.

Magnetic flux Total magnetic effect in a given area, defined as the product of the magnetic field strength and the area (Sec. 15-8).

Magnetic inclination The angle that a magnetic needle makes with the horizontal if it is free to turn in all directions; commonly known as "dip."

Magnetic north pole The point where a free magnetic needle would point vertically downward.

Nondelineable Something that, by its very nature, cannot be depicted in a drawing or by means of a mechanical model; hence it cannot be described in words, and has to be defined operationally.

Soft iron A type of iron that can be strongly magnetized by induction, but which returns to its normal state when the inducing influence is removed; pure iron, which is also mechanically soft, is an example.

Solenoid A coil of wire having a length several times its diameter; when carrying an electric current it behaves in a manner analogous to a bar magnet.

EXERCISES

1. Outline the early history of the magnetic compass, from the earliest known references to William Gilbert.

2. Tabulate the principal similarities and the principal differences between magnetism and electrostatics.

3. Compile a brief list of ferromagnetic materials. Which of these can be permanently magnetized, and which cannot?

4. Outline briefly the domain theory of ferromagnetism.

5. Ferromagnetic materials lose their characteristic properties when they are heated, at temperatures still well below the melting point. Suggest a reason for this. Could a liquid ever be ferromagnetic?

6. Define "magnetic field," and "magnetic field strength." What is the general significance of the term "field" as used here? Name two other types of field.

7. A common experiment in magnetism is to sprinkle iron filings over a magnet, and drawings of patterns produced in this way are found in most textbooks of elementary physics. What do these patterns actually display? Sketch the type of pattern produced by a simple bar magnet.

8. What are the declination and inclination when referring to the earth's magnetism? Find out the approximate values of these quantities for your own area.

9. Show by means of a diagram that the earth's magnetic field is roughly the same as that of a bar magnet located deep in the interior.

10. Give three reasons why the earth's field could not be caused by an actual magnet inside the sphere.

11. Describe simple experiments to illustrate the magnetic field produced by an electric current, and the reaction of the field upon a current. Give two or three practical applications of these effects.

12. State the two direction rules, for the field produced by a current, and for the force exerted by a field upon a current.

13. Use the direction rules to show that electric currents flowing in the same direction will attract each other, and that currents flowing in opposite directions will repel each other.

14. Define "magnetic flux," and explain how flux is used as a measure of the strength of a bar magnet.

15. Show by simple diagrams how an electromagnet would be designed to (a) produce a strong magnetic field for experimental purposes; (b) produce a powerful lifting force. What kinds of materials would be used for the cores in these magnets?

16. What kinds of materials are used to make strong permanent magnets? How are they magnetized?

induced currents

If an electric current produces magnetism, then there ought to be some way in which magnetism produces electricity. So argued many scientists in the early years of the nineteenth century, following the discoveries of Oersted and Ampère, but for several years nobody succeeded in producing any such effect. Finally, in 1830, Henry° tried winding an extra loop of wire around the middle of a large electromagnet, and connecting the loop to a galvanometer. Whenever the magnet was turned on or off a

---

° Joseph Henry (1799–1878) was professor of mathematics at Albany Academy, and later secretary of the Smithsonian Institution in Washington. Michael Faraday (1791–1867) was director of the Royal Institution in London, England, and as such had more opportunity than Henry to display his great skill and versatility in experimentation. Both men are credited with other discoveries besides that of the induced current in a secondary coil, and both have had electric units named after them. Henry's work on the design of electromagnets was the basis for the invention of the electric telegraph, by Samuel Morse. He also studied the effects of self-induction, the voltage set up in a coil when the current is changing through the same coil, and the unit of self-inductance is called a henry. Faraday did experiments in electrostatics, and was the first to use the concept of lines of force; the unit of electric capacitance, the farad, is named after him. He also studied electrolysis and formulated the laws of that phenomenon (Sec. 21-1).

momentary current flowed through the extra loop and the galvanometer. In the following year Faraday, in England, made a similar discovery independently, and performed a number of experiments to study the phenomenon further. Henry and Faraday both arrived at the correct conclusion, and realized that it is the electric *current*, charge in motion, which produces the magnetic field, and so the magnetism would have to be in motion in order to produce electrical effects. But since there is no natural magnetic current, it would either have to be produced by moving a magnet or possibly simulated by magnetizing and demagnetizing a coil.

The series of experiments performed by Henry and Faraday are conveniently summarized in a modern laboratory demonstration (Fig. 16-1). A large solenoid (hereafter referred to as the secondary coil) is connected to a galvanometer, which is capable of detecting small currents, to form a closed circuit in which there is no battery or other source of EMF. The north pole of a bar magnet is plunged into the coil, and the galvanometer is deflected, but soon returns to zero, showing that an electric current passed momentarily. When the magnet is removed, the galvanometer is momentarily deflected the other way; when the south pole of the magnet is used, the same effects are observed, but in the opposite direction, as might be expected.

Substitute for the bar magnet a small coil (designated as the primary coil) which is connected to a battery. Inserting this into the secondary coil produces similar effects to those caused by the bar magnet, but the galvanometer deflection will probably be much less. Leave the primary coil inside the secondary, and open and close the battery circuit; closing the circuit produces the same effect as inserting the coil, opening the circuit is equivalent to removing the coil. Use an iron core inside the primary coil, and the effects are greatly enhanced, probably to the point where the gal-

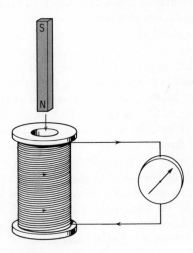

FIG. 16-1

Simple demonstration of induced currents.

vanometer is thrown right off its scale. Finally, insert the iron-cored coil quite slowly. This will produce a small deflection of the galvanometer, which can be maintained as long as the iron-cored primary is still moving.

The results of these experiments can be summed up in a few words: Whenever any change is made in the magnetic field inside the large secondary coil there is an *induced current* in the secondary circuit, the current flowing only while the change is taking place.

16-2   The Law of Induction

One more test is necessary before the results of experiments on induced currents can be expressed in the form of a quantitative law. Suppose a variable resistance is included in the secondary circuit, in series with the coil and the galvanometer. It can then be shown that the induced current is inversely proportional to the total resistance in the circuit. Therefore it is the voltage in this circuit, rather than the current, which depends upon the change in the magnetic field.

Then the *law of electromagnetic induction, Law IV of electricity and magnetism,* is:

Whenever there is a change in the magnetic field inside a closed electric circuit there is an induced electromotive force, proportional to the rate of change of the magnetic flux passing through the circuit. The direction of the induced current is always such that its magnetic field tends to oppose the change in the primary magnetic flux.

The statement about the direction means that when the north pole of the magnet is inserted into the secondary coil, the momentary induced current flows so as to make the top end of the coil north, thereby exerting a force of repulsion on the approaching magnet; when the magnet is withdrawn, the current in the coil flows so as to attract it. When the fixed primary and secondary are used, closing the primary circuit causes a current in the secondary in the opposite direction to that in the primary, so that the setting up of the magnetic flux inside the pair of coils is momentarily delayed. When the primary circuit is broken, the induced current flows in the same direction as the primary current, and tends to maintain the flux. This is actually a consequence of the law of conservation of energy, for the secondary current represents an expenditure of energy, even if this is no more than a momentary development of heat in the wire of the coil, and work must be done somewhere. Mechanical work is done against the repulsive force when the magnet is being inserted, and against the attractive force when it is being withdrawn.

16-3   The Principle of the Electric Generator

The discoveries of Henry and Faraday made it possible to develop electric current by the expenditure of mechanical work, and so they form the basis of our entire electrical industry. The original experiments produced only momentary currents, but it was rather obvious that current could be produced continuously by rotating a coil in a magnetic field, and it was only 2 years after Faraday announced the results of his experiments that a French instrument maker, Pixii, built the first electric generator. By modern standards, his machine was rather crude and inefficient, but improvements followed one after another, and the highly efficient modern generator is a direct descendant of the early machines.

The simplest practical generator consists of an iron-cored coil rotating between the poles of a permanent magnet (Fig. 16-2). Contact to the coil is made through a pair of sliding contacts (the brushes) which press against copper rings (the sliprings) attached to the two ends of the coil. This simple arrangement produces an alternating current (a-c) flowing alternately in opposite directions. When the axis of the coil is parallel to the magnetic field the flux is a maximum, and as the coil turns the flux starts to decrease. When the coil is at right angles to the field the flux is zero, and starts to increase in the opposite direction. This still produces current in the same direction in the external circuit, but when the coil passes through the position where it is once again parallel to the field, but reversed in direction, the external current reverses. The relation of the induced EMF to the position of the coil is shown in Fig. 16-3.

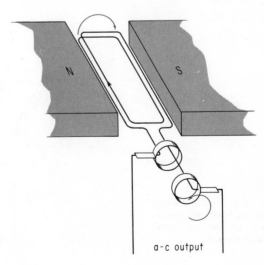

FIG. 16-2

A simple electric generator, consisting of a single rotating coil.

a-c output

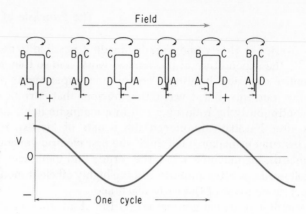

FIG. 16-3

Alternating current output of the simple generator, showing the relation of the induced EMF to the position of the coil.

16-4   *The Direct-Current Generator*

For a great many purposes, particularly for heating and lighting, it does not matter which way the current is flowing, and alternating current is perfectly satisfactory. When it comes to distributing electric power over a city or other area, alternating current has tremendous advantages, and, as most students will realize, electric power is almost always supplied to the consumer in this form. However, it is more economical to use direct current for the high voltages and large currents that are necessary in transmitting power over long distances, or by cable under the sea. Large machines for converting alternating current into direct current, and vice versa, are now being built in connection with major power projects.

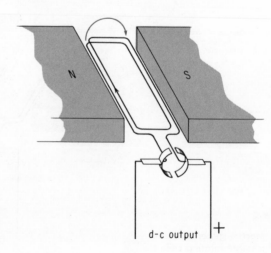

FIG. 16-4

A simple single-coil generator with a commutator, to convert alternating current into intermittent direct current.

There are certain applications for which the current must be in one definite direction, and direct current is necessary. One such process is electrolysis, and practical applications of electrolysis (such as plating metals with silver or chromium) require large currents, much larger than can reasonably be produced by means of voltaic cells. Long before electric lighting came into general use an important electroplating industry grew up, manufacturing silver plate as a low-priced substitute for solid silver utensils. In order to furnish the large currents needed, it was much cheaper to use an electric generator driven by a steam engine, than to use batteries. Thus the first large generators to be built were designed for electroplating, and produced direct current.°

The device that converts the alternating current of a simple rotating coil (Fig. 16-3) into direct current is the *commutator* (Fig. 16-4). In place of the separate sliprings, a single ring is used, divided into two sections with insulation between the sections. The ends of the coil are connected to the two sections of the commutator, and the brushes are placed on opposite sides, so that they make contact with opposite sections. Now, as the coil rotates, the connection to the external circuit is reversed at the same instant as the induced EMF in the coil, so that the current is always in the same direction, but is intermittent.

Two modifications of the simple coil and commutator shown in Fig. 16-4 lead to the modern d-c generator. A much larger magnetic field can be obtained by replacing the permanent magnet with an electromagnet, which is energized by diverting a small part of the current output of the generator through the fixed field coils. The magnetic flux is increased still further by shaping the poles of the electromagnet and the iron core of the rotating armature coil so that there is only a small air gap between them. Secondly, the EMF can be made almost uniform by using a number of coils on the armature, each coil being connected to a pair of commutator segments, so that at any instant the brushes make contact with that pair of segments where the induced EMF is a maximum.

16-5   Development of the Alternating-Current Generator

Just as the modern d-c generator is a development from the simple rotating coil with a commutator, so the single coil with sliprings has gone through several modifications in the development of the a-c generator which is the basis of the modern electrical distribution system. The first modification is the same as for the d-c generator, namely the use of an electromagnet for

---

° Very large d-c generators are used in the commercial production of aluminum, by the electrolysis of bauxite (Al_2O_3), and large aluminum plants are often located near waterfalls on important rivers, where large quantities of hydroelectric power can be produced cheaply.

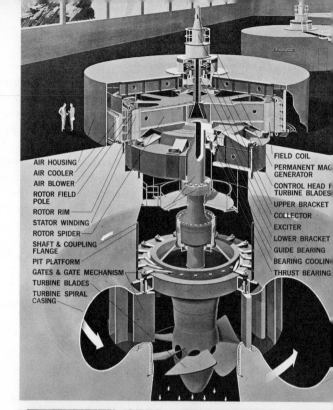

AIR HOUSING
AIR COOLER
AIR BLOWER
ROTOR FIELD POLE
ROTOR RIM
STATOR WINDING
ROTOR SPIDER
SHAFT & COUPLING FLANGE
PIT PLATFORM
GATES & GATE MECHANISM
TURBINE BLADES
TURBINE SPIRAL CASING

FIELD COIL
PERMANENT MAG GENERATOR
CONTROL HEAD F TURBINE BLADES
UPPER BRACKET
COLLECTOR
EXCITER
LOWER BRACKET
GUIDE BEARING
BEARING COOLIN
THRUST BEARING

FIG. 16-5

Top. Cutaway diagram of a modern a-c generator, driven by a water turbine in a large hydroelectric installation. Bottom. Photograph of four such machines installed at the Samuel C. Moore Power Station of the New England Power Company, Littleton, New Hampshire. (Diagram and photograph courtesy of Westinghouse Electric Corporation, East Pittsburgh, Pennsylvania.)

the field. The field magnet requires direct current in order to produce a constant magnetic field, and so this has to be provided by a small auxiliary generator.

An armature having several coils is used, but for a different reason than in the case of direct current. Experience has shown that the transmission system, and all machinery operated by the system, is less bulky and more efficient if the frequency of alternation is fairly high, and a frequency of 60 cycles per second° has become standard throughout most of North America. This means that a single-coil generator would have to rotate at a speed of 60 revolutions per second, and operating the heavy iron-cored armature of a large generator at this speed would introduce mechanical difficulties. If, however, several coils are used, say 6, with 6 pairs of poles on the field magnet, then the current alternates 6 times per revolution, and the speed need only be 10 revolutions per second.

Finally, there is in principle no reason why the coils have to rotate between the poles of a fixed magnet. The same induced EMF can be produced by rotating the magnet inside a fixed coil. The current in the rotating armature (the rotor) has to pass through the sliding contact of the brushes against the sliprings, and it is easier to make brushes which will handle the relatively small direct current of the field magnet than to make the large a-c output of the generator pass through a sliding contact. Therefore, in a large modern generator the rotor is the field magnet, and the alternating EMF is induced in the fixed coils of the stator. Figure 16-5(a) is a diagram of an a-c generator, driven by a water turbine in a hydroelectric power station. The rotating field coil is excited by a small d-c generator, mounted on the same axle as the main generator, and housed in the upper protruding section. The fixed stator windings, in which the a-c output is induced, fit closely around the poles of the rotor magnet. Figure 16-5(b) is a photograph of a set of four such generators in a large hydroelectric plant.

16-6   Current-Voltage Relations in Alternating Current

Where electricity is used for heating and lighting, and the output element in the circuit (the stove or lamp) is a simple resistance which obeys Ohm's law, the power at any instant is

$$P = VI = RI^2.$$

The heat output is the average of this quantity, taken over several cycles, and so the *effective current* (or voltage) is defined as the steady current which would produce the same amount of heat in a resistance. This is also the square root of the average value of I^2, and so it is sometimes known as

---

° The expression "60-cycle" means 60 complete repetitions per second of the cycle of EMF, as indicated in Fig. 16-3.

the root mean square (RMS) value. The relation above then holds for the average heat output as well as for the instantaneous power consumption, if V and I are the effective values. If the alternating current has the form shown in Fig. 16-3, the maximum voltage is $\sqrt{2}$ times the effective voltage. A circuit which is rated at 115 volts actually alternates between $+163$ and -163 volts.

If there are motors or similar machines in the circuit, the relation between energy output and the effective values of voltage and current is more complicated, and the useful work done can be less than VI. This is wasteful, and is bad design, so there is no need to go into details; for most practical purposes, using properly constructed equipment, the relation

$$P\text{(watts)} = V\text{(volts)} \times I\text{(amperes)}$$

is sufficiently accurate.

16-7   The Transformer and Electrical Power Systems

The great advantage of using alternating current for the distribution of electrical power from a central station to consumers in a widespread area is the ease with which the voltage can be altered by means of transformers. A simple transformer consists of two coils, having different numbers of turns, wound on the same soft iron core, very often of the form shown in Fig. 16-6. The input coil which is connected to the power supply is known as the primary, and the output coil, connected to the load, as the secondary. The alternating current in the primary sets up an alternating magnetic flux in the core. Since the core also passes through the secondary coil, the changing magnetic flux induces an EMF in the secondary.

Let the two coils have N_1 and N_2 turns, respectively. Since induced voltage is proportional to the magnetic flux multiplied by the number of turns in the coil, and since both coils enclose the same amount of flux, the primary and secondary voltages are proportional to the numbers of turns,

$$\frac{V_1}{V_2} = \frac{N_1}{N_2}.$$

FIG. 16-6

A simple transformer.

Apart from a very small loss due to heating of the wire in the transformer, the power output from the secondary is equal to the power input to the primary, and so

$$V_1 I_1 \approx V_2 I_2, \text{°}$$

or

$$\frac{I_2}{I_1} \approx \frac{V_1}{V_2} = \frac{N_1}{N_2}.$$

Nearly all small electrical devices are designed to operate at 115 or 230 volts, values which have become standard nearly everywhere.† To use higher voltages in the home would be much too hazardous, because the danger of electrocution and of fires from sparks and short circuits would be even greater than it is. However, it is not feasible to distribute electric power at 230 volts, even in the quantity required to light a small town. At this voltage the current in the main circuit would be impossibly large, and heavy copper bars would have to be used in place of the usual wires, or else there would be a very large waste of power due to heat developed in the line. The power has to be distributed at a high voltage, with a corresponding reduction in current, and then the voltage is reduced to a little over 230 volts by means of a transformer located close to each group of houses.

In order to transmit power from a large hydroelectric installation to an industrial area, still higher voltages are used, and it is possible to supply a fair-sized city 200 or 300 miles from the source, using one transmission line. The principles involved in an a-c distribution system can be clarified by referring to Fig. 16-7. The generators may be operated at 12,000 volts. Their output is fed into a bank of step-up transformers, with a turns ratio of 1:20, making the voltage on the long transmission line 240,000 volts. At a main distribution point on the outskirts of the city a bank of step-down transformers, with ratio 10:1, reduces the voltage to 24,000 and feeds this into lines leading to several substations. The substations reduce it again to 2400 volts, for the lines along the streets. Finally, small transformers, each

° The mathematical symbol $\approx$ is read "approximately equal to," and is used where small corrections have been ignored. The symbol $\sim$ means "about," and is used where the accurate value is not known, or is unimportant. Both symbols appear frequently in scientific writing.

† There is a rather curious history to the use of multiples of 115 in power systems. Early generators were designed to produce 550 volts, or some other multiple of 110, and this probably goes back to James Watt's evaluation of the horsepower as 550 foot-pounds of work per second. In a power distribution system a little heat always develops along the wires, resulting in a small voltage drop. Although the voltage at the terminals of the generator might be the proper multiple of 110, by the time the current reached the customers the voltage might be distinctly below the value for which their equipment was designed. Therefore the power companies raised the voltage to a multiple of 115, to ensure that the customers would get what they were paying for. The equipment manufacturers followed suit, and designed equipment for 115 volts, and the power companies had to raise the generator voltage again. Nowadays, in a city, in homes not too far from the power distribution point, the voltage at a wall outlet is usually somewhere between 115 and 120 volts.

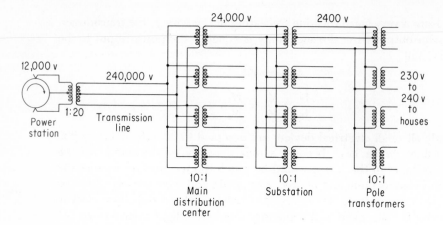

FIG. 16-7

Principles of long-distance power transmission.

serving a group of houses, reduce the voltage to somewhere between 230 and 240 volts, the difference from the theoretical value of 240 being due to small losses on all the lines.

16-8   *Electric Motors*

For a discussion of electric motors the student should refer to a textbook on electricity—we shall mention here only a few basic principles. The construction of all motors is, of course, based on the fact that a magnetic field exerts a force on a wire that is carrying an electric current, and therefore electrical power can be used to do mechanical work.

Simplest in principle is the d-c motor, which consists of an armature with several coils connected to a commutator, and rotating between the poles of an electromagnet, very similar in construction to the d-c generator. In fact, a d-c generator will run as a motor if current is supplied to it from an external source of emf, although for maximum efficiency the construction details of the motor will be somewhat different. Small household motors, designed to operate from an ordinary a-c outlet, are usually built on the principle of the d-c motor, because the direction of rotation depends on the relation between the coils and not on the direction of the current supply. However, these motors—called universal motors because they will run on either direct or alternating current—are impractical in large sizes; therefore big industrial motors are designed to run on alternating current. These are usually induction motors. In place of armature coils supplied with current through brushes, the rotor merely carries a number of closed loops of heavy copper wire. The alternating magnetic flux in the field coils induces large currents in the rotor loops, and the reaction between the induced currents and the magnetic field keeps the motor turning. The disadvantage of the induction motor is that it will run only at or near the speed for which it is designed; in the simplest case, one revolution per cycle of the a-c supply. With some designs, special starting devices have to be used to bring the motor up to speed.

16-9   A New Way of Life

There is no need to elaborate on the uses of electric power in our modern industrial society. Instead, think of a life without electricity. Think of homes and offices heated by coal fires, lighted by kerosene lamps, and without any of the mechanical conveniences which we are accustomed to obtain by flipping a switch. Think of factories operated by steam engines, with power transmitted to the machines by an intricate system of rotating overhead shafts and leather belts, instead of having each machine driven by its own electric motor, under the control of the operator. Then remember that even in the most highly developed nations of North America and Europe this state of affairs is well within the memory of the older generation.

Practical incandescent electric light bulbs were first produced by Thomas Edison in 1879. Edison's bulbs had carbon filaments, made by carbonizing thin strips of bamboo in vacuum. The modern tungsten filament lamp had to wait for methods of refining metallic tungsten and drawing it into wires, and did not come into general use until well into the twentieth century.

New York did not have electric power available commercially until 1883, when a power plant, also designed by Edison, was built to sell power to consumers for lighting offices and homes. It used generators driven by steam engines, with coal as the fuel, and the power was only distributed locally, up to a distance of about 5 miles. In 1877 a small hydroelectric plant was built at Niagara Falls, also for local consumption only; it was not until 1895 that power from Niagara reached the neighboring large cities of Toronto and Buffalo. Even after this it was 20 years or more before electric light came into general use in the home in a number of large American and European cities, and the common household appliances came into use still later. The really spectacular increase in the use of electricity and in the total capacity of central power plants came shortly after World War I. Less industrialized countries than those of America and Europe are still in the early development stage, and some have hardly relinquished the kerosene lamp.

Alternating current (a-c) Electric current in which the direction of flow is reversed at regularly recurring intervals in such a way that the total amount of charge transferred is zero.

Armature The rotating coil in a d-c motor or generator, or in other machines in which the rotation or the induction of current operates on the same principle as in a d-c machine.

Brushes The fixed terminals that make contact with a rotating coil by pressing against the sliprings or commutator on the axle of the coil.

Commutator Device for reversing the external connections to a rotating coil at the correct instant, so that in the case of a generator the output current is always in the same direction (d-c); in the case of a motor the forces that keep it rotating are always in the same direction.

Cycle One complete sequence of alternation, from maximum current in one direction to the next maximum in the same direction.

Direct current (d-c) Electric current always flowing in the same direction. Technically, the term "direct current" implies a constant current. A current which is always in the same direction, but which is fluctuating regularly, is considered to be the sum of a direct current plus an alternating current.

Effective current (or voltage) The steady current that would produce the same average rate of heating in a given resistance as does the actual alternating or fluctuating current. It is equal to the root-mean-square current.

Electromagnetic induction The production of an electric current in a closed circuit when the magnetic flux through the circuit is altered.

Galvanometer Instrument used for detecting small electric currents and estimating the relative amounts when there is no need to know the precise values.

Induced current Electric current produced by a change of magnetic flux.

Induction motor An a-c motor in which the current in the rotating coils is produced by induction, without any need for external connections.

Root-mean-square current Square root of the average value of $(current)^2$.

Rotor General term for the rotating coil in any type of electrical machinery.

Self-induction Effects caused by the induction of an electromotive force in a coil when the current carried by the same coil is changing; especially evident when a coil or electromagnet is connected to an a-c supply.

Sliprings Metal rings mounted on the axle of a rotating coil in order to make connection with an external circuit through the brushes.

Stator The stationary coils of a motor or generator.

Universal motor A motor that will run on either direct or alternating current; it operates on the same principle as a d-c motor, and most small household motors are of this type.

EXERCISES

1. What is the converse effect to that of the magnetic field produced by an electric current? Distinguish this from the reaction effect. How did Henry and Faraday discover the converse effect, and when? In what types of machine are the three effects mentioned in this exercise used?

2. In a demonstration experiment a large coil of wire is connected to a galvanometer; state what happens when: (a) a bar magnet is inserted in the coil; (b) the magnet is removed; (c) a small coil connected to a dry cell is inserted and removed; (d) the small coil is left inside the larger one, and the connection to the dry cell is broken; (e) the last two tests are repeated with a rod of soft iron inside the small coil; (f) with the small coil inside the larger coil, and connected to the dry cell, the iron rod is inserted and withdrawn; (g) test (f) is repeated with a hard steel rod in place of the soft iron; (h) test (f) is repeated slowly; (i) a small magnet is placed inside the large coil, with its axis parallel to the axis of the coil, and is rotated around the common axis; (j) the small magnet of test (i) is rotated in the perpendicular direction; (k) the large coil is stood upright, and then quickly turned upside down.

3. State Faraday's law of electromagnetic induction.

4. How could you demonstrate that it is electromotive force rather than current that is induced by a change of magnetic flux?

5. Show that the rule for direction in Faraday's law follows from the law of conservation of energy.

6. If the direction rule for induced current could be reversed by some unknown means, it would be possible to make a perpetual motion machine that would do work without any expenditure of energy. How would such a machine be arranged?

7. Explain how a simple coil rotating in a magnetic field produces an alternating current.

8. Explain the principle of the commutator in a d-c generator.

9. What was the first large-scale use of electric generators? What type were they, and how were they driven?

10. In a modern d-c motor what replaces the simple coil rotating in a magnetic field, and the simple two-section commutator?

11. In a modern a-c generator what replaces the simple rotating coil?

12. Referring to Exercises 21 to 24 at the end of Chapter 14, which of these questions (if any) would give the same answer if the numerical values given were the effective values in an a-c circuit? Assuming that direct current was implied in formulating the questions, which of them refer to devices that would not work on alternating current?

13. What is the maximum instantaneous voltage in a 240-volt a-c circuit? What is the maximum instantaneous current through a stove element that produces 1500 watts on a 240-volt circuit?

14. How would the instantaneous power fluctuate if the nominal power output is P watts?

15. What would be the ratio of the numbers of turns in the primary and secondary windings of a transformer designed to convert 6000 volts to 240 volts? If the primary current in this transformer is 5 amperes, what is the approximate value of the secondary current?

16. Why is it necessary to use the highest feasible voltage in transmitting electric power over long distances?

the empirical laws of light

17-1   Radiant Energy

Light was listed in Sec. 8-1 as one of the many forms of energy. We must now be more specific, and classify it as a form of radiant energy, or briefly, *radiation*. There are many forms of radiation, radiant heat, broadcast radio, X rays, radioactive rays, to mention only a few. They have important properties in common, which are most easily described by discussing the special case of light. The first essential property is that there is an energy source; in the case of light, the sun, or an electric light bulb. Energy flows out in all directions, is "radiated," from the source, and travels by various paths to a receiver, where it is converted into a more usable form. The receiver of light is commonly the eye or a photographic film, and in both cases the immediate conversion is to chemical energy. In the retina, the sensory membrane of the eye, there is a further conversion of the chemical energy into the electrical energy of a nerve impulse which conveys the sensation to the brain. In the film, chemical changes initiated by the light produce a permanent record. In other light-sensitive receivers, the light energy produces an electric current directly (photoelectric cell), or it is converted into heat and causes a measurable rise of temperature.

At this stage we shall not be concerned with the mechanism by which the energy is transported from the source to the receiver. Whatever the mechanism, we can imagine it as flowing along a bundle of *rays*, and we can *describe* the properties by drawing geometrical diagrams of the rays. Then the first law of light is the *law of rectilinear propagation:*

Light travels in straight lines until it meets some material object.

Straightforward evidence for the law of rectilinear propagation lies in the fact that a light source of small dimensions casts sharply defined shadows, and that the shape and location of the shadow can be determined very precisely by drawing straight-line rays (Fig. 17-1). However, like so many laws of physics, the law is not absolute, but is subject to important limitations, which will be discussed later. In principle, the law should apply to all forms of radiation, as well as to light, but again with recognized limitations.

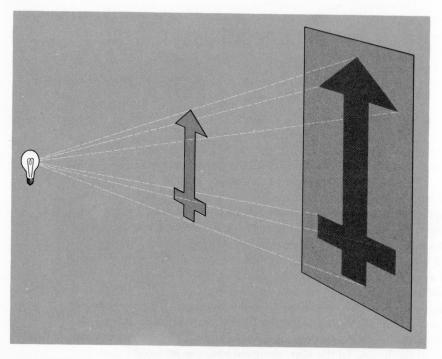

FIG. 17-1

Rectilinear propagation of light.

17-2   Light Intensity and Illumination

The *intensity of a light source* is its output, and, since light is energy, the intensity might be measured in watts.° However, all ordinary light sources produce a great deal of radiant heat as well as light, and the illuminating value of the light depends on the color of the source. A white source produces a much better illumination than a yellow or reddish source of the same total energy. It has been necessary, therefore, to devise a special arbitrary unit of light intensity, the *candlepower*. As the name implies, this was originally intended to be the intensity of an ordinary wax candle of specified size. However, an actual candle is far too variable in its output to make a satisfactory standard of measurement, and after trying several different standard sources, the International Bureau of Weights and Measures has agreed to define the candlepower as follows:

One square centimeter of blackbody (that is, an ideal black when cold), maintained at the temperature of melting platinum (1774°C), produces 60 candlepower.

In dealing with practical problems of lighting we are interested in the *illumination*, which is defined as the light energy received per second on a surface of unit area. From Fig. 17-2 it should be evident that if the distance from the light source is doubled, the energy is spread over four times the area. Generally, if the distance is increased by a factor x, the area of cross section of the beam is multiplied by x^2, so that the energy per unit area is divided by x^2. Therefore the illumination is inversely proportional to (distance)^2.† Once again, as in Newton's law of gravitation and Coulomb's law of electrical forces, we have a phenomenon in which an effect emanates from a source and spreads in all directions—once again the effect varies as the inverse square of the distance.

In the case of light (and radiation generally) there is a difference from these other point-source phenomena; the energy is rarely distributed uniformly around the source, but is different in different directions. A more useful quantity than the intensity of the source is therefore the *light flux*, which is the amount of light radiated within a given solid angle, like, for example, the beam illustrated in Fig. 17-2. The unit of light flux is the *lumen*, which is the amount of light produced by a standard candle within a cone whose base is 1 square meter at a distance of 1 meter. It follows that a standard candle that was radiating uniformly in all directions would produce 4π lumens.

° When electrical light bulbs are rated in watts, this refers to the electrical energy supplied. Only about 5 per cent of the energy output of an ordinary tungsten bulb is in the form of visible light.

† This is sometimes regarded as one of the empirical laws of light, but, since it is a simple deduction from the law of rectilinear propagation and the law of conservation of energy, it is hardly necessary to list it as a separate law.

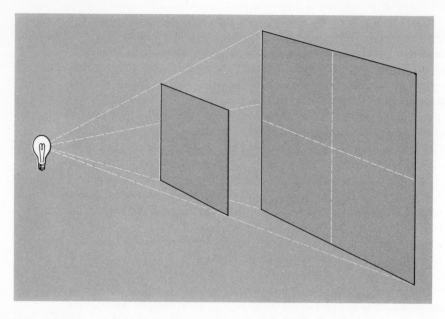

FIG. 17-2

Illumination is proportional to $1/(\text{distance})^2$.

Illumination is then measured in *lumens per square meter* or lumens per square foot. An illumination of 1 lumen per square foot is also known as a *footcandle,* because it is the illumination at a distance of 1 foot from a standard candle. It is the unit usually employed in portable lightmeters, for use in lighting surveys and in photography.

17-3   *The Law of Reflection, Optical Images*

Light travels in straight lines until it meets a material object, and we must consider next what happens when it does meet some object. The simplest case is that of reflection from a smooth surface, closely approximated by a good quality mirror, either plane or curved. The second law of propagation of light, the *law of regular reflection* (Figs. 17-3 and 17-5), is then:

Light is reflected so that the reflected and incident rays make equal angles with the normal to the reflecting surface.

The law of reflection is of great antiquity. It was certainly known to Euclid (about 300 B.C.), for his work on geometry includes a proof of the rule for finding the image of a point source produced by a plane mirror (Fig. 17-3). The rule is that the line *OI* joining the object to the image is at right angles to the mirror surface, and that *I* is the same distance behind the mirror as *O* is in front.

This raises the question of optical images, formed by mirrors of different shapes, and later by lenses and various optical instruments. The theory of images is an important branch of applied physics, known as geometrical optics because the methods used are based on geometrical construction of the light rays. In the first place, *image* can be defined as the point from which the rays entering the eye (or other receiver) diverge, or appear to diverge. Images are of two main classes, *real* and *virtual*. The image is said to be real if all the light rays actually pass through (or very close to) the image point. It is said to be virtual if the rays only appear to diverge from the image point. Images are further classified according to their size relative to the object, enlarged or reduced, and according to their attitude, erect or inverted. Another question, of concern to the designers of optical instruments, is the perfection of the image; how closely are the rays concentrated at the image point?

The image in a plane mirror is always virtual, since it is always behind the mirror, where no light actually penetrates. It is the same size as the

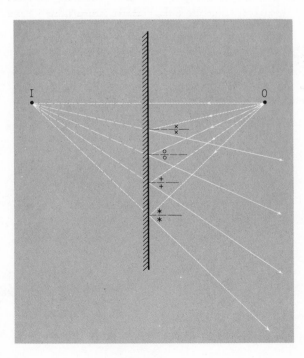

FIG. 17-3

Law of reflection at equal angles. Light coming from a small object O appears after reflection to come from the image point *I*.

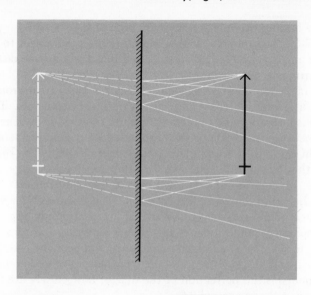

FIG. 17-4

Image in a plane mirror.

object (Fig. 17-4), and is erect but is inverted laterally; that is, right and left are interchanged. It is ideally perfect if the mirror is an ideal plane.

The concave mirror in Fig. 17-5 is also producing an erect virtual image, which in this case would be enlarged. It can produce a real image, either

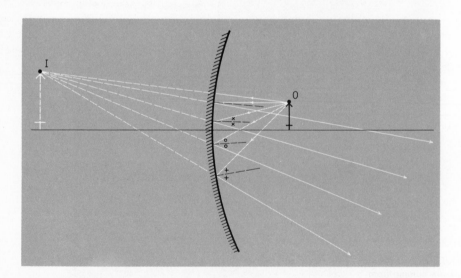

FIG. 17-5

A concave mirror producing an enlarged virtual image.

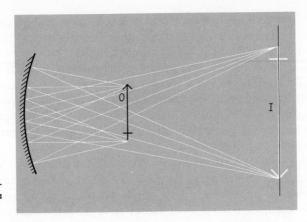

FIG. 17-6

A concave mirror producing a real image on a screen.

enlarged or reduced, and inverted (Fig. 17-6), but when real images are required, lenses are usually more convenient. Finally, it should be noted that virtual images are useful only for visual observation; in order to take a photograph or to project a picture on a screen, the image must be real.

17-4   *Diffuse Reflection: Scattering and Absorption*

When light is reflected from an irregular surface, the law of reflection may be obeyed at any point of the surface, but the reflected rays are at all sorts of angles (Fig. 17-7). There is no definite image, or at best a ghostly image such as may be seen in a polished tabletop, and what we see is the reflecting surface itself. It is therefore by diffuse reflection that we "see" nonluminous objects. If a mirror reflection were perfect, the mirror itself would be invisible, a phenomenon which serves stage magicians: "It is all done with mirrors."

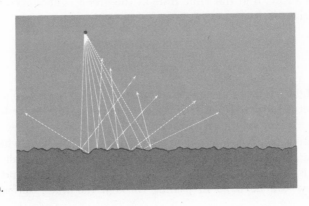

FIG. 17-7

Diffuse reflection.

When light is diffusely reflected from a collection of small particles, such as the water drops in a cloud, it is said to be *scattered*. There is always some scattering when light passes through matter, however transparent it may appear to be, for the molecules themselves always scatter a little light. We usually see the glass of a windowpane, and the magician's illusion is never perfect, but has to be enhanced by lighting effects in order to deceive the audience. If the scattering particles are very small, and particularly if they are individual molecules, blue and violet light are scattered much more strongly than red light.

The blue light of a clear summer sky is light scattered by the molecules of the atmosphere, and so in the blue of the sky we are really seeing the several miles of depth of air with which our planet is surrounded. When the sun is low on the horizon, at sunset or sunrise, the light strikes the atmosphere at an extreme angle, and has to travel a much greater distance through air. Much of the blue light is lost from the beam by scattering, and the light which penetrates the atmosphere to reach our eyes or to illuminate the clouds gives us the golds and reds of a fine weather sunset. To an astronaut, circling the earth in his space capsule, outside the atmosphere, the sky is black, and the stars can be seen even when the sun is shining brilliantly.

When light encounters matter, besides reflection and scattering, there is usually some degree of *absorption*. Both scattering and absorption represent a loss of energy from the light beam. In the former case the energy is not converted into another form, but the material which causes the scattering is seen as if it were a new source of light. When light is absorbed the energy is converted into heat or chemical energy; if the absorption is complete the object appears black. Absorption is often, one might even say usually, color-selective. An object appears red because the energy of the blue and green light is absorbed; it is a transparent red, like a piece of red glass or a bottle of wine, if the red light is transmitted; it is an opaque red, like a rose, if at the same time as the green light is absorbed, the red is diffusely reflected.

17-5   Refraction

When light passes in a regular manner from one transparent medium to another it is *refracted*. That is, in general, the light rays are bent through an angle. A simple example of refraction is seen if one pokes a stick at an angle into a pool of water. The stick appears to be bent where it enters the water, and at the same time the pool appears to be shallower than it actually is (Fig. 17-8). The rays of light traveling from the end of the stick to the eye are deviated in passing through the water surface, with the

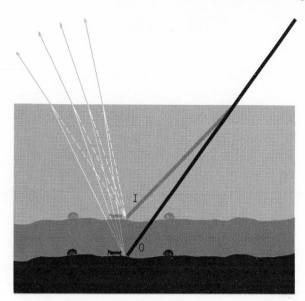

FIG. 17-8

Virtual image produced by refraction at a plane surface.

result that we see a virtual image (I) of the stick and of the bottom of the pond.

The ancients were, of course, quite familiar with the phenomenon of refraction, but the law which would permit a geometrical construction for the refracted rays eluded them. This is credited to the Dutch physicist, Willebrord Snell, in about 1620. In modern form the third law of propagation of light, the *law of refraction*, states:

If i and r are the angles of incidence and refraction, respectively, then the ratio,

$$\frac{\sin i}{\sin r} = n,$$

is constant as the angles are varied.*

The constant (n) is called the *index of refraction*, and depends on the properties of both materials. It also varies with the color of the light; the typical values given in Table 17-1 are for yellow light.

* For readers who are unfamiliar with trigonometrical notation, the geometrical construction (Fig. 17-9) which was originally given by Snell, and which follows from the modern form of the law, will prove helpful. Draw a circle around the point at which refraction occurs, to intersect the incident and refracted rays at P and Q. Draw perpendiculars, PM and QN, onto the normal to the surface. Then the ratio (PM/QN) is equal to the refractive index (n), and is constant for different rays. The diagram is correctly proportioned for light passing from air to water.

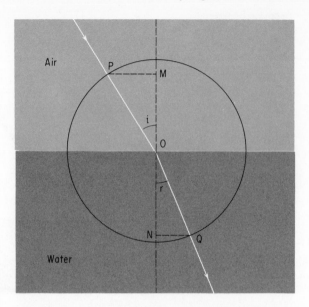

FIG. 17-9

The law of refraction.

Refraction by the atmosphere has to be taken into account in astronomical observations. There is, of course, no sharp boundary between the near vacuum of outer space and the atmosphere surrounding the earth, and so the rays are not bent at a sharp angle, as they are in passing from air to water. Instead, the rays coming from a distant star follow a continuous curve as they pass from one layer of atmosphere to another of greater density (Fig. 17-10). However, the resulting angular deviation is the same as if the rays had passed directly into the dense atmosphere near the ground. For a star on the horizon the deviation is 36 minutes of arc, and the star appears to be elevated above the horizon by this amount. The

TABLE 17-1   A FEW VALUES
OF REFRACTIVE
INDEX FOR
YELLOW LIGHT

Air to water	1.330
Air to soft (crown) glass	1.517
Air to hard (flint) glass	1.650
Water to crown glass	1.141
Air to lens of the eye	1.437
Air to diamond	2.417
Vacuum to air at normal pressure	1.00029

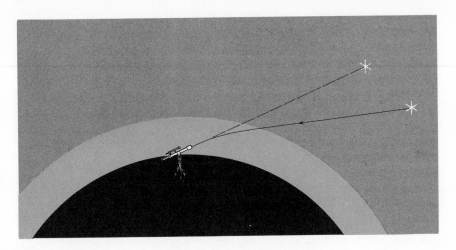

FIG. 17-10

Refraction of starlight in the atmosphere.

same occurs with the rising or setting sun, and the sun is actually a little more than its own diameter below the horizon before it completely disappears.

The three laws of propagation of light, the rectilinear law, the law of regular reflection, and the law of refraction, are empirical laws. That is, they are generalized statements of the way light behaves, without any attempt at explanation. We would like now to investigate the mechanism by which light energy is transferred, and so to formulate a theory of light, and of radiation in general, relating the empirical laws to a more fundamental principle, just as Kepler's and Galileo's laws were related to Newton's law of gravitation. This has, in fact, been a subject of much controversy, and theories of light have passed through several stages before developing into the modern form. This subject will have to be deferred for the present, and we too shall have to allow modern views to emerge gradually as we discuss a number of other phenomena besides the simple laws of propagation.

17-6   Lenses

We do not need to know more than the empirical laws in order to make a great deal of progress in practical application. Some of the most important applications center around the phenomenon of refraction by a lens, consisting in the typical case of a piece of glass bounded by two spherical surfaces. A biconvex glass lens is a *converging* lens [Fig. 17-11(a)]. Rays of

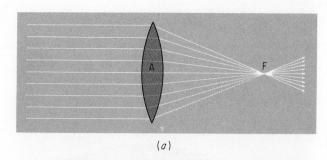

(a)

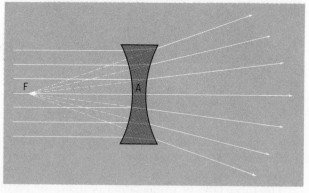

FIG. 17-11

Converging and diverging lenses.

(b)

light coming from a distant object, which are very nearly parallel when they strike the lens, are refracted at each surface of the lens, and are converged so that they pass through (or very close to) a *real focus* (F). When the incident rays are parallel, F is referred to as the principal focus, and the distance $f = AF$ is the *focal length*. A biconcave lens [Fig. 17-11(b)] diverges the light so that parallel incident rays appear, after refraction, to come from a *virtual principal focus;* the focal length is then considered to be a negative quantity.

Four basic ways in which lenses may be used are illustrated in Fig. 17-12. In (a) a converging lens produces a reduced real image of a large object; this corresponds to a simple camera or to the eye. In (b) the same lens, placed at a distance a little greater than its focal length from a small object, produces an enlarged real image, as in the case of a projection lantern. In (c) the small object is a little closer to the lens than the focal length, and the image is enlarged and virtual; this corresponds to a simple magnifying glass. Finally, (d) shows a diverging lens, which always produces a reduced virtual image of a real object. Diverging lenses are rarely used by themselves, but almost always in combination with a converging lens. For example, a diverging lens is used in eyeglasses to correct short sight. The combination of the glass diverging lens with the converging lens of the eye brings objects to a proper focus on the retina, whereas the eye lens by itself would focus the light in front of the retina.

A simple biconvex lens alone seldom produces a sharply defined image, but is subject to a number of defects known as aberrations. One of these

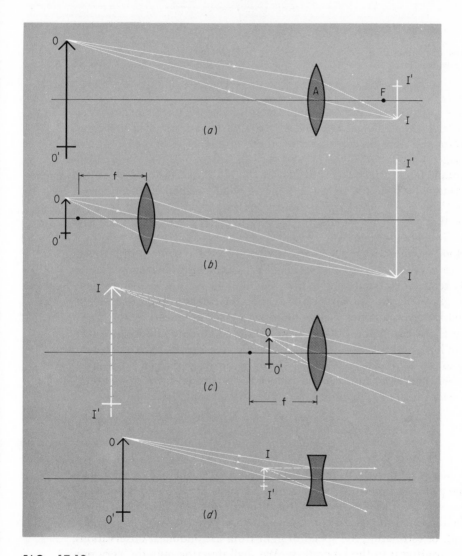

FIG. 17-12

Four ways in which simple lenses can be used.

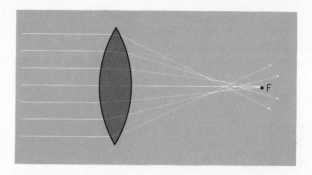

FIG. 17-13

Spherical aberration in a
simple biconvex lens.

effects—spherical aberration—is illustrated in Fig. 17-13. Light rays passing through the center of the lens are brought to the principal focus, but
rays refracted near the rim are converged too much, with the result that
the image of a point of light is a more or less fuzzy spot. The focal length
of a simple lens varies with the color of the light, due to the variation in
the refractive index of the glass, producing what is called chromatic aberration. There are also various distortions produced in trying to focus
objects that are not on the axis of the lens, in order to take in a wide field
of view in a photograph.

A good camera and a good microscope always have composite lenses,
made of several separate pieces of glass. Chromatic aberration can be
greatly reduced by combining a diverging flint-glass lens with a converging
crown-glass lens. If the curvatures of the surfaces are properly selected,
the flint lens compensates the variation with color produced by the crown
lens, without eliminating the focusing effect. The combination is a converging lens, and is described as achromatic—no color. By adding more
lenses to the combination—possibly using a third type of glass—spherical
aberration and distortion can be reduced, permitting a wider aperture°
and a wider field of view than is possible with a simple lens.

17-7   The Velocity of Light

Light energy takes time to travel from the source to the eye or the photographic plate, and the speed with which it travels through empty space (or
in an evacuated tube in the laboratory) turns out to be one of the important fundamental numerical constants of nature. We shall not discuss early
methods of estimating the speed of light from astronomical observations,
or of measuring it in the laboratory. We shall describe only the very pre-

° The lens aperture is usually stated by giving the width of the lens opening, or of the
adjustable diaphragm, as a fraction of the focal length. For example, if a lens is rated as f2.8
(which should be f/2.8) it means that the opening is 1/2.8 of the focal length.

cise measurements made by Michelson° at various times between 1915 and 1930.

The main part of the apparatus was set up near the astronomical observatory on top of Mt. Wilson, in California. Here light from a bright source (S, Fig. 17-14) was reflected from the polished face (A) of a very precisely ground, octagonal steel block. From here mirrors (B, C) reflected the light to a large concave mirror (D), which projected it as a parallel beam to the top of Mt. San Antonio, 22 miles away. Here the light was received by mirrors E and F and reflected back over very nearly but not quite the same path, so that the return beam was reflected by mirrors G and H to the face (J) of the steel block, and finally into the viewing telescope (K).

When all these mirrors had been properly adjusted, the steel block was set in rotation, so that a flash of light was transmitted to the distant mountain every time a face of the block came into the correct position. The light took a certain time (about $\frac{1}{4240}$ second) to travel the 44 miles to Mt. San Antonio and back, so that, in general, face (J) of the block would be out of position when the flashes returned, and nothing would be seen in the telescope. Now the speed of rotation was adjusted so that the next face (J')

° Albert A. Michelson (1852–1931) taught physics for a while at the Case School of Applied Science in Cleveland, and later at the U.S. Naval Academy. When the University of Chicago was established in 1891 he became professor of physics there, and held that post for many years. He is renowned for the extreme precision of his experiments, and his measurement of the velocity of light, with result correct to six figures, is one of the most elaborate and precise physical measurements ever made.

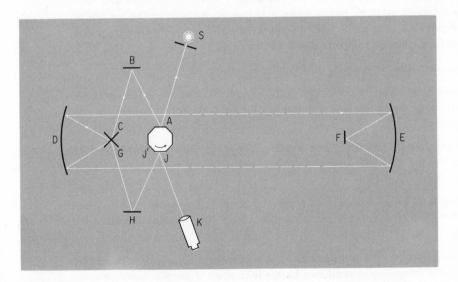

FIG. 17-14

Michelson's measurement of the speed of light.

came into position at the precise instant that the return flash hit it, and the light was once again seen in the telescope. Thus the time required for light to travel 44 miles was equal to the time required for the steel block to turn through ⅛ of a revolution. To get the correct return of the light beam, the block had to rotate at about 530 revolutions per second. Its speed was measured by comparison with a standard astronomical clock, and had to be held constant for at least 100,000 revolutions.°

As a result of Michelson's measurements, and other, more recent experiments, the speed of light in vacuum is now given in tables of physical constants as 299,796 kilometers per second, or 186,285 miles per second. Light from the moon therefore takes about 1.2 seconds to reach the earth; light from the sun takes about 8½ minutes.

GLOSSARY

Absorption Conversion of part of the energy of a beam of radiation into heat (or some other form) as it passes through a material, or is reflected by a surface.

Achromatic lens Lens in which the differences of focal length for different colors are compensated, so that all colors are brought very nearly to the same focus.

Blackbody Technically, a body that completely absorbs the light and heat radiation falling upon it; hence when it is heated it radiates the maximum amount possible at the given temperature; closely approximated by a dull black surface, such as that of a piece of charcoal.

Candlepower Unit of intensity of a light source (Sec. 17-2).

Chromatic aberration Imperfection of the images produced by a lens because the material of which the lens is made has different refractive indices for different colors.

Converging lens Lens which concentrates a parallel beam (approximately) into a point; the principal focus is then real, and the focal length is considered to be positive.

Diverging lens Lens which causes a parallel beam to appear to diverge from a point; the principal focus is virtual, and the focal length is considered to be negative.

Focus, focal length The principal focus of a lens (or a spherical or parabolic mirror) is the image point produced by the lens when a parallel beam, travel-

° To get the required accuracy, the distance of 22 miles between the two mountains had to be known to within about 3 inches; a special survey team spent several months determining the distance.

ing parallel to the axis of the lens, is incident upon it; the focal length of a simple lens is the distance from the center of the lens to the principal focus.

Footcandle   Unit of illumination; the illumination received at a distance of 1 foot from a source of 1 candlepower intensity.

Geometrical optics   That part of the theory of light that employs geometrical constructions of light rays, based upon the three laws of propagation; essential to the design of optical instruments.

Illumination   The amount of light energy received per unit area.

Lens aperture   Ratio of the diameter of the lens opening to the focal length; the aperture number on a camera is the reciprocal of this quantity.

Light intensity   A measure of the light energy produced by a source, taking color values into account.

Lumen   Unit of light flux, which is the total amount of light energy emitted within a given cone; a standard candle, radiating equally in all directions, produces 4π lumens.

Parallel beam   Beam of radiation in which the rays are all parallel.

Radiation   The emission of energy from a source, and its propagation in all directions through the surrounding space; light, radiant heat, radio waves, and radioactive emissions are examples.

Real image   One in which the light is actually concentrated at the image point.

Refraction   Bending of the light rays when they pass from one transparent material to another.

Refractive index   Quantity that measures the amount of refraction; defined as the ratio of the sine of the angle of incidence to the sine of the angle of refraction (Sec. 17-5).

Scattering   When light is diffusely reflected in all directions by small particles, without loss of energy, as it passes through a material, it is said to be scattered.

Spherical aberration   Imperfection of the images produced by a lens due to the fact that the lens surfaces are portions of spheres.

Virtual image   One in which the light rays only appear to diverge from the image point, without actually passing through it.

EXERCISES

1. What are the three essential parts to any observation of radiation?
2. What is your eye actually receiving when you see yourself in a mirror?

3. Trace the various conversions of energy when you see a picture illuminated by an electric light.

4. Show that the law which states that the illumination is inversely proportional to the square of the distance from the source follows from the conservation of energy.

5. Name and define the standard unit of light intensity. Why has it been necessary to introduce an arbitrary unit of this quantity?

6. What is the illumination at a distance of 5 feet from a source of 100 candlepower?

7. How close to a 50 candlepower source would you have to be in order to receive 10 footcandles?

8. In Exercises 6 and 7 would the answers be greater or less: (a) If the source were a desk lamp with a reflector, and the illuminated surface were directly under the lamp? (b) If the illuminated surface were inclined to the beam of light?

9. State the three laws of propagation of light.

10. A man stands 3 feet away from a wall mirror; how far away from him is his image?

11. What is the minimum height of a wall mirror such that a man 6 feet tall can see his entire body? How high above the floor would the mirror have to be placed? How are these answers affected by the distance that the man stands away from the mirror?

12. Draw the geometrical constructions for three different rays of light passing at different angles from air to glass of refractive index 1.5.

13. A fish in a pond sees a man standing on the bank at the water's edge; where, from the fish-eye-view, does the man appear to be? Does he appear taller or shorter than normal? (The answer to this question can be deduced by drawing a diagram roughly to scale.)

14. Draw a diagram to show that when light is passing from one medium to another of lower refractive index (for example, from water to air) the rays cannot emerge if they strike the surface at an angle greater than a certain value. What happens to the rays that strike the surface at greater angles?

15. Explain with the aid of a diagram why it is that a pool seems shallower than it actually is, when you are looking straight downward into it.

16. Why is the sky blue on a sunny day? and why is the sunset red?

17. What happens to produce the color when you look through a piece of red glass? when you look at a red painted wall?

18. State what type of lens, convex or concave, is used in the following cases: (a) to project a lantern slide on a screen; (b) to photograph a tiny object; (c) to look at a tiny object; (d) to correct the vision of a person who cannot see clearly objects more than a few feet away.

19. In the first three cases of Exercise 18, where should the object be placed with respect to the principal focus of the lens?

20. Why is it unsatisfactory to use a simple lens made of one piece of glass in a good camera?

21. Describe briefly the principle of Michelson's method of measuring the velocity of light. Where was the experiment carried out? Approximately how long did it take the light flashes to return to the transmitting point?

22. Michelson's measurement of the velocity was precise to 1 part in 100,000; what is the maximum error that could be permitted in determining the distance the light had to travel?

23. Calculate as precisely as the data permit the average time required for a radar echo to return from the moon.

CHAPTER **18**   ## waves

When one speaks of waves, the first things that come to mind are ocean waves or ripples on a pond. One easily realizes that an ocean wave, rolling along the surface of the sea, carries energy. The waves are set in motion by the wind, and if there is a wide stretch of open sea they continue to roll long after the wind has died down, or they may travel into a calm area, miles away from the storm which started them. Finally the waves reach the land, where they may possibly break upon a shelving beach. As they break they stir up the sand, or even shift large stones. The waves do work upon the beach; the wind did work upon the water in setting the waves in motion. But there is no flow of water in the open sea; the surface merely rises and falls as the wave passes over it. Even when a wave arrives at the shore, and water rolls up on the beach, it promptly flows back again into the trough of the next wave. What is transported by the wave is the state of motion—and *energy*—energy which came originally from the kinetic energy of the wind, and which later stirred the sand on a beach hundreds of miles away.

There are many other types of waves known in nature, besides waves on a body of water, and they provide some of the most important mechanisms for radiation of energy from a source. Therefore we must now examine the characteristic properties of wave motion in general, and the specific properties of some of the more important types of waves.

A simple example will serve to illustrate the principle of wave motion. Imagine a long rope attached to a flexible support (S, Fig. 18-1) at one end, and kept taut by a weight (W) hanging over a pulley. Suppose S is pulled aside and then released. The bending of the end of the rope sets up forces in the neighboring portion. This portion has inertia, and it takes a certain time for it to respond. When the second portion does respond it sets up forces in the next portion, and so on all the way along the rope. The result is that a pulse travels along the rope, with a definite speed, which depends on the mass per unit length of rope and on the stretching force applied to it.

Finally the pulse reaches the pulley, where it can exert a force on the weight (W) and set it in motion. Energy supplied to the rope at one end is received at the far end after a certain time interval, although some of the energy has been dissipated through friction in the material of the rope. The rope that transmitted the energy has suffered no permanent change or displacement; after the pulse has passed it is just as it was before.

Transmission of a wave in the form of a single pulse is not very common, and is of little interest. The more important types of wave motion in nature are continuous waves, which can be exemplified in the case of the stretched rope if we imagine the support (S) to be set in continuous vibration [Fig. 18-1(b)]. Every portion of the rope is set in vibration in its turn,

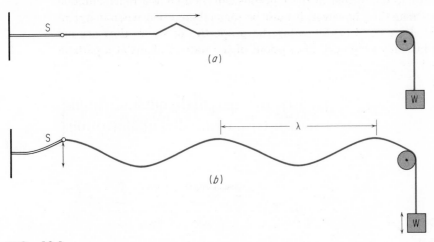

FIG. 18-1

Waves in a long rope: (a) a single pulse; (b) a continuous train of waves.

and finally the weight (W) at the far end is also caused to vibrate. Under the proper circumstances there can be a continuous flow of energy from S, which can be considered a source, to W, considered a receiver.

18-2   *Transverse and Longitudinal Waves*

The wave in the rope is classed as a *transverse,* mechanical wave. It is transverse because the particles oscillate at right angles to the direction in which the wave is traveling. It is mechanical because mechanical forces are exerted upon the particles of the rope, and these move in response, according to Newton's laws of motion.

A wave motion is classed as *longitudinal* if the particles oscillate back and forth in the same direction in which the wave is traveling. A longitudinal, mechanical wave can be set up in a long spring (Fig. 18-2) which is alternately compressed and stretched. Then a continuous train of waves of compression travels along the spring, and as the waves pass over the coils of the spring these are set in vibration in a direction parallel to the length of the spring. Each coil does work on the next, and again there is a continuous flow of energy, which can be made to do work at the far end.

Even though the motion of the coils of the spring is longitudinal, the wave is frequently represented graphically as if it were transverse. The upper curve in Fig. 18-2 shows the displacement of the coils from their normal positions, positive for displacement to the right, negative to the left. The lower curve shows the forces in the spring, positive for compression, negative for expansion. Either of these graphs can be used as a representation of the wave motion; however, it must be remembered that when diagrams of this kind are used in discussing the properties of waves they are not pictures but only graphical descriptions of the state of affairs at a particular instant.

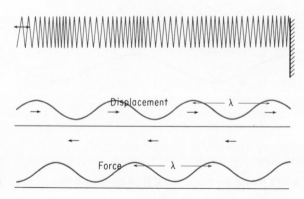

FIG. 18-2

Longitudinal wave in a spring: graph of the displacement; graph of the forces.

Whatever the type of wave, if it is produced by regular vibrations in a source, or by any kind of regular alternation, it can be characterized by three related quantities.

The *frequency* is the number of vibrations per second, where a complete vibration, or *cycle* is always considered to be from one extreme of the motion across to the other extreme and back to the starting point. Frequency (f) is usually stated in cycles per second, or simply "cycles,"[*] with the "per second" implied. The frequency is determined by the source, and must, of course, be the same at all points along the wave.

The *wavelength* is the distance between successive crests of the wave. Or, in the case of a longitudinal wave, for example, it is the distance between successive points where the displacement from normal positions is a maximum, or between points where the compression is a maximum. It is conventionally denoted by the Greek letter (λ) and is indicated in the diagrams in Fig. 18-2.

The *wave velocity* (V) is the speed with which the crests appear to travel. Now, in 1 second the source sends out f waves, each λ meters in length. When 1 second has elapsed, the crest of the first wave must be at a distance of $f\lambda$ meters from the source. But the distance the crest has traveled in 1 second is just the velocity, and therefore we must have

$$V = f\lambda,$$

or

(velocity) = (frequency) × (wavelength).

It has long been recognized that sound is transmitted through the air by means of longitudinal, mechanical waves. When the prongs of a tuning fork (Fig. 18-3) move outward, the air in front of them is compressed; when they move inward, the air can expand. As the prongs move back and forth in regular vibration, a train of compression waves is sent out, similar to the waves in the long spring, except that in this case waves are transmitted in all directions around the tuning fork.

The efficiency with which the vibrations can be set up in the air—and therefore the amount of energy transmitted and the loudness of the sound —depends on the surface area of the vibrating source. In order to hear distinctly the sound produced by a tuning fork, the fork has to be mounted on a hollow wooden box, or else its stem has to be pressed against a table

[*] The term "cycle" is often used with metric prefixes; a kilocycle is 1000 repetitions per second; a megacycle is 1,000,000 repetitions.

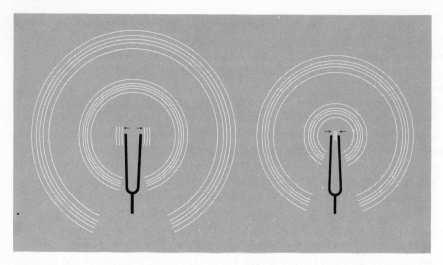

FIG. 18-3

Sound waves produced by a tuning fork.

top, so that a large area is set in vibration. Similarly, the sound of a violin string could not be heard more than a few feet away if the string were not mounted on the body of the instrument.

The velocity of sound in air is about 1100 feet per second. This does not depend on the atmospheric pressure, but it does vary with temperature, the velocity being proportional to the square root of the absolute temperature. The velocity can be estimated by observing the time required for the echo to return from the wall of a large, distant building, or from a steep cliff, but specially designed laboratory experiments furnish much more precise measurements.

What we recognize as "pitch" in a musical note, or somewhat less definitely in any sound, is directly related to the frequency of the sound waves. Audible sounds vary in frequency from about 20 cycles for the low-pitched rumble of the deepest notes on an organ to some 20,000 cycles for the highest pitched squeal. These limits vary very much for different people, and should only be taken as rough estimates. Using the relation of the last section, the corresponding wavelengths would be 55 feet for the rumble, and 0.66 inch for the squeal.

18-5   Resonance

Most things have one or more natural frequencies of oscillation. A solid body has its proper frequencies of mechanical vibration. In a long tube filled with air the natural frequencies are such that a longitudinal sound wave set up at one end and reflected from the far end reaches the source just as a new wave is leaving. The incident and reflected waves then combine to set the air column in oscillation, in what is called a *standing wave*. If the tube is closed at the far end, its length is just ¼, ¾, ⁵⁄₄, etc., times the wavelength of the standing wave (Fig. 18-4), and this rule determines the notes produced by the corresponding form of organ pipe.

If a body is exposed in any way to oscillations of its own natural frequency, sympathetic vibrations will be set up in it. For example, if two identical tuning forks are placed close together, and one of them is struck with a hammer, the other will vibrate in sympathy, or in *resonance*. Body parts of an automobile sometimes resonate to a particular frequency of the engine, and produce an unpleasant rattle when the car is traveling at a certain definite speed.

Figure 18-4 illustrates also a simple method of measuring the wavelength of a sound. A long tube is mounted with one end submerged in a deep vessel of water, so that the length of the air column can be varied by raising or lowering the tube. If a vibrating tuning fork is held over the open end of the tube, and the water level is slowly lowered, the air column will

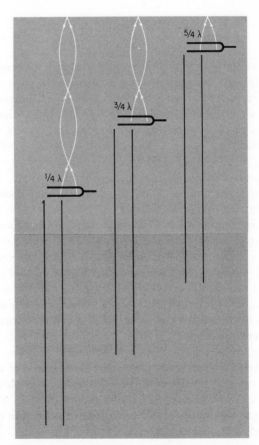

FIG. 18-4

Resonance in an air column of adjustable length.

be set in vibration by resonance when its length is equal to ¼ or ¾ of the wavelength of the sound. The vibrating air column is a much more efficient radiator of sound energy than the fork itself; consequently, when resonance occurs the sound becomes noticeably louder, and the resonance lengths can be easily determined.

In sound recording and reproducing equipment resonance is usually undesirable. Moving mechanical parts, such as the diaphragm of a microphone or the arm of a record player, have to be made as light as is feasible, so that their natural frequencies will be very high. They will then respond without resonance to all frequencies over a wide range, and will follow faithfully the oscillations of the incoming sound waves. On the other hand, resonance is essential in a radio receiver. An electrical circuit may also have its natural frequency, corresponding to the alternating current oscillations which would be set up in it by a sudden impulse, such as an electric spark. The function of the tuning condenser in a radio receiver is to make the circuit which picks up the radio waves resonate to the incoming signal. The receiver then becomes very sensitive to the required frequency, but rejects other frequencies.

18-6   Reflection and Refraction of Waves

Before we can argue whether a certain kind of energy (light, for example) is radiated by means of a wave motion or by some other mechanism, we must demonstrate that a beam of waves will be reflected and refracted according to the empirical laws governing these phenomena. In the case of reflection this is not difficult. Figure 18-5 shows waves radiating in all directions from a source (S) and striking a plane reflecting surface where they are turned back on themselves so that they appear to radiate from an image point at I. They may be any kind of waves, sound, water ripples, radio, light; the arguments to follow are perfectly general.

The law of reflection was stated in terms of rays extending in straight lines from the source, but we must bear in mind that this was an artificial geometrical device, introduced as a means of describing the behavior. If the wave velocity is the same in all directions, the wave fronts (that is, the successive crests) are spheres, and the geometrical rays can be identified with the radii of these spheres. Since the radii of a sphere are always at right angles to the surface, we can state a more general rule for drawing the rays that describe the behavior of a beam of waves; they are simply a set of lines drawn at right angles to the wave fronts, and therefore in the direction in which the wave is traveling. Furthermore, since we can always treat a very small portion of the surface of a sphere as if it were flat, we can restrict the argument to the case of "plane waves," where the wave fronts are a series of parallel planes (Fig. 18-6). The rays will then also be parallel, and so this corresponds to the case of a parallel beam, as discussed in several examples in Chapter 17.

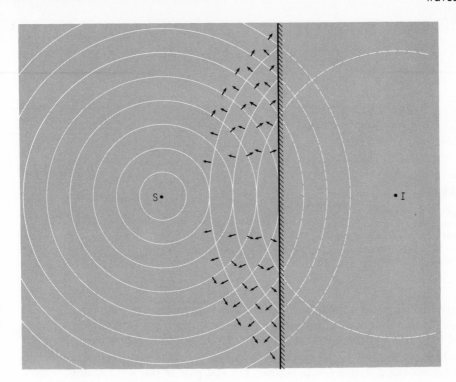

FIG. 18-5

Reflection of the waves from a point source.

The first portion of the wave strikes the surface at O, is reflected, and travels the distance OC in the same time as the last portion of the incident wave travels the distance BP. Therefore $OC = BP$. The formal geometrical proof that this makes the angles AON and NOC equal is hardly necessary; it is obvious from the figure. Waves therefore obey the law of reflection at equal angles.

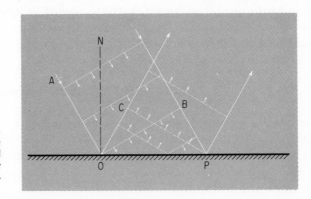

FIG. 18-6

Reflection of plane waves. OB is the incident wave front, CP is the reflected wave front, and the short arrows represent the corresponding rays.

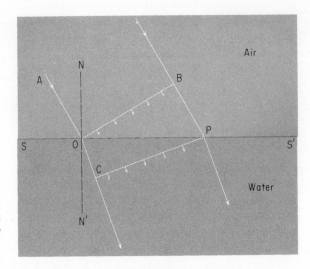

FIG. 18-7

Refraction of waves which are slowed down when they pass through the surface *SS'* separating two transparent media.

Figure 18-7 shows that the refraction of waves passing from one medium to another is due to a change in velocity. As a concrete example one might think of light passing from air, where the velocity is V_1, to water, where it is V_2, which is less than V_1. Now the first part of the wave is refracted at O, and travels the distance OC in water. The last part of the wave is still in air, and travels the distance BP in the same time. Therefore

$$\frac{BP}{OC} = \frac{V_1}{V_2}.$$

From this it can be shown to follow that

$$\frac{\sin(AON)}{\sin(N'OC)} = \frac{BP}{AC} = \frac{V_1}{V_2} = n \text{ (a constant)}.$$

Waves are therefore refracted according to Snell's law, and the index of refraction is simply equal to the ratio of the velocities. If the wave is slowed down in passing through the surface, the beam of waves will be refracted into the second medium, toward the normal, as light is in passing from air to water. Conversely, if the waves travel faster in the second medium, the beam will be refracted away from the normal.

18-7   *Interference and Diffraction of Waves*

Suppose two wave trains, of exactly the same frequency and wavelength, fall together on the same receiver. If two wave crests arrive at the same instant, as in Fig. 18-8(a), the forces exerted on the receiver will be doubled, and the effect is as if there were a combined wave of double the amplitude. If the troughs of one wave strike the receiver at the same instant as the crests of the other wave, the forces on the receiver will be equal and opposite at every instant, and the resultant effect will be nil [Fig. 18-8(b)].

Waves that combine their effects in this way are said to *interfere;* if they add as in case (a) it is said to be constructive interference, and if they oppose as in (b) it is destructive interference. Destructive interference is complete only if the two waves are of the same amplitude as well as the same frequency. In actuality, the waves are usually unequal in amplitude, and the destructive interference is only partial.

Interference effects can be produced in many different ways, for example, by a reflection, where there can be interference between the wave reflected from some surface and the wave received directly from the source. This can be nicely demonstrated by means of sound waves. If a tuning fork of fairly high frequency is held a few feet away from a flat surface, such as a smooth wall or a blackboard, there will be a strong echo. At some places in the room the echo will interfere destructively with the direct sound and the fork will hardly be heard; at other places the sound will be augmented by the echo. If the fork is now moved slowly toward or away from the wall, the interference pattern will change, and a listener at any particular spot in the room will hear the sound rise and fall as the pattern passes over him.

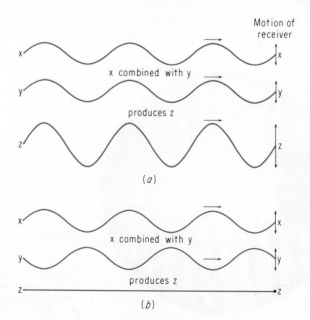

FIG. 18-8

Interference of two trains of waves: (a) constructive; (b) destructive.

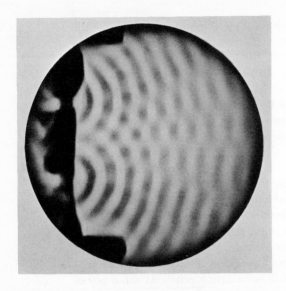

FIG. 18-9

Diffraction and interference of water ripples after passing through a pair of slits. (Photograph courtesy of Griffin and George Ltd., Wembley, England.)

Interference effects also accompany another phenomenon that is typical of wave motion, that of *diffraction*. If an obstacle is placed in the path of a beam of waves the outlines of the shadow are never ideally sharp; there is a limitation on the law of rectilinear propagation, and the waves bend more or less into the region behind the obstacle. One can think of the edge of the obstacle as providing a new, "secondary" source of the wave disturbance, and then there may be interference between diffracted waves coming from the edge and the direct wave from the original source, or between diffracted waves coming from opposite edges.

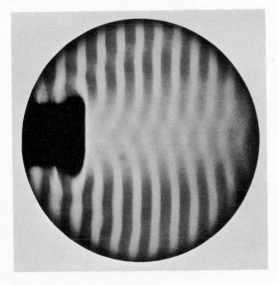

FIG. 18-10

Diffraction of water ripples as they pass a small obstacle. (Photograph courtesy of Griffin and George Ltd., Wembley, England.)

Interference and diffraction effects can be beautifully illustrated by means of ripples on water or on mercury, and Figs. 18-9 and 18-10 are photographs of water ripples of short wavelength. These photographs were obtained by illuminating the surface across which the ripples were traveling with a flashing light of exactly the same frequency as the tuning fork that was producing the ripples. Then the ripple pattern is exactly the same at every successive light flash, and the waves appear to stand still.

18-8   Wave Properties of Light

The first thorough discussion of the properties of waves was given by the Dutch physicist, Christian Huygens, in 1678, along with the hypothesis that light is transmitted by some form of wave motion. It is obvious that sound is a wave phenomenon, because in the case of sound there is an actual material medium, the air, which is set in vibration by the waves, and these vibrations can be directly observed. On the other hand, the wave nature of light is not at all obvious. A little before Huygens' work was published, Isaac Newton had put forward the alternative hypothesis that a beam of light consists of a stream of small "corpuscles," and there arose another of the great controversies that from time to time have interrupted the smooth flow of scientific discovery. The controversy over Huygens' wave theory and Newton's corpuscular theory is as famous in its way as that over the geocentric and heliocentric views of the solar system, and it was not to be finally resolved for over a hundred years.

Both theories led to the correct laws of reflection and refraction, for Newton was able to explain these on the basis of his corpuscles, by assuming them to be repelled by a mirror, and to be attracted by a transparent material such as water or glass. As they were originally presented, both theories had rather obvious difficulties. If there were forces exerted on Newton's corpuscles when they approached a reflecting or refracting surface, then it seemed that they must have mass, and yet it was impossible to detect any loss of mass from a source which is emitting light, or any gain of mass when light is absorbed. On the other hand, it seemed necessary to ascribe to the medium which might carry Huygens' waves quite impossible properties of rigidity and weightlessness.

When two theories compete we look for a crucial test to decide between them. One obvious distinction between the two theories of light concerns the velocity of transmission in a refracting medium such as water. According to Huygens, the velocity in water should be less than in air; according to Newton, it should be greater. However, it was 150 years before anybody succeeded in making a direct measurement of the velocity in water, by which time it had been firmly established that light involves waves of some kind.

The phenomenon that finally decided the controversy in favor of Huygens' waves is that of diffraction and interference. Waves, of any kind,

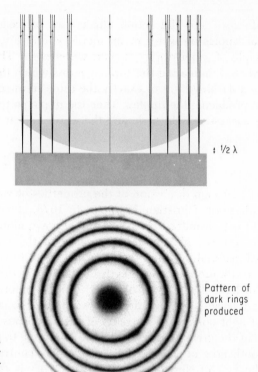

‡ ½ λ

Pattern of
dark rings
produced

FIG. 18-11

Interference between reflections
from the two sides of the film of air
formed between a lens and a flat
plate; the so-called Newton's rings
experiment.

must interfere under the proper experimental conditions, but in the case of
light the wavelength is very short, and the conditions necessary to observe
the interference in practice can be quite exacting. Actually, Newton himself, in his later years, described both diffraction effects and the interference effects that take place between the reflections from the two sides of a
thin film (Fig. 18-11). However, he gave a possible explanation of a way in
which his light corpuscles could produce these particular "appearances,"
and his authority was so great that for many years his successors seem to
have accepted his views without critical examination.°

Finally in 1801 Thomas Young, one of the very few advocates of the
wave theory in this period, performed an experiment in which the interference effect was unmistakable (Fig. 18-12). A fine slit (S) acts as a source
from which light flows in all directions, to fall on a second screen in which
there are two fine slits (S_1, S_2). These act as secondary sources, and waves
spreading out from them are superposed in the same way as the ripples in
Fig. 18-9. If a screen or a photographic plate is inserted in the area where

° Reading the description of these experiments in *Opticks*, the last book Newton wrote before
his death, leaves the impression that he himself was on the verge of discovering light waves.

the waves overlap, it will be crossed with a series of light and dark bands, as shown to the right of the figure.

A great many contemporary physicists were not convinced even by this demonstration, since diffraction at the slits was involved, and Newton had "explained" diffraction. It was not until Fresnel a little later produced interference effects independent of any diffraction that the wave theory began to be generally accepted. In one of Fresnel's experiments the light from a fine slit was reflected off a pair of mirrors inclined at a very small angle (Fig. 18-13). Thus the two interfering beams obeyed the laws of propagation, without diffraction, and the point was proved.

Interference experiments, besides demonstrating the wave nature of light, provide a means of calculating the wavelength, with great precision in the best modern techniques (cf. Sec. 5-2). It is found that the wavelength varies with the color, from about 0.00004 centimeter for deep violet to 0.000078 centimeter for the deepest visible red. There is no way of measuring the frequency directly; it has to be deduced from the relation between velocity,

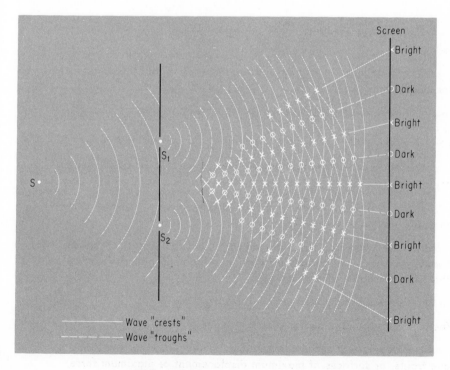

FIG. 18-12

Thomas Young's experiment, showing interference between the light waves diffracted at a pair of fine slits.

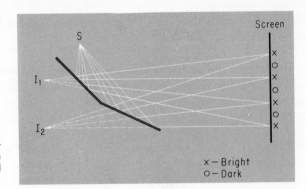

FIG. 18-13

Fresnel's experiment, showing interference between the light waves reflected from two mirrors.

wavelength and frequency (Sec. 18-3). Since the velocity of light is very nearly 3×10^8 meters per second, the frequency ranges from 7.5×10^{14} cycles for violet to 3.8×10^{14} for red.

GLOSSARY

Corpuscular theory The theory that light energy is transmitted by a stream of small particles.

Diffraction The bending of waves around an obstacle, so that the shadows are never ideally sharp.

Frequency Number of periodic repetitions, measured in cycles per second, where a cycle is a complete oscillation from one maximum to the next maximum in the same direction.

Interference Effect produced by superposing two or more waves of the same frequency.

Longitudinal wave Wave in which the motion and the forces are in the same direction as the wave is traveling.

Mechanical wave Wave in a material medium, in which the state of motion and the energy are transmitted from one portion of the medium to the next by forces that obey Newton's laws of motion.

Medium The substance through which a wave is traveling.

Pitch The pitch of a sound is measured by its frequency.

Plane wave Wave through a three-dimensional medium in which the successive wave fronts, or surfaces of maximum displacement or maximum force, are planes; a beam of plane waves is the same as a beam of parallel rays.

Propagation The travel of waves through or along a medium.

Resonance The phenomenon of a body being set in vibration by waves that have a frequency the same, or nearly the same, as the natural vibration frequency of the body.

Standing wave Wave in which all the particles (or forces) along the length of the wave reach their maxima at the same instant, so that there is no apparent propagation; usually produced by the combination of a forward wave with a return wave reflected along the same path.

Transverse wave Wave in which the motion and the forces (or the fields) are perpendicular to the direction of propagation.

Wavelength Distance, measured along the direction of propagation of a wave, from one maximum to the next maximum in the same direction (that is, from crest to crest).

EXERCISES

1. Describe how a wave motion transmits energy in (a) the case of a water wave, and (b) the case of a sound wave.

2. Distinguish between the two types of mechanical wave; give examples of each.

3. State and prove the relation between velocity, frequency, and wavelength for any type of wave.

4. Find: (a) the wavelength in normal air of the note middle A (frequency 440 cycles); (b) the velocity of sound in water, if middle A produces a wavelength of 3.25 meters; (c) the frequency of yellow-green light of wavelength 0.000055 centimeter; (d) the wavelength of a 12-megacycle radio wave; (e) the wavelength of an earthquake wave with an oscillation period of 6 seconds, traveling 10 kilometers per second.

5. Explain how the velocity of sound in air can be measured by observing resonance in a pipe of adjustable length.

6. Show that waves reflected from a plane surface will obey the empirical law of reflection of light.

7. Draw a diagram to illustrate how the rays are related to the wave front in a wave that is spreading out in all directions from a source.

8. Demonstrate by means of a diagram that waves will be refracted when they pass from one medium to another medium in which the velocity is different.

9. Calculate approximately the velocity of yellow light in water.

10. How does the velocity of light in glass vary with the color? with the frequency?

11. Try to find a simple piece of evidence that the velocity of sound in air is the same for all frequencies.

12. Describe either a natural phenomenon or a simple experiment which demonstrates interference (a) of sound waves, (b) of water waves.

13. What were the two competing theories of light that were current in the eighteenth century? Who was chiefly responsible for each theory? Name three things that would have been decisive if they had been known and understood at the time.

14. What is diffraction? Give some simple examples.

15. Describe the experiment performed by Thomas Young in 1801. Why did many of Young's contemporaries refuse to accept his conclusion?

16. Describe one of the decisive experiments performed by Fresnel.

17. Explain how the colors are produced in a thin transparent film, such as the wall of a soap bubble.

the spectrum and what it shows

19-1   The Spectrum and the Prism Spectrograph

The refractive index of a transparent material depends on the frequency or the wavelength of the light; normally it increases as the frequency increases, or as the wavelength decreases. The color of visible light also depends on the wavelength; beginning with the longest wavelengths in the deep red, we observe in succession all the colors of the rainbow, from red through orange, yellow, green, blue to violet, with the shortest visible wavelengths. It follows that if the light from a source that is producing many different wavelengths (as most sources do) is passed through a glass prism (Fig. 19-1), the different colors will be refracted differently, red the least and violet the most, and the light will be spread out into a *spectrum*.

To display the spectrum as clearly as possible, without too much overlapping of colors, it is necessary to place a fine slit in front of the source, and then to use a lens to project the light as a nearly parallel beam onto the prism. A second lens beyond the prism focuses the light on a screen or a photographic plate. The focal length of the lenses also depends on the

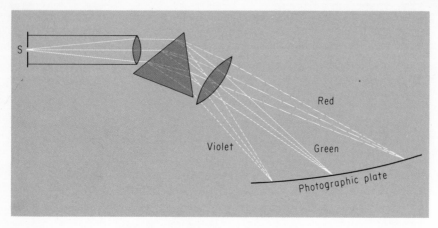

FIG. 19-1

Principle of the prism spectrograph.

wavelength, the short wavelength violet being focused closer to the lens than the long wavelength red. To allow for this the spectrum is usually received on a photographic plate set at an angle to the beam, and slightly curved. This device is known as a *spectrograph*—a most important laboratory tool. What the instrument actually produces on the screen or plate is a series of images of the fine slit, each image produced by light of a single pure color or wavelength. The result can readily be interpreted to give a list of the wavelengths produced by the light source, and these can yield a great deal of information about the nature of the source.

When the spectrograph is used photographically, the list of wavelengths is not limited to those of the visible colors, and the spectrum recorded on the photographic plate extends well beyond the visible limits of wavelength, 7800 angstrom units* in the red to 4000 Å in the violet. On the long wave side, deflected less than the red, lies the *infrared*, which can be photographed with specially prepared plates to wavelengths of about 11,000 Å. At the other end, deflected more than the violet, lies the short wavelength *ultraviolet*, to which photographic plates are sensitive without special treatment. For a great many purposes the information that can be deduced from the spectrum is incomplete unless the ultraviolet is recorded as far down the wavelength scale as possible. Glass is opaque to waves only a little shorter than the visible violet, and so laboratory spectrographs are frequently made with prisms and lenses of quartz, which is transparent to about 1800 Å, cutting off the spectrum at nearly the same place as does the air (Sec. 20-5).

---

* It has become customary to list wavelengths of the spectrum in *angstrom units* (Å). One Å = 10^{-8} centimeter, so the limits quoted are from 0.000078 to 0.000040 centimeter.

19-2   *The Diffraction Grating*

A spectrum can also be produced by means of a *diffraction grating,* which has many advantages, particularly in permitting very precise measurements of the wavelengths present in the spectrum, as long as there is plenty of light to work with. The grating consists, in principle, of a large number of closely spaced parallel slits (Fig. 19-2), which can be obtained by ruling lines on glass with a fine diamond point. Gratings have been made with as many as 40,000 lines to the inch, over a width of 6 inches, producing 240,000 lines in all.

The diffraction pattern produced by a pair of slits was illustrated in Sec. 18-7. Adding more slits makes the maxima in the diffraction pattern brighter and narrower; decreasing the distance between the slits increases the distance between the maxima. When there are several thousand closely spaced slits, the pattern produced with light of a definite wavelength consists only of a few narrow lines. Finally, if the light is that of an ordinary source with many wavelengths, each maximum of the diffraction pattern becomes a clearly defined spectrum. Moreover, a diffraction grating can be made self-focusing, by ruling the lines on the inside of a concave mirror,° so that the lenses necessary with a prism spectrograph can be eliminated. Another advantage is that concave reflection gratings can be used throughout the wavelength range from the longest infrared to the shortest ultraviolet. By working in vacuum, they can even be used to study wavelengths between those of ultraviolet and those of X rays, in the range where air is almost completely opaque.

° Concave gratings are usually ruled on polished speculum metal.

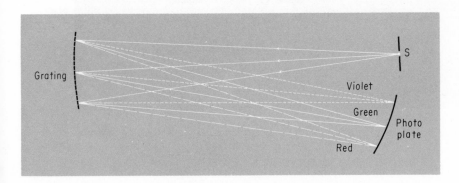

FIG. 19-2

A concave, self-focusing diffraction grating.

In the first place, a spectrum gives us important information concerning the general nature of the source—whether it is solid or gaseous, and if it is gaseous whether the gas consists of single atoms or of molecules composed of two or more atoms.

In the mercury vapor lamps used for street lighting in many cities, the light is produced by passing an electric current through mercury vapor in a glass tube. Again, in the neon signs, which give such brilliance to the downtown areas in any large city, the letters and figures are formed from glass tubes filled with a gas° through which an electric current can be passed.

In either mercury vapor or neon gas the ultimate sources of the light are mercury or neon atoms, "excited," that is, set into electrical oscillation, by the electric current. The atoms of any chemical element have a characteristic structure, and hence have characteristic oscillation frequencies. The light from sources such as those described contains only these definite frequencies, and so the spectrum consists of sharply defined bright lines (Fig. 19-3), although the number of lines may be quite large.

There are only a few chemical elements that can be obtained as gases or vapors of single atoms, to be used in a glass tube. However, there are other

° Only the brilliant red signs actually contain neon gas; other gases and mixtures of gases are used to produce other colors.

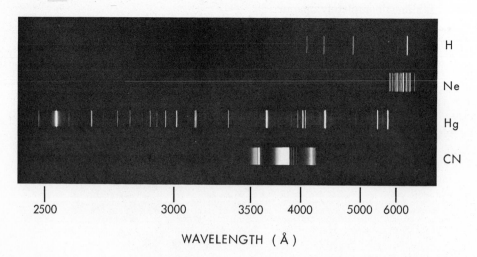

WAVELENGTH (Å)

FIG. 19-3

Photographs of emission spectra produced by gases and vapors; (H) hydrogen; (Ne) neon; (Hg) mercury; (CN) cyanogen. (Photographs by G. E. Shipley, University of Alberta.)

ways in which bright-line spectra can be obtained; one of the simplest is to make an electric spark jump between two metal terminals, in the open air. The heat of the spark vaporizes a little of the metal, and it happens that in nearly all cases the atoms of the metal are more easily excited into oscillation than are the molecules of the air. The spectrum of the light from the spark therefore shows the bright lines which are characteristic of the metallic elements present in the terminals. In this and other ways the atomic spectra of all the stable chemical elements have been studied and their characteristic wavelengths tabulated. If, therefore, we find a source of light giving a bright-line spectrum we immediately recognize two things; we deduce that the source is gaseous in nature, and we identify the chemical elements that are present in it.

19-4   The Continuous Spectrum of Heat Radiation

A great many common light sources are solid (or sometimes liquid) as for example, the tungsten filament of an ordinary electric light bulb. In this case the atoms are closely packed together, and they have no room to develop their characteristic oscillation frequencies. All frequencies are possible, and the spectrum shows a continuous gradation of color, from red to violet, without any characteristic lines.

A continuous spectrum tells us very little about the materials present in the source, but it is not without interest, for it turns out that we can deduce from it the temperature of the source. A "red-hot" stove gives most of its energy in the form of long wavelength infrared radiation; only a little overlaps into the red end of the visible spectrum; the blue and violet are practically absent. A "white-hot" tungsten bulb gives a much larger proportion of its energy in the form of visible light, and it looks white in comparison with the stove because its spectrum contains a fair amount of blue with some violet; the higher the temperature of the source, the farther the spectrum extends into the shorter wavelengths of violet and ultraviolet.

If the source of the light is a *blackbody*, which is defined as a body which when cold would absorb all the radiant energy falling upon it,* the temperature radiation when it is hot obeys two well established laws of heat radiation. The first law concerns the total energy produced, and is usually known as *Stefan's law:*

The radiation from a blackbody is proportional to the fourth power of the absolute temperature.

---

* Blackbody radiation is fairly well approximated when a dark, opaque material is heated, especially a block of carbon.

Using the most recent value of the proportionality constant, the radiation from a blackbody at temperature $T°K$ is $5.673 \times 10^{-8} T^4$ watts per square meter of surface.

The second law, known as *Wien's law*, concerns the effective wavelength of the radiation:

If the intensity of the radiation in different parts of the spectrum is plotted against the wavelength, for sources at different temperatures, a series of curves such as those in Fig. 19-4 is obtained. Then

The wavelength at which the maximum intensity occurs is inversely proportional to the absolute temperature,

or

$$\lambda_{\max} T = \text{constant.}$$

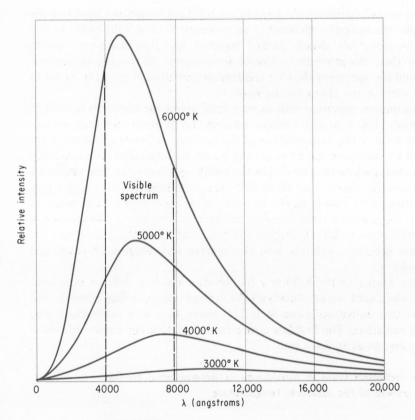

FIG. 19-4

Intensity at different wavelengths from blackbodies at different temperatures.

For example, the light from an old-fashioned kerosene lamp gives a continuous spectrum, with the intensity maximum at a wavelength of about 0.0002 centimeter in the infrared. From this it can be deduced that the light comes not so much from burning gases as from solid particles of soot that are carried upward in the flame, at a temperature of about 1500°K.

19-5   Band Spectra of Molecules

This chapter would not be complete without a brief reference to the distinctive appearance of the spectrum produced by a gaseous source when the gas is composed of molecules rather than of single atoms. Figure 19-3 includes a photograph of the spectrum of cyanogen produced by an electric spark between carbon terminals. Since the source is gaseous it produces lines of definite frequency, but there are a very large number of lines and they are grouped into *bands* that give the spectrum its fluted appearance. This should be contrasted with the spectrum of mercury in which there is no obvious regularity in the arrangement of the lines.* The band spectrum in Fig. 19-3 is characteristic of the molecule CN, and the banded appearance always indicates the presence of molecules.

19-6   Absorption Spectra

In the various spectra discussed so far, we have been interested in the wavelengths produced by the light source. We get a distinctive difference in the appearance of the spectrum if we take the light from a source that produces a continuous spectrum and pass it through various materials; the result is characteristic of the intervening material rather than of the source.

In Fig. 19-5 the light from an ordinary tungsten electric light bulb is depicted passing through a glass tube containing sodium vapor before it enters the spectrograph. The sodium atom has two closely spaced frequencies that correspond to a pair of spectrum lines in the orange-yellow,† of wavelengths 5890 and 5896 Å. Since these wavelengths are present in the light from the original source, the sodium atoms are set into oscillation by resonance.‡ The atoms radiate in all directions, and so the energy of these particular wavelengths is abstracted, or *absorbed,* from the original beam.

---

* Of course there must be rules governing the arrangement of the lines in an atomic spectrum, or we would not always get the same spectrum from the same element. However, the rules are far from obvious, and it took the combined efforts of many physicists over a period of more than half a century to work out the systematics of line spectra. It is a vast subject, and the details cannot possibly be given here.

† These spectrum lines provide the brilliant color when common salt is thrown on a fire, or in the light from a sodium vapor lamp.

‡ We are here arguing by analogy, and, as usual, analogies only tell part of the truth. It is not quite correct to speak of atoms oscillating in resonance (cf. Sec. 33-4).

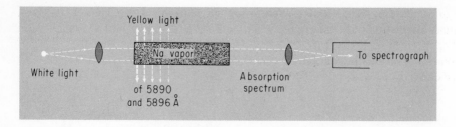

FIG. 19-5

Production of resonance absorption when a beam of light passes through sodium vapor.

A photograph of the spectrum now shows a pair of dark lines against a bright background, located precisely where the bright lines of a sodium vapor source would appear. The result is classed as a dark-line absorption spectrum.

In the case described the light absorbed is immediately reradiated. The energy of the sodium resonance frequencies has not been converted; it has merely been redistributed, and so lost to the original beam. In other cases where light of certain frequencies is absorbed, there may be a conversion of energy, possibly into heat or chemical energy. Or there can be a partial conversion, and the light which is reradiated may have a different frequency from that which was absorbed. Moreover, absorption spectra can show the same general types as emission spectra; dark lines when the absorbing material is an atomic vapor as in the case of sodium; bands, with the distinctive fluted appearance dark against the bright background, in the case of gas molecules; continuous absorption over a broad region of the spectrum, in the case of something like a piece of colored glass.

19-7   Spectrum of the Sun

Figure 19-6 is a photograph of a portion of the spectrum of the sun, with an emission spectrum of iron beside it on the same plate. The solar spectrum is clearly of the dark-line absorption type. Moreover, many of the dark lines correspond precisely to the bright lines of the iron spectrum. We can conclude immediately that light from a continuous spectrum source has passed through a region that contains, among other things, large quantities of iron vapor.

From the observation that the continuous background in the sun's spectrum has its maximum intensity at about 4900 Å in the yellow-green, we could estimate the temperature by the use of Wien's law (Sec. 19-4). We also know the total energy the sun is producing, and so we can also use Stefan's law of total radiation to estimate the temperature. The two estimates do not quite agree, because the sun is not quite a blackbody, and also because different layers must be at different temperatures. The second method is probably the more realistic, and gives an "effective" surface temperature of 5740°K, or about 9900°F.

At this temperature every conceivable material must be gaseous, and so we arrive at the following picture of the structure and composition of the sun. The main bulk must be a great sphere of incandescent gas, not burning in the usual sense of the word as the ancients thought it must be, but maintained at a high temperature by some internal source of energy (Sec. 31-2). This main body, technically known as the photosphere, is the source of the light, and produces a continuous spectrum because its density is comparable to that of ordinary solids and liquids. The photosphere merges gradually, without any clearly defined boundary, into a cooler and less dense atmosphere, which absorbs light from the photosphere and produces the dark lines in the spectrum.

The dark lines can be identified with emission lines of well-known chemical elements, as in the case of iron in Fig. 19-6, and so the composition of the sun's atmosphere can be determined. Of the 88 distinct elements that occur naturally on earth some 70 have been identified in the sun by means of their spectrum lines. The others are all scarce elements, which occur only in minute quantities on earth, and there is every reason to believe that they also occur on the sun in quantities too small to detect by means of the spectrum. The elements that appear to be most prominent are the simple gases, hydrogen and helium, and the common metals such as iron, magnesium, calcium, and sodium. That it is the line spectrum that is observed shows that these are almost all in the atomic form, as is to be expected, because at 5740°K all ordinary chemical compounds would be dissociated into their constituent elements. The occurrence of faint molecular bands shows, however, that certain compounds can still exist in small quantities at the temperature of the sun; in particular, titanium oxide and certain simple carbon compounds have been detected.

FIG. 19-6

A portion of the spectrum of the sun, compared with the emission spectrum of iron. (Photograph from Mt. Wilson Observatory.)

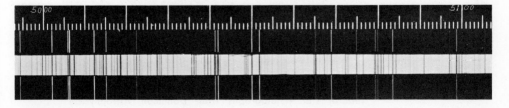

19-8   *Spectra of the Stars*

Figure 19-7 shows spectra of a few selected stars. These are all of the same dark-line type as that of the sun, showing that in general stars possess a luminous photosphere surrounded by an atmosphere, like the sun. However, a superficial look at the photographs in the figure seems to suggest that they vary greatly in composition. It turns out that this conclusion is quite wrong, and that the reason different lines appear in different spectra is that the effective surface temperatures are very different. The spectra at the top are of stars that are much hotter than the sun, and that appear blue in comparison; those at the bottom are of comparatively cool, red stars.

It happens that the sun is just at the right temperature to bring out the spectra of the metals most effectively. At a higher temperature hydrogen and helium show themselves more distinctly, and the metals are suppressed. At temperatures lower than that of the sun hydrogen only appears faintly, and molecular bands appear, to become the most prominent feature in the coolest red stars. Careful comparison of the lines of different elements, taking the temperature into account, has shown that the majority of stars have compositions similar to that of the sun, and that of the component elements hydrogen is by far the most abundant, whether or not it produces the strongest lines in the spectrum; helium is second and exceeds the total of all the remaining elements put together.

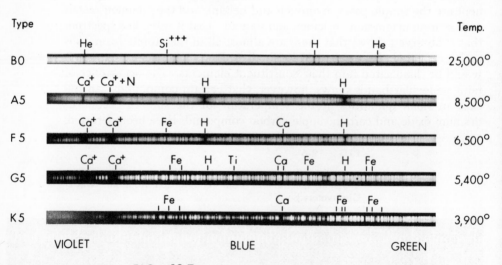

FIG. 19-7

Spectra of some selected stars; the spectrum at the top is that of a very hot, bluish star, that at the bottom of a relatively cool, reddish star. (Photographs from Dominion Astrophysical Observatory, Victoria, B. C.)

19-9   *The Doppler Effect*

There is a general property of waves which we have not yet discussed, and which is of particular importance in connection with spectra, especially with the spectra of the heavenly bodies. This is the apparent change in wavelength and frequency when either the source or the receiver are in motion. It was first thoroughly discussed by an Austrian physicist, Johann Doppler, in 1842, and has been known ever since as the Doppler effect.

Suppose we have a source (S, Fig. 19-8) which is moving to the right with a speed v, and which at the same time is sending out waves of sound, radio, or light with a wave velocity V and a frequency f. When the wave (1) was sent out the source was at S_1; when wave (2) was emitted the source had moved to S_2, and so on. It is clear from the diagram that the waves will be crowded together in front of the source, and will be spread out behind it. Let $\lambda_0 = V/f$ be the wavelength that we would observe if the

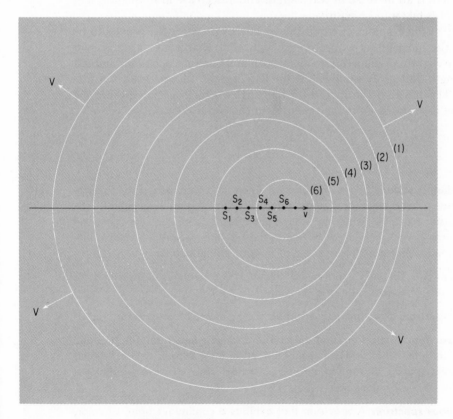

FIG.   19-8

Doppler effect, the apparent change in wavelength of waves coming from a moving source.

source were stationary, and let λ be the apparent wavelength when the source is approaching. The difference, $\lambda_0 - \lambda$, must be equal to the distance $S_1 S_2$, which the source moves during one period of its vibration, that is, during the time $1/f$. Therefore

$$\lambda_0 - \lambda = \frac{v}{f} = \frac{v}{V}\lambda_0.$$

It can be shown that we would observe exactly the same change of wavelength if the source were fixed, and the receiver were moving with a speed v. Moreover, there is no effect if either the source or the receiver is moving transversely, across the line of sight. The change in wavelength, or Doppler shift, therefore depends only on the component in the line of sight of the *relative* velocity of source and receiver. If they are approaching each other there is a decrease in wavelength and an increase in frequency, and the effect is considered to be negative; if they are receding from each other there is an increase in wavelength and a decrease in frequency, and the effect is taken to be positive.

Study of the Doppler effect in the spectra of the stars has proved to be one of the most useful astronomical tools. For almost all stars the dark lines are slightly displaced from their normal laboratory positions, and the wavelength shift gives immediately the line-of-sight velocity relative to the earth. This has to be corrected for the earth's orbital motion around the sun, and then the star's motion relative to the sun is known.

GLOSSARY

Absorption spectrum Spectrum obtained when the light entering the spectrograph has passed through a medium that absorbs certain frequencies. The term is used especially when the source produces a continuous spectrum and the absorbing medium is a gas or vapor; the resulting spectrum contains dark lines or bands that are characteristic of the absorbing medium.

Ångstrom unit The unit, equal to 10^{-10} meter, commonly used for listing the wavelengths of spectrum lines; abbreviated Å.

Atomic spectrum Spectrum characteristic of free atoms of an element.

Band spectrum A spectrum that consists of a large number of lines crowded so close together that under low magnification they appear to be grouped into bands spaced at regular intervals; characteristic of gases containing molecules of two or more atoms (Sec. 19-5).

Continuous spectrum A spectrum that exhibits a continuous band of color, showing that the source is producing all possible frequencies over a wide range; characteristic of heated solids and liquids, or of hot gases at a high density.

Diffraction grating A device consisting of a large number of closely spaced parallel slits or grooves, usually made by ruling with a diamond point on glass or metal, often on the inside of a concave mirror; used in spectrographs in place of a prism.

Doppler effect The apparent change in frequency and wavelength of light or of sound, when the source and the observer are moving relative to one another.

Infrared That portion of the radiation spectrum that has longer wavelengths and lower frequencies than those of visible red light; it is physically of the same nature as light, but is deflected less than the red in a prism spectrograph.

Line spectrum Spectrum that consists of a number of discrete sharp lines, usually without any obvious pattern; characteristic of gases and vapors that contain free atoms rather than molecules.

Molecular spectrum Spectrum characteristic of a gas or vapor that contains polyatomic molecules; synonymous with band spectrum.

Spectrograph Instrument designed to photograph, or otherwise record, the spectrum of a light source.

Spectroscope Instrument designed for the visual examination of spectra.

Spectrum Originally, the band of color produced by passing light through a prism. It should be considered as a means of determining the frequencies present in the light, and is then extended by analogy to include all the frequencies, whether they produce visible colors or not.

Ultraviolet Radiation with shorter wavelengths and higher frequencies than those of the visible violet.

EXERCISES

1. Indicate on a simple diagram the essential parts of a prism spectrograph, and name the function of each part.

2. What range of wavelengths is covered by visible light? What determines the upper and lower limits?

3. What is a concave grating? What are some of the advantages of a grating spectrograph, compared with the prism type?

4. What are the special characteristics of a source that is producing a line spectrum?

5. Suggest methods of obtaining the line spectra of each of the following elements: argon, hydrogen, mercury, sodium, iron.

6. What would you expect to see in the spectrum of an electric discharge through oxygen gas?

7. State Stefan's law of radiation. Explain briefly what it refers to, and how it can be used to deduce information about the source of radiation.

8. We speak of things being "red-hot" or "white-hot." State the physical law that is involved here. Explain how this law relates the color of the light from a hot source to the temperature. What must be the nature of the source in order that an accurate value of the temperature can be deduced in this way?

9. What can you deduce about the nature of the source from the appearance of the spectrum in each of the following cases: (a) The spectrum consists of a few bright lines in the visible and ultraviolet, with no obvious regularity in the arrangement. (b) The spectrum shows a continuous band of color, strong in the red, and fading out in the blue, with several dark lines superposed on it. (c) The appearance is the same as in (b), except that the lines are bright. (d) The spectrum consists of a number of equally spaced bands. (e) The spectrum shows a continuous background, strongest in the yellow, crossed by a great many dark lines; when placed beside a spectrum of iron, each line of the latter has a corresponding dark line in the unknown spectrum, but the dark lines are all shifted a little bit toward the red, as compared with the lines in the laboratory spectrum of iron. (f) The spectrum is continuous, and strongest in the blue, with a few prominent dark lines.

10. Describe what is seen in the spectrum of sunlight, and explain how this spectrum is produced.

11. What is the surface temperature of the sun? Describe two ways in which this can be estimated.

12. What elements exist in the sun? Which elements appear to be the most abundant, and which actually are the most abundant? Why is there a difference between the appearance and the fact? Are there any compounds in the sun?

13. A superficial examination of the spectra of a number of bright stars seems to indicate that they are very different in composition. Is this conclusion correct? If not, what is the reason for the apparent difference?

14. Explain qualitatively how the Doppler effect is produced when (a) a source of light is approaching you, and (b) you are approaching the source. There is a fundamental principle of physics according to which there cannot be any difference in the appearance of the spectrum in the two cases. State this principle, and give another example of its application.

15. In a certain spectrum the two sodium lines that normally have wavelengths of 5890 and 5896 Å are found at 5893 and 5899 on the wavelength scale. Estimate the velocity of the source in meters per second and in miles per hour. In what direction is the source moving?

16. How fast would a source of sound have to be traveling so that the pitch would be raised by a semitone? (Notes that differ in pitch by a semitone have frequencies very nearly in the ratio 16:15.)

electromagnetic radiation

The evidence discussed in Chapter 18 showed that light energy is transmitted by some kind of a wave. There is further evidence, in the phenomenon of *polarization*, that the waves belong to the transverse class. There are a great many crystals whose refractive indices are different for light waves vibrating in different directions, and in the case of a colored crystal the color may depend on the direction of vibration of the light. An extreme case is iodosulfate of quinine, which crystallizes in long needles, and which is nearly colorless if the light is vibrating parallel to the length of the needles, deep purple if it is vibrating at right angles to the needles. The material sold commercially as Polaroid consists of sheets of celluloid, coated with tiny crystals of the iodosulfate, laid down in such a way that the needles are all parallel.

To use an analogy solely for the purpose of explaining what polarization means, let us imagine that the Polaroid sheet comprises a lot of parallel slots, so that a transverse wave can pass through it if the vibrations are parallel to the slots, but will be stopped if the vibrations are at right angles to the

317

slots. Now, a beam of light from any ordinary source is actually being produced by a great many different atoms. The light from any one atom will have a definite direction of vibration, but the beam will contain all sorts of vibrations, all of them, however, lying in a plane at right angles to the direction in which the beam is traveling, as shown on the left of Fig. 20-1. If this beam falls on a sheet of Polaroid in which the "slots" are vertical, vertical vibrations will pass through, and horizontal vibrations will be stopped. For vibrations inclined to the slots, a portion of the light will get through and will be forced to vibrate vertically. Therefore the light emerging from the Polaroid is all vibrating vertically, and contains on the average half the intensity of the original beam. The beam is now said to be *polarized;* that is, it has a definite direction of vibration.

The eye has no mechanism for distinguishing direction of vibration; the polarized beam *looks* like any other. To show that the light is polarized we must look through another sheet of Polaroid, and rotate it. When the slots of the second Polaroid are horizontal, as shown in the figure, the light from the first Polaroid cannot get through. If the second sheet is turned parallel to the first one, light is transmitted. Therefore the test for polarization of the light is to look through a piece of Polaroid (or some other similar device) and notice whether the intensity changes when the Polaroid is rotated. The proof that light waves are transverse is that polarization effects occur, for if the waves were longitudinal, the direction of vibration would already be fixed, and there could be no effects such as those produced by rotating the Polaroids.

Light reflected at an angle from any surface is partly polarized, with vibrations mostly parallel to the surface. Light from the blue sky is also partly polarized, with vibrations at right angles to the sun's rays. The purpose of Polaroid sunglasses, besides reducing the intensity of the light, is to cut off much of the reflected light from the road or the distant sky, and so reduce the glare.

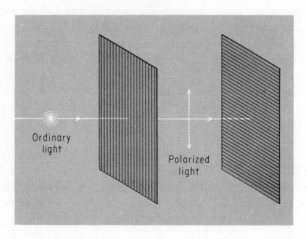

Ordinary
light

Polarized
light

FIG. 20-1

How "crossed" Polaroids
cut off a beam of light.

20-2   *Maxwell and the Electromagnetic Theory of Light*

The experiments on interference and on polarization demonstrated that light involves some kind of a transverse wave, but the mechanism of the wave remained mysterious. In 1861 Maxwell published the first of his epoch-making papers on the theory of electricity and magnetism, which culminated in his great work, *Treatise on Electricity and Magnetism,* in 1873. In this work he collected all the different laws—Coulomb's law of force, the law of magnetic field around a current, the law of induction—and organized them into a consistent whole on a sound mathematical basis, just as Isaac Newton had organized the science of mechanics. In doing so, he made an important new contribution. An electric current in a wire produces a magnetic field; a varying magnetic field produces an EMF in a closed circuit. These are not precise converses; also, what about cases where there is no actual closed circuit, so that there is no real flow of current, but only a varying electric field? In the case of electromagnetic induction, when there is no actual circuit in which the current might flow, the induced EMF really represents an electric field in space. For reasons of symmetry between the laws of electricity and those of magnetism, Maxwell argued that any varying electric field must produce a magnetic field:

A varying magnetic field in space produces an electric field (mathematically equivalent to Faraday's law of induction);

conversely,

A varying electric field produces a magnetic field (Maxwell).

From these two laws Maxwell predicted theoretically that a change in the electric and magnetic conditions of a circuit would not be observed instantly at a distant point, but that the effects of the change would travel outward from the source with a finite velocity, which he computed and found to be very nearly equal to the measured velocity of light. Moreover, since electric and magnetic fields involve a form of potential energy, this energy has to be provided by the source, and has to flow outward into the field with the same velocity.

In particular, if the source is oscillating with a definite frequency, so that it is continually varying, a continuous train of alternating fields must flow outward into the surrounding medium. This will exhibit the essential characteristics of a wavelike phenomenon, namely, a definite frequency and velocity, and therefore a definite wavelength. Moreover, if the frequency of oscillation is high enough, so that the fluctuations of field are rapid, the flow of energy can be considerable, and so the *electromagnetic waves* can transport energy. In this, Maxwell not only predicted the existence of what we now know as a radio wave, produced by an electric circuit, but he also made the suggestion, abundantly confirmed by later developments, that light waves might be electromagnetic in nature, produced by electrical oscillations within the atoms and molecules which are the ultimate sources of the light.

20-3   The Mysterious Ether

Huygens, who originated the wave theory of light, Fresnel, who finally established its validity by his experiments, and nearly all physicists throughout the eighteenth and nineteenth centuries, thought that the light waves must be actual vibrations of a mysterious medium known as the *ether*,° which was supposed to pervade all space, both the empty space between the stars and the interstices between the atoms of matter. Maxwell himself was a firm believer in the ether, and in part of his theory he discussed electric and magnetic fields in terms of stresses set up in the ether. He therefore still thought of light waves as something rather like transverse vibrations in an actual elastic medium, but suggested only that the oscillating stresses set up by a light wave were of the same nature as those set up around a charged body or a current-carrying wire. This part of his theory has had to be abandoned, but Maxwell's ether stresses were only an appendage to his general mathematical treatment, and rejecting them does not detract from the usefulness of his basic work. Maxwell's mathematics are still the foundation of all theoretical discussions in electricity and magnetism, and still provide the connecting link between those phenomena and the phenomena of light. Along with Newton's laws of mechanics, Maxwell's laws of electricity and magnetism constitute the basis of so-called *classical physics*.

Unfortunately for those who, in the nineteenth century, sought for mechanistic explanations of all nature, the ether had to have extraordinary properties. The velocity of transverse mechanical waves in any medium depends upon the ratio of rigidity to density, and in order to transmit waves at 300,000 kilometers per second, the rigidity would have to be greater than that of steel, while the density was less than that of the best laboratory "vacuum." However, the controversy which finally disposed of the ether concerned the question whether it was fixed in space, as seemed to be required by astronomical observations, or whether it was carried along with the earth, as seemed to be required by laboratory experiments on refraction.

° No connection, of course, with the organic chemical known by the same name.

In 1887 Michelson and Morley, then at the Case School of Applied Science, devised a very sensitive method of comparing the velocity of light in different directions in space. If the ether were fixed, with the earth swimming through it without any friction, the velocity of light in an east-west direction should be different from that in a north-south direction. The experiment showed no difference—a result that might have been expected on the ground that there can be no way of detecting the earth's motion through space by experiments carried out upon the earth without observations of some other body. The final conclusion, later further clari-fied by Einstein in his theory of relativity (Sec. 33-10), is that the ether does not exist, or if it does exist there is no possible way of detecting it, and so we might as well ignore it.

In the end we have to say that light energy is transmitted by electro-magnetic waves, but this does not bring us any closer to a nice descriptive picture of the mechanism. The light beam has wavelike properties, for there is a definite frequency which is the same at all points along the beam, and the energy is propagated with a definite velocity. The beam displays the phenomena of diffraction and interference, and there is a measurable wavelength. Light can be polarized and so its wavelike properties corre-spond to those of the transverse class. We find in fact that the electric field, the magnetic field, and the direction of propagation are mutually at right angles, and that the electric field corresponds to what was described in Sec. 20-1 as the "direction of vibration." However, we should avoid thinking of a light wave as if it were anything like a transverse wave in a rope or like a water wave. All we can say is that it involves rapidly oscil-lating electric and magnetic fields, and we have to leave it at that. Both the fields and the light wave are nondelineable—they cannot be pictured or described in words. If we use a wavy line in discussing certain of the properties of light, all we are really doing is drawing a graph of the elec-tric field strength associated with the wave.

20-4   Waves From an Oscillating Electric Circuit

Electromagnetic radiation produced by oscillations in an electric circuit was first observed experimentally by a German physicist, Heinrich Hertz, in 1886, using the apparatus illustrated in Fig. 20-2. Electric charge would build up on the large plates until a spark jumped across the gap to discharge them. This would produce a surge of current, and therefore a rapid change of the magnetic flux threading the circuit. This in turn would produce an induced EMF, which would recharge the plates in the opposite direction. The result was that every time the spark coil produced a spark in the gap, charge oscillated back and forth between the plates with a frequency which depended upon their dimensions, and which in Hertz' apparatus

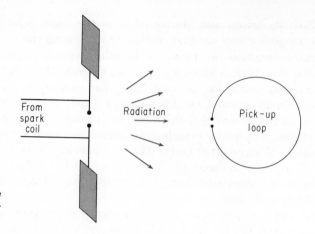

FIG. 20-2

Hertz' experiment on the production of electromagnetic waves.

was about 3×10^8 cycles per second.* As Maxwell had predicted, the varying electric and magnetic fields produced electromagnetic waves, with a flow of energy, in the region around the oscillating circuit. The waves, in their turn, set up oscillations in another circuit, some distance away. As receiving circuit, Hertz used a loop of wire with a small gap, and observed tiny sparks across this gap whenever oscillations occurred in the principal circuit.

*In modern radio practice an oscillating circuit usually contains a coil and a condenser consisting of two or more plates separated by a thin layer of air or insulating material (Fig. 20-3). As the plates discharge through the coil, the varying current induces an EMF. This tends to keep the current flowing, which in turn recharges the plates in the opposite direction, so that charge oscillates back and forth between the plates, with a definite frequency determined by the dimensions of the coil and condenser. A source of energy, provided with the help of a radio tube or a transistor, keeps the circuit in continual oscillation.

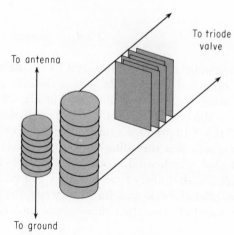

FIG. 20-3

A circuit containing a coil and a condenser; oscillations of a definite frequency are set up and induce corresponding oscillations in the antenna.

Hertz demonstrated that the effects he was observing were in fact due to the propagation of waves with a finite velocity by showing that they could be reflected off a wall, and that they could be diffracted and could interfere like sound or light waves. He was able to measure the wavelength, which was about 1 meter. However, he made no suggestions for any practical uses of the waves, and he could have had no inkling of the impact his electromagnetic waves were going to have on society in the next 50 years or so, through the development of radio and eventually of television. These developments had, indeed, to wait for another basic discovery, that of the free electron, and for another technical invention, that of the radio tube.

Although we must credit Hertz with the first production and study of what we now know as radio waves, his apparatus would have been very inefficient as a transmitter. To radiate any appreciable amount of energy the oscillating electric circuit has to be connected to an antenna, rather as a vibrating tuning fork has to be mounted on a sounding box. The simplest type of antenna, and a very efficient radiator, is a vertical steel mast, as actually used by many radio broadcast stations. We then have the situation illustrated in Fig. 20-4, where the generator which produces the electrical oscillations is represented by a "black box,"* connected to the

* The term "black box" is common slang among physicists, to indicate a piece of complicated apparatus, usually purchased complete from an electronics company, when they are not concerned with what goes on inside the box, but only in using its output as an experimental tool.

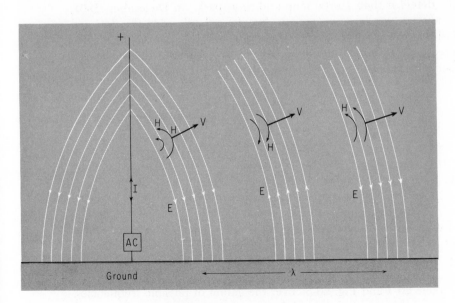

FIG. 20-4

Radiation of electromagnetic waves, caused by electrical oscillations in a vertical antenna.

vertical antenna. The free end of the antenna is charged alternately positive and negative by the generator, so that when it is positive an electric field is directed from the top of the mast toward ground. At the same time the current flowing in the antenna sets up a magnetic field, whose lines of force are horizontal circles around the mast. As these fields are being set up, energy must flow out from the mast with velocity c, equal to the velocity of light. Then the current and the charge on the antenna change sign, and fields in the reverse direction begin to build up. In the meantime the previous fields are still traveling outward; they break off, so to speak, from the antenna which originated them, and travel on into space, carrying the radiated energy. Since the direction of propagation of the waves is at right angles to the plane in which the electric and magnetic fields lie, most of the energy is radiated horizontally all around the mast; very little is transmitted vertically, parallel to the length of the antenna. It should be noted also that the waves are polarized, with the electric field vertical, parallel to the antenna.

The name usually associated with the invention of "wireless," and with the beginnings of the radio industry, is that of the Italian engineer, Guglielmo Marconi (1874–1937), rather than that of Maxwell who predicted the existence of electromagnetic waves, or of Hertz who first succeeded in producing them. We owe to Marconi the idea of using the waves to transmit messages without the aid of conducting wires, the idea of the antenna to increase the efficiency of radiation, and a much more sensitive detector than Hertz' loop and tiny spark. In December, 1901, waves radiated by a large antenna in Newfoundland, using the dots and dashes of the Morse telegraphic code, were picked up by Marconi's sensitive detector in Ireland, 1500 miles away. By prearrangement, the first signal sent and received consisted of the three dots of the Morse letter "S".

20-5   *The Complete Electromagnetic Spectrum*

Light, with wavelengths of about 5×10^{-5} centimeter, Hertz' meter-long waves, the waves of a kilometer and more in length that were used by Marconi to span the Atlantic Ocean, are all electromagnetic radiations. They all have the characteristic wave properties, they all travel with the same velocity in a vacuum, and they are all produced by electrical oscillations of some kind. Oscillations of other frequencies must produce waves in other wavelength ranges, and each range may have its special uses. There is no need to give an account of the historical details of the various radiation phenomena which have been proved to involve electromagnetic waves. Table 20-1 and Fig. 20-5 cover the gamut of possible frequencies. There is a continuous gradation of the wave properties, and different frequency ranges differ only in the methods of producing and detecting the waves, and in the physical phenomena with which they are associated.

TABLE 20-1   DIFFERENT KINDS OF ELECTROMAGNETIC WAVES

Frequency Range (in cycles)	Kind of Wave and Practical Uses	Wavelength Range
25 to 1,000	Alternating current electric circuits (the waves are not used but can cause radio interference).	12,000 to 300 kilometers
100,000 to 10,000,000	Radio, used mainly for communication, including commercial broadcasting.	3,000 to 30 meters
10^7 to 3×10^{10}	High frequency, used mainly for television and radar.	30 meters to 1 centimeter
	Overlap slightly with:	
2×10^{10} to 3.9×10^{14}	Infrared, produced mainly by hot bodies and including radiant heat, detected by heating effects, also some vibrations of molecules.	1.5 to 7.8×10^{-5} centimeter
2.7×10^{14}	Longest wavelength that can be photographed.	11×10^{-5} centimeter
	Physical properties merge continuously into:	
3.9×10^{14} to 7.5×10^{14}	Visible light, the narrow range which alone affects the eyes of mammals.	7.8×10^{-5} to 4×10^{-5} centimeter
	Physically similar to:	
7.5×10^{14} to 16×10^{14}	Ultraviolet, produced in the same way as visible light, and easily photographed.	4×10^{-5} to 1.85×10^{-5} centimeter
16×10^{14} to about 3×10^{17}	Range over which air is almost completely opaque, and therefore of little practical use.	1.85×10^{-5} to 10^{-7} centimeter
3×10^{17} to 10^{20}	X rays, including those used in medicine.	10^{-7} to 3×10^{-10} centimeter
	Overlap with:	
10^{19} to 10^{21}	Gamma rays, produced by radioactive materials.	3×10^{-9} to 3×10^{-11} centimeter

20-6   *Infrared Radiation*

Figure 20-5 shows that visible light covers only a very small fraction of the whole range of possible frequencies. The visible range is limited on the long wavelength side by the longest waves which can excite chemical effects in the retina of the mammalian eye, about 7800 Å in the deep red. It is limited on the short wavelength side, at about 4000 Å in the violet, by absorption in the cornea, which is opaque to shorter waves. As far as the source that produces the light and the physical properties of the waves are concerned, these limits are purely accidental, and the spectrum of a light source extends some distance beyond either end until limitations of the source, of the prism, or of the method of detection are encountered.

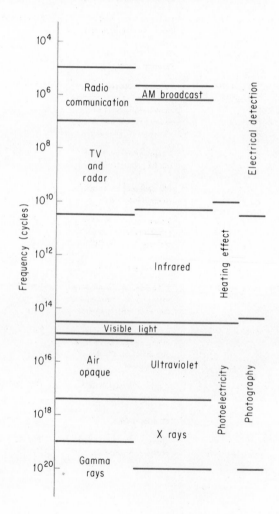

FIG. 20-5

Frequency ranges of electromagnetic radiation.

FIG. 20-6

An infrared photo-graph, compared with the same scene taken in ordinary light. (Photographs by J. Salt, University of Alberta.)

Waves longer than the visible red are referred to as infrared, because they have lower frequencies than the red. As indicated in the table, they are associated mainly with heat radiation, especially with long wavelengths up to a millimeter or more. However, they do have some properties which are physically the same as those of visible light. The shorter infrared waves affect specially treated photographic film, and photographs taken with infrared radiation show some interesting effects. Scattering by small particles in the atmosphere is very much stronger for short wavelengths (Sec. 17-4), and so infrared will penetrate a fog or smoky haze which completely obscures ordinary white light. Figure 20-6 includes a photograph of a landscape taken with a film sensitive to infrared, using a filter which cuts out most of the visible spectrum. In the infrared photograph the blue sky appears black, making the clouds stand out in strong contrast. But the most striking feature is that the trees appear bright; the chlorophyll in the leaves, which absorbs red and reflects green, also reflects strongly in the infrared just beyond the visible limit.

The characteristic spectra of atoms and molecules extend well into the infrared, and this wavelength range is particularly interesting for the absorption spectra of many organic liquids, providing useful identification tests. Beyond 11,000 Å photography is useless, and the radiation has to be detected by means of a sensitive thermometer.

20-7   Ultraviolet "Light"

The region of frequencies greater than the visible violet is known as ultraviolet, and these waves are found beyond the violet in an ordinary prism spectrograph. This frequency range is of utmost interest to the spectroscopist because it covers the characteristic identification spectra of a great many atoms. However, the more general interest in ultraviolet radiation is due to its ability to cause many kinds of *photochemical reactions,* in which radiant energy is directly converted into chemical energy.

One such reaction is, of course, that which occurs in silver bromide in the photographic process. The photographic emulsion on the film contains thousands of minute silver bromide crystals. The direct action of the light reduces the silver bromide and produces a tiny speck of free silver on the surface of the crystal. The developer is a chemical which attacks silver bromide only in the presence of metallic silver, so that when the exposed film is placed in the developing solution, the reduction of silver bromide to silver continues in only those grains which were previously affected by the light. The fixing solution dissolves away any silver bromide which remained unaffected, leaving the picture in the form of a black deposit of metallic silver. It is a frequent, but not exclusive, feature of photochemical reactions that they are caused by any wavelength shorter than a certain definite limit, and this is true of the photographic process, where the primary action on the silver bromide takes place with any wavelength shorter than about 5500 Å in the yellow-green. The limit can be extended to longer wavelengths by saturating the film with a dye that absorbs the light to be photographed.

Other photochemical reactions that have already been mentioned are photosynthesis in the chlorophyll of green plants, and the production of ozone in the upper atmosphere. Still others of interest are the production of the brown pigment known as melanin by the effect of violet and ultraviolet radiation on the skin of white people, and the production of vitamin D, directly in the human skin and indirectly in various foodstuffs.

Another important radiation phenomenon is *fluorescence,* which means in general the absorption of one wavelength, and reradiation of part of the energy at a longer wavelength. This can occur in any part of the wavelength range, but the cases of especial interest are those in which very short wavelengths excite radiation in the visible range. For example, there are a number of materials that emit visible light under the influence of X rays, and this effect finds useful application in the *fluoroscope* used by radiologists to make visual examination of the internal organs of the body.

Similarly, invisible ultraviolet radiation excites visible fluorescence in a great many materials, often producing brilliant colors. Many of the applications of this phenomenon are more spectacular than useful, where "black light" from a source strong in ultraviolet is passed through a filter that absorbs most of the visible spectrum, and then is used to excite brilliantly colored fluorescence in suitable active materials. However, most natural phenomena find a practical application sooner or later, and this is no exception. In fluorescent lighting, used so extensively in large buildings, the source of the energy is an electric current carried by mercury ions in a partially evacuated tube. Initially, the light is that of the characteristic line spectrum of mercury, with strong emission lines in the green and blue, and some in the yellow, but very weak in the red, so that the light from the mercury alone has a harsh blue-green quality. But mercury also emits very strongly in the ultraviolet, at a wavelength of 2536 Å. The energy of this radiation, which would otherwise be wasted for illumination purposes, excites fluorescence in a suitable material coated on the inside of the glass tube, not only giving a pleasanter quality to the light but conserving energy as well.

20-9   *X rays*

For practical purposes the short wavelength limit of the ultraviolet is 1850 Å, the point at which the strong absorption bands of oxygen gas begin. For wavelengths a little less than this, oxygen absorbs so strongly that a millimeter thickness of air at ordinary pressures is almost completely opaque. At wavelengths somewhat beyond the oxygen limit all other materials that we usually think of as transparent also absorb almost completely. However, an electric spark between metal terminals can still produce radiation in this wavelength range, and the radiation can still be detected by a photographic plate. The range has, therefore, been explored experimentally by using reflecting diffraction gratings to form the spectrum and by working entirely in vacuum, but so far there are no practical uses for the "vacuum ultraviolet."

At very much shorter wavelengths, beginning about 10 Å, all light materials again become more or less transparent, and we enter the X-ray range. X rays of wavelength much longer than 10 Å can be produced, and X-ray spectra extend far into the range where experiments have to be carried out in vacuum, overlapping with the vacuum ultraviolet. Around 100 to 200 Å the only distinction between X rays and ultraviolet light lies in the way in which the radiations are produced, but this range is only of academic interest.

X rays were first observed by Wilhelm Roentgen, in Germany, in 1895, when he was studying electrical discharges in gases at very low pressure. He found, more or less by accident, that when the charged particles that carried the current (the cathode rays, or free electrons, Sec. 21-2) impinged on the glass wall of a tube, or on a solid "target" within the tube (Fig. 20-7), they produced some kind of radiation which passed through the glass and could be detected some distance away, either by photography or because they excited fluorescence in various materials. Because he was unable to establish the nature of this new radiation he referred to them as "X rays," and the term has persisted in popular usage, although many scientists prefer to call them Roentgen rays, after the discoverer.

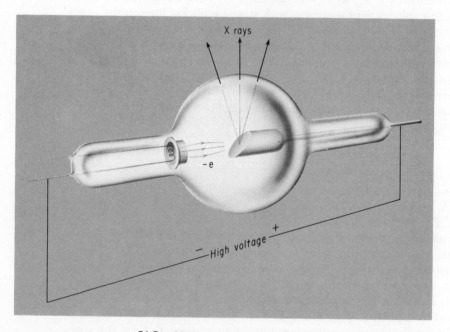

FIG. 20-7

An early type of X-ray tube; cathode rays from the high-voltage negative terminal are concentrated on a solid target, where the impact produces the X rays.

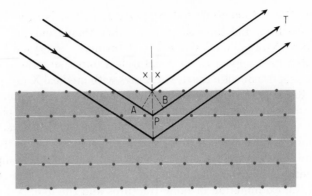

FIG. 20-8

Selective reflection of X rays from the interior planes of a crystal.

X rays are only very slightly refracted, so slightly that it was many years after Roentgen's discovery before refraction by a prism was observed. Neither are they reflected in the usual sense, or diffracted in the type of experiment used to demonstrate the wave nature of light. As a result the usual controversy over the nature of the radiation arose. However, interference effects were eventually found, proving that the X rays have wavelike properties and providing a means of measuring the wavelength.

The interference is observed in a special type of reflection which occurs when X rays fall on a crystal, with its regular arrangement of atoms and molecules. The atoms of the crystal can be considered to be arranged in regular parallel planes, as shown in Fig. 20-8. A beam of X rays will not be appreciably reflected from the surface of the crystal, but will penetrate, and there will be a very weak reflection from each successive plane of atoms. If the difference in the paths which different reflections have followed (the distance *APB* in the figure) is a whole number of wavelengths, the weak reflections from the different planes reinforce each other and may combine to produce an observable intensity in the direction *PBT*. The reflection obeys the law of equal angles, but it takes place only at particular values of the angle, depending on the wavelength of the X rays and on the distance between the crystal planes.

If the distance between the planes of atoms is known, or can be calculated, the experiment provides a method of producing X-ray spectra, and of measuring their wavelengths. As in the case of light, there are both continuous and line spectra. The latter depend on the elements present in the target of the X-ray tube, only very slightly affected by the chemical combination in which these elements occur, and so X-ray spectra can sometimes be useful in identifying elements. If X rays with a known line spectrum are used, the experiments provide a means of measuring the distance between the crystal planes; the ability to obtain these measurements has led to the development of a very efficient method of crystal analysis. It is not necessary to have perfect crystals, because the reflections take place from the internal planes rather than from the surface. It is possible by X-ray crystal analysis to determine the crystal form of many materials which appear to be structureless under superficial examination.

Most people associate the use of X rays with medical X-ray photography. It was Roentgen himself who discovered that the rays would penetrate more readily through flesh than through bone, and he took photographs of bone structures, and suggested how the rays could be used by medical practitioners. The medical profession responded readily to the useful new tool, and long before the nature of the rays was properly understood by the scientists, they were being used in hospitals, with rather crude apparatus, for the examination of bone fractures and the like. What makes the use of X rays for medical diagnosis possible is the fact that the absorption of short wavelength X rays by different materials increases with the atomic weight of the elements present: bone contains calcium and phosphorus, whereas the soft parts of the body are composed mainly of lighter elements, so that the bones absorb the X rays more than the flesh, and show light against a darker background in the photograph. It should be noted that X-ray photographs are really shadowgraphs. Since there is only very slight

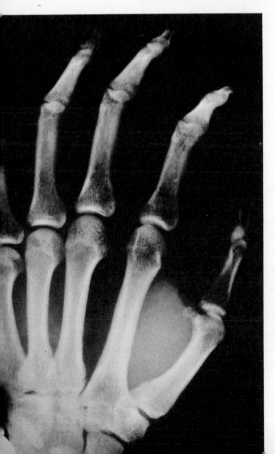

FIG. 20-9

An X-ray photograph; an original negative showing the bones light against the background of the surrounding flesh. Note the deposit in the finger joints, evidence of arthritis. (Courtesy of Dr. H. E. Duggan, University of Alberta Hospital.)

refraction and reflection, X rays cannot be focused by lenses or spherical mirrors. Good photographs require a source which comes as near as possible to being a small point, so that the shadows will be sharply defined.

GLOSSARY

Antenna Conductor in which electrical oscillations in the radio range can be set up, so that it acts as a source or receiver of electromagnetic waves.

Black box Term employed by physicists to refer to a complicated piece of electronic equipment used as an instrument in their experiments; the detailed circuitry of the equipment is regarded as if it were hidden in a "black box."

Classical physics The aggregate of scientific knowledge, both experimental and theoretical, that is based on Newton's laws of mechanics and Maxwell's laws of electricity and magnetism. It deals essentially with macroscopic (large-scale) phenomena and with continuous quantities, and the basic principles were all developed before the year 1900.

Condenser In electricity, a device consisting of a pair of conducting surfaces of large area separated by a thin layer of insulating material; large charges can be accumulated on the surfaces because each of them attracts charge of the opposite sign to the other surface.

Electromagnetic radiation Radiation of energy from a source by means of electromagnetic waves.

Electromagnetic wave A wave in which the energy is transmitted by oscillating electric and magnetic fields; in a vacuum the wave travels with a velocity equal to that of light, regardless of the frequency.

Fluorescence The emission of radiation when the energy required to excite it is provided by the absorption of radiation of a shorter wavelength, coming from a different source.

Fluoroscope Instrument used to make X rays visible by causing them to excite visible fluorescence on a suitable screen.

Photochemical reaction A reaction that takes place only when one of the molecules concerned is excited by the absorption of light energy.

Polarization The act of causing transverse waves to vibrate in a definite direction at right angles to the direction of propagation.

Polarized light Light in which the oscillating electric fields are all in a definite direction; the term can be used of any type of electromagnetic wave.

Polaroid Trade name for a material that is manufactured in sheet form, and that has the property of transmitting light only when the electric field is in a specified direction in the sheet; used for producing and detecting polarized light.

Roentgen rays Alternative term for X rays; after the original discoverer.

EXERCISES

1. How does the material known as Polaroid produce polarization effects?

2. How can you find out whether a beam of light is polarized, and whether the polarization is total or only partial? How is the preferred direction of the electric field indicated?

3. State what you would observe in applying the tests of Exercise 2 to: (a) the sun; (b) sunlight shining on a paved road; (c) the sparkle of the waves on a sunny day; (d) your own reflection in a mirror; (e) the moon; (f) an electric light bulb; (g) the blue sky.

4. Outline Maxwell's important contributions to the theory of electricity and magnetism, besides organizing the subject into a consistent whole.

5. Summarize as well as you can the evidence that light is transmitted by electromagnetic waves.

6. Describe briefly the essential features of the attempt by Michelson and Morley to detect the ether.

7. We often try to explain interference effects by drawing the light rays as wavy lines; what do the wavy lines represent?

8. Give an outline of the events leading to the first successful transmission of a wireless message.

9. How does the combination of a coil and a condenser function in producing oscillations of a definite frequency in an electric circuit?

10. Describe how oscillations in an antenna produce electromagnetic waves. How are the waves polarized when the antenna is a vertical wire? when it is a horizontal rod with a gap in the middle? Would you expect the latter type of antenna to transmit equally well in all directions?

11. How are radio waves of suitable frequencies transmitted around the curve of the earth?

12. What determines the range of wavelengths that can be photographed? What determines the wavelength range of visible light?

13. In a photograph taken with infrared light why do the trees appear bright against the dark background of the sky? Would a cumulus cloud be bright or dark in the photograph?

14. Electromagnetic waves 5×10^{-5} centimeter in length are visible light; what are waves of each of the following lengths: (a) 1 meter; (b) 0.001 centimeter; (c) 10^{-8}

centimeter; (d) 10^{-5} centimeter; (e) 1 kilometer. Give for each case one way in which the waves might be produced and one way in which they might be detected.

15. Describe briefly the chemical reactions involved in the exposure, developing, and fixing of a photographic film.

16. Give several examples of photochemical reactions other than those involved in photography and photosynthesis.

17. Name some of the practical applications of fluorescence, produced (a) by ultraviolet light, (b) by X rays.

18. Describe what you would expect to see if you looked through a spectroscope at: (a) a red neon sign; (b) a fluorescent lamp of the type commonly used in offices and factories; (c) a mercury street light.

19. Who discovered X rays, and when? How did they acquire their popular name?

20. Why is there no lens in an X-ray camera? Why does the bony skeleton show on an X-ray photograph? Are X rays ever reflected or refracted?

21. Explain with the help of a diagram how X rays show interference effects in a crystal.

22. The phenomenon referred to in Exercise 21 has led to two apparently unrelated specialties in experimental physics. Explain briefly the two different things that can be studied in this way.

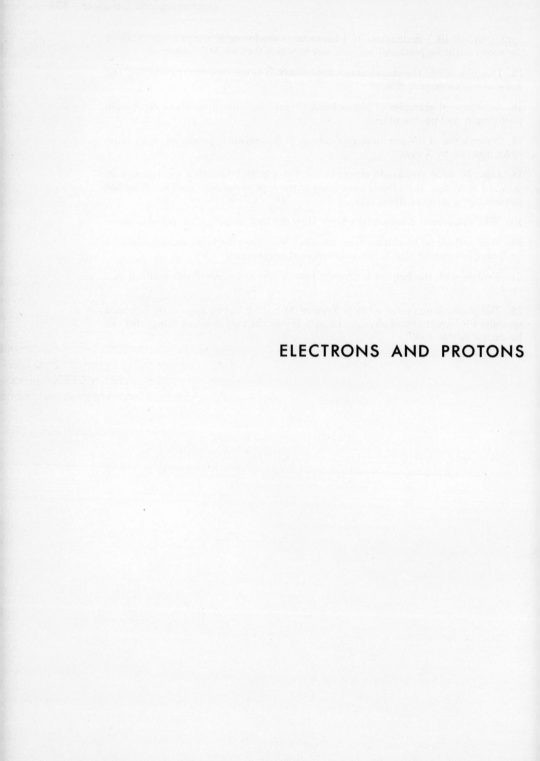

ELECTRONS AND PROTONS

part five

Most of the mass of the atom is concentrated in a minute positively charged nucleus, which is surrounded by a cloud of negatively charged electrons.

—RUTHERFORD (1911)

the electron

Electrolysis—already mentioned briefly in Secs. 14-5 and 16-4—is the phenomenon in which the passage of an electric current through an ionic solution causes chemical reactions to take place, with the deposition of different materials at the positive and negative terminals. We now have need of the *law of electrolysis,* which was discovered by Michael Faraday in 1834. The law can be stated in modern terms as follows:

The number of molecular weights of any ion deposited by electrolysis is proportional to the amount of electric charge passing through the solution, and inversely proportional to the charge number of the ion.

Numerically, using the currently accepted value of the *Faraday constant,* the deposit of a mole of any singly charged ion is accompanied by the passage of 96,488 coulombs of electric charge. A mole of doubly charged ions carries twice this quantity of charge, and so on. The simplest explanation of Faraday's empirical law is that the individual ions of a particular element or radical all carry the same amount of electric charge, e coulombs

339

for all singly charged ions (positive or negative), 2e coulombs for all doubly charged ions, etc. It follows that, like mass, *electric charge is a discontinuous quantity*, and occurs only in positive or negative multiples of e. Just as the smallest possible change in the mass of a body is represented by the addition or removal of one atom, the smallest possible increase or decrease in its charge is one *electron.*°

21-2   *Cathode Rays*

In the latter years of the nineteenth century a number of physicists became interested in the phenomena that accompany the passage of electricity through gases at low pressure. If a high voltage is applied between a pair of separate terminals in air at atmospheric pressure, a spark will jump a certain definite distance, depending on the electric field strength near the terminals. If the gas is confined in a glass *discharge tube,* having terminals sealed into the ends, and the pressure is reduced, the spark will jump much greater distances and take the form of colored streamers extending the length of the tube [Fig. 21-1(a)]. As the pressure is reduced still further by means of a vacuum pump—to 1 or 2 millimeters of mercury—the streamers spread out and fill the whole tube with a brilliant glow. † It was obvious to those studying the phenomena in the late 1800's that at this stage the electric current in the tube is carried by charged gas ions, and that electrical disturbances of these ions are responsible for the light.

As the pressure is further reduced, the glow breaks up into a number of striations and a dark space appears between the negative terminal (the *cathode*) and the beginning of the glow [Fig. 21-1(b)]; a little later a second area of bright glow, of a different color, develops immediately around the cathode. In the next stage, at a pressure of perhaps 10^{-4} millimeter, the original glow disappears altogether and the dark space reaches the positive terminal (the *anode*); the cathode glow then faintly fills most of the tube.

It is at this stage that the so-called *cathode rays* begin to appear, giving an effect of some kind of radiation emanating from the cathode, traveling down the tube from negative to positive, exciting the faint bluish glow as it passes, and finally causing the glass walls of the tube to glow when it impinges upon them. That this is indeed the case is readily demonstrated by a study of the qualitative properties of the rays, as follows:

1. They normally travel in straight lines, as is shown by the fact that they cast sharp shadows of an obstacle upon the end of the tube (Fig. 21-2).

° The first use of the term *electron* for the indivisible unit, or atom, of electric charge occurs in a paper published in 1891 by an Irish physicist, G. J. Stoney. However, he did not, at this time, think of electrons as discrete particles, capable of independent existence, unattached to an atom.

† It is at this stage of pressure that a neon sign functions. With a suitable voltage, provided by a small step-up transformer, the discharge will travel several feet, following all the curves of the tube. At this stage also the spectrum of the gas is most efficiently produced.

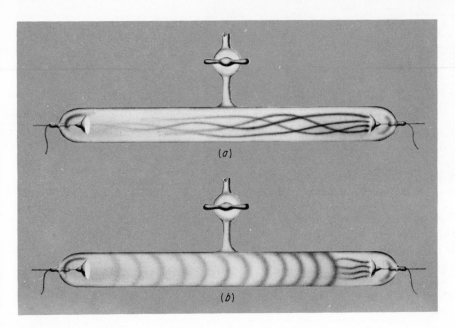

FIG. 21-1

Two stages of the discharge as the gas pressure in a discharge
tube is reduced.

2. They are themselves invisible, but they excite any gas molecules
remaining in the tube to produce light (the blue glow), and they cause
many solid materials to fluoresce, including ordinary glass, accounting for
the glow on the walls of the tube.

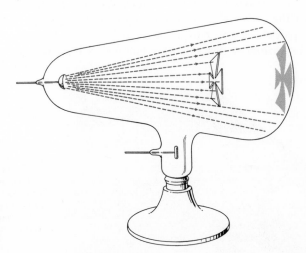

FIG. 21-2

Cathode rays traveling
down a tube in straight
lines cast sharp shadows.

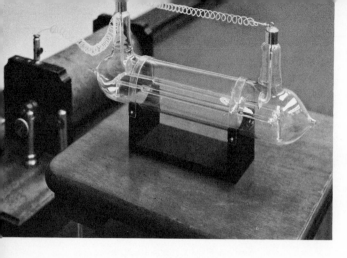

FIG. 21-3

The cathode-ray beam exerts a force on a paddle wheel, and therefore carries energy. (Photograph by J. Salt, University of Alberta.)

3. They affect a photographic plate.

4. They carry energy, for if they impinge on a thin strip of metal they make it red-hot, and they can cause a little paddle wheel inserted in the tube to rotate (Fig. 21-3).

5. They are deflected by electric and magnetic fields (Fig. 21-4).

6. When they strike a solid target they excite it to produce X rays (Sec. 20-9).

21-3   Thomson's Experiment on Cathode Rays and the Identification of the Electron

The fact that the cathode rays are deflected by electric and magnetic fields shows that they are a stream of charged particles, rather than some new kind of wave radiation. The stream of particles is obviously traveling from negative to positive in the tube, but if we apply the left-hand rule (Sec. 15-7) as if the current were flowing in the conventional direction from positive to negative, we get the correct direction for the deflection. It follows that the cathode-ray beam is a stream of negative electricity, that is, that the particles are negatively charged.

The experiments described so far are qualitative, but in 1897 J. J.

FIG. 21-4

Deflection of the cathode-ray beam by a magnet. (Photograph by J. Salt, University of Alberta.)

Thomson° measured the electric and magnetic deflections quantitatively. He produced a narrow beam of cathode rays in a long tube by passing them through a hole in the anode (Fig. 21-5). To this beam he applied an electric field by means of a pair of charged plates sealed into the tube, so that the cathode-ray particles were deflected through an angle, which could be measured on the fluorescent screen at the end of the tube. He then brought the beam back to its original position by applying a magnetic field at right angles to the electric field. The electric and magnetic forces on the particles were now equal and opposite; it was also possible to measure the deflection produced by either force alone.

From these measurements Thomson could calculate the velocity of the particles in the cathode-ray beam, and the ratio of their charge to their mass, the quantity e/m, which is now recognized as diagnostic of the nature of the particle in all experiments of this type. He could not, however, determine separately the charge and the mass, because what is really determined by measuring the deflection is the acceleration, which is the ratio of the force to the mass. Both forces are proportional to the charge, e, and so both accelerations are proportional to e/m. The result of Thomson's measurement was that e/m for cathode rays is approximately 1800 times† the corresponding value for hydrogen ions, which can be obtained from

° J. J. Thomson (1856–1940) was for many years professor of physics and director of the Cavendish Laboratory at the University of Cambridge, where he provided the inspiration for a long succession of younger physicists.
† Modern value 1837.6.

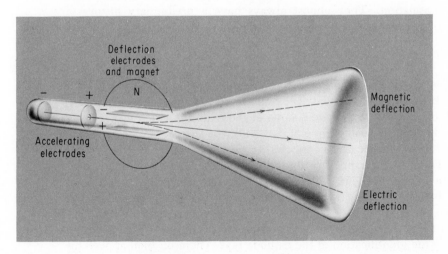

FIG. 21-5

J. J. Thomson's experiment to determine the value of e/m for cathode rays. N indicates the north pole of the magnet.

experiments on electrolysis. This could mean either that the charge was many times the ionic charge in electrolysis or that the mass was very much smaller than the mass of any atom. Because the ionic charge was known to be a basic unit, the atomic unit of electricity, it seemed much more likely that Thomson's cathode-ray particles were a new particle of extremely small mass, and they were recognized as such from the start. It was not long before the term "electron" came to be transferred from the unit of charge to the actual particle.

Thomson also established that the value of e/m for the cathode rays was the same regardless of what gas might be used in the discharge tube in which the rays were produced, a special case of the more general fact, established soon afterward, that all electrons are identical, wherever they may be found. As a result of these experiments Thomson is usually credited with the "discovery of the electron," and the date 1897 is taken as one of the great landmarks, or turning points in the history of physics. The latter is certainly true, for along with the nearly simultaneous discovery of radioactivity, the identification of the cathode ray as a new particle of very small mass—a constituent part of all matter—meant that atoms could no longer be considered as indivisible units, and studies of atomic structure became possible, with far-reaching consequences for the science of our own time. However, Thomson did not so much *discover* the electron as identify its nature; the term electron was already in use for the unit of charge, and cathode rays were already well known. This is not to detract from Thomson's experiments, which indeed were of the utmost importance to science, but only to emphasize that the great turning-point discoveries have rarely been made in isolation. They almost always have a preliminary history of observations made by many different workers.

21-4   *The Thermionic Effect*

In the course of Edison's work on the development of the electric light bulb, a blackening of the glass occasionally created problems. Thinking that he might be able to collect some of the material which was causing the blackening, he sealed a metal plate into the side of one of his bulbs. When this extra plate was connected to the positive side of the battery that provided the current for the bulb, a small current passed between the plate and the filament; when it was connected to the negative terminal of the battery, nothing happened. The plate was therefore collecting negative charge.° This observation was not understood at the time and was not followed up until after Thomson had performed his first experiments on the identification of the cathode rays. Thomson then applied his method of electric and magnetic deflections to identify whatever it was

---

° The blackening of old electric light bulbs is simply due to very slow evaporation of the material of the filament, and has nothing to do with the effect observed by Edison in this experiment.

that was being given off by the filament in Edison's bulbs, and found that it gave the same value of e/m as the cathode rays from a gas discharge. The *thermionic emission,* as it came to be called, proved to be evaporation of electrons from the filament, and further experiments showed that it occurred to some extent from any hot metal.

Thus the modern cathode-ray tube was born, for thermionic emission gives a much more reliable and much more easily controlled source of electrons for the cathode-ray beam (and for the radio tube which was soon to follow) than does a gas discharge. A modern tube is shown in Fig. 21-6. A specially treated tungsten filament acts as cathode and provides a copious supply of electrons when raised to a dull red heat. A variable potential applied to the grid attracts or repels electrons and controls the current in the tube. Electrons passing between the wires of the grid are accelerated by a high positive potential on the anode, and emerge from the hole in the latter with a definite velocity, determined by the work done upon them in passing from filament to anode. The tube is evacuated to the highest possible vacuum, so that gas molecules will not interfere with the electron beam.

The accurately controlled electrons produced by the combination of

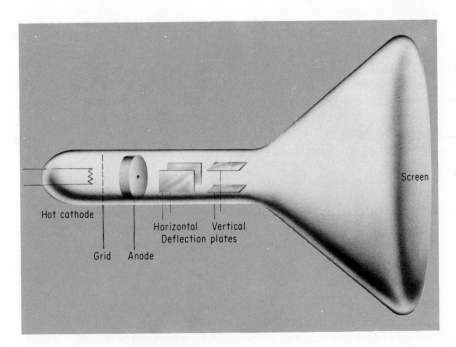

FIG. 21-6

Modern cathode-ray tube for studying details of a varying electric potential.

filament, grid, and anode can be used in many different ways. In the cathode-ray tube illustrated two pairs of plates are provided, and electric fields set up between these plates deflect the beam horizontally and vertically, respectively. The beam finally impinges on a fluorescent coating on the end of the tube, so that horizontal and vertical deflections can be measured, and the potentials applied to the deflecting plates can be studied. A tube of this type is an indispensable tool for the electronics engineer for studying the precise form of the oscillating voltages in his circuits.

The picture tube of a television receiver is a cathode-ray tube, essentially operating on the principle illustrated in Fig. 21-6. The two pairs of deflection plates are used to make the spot traverse the screen in a series of parallel lines so that the whole screen is covered 30 times per second. The rate at which the spot moves and the regular repetitions are controlled by a special signal sent out from the broadcast station, along with the "video" and "audio" signals, so as to synchronize with the scanning mechanism in the television camera. The video signal is applied to the grid of the cathode-ray tube, and varies the current in the tube, so as to control the brightness of the moving spot, and write the picture.

21-5   Millikan and the Electronic Charge

Although Thomson's experiment is basic to modern methods of identifying small charged particles, it could not determine the mass and charge of the cathode rays separately, but only the ratio e/m. In order to find the actual value of the electron charge a different method was necessary. The classical experiment in this field, and the first accurate measurement of the charge (e) was performed by Robert A. Millikan at the University of Chicago, during the years 1913–1917, and has become known as the oil-drop experiment.

By means of an atomizer, Millikan introduced small drops of oil° into the upper half of a metal box, as shown in Fig. 21-7. In this space the drops settled slowly through the air, and a few of them fell through the hole in the partition into the lower space, where they were subject to an electric field set up between the partition and a metal plate below. Here particular drops could be picked out, and watched through a microscope. The drops were negatively charged by friction in passing through the atomizer nozzle, and so when they were in the electric field they were repelled by the lower negative plate. By adjusting the potential on this plate, drops could be held very nearly steady, forced to move upward, or allowed to fall very slowly, so that a selected drop could be watched for several minutes.

When small drops are moving through air they very soon attain a constant

---

° Oil was chosen because the drops would evaporate very slowly and would not change in mass during the course of an observation. Mercury drops were also used in some of the experiments.

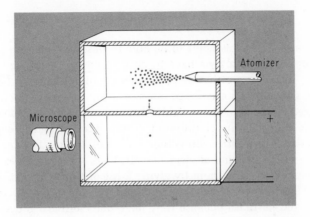

FIG. 21-7

Millikan's oil-drop experiment.

velocity, when the air friction, which is proportional to the velocity, is equal and opposite to the applied force, of gravity or of the electric field. By measuring the rate of fall of a drop when there was no electric field applied, its weight and size could be determined. Knowing these, the force exerted by the electric field could be measured when the drop was moving slowly up or down, and so the charge on the drop could be calculated. In a great many separate measurements, this charge was always an integral multiple of the quantity (as given today),

$$e = 1.6020 \times 10^{-19} \text{ coulomb.}$$

This then must be the numerical value of the charge on the electron, or, strictly speaking, it is the indivisible unit of charge whose existence had been deduced from the laws of electrolysis.

When the charge is known, its value can be combined with the value of e/m found in experiments of the Thomson type, involving magnetic deflections, to give the mass of the cathode-ray electron:

$$m = 9.107 \times 10^{-28} \text{ gram.}$$

Knowing the electron charge also provides an indirect method of calculating Avogadro's number (N), the number of molecules in a gram-molecular weight of any compound (Sec. 11-3). When a mole of material is collected in an electrolysis experiment (Sec. 21-1) N individual ions are collected, and, if each of these carries a single electronic charge (e), the total charge passed through the solution must be Ne. But this is just the Faraday constant (F), and therefore

$$N = \frac{F}{e} = \frac{96{,}488 \text{ coulombs per mole}}{1.6020 \times 10^{-19} \text{ coulomb}}$$

$$= 6.023 \times 10^{23} \text{ molecules per mole.}$$

This result is much more precise and reliable than those derived from experiments with gases, or from studies of the Brownian movement of small particles.

21-6   *Four Manifestations of the Electron*

One would like at this point to be able to describe what an electron looks like, but unfortunately we have to do without the aesthetic satisfaction of drawing its picture, either actually or mentally. Electrons have a definite electric charge, and a definite mass (as long as their velocities are small compared to the velocity of light). However, the size and shape appear to be quite different under different circumstances, and it is preferable to ignore these properties altogether, and not to use the terms "size" or "shape" when speaking of electrons. Instead, we should treat them operationally, and describe them by giving a list of those properties that can be observed, or can be deduced from the effects they produce. Primarily they are charged particles because they have mass and are affected by electric and magnetic fields, but under some circumstances they have wavelike properties (Sec. 33-7). In their particle-like properties they certainly do not behave as nice neat spheres, because they have angular momentum somewhat as if they were spinning like a top, and because they sometimes behave as tiny magnets.*

To summarize the situation, there are four principal ways in which electrons can make their presence evident, with quite different properties, so that one might think we were dealing with four different things, and yet a given electron can readily pass from one manifestation to another, showing that we have just one omnipresent entity.

First, the electron is the *indivisible unit of electric charge,* deduced from the facts of electrolysis and confirmed by Millikan's oil-drop experiment, with the result that electric charge, like mass, is a discontinuous quantity.

Secondly, electrons can appear as discrete, *free particles,* in the cathode-ray beam.

Thirdly, electrons are a constituent part, and an essential *building block in all atoms,* for they can be obtained from any material, and are identical, whatever their origin. It is evident, also, that the electrons within the atoms are responsible for the emission of the electromagnetic waves we know as light, although it is too simple and too mechanistic a picture to think of the electrons as simply vibrating inside an atom.

Finally, it is the electrons which carry the current in electrical conduction by a metal, and so it is they which constitute the *electric fluid* postulated in the early theories of electrical charging and conduction.

That an electron can be at one instant a free particle in a cathode-ray tube, at another instant a part of the electric fluid in a wire, and then emerge attached to an atom to form a negative ion in an electrolytic solution is shown by the continuity of the current in a cathode-ray tube or radio tube circuit. In a circuit containing a radio tube and a battery the current continues to flow as long as the filament is kept hot and the proper poten-

---

* Space will not permit a discussion of the details of these two properties. They are deduced from certain effects observed in atomic spectra, and in the magnetization of iron.

tial is maintained across the tube. Electrons must, therefore, circulate continuously in the circuit, crossing the tube from the negative cathode to the positive anode, traveling through the wire to the positive terminal of the battery, crossing the battery attached to negative electrolytic ions, and returning to the cathode of the tube through the other wire, to replenish the supply evaporated from the filament through the thermionic effect.

21-7   Diode and Triode Tubes

Out of the identification of the electron and the discovery of thermionic emission there has grown the flourishing branch of applied science known as *electronics*. One usually thinks of it in terms of modern communications, radio and television, whereby we can be in almost instant communication with any part of the world, and even see what is going on thousands of miles away. However, there are hundreds of other applications, in other branches of science as well as in industry. All of these are founded basically upon the diode and triode tubes and their modifications, and upon the high-frequency a-c circuit. Space will not permit any detailed discussion, beyond a brief description of the two main types of tubes and their basic functions.

The *diode tube* consists merely of a heated cathode as a source of electrons, and an anode to which is applied a positive potential to attract the electrons. Basically it is a rectifier, converting alternating current into an intermittent direct current, because the electrons can only pass through it in one direction, from cathode to anode. The diode was first used by J. A. Fleming in 1904, as a detector of electromagnetic waves, more sensitive than the early detectors used by Hertz and Marconi, because the direct current, even if intermittent, will operate a telegraphic relay, whereas the original alternating current will not.

The spectacular advances in electronics began with the invention of the *triode tube*, which was patented by Lee de Forest in 1906. In the triode a grid of fine wires is placed around the hot cathode, to control the current through the tube in the manner already described for the cathode-ray tube. Fundamentally the triode is an amplifier. If it is connected as shown in Fig. 21-8 an a-c voltage of very small amplitude can be super-

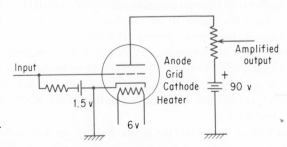

FIG. 21-8

A simple triode-tube amplifier.

posed on the potential of the grid battery. This makes the current through the tube, although still unidirectional, fluctuate around its mean with the frequency of the "signal" applied to the grid. The voltage drop across the resistance in the anode circuit will then follow all the details of the fluctuations on the grid, and so provide an amplified output.

It is the extreme versatility of the triode tube and its more modern modifications which have led to the host of applications of electronics. The tube can be used as a simple amplifier, as indicated, when it will respond to a wide range of frequencies. It can be used as a "tuned amplifier," by incorporating along with it a resonant circuit; it will then amplify effectively only the particular frequency to which it is tuned. Because its output is unidirectional it can combine the functions of amplifier and detector. If a portion of the output is used to induce voltage fluctuations on the grid, the valve can act as a generator of high-frequency alternating current, with frequency determined by the resonance frequency of the circuit to which the valve is connected. Therefore large triodes, handling large currents and large quantities of power, are central to the radio transmitter as well as to the receiver.

21-8   Science and Technology

In the scientific method the order of events is supposed to be, first, observation and the formation of a hypothesis or theory, then prediction of new observations and their confirmation by experiment, and finally, practical use of the discovery for industrial purposes or to improve our standard of living. The first stages are usually considered as belonging to the field of "pure science," and the last stage to "applied science," or technology. It is interesting to see whether this is a valid generalization, and whether we can make a clear distinction between science and technology. We then find cases where the "pure" and the "applied" merge inextricably, cases where the technology has come first, and, above all, cases where technical advances in one field have paved the way for scientific discovery in a different field. It is doubtful if we can find even one field existing in isolation as a nicely wrapped package with events in their supposedly proper sequence.

In this and the previous chapter we have discussed two fundamental discoveries, those of the electromagnetic wave and of the electron. These two fields, basically quite different, have reacted one upon the other at every stage of their development. If we had known nothing about electrons and the uses of electronic devices, radio communication would still be the dot-and-dash wireless of Marconi. If radio had not required high-frequency alternating currents, and sensitive means of handling and detecting them, the triode tube, with all its modifications, would probably never have been invented.

To what extent do these two fields depend on still earlier science and invention? It goes without saying that both of them require a knowledge and thorough understanding of the laws of electricity, quite apart from the fact that it was Maxwell's prediction of the existence of electromagnetic waves that led to the development of wireless in the first place. However, there is one purely mechanical invention without which the whole field of electronics would have been impossible. This is the vacuum pump, and not only electronics but also many other developments in modern atomic science have been made possible by successive improvements in vacuum technology, producing continually better and better vacuums. At one stage of the development of vacuum techniques, say that of about the mid-nineteenth century, intensive study of electrical discharges in gases became possible, leading to some of the early discoveries in spectroscopy. Then improved pumps, producing a higher vacuum, led directly to the discovery of gas-produced cathode rays, and so to the identification of the free electron. A still better vacuum and the hot filament could replace the gas discharge as a source of free electrons, with immediate improvements in methods of controlling the electron beam. Only when vacuum pumps reached this stage of efficiency did the triode and the modern cathode-ray tube become possible.

Then applications were found for the triode tube not only in communications and in industry, but also in any modern scientific laboratory—as an essential tool. Electronic devices have made possible modern methods of studying the rays from radioactive materials, and so have contributed to discoveries in subatomic physics. They have found uses in the biological laboratory, and particularly in medicine, for example, for detecting and amplifying the minute electrical impulses which transmit messages along a nerve, and so in a way biologists have come full circle, back to Galvani's frog. The modern X-ray tube, producing a reliable and precisely controlled beam, is also dependent upon vacuum techniques and upon electronics. The X-ray tube in its turn has led, among its many uses, to new discoveries in chemistry, for the elucidation of the functions of DNA (Sec. 13-7) could not have been accomplished without X-ray analysis. So technology and pure science can never be entirely separated.

Actually technology is far older than pure science, especially in mechanics, in heat and energy, and in chemistry. Men were using mechanical devices, the wheel and the pulley, the lever, the water pump, and the siphon, long before Galileo and Newton laid the foundations of modern science by stating the laws of mechanics. The *controlled* use of fire goes back to the dim Stone Age. Even the smelting of metals precedes written history, and antedates by thousands of years the scientific understanding of chemical combination and of the processes of oxidation and reduction. It is only in fields like electricity or atomic physics, where the development has taken place entirely since the seventeenth century—when science began to come into its own—that the pure science has come before the technical application.

GLOSSARY

Amplifier Device that increases the amplitude of a sound vibration or an electrical oscillation without altering the frequency.

Anode Positive terminal of a discharge tube or an electrolytic cell.

Cathode Negative terminal of a discharge tube or an electrolytic cell.

Cathode rays Stream of negatively charged particles (now known to be electrons) projected from the cathode in a vacuum tube.

Diode Vacuum tube containing two electrodes, a hot cathode as a source of electrons, and an anode; basically a rectifier that passes current in one direction only.

Discharge tube Glass tube containing a gas at low pressure, with two or more electrodes sealed inside so that an electric current can be passed through the gas, to excite it to produce light.

Electrode Any terminal by means of which electrical connection is made to the gas in a discharge tube or to the fluid in an electrolytic cell; usually made of metal and connected to a wire that is sealed into the wall of the tube.

Faraday constant The electric charge transported when a gram-molecular weight of a singly charged ion is deposited in electrolysis.

Grid (of a triode or cathode-ray tube) Electrode composed of a number of fine wires or a piece of netting, placed close to the cathode; the potential on the grid controls the current through the tube without preventing the electrons from reaching the anode.

Hot cathode Cathode that is heated to produce a stream of electrons by thermionic emission.

Oil-drop experiment Experiment performed by Millikan to determine the electronic charge, by measuring the electrostatic charges on tiny drops of oil.

Rectifier Device that passes electric current only in one direction, so that it converts alternating current into intermittent direct current.

Specific charge, e/m The ratio of electric charge to mass for electrons, ions, and other charged particles; the quantity that is measured in a magnetic deflection experiment, and that is diagnostic of the nature of the particle.

Thermionic effect Emission of free electrons by evaporation from a hot metal.

Triode Vacuum tube with three electrodes, cathode, grid to control the current, and anode; the triode and its modifications are basic to nearly all electronic circuits.

1. State Faraday's law of electrolysis, and explain how the law follows from the hypothesis that there is a fundamental, indivisible unit of electric charge.

2. Calculate the charge transferred when 1 gram of silver is deposited in electrolysis.

3. Describe briefly the successive appearances as the air is pumped out of a discharge tube.

4. Compile a list of the important properties of cathode rays.

5. Which of the effects listed in Exercise 4 could be produced either by a stream of particles or by a beam of electromagnetic waves? Which are suggestive of particles, and which are decisive in favor of particles?

6. Demonstrate with the aid of the electromagnetic direction rules that the cathode-ray particles are negatively charged.

7. Describe briefly the experiment performed by Thomson on cathode rays. Precisely what was measured in this experiment? In what sense is Thomson credited with the discovery of the electron?

8. Why is it not feasible to measure separately the charge and the mass of free electrons? How are these quantities deduced, and what assumption has to be made in order to permit the deduction?

9. What is the evidence that all electrons are alike, whatever their origin?

10. Explain the function of the grid in a cathode-ray tube or a triode.

11. How is the velocity of the electrons controlled in a modern cathode-ray tube?

12. Calculate the work done on an electron by a potential of 100 volts. Calculate the velocity acquired by the electron.

13. Calculate the velocity a proton would acquire when accelerated by a potential of 100 volts.

14. Give a short description of Millikan's oil-drop experiment. What was actually measured in this experiment?

15. How can one estimate the size and mass of particles that are seen only as little points of light, even under a powerful microscope?

16. Concerning the several manifestations of the electron, describe briefly experiments that show: (a) that the electron which enters into the structure of all atoms is the same as the indivisible unit of electric charge; (b) that the electrons which conduct the current through a wire can attach themselves to atoms to form negative ions in an electrolytic cell; (c) that an electron which is at one time attached to a molecule in a gas discharge tube can later be evaporated from the hot cathode of a radio tube.

17. Explain how a triode acts as an amplifier of sound.

18. Explain what happens when you tune your radio to different stations.

inside the atom

In 1896 Henri Becquerel, of the Conservatoire des Arts et Métiers in Paris, was studying fluorescence and similar phenomena in uranium compounds, and found that they would affect a photographic plate whether they had been exposed to light or not. However, the radiation which was given off by these compounds in the dark was not ordinary light, but was more like the X rays which Roentgen had recently observed coming from a cathode-ray tube (Sec. 20-9). Like X rays, the new uranium radiation would pass through many normally opaque materials, such as the black paper in which the photographic plates were wrapped, but only weakly through heavier materials like metals. It would also discharge a gold-leaf electroscope (Sec. 14-2), by ionizing the surrounding air, and this instrument soon became one of the most useful tools for detecting and studying the new radiation.

Becquerel did not follow up this discovery himself. That task was left for Marie Sklodowska Curie, from Warsaw, Poland, who was studying at the Sorbonne in Paris, and her husband, Pierre Curie, then professor in the

School of Physics and Chemistry, and shortly to be appointed to the Sorbonne. The Curies found that the activity of uranium compounds, as measured by the rate at which they discharged the electroscope, was proportional to the amount of uranium present, regardless of the elements with which it was combined. They observed that thorium behaved in the same way as uranium; then they discovered a sample of untreated uranium ore, consisting of the mineral known as pitchblende, which proved to be actually more active than pure uranium. It was evident that there must be another, previously unknown active element present in the pitchblende, and so they obtained several tons of this material from the waste of a silver mine in Bohemia, and proceeded to hunt for active materials in it. In the course of some 3 or 4 years of painstaking chemical treatment, following each stage of the chemistry with the electroscope to see where the *radioactivity* had gone, they succeeded in identifying two highly active elements, which they named polonium and radium, and in extracting about a tenth of a gram of pure radium chloride. Radium was identified as belonging to group II of the periodic table, along with barium, and its atomic weight was estimated.°

Pierre Curie was killed in a traffic accident in 1906, and Marie was shortly appointed to succeed him at the Sorbonne, where she continued her studies of the chemistry of radium and other radioactive elements. She became interested also in the medical uses of radium, for the treatment of cancer and similar diseases, and soon achieved worldwide fame, one of the few women ever to attain to the front rank in the world of science.

22-2   *The Three Kinds of Rays*

We owe to the Curies, and particularly to Marie Curie, the isolation of elemental radium and much of the chemistry of radioactivity, but we owe a great deal of the early physics of the subject to Ernest Rutherford† and his collaborators. At an early stage it was discovered that there are three distinct kinds of radiation produced by radioactive materials, although pure, freshly prepared radioactive elements do not produce all three at once. The three types of rays are easily distinguished by the extent to which they penetrate different materials and by the intensity of the ionization which they produce in air. They are designated by the first three letters of the Greek alphabet, alpha (α), beta (β), gamma (γ).

° For the original discovery, and for the isolation of radium, Becquerel and the two Curies shared the 1903 Nobel prize.

† Rutherford was a New Zealander, who studied in England under the famous J. J. Thomson. He worked for a time at McGill University in Montreal, and it was there that his first experiments on radioactivity were performed. Later he returned to England, to the University of Manchester, and finally succeeded Thomson as Professor of Physics at Cambridge. He was honored first by a knighthood and later by a peerage, so that he is usually referred to as Lord Rutherford.

Alpha rays cause intense ionization, but are quite easily stopped, by a few thicknesses of aluminum foil. In air they travel a certain definite distance, up to about 15 centimeters, depending upon their initial energy. Because of their intense ionization, they can produce severe surface burns in the skin; radioactive materials should never be handled with bare hands.

Beta rays are much less ionizing than alpha rays, but penetrate to much greater distances, up to a millimeter or more in light metals like aluminum and to several meters in air. They are not a serious danger, because protection against them requires only that radioactive materials be kept in a container of reasonable thickness.

Gamma rays are extremely penetrating, but cause only relatively weak ionization. It is the gamma rays which, on the one hand, have therapeutic properties, but, on the other hand, are the source of danger when handling radioactive materials in large quantities. This is because gamma rays penetrate deeply to all parts of the body, and can destroy living cells wherever they penetrate. Active, growing cells are more susceptible than mature cells, and so under some circumstances it is possible to adjust the exposure to gamma rays (or to X rays) so that a malignant cancerous growth is killed without doing too much damage to the surrounding tissue. Healthy, growing cells, the reproductive cells, the blood-producing cells of the bone marrow, and so forth, should be protected from gamma rays at all times.

22-3   Identification of the Three Rays

One of Rutherford's first efforts was to identify the three types of radiation, using the deflection in a magnetic field in somewhat the same manner as Thomson used it to identify the cathode ray. The results of a long series of actual experiments can be conveniently summarized, and most easily understood by thinking of the imaginary, idealized experiment illustrated in Fig. 22-1. Imagine a small quantity of radioactive material placed in the bottom of a hole in a lead block, so that the rays emerge vertically upward from the hole. The block is placed in a strong magnetic field, with the lines of force pointing away from the observer.

The alpha rays are deflected slightly to the left, showing that they are positively charged particles, carrying a large momentum and kinetic energy. Measurement of the deflection shows that they have an e/m value approximately half that for hydrogen ions. Rutherford identified them as helium ions carrying two units of electric charge (He^{++}); he also demonstrated that helium gas accumulates wherever radioactive materials are producing alpha rays. Later the rays proved to be bare nuclei of helium atoms, devoid of the electrons with which the nuclei are normally surrounded.

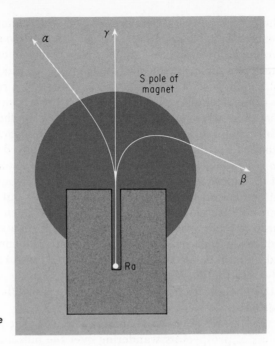

FIG. 22-1

Magnetic deflection of the three
types of radioactive rays.

The beta rays are deflected quite strongly to the right, showing that they
are negative particles, with a smaller momentum. Measurement identified
them as electrons traveling with a high velocity, but with momentum less
than that of the alpha rays because of their much smaller mass.

The gamma rays are not affected by a magnetic field, and so Rutherford
assumed them to be short electromagnetic waves, similar in nature to
X rays, and this has been abundantly proved by later evidence.

22-4   Detection of Single Particles

It is impossible ever to see single atomic particles, or to photograph them
with ordinary light, even with the most powerful microscope conceivable,
because an object of dimensions smaller than about half the wavelength of
the light cannot project an optical image. However, a single atomic particle can produce a detectable effect in several different ways, if the particle
is electrically charged, and if it is traveling with a high enough velocity.
As a result, methods of tracing and counting single particles have been
devised and have become routine laboratory technique in modern atomic
physics.

All three types of radiation from radioactive elements cause visible fluorescence in suitable materials. When Rutherford looked at the fluorescence produced by alpha rays under a low-power microscope, he found that instead of a uniform glow like the fluorescence produced by X rays or ultraviolet light, that of the alpha rays consisted of a rapid succession of discrete splashes of light, which he called *scintillations*. He was able to prove that these were the result of impacts upon the fluorescent screen of individual alpha particles, and so by watching scintillations Rutherford was able actually to count the number of particles emitted in different directions from a radioactive source, and he used this counting technique in many of his experiments. The laborious method of counting scintillations under an optical microscope has become obsolete, but scintillation techniques are still useful. A photoelectric "eye" has been developed, which is so sensitive that it will respond to the light from a single scintillation, and produce a minute pulse of electric current. The current pulses can be amplified, and can be used to actuate any desired type of electrical recorder. Naturally, *scintillation counters* are not limited to the detection of alpha rays, but can be used to record the impacts of many different kinds of high-speed particles.

Most readers will have heard of an instrument called a *Geiger counter*, in accounts of prospectors wandering over the hills looking for uranium ore, or of a hospital technician hunting for a lost radium capsule among the refuse. This instrument, invented by H. Geiger working in Rutherford's laboratory, can be made in several different forms, of which that shown in Fig. 22-2 is typical. A metal tube filled with a suitable gas at a pressure of a few centimeters of mercury has a fine insulated wire down the center. A potential of 1000 volts or so between the wire and the tube causes a strong electric field around the wire, and this is adjusted so that an electric discharge is almost ready to pass. If a high-speed particle passes through the tube, producing ions in the gas, the incipient discharge is triggered; a

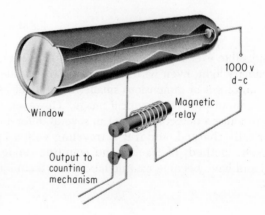

FIG. 22-2

A Geiger counter for detecting single high-speed particles.

pulse of current flows for an instant in the circuit and can be used to produce an audible click in a pair of earphones, or to actuate an electrical counter. The instrument shown in the figure has a thin window to allow alpha particles of low penetrating power to enter the tube. However, one of the advantages of the Geiger counter is that it can be used to detect gamma rays, in which case the window is unnecessary. The instrument will then respond to a sample of radium many feet distant, or to a deposit of radioactive ore buried under several feet of rock and soil.

It may sound anomalous to speak of "counting" single gamma rays, which are classed as electromagnetic waves. However, the burst of gamma radiation emitted from one atom in one event has many of the properties which, from a mechanical point of view, one would associate with an uncharged mass particle (Sec. 33-6).° Gamma rays produce directly only a very weak ionization in the gas. However, a gamma ray passing through a Geiger tube may cause an electron to be ejected from the metal wall, and the electron will then ionize the gas, and trigger the counter.

22-5   Tracks of High-Speed Particles

Useful as the scintillation counter and the Geiger counter may be for recording numbers of particles or for detecting the presence of radioactive materials, a more interesting and more informative method of studying individual charged particles is the *cloud chamber,* invented by C. T. R. Wilson at Cambridge in 1912. When the pressure of water vapor in moist air reaches the saturation point, the vapor normally condenses and forms a cloud. However, the tiny droplets that constitute the first stage of the cloud cannot form in isolation, but have to condense *on* something. In ordinary atmospheric clouds the droplets form around dust particles, which are always present, but charged gas ions can also attract water molecules and act as efficient condensation centers.

The Wilson cloud chamber (Fig. 22-3) takes advantage of this property of cloud formation to make visible the path along which a high-speed charged particle has recently passed. A close-fitting piston slides in a cylinder with a glass top, the space above the piston being filled with moist air. When an alpha particle passes through the chamber it leaves gas ions all along its path, possibly several thousand in number. If the piston is drawn down sharply immediately after the particle has passed, before the ions have had a chance to diffuse, the air expands and cools and the moisture condenses on the gas ions, outlining the path of the alpha particle by a thickly populated row of cloud droplets. In a continuous operation the piston is geared to a motion-picture camera, photographing the cloud

---

° When the particle-like properties of gamma rays or X rays are in evidence, the burst of radiation from a single atomic event is called a *photon.*

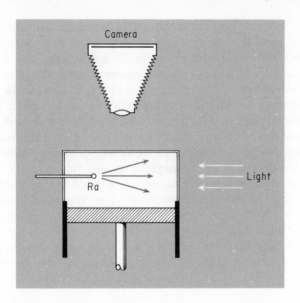

FIG. 22-3
Wilson cloud chamber.

in the chamber immediately after each expansion. The photographs can then be studied at leisure, to look for interesting events.

Figure 22-4 is a photograph of the cloud tracks produced by a beam of alpha rays in moist Freon gas, with a radioactive source mounted inside the chamber. The tracks are all approximately the same length, showing

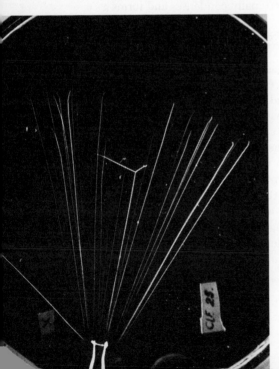

FIG. 22-4

Cloud tracks produced by alpha particles, showing one collision event. (Photograph courtesy of J. K. Bøggild, Institute for Theoretical Physics, Copenhagen, Denmark.)

the definite range of alpha particles in a gas, and are nearly all straight throughout their length, except for a possible slight hook near the end. This photograph shows one interesting event; the branched track is the result of a head-on collision between an alpha particle and the nucleus of a fluorine atom.

Another device which is similar in principle to the cloud chamber is the *bubble chamber*. If a liquid is a fraction of a degree below the boiling point, and a high-speed charged particle passes through it, tiny bubbles form along the track left by the particle and make it visible. Liquid hydrogen is commonly used in the bubble chamber; it has the special advantage that collisions with hydrogen atoms frequently occur and help to identify the particle which caused the track (cf. Sec. 34-4). In either the cloud chamber or the bubble chamber the density of cloud drops or bubbles along the track depends on the charge and velocity of the particle, while the length of the track depends on the energy. It is also possible to apply a magnetic field to the chamber and cause the particles to travel in circular arcs. The particle which made any particular track can thus be identified and its momentum and energy measured. If there is a collision, and a forked track, the law of conservation of momentum must be obeyed, and deductions made from the nature of the track can be confirmed.

22-6   *Rutherford and the Nuclear Atom*

The discoveries of the electron and of radioactivity showed that an atom must be a composite structure, containing negative electrons and sufficient positive charge to balance the electrons and make the whole electrically neutral. Since the electrons are known to be light particles, the mass of the atom must be associated principally with the positive charge, but in the early 1900's nothing was known about where the mass and the positive charge were located. Some physicists held that the mass must be distributed throughout the atom; others that it must be concentrated in a small nucleus, with the electrons revolving around the nucleus like planets around the sun. Either theory could account for the facts which were known at the time, for radioactivity and for the existence of the electron.

When a dispute of this kind arises, the thing to do is to devise an experiment for which the competing theories predict distinctly different results. Rutherford decided that an experiment on the passage of alpha particles through matter could be decisive. Consider an alpha particle passing through a thin layer of solid material; in the actual experiment gold foil and similar materials were used. The alpha particle, being comparable in mass to the atoms, is practically unaffected by the very much lighter electrons, but may be deflected from its straight-line path by the repulsion of the positive parts of the atoms. If the positive charge and mass were distributed throughout a sphere of atomic dimensions, the alpha particle would be slightly deflected by each gold atom, and would follow an irregular path through the foil. Rutherford calculated that the combination of many small deflections would produce an overall average deflection of a few degrees, so that all the alpha particles would be deflected, none very much, and the distribution in angle of the particles emerging from the foil would be of the form (a) shown in Fig. 22-5.

On the other hand, if the positive charge and mass were concentrated in a small nucleus in the center of the atom, most of the alpha particles would go right through the foil without passing close enough to a positive charge to be deflected appreciably. A few would approach closely to the nucleus of a gold atom, would be strongly repelled and would be deflected through a large angle as indicated in Fig. 22-6, some particles even being turned backward. The chance of a particle approaching closely to two nuclei in the foil, and being deflected twice, would be completely negligible, and the distribution in angle of the emerging particles would be as shown as (b) in Fig. 22-5.

Rutherford's experiment is illustrated in Fig. 22-7. The source was a speck of polonium, which emits only alpha particles, having a range in normal air of 3.87 centimeters. The number of particles per second produced by the source was determined, and then the gold foil was inserted. Particles which had been deflected in passing through the foil were received on a small fluorescent screen, which could be placed in different positions and which could be studied by a microscope. The numbers of particles

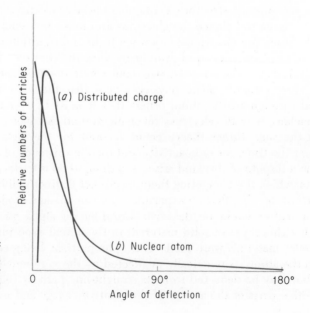

FIG. 22-5

Distribution in angle of scattered alpha particles according to two different assumptions concerning the nature of the atom.

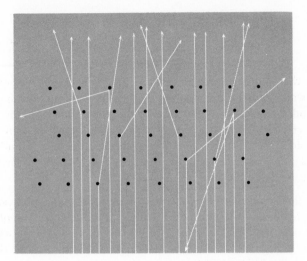

FIG. 22-6

Alpha particles passing through matter in which the positive charges are concentrated in small nuclei.

received in different screen positions were determined by the laborious method of counting scintillations, and so the fraction of the original beam which had been deflected through any given angle could be determined.

The results of the experiment were unmistakable; the distribution in angle of the particles scattered by the foil was of the form computed for a nuclear atom, with the positive charge and mass concentrated in the center. It was possible also to place an upper limit on the size of the nucleus, for particles which had been turned almost directly back by a close encounter with a gold nucleus occurred in the expected numbers. In order to be so strongly deflected, these particles must have come within about 10^{-12} centimeter of a gold nucleus without actually hitting it. The nucleus must therefore be smaller than this limit, and must have a diameter not more than about 1/100,000 of the diameter of the atom.* No matter how solid

° Later experiments, in which actual collisions with nuclei did occur, showed that nuclei are only a little smaller than Rutherford's limiting size. Complete atoms range in diameter from about 1 to 5×10^{-8} centimeter, and nuclei are about 100,000 times smaller.

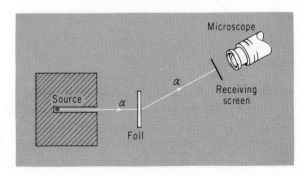

FIG. 22-7

Rutherford's experiment on the scattering of alpha particles by thin metal foils.

a piece of matter may appear to be, almost the whole of its volume is accounted for by the electron clouds, with plenty of empty space; the mass is nearly all concentrated in the tiny nuclei, which occupy only something like 10^{-15} of the total volume.

From the precise numerical results of his scattering experiments Rutherford was able, finally, to calculate the positive charge on the gold nucleus, and found it to be very close to $79e$, where e is the electronic charge. The normal, electrically neutral gold atom must therefore contain 79 electrons. Now, gold is the 79th element in the modern form of Mendeleev's periodic table, and so from this and other evidence, which we shall not discuss in detail, we have the simple rule:

The *atomic number of an element*, which determines its position in the periodic table, and therefore its chemical properties, *is none other than the number of units of positive charge on the nucleus;* this must, in turn, be equal to the number of electrons in the neutral atom. It is, therefore, the nuclear charge that ultimately determines what an element is.

22-7   The Physical Basis of Chemical Combination

Knowing the number of electrons in the atom of any element, and knowing the importance of this number in determining the chemical properties, the question arises whether we can learn anything about the structure of the atom, particularly about the way in which the electrons are arranged. We cannot do more here than state some of the results which have been deduced, partly from theory, and partly from the accumulation of experimental evidence, through studies of the spectra of the elements, both optical spectra and characteristic X-ray spectra, as well as through the evidence of the periodic table itself.

In a heavy element the electrons are arranged in a series of shells, containing successively 2, 8, 18, 32, 18 electrons, with a certain number left over on the outside. For example, gold has these 78, with one left over, making up the total of 79. The successive filling of the shells, as the atomic number increases, determines the periodicity of the table, with its short periods of 8 elements, the long periods of 18, and the one special period of 32 which includes the rare earth elements (Sec. 9-11). The electron shells are further divided into subshells° of 2, 6, 10, 14, to make up the 32 of the largest, fourth shell. A configuration of eight electrons has a peculiar stability, whether it is the second complete shell of eight, or whether it comprises the first two subshells of one of the larger, outer shells.

° In older descriptions the electrons are assigned to definite elliptical orbits, of fairly definite shapes and sizes, corresponding to the subshells. This produces much too mechanistic a picture and is misleading. The reader who does not wish to delve into the mathematical theory should think of the shells merely as clouds of negative charge containing specified numbers of electrons.

We are now in a position to understand better some of the facts of chemistry, already described in Chapters 9 and 13, particularly the formation of positive ions in solution, and the two principal types of chemical combination, the ionic bond and the covalent bond. In general, the chemical properties can be associated with the number of electrons outside the last complete shell, although there can be irregularities when the atom has an incomplete inner shell. The number of electrons involved (referred to as the *valence electrons*) never exceeds eight, because as soon as a stable group of eight is formed in the outer shell a new shell is started.

As examples of strong ionic bonding we may think of compounds of the sodium chloride type. The alkali metals, sodium, potassium, etc., all have one electron outside a shell of eight. The one valence electron is easily removed, either in the gas state or in solution, but it is much more difficult to disturb the underlying stable group of eight. The alkalies therefore form singly charged positive ions, Na^+, etc. The halogens, fluorine, chlorine, etc., all have outer shells of seven electrons; they need one more to make the stable configuration of eight. In the gas state they may sometimes lose an electron and form positive ions, but in solution they pick up the electron needed to make a stable outer shell, and so they form singly charged negative ions, F^-, Cl^-, etc. When an alkali and a halogen combine to form a compound of the NaCl type, the easily detached electron from the sodium fits itself into the gap in the outer shell of a chlorine, as indicated in Fig. 22-8. The compound is then held together by electrical attraction between the positive and negative ions. All the electrons in the solid are in stable complete shells, and the result is a stable crystalline solid, and an electrical insulator.

Similar considerations apply to the metals of the alkaline earth group (magnesium, calcium, etc.) which have two electrons outside a shell of eight and readily form doubly charged positive ions, to oxygen and sulfur which have six electrons in their outer shells and so can readily accept two more to form doubly charged negative ions, and to oxides and sulfides like MgO and CaS. An exception to the rule that an element with one valence electron should form singly charged positive ions occurs in copper which has 1 electron outside a shell of 18. One on top of 18 is more strongly bound than one on top of 8, and at the same time the 18 are less strongly bound together than the particularly stable 8. It is fairly easy to remove two electrons from the copper atom and so it forms many compounds in which it behaves as a doubly charged positive ion. Silver and gold, which also have 1 electron on top of 18, obey the rule and form singly charged ions. For elements with three, four, or five valence electrons and for elements with incomplete inner shells there are no simple ionization rules; we can say only that elements with similar electron arrangements have similar properties.

In marked contrast to the elements that form ionic compounds are the inert gases, neon, argon, etc., which all have stable outer shells of eight

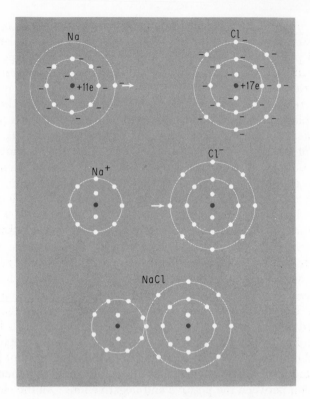

FIG. 22-8

Ionic bonding in NaCl. (The arrangement of the electrons is schematic only.)

electrons.° They therefore do not readily lose electrons to form positive ions, nor accept electrons to form negative ions; they have no naturally occurring chemical compounds; they are all monatomic gases that liquefy only at low temperatures.

In metals, most of which behave as positive ions in forming compounds, some of the valence electrons are set free when the metal solidifies, and can wander between the positive ions that make up the bulk of the material. These free *conduction electrons* are then available to constitute the electric fluid, and to make the metal a conductor. At the same time they form a negatively charged cloud within the metal, acting as an attractive binder to hold the positive ions together.

22-8   *Electron Structure of Covalent Bonds*

The simplest case of covalent bonding occurs in the hydrogen molecule (H_2, Fig. 22-9). The two electrons from the two hydrogen atoms combine to form a common configuration around the center of gravity of the two

---

° Helium, the lightest inert gas, has only two electrons, forming the stable pair of the first complete shell; the same considerations apply.

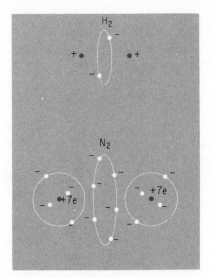

FIG. 22-9

Schematic electron arrangements in the hydrogen (H_2) and nitrogen (N_2) molecules.

nuclei. The binding force that holds the molecule together arises from the strong tendency of electrons to pair together; it has analogies with a magnetic rather than an electrostatic attraction. The pairing and shell properties of the electrons are fully occupied; the resulting molecule is very stable and has little tendency to combine as a unit with anything else. Ordinary hydrogen is therefore a diatomic gas; its molecules cohere to form a liquid only at $-253°C$, and a still lower temperature is required to solidify it. Similar considerations apply to nitrogen gas (N_2, Fig. 22-9) and to oxygen (O_2).

The peculiar properties of carbon (Sec. 13-2) can now be associated with the tendency of its four valence electrons to form covalent bonds, rather than becoming detached from the carbon nucleus to form a positive ion. For example, the electron arrangement in the ethane molecule (C_2H_6) is indicated schematically in Fig. 22-10. A pair of electrons, one from each

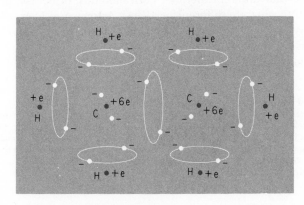

FIG. 22-10

Schematic electron arrangement in the ethane (C_2H_6) molecule.

carbon, holds the structure together; three other electrons from each carbon pair with the electrons of the six hydrogens. The positive hydrogen nuclei are close to the surface of the structure, and can easily be substituted by some other atom or radical.

22-9   *Isotopes*

Following his success in identifying the electron, Thomson applied a similar method of electric and magnetic deflections to the identification of the positively charged particles in a gas discharge. As expected, he found that the values of e/m corresponded with those for atoms and molecules carrying one or two units of charge. They were, therefore, positive ions of the gases known to be present. However, in 1912 he found that a gas discharge in neon gave two distinct kinds of positive ion, with atomic weights of 20 and 22, respectively, occurring in the proportion of about 10 to 1. Ordinary neon has an atomic weight of 20.2, and the conclusion was that the neon found in the atmosphere is a mixture of two gases having almost identical properties, both of them being chemically inert.

A little earlier Rutherford and Soddy had found among the radioactive elements some that had different radioactive properties and different atomic weights, but could not be separated chemically. Soddy decided that these should not be considered as different elements, but rather as different varieties of the same element, and he coined the name *isotope*° for them because they had to be assigned to the same position in the periodic table. Thomson's discovery in neon now suggested that isotopes might occur among the light elements as well as among the heavy radioactive elements.

Studies of pure science in England were interrupted by World War I, but in 1919 F. W. Aston at Cambridge developed a method for the separation of positive ions having different masses (strictly, different values of e/m), and for measurement of the masses of individual particles.† About the same time, A. J. Dempster at Chicago accomplished the same purpose by a somewhat different method; both methods, of course, used magnetic deflection to separate different particles. Aston's and Dempster's methods soon developed into routine experiments, which could be applied to a wide variety of materials. Between them they studied most of the common elements, and found that most of them are mixtures of two or more isotopes.

° Derived from the Greek *isos*, equal, and *topos*, place.

† In Aston's method the particles were detected photographically. After separation by the magnetic field, particles of different masses produced sharp lines on the plate, giving an appearance similar to a line spectrum. Aston therefore referred to his apparatus as a *mass spectrograph*, and the name has persisted, although the photographic method is now seldom used, the particles being detected electrically. Mass spectrographs are now standard equipment in many physics and chemistry laboratories (see Fig. 22-11).

The instrument which separates the different isotopes of an element can also be used to make precise measurements of the atomic weights of the individual isotopes. In all cases these are very close to, but not exactly, integers when compared with the carbon 12 standard. All atomic nuclei therefore have masses near to multiples of a definite unit, which is a little less than the mass of a hydrogen nucleus.° It follows that nuclei are composite structures made up of a finite number of units. One building block is certainly the hydrogen nucleus, commonly referred to as a *proton.* The closest integer to the precise atomic weight, that is, the number of mass units in the nucleus, is known as the *mass number.* When it is necessary to distinguish different isotopes in chemical symbols, the mass number is written as a superscript, as Ne^{20}, Ne^{22}.

22-10   *Preparation of Pure Samples of an Isotope*

The atomic weight of an element as determined chemically represents the average value of the mixture of isotopes which is normally found in nature. Different isotopes of an element have identical chemical properties, except for small differences in the rates at which chemical reactions proceed. They are only very slightly separated by any chemical process, and so the proportion of the different isotopes in any element, as it is found naturally in the earth's crust, is very nearly constant. However, the isotopes can be separated by physical processes which depend upon the masses of the atomic or molecular particles, and nearly pure samples of single isotopes of many of the elements have been prepared. Complete separation can, of course, be effected by magnetic deflection, and actually takes place in a mass spectrograph. This device has been used to prepare samples of pure isotopes, but it is a very slow and expensive process to collect the particles from a mass spectrograph, in large enough quantities to weigh and handle.

° The small deviations of atomic masses from whole numbers are related to the potential energy of the forces that hold the nucleus together, through the mass-energy relation.

FIG. **22-11**

A modern mass spectrograph. In this instrument the deflection angle is fixed and particles of different masses are deflected into the collector by varying the current in the electromagnet. (Photograph by J. Salt, University of Alberta.)

A more practical method depends on a difference in the rate of diffusion, either of gas molecules or of ions in solution. In a gas, molecules containing the lighter isotope will travel, on the average, with a somewhat higher velocity, and will diffuse more rapidly. For example, when it was required to separate large quantities of uranium 235 (useful for atomic explosions and for nuclear atomic power installations) from the more abundant U^{238}, a large plant was built at Oak Ridge, Tennessee, to employ the diffusion method. In this process uranium hexafluoride (UF_6), which is a gas at ordinary temperatures, is passed slowly through a long tube, and the lighter fraction, containing the U^{235}, tends to diffuse to the walls more rapidly than the heavier fraction. Gas skimmed off near the walls contains a little more U^{235} than normal, and if the process is repeated many times nearly pure $U^{235}F_6$ can be obtained.

Another method depends on the fact that in the liquid state different isotopes have slightly different boiling points, the lighter and faster moving molecules evaporating more readily than the heavier ones. The principle underlying this method is being applied successfully in large-scale operations to separate heavy hydrogen (H^2, also known as deuterium, D) from the normal mixture, which contains one part in 6500 by volume of the heavy isotope. Liquid deuterium boils at 23.5°K, ordinary hydrogen at 20.4°. The mixed liquid is allowed to trickle down through a long column packed with glass beads or metal foil so as to present a large surface area for the liquid to flow across. Hydrogen gas flows slowly up the column, and evaporates the liquid as they meet. The heavy isotope is the last to evaporate, and under proper conditions nearly pure liquid deuterium collects at the bottom of the column.

GLOSSARY

Alpha (α) *rays* Heavy positive particles ejected from natural radioactive elements; they prove to be the nuclei of helium atoms.

Atomic number The order number of an element in the periodic table; equal to the number of units of positive charge on the nucleus, and hence to the number of electrons in the neutral atom.

Beta (β) *rays* Negative electrons ejected from radioactive elements.

Bubble chamber Device for displaying the paths of high-speed charged particles by passing them through a liquid that is a fraction of a degree below its boiling point; the path of a particle is shown by a line of small bubbles.

Cloud chamber Device for displaying the paths of charged particles by passing them through a gas that is supersaturated with moisture; the path of a particle is shown by a line of droplets that have condensed on the ions that were produced by the particle as it passed.

Conduction electrons The electrons that constitute the electric fluid and carry the current in a metallic conductor; they are set free to wander through the metal when it is in the liquid or solid state.

Electron shells The series of concentric spherical shells into which the electrons of an atom are grouped; complete shells contain definite numbers (2, 8, 18, 32) of electrons.

Freon Trade name for CCl_2F_2, a gas with a boiling point of $-28°C$ so that it is easily condensed under pressure; used as the coolant in household refrigerators and as the solvent in spray bombs.

Gamma (γ) *rays* Electromagnetic waves of very high frequency produced by radioactive elements, along with the ejection of particles.

Geiger counter Device that detects and counts single charged particles by causing them to trigger a momentary gas discharge.

Heavy hydrogen The isotope of hydrogen with atomic weight approximately 2; also known as deuterium.

Mass number The nearest integer to the atomic weight of an individual isotope; equal to the number of particles (protons and neutrons) in a composite nucleus.

Mass spectrograph Device for determining the masses of atomic particles, and for separating a mixture of particles according to their masses.

Range The distance that charged particles can travel through air at $0°C$ and standard atmospheric pressure; alpha particles ejected from a particular radioactive isotope all have very nearly the same range.

Scintillation In the study of radioactivity, the flash of light produced when a single alpha particle strikes a fluorescent screen; it is visible under a low-power microscope.

Scintillation counter Device for counting charged particles by recording the electrical impulses produced when the light from single scintillations is received by a sensitive photoelectric cell.

Valence electrons Those in the outermost electron shell of an atom.

EXERCISES

1. Outline the story of the discovery of radioactivity by Becquerel and the Curies.

2. How can an electroscope be used to measure the amount of uranium in a sample of ore?

3. Describe the distinguishing properties of alpha, beta, and gamma rays—penetration, ionization, and magnetic deflection.

4. Describe briefly the biological effects of the three types of rays.

5. Calculate the value of e/m for alpha rays, and compare this with the value for free electrons. Who first used the measurement of e/m to identify the alpha ray, and when?

6. Explain the principles involved in the detection and study of single charged particles by: (a) scintillations; (b) the Geiger counter; (c) cloud chambers; (d) bubble tracks.

7. (a) How are alpha particles passing through matter affected by the nuclei of the atoms? (b) How would they be affected if the positive charge and the mass of an atom were distributed over the whole volume of the atom? (c) How are alpha particles affected by the electrons in the material?

8. Describe briefly Rutherford's experiment on the scattering of alpha particles by thin metal foils. Explain how the results of this experiment gave an upper limit to the size of the nucleus.

9. The radius of a gold atom is approximately 1.40×10^{-8} centimeter, and the radius of the nucleus is approximately 8.7×10^{-13} centimeter. What fraction of the volume is in the nucleus? Estimate the density of matter in the nucleus.

10. Outline the evidence that radioactivity is a property of the atomic nucleus.

11. Explain the connection between the three different meanings of the term "atomic number." (See *Glossary*.)

12. In the table of the elements why do chemical and physical properties repeat after 8 or 18 elements?

13. Explain the connection between the number of valence electrons and the chemical properties for each of the following elements: sodium, calcium, oxygen, carbon, bromine, silver, radium.

14. How do electrons form a covalent bond?

15. How was it first discovered that many elements are a mixture of isotopes?

16. Explain the principles involved in two different methods of extracting nearly pure samples of the isotopes of an element.

17. Estimate the approximate proportions of Cl^{35} and Cl^{37} in natural chlorine, assuming that these are the only stable isotopes.

18. List as many as you can of the properties of an element in bulk that depend on the mass of its atoms.

19. State two reasons for believing that the nuclei of heavy atoms are composite structures. If they are composite structures, why are their masses not precisely equal to the sum of the masses of the parts?

nuclear chemistry

23-1   *Radioactive Disintegration*

The activity of uranium or radium salts is strictly proportional to the amount of the active element the salt contains, and is unaffected by any ordinary chemical or physical changes in the material. As soon, therefore, as it was established that the atom is of the nuclear type, and that it is the cloud of electrons surrounding the nucleus that determines the ordinary chemical and physical properties, it also became evident that radioactivity is a property of the central nucleus. Since it is the number of units of positive charge on the nucleus that determines what an element is, and its position in the periodic table, any change in that charge means that we have a new element. Ejection of a charged alpha or beta particle from the nucleus therefore means the conversion of an atom of the radioactive element into something different, according to the following rules:

Ejection of an alpha particle, with charge $+2e$ and mass 4 units, reduces the nuclear charge by two units, and the mass number by four. The new element lies two places lower in the periodic table.

Ejection of a negatively charged beta particle, with negligible mass on the atomic scale, increases the nuclear charge by one unit, and so produces the next higher element in the table, without any change in the mass number.

With a very few exceptions, a given element produces either alpha or beta particles, and in the few cases where an element can produce either, it never produces both at once. The gamma radiation is incidental to the ejection of the alpha or beta particles; the ejection of the particle may cause the nucleus to be left in an excited state so that it may emit a burst of electromagnetic radiation (a photon).

In the heavy, natural radioactive elements, a particular nucleus goes through a whole series of transformations before it finally settles down to a stable form, which is in all cases an isotope of lead. Since the changes of mass are always by ejection of an alpha particle, which has four units, the elements in a given series must have mass numbers differing in steps of four. The most important *radioactive series* is that which contains uranium and radium as two of its members (Table 23-1), and in which all the masses are of the form $4n+2$. Members of two other series are found in the earth's crust, the thorium series with masses of the form $4n$, and the comparatively rare actinium series with masses $4n+3$. The $4n+1$ series is known only through elements produced artificially; some of its members may have existed in the primeval nebular cloud from which the solar system was born, but they have all disappeared long ago.

It is convenient to think of the emission of a particle from a natural radioactive element as a spontaneous *nuclear reaction,* and to indicate it by a symbolism analogous with a chemical equation. For example, radium itself ejects an alpha particle and transforms into the inert gas, radon, as indicated in the nuclear reaction equation,

$$_{88}\text{Ra}^{226} \longrightarrow {_{86}}\text{Rn}^{222} + {_2}\text{He}^4 + \text{Q(energy)}.$$

The superscripts give the mass numbers of the isotopes involved, and the subscripts the atomic numbers or nuclear charges; both of these must, of course, balance on the two sides of the equation. The alpha particle is here indicated by its chemical symbol, $_2\text{He}^4$, because it is, after all, the nucleus of a helium atom, and after it has come to rest it picks up a pair of electrons and becomes an ordinary atom of helium gas. The term (Q) on the right-hand side of the equation does not denote a particle, but is included to indicate the fact that a large amount of energy is released in the reaction. This energy appears primarily in the form of kinetic energy of the ejected particle, but may include also the energy of a photon of gamma radiation.

Similarly, the equation,

$$_{82}\text{Pb}^{210} \longrightarrow {_{83}}\text{Bi}^{210} + e^- + \text{Q,}$$

TABLE 23-1   **THE URANIUM-RADIUM SERIES**

92   **Uranium   238**
α $\downarrow$ 4.498×10^9 yr

90   **Thorium   234**
β $\downarrow$ 24.1 d

91   **Protactinium   234**
β $\downarrow$ 1.175 min

92   **Uranium   234**
α $\downarrow$ 248,000 yr

90   **Thorium   230**
α $\downarrow$ 80,000 yr

88   **Radium   226**
α $\downarrow$ 1620 yr

86   **Radon   222**
α $\downarrow$ 3.825 d

84   **Polonium   218**
α $\downarrow$ 3.05 min

82   **Lead   214**
β $\downarrow$ 26.8 min

83   **Bismuth   214**
α ⟋ β ⟍   19.7 min

81   **Thallium   210**   84   **Polonium   214**
β ⟍   1.32 min α ⟋ 1.64×10^{-4} sec

82   **Lead   210**
β $\downarrow$ 19.4 yr

83   **Bismuth   210**
β $\downarrow$ 26,000 yr

84   **Polonium   210**
α $\downarrow$ 138.4 d

82   **Lead   206**

STABLE

describes one of the beta-particle emissions which occurs in the radium series, e^- being the symbol for a negative electron of negligible mass.

23-2   *Energy of Nuclear Reactions*

The energy released in a nuclear transformation is eventually converted into heat, as the ejected particle is brought to rest by collisions with atoms of the surrounding material, and as the gamma ray is absorbed. One of the earliest observations, after the discovery of radioactivity and the isolation of radium, was the large amount of heat produced by any radioactive element; a gram of pure radium produces about 100 calories of heat per hour, and keeps this up for many years without any evident decrease in the rate.

The custom has arisen of stating the energy involved in a single atomic or molecular event in *electron-volts,* one electron-volt being the kinetic energy acquired by an electron in passing through a potential difference of one volt.* Since the work done on an electron by a potential of V volts is Ve joules, where e is the electron charge, equal to 1.602×10^{-19} coulomb,

1 electron-volt $= 1.602 \times 10^{-19}$ joule.

The energy exchanged, either absorbed or released, in an ordinary chemical reaction can be anything up to 3 or 4 electron-volts per molecule. The energies required to produce singly charged positive ions of the different elements, that is, to detach an electron from the outermost shell, range from 3 to 25 electron-volts. By way of contrast, the energy released when an atom of radium is transformed into radon and helium is 6.5 *million* electron-volts (abbreviated Mev). The tremendous concentration of energy in single nuclear events must be kept in mind throughout what follows.

This energy is related to a change in mass by Einstein's famous mass-energy equation,

$$E = mc^2,$$

where E is the energy produced or absorbed, m is the loss or gain of mass, and c is the velocity of light in meters per second. Thus a loss of mass of 1 kilogram corresponds to a gain of energy of nearly 9×10^{16} joules.

23-3   The Law of Radioactive Decay

When a radioactive element ejects an alpha or beta particle and is transformed into an atom of a different element, the new element has different chemical properties and can be separated from the parent material; the atoms which have given off their particles are lost to the original supply. The number of particles ejected per second, the *activity,* is strictly proportional to the amount of parent material present, and it follows that in any specified interval of time a definite fraction of the parent element is transformed.

* The custom has its origin in an early type of experiment in atomic physics, in which a controlled beam of cathode rays was used to initiate various atomic events. For example, the energy required to ionize a gas molecule was determined by measuring the voltage that had to be applied to a beam of cathode rays in order to bring them to the point where they would produce ions in the gas. The voltage necessary is referred to as the ionization potential of the gas.

The time required for one-half of a radioactive element to be transformed into the next element in the series is called the *half-life*. It is a characteristic constant of the radioactive isotope concerned, and is the same regardless of the amount initially present.

For example, the radioactive inert gas, radon 222 (itself the daughter product of radium) produces alpha particles and transforms into an isotope of polonium, which is a semimetallic solid. The polonium can be collected on a charged metal plate exposed to the radon gas, and removed, while the radon gradually disappears. Radon has a half-life of 3.825 days, so suppose we start with N_1 atoms of the gas; then after 3.825 days half of it will have transformed into polonium 218, and there will be $N_1/2$ atoms of radon left. After another 3.825 days half of that will have been transformed, and there will be $N_1/4$ atoms left, and so on. If we plot the number of radon atoms against the time in days we get the curve shown in Fig. 23-1, in which the ordinate is reduced by half in each half-life interval. In theory the radon never completely disappears, but after 10 half-lives, say, the amount is only $1/1024$ of the amount we started with, and may be too small to detect.

The half-lives of different radioactive isotopes vary from a fraction of a second to several billion years, those of the elements of the uranium-radium series being given in Table 23-1. Naturally, only isotopes with moderate half-lives, like radon 222, can be watched as they decay, and their lives measured directly. Very short and very long half-lives have to be deduced indirectly; in the case of the long-lived isotopes by measuring the present activity of a known quantity of the element. Each of the three series of heavy radioactive elements that are found in the earth's crust has one very long-lived parent. For example, uranium 238, the parent of the uranium-radium series, has a half-life of 4.498 billion years, some 10,000 times longer than any of the isotopes derived from it. If a uranium compound is left to itself for a long time, as it is in a rock which was solidified

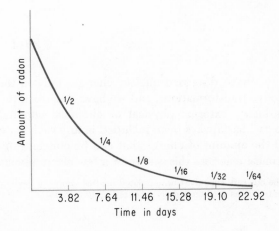

FIG. 23-1

Decay curve of radon 222.

millions of years ago, all the members of the series will accumulate in amounts proportional to their half-lives, and will be found alongside the uranium. In this series, radium, with a half-life of 1620 years, is longer lived than its immediate descendants, and forms the parent of a sort of subseries.*
In a natural uranium ore every gram-molecular weight (238 grams) of uranium 238 will be accompanied by 1620/4,498,000,000 of a gram-molecular weight of radium 226, which works out to 0.00008 gram.

It is important to notice that the discovery of the law of radioactive decay introduced a new, and at the time quite unexpected, feature into physical law—the feature of probability. The law that the number of atoms which decay in a given time is strictly proportional to the amount of the element present to begin with can be restated in a different form, which is mathematically equivalent, and leads to the same decay curve (Fig. 23-1):

There is a definite probability that a selected atom will decay within the next second, and this probability is not affected by any ordinary physical or chemical processes carried out upon the material.

This means that, just as a life insurance company can predict with reasonable accuracy how many persons out of a population of a million will die within the year, so here we can predict, much more accurately than the insurance company, how many atoms in a piece of uranium will decay in the next year. But the insurance company cannot say which individuals will die, and neither can we say which uranium atoms will decay. Concerning an individual, the insurance tables cannot say when he will die, but only that he has a life expectancy of so many years; concerning a selected atom, we cannot say when it will start its series of transformations, but only that there is an even chance that it will do so within the next half-life period.

23-4   *Induced Nuclear Reactions*

So far we have discussed nuclear changes only in terms of spontaneous radioactive transformations, and we have described them as unaffected by any ordinary, external physical or chemical conditions. But the word "ordinary" has always been included in any such statement. It is a question of the amount of energy that can be concentrated on a single atom. In chemical reactions this is at most a few electron-volts, in a gas discharge

---

* In the 60 years since the Curies isolated the first sample of nearly pure radium, a little over 1 per cent of it has gone through its series of transformations.

tube or a cathode-ray beam it can be considerably more; in a physical process such as heating, even to temperatures far above the melting point, it is less. However, if we can concentrate on one atom an energy of a few million electron-volts, an amount comparable with that released in a radioactive disintegration, things are very different. It is then possible to induce, by external means, changes in the atomic nucleus.

One way of concentrating large amounts of energy on single atoms is to bombard a material with high-speed charged particles of atomic mass, and one source of such particles is the alpha-ray beam itself. In 1919 Rutherford was studying the passage of alpha rays through some of the light elements, in a continuation of the experiments he had already carried out with silver and gold foils (Sec. 22-6). When he bombarded nitrogen gas with the alpha particles, he found a few particles ejected, in all directions, with ranges much greater than those of the alpha particles themselves, and he soon succeeded in showing that these were *protons,* or singly charged nuclei of hydrogen atoms, $_1H^1$ in the notation used to describe nuclear events. He soon found that protons could be produced in a similar manner from other light elements. Soon, also, a few examples of such events were found among the photographs taken of the tracks left by charged particles in a Wilson cloud chamber (Sec. 22-5).

In these photographs the tracks left by the protons could be distinguished from those of the alpha particles by the density of droplets along the paths. The nucleus recoiling from the collision was shown by a thick, short spur to the track. From a study of the momentum relations in events of this type, and from other evidence, it was established that the alpha particle had penetrated the repulsive electric field surrounding the nitrogen nucleus, and had made a direct hit upon the latter, with the result that a nuclear transformation had taken place, as described by the equation,

$$_7N^{14} + {}_2He^4 + Q_1 \longrightarrow {}_8O^{17} + {}_1H^1 + Q_2.$$

In this equation energy terms have been included on both sides to indicate that the bombarding particle must have a large energy in order to overcome the electrical repulsion of the nucleus and make an actual collision. In this particular case Q_2 is less than Q_1, so that there is a net loss of kinetic energy. This has been converted into the energy of mass, the combined precise masses of oxygen and hydrogen being greater than that of the nitrogen and helium. In a few other cases there is a decrease in the precise total mass, and a gain of kinetic energy, which, of course, is ultimately converted into heat.

The dream of the medieval alchemists, of converting one element into another, had actually come true, but in a manner and under circumstances which they could not possibly have conceived, and with consequences totally different from their idea of turning base metal into noble gold.

It was obvious from Rutherford's discovery, described in the last section, that, if alpha particles from a radioactive source would induce nuclear reactions, other charged particles of comparable energy must do the same. The trick was to accelerate particles to the necessary velocities, using, for example, protons obtained as positive ions from hydrogen gas, or alpha particles produced artificially from helium gas. Several different types of machines have been built for this purpose; only a few outstanding ones can be described here. They are what have been popularized as "atom smashers," and machines producing particles with energies in the million-electron-volt range are now commonplace. In spite of their size and cost, many machines designed for this energy range have not only been built for government research centers, but are found in physics laboratories of universities all over the world.

It must be emphasized that, from an energy point of view, these machines are extremely inefficient. There may be a gain of energy in some of the nuclear reactions which take place in them, but this is only a very small fraction of the amount of energy which has to be poured into the machine in order to produce a useful beam of high-speed particles. They therefore have no direct relation to the production of nuclear atomic energy; that is another story, which will be discussed in the next chapter.

Particle accelerators, to give them a more sophisticated name, fall into two general classes: those which actually produce potential differences of a

FIG. 23-2

The 6 million electron-volt Van de Graaff accelerator at the University of Alberta, built by High Voltage Engineering Corporation. (Photograph by J. Salt, University of Alberta.)

few million volts, and those which accelerate the particles in steps, by making them pass many times in succession through a small potential difference until they have acquired the necessary energy. The most successful machine of the former type is the Van de Graaff accelerator, called after its inventor. This is a modified electrostatic machine, which charges a large metal sphere to a potential of several million volts. The sphere and charging device are housed in a large steel tank, in a chemically inactive gas at several atmospheres pressure, in order to prevent sparks from jumping to surrounding objects. The high voltage is applied directly to positive ions in a long evacuated tube, and the resulting beam of high-speed particles can be used to induce many kinds of nuclear reaction in suitable targets.

For energies greater than about 10 million electron-volts, acceleration in successive steps is the only feasible method. The original machine of this type was the *cyclotron*, which was built by E. O. Lawrence at the University of California in 1933, and which earned for him a Nobel prize. In this machine protons are introduced into a vacuum chamber between the poles of a large electromagnet. The magnetic field causes the protons to whirl around and around in circular orbits, the radius of the orbit getting larger and larger as the protons gain speed (Fig. 23-3), while the time required to

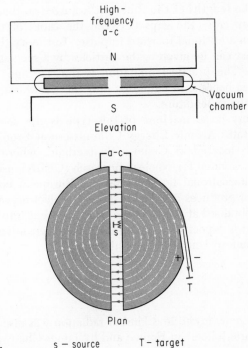

FIG. 23-3

Principle of the cyclotron accelerator.   s — source   T- target describe the orbit remains constant. Inside the vacuum chamber is a pair of electrodes, shaped like a flat circular tin cut in half along a diameter. As long as the protons are inside either half of this box there is no electrical force on them, but when they cross the gap between the two half-boxes they are subject to an electric potential. A high-frequency alternating potential of some 10,000 volts is applied between the electrodes, and the frequency is synchronized to be the same as the frequency with which the protons describe their magnetic orbits, so that every time the protons cross the gap, the potential is in the right direction to give them an additional forward kick and increase their speed. In a large cyclotron the protons may whirl around several hundred times, and travel a quarter of a mile or so, before they reach the outer limits of the magnetic field. Finally, they enter the space between an extra pair of charged plates, which deflect them out of the magnet and direct them onto a target where they can produce nuclear reactions.

The synchronization in the original Lawrence cyclotron fails when the speed of the particles approaches that of light, which happens for protons when the energy is about 20 million electron-volts. The cyclotron has been modified to produce higher energies, but the highest energies now available— in the billion-electron-volt range—are produced by various forms of *linear accelerator*. In this type of machine the particles are constrained by suit-ably placed magnets to follow a very long path through a series of metal tubes. The lengths of the tubes are adjusted so that as the particles gain speed they cross the gaps between the tubes at the correct instant to receive an additional forward impulse. In theory there is no limit to the energy that can be given to the particles by a succession of properly timed impulses. The practical limitation is the size and cost of the machine, which soon become so large that only the wealthiest national governments can bear the expenditure.

One very large machine of this type is the accelerator built by the United States Atomic Energy Commission at Brookhaven, Long Island; another is located at Geneva, Switzerland, where it was built by the European Council for Nuclear Research (CERN), using funds contributed to this international body by several European countries. The CERN accelerator produces particles of 33×10^9 electron-volts energy—the high-est ever obtained at the time the machine went into operation. An accel-erator that is expected to attain 45×10^9 electron-volts is under construc-tion at Stanford University, in California.

23-6   Neutrons

In 1932 a new, mysterious kind of radiation was discovered independently by the Curie-Joliots[*] in France and by James Chadwick in England. They

[*] Irène, daughter of Marie and Pierre Curie, and her husband, Frédéric Joliot.

were studying the secondary radiation which is given off by light elements, particularly beryllium and boron, when they are bombarded by alpha particles, and nuclear reactions take place. In order to determine the range of the particles ejected in the reaction (which were expected to be protons, as in Rutherford's experiments) they inserted different absorbing materials, and found that, when a material rich in hydrogen, such as paraffin wax, was used as the absorber the number of long-range particles received in the detector was actually increased.

A slight modification of the original experiment, illustrated in Fig. 23-4, showed clearly that the increased activity was due to protons coming from the paraffin. An alpha particle hits the beryllium; a proton is ejected from the paraffin! Obviously, something which did not affect the type of detector they were using had traveled from the beryllium to the paraffin, and had there collided with the nucleus of a hydrogen atom. Chadwick soon came to the conclusion that the only thing that could have an appropriate amount of energy to have been formed in a nuclear reaction between an alpha particle and a beryllium nucleus, and have enough momentum to knock a proton out of the paraffin with the observed velocity, must be a particle with a mass about the same as that of a proton. Since it produced no ionization along its own path, it must be uncharged, and so he gave this newly discovered particle the name *neutron*.

The reaction of the beryllium, which produces the neutrons, is described by the equation

$$_4\text{Be}^9 + _2\text{He}^4 + \text{Q}_1 \longrightarrow _6\text{C}^{12} + _0\text{n}^1 + \text{Q}_2,$$

where $_0\text{n}^1$ denotes the neutron, of charge 0 and mass 1 unit. The reaction in the paraffin is a simple collision between the neutron and one of the protons in a paraffin molecule, like the collision between two billiard balls. In simple collisions between two particles of nearly the same mass, if the

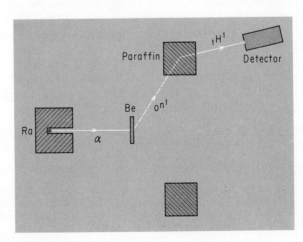

FIG. 23-4

Schematic diagram of the type of experiment that led to the discovery of the neutron.

collision is head on the incident particle is stopped and the particle which is struck carries on with the same energy and momentum as the incident particle. If the collision is not quite head on, the two particles share the energy and momentum, and fly off at different angles. On the average, the incident particles lose half their energy when they collide with stationary particles of the same mass.

The uncharged neutrons have no effect on the electrons of any material through which they pass. They go right through the atoms without giving up any energy until they make a close collision with a nucleus, and so they can travel large distances through matter, and are more penetrating than even the most energetic gamma rays. When they do hit a nucleus they may simply rebound, in a billiard-ball type of collision, or they may be absorbed into the nucleus and cause a nuclear reaction. When a beam of neutrons passes through a considerable thickness of material, like the paraffin, containing large numbers of light atoms with which they do not readily react, they lose energy through the simple collisions, until eventually their velocities are reduced to little more than those of gas molecules.* These "slow" neutrons can still penetrate through the electron shells of any atom, and hit the nucleus. When they do so they are even more likely to be absorbed, and to cause a reaction, than are the "fast" neutrons of the original beam. Slow neutrons are therefore especially effective in producing nuclear reactions.

Since neutrons do not themselves cause any ionization, the question arises of methods of detecting and measuring a neutron beam. The ejection of protons from paraffin, which led to the original discovery, is of course one method, but it is clumsy. A method that is much used nowadays is to line the inside of a Geiger counter with a material (lithium and boron are effective) in which the neutrons readily produce reactions; the counter then responds to the products of the reaction. There is also the question of measuring the energy of the neutrons. Again, the usual method of magnetic deflection is useless with uncharged particles. However, it has been found feasible—and very effective—to measure the velocity directly, by actually measuring the time required for a burst of neutrons to travel a known distance.

23-7   Nuclear Structure

Quite early in the history of the modern atomic theory it was suggested that the atoms of the different chemical elements might all be made up

---

* The material that is used to slow down a beam of neutrons in this way is referred to as a moderator. Neutrons only react weakly with ordinary hydrogen, and so any hydrogen-rich material can be used as a moderator. However, they react hardly at all with the heavy isotope of hydrogen (deuterium, $_1H^2$), with ordinary oxygen 16, or with carbon 12. "Heavy water," water made with deuterium in place of ordinary hydrogen, has proved to be the best neutron moderator of all. It can now be obtained in large quantities.

from a small number of more fundamental particles, of which the hydrogen atom was probably one. In the nineteenth century this was little more than a speculative suggestion, very similar to the Greek concept of atomism. It fell into disrepute for a time, because there are a number of elements (chlorine, for example) whose chemical atomic weights are not even approximately multiples of that of hydrogen. The study of radioactivity, and the confirmation of the nuclear type of atom, made it quite clear that the nucleus is a composite structure. Then the discovery of isotopes, with individual atomic weights which are very close to integers, revived the hypothesis of a fundamental mass unit, probably the proton. The fact that the mass unit is somewhat less than the mass of a free proton presented no serious difficulty, because theory showed that there would be a loss of mass when charged particles are closely packed together.

At first it was assumed, rather naturally, that the nuclei of heavier atoms were composed of positively charged protons, held together by negative electrons. However, after the uncharged neutron was discovered, and its properties became known, it became evident that protons and neutrons, rather than protons and electrons, were the building blocks of heavier nuclei.° For example, the alpha particle, $_2\text{He}^4$, contains two protons to give it a charge of two units, and two neutrons to make up the mass of four units. This apparently is a very stable combination, and so can be ejected as a single particle from the heavy radioactive elements. As another example, the nucleus of a uranium atom, $_{92}\text{U}^{238}$, contains 92 protons to provide the charge of $92e$, and 146 neutrons to make the mass up to 238 units.

If the electron is not one of the building blocks within the nucleus, how is it that electrons are ejected as beta particles, from some specific radioactive elements? It has been discovered that the neutron itself is radioactive, with a half-life of 13 minutes, so that unless something else happens to it in the meantime, it converts spontaneously into a proton, with the emission of a beta particle and a gamma-ray photon. Apparently this can happen to one of the neutrons inside a heavy atom, and so give rise to the beta rays of natural radioactivity.

Again, if there are no negative electrons to provide the cement, what holds heavy nuclei together in spite of the strong electrostatic repulsion between the closely packed protons? Apparently there are very strong attractive forces between both protons and neutrons, which act only when they are very close together. These forces are of a new kind, not related to electric or magnetic attractions, and very much stronger than the latter within their range of action. They are still somewhat mysterious and there is no simple law of the variation of nuclear attractions with distance. It is the conversion of mass into potential energy of these nuclear forces that accounts for the apparent loss of mass when protons and neutrons are

° Detailed discussion of the experimental evidence which makes this clear would take too much space. Let it suffice to say that it has to do with the proper balancing of the angular momentum and magnetic properties of the particles concerned.

packed together, and conversely there is a conversion of nuclear potential energy into kinetic energy and gamma-ray energy when radioactive emission takes place.

23-8   "Artificial" Radioactive Isotopes

Between the bombardment of all sorts of materials by natural alpha particles or by charged particles from accelerators, and the reactions induced by fast and slow neutrons, literally thousands of nuclear reactions have now been observed and described in scientific journals. Some of the most interesting reactions are those in which the product nucleus is radioactive, with a half-life of a few hours or days. These include the several isotopes of elements heavier than uranium, all those up to lawrencium (number 103) having been found among the products of bombardment of the natural heavy elements. But they also include a large number of isotopes of the familiar light elements. For example, there is a radioactive phosphorus, $_{15}P^{32}$, which emits beta particles with a half-life of 14.3 days, and which can be produced by the following reaction:

$$_{16}S^{32} + _{0}n^{1} \longrightarrow _{15}P^{32} + _{1}H^{1}.$$

Radioactive isotopes of medium lifetime, produced in this way, are truly man-made elements.° Only very few of them have been found in nature; carbon 14 and plutonium 239, for example, are produced in minute quantities by bombardment with the cosmic rays that are always entering the atmosphere, or by stray neutrons. However, some radioactive isotopes can be manufactured in considerable quantity by neutron reactions in a nuclear reactor (Sec. 24-3), and they have found many uses. For example, cobalt 60, which emits beta and gamma rays with a half-life of 5.25 years, is widely used as a relatively inexpensive substitute for radium in the treatment of malignant tumors.

One of the most interesting uses of manufactured isotopes is that as *radioactive tracers,* sometimes referred to as "tagged atoms." When it is desired to find out just what happens to a certain element in the metabolism of the body, in the growth of plants, or in chemical research, a little of a radioactive isotope can be added to the natural inactive element, and this can be followed with a Geiger counter or some other instrument that detects the radioactive emission produced. For example, iodine is essential to the proper functioning of the thyroid gland, and if some radioactive iodine is taken into the body it soon finds its way to the thyroid. Study of the way in which the radio-iodine is utilized can help greatly in diagnosis of thyroid disorders. Again, cobalt is an essential ingredient of vitamin B_{12},

°Two light elements, technetium, number 43, and promethium, number 61, have no stable isotopes, and are known only as manufactured radioactive atoms.

and this vitamin, in turn, is necessary before the bone marrow will make red blood corpuscles in the proper quantity. A study of what happens after taking a dose of radioactive cobalt 56 can show whether the body is producing vitamin B_{12} properly, and helps in the diagnosis of certain types of anemia, or red corpuscle deficiency. In agriculture, by adding some phosphorus 32 to fertilizers and observing when and where this appears in the plants, it has been possible to find out what conditions are necessary for the crops to make the most efficient use of the fertilizer.

23-9   *Positrons*

So far in this account we have recognized three different "fundamental" particles, the neutron, the positively charged proton, and the negative electron. The evidence seems clear that these three are the building blocks of all ordinary matter, protons and neutrons in the nucleus, electrons in the outer cloud which makes up most of the volume of an atom. Mass and electric charge are discontinuous quantities, protons and neutrons providing the basic units of mass apart from the fact that the potential energy of the nuclear forces accounts for small variations in their apparent mass when they are closely packed together. As far as we can tell from the most precise experiments the electric charges on the proton and on the electron are exactly equal and opposite, so that the charge value, 1.6020×10^{-19} coulomb, appears to be a true basic unit, not subject to variations like the unit of mass.

In the last 30 years a number of other things have been observed, which appear to be single particles, but which have only a very temporary existence. Many of these were first identified in the tracks of droplets left by cosmic rays passing through a cloud chamber.° The first of these unstable particles to be discovered was the *positron*, or positively charged electron. In 1928 Paul Dirac of Cambridge University developed a theoretical method of treating electrons which seemed to fit in very well with their observed properties, including the fact that they have a "spin," or an intrinsic angular momentum, and behave like tiny magnets (Sec. 34-3). Dirac's equations, however, had a symmetrical feature,† which suggested the possibility of a particle opposite in all respects to the electron, specifically as regards its having a positive charge.

In 1932 C. D. Anderson of the California Institute of Technology found such a particle in a cloud photograph of cosmic rays passing through a strong magnetic field. Because the particle was slowed down in passing through a lead plate inserted in the cloud chamber, the direction in which

---

° Cosmic rays, and "strange" particles in general, will be discussed further in Chapter 34.

† There is an analogy with the algebraic equation, $x^2 = a$, which has two solutions, $x = +\sqrt{a}$, and $x = -\sqrt{a}$.

it was traveling could be traced; the deflection produced by the magnetic field showed that it must have a mass similar to that of an ordinary electron, but be positively charged. Positrons are now known to be produced quite frequently, in at least two distinct ways. When a gamma-ray or X-ray photon of sufficiently high energy hits a heavy atom a positron and an ordinary negative electron can be simultaneously created, so that there is a direct conversion of the electromagnetic energy of the gamma ray into mass (Fig. 23-5).[*]

The other common source of positrons is radioactive emission from certain artificially produced unstable isotopes. For example, sodium 22 decays with a half-life of 2.6 years, in the reaction

$$_{11}\text{Na}^{22} \longrightarrow {}_{10}\text{Ne}^{22} + \text{e}^+ + \text{Q}.$$

Positrons cannot last very long; in passing through matter they very soon encounter a negative electron, and the two annihilate each other, the mass disappearing in a spurt of gamma-ray energy.

23-10   Neutrinos

No account of nuclear reactions can be complete without reference to the mysterious *neutrino*, or little neutron. When a radioactive element decays by emission of beta particles (negative or positive electrons) there is, in general, an apparent violation of the laws of conservation of energy and momentum. The energy computed by Einstein's relation from the loss of mass is greater than the combined energy of the ejected beta particle and the gamma ray which usually accompanies it. Moreover, the combined energy is not a definite quantity, but can take any value up to a maximum

[*] In order to produce an electron-positron pair, the gamma-ray photon must have an energy at least equal to $2\,m_0c^2$, where m_0 is the mass of the electron. This works out to 1.0216 million electron-volts.

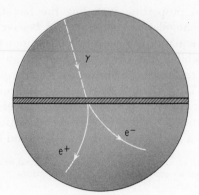

FIG. 23-5

Production of an electron-positron pair when a gamma ray is absorbed in a lead plate; diagram of the type of track observed in a cloud chamber with a magnetic field; the gamma ray leaves no track and its presence is deduced.

limit, which is equal to the computed energy production of the reaction. In 1930, therefore, Wolfgang Pauli hypothesized that the excess energy must be carried off by a third particle which was also emitted in the reaction, and he deduced what the properties of this particle must be.

Pauli's particle, now recognized as a neutrino, has neither electric charge nor mass in the ordinary sense, but it carries energy and momentum by virtue of the fact that it is traveling with the velocity of light. In this respect it is like a gamma-ray photon, but it has none of the other characteristics of electromagnetic radiation. Because neutrinos have no charge, no true mass, and no electromagnetic field like that of a gamma ray, they are the most highly penetrating of all known particles, and can pass through miles of dense matter without doing anything. They do, however, have a "spin," an intrinsic angular momentum like that of the electron, and by virtue of this there is a very small probability that they may interact with an atomic nucleus when they pass close to it, and so cause a nuclear reaction.

In 1956 Frederick Reines and Clyde Cowan of Los Alamos exposed a very large scintillation counter to an atomic reactor in which many beta-particle disintegrations were going on, so that the production of a large number of neutrinos was anticipated. As a result they observed rare events in which protons were apparently converted into neutrons plus positrons— the reverse process to neutron decay. Since this involves an increase of mass it requires energy, and they were able to demonstrate that the necessary energy could only come from the absorption of a neutrino.

GLOSSARY

Accelerator Machine in which charged particles are given energies great enough to enable them to cause nuclear reactions.

Artificial radioactivity Radioactive emission from an isotope which is manufactured by an induced nuclear reaction, and which does not occur in nature.

Atom smasher Popular term for a particle accelerator that can cause nuclear reactions.

Cosmic rays High-energy particles and photons that are continually entering the earth's atmosphere from somewhere in outer space.

Cyclotron Machine for accelerating particles by making them describe many circular orbits between the poles of an electromagnet, and giving them a forward impulse at each half orbit; capable of producing energies in the 10 million electron-volt range.

Electron-volt The energy acquired by a particle having one electronic charge when it is acted upon by a potential of 1 volt; the unit used to state the energy of a single particle, or the energy involved in a single atomic reaction.

Half-life The time during which one half of a sample of a radioactive isotope will disintegrate.

Induced nuclear reactions Changes in the nuclei of atoms caused by bombardment with high-speed charged particles or with neutrons.

Ionization potential The energy in electron-volts required to ionize an atom or molecule.

Linear accelerator Machine for accelerating charged particles to high energies by passing them through a succession of electrodes, so spaced that the particle receives an additional forward impulse at each electrode; theoretically capable of producing particles of any desired energy.

Mev Abbreviation for million electron-volts.

Moderator (of neutrons) Material in which the energies of neutrons are reduced to a few electron-volts by successive elastic collisions with atomic nuclei in the material.

Neutrino Particle that possesses neither intrinsic mass nor electric charge; it is produced in certain types of nuclear reaction, and carries energy and momentum by virtue of the fact that it travels with the speed of light.

Neutron Uncharged particle with a mass approximately equal to that of a proton (or hydrogen nucleus).

Nuclear reaction Any reaction in which the nuclei of the atoms are affected, so that the elements or isotopes produced are different from those entering into the reaction.

Nuclear reactor Device in which nuclear reactions proceed spontaneously in a self-sustaining chain reaction, but at a controlled rate rather than explosively, as in an atomic bomb (Sec. 24-3).

Photon Quantum of electromagnetic waves produced by one atom at one time (Sec. 33-1); the term is used especially when the particle-like properties of the quantum are in evidence.

Positron Positively charged particle with mass equal to that of an electron; produced in certain radioactive transformations, or by the conversion of a gamma-ray photon into a positron-electron pair.

Radioactive decay or disintegration Conversion of a radioactive isotope into an isotope of a different element by the spontaneous emission of a charged particle from the nucleus.

Radioactive series A succession of disintegrations that a radioactive isotope may undergo before settling into a stable state; used particularly of the heavy, natural radioactive elements.

Radioactive tracer A radioactive isotope that can be added to an element in order to trace it through a series of chemical reactions (especially biological reactions), by observing what happens to the radioactivity.

Slow neutrons Neutrons whose energies have been reduced to values comparable with those of gas molecules by collisions with the nuclei in a moderator.

Spin In atomic physics, the intrinsic angular momentum possessed by electrons and by many other atomic particles.

Tagged atoms Popular term for radioactive tracers.

Van de Graaff accelerator Particle accelerator in which high energies are obtained by the direct application of a high voltage, obtained through electrostatic charging; useful for energies of 1 to 10 million electron-volts.

EXERCISES

1. State and explain the rules for the radioactive transformations caused by the emission of: (a) an alpha particle; (b) a beta particle; (c) a positron.

2. Why do all the isotopes of the uranium-radium series have mass numbers of the form $4n + 2$? Illustrate your answer by giving a portion of the series, from radium 226 to lead.

3. Write the nuclear reaction equations for each of the following: (a) emission of alpha rays from radon 222; (b) bombardment of aluminum 27 with alpha rays, resulting in the ejection of protons; (c) production of neutrons by bombarding beryllium 9 with deuterons (nuclei of deuterium atoms); (d) production of sodium 22 by bombarding magnesium 24 with deuterons, and subsequent decay of sodium 22 by emission of positrons.

4. Calculate the net loss of mass when a nucleus of radium 226 ejects an alpha particle with an energy of 4.61 million electron-volts. Express the result both in kilograms and in atomic mass units.

5. Explain how the concepts of (a) a definite half-life for a radioactive isotope, (b) a definite probability of disintegration, (c) an activity strictly proportional to the amount of isotope present, are all connected, and are all expressions of the principle that radioactivity is a spontaneous property of the atomic nucleus.

6. Why is there always a definite proportion of radium to uranium in a natural uranium ore? How much radium would there be in a sample of ore that contained 100 kilograms of uranium 238? How much polonium 210?

7. Where radium is used for radiotherapy treatments radon gas is extracted from the main radium supply and sealed in tiny gold tubes. Suppose such a tube contained ¹⁄₁₀ cubic millimeter of radon, how much would be left after 15.3 days? What would be the most abundant isotope in the deposit on the inside of the tube at that time? Just after the radon is extracted, how would its alpha-particle activity compare with that of the radium 226 left behind?

8. Describe two types of particle accelerator: (a) one that produces the required voltage directly; (b) one that accelerates the particles in steps.

9. Explain the principle of an accelerator designed to produce particles with the highest feasible energies, in the billion-electron-volt range.

10. What is the energy in joules of the particles produced in the CERN accelerator?

11. Describe how neutrons were first discovered. When the effect was first observed, it was thought that it might be due to gamma rays; how was this suggestion disproved?

12. Name briefly the three important things that a neutron can do after leaving the source.

13. How are neutrons detected, and how is the velocity of neutrons measured?

14. State the number of protons and neutrons in each of the following nuclei: nitrogen 14, neon 22, chlorine 37, nickel 60, gold 197, uranium 238.

15. How are nuclei stable in spite of the repulsion between their protons? How can one calculate the total binding energy of a heavy nucleus?

16. Describe briefly some of the uses of artificial radioactive isotopes, (a) for radiotherapy, (b) in industry.

17. How are radioactive tracers used? Give examples.

18. Why do we believe that a composite nucleus is constructed of protons and neutrons, rather than some other particles, such as electrons?

19. How was the positron first discovered? Where, if anywhere, do positrons occur in nature? How are they produced artificially?

20. Calculate the energy in electron-volts required to produce the mass of a positron-electron pair.

21. Why was it necessary to postulate the existence of a neutrino? What do neutrinos do after they are produced in a nuclear reaction?

22. Which of the elements listed in the periodic table are known only in an artificially produced unstable form? Which are unstable, but occur in the earth's crust? Which are normally stable, but have naturally occurring unstable isotopes?

nuclear atomic energy

From the time that the principles of radioactivity began to be understood, and scientists realized that mass and energy are mutually convertible, it became obvious that atomic nuclei contained a vast store of energy which might someday be tapped. It was obvious, too, that nuclear reactions of some kind, with loss of mass, must be the source of the energy which the sun and stars pour out continuously throughout their long lifetime (Sec. 31-2). However, it was not until 1939 that a process was discovered that led to a method of utilizing nuclear energy on earth. For this purpose natural radioactivity is useless, because uranium and other radioactive elements are comparatively rare, and there is no known way of increasing the rate at which they release their energy. The kind of nuclear reaction which is produced by bombardment with high-speed charged particles is useless because the energy required to run the accelerating machine is far greater than that produced by the reaction.

In February, 1939, Otto Hahn, Fritz Strassmann, and Lise Meitner, in Germany, announced the discovery that one of the products of the action

393

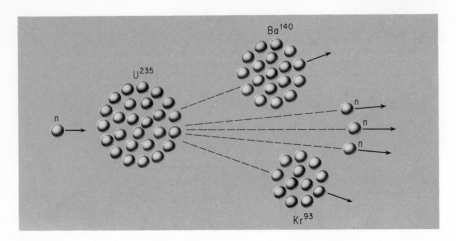

FIG. 24-1

Fission of a uranium 235 nucleus.

of neutrons on uranium is unmistakably a radioactive isotope of barium, later identified as $_{56}Ba^{140}$. A little before this it had been observed that neutrons induced some kind of "artificial" radioactivity in uranium, but the details were obscure, and it had been supposed that new elements, heavier than uranium, were being produced. This does indeed happen under some circumstances, and elements beyond uranium in the table are now well known, but what Hahn and the others had discovered was something quite different. Instead of giving off a proton or some other simple particle, the uranium nucleus, when struck by a neutron, had split into two roughly equal parts, as indicated in Fig. 24-1.

It was soon established that it is the relatively rare light isotope of uranium, U^{235}, which breaks up in this way under influence of slow neutrons. The *fission*, as it came to be called, can occur in many different ways, among which the diagram shows only one possible example, isotopes of atomic number ranging from 30 to 60 having been observed among the "fission fragments." Fission also occurs in several other heavy nuclei, a particularly important case being that of plutonium 239. The details are unimportant for our purposes. The important factors are that there are always two or three fast neutrons ejected, that the immediate fission fragments always contain too many neutrons to balance the number of protons, and so are highly radioactive, producing several beta particles and gamma rays before settling down to stable atoms, and finally that the total amount of energy released, including that produced by the radioactivity of the fragments, is very large, approximately 200 million electron-volts, as compared with the 10 million electron-volts or so of ordinary radioactive emission.

24-2   *Chain Reactions and Nuclear Explosions*

Before the store of energy contained in atomic nuclei could be tapped it was necessary to find a reaction which would be self-sustaining, or, to use a term which is particularly apt in this case, a *chain reaction*. For example, ordinary combustion is a self-sustaining reaction. In order to light a fire, a piece of flammable material has to be heated to a certain critical temperature in the presence of a plentiful supply of oxygen. Then the heat produced by the burning of the first piece heats the surrounding material to the ignition point, and the fire spreads. The lighted match acts as a trigger to start the reaction, which then continues of its own accord. If the heat produced in the burning of the first piece is not enough, or if the heat is carried away too quickly, the fire goes out. The difference between simple combustion and a conventional explosion, such as that of dynamite or TNT, lies in the rate at which the reaction spreads, once it is started.

When the discovery of nuclear fission was announced, quite publicly, in the course of the normal international exchange of scientific information, it was obvious to any competent physicist that here was the first essential for a self-sustaining chain reaction, which could release tremendous amounts of nuclear energy, because each primary neutron produces two or more secondary neutrons, and these could collide with other uranium nuclei in the surrounding material, and cause the reaction to spread of its own accord, as indicated in Fig. 24-2. There were, however, serious difficulties to be overcome before a chain reaction could be achieved. The neutrons produced by fission are fast neutrons, with a high penetrating power. In a

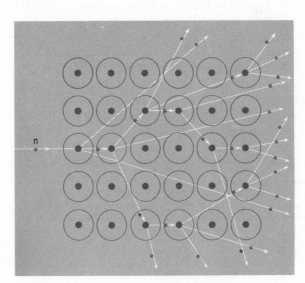

FIG. 24-2

How a chain reaction causes an explosion in a sufficiently large mass of fissionable material.

small lump of material most of these "secondary" neutrons escape before they have a chance to hit a U^{235} nucleus, and cause another fission. The reaction ceases, just as a candle flame goes out when one blows on it and drives away the hot gases. There must, therefore, be a critical mass (which turned out later to be a few kilograms of pure U^{235} or plutonium) such that for every primary neutron entering the material at least one secondary neutron is caught, and causes fission. With more than the critical mass in one lump there would be a violent explosion; with less than the critical mass nothing much would happen, and the material would be perfectly safe to handle, apart from the precautions necessary in handling any radioactive material. Thus one of the first problems which would have to be solved was to obtain enough of the rare fissionable materials, U^{235} or Pu^{239}, to accumulate a critical mass.

When these facts became clear to the scientific world early in 1939, it was obvious to any student of the international scene that war with Nazi Germany and her satellites was imminent, and that the United States would be drawn into it sooner or later, in spite of the strong sentiment that America should remain aloof from European affairs. It was at this point that a group of atomic scientists persuaded the aging Professor Einstein to write his famous letter to President Franklin Roosevelt, explaining the possibilities inherent in the discovery of nuclear fission, and suggesting that the Germans would probably seize upon it to produce a weapon of devastating power. A veil of the strictest secrecy was lowered over any further nuclear research, and two teams of scientists went quietly to work behind locked doors to try and solve the practical problems involved in the utilization of nuclear fission. The American team worked first at Chicago and later at Los Alamos in the New Mexican desert, with the help of several famous scientists, Enrico Fermi, Niels Bohr, and others, who had become refugees from totalitarianism. A British-Canadian team worked first in Montreal and later at Chalk River, near Ottawa.° Physicists everywhere knew what was going on, and why. Only the practical details could be kept secret, so that much of what is described here did not become general knowledge until after the first atomic bombs had been dropped on Hiroshima and Nagasaki, to bring to a swift conclusion the war with Japan.

How does a nuclear explosion work? The details of construction of nuclear weapons are, of course, still military secrets, but the principles involved have long ago become general scientific knowledge. There must

---

° A curious situation developed, most unusual in the world of science. The code word for the American team was "Manhattan Project," and the British-Canadian effort had a similar code name. One might ask for news of a friend, and the answer might be, "He's gone to Manhattan." The conversation was immediately dropped, and no further questions were asked, because one knew that they could not and would not be answered. There is an interesting and very human account of the secrecy conditions of the early 1940's in Laura Fermi's biography of her famous husband, *Atoms in the Family*.

In Germany, where fission was first observed, there was no intensive effort to exploit it for military purposes, apparently because Hitler did not believe it feasible.

be two or more well-separated pieces of fissionable material, uranium 235 or plutonium, each of which is smaller than the critical size necessary for a chain reaction, but such that the total mass is greater than critical. To set off the explosion these must be brought together very rapidly, and held for the second or so that it takes for the chain reaction to spread throughout the mass. This can be done in several ways. One method, for example, is to make one piece of plutonium in the shape of a bullet and the other in the shape of a cup into which the bullet just fits; the bullet is fired into the cup by a charge of conventional explosive. No source of neutrons is necessary to trigger the reaction, once the critical mass is assembled, because there are always cosmic ray neutrons present in the atmosphere. When the chain reaction starts, the temperature of the plutonium goes up to several million degrees Kelvin within a second or so. Everything, including the material of the bomb itself, is almost instantly vaporized into high-pressure gas, and the wave of heat and pressure energy spreads out to do the physical damage. To this extent a nuclear explosion of the "A-bomb" type is simply an explosion on a huge scale, and it has in fact been suggested that plutonium explosions might be used in very large rock-blasting operations, or to release petroleum that is trapped underground in rock or sand.

The energy theoretically available from the nuclear fission of a kilogram of plutonium is equivalent to that obtained by burning 700,000 kilograms of pure hydrogen, which, weight for weight, is the most energetic ordinary fuel we have. There is no practical way of utilizing all this energy before the reaction stops, or the mass of plutonium vaporizes, but still the explosion of a few kilograms of plutonium in the early atomic bombs produced as much heat and blast as 20,000 tons of TNT. However, the new and alarming feature of a nuclear explosion as compared with that of a very large quantity of conventional chemical explosive is the high-energy radiation produced in the form of highly penetrating gamma rays and neutrons. This radiation can cause death to any living thing over a large area, and over a still more widespread area it can—through its effect on the reproductive cells—cause an unknown amount of damage to generations yet unborn.

24-3   *The Nuclear Atomic Pile*

The first successful use of the fission reaction was actually not an explosion, but a *controlled chain reaction,* of the type which has since become useful as a source of electric power. In this case the number of secondary neutrons captured must be just the right amount to keep the reaction going at a moderate, but controlled rate. Fermi decided that this could be done with sufficiently large quantity of natural uranium, containing U^{238}

as well as the fissionable U^{235}. A team of scientists, engineers, and technicians worked under his direction underneath the football stands at the
University of Chicago, where they assembled the first *atomic pile* (technically described nowadays as a *nuclear reactor*). In late 1942 this was completed, and on December 2nd of that year Fermi turned on the controls,
and, true to his prediction, the uranium started to react, and continued to
do so as long as required. Still, it was over 2 years before the first test bomb
was exploded in the New Mexican desert. This delay was due to the fact
that a number of other technical problems had to be solved; there was also
an insufficient quantity of plutonium accumulated from the reactions in
the Chicago pile, or, alternatively, of pure U^{235} by the laborious process of
isotope separation.°

The principle of the nuclear reactor is illustrated in Fig. 24-3. First we
must have the nuclear fuel, which, in a large reactor like the original
Chicago pile, can be natural uranium, consisting of 0.7 per cent fissionable
U^{235} and 99.3 per cent common U^{238}. This is usually in the form of rods
of uranium metal, and the total amount must, of course, exceed the critical
mass necessary to maintain the chain reaction. Now, the fission of U^{235} is
most efficiently caused by "slow" neutrons, with energies of some 20 to 30
electron-volts. So we must have a *moderator*, to catch the fast neutrons
ejected in the fission reaction, slow them down, and reflect a sufficient
number of them back into the uranium rods. In the original Chicago pile
the moderator consisted of blocks of very pure carbon, but heavy water,
D$_2$O, containing the heavy isotope of hydrogen, has been found to be
more effective.

There must be a control, consisting of some material that reacts readily
with neutrons, and so removes a lot of them from circulation. An effective

° Both methods were used for the bombs dropped on Japan in 1945, and both are still
employed to obtain fuel for power production by nuclear energy.

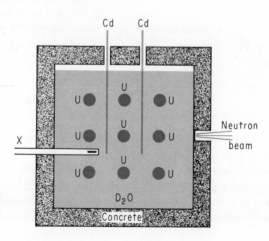

FIG. 24-3

Schematic diagram of a nuclear reactor, commonly known as an
atomic pile.

control consists of a few rods or sheets of cadmium, which can be raised or lowered in the pool of heavy water. When the cadmium sheets are down, they absorb excess neutrons and prevent the chain reaction from taking place. As they are slowly withdrawn from the pool a point is reached such that for every primary neutron precisely one of the two or three secondary neutrons misses the cadmium, is slowed down by the moderator, and finds another U^{235} nucleus. The reaction then becomes self-sustaining, but steadily, without any explosive tendency. Raise the control sheets a little too far, and the temperature inside the reactor starts to rise. Automatic sensors, connected to the machinery which raises and lowers the controls, then go into action and restore the stable safe condition. Finally, the whole structure is surrounded by a thick wall of concrete, to protect the operators and research workers from the stray neutrons and high-energy gamma rays that are continually escaping from the reactor.

The first reactors were built for experimental purposes rather than for the generation of electric power. They are operated with an energy output just enough above the critical rate to make the reaction self-sustaining, and the temperature is not allowed to rise more than a few degrees above that of the surroundings. Such a reactor is the most copious source yet known of neutrons for all sorts of purposes. For experiments in nuclear physics, to be carried on outside the reactor proper, a beam of fast and slow neutrons can be obtained from a hole in the concrete protecting wall. For the production of artificial radioactive isotopes in quantity, the raw material can be exposed to intense neutron radiation by inserting it through a tube right into the reactor, as at X in Fig. 24-3.

One of the most important by-products of a natural uranium reactor is the production of large quantities of fissionable plutonium. Some of the fast neutrons from the initial fission reaction in U^{235} act on the much more abundant U^{238} to cause the simple nuclear reaction

$$_{92}U^{238} + _{0}n^{1} \longrightarrow _{92}U^{239}.$$

The U^{239} decays spontaneously by the emission of a beta particle, with a half-life of 23.5 minutes, to produce $_{93}Np^{239}$ (neptunium). This in turn decays with a half-life of 2.33 days to produce the plutonium, $_{94}Pu^{239}$. Plutonium 239 is fairly stable, having a radioactive half-life of 24,000 years, and it occurs in minute quantities in nature from the action of cosmic-ray neutrons on natural uranium. However, the plutonium which is used for nuclear explosions and for small power-producing reactors is truly a man-made element. After a natural uranium reactor has been running for some time it is shut down, the uranium fuel rods are removed, and the plutonium (and fission products) which have accumulated are extracted chemically. Incidentally, great care must be exercised in handling plutonium and many of its compounds—they are not only radioactive, but also extremely poisonous, in the ordinary chemical sense.

Figure 24-4 is a graph of the precise atomic weights of the known stable isotopes, divided by their mass numbers, so that it represents the average mass per nuclear particle. The horizontal line drawn at the value unity represents isotopes which have precisely one atomic mass unit per particle. This line necessarily passes through carbon 12, which has six protons and six neutrons, because its atomic weight is exactly 12.000 . . . by definition. Isotopes represented by points below the line have less mass per particle than carbon, those above the line have more. There are many local irregularities in the detailed graph, but there is a general trend, shown by the shaded band in the figure. The diagram shows that the mass per particle is a minimum in the neighborhood of iron. If elements heavier than iron are involved in a nuclear reaction which moves them to a lower position in the periodic table, they usually lose mass, and so generate energy. Thus, natural radioactivity and fission of heavy elements both cause a reduction in the mass per particle, and produce energy. For elements lighter than iron the reverse is usually true, and they lose mass when a reaction moves them toward higher atomic numbers. The steepest part of the graph

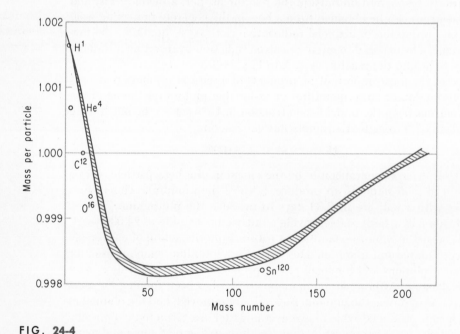

FIG. 24-4

Graph of the mass per nuclear particle in the different isotopes. The vertical scale is compressed toward large deviations from the value unity. The circles represent exceptionally stable isotopes.

occurs among elements lighter than neon, particularly the isotopes of hydrogen and helium. Isotopes of these elements lose an appreciable fraction of their mass when their nuclei combine, or are synthesized, into the nuclei of heavier elements, the most conspicuous case being the synthesis of four hydrogen nuclei, or simple protons, into a helium nucleus, or alpha particle.

Reactions in which two light nuclei combine to produce a heavier nucleus, with a net conversion of mass into energy, are known as *fusion reactions,* and two of several that have been observed to take place are

$$_1\text{H}^1 + {_1\text{H}^1} \longrightarrow {_1\text{H}^2} + \text{e}^+ + \text{Q},$$
$$_1\text{H}^2 + {_1\text{H}^3} \longrightarrow {_2\text{He}^4} + {_0\text{n}^1} + \text{Q}.$$

Since both particles entering into the reaction are positively charged, one of them at least must be traveling with a high velocity so that they can approach close enough to react. In laboratory studies this is attained in some form of particle accelerator. However, it turns out that in a gas at a temperature of a few million degrees an appreciable fraction of the atoms have sufficient energy to make close collisions, and react. If the mass of material is large enough, the atoms which first react produce sufficient energy to maintain the very high temperature, and the reaction becomes self-sustaining for the same reason that an ordinary flame is self-sustaining, or the reaction may even spread explosively. Fusion reactions of light nuclei which take place under these conditions of high temperature are referred to as *thermonuclear reactions.* There is no doubt that they are taking place naturally, all the time, in the deep interior of the sun and stars. They are also the source of the energy in the explosion of a thermonuclear bomb, or "H-bomb."

To effect a thermonuclear explosion it is necessary to have a fairly large mass (there is no theoretical *upper* limit) of materials which can combine in a fusion reaction, with the materials for a plutonium fission explosion embedded in the center. Explosion of the plutonium raises the temperature locally to the million-degree range, and ignites the fusion reaction. In a fraction of a second the whole mass explodes, producing heat and blast equivalent to several million tons of TNT,° and sufficient penetrating radiation and radioactive dust (called fallout) to cause death and injury over an area of several hundred square miles. The fallout, which spreads over a wide area, comes not only from the explosive material itself, but also from nearby material which is rendered radioactive by secondary nuclear reactions induced by the intense gamma rays. The nearby material may be part of the case which enclosed the bomb, and the so-called "clean bomb" is one in which this source of fallout is reduced to a minimum.

° The term "megaton," as applied to thermonuclear weapons, means an explosive energy equal to that of a million tons of TNT.

So far, no satisfactory method has been found of controlling the rate of a fusion reaction so that it could be used for the peaceful production of power. For this purpose, the reacting material, which is in the form of gas at a temperature of a million degrees and a very high pressure, would have to be confined in a limited volume in order to make the reaction self-sustaining. Obviously, no ordinary container could withstand these temperatures, but, because the gas would be completely ionized, it is theoretically possible to confine it by means of a suitably shaped magnetic field. At the time of writing, this has been done only on a very small scale, but human ingenuity will probably find a way of confining enough high-temperature ionized gas to produce a fusion reaction. If this can be achieved at reasonable cost, the world energy problem can be solved, for the ingredients of such a reaction are in almost unlimited supply in the sea.

24-5   The Production of Nuclear Power

In discussing the use of nuclear energy for the production of useful power, we can think of two types of application. The first is in very large electric generating plants, now becoming important in a few parts of the world, where there is very little available waterpower, and where coal is beginning to get scarce. Nuclear power plants of this type can operate in essentially the same manner as the nuclear reactor described in Sec. 24-3, using natural uranium as the fuel, and producing plutonium as a by-product. However, a power-producing reactor must operate at a fairly high temperature, and generate large quantities of heat. The problem is how to use that heat energy to drive a set of electric generators. The nuclear energy cannot be used to produce steam directly. That is, the reactor cannot simply be inserted into a large steam boiler, because the steam produced would be radioactive and would contaminate everything with which it came in contact with a cumulative source of radiation which before long would reach dangerous levels. The heat must, therefore, be transmitted from the reactor to the steam boiler by means of a fluid *heat exchanger*.

The principle of the heat exchanger is illustrated in Fig. 24-5. The heat is transmitted from the reactor to the boiler by means of fluid which is kept circulating in a closed system of pipes. The fluid can be water under a pressure high enough to prevent it being converted into steam, or it can be a liquid with a high boiling point, because the higher the temperature at this stage the more efficient the whole operation. The circulating fluid passes through a coil built into the moderator which surrounds the reactor proper, where it collects the heat of the nuclear reactions. It then passes through another coil attached to the steam boiler, and gives up its heat to produce steam, which can be used to turn the turbines that drive the electric generators.

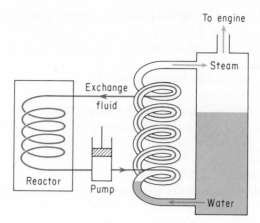

FIG. 24-5

Principle of the heat-exchange system
in a nuclear power plant.

The first nuclear power plant, designed to produce electric power on a useful scale, was built at Calder Hall in the north of England, and went into operation in 1956. Since then, several more have been built in England, where shortage of electric power is a very serious problem, a number have gone into operation in the United States and in the Soviet Union, and others are being built in many places where there is a scarcity of water-power and fossil fuel.* At present, nuclear power from a uranium reactor cannot compete in cost with waterpower where this is plentiful, or with coal unless this has to be transported long distances. The initial cost of a nuclear power plant is comparable with that of a hydroelectric plant; both being considerably higher than that of building a coal-burning plant. Although the cost of the uranium fuel is much less than that of an equivalent amount of coal or oil—transportation costs are negligible, because a single charge of uranium lasts for several months—the disposal of the highly radioactive waste products is a serious problem which greatly increases the operating cost.

The other type of nuclear power plant that is becoming ever more useful is the comparatively small portable unit, such as that in a nuclear submarine, enabling the vessel to remain submerged for weeks or even months, because there are no batteries to be recharged, and no need for any air-consuming internal combustion engine. Nuclear power is useful in surface ships required to make long voyages in seas far from any conventional fuel supply, such as the icebreaker that was recently built by the Soviet Union for service along their great stretch of Arctic coast. Another use for units

* There are large power reactors in operation or under construction in China, in France and other European countries, in Canada, and in India. All these reactors produce plutonium which could be used for atomic weapons. One of the principal functions of the International Atomic Energy Commission—so-called Atoms-for-Peace—is to promote the construction of power reactors and to devise and encourage peaceful uses for the plutonium in countries that will cooperate in the program.

of this type is to provide heat and electric power at remote settlements, such as research stations in the Antarctic, or government outposts in the Far North, where the transportation of fuel is a large item in the maintenance cost.

These small units have as their source of energy a reactor that is fueled with pure plutonium, or with "enriched" uranium, in which the fissionable isotope U^{235} has been artificially concentrated. The principle of operation is the same as in a large powerplant reactor, and similar methods have to be used to transfer the heat from the reactor to the steam turbine or other unit where it is to be used, but the critical size necessary to make the nuclear reaction self-sustaining is very much less. The greatest part of the bulk and weight is in the shielding which is necessary, in a ship, for example, to protect the men from the radiation produced in the reactor. This makes nuclear energy impractical at present for airplanes or automobiles, although a small unshielded nuclear unit has been used as the source of power for an unmanned satellite in its orbit around the earth.

24-6   Problems of Radioactive Contamination

All high-energy penetrating radiation is potentially dangerous to living organisms. Gamma rays cause ionization within the body, and this may disrupt some of the molecules. Neutrons collide with nuclei in the body, and this also disrupts molecules, either directly or through the ionization caused by the recoil particles. A living cell can tolerate the destruction of a few of its molecules, and repair the damage, but if enough molecules are disrupted the cell dies. The body can tolerate destruction of some of its cells, but if enough are destroyed the resulting chemical changes can cause serious illness; with a higher degree of destruction death results, especially if the damage occurs in one of the vital organs. Even if a cell is not killed, radiation damage can cause it to "run wild," cease performing its normal function, and multiply indiscriminately, and this could be the beginning of a malignant cancerous growth. Finally, any level of damage to the cells of the reproductive organs can cause mutations in the genes, and so affect the inherited characteristics of the next generation, probably with detrimental results.

From the very beginnings of life upon earth, all living things have been subjected to small amounts of radiation, from cosmic rays and from radioactive substances in the soil. This is believed to be one of the causes of the natural gene mutations which are continually taking place, and without which life could not have evolved over the ages in the way that it has. However, for most human beings today the natural radiation which cannot be avoided is augmented by X-ray examinations and the like. In the opinion of the experts, the amount of radiation which the average person receives, due to cosmic rays, medical X rays, stray radioactivity, and anything else, is still far below the level at which any serious damage is likely, but technicians working with X rays or radioactive materials have to take every precaution not to get an overexposure. We should remember, too, that radiation damage is cumulative; small doses every day are almost as bad as the same amount in one large dose.

Any large-scale nuclear reaction, either an explosion or a controlled reaction for the production of power, produces large quantities of radioactive isotopes of many different kinds, some of which have half-lives measured in years. In the case of an explosion taking place on or near the ground, the radioactive material produced by the reaction itself is increased by particles of earth drawn up into the atmosphere, and rendered radioactive by the intense neutron and gamma radiation to which they have been subjected. This material gradually settles to the ground, or is brought down by rain and snow, and constitutes the delayed radioactive fallout. Most of the radioactivity decays fairly rapidly and never travels very far from the locality of the explosion, but some of it persists, not only because it involves long-lived isotopes, but also because particles remain suspended in the atmosphere, and are carried all the way around the world by the high-altitude westerly winds.

Tests of large nuclear weapons carried out in the years before 1963 contaminated the atmosphere throughout the North Temperate Zone, so that long after the explosions took place, and in places far removed from the test localities, measurements of the radioactive content of the atmosphere and of the rain or snow gave values several times that normally found from cosmic rays and natural radioactivity.° The amount was still well below that which the experts consider "safe," in the sense that it is extremely unlikely that it would cause any actual deaths, but we do not know how many deleterious gene mutations it may have caused.

One other very serious problem has still not found a completely satisfactory solution; how are the large quantities of highly radioactive waste material from nuclear power plants to be disposed of in safety? A nuclear reactor is continually producing fission products and other highly radioactive isotopes; the reactor has to be shut down periodically, and these

---

° Public alarm at this time centered largely around the danger of strontium 90 (which has a half-life of 25 years), and around the fact that measurable quantities of this isotope were being found in milk. Strontium 90 is only one of a number of long-lived radioactive substances included in the general contamination, but it is particularly dangerous because it is absorbed in the bones of growing children, so that the child remains exposed to radioactivity until the strontium in its bones decays. Testing milk for strontium 90 is a convenient way of estimating the accumulated fallout in a given region. When the level of atmospheric contamination has been high, long-lived isotopes settle on the grass of the pasture fields. The cattle eat the grass, and a certain fraction of the strontium turns up in the milk they produce. Actually, the total radioactive contamination per unit mass of material will be less in the cow's body than in the grass, less in the milk than in the cow, and less in the child than in the milk it consumes. However, the milk provides a convenient test indicator, and is the subject of much publicity when the results of tests are reported.

materials removed. At present the radioactive waste, which has to be handled with the utmost care in order to protect the workers, is stored for a while behind heavy concrete walls in order to "cool," that is, to allow time for the short-lived isotopes to decay. Still highly radioactive, the material is then transferred to some permanent storage where its radiations cannot do any harm. This may be in concrete vaults deep underground, or it has been suggested that it might be encased in concrete and sunk in the ocean. This is a costly operation, and is one of the main reasons why nuclear power can only compete with waterpower or conventional fuel under special circumstances. So far, the amount of radioactive waste which has had to be buried somewhere is not large, but in time it may become very large indeed, and disposal will then be a very serious problem, to say nothing of the danger that at any stage of the process some of the material might escape, and contaminate an inhabited area.

GLOSSARY

Atomic pile Term used at first for what is now known as a nuclear reactor; so called because the first reactor was constructed in a pile of graphite blocks.

Chain reaction One in which the energy produced by the first atoms to react provides the trigger to initiate more reactions, so that once the process is started it becomes self-sustaining; lighting a fire is a simple, familiar example.

Critical mass In connection with nuclear reactions, the mass that is just sufficient to make the reaction self-sustaining (Sec. 24-2).

Enriched uranium Uranium in which the proportion of the fissionable isotope, U^{235}, has been artificially increased.

Fission products Isotopes produced in a nuclear reactor or a nuclear explosion by the fission of the nuclear fuel; most fission products are radioactive.

Fissionable materials Isotopes of the heavy elements that are subject to fission when bombarded with neutrons.

Fusion reactions Reactions in which two light nuclei combine to produce a heavier nucleus.

Heat exchanger Device for transferring heat energy from one fluid to another without direct contact, so that the fluids do not mix.

Heavy water Water in which most of the hydrogen has been replaced by the isotope of mass 2; deuterium oxide, D_2O.

Megaton Literally, a million tons; applied to a nuclear explosion that produces energy equivalent to that of a million tons of TNT.

Nuclear fission Reaction in which the nucleus of a heavy atom splits into two roughly equal parts, producing isotopes of two lighter elements, accompanied by the ejection of two or more neutrons.

Nuclear fuel Material that provides the source of the energy in a nuclear reactor; usually uranium or plutonium.

Radioactive fallout Radioactive isotopes projected into the atmosphere by a nuclear explosion, later to fall to the ground; fallout can be transported long distances by the wind.

Thermonuclear reactions Reactions taking place in a gas at a very high temperature, when the kinetic energy of the gas atoms is sufficient to cause a nuclear reaction when two atoms collide; such reactions take place naturally in the sun and stars, and are the source of the explosive energy of a hydrogen bomb.

EXERCISES

1. Explain why it is impractical to use as a source of electrical power: (a) the energy of radioactive emission; (b) the energy of the reactions that take place in a particle accelerator.

2. How and when was nuclear fission discovered?

3. Explain how nuclear fission can give rise to a chain reaction. Why is a critical mass necessary?

4. Who built the first nuclear reactor? When, where, and why?

5. Describe the essential features of a reactor that uses natural uranium as the fuel. How is the energy output controlled?

6. What causes the physical damage in a nuclear explosion?

7. The average amount of energy produced in the fission of a heavy nucleus is approximately 220 million electron-volts. Calculate the energy in joules produced by the complete fission of a kilogram of uranium 235. Calculate the equivalent amount of gasoline, if burning 1 kilogram of gasoline produces 11,500 kilocalories of heat.

8. What are some of the peaceful uses of a low-energy nuclear reactor?

9. What is plutonium? How is it produced? Give some of its properties.

10. Which elements can produce energy by fission, and which might produce energy by fusion?

11. Give examples of fusion reactions.

12. What is the difference between an induced fusion reaction and a thermonuclear reaction?

13. Describe briefly the essential features of a small nuclear power plant, such as might be used in a nuclear submarine.

14. Which are likely to be the most expensive to build and to operate, a large nuclear power plant, a hydroelectric plant, or a coal-fired power plant?

15. Under what conditions are nuclear power plants practical?

16. Disposal of the waste is a serious problem in the utilization of nuclear power. What does this waste consist of? What are some of the possible methods of disposal? Is there any practical use for any of the waste products?

17. Describe briefly the biological effects that can be caused by the products of nuclear reactions.

18. Discuss briefly the problem of the fallout from nuclear explosions.

REVIEW EXERCISES FOR CHAPTERS 14 THROUGH 24

1. What were the important contributions to science of each of the following, and what was the approximate date: Michael Faraday, Alessandro Volta, James Clerk Maxwell, William Gilbert, Joseph Henry, Albert Michelson, Christian Huygens, J. J. Thomson, Robert Millikan, Marie Curie, Ernest Rutherford?

2. Give four phenomena in which the effects decrease inversely as the square of the distance from a center. Explain why these quite different phenomena all obey the same law of distance.

3. Give examples of concepts that can only be defined operationally.

4. Give examples of entities that are apparently real and yet cannot be pictured or described in words.

5. State the law of electromagnetic induction. Explain how it lies at the basis of the entire electrical industry.

6. Write a brief historical account of the development and expansion of the use of electricity.

7. Explain how energy can be transmitted by a wave motion, and give three different forms of wave motion that occur in nature. Give one example of radiation that is *not* transmitted by waves.

8. Give examples of resonance occurring in: (a) sound; (b) mechanical vibration; (c) light; (d) an electric circuit.

9. Explain how interference occurs in a wave motion, and give examples of interference phenomena in: (a) sound; (b) light; (c) X rays.

10. Explain what is meant by diffraction, and give examples of this phenomenon.

11. Describe the principal features of the spectra of: (a) a discharge in air at low pressure; (b) an electric light bulb; (c) the sun; (d) a bright bluish star; (e) a red star; (f) the planet Venus; (g) an electric spark between copper terminals.

12. Discuss how improvements in the vacuum pump led to new fundamental scientific discoveries. Give other examples of new discoveries that were dependent on improvement in technology.

13. Explain the following terms: Avogadro's number, mole, Faraday constant, atomic number, isotope, mass number.

14. State and explain the connection between (a) the Faraday constant and the electronic charge; (b) Avogadro's number and the mass of a proton; (c) Millikan's oil-drop experiment and the mass of the electron.

15. Describe briefly five different methods of detecting single atomic particles.

16. Explain the principle of the periodic table of the elements. How many elements should there be in each row of the table, and why? How can we be sure that there are no unknown light elements?

17. List the different fundamental particles which have been encountered in your study up to this point, and give the essential properties of each. Which of them enter into the structure of a heavy atom, and how? Which of them were predicted to exist before they were discovered, and why?

18. Compile a table comparing approximately the energies involved in: (a) a gas molecule in the atmosphere; (b) an atom in the atmosphere of the sun; (c) an atom in the interior of the sun; (d) an energetic chemical reaction, such as the oxidation of a molecule of methane; (e) the ionization of an atom; (f) an electron that is about to produce an X-ray photon; (g) radioactive emission; (h) fission of a heavy nucleus; (i) the maximum particle energy that has so far been produced in an accelerator.

19. Write a short essay on the peaceful uses of nuclear atomic energy—how it can be produced, its advantages and its limitations.

THE CHANGING COSMOS

part six

"The world is ever changing, but always and everywhere the same."

writing the earth's history

25-1   ***The Principle of Uniform Evolution***

"The world is ever changing": Mountains are thrust up, and worn down again; continents rise or shift, and dry land emerges from the sea; the sea invades areas which were once dry land. On the cosmic scale, stars are born and die; planetary systems like our own solar system are formed from clouds of dust, then may be swallowed up by an exploding star. On the other hand, for long ages there have been stars in the sky. For long ages there has been a planet Earth, with mountains and rivers and seas, and we have every reason to believe that there will still be a planet Earth for long ages to come. For at least two-thirds of the earth's history there have been living things upon it, changing in outward form, and gradually developing from a few types of single-celled organisms to the tremendous variety we see today.

Yet the world is "always and everywhere the same." This is what geologists imply when they speak of the *principle of uniformity.* It means that the forces which thrust up the mountains, and the causes of erosion which wear them down again, have always been acting in the same way—ever since the world was formed. The processes which, only a few million years ago, formed the great Himalaya mountains of Asia, are of the same nature

413

as those which, aeons ago, produced the mountains of the Canadian Shield, now worn down to little more than rolling hills. In the living sphere, our human bodies are made of the same types of complex carbon-based molecules, and are subject to the same laws of chemistry, as the most primitive single cell.

On the cosmic scale, apart from the possibility that the creation of the cosmos was a unique event,* uniformity means that the *laws* of nature have always been the same, that they are now the same everywhere in the cosmos, and that they always will be the same. Stars everywhere shine by virtue of the energy produced in a few types of nuclear reaction. All planetary systems, including our own, revolve around their parent stars in conformity with Newton's law of universal gravitation.

If we accept the principle that the laws of nature are "always and everywhere the same"—and we must remember that the sciences of historical geology and of cosmology are meaningless unless we do accept it†— it follows that evolution, both of the stars and of life upon earth, has been a continuous process, subject at all stages to the laws of physics and chemistry. The rate of evolution may have varied, for there is evidence that there have been long periods of slow, gradual change, and other periods of relatively rapid change, but the uniform course of evolution can never have been interrupted.

The cosmos has sometimes been compared with a cataract in a great river. The molecules of water change, waves break and re-form as the water flows over the rocks, the flow and turbulence increase when the river is in flood, and slow down in the dry season of the year. Yet it is always the same river, and a picture of it today would not differ much from one made 100 years ago.

In opposition to the principle of uniform evolution we have the once widely held theory of *catastrophism,* that the changes in the configuration of the mountains and in the living things which inhabited the earth— changes whose occurrence cannot be disputed because the evidence is clear—happened abruptly in a series of catastrophic events, of which the biblical flood was thought to be the most recent example. Along with catastrophism in evolution, which requires the laws of physics to have been suspended or temporarily altered at certain periods of time, we have the idea that the laws may differ at different locations in space. This is no longer believed, but it was an important part of the thinking of Aristotle and of the medieval scholastic philosophers that the sun and stars were in essence different from the earth, and that they were made of some more refined, more "perfect" material than gross earth and stone. The concept of perfection of the heavenly bodies received its deathblow when Isaac

---

* This is only a possibility; the cosmos may have existed from all time (see Sec. 31-8).

† Cosmology is the branch of astronomy that deals with the evolution of the stars and of the cosmos as a whole.

Newton showed that the moon and the planets obey the same law of gravitation as a falling stone.

Nobody today seriously questions the proposition that the basic laws of physics, the law of gravitation, the laws of conservation of energy and momentum, the laws of electricity, and many others are the same everywhere in the cosmos—that they were the same yesterday, and that they will be the same tomorrow as they are today.

25-2   *The Role of Deduction in Modern Science*

So far in this work we have been concerned mainly with the discovery of the laws of nature. The science of astronomy played a very important role in the early days of the scientific revolution in helping to arrive at the fundamental laws of gravitation and of mechanics generally, through the work of such men as Kepler, Galileo, and Newton. Geology has played a similar role in its time, through the discoveries of William Smith, Lyell, and others who in the early nineteenth century showed how to work out the succession of strata (or layers of rock) in the earth's crust, and through Charles Darwin, the father of our modern theories of the continuous evolution of living things.

To a great extent, however, modern astronomy and geology have taken a different turn, and no longer are they concerned, primarily, with the discovery of new laws and principles. For the most part astronomers now ask the question: "What can we deduce about the stars and about the cosmos by assuming the validity of the laws of physics which have been established through laboratory experiment?" And the answer is: "A simply amazing amount."

It will probably be only a few years before the first expedition lands on the moon, or on one of the closer planets, to study it at first hand. However, even if a rocket ship could be accelerated to a speed approaching that of light it would take it over 4 years to reach the nearest true star. The stars are forever out of reach of close inspection, much less are they accessible to any kind of experimentation. The only contact we have, or can ever hope to have, with the stars, and beyond the visible stars, with the outer reaches of the cosmos, is through the radiation we receive from them in the form of light, or other types of electromagnetic waves. Everything we know about a particular star has to be deduced from its radiation, mainly from the little spark of light that we pick up and analyze in a telescope, for the stars are so far away that not even the largest of them can be seen as anything more than a point. The analysis of that spark of light, and the deduction from it of facts about the star from which it came, is an intriguing detective story.

The same applies, in a somewhat different form, and perhaps to a different degree, to anything which is inaccessible to direct observation and to experiment, for example, to the interior of our own earth, and to the past history of the earth. These are the contributions of geophysics, and of historical geology. Again, we have to accumulate whatever information we can from observations made at a distance, in space or in time, assume the laws of physics, and use the present observations and the laws to deduce what the earth is like inside, what it was like a billion years ago, and when and how it was born.

25-3   *Evidence of Change in the Earth's Crust*

We do not have to look far to realize that the great mountain ranges of the earth are slowly being worn down, and their material being deposited on the plains or carried away into the ocean. Signs of erosion are everywhere, from the little gullies left in a sloping plowed field after a heavy rain, through the ravines cut by a mountain stream, to the deep gorges which are sometimes carved out by a great river, like that of the Niagara River below its famous falls. We have only to dip a little water out of a river like the Mississippi or the Nile when it is in flood, to realize that it is carrying away tremendous quantities of silt and sand. This material must be deposited when the flowing water slows down, and eventually comes to rest in a sea or lake. It is not hard to find evidence that recently deposited material is building up the land in low-lying areas. For example, study of a map of an area such as the Mississippi Delta shows that silt carried down by the river has formed several tongues of dry land which extend far out into the Gulf of Mexico, and which continually grow, year after year. Or, on a smaller scale, we can look at the floodplain which is formed by the deposits of a rushing mountain river when it encounters a more level area, and flows out over it.

FIG. 25-1

V-shaped ravine of a vigorous mountain stream, Banff National Park. (Photograph by author.)

FIG. 25-2

The Niagara River gorge. (Photograph by F. B. Taylor, U.S. Geological Survey.)

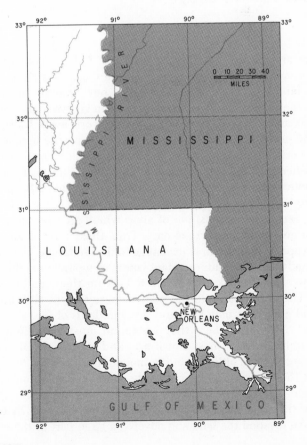

FIG. 25-3

Map of the Mississippi River Delta.

FIG. 25-4

Typical flood plain along the course of a mountain river, the
Bow River near Banff in the Canadian Rockies. (Photograph by
B. G. Wilson, University of Calgary.)

These are gradual, continuous changes. Other, more drastic changes
occur in mountainous regions or along the banks of a river, when there is
a great landslide, or when a river cuts a new channel through a neck of
land, as the Mississippi has several times been known to do. Again, all along
our seacoasts, cliffs are continually being worn away by the waves, and
sand and gravel are continually being piled up on the beaches.

If the existing mountains are continually being worn down, and eventually washed into the sea, new mountains must continually be forming, or
the whole surface of the earth would long ago have been reduced to a
nearly uniform level. It is not quite so easy to find obvious, visible evidence
of new, recent mountains, nor of areas which are even now slowly rising,
to form new mountains some day. True, there are volcanoes, and a volcanic eruption makes a drastic change in the landscape, but this is only one
cause, and a relatively unimportant cause, of mountain building. However,
there are signs if one knows where to look for them, and how to interpret
them. There are places in the world where sea-cut cliffs and beaches of
sand and gravel are now high and dry, hundreds of feet above the present
sea level. The land where they are found must have risen from the sea
within quite recent times. Fossil fish, and other signs of ocean life have
been found at high altitudes in the mountainsides of the Swiss Alps, showing that these mountains must have been under the sea only a few million
years ago. The tremendous beds of fossiliferous sandstone which underlie
much of the great central plains of North America show that the sea must
once have invaded the land and covered a large part of the continent.

25-4   Types of Rock

In order to understand how a geologist deduces the history of a region from his observations one needs to know something about the different types of rock, and the ways in which they were probably formed. Ability to recognize rock types in the field can only be acquired by handling and studying actual samples. Moreover, the list given here is far from complete; a geologist would recognize subdivisions of these types, and other comparatively rare types that we have not included.

First of all, there are three main classes of rock:

Sedimentary rocks have been laid down by the action of water or wind, and then have been cemented into solid rock by pressure and chemical action. They usually occur in distinguishable layers, and they may be the result of erosion of preexisting mountains, and transport of the material by rivers or by wind, or they may be of biological origin. In the former case sandlike grains can be recognized on close examination; in the latter case the microscope will usually show fragments of broken shells and skeletons of the organisms involved. It is in the sedimentary rocks that recognizable fossils are found, and so they are particularly significant in discussions of geological history.

Igneous rocks have been solidified from molten material. They may be "extrusive," where the melt from an active volcano has spread out over the surrounding area, and has solidified upon the surface, in the presence of oxygen. They may be "intrusive," where molten material has welled up under the surface layers without actually emerging into the air.

Metamorphic rocks have been subjected to pressure and heat after being deposited, without actually being remelted. This has changed their crystal structure and chemical composition in ways that can be recognized by the expert.

25-5   Sediments and Their Origin

Sedimentary rocks are subclassified according to their grain size and origin. Among those rocks which are the products of earlier erosion, that of the finest grain is classified as *shale,* which is solidified mud or clay, and which usually occurs in well-marked thin layers. It is usually waterborne, and must have been deposited in still water, where there was an opportunity for the finest particles to sink to the bottom. An extensive layer of shale therefore suggests an ancient lake bed, or, if it is adjacent to an ancient sea, it might mark the delta of a large river. Coarser grains of mineral origin produce *sandstone,* which, as the name suggests, is formed by the cementing together of grains of sand, as is obvious from the examination of a sample. An extensive layer of sandstone may mark the bed of an

FIG. 25-5

Folded beds of limestone showing on a mountainside (the Rocky Mountains near Banff, Alberta). (Photograph by author.)

ancient shallow sea, where tidal currents and wave action have kept the sediment-laden water stirred up enough to carry away the very fine-grained material, while allowing the coarser sand to sink to the bottom. On the other hand, sandstone can sometimes be a wind-borne deposit, marking a former sandy desert, or a widespread area of sand dunes. A pebbly beach, or a gravelly sandbar in a river forms a *conglomerate*, when recognizable pebbles and small stones are cemented together by smaller grains. Wind- and waterborne deposits are usually more or less sorted according to grain size, from the fine clays and silts which harden into shale, to the pebbles of a wave-beaten beach. An unsorted conglomerate, containing everything from fine sand to fair-sized boulders, is likely to have been carried by moving ice, and to mark the site of an ancient glacier.

The most important rock of biological origin is *limestone*. It is formed by myriads of tiny creatures inhabiting the sea—they die and their bodies sink to the bottom, where the soft parts decay and are lost, leaving the shells or skeletons, composed largely of calcium carbonate, which is also an essential constituent of mammalian bones. In any deep ocean today, the remains of countless creatures which have died within fairly recent times form a thick layer of soft ooze. As this is buried and compressed by more and more accumulation on top, it too will harden into a rock rich in calcium carbonate. Limestone is therefore characteristic of the bed of an ancient ocean. Deposits several hundred feet in thickness occur, and must represent accumulations of many millions of years. Although they were initially deposited in horizontal layers, some of them are now found high in mountains and are folded into elaborate curved patterns. The limestone beds—the way in which they are inclined or folded, and the identifiable fossils which they may contain—provide important clues to the age of a mountain system, and to the way in which it was thrust up. Similar in origin to limestone, but much softer and almost white instead of various shades of gray, is *chalk*, which contains large quantities of silica. It occurs in thick beds in many parts of the world, typically in England. Geologically speaking, *coal* also has to be classed as a sedimentary rock of biological origin. It comes from the remains of plant life which have decayed and lost a great deal of their more volatile constituents, leaving behind solid materials rich in carbon.

25-6   *Igneous and Metamorphic Rocks*

The commonest igneous rock to be found on or near the surface, where it can be conveniently studied, is *granite,* which is a hard, rather coarse-grained material, usually gray to pink in color, and mottled. It shows that it has been solidified from a melt because it contains distinct crystals of

FIG. 25-6

Map showing the Canadian Shield, a very ancient mountain system that is now worn down to little more than rolling hills. It has remained above sea level for at least a billion years, and has only a thin layer of recent soil on top of the granite cores of the ancient mountains.

minerals that are not soluble in water,° particularly feldspar, which is mainly aluminum silicate, and quartz, which is nearly pure silicon dioxide (silica). Deep boreholes, combined with geophysical evidence (Sec. 27-5), show that granite and similar rocks probably underlie most of the continental areas of the earth. This widespread layer is usually a very ancient structure; it comes to the surface in a few places, where aeons ago it was uplifted in the formation of a mountain range, now worn down again almost to a level plain. Younger mountain ranges, showing their comparative youth by the fact that they are still high mountains, sometimes have granite cores, formed by the intrusion of molten material during the mountain-building process.

We shall not describe other, less abundant types of intrusive igneous rock, or the different varieties of extrusive *lava;* their classification is a matter for the expert. The lavas are primarily the products of volcanic erruptions, and show by their fine-grained structure that they have cooled rapidly, after being extruded onto the surface. Only one other igneous rock needs to be described: *basalt,* a very heavy fine-grained rock, almost black in color. Where it is found exposed on the surface it is usually a solidified lava flow, but its importance for what follows is that a rock very similar to basalt appears to underlie the beds of all the deep oceans, and may be part of the primeval crust of the earth.

The metamorphic rocks are less abundant than either the sediments or the igneous rocks. Their presence is evidence that a layer of rock has been deeply buried, to a depth where high temperatures and pressures have been encountered, and then has been uplifted again. This must take a long time, and the recrystallization which is characteristic of the metamorphosis is also a slow process, so that metamorphic rocks are likely to be old, except in rare cases where they have been heated by close association with a volcano. Two typical varieties are marble, which is a metamorphosed limestone, and slate, which is derived from shale, and shows its origin by its laminated structure.

25-7   Compiling the Geological Record

In the late eighteenth and early nineteenth centuries there was much discussion among naturalists about the significance of the fossils which were being found in rocky cliffs in many parts of the world, about the reasons for the different strata of rock which were evident in many of the cliffs, and about the way in which the earth itself had been formed. Except for a very few extremists, there was general agreement that fossils were the remains of creatures that had once lived in the sea, or roamed over the land, but there was no agreement about when these creatures had lived, about why many of them were different from any creature alive today, or

---

° A "mineral," as opposed to a rock, is a material of fairly definite chemical composition. Rocks like granite are composed of grains of many different minerals.

about the interpretation of the rock strata. Opinions varied all the way from those of men who insisted upon a succession of sudden catastrophic floods, in which all existing life had been overwhelmed and buried under sand and silt, to those who believed in an orderly evolution of life, and in the formation of rocks by the same gradual forces of erosion and deposition that we can see in action in the present-day world. Among the "uniformists," who accepted the principle of orderly evolution, both of living things and of the earth's crust, there were several different theories about the way in which this might have happened. Nobody had enough factual evidence to back up a proposed theory, and controversy raged.

One whose ideas were very close to those we accept today was a British engineer, William Smith, who was engaged in constructing canals. He was struck by the orderly sequence of strata in the banks of canal cuttings, and in the fact that successive layers contained slightly different fossils. In 1799 he published a paper in which he proposed using fossil types to correlate strata in different areas, and to establish the order in which the different strata had been laid down. In the following years he succeeded in tracing some of the layers over a large part of England, and in compiling a chart showing the succession of strata in that country, from the oldest at the bottom to the youngest at the top. A little later another Englishman, Charles Lyell, traveled widely, studied cliffsides wherever he went, and applied similar methods to compile a geological history of much of Europe, which was published in a series of works in 1830–1850. From

FIG. 25-7

Part of the bank of the Grand Canyon of the Colorado River, showing the sequence of strata of different ages. (Photograph by L. F. Noble, U.S. Geological Survey.)

this time most geologists accepted the principle that the methods of *stratigraphy*, based on the study of fossils, could be used to compile a sequence which would give both a history of the earth's crust, and at the same time a history of the evolution of living things.°

The compilation of the history of the earth's crust has now been extended over the whole world, by the study of the sedimentary rocks, not only in cuttings, river banks, and cliffs, but also in high mountains where the original strata have been uplifted and tilted, in mines, and in deep borings in the search for oil and useful minerals. The principles involved are still the same as those used by Smith and Lyell on a smaller scale; in the sequence of sedimentary strata from any one place the bottommost are the oldest; strata from different places, which contain similar populations of fossils, are approximately the same age.†

No one locality provides a complete cross section, for it will at one time have accumulated sediment, and at another time it will have been high and dry. A cliffside in one area gives a few layers of the sequence. Some of these layers correlate, through the fossil population, with part of the cross section from another locality, and so the total sequence is extended, up or down as the case may be. Still another locality provides data to fill in a gap in the sequence from the first locality, for there has probably been a time when no deposits were laid down there. Gradually, the whole worldwide sequence is built up, by taking a bit from here and a bit from there, and piecing all the various bits together.

GLOSSARY

Basalt A heavy, fine-grained igneous rock, dark gray to black in color.

Canadian Shield A broad band of very ancient rocks that covers much of central and northeastern Canada (Fig. 25-6); it consists mainly of the granite roots of an ancient mountain system, and is the oldest part of North America.

Catastrophism The theory that changes in the population of the earth—shown by differences in the fossils in different rock strata—were due to a succession of sudden catastrophes.

° However, Charles Darwin's *Origin of Species*, published in 1859, was still able to arouse a storm of controversy over biological evolution. Many theologians still insisted upon a sequence of catastrophes, and of acts of special creation, including particularly that of Man. Darwin's theory that man, *Homo sapiens*, constituted a biological species that had evolved by natural processes through a long sequence of "lower" types, seemed to the nineteenth-century theologian to upset all religious doctrine. Even among scientists who accepted the principle of evolution there was heated controversy over Darwin's theory of the machinery of evolution, particularly over the natural selection of small favorable mutations for which Darwin could not account.

† In correlating strata from different localities it is not sufficient to find one identical species of fossil. It is essential that the whole population be similar, although not necessarily identical, for the population will depend on climatic and other conditions at the time the sediment was deposited. One population may be oceanic in nature; another of the same age may consist of land animals and plants; still another may be a mixture of species living originally in marshes or shallow water.

Chalk A soft white sedimentary rock, composed largely of the remains of microscopic organisms whose skeletons contained large quantities of silica.

Conglomerate Sedimentary rock formed from materials that have been eroded from older rocks; contains particles of all sizes from fine sand to boulders.

Cosmology Branch of astronomy that is concerned with the origin and history of the cosmos.

Delta Deposit formed around the mouth of a river; characteristically takes the form of a Greek letter Δ, and is intersected by several branches of the river (see Fig. 25-3).

Extrusive rock Igneous rock that is the result of molten material flowing over the surface of the earth and solidifying in the presence of air.

Floodplain Portion of a river valley that is subject to periodic flooding; characterized by a deposit of silt and fine sand.

Fossiliferous Term applied to rock that contains identifiable fossils.

Geophysics The application of physical methods to the study of the structure of the earth.

Granite A coarse-grained igneous rock, pink to gray in color, containing many easily visible crystals.

Igneous rocks Rocks formed by the solidification of molten material.

Intrusive rocks Igneous rocks that have solidified from pockets of molten material inside the earth's crust, without exposure to the air.

Lava Molten material flowing from a volcano; also the same material after it has solidified into rock.

Limestone A moderately hard sedimentary rock, usually gray in color, composed mainly of calcium carbonate from the shells and skeletons of marine organisms.

Magma Molten material that occurs in pockets in the earth's crust, or just beneath the crust; the source of lava for volcanic eruptions.

Marble A hard crystalline rock, metamorphosed from limestone by heat and pressure.

Metamorphic rocks Rocks that have been altered in structure and appearance by heat and pressure without actual melting.

Primeval crust and rocks The original crust that formed when the earth first solidified; no part of it still remains near the surface, but it probably underlies the deep oceans and the known rocks of the continents.

Sandstone A sedimentary rock formed by the deposition of material eroded from older rocks; shows visible grains, the size of sand particles.

Sedimentary rocks Rocks formed by the hardening of material that has been deposited in layers by any transporting agency.

Shale A fine-grained sedimentary rock formed by the hardening of clay or silt.

Silt Muddy material transported by a river and deposited along the riverbed or near the mouth.

Slate A fine-grained hard rock that results from the metamorphosis of shale; it usually occurs in well-marked thin layers, and is easily split.

Stratigraphy The study of rock layers and the deduction therefrom of the geological history of a region.

Stratum A layer of rock of one uniform type, occurring in the earth's crust.

Uniformity In geology and cosmology, the principle that the laws of nature, and therefore the processes involved in evolution, are the same everywhere, and have always been the same.

EXERCISES

1. Discuss briefly the principle of uniformity as applied to: (a) the history of the earth's crust; (b) biological evolution; (c) the cosmos.

2. How much of the cosmos is available for direct observation?

3. Describe briefly geographical features that demonstrate that the hills are continually being worn down and the material transported large distances.

4. Describe geographical features and phenomena that show: (a) that new mountains are being formed; (b) that extensive areas of the continents are rising or falling; (c) that the oceans have at times been shallower than they are at present; (d) that areas that are now mountainous were once under the sea.

5. Name and describe briefly the three principal classes of rock.

6. Distinguish between intrusive and extrusive rocks, with examples.

7. State the principal characteristics of the following types of rock: sandstone, granite, soft lava, shale, limestone, marble, conglomerate. To which classes do they belong? Where and how are they likely to have been formed?

8. Suggest ways in which one could identify a rock that was deposited: (a) by running water; (b) by the wind; (c) by a glacier; (d) in the depths of the ocean; (e) on a beach of an ocean or a lake.

9. Where, how, and when did the science of stratigraphy originate?

10. Explain how a sequence of strata is compiled.

11. Explain how stratigraphy permits deductions about: (a) the geological history of a region; (b) the climatic history; (c) the course of biological evolution.

12. Write brief accounts of the two controversies that arose in the nineteenth century as a result of geological observations: (a) the controversy between the catastrophists and the uniformists; (b) the controversy over Darwin's theory of evolution.

the story of evolution written in the rocks

26-1   *Geological Eras and Revolutions*

Geologists divide the historical record of the earth's crust, as derived by correlation of the fossil-bearing sediments, into six *eras*, as shown in the illustration at the top of pp. 428–429.

The *revolutions* which divide the eras mark times in the earth's history when there seem to have been sudden widespread and quite significant changes in the population of living things, as shown by marked differences in the fossil population between layers of sediment which are quite close together in the complete geological record.° For example, during the Rocky Mountain revolution, 63 million years ago, the dinosaurs, the great reptiles that had dominated the scene for 160 million years, became extinct, and the mammals took over. On the other hand, throughout the Mesozoic era there was a continuous, gradual development of the reptiles, as well as of plants and of other forms of animal life, such as the insects. The revolutions provide convenient reference points to mark the major

° This applies mainly to the population of land animals. Ever since the first vertebrate fish appeared, in the middle Paleozoic, there have been fish in the sea.

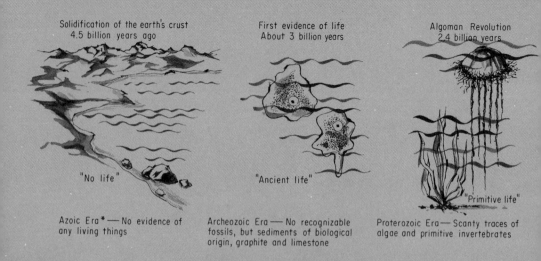

Solidification of the earth's crust
4.5 billion years ago

"No life"

Azoic Era*— No evidence of
any living things

First evidence of life
About 3 billion years

"Ancient life"

Archeozoic Era — No recognizable
fossils, but sediments of biological
origin, graphite and limestone

Algoman Revolution
2.4 billion years

"Primitive life"

Proterozoic Era — Scanty traces of
algae and primitive invertebrates

divisions of geological history. However, since scientists have learned to appreciate the very long time span covered by the record, they have realized that the revolution intervals were not interruptions to the orderly course of evolution, but merely periods when the overall zoological pattern changed relatively quickly, with rather noticeable results. Forms which were once important, like the dinosaurs, disappeared, but the discovery of many transition types has shown that no new forms suddenly appeared. Forms which became abundant after a revolution had transitional ancestors, although these might have been insignificant creatures, comparatively few in number.

The biological revolutions seem to have coincided approximately with periods of intense mountain-building activity, which, throughout the earth's history, have alternated with long periods of relative quiet, so that the transition intervals have been named after major mountain systems which were thrust up at about the same times.† However, there have been other periods of widespread mountain activity, which did not coincide with any important biological change, and it is hard to see how there could be any cause-and-effect relationship between the mountains and the living forms. The causes are obscure in both cases. We do not know why periods of activity in the earth's crust and periods of quiet should have

* From the Greek *an*–, without, and *zoe*, life. The names of the other eras have similar origins, as indicated by the words within quotation marks.

† Geologists are not always in agreement on the names assigned to the revolutionary transition periods; we have here followed the practice of the majority in North America. There are some indications that we are passing through a period of mountain building. Whether or not this is also a "revolution" we cannot say; we are too close to it to see it in proper perspective. Perhaps, if geologists a million years from now are still talking about eras and revolutions, they may call the period just past the "Himalayan" or "Alpine" revolution, and speak of it as ushering in the age of dominance by man.

Killarney Revolution
600 million years

"Old life"

Paleozoic Era— Abundant fossils, at first of marine invertebrates, later including fishes and the first land animals

Appalachian Revolution
220 million years

"Middle life"

Mesozoic Era — Age of reptile dominance, first birds and mammals

Rocky Mountain Revolution
63 million years

"Recent life"

Cenozoic Era — Mammals and flowering plants abundant, emergence of man

alternated; we do not know what combinations of causes may have led to the biological revolutions. Climatic changes, such as a period of dry, semi-arid conditions, probably had something to do with the latter, but it is hard to see how this could have happened at nearly the same time all over the world,* or to see the connection between the general climatic change and the formation of mountain ranges.

26-2   *Dating the Geological Record*

The illustration at the top of pp. 428–429 gives some figures for the time elapsed since the beginning of each of the six geological eras, and the relative times are shown to scale in Fig. 26-1. In this diagram the time since the arrival of man on earth is represented by something less than the thickness of the line which bounds the top of the Cenozoic era. For a long time geologists and physicists have been trying to estimate the duration of the different eras, as well as the total age of the earth, and it has seemed that every fresh estimate has made the earth older, and the time required for any geological change longer.† Now, however, methods have been refined to the point where the age of any rock stratum can be determined quite accurately.

The thicknesses of rock strata give some idea of the relative duration of different geological periods, in any one area. However, reasonably precise

---

* There is evidence that there have been changes in the composition of the atmosphere, and that the rate of evolution was speeded up during periods when the oxygen content was high. This, of course, would happen simultaneously all over the world.

† We shall not discuss in detail early methods of estimating the age of the earth, based upon the time required for sedimentary strata to accumulate, or the time required for salt to accumulate in the sea. All such estimates gave ages far too low.

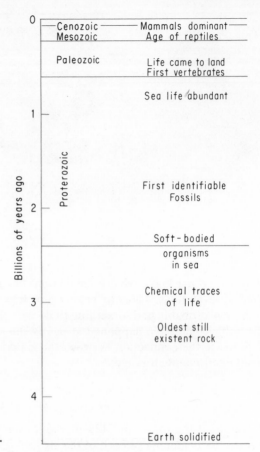

FIG. 26-1

The time scale of geological history.

ages, such as those quoted in the table and the figure, have been based on the decay of radioactive elements that are present in small quantities in most types of rock. The several radioactive transformations that are useful for this purpose are listed in Table 26-1. For a reliable determination one must work with single isotopes of the elements concerned and determine the quantities present in the rock by means of a mass spectrograph, using grains of definite minerals picked out from a sample of igneous rock.

In Fig. 26-2 the curve represents the decay of one of the original radioactive elements, say, uranium 238. The amount of uranium present when the rock solidified is represented by the initial value, N_0, at time zero. After t years the proportion of lead 206 to uranium 238 is represented by the ratio AB/BC on the diagram. If this ratio can be accurately determined at the present time, the value can be fitted onto the curve, and the age t can be calculated. There are, however, several sources of uncertainty. For example, in the uranium-lead or thorium-lead methods there was probably

TABLE 26-1   **RADIOACTIVE TRANSFORMATIONS WHICH CAN BE USED FOR DATING PURPOSES**

Elements Compared	Overall Reaction	Half-life
Uranium-lead	$U^{238} \longrightarrow Pb^{206} + 8\ He^4$	4.50 billion years
	$U^{235} \longrightarrow Pb^{207} + 7\ He^4$	713 million years
Thorium-lead	$Th^{232} \longrightarrow Pb^{208} + 6\ He^4$	13.9 billion years
Potassium-argon	$_{19}K^{40} + e^- \longrightarrow {}_{18}A^{40}$	1.29 billion years
Rubidium-strontium	$_{37}Rb^{87} \longrightarrow {}_{38}Sr^{87} + e^-$	50 billion years
Carbon 14-carbon 12	$_6C^{14} \longrightarrow {}_7N^{14} + e^-$	5700 years

some lead present with the radioactive element in the molten material from which the rock was formed.

In the potassium-argon reaction a potassium nucleus absorbs one of its own outer electrons, converts to argon 40, and ejects a gamma ray. Only 11.1 per cent of the potassium 40 reacts in this way; the remainder emits beta rays and converts to calcium 40, which cannot be distinguished from the calcium that is abundant in almost all rocks. The uncertainty in this case is that some of the argon, which is a gas, may have escaped in the course of time. However, experience has shown that in certain minerals, mica in particular, the newly formed argon atoms are trapped in the crystal, and so the argon slowly accumulates over the ages.

The analysis of carbon 14 serves to date recent deposits, either of partly decomposed natural biological materials, or of archeological collections. Carbon 14 is continually being produced in the atmosphere by the action

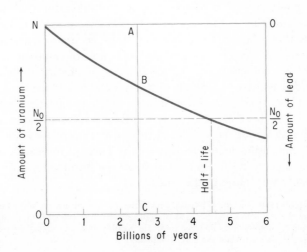

FIG. 26-2

Radioactive clock method of determining geological ages.

of cosmic-ray neutrons on nitrogen, and it mixes with the ordinary carbon dioxide to form $C^{14}O_2$. Living plants absorb the mixture, and animals in turn eat the plants, so that in any *living* organism the carbon compounds which make up a large part of its structure contain a definite proportion of radioactive carbon 14 along with the ordinary carbon 12. When the organism dies, its metabolism ceases, no fresh carbon is absorbed, and the carbon 14 which accumulated during its lifetime starts to decay. The ratio of C^{14} to C^{12} at any later date is therefore a reliable indicator of the age of the deposit in which the dead organism is found.

The carbon 14 method is useful for ages up to about 50,000 years. The potassium-argon method is useful for ages greater than 50,000 years, although for very great ages, a combination of the lead methods is better.

26-3   *The Age of the Earth*

The oldest terrestrial rock which has so far been dated by the radioactive method is a sample from South Africa whose age is placed at 3.3 billion years. This, and other very ancient rocks which have been found in various places, do not appear to be part of the original crust of the earth, and geologists now believe that none of the primeval plutonic° rocks still remain close to the surface, where they would be accessible to study. All of the original land surface has been worn away by erosion, and such of the original rocks as may still remain are deeply buried, either beneath the deep ocean or in the lowermost layers of the crust. The question therefore arises of the age of the earth itself, by which we mean the time since it first solidified out of the cloud of dust and gas from which the sun and its family of planets must have been formed.

The point in time when the original solidification took place is not as easy to determine as the age of a specific igneous rock, and it is only quite recently that a figure that is believed to be accurate has been determined. The procedure involves an intercomparison of the amounts of the different lead isotopes in lead ores obtained from rocks of various, known ages. We cannot discuss here the details of the calculation, which is contingent upon lead 204 being part of the original material from which the earth was formed, whereas the other isotopes are apparently products of uranium and thorium, formed at different rates. Several recent determinations, made in different laboratories, using materials from many parts of the earth, all give nearly the same age, and the average of these measurements, 4.55 billion years, is probably very close to the truth.

° Geologists refer to layers of igneous rock which cover a large area, and which appear to have been formed deep within the earth, as plutonic, after the Greek god, Pluto, who was supposed to rule over the underworld. Plutonic rocks are possibly, but not necessarily, part of the original, primeval crust, formed when the earth solidified.

Meteorites which have fallen upon the earth at various times have also been dated by the radioactive clock method, and in most cases the calculated ages are just about 4½ billion years. It seems, therefore, that an estimate of 4.55 to 4.60 billion years not only establishes the age since the earth solidified, but that it also comes close to the age of the solar system as a whole, including that of the sun itself. This conjecture is not unreasonable, because we can be fairly certain that, once the cloud from which the solar system originated started to contract to form the sun, and the pieces which formed the planets broke off from it, completion of the process would have been comparatively rapid. Perhaps it took only a few million years—a very short time on the cosmic scale.

26-4   Precambrian Times

Geologists often lump the first three eras of geological time together, under the term *Precambrian*, meaning all that time before the Cambrian,* which is the first period of the Paleozoic era. This comprises about 85 per cent of the earth's history, and only toward the end of that time did living creatures become sufficiently highly developed to leave behind fossils that can be identified and classified into their biological families.

The first 1½ billion years are the *Azoic era*, of which very little is known, since very few rocks of Azoic age remain, and most of those are igneous or metamorphic. However, the existence of a few sediments, and of metamorphic rocks which seem to have a sedimentary origin, shows that the cycle of mountain building and erosion had already commenced. The few Azoic rocks which have been studied contain no identifiable traces of life. We have to think of a rugged landscape, with the land completely barren of life, but drenched in rain from time to time, and intersected by mighty rivers, just as the world is today. We can surmise that the rain and the rivers wore down the original mountains almost to a level plain, that wide areas of sand and clay were deposited, to harden into sandstone and shale, that new mountain ranges were thrust up, to be eroded in their turn, and that all this probably happened several times before life appeared on the earth. We know nothing of the detailed history; all but the sketchiest traces have been obliterated long ago.

The *Archeozoic era* began about 3 billion years ago. Its beginning is only vaguely marked (and is ignored by some geologists), but there is evidence in northern Canada, in South Africa and in a few other places of extensive mountain-building activity at about this time. Rocks of Archeo-

---

* Subdivisions of the eras are known as periods, and the periods of the Paleozoic are named after areas where rocks of the corresponding age are found. For example, Cambrian comes from the Latin name for Wales, in Britain, called *Cambria* by the Romans. Space will not permit details of the different periods.

zoic age, mostly plutonic granites, are found on or near the surface in areas which can be identified as the primitive cores of the major continents. These are the so-called shields, of which the best known is the Canadian Shield (Fig. 25-6), although there are similar areas in other parts of the world. We know very little, except by conjecture, about Archeozoic life. Living organisms must have been fairly abundant toward the end of the era, at least in the sea, for in several places beds of limestone alternate with layers of other sediments or metamorphic rocks. These limestones are almost certainly the remains of tiny, primitive single-celled organisms which swam in the Archeozoic seas, and which had already evolved to the stage where they were secreting calcium carbonate to form protective shells or rigid skeletons. There are also occasional deposits of graphite, nearly pure carbon which is probably a metamorphosed form of organic carbon, and which indicates the existence of vegetable life, probably primitive algae. Whether any living things had yet emerged from the sea is a matter of pure conjecture; there is no evidence, and probably the land was still completely barren.

The third era of the geological sequence, the *Proterozoic*, is taken to have started after the first extensive mountain activity shown in the Canadian Shield. This took place about 2400 million years ago, and the era lasted 1800 million years, or 40 per cent of geological time. It terminated with a fairly well-marked biological revolution, at about the same time as a great range of mountains was thrust up. These are known to geologists as the Grenville Mountains, and they extended from Minnesota, across the area where Lakes Superior and Huron are now, into northern New York State. They are almost completely eroded, and little remains of them except their granite roots, which form the low hills along the southern portion of the Canadian Shield.

In North America, rocks of Proterozoic age are found close to the surface in an irregular zone all around the border of the Shield, and in some places within the Shield, where they overlie the granite. To the west, borings show that they extend some distance underneath the younger sediments which cover the Great Plains. These Proterozoic rocks are mostly sediments, which have been altered more by pressure and chemical action than by heat.° They are the oldest rocks that contain fossils that can be identified and assigned to their places in a biological classification. Most of the fossils are algae, or seaweeds, of several types. Animal remains are scanty, but primitive corals and sponges have been found, along with a few minute shellfish. Worms must have been present, because casts and lime-lined burrows, similar to those now being formed by seashore worms,

° The great iron deposits of the Mesabi Range in Minnesota, and of Labrador, are Proterozoic sediments. They probably came from iron-rich biological material. In the billion years or more since the sediments were laid down, other minerals have gradually been dissolved, leaving the insoluble iron compounds.

are quite common. Actually we can conjecture that by this time life was quite abundant in the sea and along the tidal shores, but most Proterozoic animals were probably soft-bodied creatures which left no fossilized remains. There may even have been a few primitive plants on the land, because fossils have been found which have been identified as fungus spores.

26-5   How Did Life Begin?

Some time during the first billion years or so of the earth's history a *first* living thing must have appeared in the sea. Just how it was formed, or when it appeared we do not know, since it left no trace in the rocks, but we are justified in indulging in a little informed speculation. Any question about the origin of life on earth—or about the possibility of life on other worlds —is meaningless until we decide what we mean by "living." Here we shall limit our discussion to organisms that have material bodies, possessing mass, and built up of molecules constructed from the 82 stable elements. Whether there exist conscious beings who do not possess material bodies is a matter of religion and philosophy, and does not fall within the province of physical science.

The boundary between the living and nonliving is rather vague, and different writers have allocated it to different stages of complexity of organic development. However, most would agree that an organism must be capable of two very fundamental activities before we can say that it is alive. It must be able to grow, by taking material from its environment and by adding the molecules, or parts thereof, to its own structure. It must be able to reproduce, and make more or less faithful copies of itself. If we accept this, and consider these two requirements as providing an operational definition of "life," we have to consider the self-reproducing molecules (Sec. 13-7) as living, and place the boundary somewhere between a detached speck of protein and a DNA molecule. Some writers would demand a higher degree of organization, say that of a single-celled bacterium or possibly a virus particle. However, whatever we may take to be the lowest and most primitive possible form of life, it certainly requires complex organic molecules, based upon the special chemical properties of the carbon atom.

In the world today, life lives upon life. All living organisms we know anything about, if they do not actually devour the cell structure of other living things, at least require the existence of molecules which were once part of another living body before they can grow and reproduce their kind. For example, think of the simplest kind of single-celled animal. We can assemble in a test tube all the ingredient molecules necessary to construct the protoplasm of the animal cell, but nothing happens, there is no *organism*, until we introduce into the mixture a germ or a spore derived from a living parent. It takes the spore, probably containing DNA or RNA, to control the gathering together, or *organization,* of the ingredients necessary to form the living cell.

The *first* growing, reproducing organism, possibly a simple form of RNA molecule, must have come into existence, out of nonliving carbon compounds, without the aid of any germ or spore. In order to speculate whether this could have happened naturally, we must appeal to the laws of chemical equilibrium to ask what kinds of molecules would have been present in the primeval ocean, before there were any living things that could die and leave behind organic molecules. There would have been plenty of the common elements, carbon, hydrogen, oxygen, nitrogen, and the commoner metals, and almost all of these would have been bound together into molecules of their simple stable compounds, the light hydrocarbons, ammonia, carbon dioxide, common metallic salts, and the like. Such compounds as simple alcohols would be present, but anything more complex would be extremely rare. We have to suppose, however, that ordinary chemical reactions produced a few molecules having the degree of complexity of adenine and the like. The question then is: "Could a few such molecules come together, in the presence of the other proper ingredients, and combine to form a very simple RNA molecule?"

As long as the simplest self-reproducing organism we knew anything about was a bacterium with a definite cell structure, or at the very least a virus particle, it seemed extremely unlikely that the proper ingredient molecules could happen, *by chance,* to bump into one another all at once, and adhere long enough to form even the simplest kind of cell. Many people therefore thought that the first appearance of life on the earth required a special act of creation, perhaps operating through some law that was still unknown to natural science. This may still be true, but since the discovery of the properties of RNA and DNA it seems quite possible that the proper ingredients could have come together in the natural course of the random wanderings of the molecules. Remember that we have a very long time during which this extremely rare event might have happened. In theory, it need only have happened once, during the billion years of Azoic time, in all the oceans of the world, although it seems more likely that there would have been a number of abortive attempts at the formation of a "prelife" organism, which disintegrated without coming to anything. There might, too, have been several, widely separated successful attempts. Once a properly constructed, self-reproducing molecule was formed, it would start to make copies of itself, and before very long there would be a little speck of "living" material. This could break up, and provide the spores to act as centers for more living specks, and life would multiply in the sea where it first appeared. Cosmic rays would bombard the genelike molecules and cause mutations, so that many different types would develop. In the course of a hundred million years or so one would turn up which was capable of synthesizing proteins and collecting around itself the proper ingredients to construct a differentiated living cell, with protoplasm and a nucleus. The evolutionary sequence of living forms would finally have commenced. If this conjectured sequence of events is more or less correct, all things living today are the descendants of a few self-reproducing molecules which appeared spontaneously in the sea some time during the first billion years of the earth's history.

26-6   *The Paleozoic Era*

Throughout the last three eras of geological time there has been an abundance of living organisms, both plant and animal. Sedimentary rocks formed during this portion of the earth's history contain many fossils which can be recognized and classified, so that sediments from different areas can be correlated, and a detailed geological record can be constructed. We shall describe only a few of the most important landmarks in the biological evolution of which the fossil record is the evidence.

About 600 million years ago there appeared in the sea a number of creatures which were a distinct evolutionary advance upon anything known from Proterozoic rocks. These had a well-developed multicellular structure, with distinctly differentiated cells, performing distinct functions. They had mouths and a digestive tract; they had sense organs, particularly feelers, and some of them had composite eyes like those of a fly; many of them had jointed legs and a tail, and could swim. Most important for geological history, a great many of these new creatures had shells, sometimes calcareous like those of an oyster or a snail, sometimes made of chitin like the shell of a crab or the outer covering of an insect. It is of these shell-bearing animals that we know most, because the hard parts were preserved and formed easily identifiable fossils. These animals had tremendous advantages over their Proterozoic ancestors in the race for survival, so that many different types prospered and multiplied, and before long the sea was thickly populated. This constitutes the first clearly marked biological revolution. In late Proterozoic rocks there are only a few scanty fossil remains, of seaweeds and a few soft-bodied animals. In early Paleozoic strata, only a few layers higher in the geological sequence, fossils are abundant, and most of them are of the new animal types.

The most prolific of the early Paleozoic animals was the trilobite, two examples of which are shown in Fig. 26-3. Its ancestor is obscure, and there are none living today, but for a long time it was the dominant creature in the early Paleozoic seas. Its body parts were well differentiated into head and mouth, flesh, and a digestive system. It had a jointed shell of several segments, with a pair of primitive legs projecting from each segment, so that it could roam in search of food, which it found with the aid

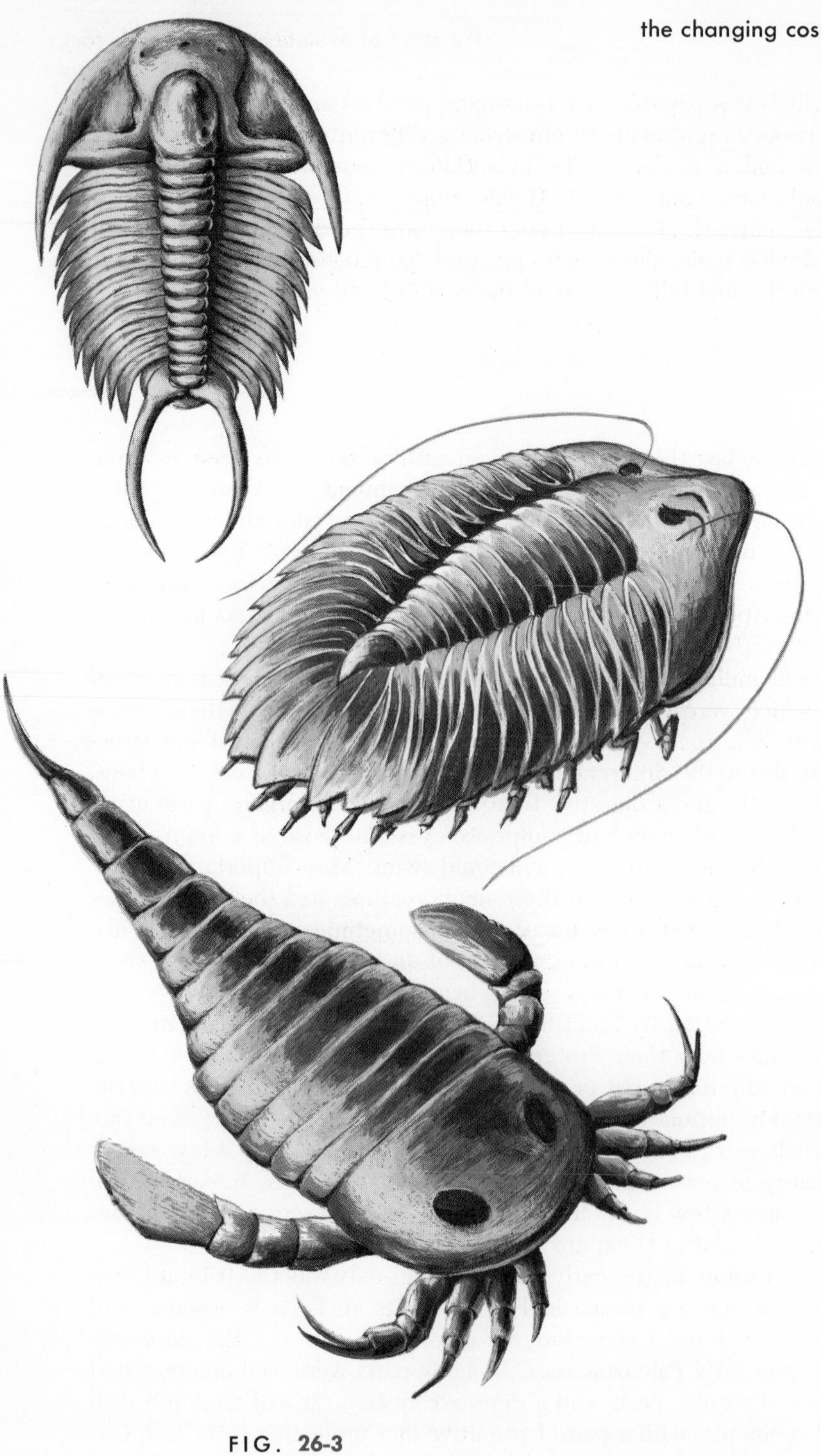

FIG. 26-3

Early Paleozoic trilobites and a contemporary eurypterid.
(Figures after R. C. Moore, *Introduction to Historical Geology*,
2nd ed., and from reconstructions in the Buffalo Museum of
Science.)

of a pair of compound eyes and a pair of long tentacles attached to its head. In size, most of the trilobites ranged from 1 to 6 inches, although some later specimens attained a length of 2 feet.

Besides the trilobites, early Paleozoic strata show shrimplike creatures, corals, and several types of shellfish. Soft-bodied animals like jellyfish, sea slugs, and worms must have been much more numerous than the fossil evidence suggests, for these animals would usually perish without leaving traces in the rocks. Vegetable life must also have been abundant, and the oxygen-carbon cycle, based upon photosynthesis, must have been well established, although direct evidence of plants is scanty, and what there is shows little advance over the Proterozoic algae. However, all these creatures and plants still lived in the sea; for a long time yet the land must have been almost, if not completely barren.

FIG. 26-4

Life in the sea 500 million years ago. (After J. Augusta and Z. Burian, *Prehistoric Animals,* Prague, Czechoslovakia.)

For an estimated 380 million years the sequence of strata shows an orderly and continuous evolution of living forms, without any revolutionary discontinuity. Species die out, and new species appear, always with a trend toward greater specialization and greater complexity, often accompanied by greater size. Late Paleozoic populations are therefore very different from those at the beginning of the era, and are classified by the geologists as belonging to different "periods." Of the many developments which took place we shall discuss only two which are of special significance to us: the development of vertebrates and the migration of living things from their primeval home in the sea on to the land. To some extent the two run parallel, because the vertebrate amphibian was one of the animals which learned to live on land, and breathe air.

Gradually, during the first 150 million years or so of the Paleozoic era, the tidal beaches became populated, and many species became accustomed to spending part of their life exposed to the air, when the tide receded. At first, the animals which lived in the tidal zone closed their shells and drew in their tentacles at low tide, and simply waited for the water to return, as many seashore creatures still do. But slowly green plants containing chlorophyll spread toward the high-tide line, where they spent only a small part of their life under water. Other plants spread from the ocean up the rivers into the freshwater lakes and marshes, and eventually reached areas where they were liable to be left on dry ground when the water level in the marsh was low. Some species developed the ability to use gaseous carbon dioxide and water vapor, and became land-based, although the fluids in their cells retained a composition similar to that of seawater, as our own body cells still have to this day. When plant life invaded the land, animal life soon followed, and air-breathing animals developed. The first of these were invertebrates, especially millipedes, many-legged worms which are distantly related to the trilobites, and scorpions, which are clearly descended from large sea creatures known as eurypterids (Fig. 26-3).

The origin of the vertebrates is somewhat obscure. It is certain that they did not descend from any of the trilobites or other creatures that were prevalent in early Paleozoic seas. The ancestor appears to be some type of lowly wormlike creature; it may have been fairly abundant even in the late Proterozoic, but very few traces of it have been found because the soft bodies were rarely fossilized. This is an example of something that has often happened in evolutionary history. A type of creature that is relatively simple in structure and not highly specialized may be unimportant in one era, yet may become the ancestor of a dominant type in a later era. Precisely because it is unspecialized and is not overdeveloped in size, the lowly creature is adaptable; it can survive when there is a change in climate, or it can spread into a new environment that was previously sparsely inhabited.

At some stage, very early in the history of living things, our wormlike ancestor developed a central nerve running the length of the body, to communicate sense impressions. This needed protection, and the beginnings of an internal skeleton developed, rather than the external shell borne by most of the worm's contemporaries. At first the internal skeleton was merely a cartilaginous spinal cord, as found in the very earliest fish, and still found today in the lowest orders of chordates. Gradually, the spinal cord hardened into a proper backbone and skeletal appendages developed, to give rise eventually to the skull and jaws, and the bones of the limbs.

The first true fish seem to have developed in the freshwater lakes and rivers; only later did they spread to the ocean, where they were abundant by the middle Paleozoic. They were of two main types, those with fins

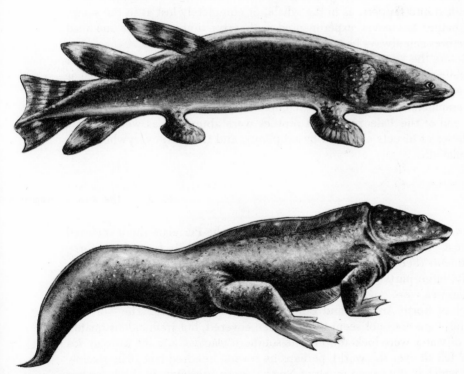

FIG. 26-5

A crossopterygian (lobe-finned) fish and an early amphibian. (From reconstructions in the American Museum of Natural History, New York, and the Chicago Natural History Museum.)

composed of spiny rays like most fish today, and those with their lateral fins mounted on short fleshy appendages (technically known as lobe-finned fish, or crossopterygians). Lobe-finned fish are rare today, but they must once have been well represented, for theirs is the main line of descent which led to the land-living mammal. They lived mostly in shallow fresh water, and with their lobed fins they could crawl, slowly, from one pond to another, and by absorbing oxygen through their swim bladders they could survive long periods out of the water, like the Australian lungfish today. About the middle of the Paleozoic there appeared a descendant of the lungfish which, when it reached maturity, had toes instead of spines on its short limbs, and a functioning lung. It was an amphibian, and in its early stages of growth it still had to live in water, like a modern tadpole.

It is worth noting that the basic structure of the land vertebrates was established at this time, and has never changed. From the first amphibian to modern man the pattern has always been an articulated backbone, with a skull at one end, to protect the nervous system, ribs to protect the lungs and heart, four limbs with five digits on each limb. Limbs may have been modified into flippers, as in the whale, or completely lost as in the snake, but nature has never experimented with extra limbs, and the modified structures can always be traced to their amphibian ancestry.

Before the vertebrate conquest of the land would be complete the soft amphibian egg had to acquire a protective shell, so that the egg as well as the adult animal could survive exposure to the air. When this happened the amphibian became a reptile, completely independent of the water. By the end of the Paleozoic small reptiles were abundant, as well as many varieties of insects and land-based plants, and the land everywhere was populated.

26-8 *The Age of Reptiles*

In the late Paleozoic, in the period known as the Permian, there occurred a great "ice age," of which we have clear evidence in typical ice-borne sediments (Sec. 28-5). At various times, although perhaps not simultaneously, large parts of Australia, India, South Africa, South America, and Antarctica were covered by a great sheet of ice, like that which covered much of North America and Europe in more recent times. The Northern Hemisphere does not seem to have been covered, but tremendous quantities of water were locked up in the southern glaciers, and the average sea level fell all over the world, perhaps by several hundred feet. The shallow seas which had covered much of North America throughout the Paleozoic —in different areas at different times—became almost dry. Life had to adapt, and so we find land dwellers multiplying at the expense of swamp and shallow-sea types, and the next younger strata of the continental areas show a very different population.* It was at about this time that the Appalachian Mountains of the eastern United States were formed, and so the relatively rapid biological change is known as the Appalachian revolution.

The geological era which followed the Permian ice age and the Appalachian revolution is the Mesozoic; it lasted 160 million years, and is characterized by the dominance of reptiles. In the late Paleozoic the reptiles had been small and not highly developed or specialized; nevertheless, they were able to take over when the sea receded and many amphibians could not find water in which to lay their eggs. Evolution never revives an extinct type. When the seas returned in the early Mesozoic, the reptiles continued to flourish and to dominate the animal scene.

This is the age of the dinosaurs, the great reptiles which appeared in the early Mesozoic, multiplied and developed into a host of different species, and suddenly disappeared at the end of the era, at about the time the major chain of the Rocky Mountains was formed, 63 million years ago. Their remains are found all over the world, wherever there was dry land or shallow marsh in Mesozoic times. In the sandstones which underlie much of the great central plain of North America, and which are exposed in the badlands† along some of the river valleys, there have been found not only

* Oceanic life naturally continued in the reduced seas, and when the ice melted and the sea rose again, the fish and marine invertebrates spread once again, without any drastic change in the characteristic types, many of which still flourish today.

† This is the term given to sandstones which have been eroded into fantastic shapes by wind and rain (Fig. 26-6). There are extensive areas of badlands in the Dakotas, in Wyoming, and in western Canada.

FIG. 26-6

Eroded sandstone in the badlands of the Red Deer River, Dinosaur Provincial Park, Alberta. (Photograph by author.)

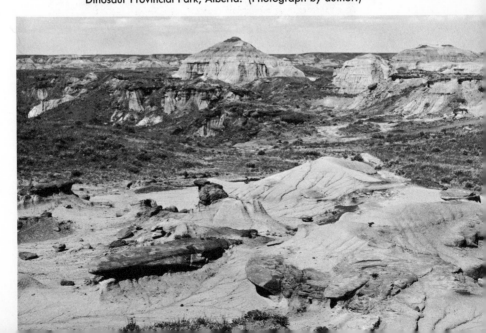

FIG. 26-7

A Mesozoic forest of giant ferns and conifers. (From reconstruction in the Chicago Natural History Museum.)

FIG. 26-8

Reconstruction of *Bronto-saurus*, the largest four-legged animal that ever lived. (Calgary Zoo, Calgary, Alberta; photograph by J. D. Cahoon, Calgary.)

dinosaur skeletons but also extensive layers of broken reptilian bones. These, along with petrified tree trunks and beds of soft coal, show that the area must, at several different times, have been covered with luxuriant marshy vegetation, and populated by hordes of reptiles.

Many different species of reptiles developed during the Mesozoic. Except for some present-day whales, these four-legged animals included the largest creatures that have ever lived. The giants were clumsy, slow-moving herbivores, inhabiting the luxuriant swamps. Others were carnivores, as is evident from their tooth structure; they could apparently run rapidly on their two hind legs, using their much smaller forelimbs to seize their prey. Most dinosaurs seem to have been covered with scales, but some grew a heavy coat of armor which developed into fantastic forms of bony plates, spurs, and finlike crests. Some even returned to their ancestral home in the sea, developed flippers and a swimming tail, and flourished abundantly, preying upon the fish, as does a killer whale. Still others developed membranous wings attached to overgrown forefeet, like the wings of a bat, and learned to fly. In some of the flying lizards the scales turned into feathers, and by the middle Mesozoic we find true birds, with feathered wings and tails, but still retaining lizardlike jaws and teeth.

FIG. 26-9

Models of the great carnivorous dinosaur, *Tyrannosaurus rex* (Calgary Zoo), and *Styracosaurus* (Dinosaur Provincial Park, Alberta); photographs by author.

FIG. 26-10

Flying reptile, *Dimorphodon* (from reconstruction in the American Museum of Natural History, New York); and primitive bird, *Archeopteryx*, from the middle Mesozoic (after J. Augusta and Z. Burian, *Prehistoric Animals*, Prague, Czechoslovakia).

Some 63 million years ago there occurred another of those relatively sudden changes in the animal population of the world that are described as revolutions. The great reptiles which had dominated the scene all through the Mesozoic rapidly disappeared, leaving only the comparatively unimportant lizards and snakes we know today, along with a few crocodiles and alligators in tropical swamps. The birds continued to multiply and flourish, but on land reptiles gave way to the warm-blooded mammals, who quickly differentiated into many different families, and soon spread over the whole earth, just as the reptiles had done in the early Mesozoic. This last era, the *Cenozoic*, in which we still live, is therefore the age of mammalian dominance.

It is interesting to speculate why the dinosaurs so quickly became extinct; as far as North America is concerned, the causes are fairly clear, but why did it happen all over the world—and in the sea—at about the same time? The forces that produced the Rocky Mountains apparently also uplifted the great central plain, resulting in a significant change in the climatic pattern. Areas that had been shallow seas or lakes, or luxuriant swamps, dried out and acquired a less humid, continental type of climate, with a greater contrast between summer and winter. The cold-blooded, overgrown and overspecialized, and rather small-brained reptiles could not adapt to the changed conditions. Long before this happened there had existed small furry animals, probably warm-blooded, and certainly to be classed as primitive mammals. Most of them were marsupials, carrying their young in pouches like the modern opossum, which they resembled in other respects as well.°

Probably mammals were much more numerous in the late Mesozoic than the fossil evidence suggests, for warm blood, a fur coat, omnivorous eating habits, and efficient care of their young would enable them to flourish in dry upland areas where the dinosaurs could not survive. Here the early mammals would die under conditions such that their skeletons were rarely preserved intact, and only a few fossil specimens have remained as proof of their existence at this early date. As a consequence of the change in climate the small mammals began to penetrate the haunts of the dinosaurs, and it is quite likely that the active little animals actually contributed to the downfall of the great, clumsy reptiles by devouring their unprotected eggs.

We think of the Cenozoic era as the age of mammal dominance, but this is by no means the whole story. Fish are as plentiful as they ever were in the sea and lakes and rivers. The tidal margins of the oceans still support

---

° The primitive mammals do not seem to have descended from any reptile, but to have come directly from the amphibian, through a collateral line of descent. Another very ancient mammalian family is that of the anteaters.

FIG. 26-11

Mammals of the early Cenozoic: *Ectoconus*, a possible ancestor of modern cattle (from reconstruction in the American Museum of Natural History, New York); *Uintathere*, allied to the rhinoceros (after J. Augusta and Z. Burian, *Prehistoric Animals*, Prague, Czechoslovakia); primitive horse (from reconstruction in the Chicago Natural History Museum).

a host of invertebrates, some of which have survived with very little change from the early Paleozoic; other ancient species have actually increased in abundance. Plants as well as animals have multiplied and diversified, and have developed forms suited for a dry upland climate, bearing hard-coated seeds that can survive a rigorous winter or long spells of dry weather. The dominant mammal, including man, has a serious rival in the insect and related species. Flying insects are first noted in the middle Paleozoic; they almost disappeared in the early Mesozoic, but later they multiplied again and are probably more abundant now than ever— and certainly more diversified.

The Cenozoic era is also the age when, for the first time, there appeared on earth creatures that could think and reason. The most primitive mammals, as well as all present-day birds, have much more highly developed nervous systems and brains than those of any reptile. This is true, for example, when we compare a porpoise with the Mesozoic ichthyosaur that lived the same kind of aquatic life; a porpoise is a highly intelligent animal, very different from a lizard which was probably capable only of responding directly to a stimulus through inherited instincts. The trend toward brain size and reasoning power has continued until it culminated in man. Now one species, *Homo sapiens,* has dominated most of the world, and has even changed the physical features of large areas by cultivation and by building.

How old is man? The evidence of early man and of his line of descent has been scanty, but recent discoveries in Africa make it clear that the genus

FIG. 26-12

Homo sapiens begins to use tools and fire. (After J. Augusta and Z. Burian, *Prehistoric Man*, Prague, Czechoslovakia.)

Homo is much older than was once thought.° The *primates*—including certain primitive types as well as monkeys, apes, and man—appeared very early in the Cenozoic. They are distinguished by comparatively large brains, eyes in the front of the head to give binocular vision, and limbs with five jointed digits—the forerunner of the efficient hand of man. Early primates seem to have been tree-dwellers, but some 10 or 20 million years ago a species of primate, Proconsul, took to the ground, using his hind limbs primarily to run and his forelimbs to grasp. A number of different subhuman types then developed—*Australopithecus* (southern ape), *Pithecanthropus* (ape-man), and others. These various hominids have disappeared,

° The Olduvai Gorge in Tanzania has been the source of much useful evidence. Caves in this valley have yielded bones identified as belonging to both hominids and primitive humans, as well as ancient stone implements. The relative ages of different specimens are indicated by the depths at which they are found in the cliffs.

leaving finally one species of true men, with highly developed brains exhibiting imagination and artistic ability, walking upright, and endowed with the ability to fashion tools instead of merely picking up stones and clubs to serve as weapons.

We cannot close this account without noting the way the rate of evolution has accelerated, and the extraordinary speed of the more recent developments. The earth spun in space for about a billion years before any living thing appeared upon it; then another 3 billion years elapsed before a vertebrate animal developed. Only about 60 million years ago the dinosaurs disappeared, the mammals took over, and the first primate appeared. About 2 million years seems to be a reasonable estimate for the first member of the genus *Homo*—a four-thousandth part of the earth's history. However, it is only within the last 20,000 years, one hundredth of his own history, that man has cultivated the earth. Civilization, and the ability to pass on knowledge by written records, has covered only a quarter of that. Finally, we cannot say that man has become truly dominant until almost our own times, with the age of electricity, the exploitation of natural resources, and the invasion of the entire globe from the sky above to the depths of the sea. This period of domination extends over perhaps 100 years, $\frac{1}{40,000,000}$ part of the earth's history, and the earth, as a planet of the solar system, has a future at least as long as its past!

GLOSSARY

Algae Plants belonging to a primitive order, having no flowers or true seeds; most algae are aquatic, and the seaweeds are the most familiar examples.

Amphibian Animal that lives partly in water and partly on land; typically, an amphibian lays unprotected eggs in water, where the young hatch and spend some time before emerging into the air; toads, frogs, and the lizardlike salamanders are the commonest modern examples.

Archeozoic The second geological era; the first that shows chemical evidence of life.

Azoic The first geological era, with no evidence of life.

Badlands Extensive areas of exposed sandstone that has been eroded into fantastic shapes by wind and rain.

Calcareous Composed largely of calcium carbonate; the term is used of shells and bony skeletons to distinguish them from other types of hard biological structures.

Cambrian First period of the Paleozoic era.

Cenozoic The sixth geological era, in which we still live; marked on land by the dominance of flowering plants and mammals.

Chitin A hard proteinlike material that forms the outer covering of insects and of many aquatic creatures, such as crabs and lobsters.

Chordate Animal with an internal skeleton; the term includes both the vertebrates and more primitive types that have only a tough cord in place of a true backbone.

Era Major division of geological time.

Eurypterid Marine animal that looks rather like a scorpion; common in the early Paleozoic (see Fig. 26-3).

Hominid Term applied to several extinct species of manlike primates that cannot be classified as belonging to the genus *Homo*.

Ichthyosaur Fish-lizard; an air-breathing reptile of the Mesozoic era that took to a life in the sea and developed a body shaped like that of a fish.

Lobe-finned fish, or crossopterygian Fish whose fins were attached to the body by fleshy appendages; Paleozoic fish of this type were evidently the ancestors of the amphibians.

Marsupial Mammal whose young are carried in a pouch of skin attached to the mother's abdomen; one of the oldest orders of mammals, represented today by the opossum in America and by the kangaroo and its relatives in Australia.

Mesozoic The fifth geological era; marked on land by the dominance of reptiles in the animal kingdom.

Paleozoic The fourth geological era; the first era that left an abundance of fossils so that the course of evolution can be traced through the era.

Period In geology, a subdivision of an era, showing a characteristic population of fossils.

Permian Last period of the Paleozoic era, marked partly by an extensive ice age in the Southern Hemisphere.

Plutonic Term applied to extensive layers of igneous rock that evidently solidified deep within the earth's crust.

Precambrian Inclusive term applied to all of geological time before the Cambrian, the first period of the Paleozoic era; includes the first three eras.

Primates The order of mammals that, along with a few more primitive species, includes the monkeys, apes, extinct subhumans, and man.

Proterozoic The third geological era; the first that left identifiable fossils.

Revolution In geology, a relatively rapid change in the fossil population, marking the end of one era and the beginning of the next.

Trilobites A group of marine invertebrates that became abundant during the early Paleozoic, but are now extinct (see Fig. 26-3).

Vertebrate Animal that possesses a definite backbone.

EXERCISES

1. Name the six geological eras, and outline the characteristics of life during each era.

2. Explain the term "revolution" as used in the history of evolution, and give examples. Why are the revolutions named after mountain systems?

3. Try to suggest how there might be connections between mountain building, worldwide climate, and biological revolution.

4. Explain how the age of a rock stratum can be determined by analysis of the radioactivity it contains. What radioactive elements are suitable for this purpose, and by what reactions do they decay?

5. In a certain sample of rock the proportion of lead 206 to uranium 238 was found to be 1 to 5; estimate the age of this rock by scaling Fig. 26-2.

6. What are the uncertain factors in the different methods of radioactive dating? Why is it necessary to use an igneous rock rather than a sediment?

7. Explain the principles of the radiocarbon method of dating recent deposits.

8. Charcoal from a long-buried campfire was found to contain just one-eighth as much radiocarbon as modern wood; approximately at what date was the campfire used?

9. Discuss briefly the problems of estimating the age (a) of the earth itself, (b) of a meteorite, (c) of the solar system.

10. What is the evidence that life was already abundant 2½ billion years ago?

11. What kinds of living organisms probably existed when the Proterozoic era was well advanced, about 1 billion years ago? Which of these left identifiable traces and which did not?

12. Outline a reasonable theory of the way in which life on earth might have originated.

13. What type of organism is likely to have been our Paleozoic ancestor? List as many as you can of the forms through which the line of descent appears to have passed, from the Paleozoic to *Homo sapiens*.

14. What distinguishes the early Paleozoic era from the late Proterozoic? What gave the new types that appeared about this time such an advantage over their predecessors?

15. Does the fossil record from the early Paleozoic give a reliable census of living forms at the time? Give reasons for your answer.

16. About when did photosynthesis become an important factor in the life cycle?

17. What are the oldest living things that are known by fossil evidence to have invaded the dry land, and about when did this probably happen?

18. Outline the important changes that took place in the plant and animal populations during the course of the Paleozoic era.

19. Outline the most significant changes that took place during the Appalachian revolution that ushered in the Mesozoic era.

20. What appears to have happened in the sea just before and during the Appalachian revolution, and during the Mesozoic era?

21. Discuss briefly some of the theories concerning the rapid disappearance of the dinosaur at the end of the Mesozoic era.

22. Outline briefly the evolution of the mammal during the late Mesozoic and early Cenozoic eras.

23. List some of the important stages in the development of brain and the ability to reason.

the not-so-solid earth

The evidence for the earth's history which has been discussed in the last two chapters has been based upon the study of rocks exposed in the banks of a river canyon, or on the slopes of an eroded mountain, occasionally supplemented by samples taken from deep mines, or from drilled oil wells. The deepest well which has so far been drilled is about 5 miles, a little less than the highest mountain or the deepest ocean. But the radius of the earth is 3960 miles, and so we have direct evidence of only a very small fraction of it. The deepest wells and the highest mountains show everywhere rocks of the types described in Sec. 25-4. These have an average density of about 2.5 to 3.3 times the density of water, whereas the earth as a whole has a density of 5.522 (Sec. 6-4). The interior must be quite different from the thin surface crust which we can explore directly, but we have to depend upon indirect evidence to learn anything about it.

Since we cannot examine the interior of the earth directly, we need some kind of a probe which will penetrate the earth, and produce information from which we can make deductions. So far the most useful probe has been the wave that is sent out in all directions from an earthquake, either a natural earthquake or a large artificial explosion. Most of what will be described in this chapter about the earth's interior has, therefore, been deduced from studies of earthquakes. However, anything we deduce from earthquake studies must be consistent with other well-established facts, for example, with the mean density already mentioned, and with the fact that the earth has a magnetic field similar to that which would be produced by a large bar magnet buried deep within it (Sec. 15-6).

As we go down in any deep mine the temperature increases at a rate of about 30°C per kilometer. We know, too, that there must be pockets of molten magma to provide material for active volcanoes at various places, and other local sources of heat to provide boiling water and steam for geysers and hot springs. Any theory of the earth's interior must, therefore, allow for a high temperature, but just how high is difficult to estimate. The rate of increase of temperature as we go down the mine, combined with a knowledge of the heat conductivity of ordinary rock, tells us how much heat is continually flowing outward from the interior, to be lost eventually by radiation from the surface. If the earth as a whole contains about the same amount of radioactive material as meteorites, there will be just enough heat produced in the interior to account for the flow of heat through the upper crust. If we assume that the interior material has about the same heat conductivity as ordinary rock, we can then calculate what the temperature must be at the center. This works out to somewhere around 5000°K, but there are too many "if's" in the calculation to place much confidence in the actual figure; we are sure only that it is hot.

27-2   Earthquakes

Besides the disastrous earthquakes that occur from time to time, quake-prone regions such as Japan or California experience frequent "tremors," which can be felt, but which do not harm well-constructed buildings. Many more are observed by means of sensitive instruments. However, we are primarily interested in events vigorous enough to be detected thousands of miles away. These are the happenings which properly deserve the name "earthquake," and by far the most important cause is slippage of the earth's crust along a geological fault.

Figure 27-1 shows a typical fault, a crack where corresponding strata on the two sides have been shifted relative to each other. Most dislocations of this kind are local, but in some cases faults can be traced for several hundred miles along the surface, and must extend downward through all the rock layers to a depth of several miles. In the course of mountain-building activity forces may tend to uplift the strata on one side of the fault, and

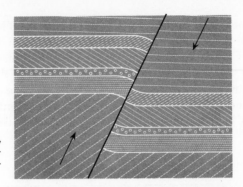

FIG. 27-1

Warped strata along a geological fault, such as might produce a major earthquake; the bending is greatly exaggerated.

depress those on the other side. Large layers of rock are slightly flexible, and the forces tend to warp the strata as shown in the figure. After a time the stresses set up in the bent rock layers become more than the rock can stand, and it has to give at its weakest point—the fault. There is another slippage along the fault, and the strata spring back to their unstressed positions.

When the stressed rock lets go, a vibration is set up and acts as a source of waves, which travel out through the rock and along the surface of the ground. It is the vibration and the waves that constitute the "quake," and do the damage, if any. The great Alaska earthquake of March 28, 1964, one of the most powerful ever recorded in North America, was the result of a slip of this kind. The arc of the Aleutian Islands, which extend from the southwest tip of Alaska, marks a narrow mountainous ridge, with a deep ocean trench on the outer side of the arc (Fig. 27-2). The same structure continues along the Alaskan coast, and the entire region is a zone of weakness in the earth's crust, shown on the mainland by several well-marked faults, lying east and west, roughly parallel to the coast. It was one of these faults, passing near the city of Anchorage, that slipped along a great part of its length and caused the damage, producing waves which were detected all over the world.

At least 95 per cent of the important earthquakes that have been recorded have occurred in two well-marked zones, which extend all the way around the world (Fig. 27-3), close to some of the youngest and highest mountain ranges; the very fact that earthquakes are frequent in these zones indicates that the mountains are still rising. The more important zone is that which more or less surrounds the Pacific Ocean. It includes the zone of weakness of the Aleutian Islands and southern Alaska. It has skipped British Columbia and the Northwest States during historical times, but there has clearly been activity there within the last 1000 years. It is active again in California and Mexico, all down the west coast of South America, and in parts of the Antarctic continent. It continues through New Zealand, the island chains of the southwest Pacific, the Philippines and Japan, to close the circle. The second, less important zone joins the circum-Pacific zone in Central America, includes the West Indies, cuts across the North Atlantic, follows the great mountain ranges of the Alps and Himalayas across Europe and Asia, and joins the Pacific zone again in Indonesia. The same zones contain most of the world's active and recently extinct volcanoes, for both volcanoes and earthquakes are evidence of active mountain building.

FIG. 27-2

The zone of weakness along the Aleutian arc and southern Alaska; heights and depths in feet.

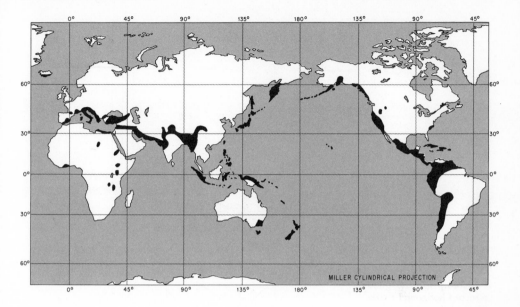

FIG. 27-3

Principal earthquake zones of the world.

27-3   Propagation and Detection of Earthquake Waves

The shock of an important earthquake produces three distinct kinds of waves, which travel out in all directions from the *focus*, the center of maximum disturbance. Two of these travel through the body of the earth. The first, which travels fastest and therefore arrives first at any detecting station, is known as the P (primary) wave. It is a longitudinal wave, of the same mechanical nature as a sound wave, traveling with a velocity of 4 to 8.5 miles per second. The next disturbance to arrive is the S (secondary) wave, which also travels through the earth, and consists of transverse vibrations. Finally, the L wave (Love, after the scientist who first studied this type of wave) arrives, traveling over the surface with a motion something like that of a water wave. The L wave is usually the most intense of the three by far, and is the one which may do damage, even at a considerable distance from the earthquake focus.

The P and S waves, since they travel through the earth, are refracted when they pass from one layer of rock to another layer of different density and elasticity (Sec. 27-5). They are also partially reflected at a discontinuity between two layers. If there is a gradual change in properties as we go to greater and greater depths, without any definite discontinuity, the

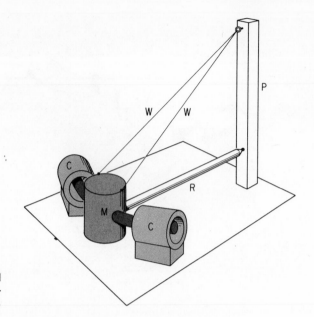

FIG. 27-4

A seismograph designed to record horizontal movements of the earth's crust.

waves are refracted continuously and follow a curved path. It is from these reflections and refractions that we can deduce information about the interior of the earth.

The waves from distant earthquakes are detected by means of instruments known as *seismographs,* one type of which is illustrated in Fig. 27-4. A heavy mass (M) is suspended by means of a pair of wires (W) and a hinged rod (R) from a rigid post (P) which is set into the ground, well below the soft surface soil. The post is slightly tilted, so that the mass and rod swing from it like a gate, but return to their normal position after being disturbed. When an earthquake wave arrives the base of the instrument and the post are set in motion, but the heavy mass tends to remain at rest, and so appears to swing relative to the post. Soft iron armatures attached to the swinging mass move inside a pair of pickup coils (CC), and induce a current whenever relative motion occurs. The current can be used to operate any kind of electrical recording equipment, and so produce a record of the movements of the ground. Figure 27-5(a) is part of a record of the Alaska earthquake, made at the seismograph station at Leduc, Alberta, 1500 miles away. Even at this distance the waves produced such a strong ground movement that it is hard to interpret the record, other than to locate the instant of the first arrival. The less confused record in Fig. 27-5(b) is that of an "aftershock" which occurred the next day; it shows clearly the arrival of both P and S waves.

The seismograph illustrated is designed to detect horizontal motion of the ground. A fully equipped observing station will have two instruments of this type for east-west and north-south movements, respectively. Another instrument, with a different type of suspension, will record vertical movements. Comparison of the three instruments will show how the ground was actually moving as the different types of waves passed by, and so show approximately the direction from which the waves were coming.

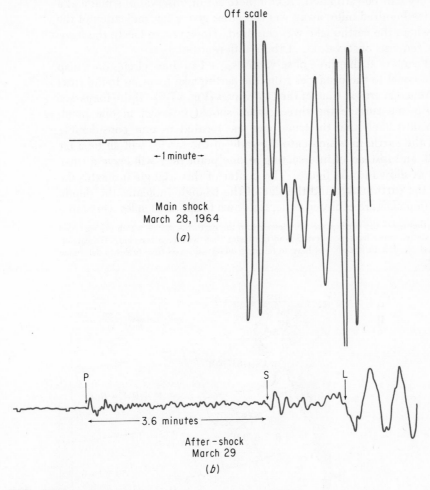

FIG. 27-5

Record of the Alaska earthquake of March, 1964, obtained at Leduc, Alberta, 1500 miles away: (a) the first wave from the principal shock; (b) an aftershock that occurred the next day. (Courtesy of E. R. Kanasewich, University of Alberta.)

27-4   *Location of the Earthquake Focus*

Long study has permitted seismologists to compile tables showing the time required for the P and S waves to travel different distances through the earth.° If the instants of first arrival of the two types of waves can be identified, and the amount by which the S wave is delayed behind the P wave can be determined, the distance of the earthquake focus from the observatory can be estimated. A complete set of observations made at a point a few hundred miles away will therefore give a fair indication of the locality where the earthquake was centered. However, to locate the focus precisely requires observations at three different points.

Taking centers at the three observatories, we can draw circles on a map with radii equal to the distances from the earthquake focus, as found from the difference in arrival time of the two waves (Fig. 27-6). If the focus was on or near the surface the three circles should intersect in one point. However, it is likely that the true focus was located at some considerable depth in the earth, in which case the radii of the circles will all be a bit too small, and instead of intersecting at one point they will leave a small triangle, as shown in the figure. The center of this triangle indicates the focus of the earthquake, and the size of the triangle indicates the depth. Most earthquakes are centered at depths down to about 40 miles, very often

° The farther away the earthquake, the deeper into the earth the waves which are recorded at a given station must have penetrated, and the faster they will have traveled. We cannot, therefore, assume definite speeds, but have to resort to empirical travel-time tables to determine the distance.

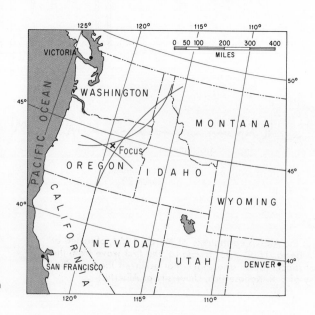

FIG. 27-6

Locating the focus of an earthquake.

near the discontinuity which marks the bottom of the earth's crust, although some have been found to have occurred as deep as 800 miles, showing that the weaknesses which produce them can be very deep-seated.

27-5   Structure of the Earth

Studies of earthquake waves have shown that the earth is comprised of three distinct concentric zones: the crust, the mantle, and the core. Outermost is the *crust*, composed of familiar types of sedimentary and igneous rock, and from 3 to 40 miles in thickness. In most places the rocky crust is covered by a thin layer of loose material, soil, sand and gravel, or oceanic ooze.

A minor earthquake or a large explosion sends out P waves through the rock, and these may be recorded at two or three observatories only 100 or 200 miles away. In this case the direct wave, which gives the first indication of the disturbance, travels entirely in the crust (*EO* in Fig. 27-7). The direct wave is then followed a little later by another P-type wave (*ERO*) that has been reflected at the sharp discontinuity between the crust and the mantle. If both the direct wave and the reflection can be picked out on the seismograph records, the time lapse between them gives the thickness of the crust at the point *R*, where the reflection occurred.* There is no reflected wave beyond the point *O'*, where the direct wave that has just reached the bottom of the crust is observed. The P-wave reflection at the bottom of the crust, and the fact that no reflection can be observed beyond a distance *EO'*, were first discovered and explained by a Yugoslavian seismologist by the name of A. Mohorovičić in 1909, and so the sudden change in properties at the bottom of the crust is known as the *Mohorovičić discontinuity* (*Moho* for short).

The P and S waves from a major earthquake, strong enough to have been recorded on seismographs all over the world, follow paths such as those shown in Fig. 27-8, lying mostly in the *mantle*, the zone which makes up 83 per cent of the earth's volume. The curved paths show that there is a continuous change in the velocities of the waves as we go to greater depths. At a depth of about 1800 miles there is another sharp discontinuity at which reflections and refractions take place, showing the existence of a definite core.

---

* There has been a scarcity of information of this type from the western plains, for local earthquakes in that area are rare. A series of very large conventional explosions, using surplus TNT from World War II, is being set off in southern Alberta. The waves from these explosions can be detected on seismographs up to 500 miles away, and will yield a lot of information about the crust underneath the plains. A similar method on a smaller scale is used by exploration geophysicists to trace strata that might contain oil, for the boundary between a sediment and an igneous rock will also reflect the waves from an explosion.

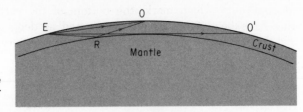

F I G . **27-7**

Paths of P waves in the
crust produced by a minor
disturbance.

In Fig. 27-8 the right half of the diagram shows the behavior of the
P waves, and the left half that of the S waves. From O_1 to O_2, and similarly on the other side, no direct P waves are observed; then beyond O_2
they are observed again, and must have passed through the core in the
manner shown. On the other hand, no S waves at all are observed at
points farther around the earth from the focus than O_3, as indicated on the
left half of the diagram. Now the S waves are transverse waves, and cannot exist in a liquid. The P waves are longitudinal, and can travel through
a liquid, but in all cases that have been studied in the laboratory the
velocity of soundlike compression waves in a liquid is considerably less
than it is in the same material in the solid state. The refraction of the
P waves when they pass from the mantle to the core is precisely in the
direction showing a lower wave velocity in the core. On both counts,
therefore, we deduce that the earth has a central core of molten liquid,
which turns out to have a radius of 2160 miles.°

Naturally, we do not know for certain what the mantle and the liquid
core are made of. However, a great many of the meteorites that fall upon

° The molten core is not, as one might think, the source of volcanic lava. This comes from
pockets of molten magma that form in a few places, either between the crust and the mantle,
or in the upper mantle.

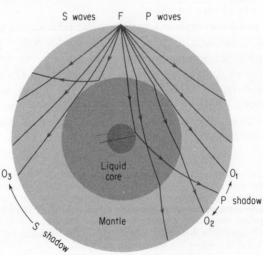

FIG. **27-8**

Cross section of the earth, showing the paths of the P waves
from an earthquake (right half
of diagram), and the S waves
(left half).

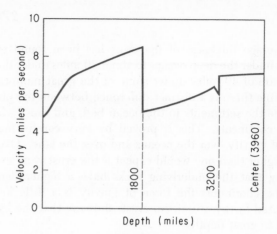

FIG. 27-9

Variation with depth of the velocity of the P waves.

the earth from time to time, and that may be the remains of an exploded planet, are composed mainly of metallic iron, with some nickel and other metals. Also, we know from analysis of the spectrum of the sun that iron is the most abundant of the moderately heavy elements. It is conjectured, therefore, that the earth's core is mainly molten iron, with other metals in the same proportion as in the metallic meteorites. Its mean density, about 11, is consistent with this conjecture, and its estimated temperature, 5000°K, is about right for the melting point of iron-nickel alloy under the very high pressure that must exist at the base of the mantle. On this theory the upper layers of the mantle would have a composition similar to that of the non-metallic meteorites that are occasionally found, and would contain large quantities of silicon—also one of the most abundant elements in the cosmos. The conjecture is, therefore, that the layers just below the crust consist mainly of silicates of iron and some of the common light metals, like magnesium, and that in lower layers of the mantle, where the earthquake evidence shows that the density increases quite rapidly with depth, the composition changes gradually to less silicon and magnesium, and to more of the heavier metals like nickel.

When the liquid core of the earth was discovered it was naturally assumed that it extended to the center. Recently, however, faint P-wave reflections have been observed in the region O_1O_2 of Fig. 27-8 where the earthquake should not have been detected at all. These apparently come from a solid inner core, 750 miles in radius, inside the main liquid core. The solid in the very center probably does not represent any significant change in composition, but exists because the extremely high pressure prevents the iron-nickel alloy from melting.

27-6   The Isostasy Principle

The average thickness of the crust has been found to vary from about 3 miles under the deep oceans to about 20 miles under the continents, with a maximum of 40 miles under some of the great mountain massifs. At the same time there is a distinct difference between the plutonic rocks which underlie the sediments in the ocean bed, and those which form the roots of the continents. This is proved by very careful measurements of the force of gravity over the oceans and over the land. Over the oceans it is a little higher than one would expect if the crust were everywhere uniform, showing that the underlying rocks have a higher density than average; over the continents the force of gravity is a little lower than could be accounted for by a uniform crust, showing that the lighter types of rock extend to great depths.

The deductions from these observations are illustrated in Fig. 27-10, which is a somewhat idealized cross section of North America, taken in about the latitude of the United States-Canadian border. The relatively thin crust under the oceans is believed to consist, underneath a layer of a few thousand feet of sediment, of a heavy basaltlike rock. This layer probably continues under the continent, but there it is overlain with a thickness of several miles of lighter granitic rock. In a few places material from the mantle seems to well up close to the surface, notably in the core of the western mountain massif.

In the diagram the continent looks like a huge mass of granite floating in the material of the mantle, with the thin layer of basalt warped so as to accommodate the great thickness of the granite. According to the principle of *isostasy,* or *isostatic equilibrium,* this is indeed the case. Although the material of the mantle behaves like a rigid solid when it is subjected to the

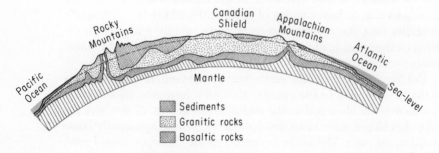

FIG. 27-10

Cross section of North America, approximately along the border between the U.S.A. and Canada; the vertical scale is greatly exaggerated and the details are somewhat simplified. (After *Imperial Oil Review.*)

sudden shock of an earthquake, and so transmits the transverse S waves, it apparently yields slowly when subjected to a steady force for a very long time. The light granite block of the continent therefore sinks in the heavier material of the mantle until the mass of material displaced is equal to the mass of the floating block, similar to an iceberg floating in water.

The isostasy principle accounts also for the slow rise and fall of extensive land areas. As a mountain range is worn down by erosion it tends to rise, along with the neighboring foothill region, to be subject to still more erosion. As the eroded material is deposited on the nearby plains, or on the shallow continental shelf that extends the granitic mass a certain distance under the ocean, these areas slowly sink. When a large part of North America was buried under several thousand feet of ice during the recent great ice ages, the crust must have been depressed well below its present level. As the most recent layer of ice melted, over the period from 20,000 to 8000 years ago, the land slowly rose again, but very slowly, so slowly that apparently the compensation is still incomplete, and the land of the north central plain and of the area around Hudson's Bay is still rising.

27-7   Origin of the Earth's Magnetism, Fossil Magnetism

If the interior of the earth consists largely of molten metal, it is not hard to understand, qualitatively, why it has the type of magnetic field that it has. There must be an appreciable difference of temperature between the upper layers of the core, just under the mantle, and the lower layers, just above the solid inner core. The inner material therefore tends to rise, and the outer material to sink, so that huge convection eddies are set up in the liquid layers. At the same time the earth is rotating on its north-south axis. Now, it can be shown that if a mass of liquid metal has an eddy motion and at the same time a rotary motion around a fixed axis, electric currents will also be set up in it, and will flow approximately in circles around the axis of rotation. We may expect, therefore, that in the liquid region between 750 and 2160 miles from the earth's center there will be weak electric currents as well as eddy currents of the material, and that the electric currents will flow more or less around the north-south axis. This is precisely the kind of electric current required to set up the magnetic field we actually observe, namely a field similar to that which would be produced by a weak bar magnet about 2000 miles long, lying in a position slightly inclined to the axis of rotation. Moreover, the convection eddies cannot be expected to remain accurately fixed, consequently the magnetic field can vary in strength and in direction, as it indeed does.

Have the earth's magnetic field and its axis of rotation always lain more or less in their present position? This is a question that was hardly even asked until recently, for it was tacitly assumed that the law of conserva-

tion of momentum would prohibit any significant change in the axis of
rotation, and in the positions of the North and South Poles, and this in spite
of the geological evidence of tropical conditions in Alaska and an ice age
in Australia. Just recently there has emerged clear evidence that the poles
have not always occupied their present positions relative to the continents.
This evidence is based on what has come to be known as *fossil magnetism*.
Most rocks contain grains of iron oxide which became magnetized when the
molten material solidified, and later, when these grains were carried away
by running water and deposited in a bed of sediment, they settled down with
their poles pointing to the magnetic north. If the layer of sediment lies
undisturbed through subsequent geological ages there is nothing to alter
the magnetization of the grains; their poles will still point to where the
north magnetic pole of the earth lay at the time the rock was formed.

One of the first places where fossil magnetism was discovered and
studied was in rock strata that are exposed in the cliffs of the Grand
Canyon of the Colorado. The magnetic grains were very carefully picked
out from a layer which was known to be about 200 million years old, and
which was still lying in its original horizontal position. The directions in
which the little magnets were lying in the rock were carefully noted, and
it was found that they pointed nowhere near the present North Pole, but
rather to a point in the Pacific Ocean about 1000 miles off the coast of
California. The north magnetic pole must have been west of California
200 million years ago!

Since this discovery was made fossil magnetism has been observed and
studied in many different parts of the world, in geological strata of many
different ages, and it has been found that the magnetic poles have varied
very much, and have even reversed themselves a number of times, the
present north magnetic pole becoming south in the magnetic sense, and
vice versa.

27-8   Drifting Continents

The study of fossil magnetism shows that in past geological ages the north
and south magnetic poles have occupied very different positions with
respect to the continental masses than they do today. This raises three different possibilities. The magnetic poles may have wandered far away from
the geographic poles. But if the earth's magnetic field is due to convection
currents set up in the liquid core, it is unlikely that the magnetic poles could
ever move very far from the axis of rotation.° Rather they must tend to
revolve irregularly around the geographical poles, as we know they have

---

° The poles could, however, reverse in direction, because the electric currents could flow
either way around the north-south axis. The observed reversals do not, therefore, affect the general conclusions of this section.

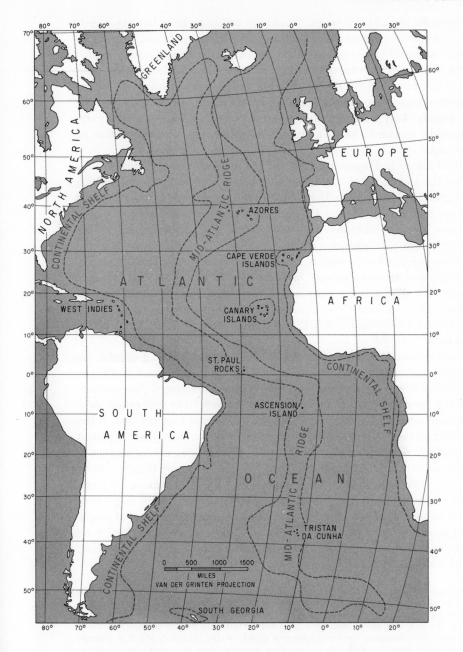

FIG. 27-11

Map showing how America and Africa might once have fitted together, and how their splitting might have left behind the Mid-Atlantic Ridge.

been doing for the last 500 years. Could the axis of rotation have changed? This is conceivable, or rather it is conceivable that the liquid core might shift one way and the mantle shift in the opposite direction just enough that the combined angular momentum of core and mantle remains fixed, although it is very hard to see what might cause such a change. The third possibility is that the great continental blocks, which appear to be floating in the mantle, may have changed their positions, while the axis of rotation actually remained fixed, as required by the law of conservation of momentum.

In 1912 Alfred L. Wegener, a German geophysicist, drew attention to the fact that the east coast of the Americas (the edge of the continental shelf, not the present shore line) is almost exactly the same shape as the west coast of Europe and Africa (Fig. 27-11), and he suggested that they might once have been joined.° Actually, he went further, and suggested that all the continents were once part of a single great land mass which was centered somewhere near where India is now, and that the Americas, Australia, Antarctica, and to some extent Africa, slowly drifted into their present positions. If this idea were right it would explain why the early stages of evolution followed almost the same course on all the continents, and why it is only in fairly recent times that any continent has had a distinctive evolutionary history.†

For a long time Wegener's suggestion fell on deaf ears, and geologists are still skeptical about the existence of a single primeval land mass. However, the idea that the granitic continental blocks have wandered over the surface of the mantle during geological time seems now to be well established. At the time when the fossil magnetism of the Grand Canyon placed the North Pole off the coast of California, similar evidence from Europe placed it somewhere north of Hawaii. The two observations are consistent if North America were then some 1000 miles closer to Europe than it is now, and if they have been drifting apart ever since. The most striking evidence comes from Australia, where it has been possible to study fossil magnetism in strata of several different geological ages. The island continent seems to have wandered all over the Southern Hemisphere, and for a long time to have been close to the South Pole, so that it could easily have become covered with ice (Fig. 27-12).

° This is actually a very old idea. It was mentioned by Francis Bacon about 1620, and by the French naturalist Buffon (1707–1788), among others.

† For example, mammalian evolution has been quite different in Australia than in the rest of the world. Native Australian mammals have never lost the marsupial habit of carrying their young in pouches, and the kangaroo has never appeared anywhere else. This indicates that Australia has had no land connection with Asia or any other continent since at least the late Mesozoic. America and Asia have been connected at several different epochs, by way of Alaska and the shallow Bering Sea, and the existence of similar animals on these continents cannot be taken as evidence of the former Transatlantic connection required by the theory of continental drift.

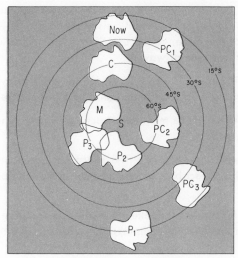

FIG. 27-12

Conjectured wanderings of Australia as indicated by fossil magnetism. (After Irving and Green, *Geophys. J.,* I [1958], 64.)

PC — Pre-Cambrian   M — Mesozoic
P — Paleozoic   C — Early Cenozoic

GLOSSARY

Aftershocks Minor shocks that follow a major earthquake, and that are due to readjustments in the disturbed area.

Continental drift Theory that the great land masses have wandered over the surface of the globe as if they are blocks of light material floating in the heavier material of the mantle.

Continental shelf Extension of the continental structure some distance under the surrounding ocean.

Fault Line where the strata of the earth's crust have fractured and one portion has shifted vertically relative to the other portion, so that corresponding layers are discontinuous across the fault.

Fossil magnetism Grains of permanently magnetized iron oxide that are found in sedimentary rocks, lying in the positions they occupied when the sediment was deposited; they point toward the position that the earth's magnetic pole occupied at the time of deposition of the rock.

Isostasy The theory that portions of the earth's crust rise or fall as material is shifted from one area to another by the processes of erosion and deposition, so that the different portions tend toward the positions of equilibrium that they would occupy if they were floating on a liquid substratum.

L wave Earthquake wave that travels over the surface; normally the third wave to arrive at a distant seismograph station, and normally the most intense of the three; called after Love, the seismologist who developed the theory of this type of wave.

Mantle The solid structure that forms the main body of the earth; overlain by the thin rocky crust, and underlain by the liquid core.

Massif An extensive mountain structure, usually consisting of several more or less parallel ranges.   '

Mohorovičić discontinuity The sharp boundary between the crust and the mantle; first described by the seismologist Mohorovičić, and known as the "Moho."

P wave Primary earthquake wave, the first to arrive at a distant seismograph station; a longitudinal compression wave traveling through the interior of the earth.

Seismograph Instrument for detecting and recording minute movements of the earth's crust, movements that are frequently caused by the waves from distant earthquakes.

Seismology The science and study of earthquakes.

S wave Secondary earthquake wave, the second to arrive at a distant station; a transverse wave traveling through the interior.

Travel-time tables Empirical tables that give the times required for the P and S waves to travel different distances through the interior of the earth.

Tremor Minor earthquake disturbance, strong enough to be felt, but not strong enough to cause appreciable damage.

EXERCISES

1. What are the principal sources of information about the interior of the earth?

2. Outline the evidence that the interior of the earth is at a high temperature. According to the present evidence, is the earth getting hotter or getting cooler?

3. Explain the most important cause of destructive earthquakes.

4. What apparently caused the great Alaskan earthquake of 1964?

5. Where do most of the major earthquakes take place?

6. Explain the mechanism and mode of propagation of the three principal types of earthquake waves.

7. Describe the construction and operation of a simple type of seismograph.

8. How is the focus of an earthquake determined?

9. Explain how the thickness of the earth's crust in a given area can be determined.

10. Outline the evidence that the earth has a liquid core.

11. There seems to be a solid inner core inside the main liquid core; explain how this is possible without the need for any significant change in composition or temperature.

12. Explain the principle of isostatic compensation; give examples of areas where this process is apparently now at work.

13. Explain how the liquid core of the earth could be the source of its magnetic field.

14. Explain what is meant by "fossil magnetism." Under what geological conditions are observations of fossil magnetism likely to produce trustworthy conclusions?

15. Discuss the theory of continental drift. What led to this idea in the first place? Outline the present evidence for the theory.

16. Discuss the manner in which mammalian evolution in Australia has taken a distinctive course, not duplicated anywhere else in the world. At about what stage of geological time did Australian evolution separate from that in the rest of the world? Explain the significance of this observation.

17. Explain briefly how seismic observations can help in the discovery of oil deposits.

CHAPTER **28** **mountains, rivers, and ice**

It is implied in everything we have so far discussed about the earth that none of the geographical and geological features of the crust are permanent. The granitic blocks which form the cores of the continents, and which come close to the surface in the continental shields, must have existed from very early times, possibly from the first solidification of the earth's crust. However, they have risen as their higher elevations have been worn down; they have sunk as they have been loaded with layers of sediment or ice; if the evidence discussed in Sec. 27-7 is reliable, they have moved around. There have always been oceans, but they have changed their boundaries as the continents changed; the Atlantic Ocean, in particular, appears to be comparatively new. Mountain ranges have been formed, and then worn away; rivers have changed their course, and new rivers have developed; new plains of sediment have been laid down; the sea has invaded areas that were once dry land, and then has receded again. In this chapter we shall discuss the causes of change, and we shall begin with mountain building (technically known as *orogenesis*), because if there were

474

no new mountain ranges formed from time to time the other geographical changes would be insignificant.

One cause of the formation of a new mountain is volcanic action, but we shall say no more about volcanoes, except to note that most of them occur in areas where other types of orogenic activity are going on, either on land or under the sea. Thus the zones of weakness where earthquakes are frequent (Fig. 27-3) are also zones of volcanic action. We are concerned here mainly with mountain ranges that are formed by widespread movements of the earth's crust. In general these are modifications or combinations of two principal types.

If the forces and the movement are mainly horizontal, as indicated in Fig. 28-1, the result is a warping of the crust, and *fold mountains* are formed, possibly with several parallel ranges. Fold mountains can be recognized by the bending and tilting of the sedimentary strata from which the range is formed (Fig. 25-5). Sometimes complete folds can be seen, sometimes only strongly tilted strata, possibly even standing on edge. The uplift is always a slow process, and erosion starts as soon as any portion is raised above the average level; the upfolds are then carved into rugged peaks by wind and rain. There is often an intrusion of igneous rock—usually granitic in nature—into the fold, so that fold mountains often have granite cores, which may be exposed in places by erosion of the overlying sediments.

If the movement of the crust is more nearly vertical, it may result merely in the uplift of a high plateau, which is then carved into some semblance of a mountain system by erosion. However, a fault may form, and then the uplifted strata may tend to slide over the remaining strata, as shown in Fig. 28-2. Erosion immediately starts; the sharp edge of the uplifted block is rarely seen, and a characteristic *block fault mountain* results. On one side the approach to the mountain top is gradual, but on the side of the fault a steep escarpment develops, intersected by rapid mountain streams and deep ravines. There is a fine example of a block fault range in the Big Horn Mountains of Wyoming, lying east of the main range of the Rockies. There is the characteristic gradual climb up from the west;

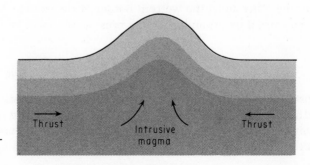

FIG. 28-1

Formation of a fold mountain.

Thrust

Intrusive magma

Thrust

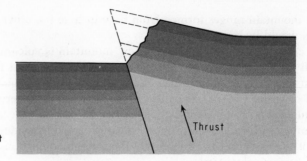

FIG. 28-2

Formation of a block fault mountain.

there is a wide, fairly level mountain top; then on the east there are precipitous canyons, with a descent of several thousand feet in a few miles.

Geologists can determine from the form of the mountain, and from the folding and tilting of the strata, the direction of the forces that caused the mountain to be uplifted. Much is therefore known about the orogenic forces that have been active at different times in different parts of the world. However, there is yet to be developed a general, consistent theory of the origin of these forces. It used to be thought that the earth is cooling and shrinking, and then the formation of mountains could be ascribed to wrinkling of the crust, like the wrinkling of the skin of a dried apple. Unfortunately, there are serious objections to this simple theory, and it does not seem tenable today. In the first place, it is doubtful if the earth is getting cooler. There is plenty of radioactive material in the interior to maintain the present temperature distribution, including the molten core, and probably the internal temperatures have been nearly constant over the last billion years. Again, if the crust is shrinking one would expect the degree of ruggedness to increase progressively, but there have been mountains from the earliest geological ages, probably as high and rugged as any that now exist.

One theory, which may account for some of the world's existing mountain systems, but probably not for all, relates mountain building to the continental drift discussed in the last chapter. For example, if the Americas are drifting westward, the series of mountain ranges that have been formed one after the other along the western border of the continental block may have been caused by crumpling of the crust as the main block advanced.

28-2   Age of a Mountain Range

Geologists assign quite definite ages to the principal mountain systems of the earth. For example, the first uplift of the main range of the Rocky Mountains is placed at the same time as the biological revolution which divides the Cenozoic from the Mesozoic, 63 million years ago. A rough idea of the relative age of different ranges can be obtained simply from their appearance. The Rockies, as the name suggests, are characterized by rugged peaks, and rapid mountain streams flowing in steep-sided V-shaped ravines. They are comparatively young mountains, but not just of yesterday, for erosion has proceeded far enough to cut them up into many separate peaks, and some of the main rivers which drain them have worn their valleys down until the valley bottom has a gentle slope, with a meandering river and wide flood plains, like the Bow Valley near Banff (Fig. 25-4).

The Coast Ranges and the Cascades which parallel the Pacific coast are much younger, and are ascribed to the middle Cenozoic. In general, they are not as high as the Rockies, and perhaps partly for this reason are less rugged, but they show the torrential mountain streams and V-shaped ravines (Fig. 25-1) characteristic of young mountains, especially on the western slope. They are less eroded than the Rockies, and the few large rivers which intersect them pass through deep canyons rather than through open valleys. It is in this mountain system that we find a series of famous volcanic peaks, Baker, Rainier, Hood, Shasta, and others. These are still younger than the mountain range from which they project, and still have the typical conical shape of volcanoes, only slightly eroded.

For an example of a very much older mountain system we may look to the Appalachian Mountains of the eastern United States, which are ascribed to about the end of the Paleozoic. They are still well-marked mountains, but they have long ago lost their rugged peaks, their steep ravines, and their typical mountain streams. Still older are the Laurentian Mountains of

FIG. 28-3

A young volcanic peak: Mt. Rainier, which is not now active as a volcano, but which is probably less than a million years old. (Photograph by B. Willis, U.S. Geological Survey.)

Quebec, which are part of the Canadian Shield. They hardly deserve the name of mountain, for they are worn down to little more than their granitic roots.

While the general appearance of the landscape affords an interesting physical contrast between mountain systems of very different ages, the geologist cannot depend upon this to estimate the age of a mountain range, and to ascribe different ranges to different periods of orogenic activity. The determination of age depends upon a careful study of the rocks in and around the mountain range, combined with the application of a few simple principles. In a fold mountain, the folding must have taken place subsequent to the deposition of the youngest sedimentary stratum found among the folds, but before the deposition of any level beds of sediment that may be found in immediately adjacent areas. The sediments can be dated quite accurately by their fossil content, and so it is often possible to fix the age of the mountain range within quite narrow limits. A volcano or a lava flow must be younger than any sediments which lie under the lava, and which may be exposed in the banks of a mountain stream.

28-3 Rivers, Young and Old

The converse process to mountain building is the wearing down of the rocks by erosion, with subsequent deposition of the eroded material at a lower level. By far the most efficient agent of erosion is rain and running water, although wind can be effective in arid areas. Even when there is neither rain nor wind, alternation of heat and cold can cause fragments to flake off a rocky mountainside—as may happen on the moon. Much of the solid material carried down from the mountains and hills finds its way into a major river, and it can then be carried hundreds of miles before it is deposited to form a layer of sediment.

Rivers, like mountains, have their history, which can be pieced together by careful study. Most of the world's great rivers have their ultimate source in mountain lakes, fed by melting snow and by frequent rains falling on the mountain tops. The lake drains through a permanent stream, which is soon joined by tributary streams from other lakes or from mountain valleys, and the water has not traveled far before it is part of a large river. In a high, rugged mountain system of recent formation, the high-lying lakes and the upper stretches of the streams and rivers must also be young. These streams are characterized by rapid torrents, taking a steep, direct course down the slope and carving out for themselves steep-sided ravines and narrow canyons. The rapid flow can transport large grains of material and can even roll boulders along the stream bed. Where the stream slackens slightly the largest grains are left behind, and so gravel bars form here and there along the river bank.

When the river leaves the mountains and flows out over a plain with a gradual slope toward the sea, it starts to meander. It is now following a wide open valley, bordered by low rolling hills, or possibly by earthern cliffs set back some distance from the river itself. This is a mature river, and its general course has probably been a drainage route as long as the plain across which it is flowing has been dry land. It is a curious fact that, when the slope of the land decreases in going from the mountain foothills to the plain, the flow gradient in the river decreases even more. Where the slope is steep the young river tends to flow directly down it. Where it is more gradual, the river tends to wander from side to side of its wide valley, forming loops, and even doubling back occasionally, so that the slope of the river bed is even more gradual than the slope of the land.

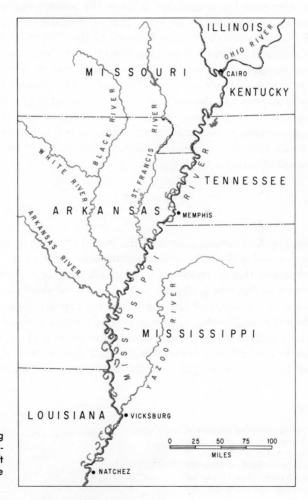

FIG. 28-4

Map of the meandering Mississippi, showing "oxbow lakes" that were left behind when a loop of the river was cut off.

Mature rivers like the Missouri-Mississippi system, the Nile in Egypt, and the Saskatchewan in western Canada, can transport vast quantities of fine sand and silt, but the current is too slow to move gravel or boulders. These rivers are characterized by shifting sand-bars as well as by their meandering course. They are subject to floods in spring and early summer, when the snow is melting in the mountains from which they draw much of their water supply, and then they may overflow their immediate banks and spread out over the flood plains of their wide open valleys. When the floods recede, quantities of silt are left behind, and so the flood plains are built up. Other transported material is carried all the way to the eventual outlet in the ocean or a lake, and is deposited in the shallow offshore waters, to form deltas like those of the Mississippi and the Nile.

There are places where a river flowing through a mountain system is actually older than the mountains. That is, the present-day river is following a drainage route established long before the mountains were thrust up. Typical examples are the Grand Canyon of the Colorado, and the deep canyons where the Columbia and the Fraser cut through the mountains of the Coast Ranges. In the case of the Columbia and the Fraser, the water draining off the older mountains to the east of the present Coast Ranges had to find an outlet to the sea. As the slow movement of the earth's crust thrust up the mountain folds, the principal rivers, instead of finding new courses, succeeded in deepening their valleys as fast as the mountains rose, and so today they still follow the original course, but through deep canyons instead of across a sloping plain.

28-4   Mountain Glaciers

In all the great mountain ranges of the world the highest peaks are perpetually covered with snow, which is compacted into ice by the weight of the fresh snow that is continually being added. Ice formed from compacted snow in this way is slightly plastic, and flows slowly under pressure, so that the lower layers of the mountain ice cap are squeezed out, and slide down the neighboring valleys as typical mountain glaciers. The moving ice of a glacier is an efficient agent of erosion, and the effects of ice can be distinguished from those of water and wind in several ways. Material of all kinds is gouged out from the rocks, and all the eroded material

FIG. 28-5

A glacial valley, showing the typical rounded formation; the snow ridge in the background is an edge of the Columbia Icefield, a remnant of the last ice age. (Banff National Park, Alberta; photograph by author.)

FIG. 28-6

A typical glacial moraine, marking the tip of a glacier that once filled the valley, now occupied by a lake. (Moraine Lake, Alberta; photograph by author.)

is carried along at the same speed. Thus the first characteristic of glacial erosion is that the deposit contains material of all sizes, from clay to large boulders. Most of the material is deposited in *moraines*, ridges that form at the tip and along the sides of the glacier, where the melting in summer is just equal to the annual advance of the ice (Fig. 28-6).

28-5   *The Great Ice Age*

The Columbia Icefield, a corner of which shows in Fig. 28-5, is a remnant of the great sheet of ice that covered much of North America about 20,000 years ago, and whose traces are easily found today. The area it covered at its maximum extent is shown in Fig. 28-7—parts of its boundary are clearly marked by a terminal moraine of which Long Island is a portion. A large part of northern Europe was covered with ice at the same time as North America, but it is significant that central Alaska and eastern Siberia, where it must have been just as cold, remained bare.

The areas which were covered can be recognized by deposits of *glacial till*—unsorted sediments which, if they are left lying long enough, will

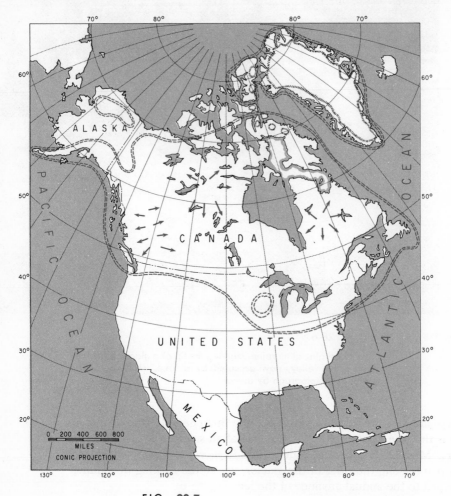

FIG. 28-7

Extent of the ice in the most recent Pleistocene glaciation, showing also the centers from which the ice spread out.

some day harden into conglomerate rocks. In some places the till is accumulated into low elongated hills known as *drumlins;* in others, streams flowing under the ice left long gravelly ridges known as *eskers*. Shallow depressions were scooped out by the ice, and today many of these are occupied by lakes, some of which have only a small trickle for an outlet, or an outlet that is not visible at all. Another evidence of former glaciation is the occurrence of erratic boulders—large rocks, sometimes weighing several tons. These particular boulders have no relation to the geological strata on top of which they are lying; they must have been carried long distances and left behind when the ice melted.

It is estimated that the ice reached a thickness of over 10,000 feet in places, and as more snow was added to the load winter after winter, the lower layers were squeezed out, as moving glaciers are squeezed out from a mountain ice cap. But there were no valleys to guide the flow, and the moving ice slid over the whole northern plain, until the southern edges of the sheet reached a warmer climate, where the ice melted away in summer as much as it advanced during the winter. Where the bedrock over which the ice moved is exposed—as it is in many places in the Canadian Shield—the direction of the ice movement is clearly delineated by parallel scratches in the rock; in other places it is shown by the direction of the esker ridges. The evidence indicates that the continental ice sheet had two main centers, one in northwestern Canada, west of Hudson Bay, and one in northern Quebec. From these two areas the ice spread out in all directions until the two sheets joined together and merged with the older Greenland ice cap and with the mountain ice cap which, by that time, had covered most of the mountains of the western United States and Canada.

Study of the Pleistocene° sediments has shown that there are four distinct layers of glacial till, separated by layers of waterborne and wind-blown sediment, containing evidence of vegetable and animal life. There have therefore been four ice ages within the last million years, separated by periods of relative warmth when the land was free from ice and vegetation could flourish. When the great ice sheets were at their maximum extent, a great deal of the world's water supply was tied up in the ice; it is estimated that the average level of the oceans must have been about 600 feet lower than it is today. North America was joined to Asia by way of Alaska, and the land connection between North and South America, the present-day isthmus of Panama, was then much wider. Other land bridges between continents and islands existed, and it must have been when the ice sheets were extensive that some of the great animal migrations took place. The horse, which evolved and developed in America, was probably driven across the Alaskan bridge into Asia by the advance of one of the ice sheets (and later became extinct in its original home, until it was reintroduced by man). Man, who probably originated in Africa and saw much of his early development in central Asia, seems to have migrated into America about the time that the last ice sheet was building up, but when there were still clear passages down the west coast and along the western border of the great plains.

° The Pleistocene is the most recent period of the Cenozoic era, and is the period in which we still live. It is usually taken to cover the last million years, and so its beginning coincides roughly with the first appearance of true men, belonging to the genus *Homo*.

It has been one of the biggest problems of geology and of earth physics to explain why large areas of the major continents have been deeply buried in ice from time to time, and a number of different theories have been proposed, each to be abandoned in turn. Any theory of the ice ages must explain why, as we look backward through geological time, the Northern Hemisphere has suffered four extensive glaciations recently, and then there is no evidence to show that any comparable phenomena have happened prior to this until the Paleozoic era, 250 million years ago. Why was there a series of successive glaciations in late Paleozoic times—similar to the recent northern series—in Australia, South Africa, and India? Why was Antarctica, located as it is immediately around the South Pole, once covered with luxuriant vegetation, as shown by extensive coal deposits? If we accept the theory of continental drift, changes in the positions of the continents relative to the North and South Poles must have had something to do with it, but it cannot be the whole story, for North America has shifted very little since the recent great glaciations.

The ice ages must have been preceded by a change in climatic conditions, affecting the entire hemisphere. This need not have been a general reduction in the temperature of the earth, or in the amount of energy received from the sun.° The area of northern Canada where the largest ice sheet originated is today a barren, arid waste—a wide stretch of *tundra*, or cold treeless plain, known to geographers as the Barren Grounds. Underneath a great deal of it is *permafrost*, or permanently frozen subsoil. Climatologically it has to be classed as a cold desert, since it has an annual rainfall of less than 10 inches. If some worldwide change in the climatic pattern could double the precipitation in the Barren Grounds—especially if the winter snowfall should be much increased—ice might again start to accumulate without any decrease in the average temperature, for the snowfall in winter might be more than could melt away during the short summer.

A recent theory of the Pleistocene glaciations, developed by Maurice Ewing and William L. Donn of Columbia University, probably approximates the truth. It involves a combination of continental drift and changes in the climatic pattern. Throughout the last million years, but not in earlier geological ages, the North Pole has been located well within the basin of the Arctic Ocean. Now the bed of this ocean has a peculiar con-

---

° When theorists cannot think of any other explanation for the formation of the ice sheets, they fall back on a general temperature drop, caused either by a change in the sun's energy, or by a change in the carbon dioxide content of the air, with a change in the blanketing effect of the atmosphere. Either or both of these phenomena may have happened, but they cannot be the sole cause of glaciation, which never occurred in both hemispheres at the same time, and which ought, according to these theories, to have been periodic throughout the earth's history, instead of happening only at a few definite epochs.

formation, which has not changed significantly during the time in question (Fig. 28-8). It is cut off from the Pacific except for the narrow, shallow Bering Strait, which has often been completely closed. It communicates with the Atlantic through the wide stretch of water between Greenland and Norway, but under this stretch there lies a submarine ridge, which

FIG. 28-8

Configuration of the Arctic and North Atlantic Oceans.

comes to the surface in Iceland and has a maximum depth of about 2000 feet. At the present time, when the only continental ice is in Greenland and Antarctica, the ocean level is fairly high and water can circulate freely between the Atlantic and the Arctic, flowing northward along the coast of Norway in the warm Gulf Stream, and southward on the west side in the cold Greenland current. The Ewing-Donn theory of periodic glaciation assumes that this circulation is slowly melting the thin layer of ice that now covers most of the Arctic Ocean. In a few thousand years, when this ice is all melted, the northeasterly winds blowing over the polar sea will become laden with moisture, instead of being cold and dry as they are at present. The precipitation in the Barren Grounds of Canada and in the tundra of northern Europe and Siberia will be greatly increased, and the conditions necessary for the formation of a new continental ice sheet will exist. As the ice accumulates, the average sea level will drop, the vigorous circulation of water between the Atlantic and the Arctic will be restricted, and the polar sea will freeze over again, to reproduce conditions similar to those of the present.

The theory predicts an alternation between periods when the Arctic Ocean was free of ice, but continental glaciers were forming, and periods when the ocean was frozen over and the ice that covered the land was melting. These periods should continue to alternate as long as the geographic North Pole lies somewhere near the center of the Arctic basin. There should have been no general glaciation in earlier ages, when the North Pole was somewhere out in the Pacific, far from any of the principal land masses. The alternation of ice and temperate conditions has happened four times so far, but that is far from providing a satisfactory confirmation of a speculative theory, and all we can say at present is that it is the most probable of the many theories that have been proposed. It would be interesting to know whether the Arctic Ocean was free of ice at the time the last glacier was forming, but of this there is no certain evidence.°

GLOSSARY

Block fault mountain   Mountain range formed mainly by the vertical uplift of an extensive area on one side of a major fault.

Drumlins   Low, elongated hills composed of glacial till left behind when the great ice sheets melted.

° Recent archeological discoveries along the shore of the Arctic Ocean indicate that it may have been a migration route for men with a fairly advanced state of culture, at about the time that the ice was accumulating. Analysis of the remains of marine life in different layers of the sediments in the bed of the Atlantic Ocean have shown that there have been marked differences in the temperature and salt content of the water at different times. This is to be expected if during certain periods the cold Greenland current failed to bring Arctic water down the American coast. Both these observations are consistent with the Ewing-Donn theory.

Erratic boulders Boulders that have been carried long distances from their place of origin, usually by the ice sheet or a glacier; they are recognized because they are composed of a different type of rock from the bedrock in the vicinity.

Eskers Ridges formed by streams flowing under the ice, and exposed when the ice melted.

Fold mountains Mountains formed mainly by horizontal compression of the earth's crust, resulting in extensive tilting and folding of the rock strata.

Glacial till Unsorted sedimentary material, containing particles of all sizes from clay to boulders, that has been deposited by glacial action, but is not yet compacted into conglomerate rock.

Meander Of a river, to follow a winding course that changes frequently, as the bank is eroded on one side, and the material deposited on the other side.

Moraine Ridge of unsorted sediment that forms across the end and along the sides of a glacier.

Orogenesis Technical term for mountain building, the process of formation of mountains by movements in the earth's crust.

Permafrost The permanently frozen subsoil found a little below the surface in subarctic regions.

Pleistocene The last and current period of the Cenozoic era; covers approximately the last million years, and coincides approximately with the time during which true men belonging to the genus *Homo* have existed, and the time of the four great ice ages.

Tundra Cold, treeless plain, as found in northern Canada and Siberia.

EXERCISES

1. What, if any, is the connection between volcanoes and earthquakes?

2. Outline the most important causes of the formation of mountains.

3. Explain how continental drift might account for the mountains of North America. Could this theory account for the Himalaya mountains of northern India?

4. Explain how it is possible to determine within fairly accurate limits the age of a mountain range. Where are some of the oldest and some of the youngest mountains of North America?

5. Describe briefly the important characteristics of a mountain stream and of a mature river.

6. How can erosion take place when there is no wind or rain, for example, on the moon?

7. How is it possible for a river to be older than the mountain range through which it flows?

8. Outline the evidence which shows that a large part of North America has been covered with ice. How do we know that this has happened four times during the Pleistocene period?

9. How can we determine when the ice melted in a particular region?

10. Central Alaska and parts of Siberia apparently remained uncovered during the last ice age; can you suggest reasons for this?

11. Look at a map of the Atlantic Ocean and estimate roughly where the shores would have been at the height of the last ice age. About where would the shores be if the ice now covering Greenland should melt?

12. There is said to have been a great ice age in the Southern Hemisphere in the late Paleozoic. Upon what types of evidence is this conclusion based?

13. The continental shelf that borders the east coast of North America is intersected by several deep submarine trenches. How might these have been formed?

evolution on other worlds

29-1   *The Nebular Theory of the Birth of the Solar System*

The earth and the meteorites that fall upon it from time to time are estimated to be 4.55 billion years old (Sec. 26-3). We can take this figure to be very nearly the age of the solar system as a whole, meaning the time since the system settled into its present configuration, with a central sun and the planets revolving around it. Since, therefore, the sun and earth and the other planets have not existed for all time, but evolved from a definite beginning, how were they formed?

A theory of the solar system which held the field for many years is that based on the *nebular hypothesis*, developed by the French mathematician and astronomer, Pierre Laplace (1749–1827). Laplace supposed that the sun and all the planets condensed from a primeval nebular cloud of gas and dust; this cloud started to rotate and assumed the form of a thin disk. According to Laplace's theory, rings separated from the main disk; these rings contracted to form the principal planets. The planets themselves were at first rotating disks, from which smaller rings separated to form the satellite moons. In the case of Saturn, which still has a thin ring of small particles around it, the formation of moons was never completed. Finally, the main central portion of the nebula contracted into a sphere, to form the sun.

To examine the nebular hypothesis, and see why it is untenable in Laplace's original form, we must review some of the facts about the structure of the solar system. The planets and their principal satellites all lie nearly in the same plane; this is consistent with the hypothesis, because a mass of gas and small particles would form a thin disk as soon as it started to contract and rotate. The planets, including the minor ones, all revolve around the sun in the same direction; with a few minor exceptions, the satellites revolve around their planets in the same direction as the planets around the sun; all the planets except Uranus (and possibly Venus) rotate on their axes in the same direction as they revolve; all this is also consistent with the hypothesis.

However, Laplace overlooked an important feature of the system—the angular momentum cannot be accounted for by his theory. The mass of the sun is about 700 times that of all the planets and all the loose material put together, but the planets, because they move swiftly in orbits far away from the center, possess most of the angular momentum. Now, at all stages of the development the total angular momentum must have remained constant, and so the original rotating disk must have had an angular momentum equal to the sum of the present values for the planets. When one of the rings that Laplace supposed to form into planets broke away from the rotating disk, it would be traveling only a very little faster than the next inner portion, and would carry away only a small fraction of the angular momentum. The main nebula, which was supposed to form the sun, would retain most of the angular momentum, and would spin faster and faster as it contracted; finally it would spin so fast that centrifugal force would counteract gravitational attraction, and the contraction would cease long before the nebula condensed into a central sphere. Another objection to Laplace's theory is that no known system of forces would cause the rings to contract lengthwise to form spherical planets.

29-2   Modern Theories of the Solar System

Because of the inconsistencies in Laplace's theory, astronomers in the early twentieth century rejected the nebular hypothesis as an explanation of the formation of the planets, although they continued to believe that the sun itself must have been formed by the contraction of a nebular cloud. There are known to be many such clouds in the Milky Way galaxy. Some have young stars embedded in them, and there is very little doubt that stars are continually being formed in this way, the sun being an earlier example. However, the consensus was that the planets must have a different origin, and must have been formed later from material ejected in some way from the sun. A popular hypothesis—repeated in many accounts of the solar system—is that there must have been a close encounter between the sun and another star, whereby a long filament of material was pulled out of the sun; from this filament the planets were supposed to have been condensed. It would be a very rare occurrence that two stars would approach close enough for this to happen, and so according to this theory only very few stars in the cosmos would possess planetary systems like our own.

However, it now appears that there is need to invoke some special mechanism to account for the sun's system of planets. In 1944 C. F. von Weizsacker showed how planets could develop in a contracting nebular cloud, not from Laplace's rings, but from local eddies that would almost certainly develop, because the cloud would be bound to be somewhat turbulent. As the cloud contracted, these eddies would break off successively, to form what have come to be known as *protoplanets*. This avoids the difficulty that the rings could not contract lengthwise, but there is still the problem of how the angular momentum of the main contracting mass or of the protoplanet eddies, or both, was transferred to the orbital motion of the planets that eventually solidified. Several reasonable mechanisms have been proposed, and it is still uncertain which is most likely to be the right one. All we can say at present is that it must have happened, or the planets and their satellites could not revolve in their present nearly circular orbits.

29-3   Growth of a Planet

Let us assume that Weizsacker's form of the nebular hypothesis, or some slight modification of it, is correct, and let us think of what must have happened as the local eddies formed into the spherical planets as they exist today. The original protoplanets were not hot, since the protosun had not yet become a self-luminous star, capable of providing life-giving energy for its family of planets. The material from which the planets were formed therefore contained many solid particles as well as large quantities of gas. Some of the larger solid particles acted as nuclei around which material collected, partly by gravitational attraction and partly by simple accretion as particles collided and adhered, until there was one central mass ready to become a true planet. Probably the mass of the original protoplanet was much greater than that of the modern spherical planet, especially in the case of the four small inner planets, for most of the gas and a great deal of the solid material would escape the accretion process, rejoin the central cloud and eventually become incorporated in the sun.

Now, when the growing nucleus approached planetary size its temperature began to increase, because as particles were attracted to the central mass, gravitational potential energy was converted into heat, and at the same time heat produced by radioactive decay had less and less chance to escape. Eventually all the solid material melted; at this point the body assumed a spherical form and became a planet, although accretion continued until most of the loose material in the vicinity was either incorporated into the planet or irretrievably lost.° Once the true planets formed, their subsequent histories were somewhat different, depending on size and distance from the sun, which by this time had become an energy-producing star.

The larger a sphere, the smaller is its surface area in comparison with its volume. Therefore, as the growing planets increased in temperature, the smaller ones lost their accumulated heat faster than the larger ones. In the case of the earth the central core is still molten, kept in that state by the heat produced by radioactive elements. In the course of time the heavier materials have sunk toward the center, so that the earth has become separated into dense liquid core, mantle, and relatively light crust. The smaller planets, Mercury, Venus, Mars, and the Moon,† all have average densities less than that of the earth, and the sorting process evidently never went as far. They must have been molten at one time and they probably have crusts, but it is not likely that any of them still have molten cores. The four great outer planets, Jupiter, Saturn, Uranus, and Neptune, all have very low average densities. They probably have central bodies similar to the earth—very likely with liquid cores—but the main bodies appear to be surrounded by great thicknesses of ice and frozen gases; this in turn is surrounded by many miles of cloudy atmosphere, so that the measured diameters are much larger than those of the massive central bodies, making the calculated densities much lower.

29-4   *Atmospheres of the Planets*

With the prospect of space flights to the moon and nearer planets one needs to know as much as possible about surface conditions on these bodies—especially about the density and composition of their atmospheres, if they have any. Again, the possibility of finding living organisms on the moon and the planets has always fascinated both serious scientists and

° Accretion is still going on in a small way, because meteors, most of which are mere grains of sand, are continually being absorbed in the earth's atmosphere, along with a few meteorites that fall to the ground.

† For the purpose of this chapter the moon should be considered as a planet. The earth-moon combination is the one case in the solar system where a planet and its satellite are comparable in size. According to the Weizsacker theory they must have formed separately from two eddies that happened to be close together in the primeval nebula, whereas all the other satellites were either formed out of the protoplanets, or were captured subsequently.

writers of science fiction. Let us see, therefore, what we can deduce about planetary atmospheres, by observation and by the use of the established laws of physics.

There are several sources of reliable information. The first is a theoretical calculation; is the gravitational attraction of the planet great enough to hold the common atmospheric gases? In the statistics of the planets (Table 3-1) we included the *escape velocity*, that is, the velocity which a body (e.g., a rocket) must have in order to escape from the gravitational attraction of the planet and fly off into space. Now, in any gas the molecules have a wide range of velocities, with average determined by the law that the mean kinetic energy is proportional to the absolute temperature (Sec. 11-4), so that the mean velocity is inversely proportional to the square root of the molecular mass. In any planetary atmosphere there will always be some gas molecules which have velocities greater than the escape velocity, but these may be very few in number. For a particular gas in the atmosphere of a particular planet, if we know the temperature we can calculate the number of molecules which come to the top of the atmosphere with velocities greater than the escape value, and so we can calculate the rate at which this particular gas will escape from the gravitational attraction of the planet, and dissipate into space.

For the earth, with an escape velocity of 7 miles per second, it turns out that any hydrogen it might have in its atmosphere would leak away in about a million years; helium would escape somewhat more slowly, but any helium included in the original protoearth would have disappeared long ago. For heavier gases there would have been only a small leakage in the whole 4.5 billion years of the earth's existence. For Mercury, with its high temperature so close to the sun, and for the moon, with its low escape velocity, very little of the common gases could have been retained. For Venus the rate of loss would be greater than for the earth, but gases as heavy as nitrogen (molecular weight 28) would be retained in considerable quantity; Mars should also retain a quantity of nitrogen and heavier gases. On the massive outer planets any of the common gases, including hydrogen, would be retained.

The first direct observation gives a clue to the total amount of atmosphere, without regard to its composition. The moon occasionally *occults* a bright star—that is, passes in front of it and hides it—and is continually occulting faint telescopic stars. If the moon had an atmosphere the light from the star would be refracted when it passed close by, as shown in Fig. 29-1; it would also be slightly dimmed. If an occultation occurred under these conditions the star would appear to "jump" away from the moon just before the moon's disk passed in front of it; it would also take a few seconds to fade out. When occultations are observed at the dark side of the crescent moon, where they can be best studied, the star disappears

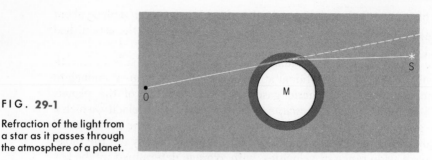

FIG. 29-1

Refraction of the light from
a star as it passes through
the atmosphere of a planet.

instantly without any change in its apparent position. From this and other
evidence it is estimated that the density of the lunar atmosphere must be
less than one millionth of that of the earth.°

Occultations of a visible star by one of the planets are extremely rare
events, but faint telescopic stars are sometimes occulted, and in the case
of Venus the predicted refraction effect has been observed. Also, when
Venus is between us and the sun, so that its illuminated surface shows only
a thin crescent, the dark side is bordered by a faint line of light, due to
sunlight scattered in the Venusian atmosphere.

If there is an atmosphere on a planet it is possible in principle to determine the composition by studying the spectrum of sunlight reflected from
the planet, for this light has passed twice through the planet's atmosphere
and should show absorption bands due to the atmospheric gases. Unfortunately this information was unobtainable until very recently for hydrogen, helium, or nitrogen, because these gases have no absorption bands in
the wavelength range that is accessible to study by the spectrographs in
ordinary astronomical observatories. In observations made before 1950 the
light under study had to pass through the earth's atmosphere. This limited
the available wavelength range, and at the same time a gas that is plentiful on earth—like oxygen—could not be detected unless it was present on
the planet in sufficient quantity to make the bands in the spectrum of the
planet measurably stronger than in the spectrum of direct sunlight. For
these reasons observations are now being made with spectrographs mounted
in rockets and satellites flying outside the earth's atmosphere.

Finally, the presence of certain gases can be inferred because they are
known to be abundant throughout the cosmos, to be in the gaseous state
at the estimated temperature of the planet, and to be heavy enough to be
retained by gravitational attraction.

The known and inferred facts about the planetary atmospheres are collected in Table 29-1, which gives the estimated density compared with that

° Recently the moon occulted the Crab Nebula, which is a strong source of short radio waves,
and refraction of these waves was observed, indicating a trace of lunar atmosphere, probably
composed of heavy gases like argon and carbon dioxide.

TABLE 29-1   THE ATMOSPHERES OF THE PLANETS

Planet	Atmospheric Density (Earth = 1)	Gases Present, in Probable Order of Abundance
Moon	less than 10^{-6}	$(CO_2$, argon)?
Mercury	less than 0.003	(N_2, CO_2)?
Venus	0.5 to 1	(N_2) CO_2
Earth	1	N_2, O_2, A, H_2O, CO_2, Ne
Mars	about 0.01	(N_2), CO_2, (A), O_2, H_2O
Jupiter		$(H_2$, He), NH_3, CH_4, (Ne, A)
Saturn		$(H_2$, He), CH_4, NH_3, (Ne, A)
Uranus		$(H_2$, He), CH_4, (Ne)
Neptune		$(H_2$, He, Ne)
Pluto		None

on earth, and the gases known or expected to be present; those merely inferred being given in parentheses.

29-5   Evolution of the Earth's Atmosphere

The earth's present atmosphere, composed mostly of nitrogen and oxygen, must be very different from that which existed when our planet first contracted into a compact sphere. By far the most abundant element in the sun and in the cosmos generally is hydrogen; helium comes next, and greatly exceeds all the heavier elements put together. The same must have been true of the primeval nebula from which the solar system was formed, and so also of the original protoearth. Nitrogen and oxygen would have been present, along with all the other common elements, but with a large excess of hydrogen they would have been combined with the latter to form ammonia gas (NH_3) and water vapor, rather than existing as nitrogen and oxygen gases. Most of the carbon would also have been combined with hydrogen, to form mainly methane (CH_4); it will be noted in Table 29-1 that the gases which have been detected in the atmospheres of the large outer planets are precisely ammonia and methane; the water in the outer layers of these planets is, of course, frozen solid.

How did the earth's atmosphere evolve from its original hydrogen, helium, and hydrogen compounds to its present composition?[*] In the first place, the free hydrogen gas and the helium would have escaped within a few million years after our planet solidified. Ammonia (molecular weight 17) and methane (16) would also escape slowly, but it is more important that

[*] This theory of the earth's atmosphere is mainly due to H. C. Urey, professor of physical chemistry at California Institute of Technology.

these gases—and water vapor as well—would be dissociated by ultraviolet light from the newly formed sun, when they drifted into the upper layers of the atmosphere. The separated hydrogen would escape into space, and in time the amount of hydrogen left would not be enough to combine with all the oxygen, nitrogen, and carbon. Then nitrogen, which does not combine readily with elements other than hydrogen and oxygen, would accumulate in the atmosphere as nitrogen gas. As for the oxygen, whose total amount on the earth greatly exceeds the total nitrogen, the history must have been somewhat different. A great deal of it remained in combination with hydrogen as liquid water, and only a part would have been set free by the dissociation process. Much of what was set free would have combined with elements of the solid crust to form silica and other oxides, with some of the nitrogen to form nitrates, or with free carbon to form carbon dioxide and carbonates. Thus only a small fraction of the total oxygen would have been set free to accumulate in the atmosphere as oxygen gas.

The whole process probably took a very long time, at least a billion years, and the separation of oxygen from water vapor is probably still going on, and probably accounts for the minute traces of free hydrogen present at great heights. The accumulation of the present atmosphere must have overlapped the development of life on earth, and during the later stages the evolution of the atmosphere must have been modified by the presence of living organisms. When primitive plants had developed sufficiently to grow through photosynthesis—far back in the Archeozoic era—the carbon dioxide in the atmosphere began to be used for plant growth and more oxygen was released, until finally a large part of the existing carbon was tied up in the organic compounds of living things, as it is today. This implies, also, that the amount of oxygen gas in the atmosphere has been increasing during most of the earth's history, and that when life began it was much less than the present 21 per cent.

29-6   Life on Other Worlds

For centuries, ever since it became known that the moon and the seven principal planets are "worlds," comparable with the earth in size, men have speculated whether there are living beings on other planets, or whether our earth is unique in that respect. Up to some 50 years ago very little was known about conditions on the other planets, or about the chemistry of life. Writers of science fiction were free to exercise their imaginations to the utmost, and they peopled the moon and the planets with all sorts of fantastic plants and animals. Among these they usually included a creature bearing some resemblance to a human being, and endowed with an intelligence far superior to our own, like the Martians in H. G. Wells' *War of the Worlds,* or the little men that some people imagine to be traveling on the so-called flying saucers that are reported from time to time.

What is the probable truth, based on intelligent speculation, using the known facts about the other planets, and about the laws of nature? If we look at the problem in this light we are bound to conclude that life is impossible on a planet which differs too greatly from our own earth in size or in temperature. At this point in the argument somebody is sure to protest that the writer is thinking of the kinds of living things with which we are familiar on earth, and that there may be other forms of life, of which we know nothing. To a certain extent the protest is justified, for we do restrict the discussion to the only kind of life we can argue about, namely, organisms possessing material bodies, capable of growth and reproduction (Sec. 26-5). Then two things are essential before any form of material living organism could develop—an abundance of carbon in an available form, and liquid water.°

The temperature condition for life restricts it to those planets whose distances from the sun are such that water is in the liquid state at least part of the time, in order that the chemical processes of metabolism can go on. It is true that, once living organisms have developed and multiplied on a planet, certain simple forms might adapt to extreme temperature conditions. There are mites that have adapted to the frigid temperatures of the Antarctic ice cap, where metabolic processes can take place only during short periods of sunlight in the summer season. There are algae that have adapted to the boiling temperatures of hot volcanic springs. However, it is extremely doubtful whether life could *originate* under such conditions. In fact, there is probably only a narrow range of temperature—even less than the range from $0°$ to $100°C$—over which living organisms could develop and evolve in anything like the profusion which we know on earth. Too cold, and all chemical processes are slowed up; only the simplest organic forms are likely to develop. Too hot, and the complicated carbon compounds from which life might originate would dissociate as fast as they were formed.

Size also needs to be considered, although less important than the temperature condition. A planet much smaller than the earth would have no atmosphere, and no water, for this too would leak away while in the

° Free oxygen in the atmosphere is not necessary. The oxygen could be in combined form—in water and carbon dioxide—and according to Urey's theory, life probably began on earth when there was only a fraction of the present quantity of oxygen in the atmosphere. It has been suggested that silicon could replace carbon on a hot planet. There are synthetic silicon compounds that are similar in structure to carbon compounds of organic origin, but it is unlikely that life could develop from silicon due to the profound difference between gaseous CO_2 and insoluble, solid SiO_2, which is quartz rock. It has also been suggested that liquid ammonia could replace water on a cold planet; this is unlikely because of the electrical properties of water, in virtue of which dissolved salts are readily ionized, promoting chemical reactions. Life might become adapted to a liquid ammonia environment, but it is hard to see how it could originate there.

state of vapor. On a planet much larger than the earth everything would weigh very much more, and the atmospheric density and pressure would be very much greater. These factors alone would not prevent some kind of living organisms, but they would be very different from anything we are familiar with. For example, for a man to walk upright would be impossible —his two legs could not support the great weight of his body. However, the main objection to life on a very large planet is based on chemical considerations. The atmosphere would contain a large excess of hydrogen, which would combine with all the other light elements, leaving no oxygen and nitrogen for the formation of complex organic molecules.

It seems that in our own solar system the earth is especially favored, and most of the other planets can be immediately eliminated. The moon is too small, and—as far as we can tell—has no water. Its *average* temperature is reasonable, but, since it takes 29½ days to rotate on its axis with respect to the sun, its surface is exposed to full sunlight without any protection by an atmosphere for 15 days at a time. During the "day" the temperature rises to well above the boiling point of water, and drops far below zero during the "night." Mercury is too close to the sun and far too hot, and probably, like the moon, has practically no atmosphere. The great outer planets are too large and are probably too cold. The asteroids and the satellites of the outer planets—along with the ninth planet, Pluto—are either too cold or too small, or both. This leaves just two possibilities, Venus and Mars, to be considered in Sec. 29-7.

If most of the other planets of our solar system are excluded as possibilities for the development of material life, what about other parts of the cosmos? If the modern form of the nebular hypothesis is the correct explanation of the origin of the solar system, then any other star which is similar to the sun in size and structure should have a family of planets revolving around it. Among all these "solar systems" there must surely be many that contain a planet about the size of the earth and about the same distance from its "sun," so that it has the right conditions for the development of life. Wherever conditions are right, and have remained right for a billion years or so, it is almost certain that life would have developed and evolved into more and more complex bodily forms. It is also reasonable to assume that, given sufficient time, intelligent beings would evolve. They might even bear some resemblance to ourselves, for the *laws* of evolution would be the same, and intelligence in a material body implies several things we ourselves possess: a brain protected by a bony skull, motor ability, manipulative skill, requiring hands as well as feet, efficient binocular vision, and communication, probably by speech. The conclusion is, therefore, that many other stars in the cosmos, perhaps as many as one in a hundred, possess planets that are inhabited by intelligent living beings.

In our own solar system the two planets besides the earth where there could be living organisms are Mars and Venus. Mars rotates on its axis in about 24.6 hours, and its axis is inclined to its orbit by about the same amount as that of the earth. Therefore Mars has days and nights and winter and summer seasons, just as we have. Since it is farther away from the sun than the earth is, the average temperature over the whole planet is less—in fact it is below the freezing point of water—but quite comfortable temperatures would be encountered during the day in summer. Mars has a measurable atmosphere; according to evidence obtained by the space probe, Mariner IV, when it passed close to the planet, the density is about 1/100 of that on earth. Spectroscopic evidence indicates that the scant atmosphere is about 90 per cent nitrogen, with the remainder largely carbon dioxide; water vapor has been detected, but there is little, if any, oxygen. The white polar caps (Sec. 3-5), which increase in size in the Martian winter, may be thin layers of hoarfrost; temporary markings that could be thin clouds have also been observed. It is possible that living organisms could exist under the dry, rarefied atmosphere, but conditions would be extremely harsh according to our standards; if there is anything living it could hardly be more than a primitive form of vegetation.°

Concerning Venus we still do not know enough to draw conclusions, largely because the planet is completely covered with dense clouds and the surface has never been observed. There is an atmosphere; the density just above the clouds is about half that of the earth's atmosphere, so that it may be about the same as that of the earth at ground level. However, the only gases of which there is definite evidence are carbon dioxide and nitrogen; oxygen and water vapor may be present in very small quantities, but this is still uncertain. With radiation received from the sun about double that on earth, Venus must have a higher average temperature, especially underneath the heavy blanket of clouds—the actual value is uncertain (Sec. 3-5). The period of rotation is so long that the "daytime" side of the planet remains sunlit for at least a month at a time. However, with the high temperature and the dense atmosphere there must be continual violent winds, keeping the atmosphere in circulation so that the temperature difference between the illuminated and dark sides is not extreme. The continual wind and the apparent absence of water vapor

---

° Seasonal color changes that have sometimes been seen on Mars have been interpreted as evidence of primitive vegetation. The reddish color of the planet comes from extensive level plains that are probably sandy deserts. It has been reported that some of these areas take on a greenish tint in the Martian spring, suggesting chlorophyll-containing plants. However, the observations of temperature and atmospheric density made by Mariner IV cast doubt on this interpretation. It has also been suggested by some observers that the polar caps may be solid carbon dioxide rather than hoarfrost. We shall probably not know the truth about life on Mars until an expedition succeeds in visiting the planet; all we can say at present is that it is possible.

have led to the theory that the clouds are not composed of water drops, but rather indicate a perpetual dust storm.

Under these conditions life on Venus seems unlikely, but the possibility cannot be ruled out entirely. Since Venus has a higher average temperature than the earth, the chemical processes involved in evolution might take place more rapidly there. If Urey's theory of the evolution of the earth's atmosphere (Sec. 29-5) is correct, Venus might formerly have had conditions suitable for the development of living organisms. If so, they might have been able to adapt to changed conditions and to survive in isolated areas.

GLOSSARY

Nebula Any object that appears as a diffuse patch of light in an astronomical telescope; particularly the clouds of gas and dust that are seen in parts of the Milky Way galaxy.

Nebular hypothesis The assumption that the sun and planets of the solar system condensed from a nebular cloud.

Occultation The obscuring of a star when the moon or a planet passes in front of it.

Protoplanet A planet in the process of formation; specifically, an eddy which, according to von Weizsacker's form of the nebular theory, broke off from the contracting nebula and started to condense into a planet.

EXERCISES

1. What are the two principal objections to Laplace's original nebular theory of the solar system? Explain how von Weizsacker overcame the objections.

2. What evidence is there that stars are still being formed by the condensation of clouds of gas?

3. Why are the sun and the planets approximately spheres? Why are they slightly flattened at the poles?

4. What would cause the temperature of a protoplanet to rise as it contracted and accumulated material, until it became molten?

5. Why is the calculated density of Jupiter very much less than that of the earth?

6. Calculate the ratio of the average velocity of hydrogen molecules at 350°K to the escape velocity from the earth; make the same calculation for oxygen molecules. What conclusions have been drawn from calculations of this kind?

7. Describe what would be seen if a star were occulted by a planet that had an atmosphere comparable with that of the earth in density.

8. Outline the existing evidence concerning the atmospheres of: (a) Venus; (b) Mars; (c) the Moon; (d) Jupiter; (e) Pluto.

9. Why is it considered an important scientific project to mount a self-recording spectrograph in an artificial satellite?

10. What gases probably existed in the protoearth at the time it broke off from the primeval nebula? What has presumably happened to them? Explain your answers briefly.

11. Describe briefly two processes by which oxygen might have accumulated in the earth's atmosphere.

12. Describe in a few words the essential requirements for the development and evolution of material living organisms on a planet.

13. It has been suggested that living organisms might use liquid ammonia in place of water on a cold planet, and might use silicon in place of carbon on a hot planet. Comment on these two suggestions.

14. Although the surface of Venus has never been seen, recent radar observations have given evidence of high mountains on the planet. How could observations of this kind be made?

15. What would living conditions probably be like on some of the other planets: Mars, Venus, the Moon, Saturn?

the detective story of the stars

About 150 B.C., the Greek astronomer, Hipparchus, working in Alexandria, compiled the first general catalogue of the "fixed" stars of which we have any record. In it he classified the stars according to an approximate scale of *magnitude,* or brightness—first magnitude for the brightest stars in his catalogue down to sixth magnitude for stars which were just visible on a clear moonless night. Nowadays it is possible to measure quite accurately the amount of energy received from a star,° and so brightness can be expressed on a precisely defined numerical scale. The scale we now use is a direct descendant of Hipparchus' ancient classification. By measurement, his first magnitude stars are about 100 times brighter, on the average, than his sixth magnitude. Therefore *a factor of* 100 *in brightness corresponds by definition to a difference in magnitude of* 5. Since the fifth root of 100 is 2.512, magnitude 1 is 2.512 times magnitude 2, $(2.512)^2$ times magni-

---

° This is not quite the same thing as the visible brightness, because a large part of the energy may be in the form of ultraviolet light, or of infrared heat radiation. We shall not take account of this technical point, but argue as if the terms "brightness" and "magnitude" referred to total energy.

TABLE 30-1   ESTIMATED
NUMBER OF
STARS IN THE
MILKY WAY
BRIGHTER THAN A
GIVEN MAGNITUDE

Magnitude	Number
5	1,600
10	300,000
15	32,000,000
20	1,000,000,000
Estimated total	100,000,000,000

tude 3, $(2.512)^5$ times magnitude 6, and so on.° Today it is possible to classify stars much more closely than the original six classes, and magnitudes are usually stated to ¹⁄₁₀₀ of a unit on the scale. Also, a few stars—not many—are brighter than the standard first magnitude and have to be assigned to magnitude 0 or even given a negative figure; the brightest true star in the sky, the Dog Star, Sirius, is listed as magnitude -1.52.

The magnitude of the faintest star that can be seen in a telescope depends largely upon the diameter of the objective lens or mirror; as the size of telescopes increases, the number of stars that can be seen or photographed gets progressively greater. The very faint stars have never been catalogued, but counts have been made of the numbers of stars on photographs of typical areas of the sky and the numbers of stars brighter than a given magnitude have been estimated, with the results shown in Table 30-1.

30-2   Distances and Proper Motions of the Stars

Figure 30-1 illustrates the modern method of determining the distance of a star by measuring the parallax effect (Sec. 2-9). We need at least three photographs of the selected star, taken against the background of faint stars, which are presumably much farther away and most of which do not show parallax. The calculation is simplest if the photographs are taken at 6-month intervals, when the earth is in the positions 1, 2, 3, in its orbit around the sun. A star that is close enough to show a measurable parallax effect is almost certain to show also a true change in position, for the stars

° It may seem ill-advised to use a scale which increases by a constant factor instead of by a constant amount. Actually it makes sense by reason of the law of experimental psychology which says that, when a stimulus is increased by constant factors, the sensation appears to increase in constant steps. A competent observer, using his eyes, judges the magnitude scale to be one of equal steps, as in fact did Hipparchus.

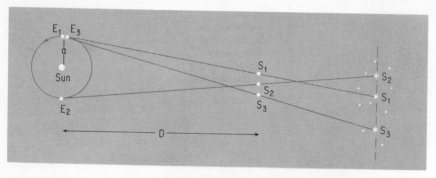

FIG. 30-1

Determination of distance and proper motion of a star (S). The apparent positions of the star relative to the faint background are shown on the right, at 6-month intervals.

are not fixed—as the ancients believed—but are moving in various directions relative to the sun. The difference in the observed angular positions of the star from photograph 1 to photograph 3 gives the *proper motion*—the apparent lateral displacement in seconds of arc per year.

The observed displacement of the star in photograph 2 as compared with the average of photographs 1 and 3 gives the parallax effect caused by observing the star from opposite sides of the earth's orbit. The distance (D) of the star can then be calculated, for the angular displacement —converted to radians—is simply equal to $2a/D$, where a is the mean distance of the earth from the sun.[*]

Finally, when the distance is known the angular proper motion can be converted to the actual velocity in miles per second. Thus the one series of observations gives both the distance of the star and the lateral component of its motion relative to the sun.

The distances of the stars are often expressed in *light-years,* the distance that light—with a velocity of 186,000 miles per second—would travel in a year. This works out to

1 light-year = 5.880 $\times$ 10^{12} miles.

In terms of this unit the closest star—a faint star in the Southern Hemisphere, known as Proxima Centauri—is 4.28 light-years from the sun; it has a parallax angle of 0.762 second. The distances of some other selected stars are given in Table 30-2.

[*] The parallax tabulated in star catalogues is defined to be the angle subtended at the star by the mean radius of the earth's orbit; this is half the angle indicated in Fig. 30-1.

TABLE 30-2   **SOME TYPICAL STARS**

Star	Class*	Apparent Magnitude	Distance (Light-years)	Absolute Brightness (Suns)	Temperature (°K)	Radius (Suns)	Mass (Suns)
Sun	MS	—	—	1	5,750	1	1
α Centauri	MS	0.33	4.31	1.15	5,500	1.12	1.1
Sirius A	MS	−1.52	8.6	60	10,700	2.25	2.44
Sirius B	WD	8.4	8.6	1/330	8,000?	0.024	0.96
β Centauri	MS	0.9	280	2,900	21,000	4.0	25
Barnard	MS	9.46	6.0	1/2,500	3,100	0.16	0.18
van Maanen	WD	12.6	78	1/7,500	7,500	0.007	0.14
Capella	G	0.9	35	96	5,500	11	4.2
Aldebaran	G	1.1	57	100	3,300	34	4
Antares	SG	1.2	350	3,500	3,100	480	30

*SG = supergiant, G = giant, MS = main sequence, WD = white dwarf.

30-3   *Absolute Magnitude*

The light received from a source is proportional to the square of the distance. Therefore, once the distance of a star has been determined it is possible to calculate the actual amount of light it is producing, as compared with our own sun. The astronomer again uses the concept of magnitude; the *absolute magnitude* is the value that would be observed if the star were moved to a distance (32.6 light-years) where its parallax angle would be 1/10 second of arc. On this scale the sun has an absolute magnitude of 4.86. If it were moved to a distance of 32.6 light-years—instead of the actual 8.5 light-minutes—it would be nicely visible as a star on a clear night and would be listed in all the catalogues, but would probably not be prominent enough to be given an individual name.

Stars vary tremendously in absolute magnitude. Sirius, which appears to be the brightest star in the sky, has an absolute magnitude of 1.3, which means that it is the equivalent of 60 suns, but is still far from the brightest. The brightest true star known is one listed as "S Doradus," which is located in an outer galaxy beyond the limits of the Milky Way, at an estimated distance of 150,000 light-years. It is −9.2 on the absolute magnitude scale, or the equivalent of about 400,000 suns, although on account of its vast distance it can be seen only in a large telescope. From this, known stars range all the way to +16, or 1/25,000 of the sun. The extremely brilliant stars are rare objects; we shall see later that they can have only a short lifetime on the cosmic time scale—a few million years—before they burn themselves out. The figures quoted seem to place the sun about midway in the scale, but actually it is quite a respectable object as stars go; there are millions brighter, but there are billions fainter.

30-4   *Temperatures and Sizes of the Stars*

We have seen in connection with the discussion of the spectra of the stars (Sec. 19-8) that there is a relation between the surface temperature and the dark lines observed in the spectrum. Once this relation was established it became possible to deduce the temperature of any star bright enough to permit its spectrum to be photographed with the aid of a large telescope. When the absolute magnitude and the surface temperature of a star are known, we can deduce its actual size, as compared with the sun which we know has a diameter of 864,900 miles. The amount of energy radiated by a star—its absolute brightness—is obviously proportional to its surface area, and therefore to its (diameter)^2. By Stefan's law of heat radiation it is also proportional to (temperature)^4, and so, using the sun as a unit of brightness or of diameter,

$$\text{brightness in suns} = (\text{diameter in suns})^2 \times \left(\frac{\text{temperature of the star}}{\text{temperature of the sun}}\right)^4.$$

In this equation everything is now known except the diameter, and so this can be deduced.

Like the absolute brightnesses, the diameters of the stars vary tremendously, from enormous supergiants several hundred times the size of the sun and big enough to engulf all the inner planets of the solar system out to far beyond the orbit of Mars, down to tiny dwarf stars actually smaller than the earth. Again the sun is midway in the scale—a typical, quite healthy specimen of the class to which the great majority of the known stars belong.

In Fig. 30-2 the absolute magnitudes of stars are plotted against their surface temperatures, in a type of diagram first used by H. N. Russell as an aid to further classification, and perhaps as a clue to the life history of the stars. When all the stars in a general catalogue are plotted on a *Russell diagram*, the great majority are found to fit into a band that extends roughly diagonally across the plot; these are known as *main sequence* stars. Toward the top left corner are points representing the brilliant, very hot, blue stars. From here the band goes continuously through bright bluish-white stars like Sirius, yellowish stars like the sun—which once again is just about in the middle—down to the host of relatively faint reddish stars that cluster thickly in the lower right corner.

Toward the upper right of the diagram a roughly oval area belongs to tremendous stars, many times the diameter of the sun. These have a low

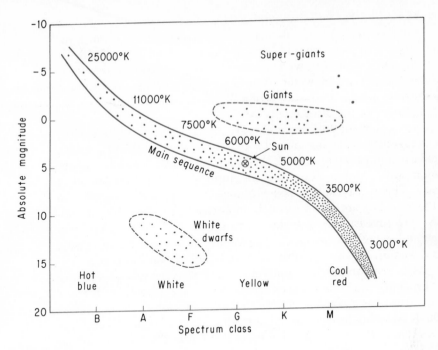

FIG. 30-2

Classification of stars according to the Russell diagram.

surface temperature—many are only red-hot—but their vast surface area places them high in the magnitude scale; they are aptly referred to as *giants* and *supergiants*. Another area in the bottom left of the diagram marks the *white dwarfs*, a group of tiny, hot stars which are inconspicuous in the sky, but which are rather important in the cosmic scheme because they are almost certainly dying stars, representing the last stage of a stellar life. A few unusual stars find places in other parts of the diagram, but the classification into giants, main sequence stars, and white dwarfs covers the majority of all the known stars.

30-5   The Dwarf Companion of Sirius

It was shown in Chapter 6 how the actual mass of the earth in tons can be calculated from the gravitational attraction it exerts upon a falling stone or upon the moon. The masses of the planets that possess satellites revolving around them can be calculated from the forces they exert on their satellites; that of the sun is calculated from the force it exerts upon the earth.

Thus we know that the sun "weighs" 2.015×10^{27} tons, although it is better to say that it contains this many tons of matter, since the term "weight" properly applies only to bodies on the surface of the earth. Since we know the sun's diameter, we can calculate that its average density is 1.410 times the density of water. Whenever we find that one celestial body is exerting a measurable attraction upon some other body, we can calculate the mass of the *attracting* body.

Now, a great many of the known stars are double. That is, there are two stars close together, revolving around a common center in elliptical orbits. A particularly interesting example is the bright star Sirius, which has a faint companion, and which is describing an elliptical orbit with a period of 50.0 years. This is classed as a *visual binary*, because it is fairly close to us and the two stars are seen separately in a telescope. The orbits of both stars have been measured; each star exerts a measurable attraction upon the other, and so both masses can be calculated. In terms of the sun's mass they are 2.44 suns for the bright Sirius A and 0.96 sun for Sirius B.

The masses are comparable, and yet Sirius B is 10 magnitudes fainter than its brilliant companion, meaning that it is producing only 1/10,000 of the light. Sirius A is a hot, slightly bluish star, with a surface temperature of 10,700°K and a brightness equivalent to 60 suns. It must have a diameter 2.25 times that of the sun, and a density of 0.59. It is a typical member of the hot end of the main sequence on the Russell diagram. Sirius B must be tiny in comparison. Unfortunately its surface temperature is not accurately known, because it is difficult to get a good spectrum of B alone, separate from that of A. However, it is a clear white in color and must have a temperature of at least 7500°K. Assuming this figure gives it a diameter of 22,000 miles, only 2.8 times that of the earth, it is a typical white dwarf. Now comes the amazing conclusion. If Sirius B contains nearly as much mass as the sun, in a sphere only 2.8 times the size of the earth, it must have a density 97,000 times that of water; a cubic foot of its material would weigh 3000 tons!

When these calculations were first made for Sirius and its small companion many people could not believe the conclusion, and thought there must be something wrong with the figures or with the assumptions on which the calculation was based. However, the only assumption is that the law of gravitation and the laws of radiation apply to Sirius just as they do to the sun and its family of planets and there is nothing wrong with either the observations of Sirius' orbit or with the arithmetic. Many other white dwarfs are now known, some with densities much greater than that of Sirius B, and we have to accept the fact that stellar material can exist with these apparently fantastic densities. The densities are indeed quite possible if most of the atoms in a white dwarf star have lost all their electrons, and are stripped down to the bare nucleus, so that the interior of the star consists of atomic nuclei and electrons, packed closely together.

30-6   *Double Stars and Stellar Masses*

In a great many cases the two stars of a pair are too close together to be seen separately in the telescope, but what appears to be a single star is shown to be double by a study of the Doppler effect in the spectrum. When the spectrum is photographed on a certain night, the lines appear double (Fig. 30-3). At this time we have one star approaching so that its spectrum lines appear shifted from their normal positions toward the violet. The spectrum lines shifted toward the red show the presence of a companion star which at that time is receding. A few days later the spectrum shows only single lines, and the stars must be moving across the line of sight. At another time the lines are again double, with the brighter star receding and the fainter approaching. Obviously it is a simple matter to

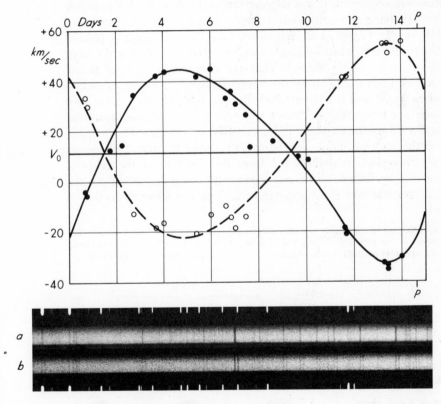

FIG.   **30-3**

The spectrum of a spectroscopic binary as seen at different times of the revolution in the orbit, with the velocity curves of the two components. (Photograph from Dominion Astrophysical Observatory, Victoria, B.C.)

ascertain the period of revolution of a *spectroscopic binary* from a series of spectra photographed on successive nights. Moreover, since the measurements of the Doppler effect give the actual orbital speeds in kilometers per second, the actual dimensions of the orbit can be calculated.

Most of the spectroscopic binary stars that have been detected have periods of only a few days, and if the stars are comparable in size with the sun the distance between them cannot be more than a few times their diameters; in fact a few appear to be almost touching. If such a system is seen more or less edge on, there is an excellent chance that the two stars will pass in front of each other and so eclipse each other twice in each revolution. A typical example of a so-called *eclipsing binary* is the bright star Algol in the constellation Perseus. Algol suddenly fades by about 1.2 magnitudes at regular intervals of 2.87 days, the time for it to fade and return again to normal being about 7 hours. Long before the spectroscopic information was obtainable it was suggested that this must be due to a dark companion revolving around the parent star in such a way as to produce a partial eclipse. In Fig. 30-4 the apparent magnitude of Algol is plotted against the time, with what we believe we are actually seeing at different times shown immediately below.° That the companion of Algol is not actually a dark body is shown by the fact that there is a slight secondary eclipse when Algol itself is in front; both are true stars, but they differ very much in surface temperature. When the information obtained from the spectrum of a binary star can be supplemented by that obtained by eclipses, not only is the mass problem completely solved, but the actual diameters of the two stars can be determined from the duration of the eclipses. Diameters of stars found in this way agree with those deduced from the absolute magnitude and the temperature and so the latter deduction is confirmed.

° Remember that we never actually see two stars in a spectroscopic or eclipsing binary. The combined effect of the pair is a single point of light; all the orbital data are deduced from changes in the apparent magnitude and from a study of the Doppler effect in the spectrum.

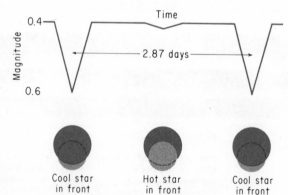

FIG. 30-4

Light curve of Algol, showing how eclipses are produced by the revolution around each other of a bright star and a relatively dark companion.

Cool star in front   Hot star in front   Cool star in front

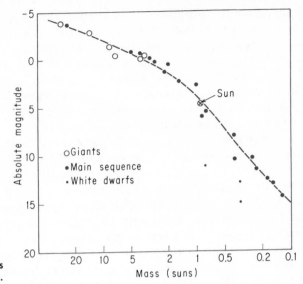

FIG. 30-5

The relation between mass and luminosity of the stars.

There must be millions of double and multiple stars that have escaped detection, because spectroscopic and eclipsing binaries will not be recognized unless their orbits are seen nearly edge on. Binaries with large orbits and periods of several years—like Sirius—can only be observed if they are close enough to the sun to show measurable proper motion. Allowing for the chances of detection, it has been estimated that at least half of the stars in the cosmos are multiple.

Double stars that have been studied have orbital periods varying all the way from less than a day to several hundred years. There are all possible combinations: pairs in which both stars belong to the main sequence; main sequence stars with white dwarf companions; pairs of giants; giants with main sequence companions. However, with all the variety of class and size, the range of *mass* is strictly limited, from about 1/10 of a sun to about 50 suns. It seems that, when a cloud of gas and dust starts to contract to form a compact body, there are limits to the mass that can become a detached, self-luminous star. Moreover, when a star forms from the cloud, its brightness depends upon its mass; there is a definite relation between observed brightness and computed mass, for all stars except the white dwarfs (Fig. 30-5).

30-7   *Star Groups and the Extension of the Distance Scale*

The ancients grouped the visible stars into constellations, which seemed to them to mark the outline of some fabulous animal or mythical hero, and to which they gave fanciful names,° like the familiar Dipper (catalogued as Ursa Major, the Great Bear), Orion, Andromeda. The constellations do not usually represent any real connection between the stars they appear to contain. However, there are many true groups of stars that do have a physical connection. Groups that belong to the Milky Way fall into two classes: fairly open, irregular groups of a few hundred stars known as *galactic clusters,* and much more compact, nearly spherical *globular clusters,* which may contain as many as a million stars.

Some of the galactic clusters are easily picked out, like the small group that has been known from ancient times as the Pleiades (Fig. 30-6). This compact group of 5 to 7 naked-eye stars—the number seen depends on the observer's eyesight—shows on a photograph to consist of about 250 closely associated stars, along with some wispy clouds of material that is not concentrated into stars. Many other galactic clusters are known, some of them being recognized only because they share a common motion relative to the sun. For example, the prominent stars of the Dipper are moving as shown in Fig. 30-7; six of them, including the pair in the "handle," share a common motion with a number of fainter stars in the same region of the sky and form a galactic cluster. Two of the familiar group have no association with the cluster, being much closer to the sun.

° The ancient constellation names are still used in star catalogues and are useful to the practical astronomer in describing the locations of stars. Naked-eye stars are catalogued by the Latin name of the constellation, with a Greek letter or a number.

FIG. 30-6

Photograph of the Pleiades, showing many more stars than are visible to the naked eye, along with wisps of nebulosity. (Photograph from Mt. Wilson Observatory.)

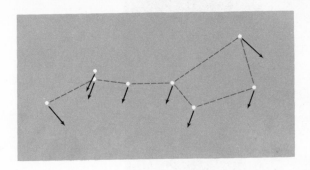

FIG. 30-7

Proper motions of the stars in the Great Dipper.

The study of galactic clusters is important because they provide groups of stars which must have a common origin and are probably of nearly the same age, so that they can furnish a clue in the problem of evolution of the stars. But they are also important because they allow us to extend the distance scale another step. Direct measurements of distance by the parallax method are of very little use beyond about 500 light-years. However, if we can estimate the absolute magnitude of a star in some way, and compare this with the measured apparent magnitude, we can deduce the distance. For main sequence stars we can determine the spectrum type and then get a rough estimate of the absolute magnitude from the Russell diagram. Applied to individual stars the distance determined from the estimated absolute magnitude is not very reliable, but, if the method is applied to all the stars of a cluster, the average gives a reasonably accurate distance for the cluster. Applied to the Pleiades, this gives an average distance for the group of 650 light-years.

For the globular clusters (Fig. 30-8), all of which are much farther away than the Pleiades, and for other galaxies—outside our own Milky Way—there is another method of determining the distance quite accurately. In a group that contains thousands of stars there will usually be a few of the very special type of bright, pulsating stars known as *Cepheid variables* after the closest and brightest of the type, δ Cephei in our own Galaxy.[°] As a Cepheid star contracts, the temperature rises; as the star expands, it falls. Therefore the brightness oscillates with a regular period, in a manner that can easily be distinguished from that of an eclipsing binary. The periods of the pulsations vary from a few hours to about 40 days, and depend upon the mass and radius of the star; therefore there is a definite relation between the period and the absolute magnitude. If a few pulsating variables can be identified in a globular cluster or an external galaxy—they often can be picked out because they are all bright stars—then the periods can be measured and the absolute magnitudes can be found from

---

[°] The Milky Way is classically known as the *Galaxy*, from the Greek word for milk. The generic term for other similar structures, like the Andromeda nebula, for example, is "galaxy" with lowercase "g."

FIG. 30-8

Globular cluster in the constellation Hercules. (Photograph from Dominion Astrophysical Observatory, Victoria, B.C.)

the period-luminosity relation. Knowing the absolute magnitude, it is a simple matter to calculate the distance.

30-8   The Milky Way

Fig. 30-9 is a photograph of the great spiral galaxy in the constellation Andromeda—it is visible to the naked eye as a hazy oval spot if you know precisely where to look—and Fig. 30-10 shows some of the star clouds in the Milky Way. Astronomers realized long ago that the Milky Way must be a vast lens-shaped collection of millions upon millions of stars, seen from the inside. When telescopes large enough to pick out individual stars in the Andromeda spiral were turned upon it and it was discovered that it, too, is a vast collection of stars, it soon became evident that it must be another "milky way" seen from the outside, and so it could be taken as a rough model of our own Galaxy.

If the Milky Way is a great spiral, with arms radiating from the central condensation—like the Andromeda galaxy—the next question is: How big is it? Unfortunately, the far side is obscured by dust, which is abundant in the direction of the presumed center, the great star clouds in the constellation Sagittarius. However, we do see globular clusters in every direction

FIG. 30-9

The great spiral galaxy in Andromeda. (Photograph from Dominion Astrophysical Observatory, Victoria, B.C.)

FIG. 30-10

Star clouds in the Milky Way; note the dark clouds of gas and dust, which obscure part of the light from distant stars. (Photograph from Mt. Wilson Observatory.)

except that of the center, and we can determine their directions and distances. Andromeda, too, has dust clouds within its center and its spiral arms, and globular clusters in its outskirts. We are therefore on fairly safe ground in ascribing to our Galaxy the structure that is shown in an idealized, much simplified form in Fig. 30-11. In the diagrams X marks the position of the sun, and all the naked-eye stars lie within the circle. The small solid circles indicate the distribution of the globular clusters from which the size of the whole was determined. The broken lines indicate the regions that cannot be seen on account of the obscuring dust.

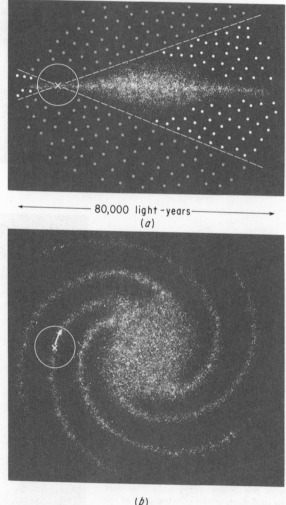

— 80,000 light-years —

(a)

(b)

FIG. 30-11

Idealized cross section and plan of the Milky Way Galaxy.

It is not surprising to find that this great collection of stars is rotating, or rather that the great majority of stars in the arms are describing nearly circular orbits around the central condensation. The rotation is therefore not like that of a wheel, but the stars near the roots of the arms are moving faster than those near the tips; it is obviously this motion that has spread the arms out into their present spiral form. By measurement of the Doppler effect of bright stars out to a distance of about 5000 light-years from the sun, the sun's orbital speed around the center has been estimated to be 200 kilometers per second. This means that it takes the sun 250 million years to travel around its galactic orbit; it has described only 18 orbits since the earth was born.

Once again we have gravitational attraction causing a body—the sun—to describe an orbit. In this case the attracting mass consists of the central galactic condensation, plus all stars that are closer to the center than the sun; those outside the sun's orbit do not contribute. If we use the figures given above for the sun's galactic orbit, we can calculate the attracting mass; we find it to be 70 billion solar masses. Since the sun is somewhat more massive than the average, and since stars in the outer limits of the Galaxy do not contribute to the net attraction, it is estimated that the Galaxy contains some 100 billion stars.

30-9   Other Galaxies, the Visible Cosmos

We have already mentioned the great spiral galaxy in the constellation Andromeda, and we have used it as an example to suggest what our Milky Way would look like if it could be seen from the outside, looking along a line inclined about 45° to the central plane. Pulsating stars of the Cepheid type can be picked out on photographs of the Andromeda galaxy, and in a great many of the similar objects which are observed, and so their distances can be found. Thus Andromeda, which is the closest large spiral, is 1,400,000 light-years away. We can measure its apparent angular width, and from this deduce its actual diameter, 130,000 light-years; it is somewhat larger than the Milky Way and one of the largest galaxies known.°

However, this great collection of stars is not the closest external galaxy. That distinction is reserved for the Magellanic Clouds, so called because they were first observed by the explorer Magellan when he passed around the tip of South America on his voyage around the world. These galaxies

° These figures may be found inconsistent with those given in older descriptions. When the pulsating star method of estimating large distances was first used there was an error in the relation between absolute magnitude and period. All distances and sizes of external galaxies that were published before 1952 are about half the correct figures. As a result, older books are liable to claim the Milky Way as the largest galaxy in the cosmos.

are easily seen on a clear night as two hazy patches of light in the Southern Hemisphere of the sky, looking like detached fragments of the Milky Way. However, they prove on examination to be about 200,000 light-years away, well outside the limits of the Milky Way, and so to be small, independent galaxies. There are six more small ones within a million light-years distance, forming a small cluster around our own. Andromeda also has a cluster of small galaxies around it, and many other examples of clusters of galaxies are known.

Besides the typical spiral galaxies there are others of many different shapes and sizes. Some, like the smaller Magellanic Cloud, are quite irregular in shape. Spirals exhibit various degrees of coiling, from the large Magellanic Cloud which shows only a suggestion of one pair of arms, through definite spirals with four or five arms, to some which are much more tightly coiled than the Andromeda.° Some show a compact elliptical or circular outline, with no arms at all. On the whole, the irregular and spiral galaxies are dusty; most of the clearly outlined elliptical galaxies are relatively clean.

Are these different characteristics signs of varying age? To be specific, are the irregular galaxies young ones, where the gas and dust clouds are only beginning to condense into stars? Then, perhaps, the tight spirals are of intermediate age, having rotated often enough to coil the arms distinctly, but still containing plenty of loose material from which more new stars can be formed; perhaps the dust-free ellipticals are very old and have used up nearly all their star-making material. It is a highly speculative problem to which we have no certain answer, but the suggestion is at least reasonable and is consistent with what we know about the ages of the stars themselves.

Large galaxies as distant as 2 or 3 *billion* light-years can be picked out— and distinguished from faint stars—on photographs taken with the 200-inch telescope at Mt. Palomar. At this distance, an entire galaxy, as large as Andromeda or the Milky Way, may appear only as bright as a star of magnitude 20, and the little speck of light we receive must have left the galaxy when the only living things on earth were tiny single-celled organisms swimming in the sea. This is the present limit of the visible cosmos. It contains hundreds of millions of galaxies, and there must be many more millions at still greater distances. Nobody knows how much farther they may extend, or whether they may not extend to infinity.

° The gas clouds in a dusty galaxy are a source of the short radio waves that are now being studied as a supplement to the study of the light from astronomical objects. These waves are not obscured by the dust and so can be detected from all parts of our own Galaxy, proving it to be a tight spiral with five distinct arms.

GLOSSARY

Absolute magnitude Figure that measures the true brightness of a star, using the magnitude scale; defined as the magnitude the star would exhibit if it were moved to a distance where its parallax angle would be $\frac{1}{10}$ second of arc.

Binary star A pair of stars revolving around each other in elliptical orbits, under the influence of their mutual gravitational attraction.

Cepheid variables Pulsating stars that exhibit a characteristic, regular variation of brightness; the period of pulsation depends on the size, and therefore there is a definite relation between period and absolute magnitude.

Constellations Apparent groupings of the visible stars; the names given them by the ancients—of heroes or animals—connote mythological beliefs and are still used when identifying and cataloguing the stars.

Eclipsing binary Double star that is recognized as such because the two stars eclipse each other at regular intervals.

Galactic cluster Group of stars in the Milky Way galaxy that evidently have a physical connection, and presumably have a common origin; may be composed of a few hundred stars.

Giant stars Comparatively cool, reddish stars with diameters about 10 to 100 times that of the sun; one of the three principal classifications that are made evident by means of the Russell diagram.

Globular clusters Compact, nearly spherical groups of stars that are found in the outskirts of the Milky Way and of other spiral galaxies; comprise many thousands of stars, in some cases over a million.

Light-year The distance light will travel in a year; equal to 5.880×10^{12} miles.

Magnitude Measure of the brightness of a star according to a conventional scale that increases in constant steps as the brightness decreases by constant factors (Sec. 30-1).

Main sequence stars The classification on the Russell diagram that comprises the great majority of known stars, including the sun; vary continuously in size, brightness, and temperature from brilliant, blue stars to faint, red stars.

Proper motion The true lateral motion of a star relative to the sun; measured in seconds of arc per year.

Russell diagram Graph on which the absolute magnitudes of the stars are plotted against their surface temperatures; used as a means of classification.

Spectroscopic binary Double star that is recognized as such because the Doppler effect in the spectrum shows that one or both of the components alternately approaches and recedes as it describes an orbit.

Spiral galaxy Galaxy of stars that shows a central condensation with two or more arms that appear to spiral outward from the center; analogous with the Milky Way.

Supergiant One of a small number of very large, reddish stars with diameters 100 or more times that of the sun.

Visual binary Double star that can be seen as such in a telescope.

White dwarfs Faint, white-hot stars, very much smaller than the sun in diameter; some are actually smaller than the earth.

EXERCISES

1. (a) What would be the approximate brightness (in suns) of a star of absolute magnitude 2.9? (b) What would be the absolute magnitude of a star of brightness one-fourth that of the sun?

2. Known stars range in absolute magnitude from -9 to $+16$, approximately. Estimate the relative range of brightness. Approximately what is the extreme range of diameters? of masses?

3. A star is observed at 6-month intervals; after the first 6 months it appears to have moved 1.52 seconds of arc in a direction parallel to the ecliptic, and at the end of the year it is 1.12 seconds from its original position. Find the parallax angle and the proper motion. Find the distance of the star in light-years.

4. Show that the actual lateral motion of a star, relative to the sun, in astronomical units per year, is equal to the proper motion divided by the parallax. Hence find the lateral component of the velocity of the star in Exercise 3, in meters per second.

5. Explain how the radius of a star can be estimated when we know its absolute magnitude and its surface temperature.

6. Outline the story of the discovery of Sirius B, the first known white dwarf. What would be the density if a mass equal to that of the sun were concentrated in a volume equal to that of the earth? How is it possible for such densities to exist?

7. For many stars the fact that they are binaries is deduced from a study of the spectrum, for others it is indicated by a regular variation in the apparent magnitude. Explain how these deductions are made. A binary star exhibits both types of variation, and at certain times the spectra of both stars are seen; compile a list of the properties of the stars that can be deduced.

8. What conditions must be fulfilled in order that a binary may be detected: (a) visually; (b) spectroscopically; (c) by the variation of magnitude.

9. What is the importance to deductive astronomy of star groups like the Pleiades? What is the evidence that some, but not all, of the stars in the Big Dipper form a similar group?

10. What are Cepheid variables? What is their importance in modern astronomy?

11. Outline the present state of knowledge about the structure of the Milky Way galaxy. Upon what types of observation is this knowledge based?

12. How has the total mass of the Galaxy been estimated?

13. Where is the closest external galaxy? Where is the nearest whose structure is similar to that of our own? What is the present state of knowledge about the most distant galaxies?

evolution in the cosmos

What are the sun and stars made of? It is essential to our hypothesis that the laws of nature and the chemical elements are the same everywhere in the cosmos; we do in fact detect the presence of well-known elements in the spectra of the stars. However, the elements must exist in a very different form from that we are familiar with, for the stars have *surface* temperatures from 3000 to 40,000°K (Sec. 30-4) and the internal temperatures must be very much higher. At these temperatures the atoms have so much kinetic energy and such high average velocities that everything behaves as if it were in the state of gas, even though the density may be greater than that of water.

The sun is pouring out energy at a rate of 5.10×10^{23} horsepower, and it is now clear that this energy is produced in the deep interior by a nuclear fusion reaction (Sec. 24-4). This has been going on with very little change in the rate for at least 4.5 billion years, and so the sun must be in an equilibrium state. The equilibrium has to be maintained under the influence of three balancing effects: the pressure caused by the gravitational forces that hold the sun together; the temperature which tends to blow it apart; and the rate at which energy is passed from layer to layer as it flows outward through the vast bulk of the sun. This last must be equal to the energy radiated from the surface. Knowing the laws of these three effects, we can work inward from the surface and calculate what the pressure and temperature in any layer must be in order to maintain equilibrium. The calculation shows that the central temperature of the sun must be about 14,000,000° K. At this temperature the atoms will not only be in the state of gas, but they will be stripped of their electrons leaving the bare nuclei. The main bulk of the sun and the stars therefore consists of a mixture of atomic nuclei and the electrons that have been stripped off.

We have seen (Sec. 30-6) that there is a relation between the total mass of a star and its absolute magnitude and this is consistent with the calculation of the internal conditions. A main sequence star that is more massive than the sun has a higher central pressure and so it must have a higher central temperature to keep it in equilibrium;° it follows that the rate of flow of energy through the star—equal to the energy radiated from the surface—is very much greater. A smaller and less massive star than the sun has a somewhat lower central temperature and radiates energy at a much lower rate; it will be a reddish star at the lower end of the main sequence. The theory is consistent with the fact that there are no known stars with masses less than about ⅒ of that of the sun, for a mass much less than this would never get hot enough for the energy-producing reactions to start, and so it would never become a self-luminous star. As a result of these calculations we are confident that we know a great deal about the interior of the sun and stars in regions where we could never conceivably make observations.

31-2   Energy of the Sun and Stars

The source of the sun's energy presents a problem that has always exercised astronomers. The ancients, rather naturally, usually assumed that it must be on fire. However, even if it were made of pure hydrogen with the appropriate amount of oxygen to combine therewith, ordinary combustion would keep it alight for only a few thousand years. In the nineteenth century, when astronomers realized that combustion was hopelessly inadequate, there was a popular theory that the source of the energy was gravitation. That is, the sun was supposed to be contracting in size so that gravitational potential energy was continually being converted into kinetic energy and thence into heat. The amount of energy which could be ob-

---

° Giant stars present a different problem, and the arguments upon which these statements are based do not apply (see Sec. 31-5).

tained in this way is surprisingly large. It could keep the sun shining for several million years; the change in the sun's diameter over the whole course of written history would be too small to measure.

However, we now know that energy of contraction—like that of combustion—is not nearly enough to keep the sun shining for the 4.55 billion years that it has been giving light and heat to the earth. In the early 1920's Sir James Jeans, professor of astronomy at Cambridge University, discussed in detail all the conceivable sources of energy. He came to the conclusion that the only source that could possibly be adequate is the conversion of mass into energy according to Einstein's relation, and that the most likely way for this to happen is the synthesis of four hydrogen atoms into a helium atom (Sec. 24-4). However, at the time very little was known about the details of nuclear reactions and it was not until scientists were able to study the reactions in the laboratory that they discovered just how the hydrogen-helium synthesis—*hydrogen-burning*—comes about. The synthesis cannot take place directly, because, even at the density that prevails at the center of the sun, the chance of four hydrogen nuclei coming together all at once is infinitesimal. The process therefore has to take place in several steps, none of which requires more than two nuclei to collide. The simplest sequence of reactions is the following:

$$\left. \begin{array}{l} {}_1H^1 + {}_1H^1 \longrightarrow {}_1H^2 + e^+ \\ {}_1H^2 + {}_1H^1 \longrightarrow {}_2He^3 + \gamma \end{array} \right\} \textbf{ twice}$$

$${}_2He^3 + {}_2He^3 \longrightarrow {}_2He^4 + {}_1H^1 + {}_1H^1.$$

Six protons ($_1H^1$) are required; two protons and a helium nucleus ($_2He^4$) are produced. The positrons (e^+) that are ejected promptly combine with free electrons in a burst of energy; the energy of the gamma rays is also absorbed and converted into heat. The net result is

$4(_1H^1) + 2e^- \longrightarrow {}_2He^4 + 28.6$ million electron-volts of heat energy.

From the results of laboratory studies of the three reactions, using particle accelerators, it is possible to calculate the rate at which they would occur in a gas at a very high temperature.° The first reaction—the synthesis of two protons—is the slowest of the three and determines the rate of the whole process. At 14,000,000°K and at the central density of the sun the calculated rate is just sufficient to provide the energy necessary to keep the sun shining. In a star with a mass of two suns or more the central temperature will be higher; the synthesis process described above is then supplemented by a different sequence of reactions,† which become

---

° Under stellar conditions the syntheses would be thermonuclear reactions (Sec. 24-4); the rate is very sensitive to temperature.

† This sequence is the so-called carbon-nitrogen cycle; it requires the presence of carbon and nitrogen as catalysts, and the synthesis of hydrogen into helium is the end result. The reactions involved in this process have been known for some time. Before the rate of the proton-proton reaction was determined, astrophysicists thought that the carbon-nitrogen cycle was the principal source of stellar energy.

very effective as the temperature increases. Massive stars therefore radiate much more energy than the sun—in some cases very much more; the theory of the production of energy is consistent with the calculation of the central temperature.

At very high temperatures, above 200 million degrees, *helium-burning* can take place. This is the synthesis of helium ($_2He^4$) into heavier elements, particularly into the common elements whose atomic masses are multiples of four: $_6C^{12}$, $_8O^{16}$, and $_{10}Ne^{20}$. These reactions also produce large quantities of energy and they are believed to be occurring in old stars of the giant class that have consumed most of their hydrogen.

31-3   Lifetime of a Star

It is estimated that a main sequence star can live on a hydrogen-burning process until about one-third of the hydrogen is consumed, because only the hydrogen near the center can be used in this way. According to spectroscopic evidence, the atoms in the sun are at present 85 per cent hydrogen. In order to provide its energy the sun is burning 4.03×10^{11} tons of hydrogen per day, but even at this rate the total supply is enough to keep it shining with very little change in its present mass and size for about 10 billion years. In that time the hydrogen content will drop to 65 per cent and a drastic readjustment will have to take place. We know the sun is about 5 billion years old, and so it must have started with 95 per cent hydrogen and must have a total lifetime as a main sequence star of 15 billion years.

The bright star, Sirius, is producing as much energy as 60 suns and is 2.44 times the sun in mass. If it also was 95 per cent hydrogen when it was born, its total possible lifetime as a main sequence star is about 1 billion years. We do not know how old it is now, but it is certainly much younger than the sun; life on earth was well advanced in its evolutionary history before Sirius started to shine. Sirius appears to be the brightest star in the sky, because it is only 8.6 light-years away, but there are many far brighter; there are some that cannot possibly last more than 2 or 3 million years. Among these there must be a number that condensed from their nebular clouds and started to shine since man appeared on earth.

31-4   Novae and Supernovae

Once in a while an inconspicuous telescopic star suddenly shines out, becomes visible to the naked eye for a few days, and then slowly fades again. It is then known as a *nova*—or new star—although we know today that novae are actually explosions taking place on old stars and there is good reason to think that they are convulsions of dying stars.

Figure 31-1 shows how the magnitude varies in a typical nova. The increase in magnitude may amount to as much as 13—an increase in brightness by a factor of 100,000. Study of the spectrum just after the outburst shows that the star is then surrounded by an expanding cloud of gas, as shown by the peculiar way in which the spectrum lines are displaced due to Doppler effect. It is estimated from the intensity of the displaced lines that in a typical case the amount of gas ejected is about $\frac{1}{1000}$ of the mass of the star. In a few days this is dissipated into space and the spectrum is again that of a normal star, but one that does not fit into any of the usual classifications on the Russell diagram. There are a few stars known to have acted as novae two or three times, and there is at least one that has had repeated small outbursts at irregular intervals of about 10 years.

Once in a very long while a star, instead of ejecting a burst of gas, simply explodes. When this happens the sudden increase in magnitude amounts to 18 or 20; at maximum the star may be the equivalent of 200 million suns. Again the fact that there has been an explosion is proved by spectroscopic study of the expanding cloud. Explosions of this kind are referred to as *supernovae;* history records just three in our Milky Way galaxy within the last 1000 years. Tycho Brahe described one that appeared in 1572, and Kepler another in 1604.

The third is the one believed to have produced the Crab Nebula (Fig. 31-2), which is identified as an expanding cloud of gas with a very hot white dwarf star in the center. We can measure the rate of increase of the apparent angular diameter and we can determine the true rate of expansion (1300 kilometers per second) by observation of the Doppler effect. From these two measurements we can calculate the true diameter of the cloud—about 4 light-years—and its distance—4500 light-years. Working backward from the rate of expansion we find that the explosion must have

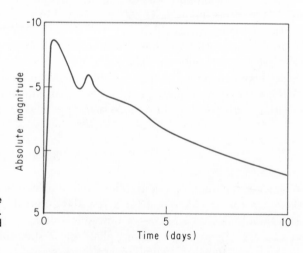

FIG. 31-1

Variation of the absolute magnitude of a typical nova. (Nova Aquilae, which had an explosion in 1918.)

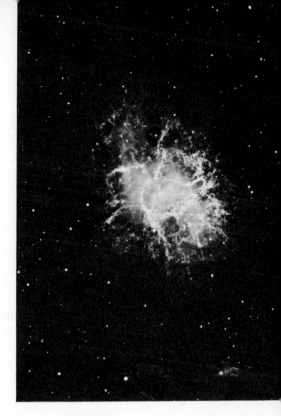

FIG. 31-2

The Crab Nebula, the remains of a star that was seen to explode in A.D. 1054. (Photograph from Mt. Palomar Observatory.)

taken place about 900 years ago (or rather the light from the explosion reached the earth then). When this was discovered old records were searched to see if anything of the kind had been observed at that time. Sure enough, Chinese and Japanese records reported what must have been a supernova, in just about the right position, in A.D. 1054. Judging from the Chinese description this must have been brighter, or closer, than the supernovae seen by Brahe and Kepler, and it is curious that there is no mention of it in European or Arab records. The supernovae of 1572 and 1604 have not been identified with any visible remains. However, the Crab Nebula is a strong source of high-frequency radio waves, and similar sources have recently been observed in the correct positions for both the later events.

A number of supernovae have been observed in other galaxies, and, judging from the frequency of their occurrence, there should be one in our own Galaxy every 300 years on the average. Some of those that have been seen in other galaxies have been almost as bright as all the other stars of the galaxy put together. If one like this should appear in our own neighborhood, say, 100 light-years away, it would be a dazzling blue-white object, 10 times brighter than the full moon.

31-5   Life and Death of a Star

We are now in a position to indulge in some informed speculation concerning the life history of a fairly large star, say, one with a mass equal to
4 suns. It starts from a nebular cloud, which is 95 per cent hydrogen gas
with some helium and with a sprinkling of the heavier elements, some of
them combined in the form of solid dust particles. The cloud starts to contract, very slowly at first, and then more and more rapidly as a central
condensation forms and the gravitational attraction increases. The temperature begins to increase, due to the conversion of gravitational potential
energy into heat, until finally the central temperature is high enough for
hydrogen-burning to begin. The final contraction, from a local condensation in an irregular cloud to a self-luminous star, must be rapid—perhaps
taking only a few thousand years—for otherwise we would observe stars
in the process of formation and only one somewhat doubtful case is actually known. The body now settles down as a stable star, with central
temperature and central energy production just sufficient to balance the
gravitational attraction. With 95 per cent hydrogen it will be on the lower
edge of the main sequence band (Fig. 30-2), but with a mass of 4 suns it
will have an absolute magnitude about zero and a surface temperature
high enough to make it slightly bluish in color (point A in Fig. 31-3).

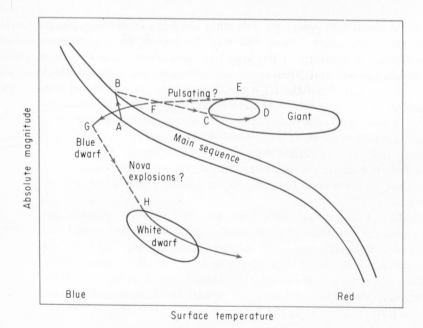

FIG. 31-3

Conjectured course of evolution of a star of four solar masses.

At this stage, if the star is rotating rapidly, it may split in two and become a binary; both stars then follow their respective evolutionary courses. Supposing that our star of 4 solar masses does not split, it starts to consume its hydrogen. As it does so the loss of mass is unimportant, but the star contracts slightly and it becomes hotter and more luminous, so that it follows the course AB on the Russell diagram, increasing in brightness by about 2 magnitudes. At B its hydrogen content is about 65 per cent; we can estimate the time required for it to cover this portion of its history —500 million years.

At B the hydrogen in the center is all converted into helium and the star has to begin forming a core composed mainly of helium. However, it is not yet hot enough to generate energy by synthesizing helium into heavier elements, and the energy is supplied by hydrogen-burning in a thin shell surrounding the helium core, both the core and the shell increasing in size as more hydrogen is consumed. Now the stars that are known to have a structure of this type are the giants. If we compute the central temperature of a giant star on the assumption that the gas mixture has a uniform composition throughout we get a value much too low to account for the energy radiated from the huge surface. In the problem of equilibrium between gravitational attraction, internal temperature, and energy production, the only solution that can give a stable star of the giant class is one with a dense helium core, an energy-producing hydrogen shell, and a vast envelope of gas of very low density, also consisting largely of hydrogen. It is conjectured, therefore, that when a star has started to form a helium core, its outer layers expand greatly, and it becomes a typical giant (C in Fig. 31-3). Its brightness cannot change much, because we know that a giant and a main sequence star of the same mass have nearly the same absolute magnitude. As the envelope of the star expands, the surface temperature drops, the color changes from blue-white to red, and the amount of energy radiated remains approximately constant. The stage BC must be covered fairly rapidly, for there are only a few known stars that fit into this part of the Russell diagram.

The course of evolution while the star is in the giant stage is uncertain; it must attain a maximum radius, and the course probably approximates to CDE in the diagram. A time must come when there is not enough hydrogen left to form the hydrogen-burning shell. The star must then contract again—converting potential energy into heat—until its central temperature is high enough for helium-burning reactions to commence. It is likely that it is in this stage of a star's lifetime that it may become unstable and start to pulsate, for it is in the region EF of the Russell diagram that we find pulsating stars, like those used to estimate the distances of other galaxies (Sec. 30-7). Whether it starts to pulsate or not, the star must convert from a typical giant to a helium star quite quickly. It must then move along the line FG, where it can live for some time by burning helium; there is a group of comparatively rare stars that occupy this region of the diagram, and that can be distinguished by their spectra from main sequence stars of the same color.

Finally, all adequate sources of energy are used up and the star must die; when it dies it must collapse into the state of fantastic density of a white dwarf (Sec. 30-5). Now there is a curious fact about white dwarfs— predicted by theory and apparently confirmed by observation—that the greater the mass, the smaller the radius. With a mass of about 1.4 suns the white dwarf state of compacted atomic nuclei would theoretically have zero radius. Obviously this cannot actually happen, and what the calculation means is that our star of 4 solar masses has to get rid of much of its substance while it is adjusting to the white dwarf state (*GH* in Fig. 31-3). There are a number of cases known of a hot white dwarf star in the center of an expanding shell of gas.° We think, therefore, that nova explosions come from dying stars that are reducing their masses so that they can settle down as white dwarfs. Why some stars do this in a succession of outbursts, some lose mass in a more or less continuous flow, whereas others die in one great supernova explosion, we do not know.

What happens in the end? A white dwarf has used up almost all its resources of nuclear atomic energy, but the amount of light and heat radiated from its tiny surface is so small that it can still keep shining for a long time. We can only conjecture that it slowly fades, and that there may exist red dwarfs, far too faint to be observed, and even completely dead black dwarfs.

What is destined to happen to stars of less than 1.4 solar masses—stars like our own sun and the billions fainter than the sun? Must they also pass through a giant stage and a helium-burning stage on their way to death as white dwarfs, but at a lower level of absolute magnitude than the course *DEFG* on the diagram? This seems likely, but we have no actual evidence. All known giants are much more massive than the sun, but this could mean only that the conjectured "subgiants" of solar mass are unobservable under present conditions. Stars of this size and brightness could only be studied in our own region of our own Galaxy, and our Galaxy is not yet old enough for its sunlike stars to have completed the main sequence stage. If stars of solar mass in a late stage of development exist in other, older galaxies we cannot as yet pick them out one by one, photograph their spectra, and study them in detail.

31-6   Quasars

Since 1960 a new astronomical mystery has emerged. Astronomical observations by means of very short radio waves have already been briefly

---

° The Crab Nebula is one such case, but there are also a number of so-called planetary nebulae, in which the expanding cloud of gas has a mass much less than that of the central star. These are thought to be the results of ordinary novae rather than of supernovae.

mentioned in connection with the tracing of the spiral arms of our Galaxy and the expanding cloud of the Crab Nebula. With regard to the latter, both theory and observation show that a cloud of turbulent, ionized gas can be a strong source of shortwave radio. We now have several types of powerful *radio telescopes*, designed to detect radio emission from astronomical objects. The most efficient is a very large parabolic reflector,° made of wire mesh, which can focus the radio waves onto a central antenna, just as the parabolic mirror of an ordinary astronomical telescope focuses light waves.

Observations with radio telescopes have shown extended clouds of gas, like the clouds of the Milky Way, but they have also shown many strong radio sources that seem to be little more than mere points, just as an ordinary star appears to be a point of light. Some of these sources have been identified with external galaxies that have peculiar features, probably associated with turbulent clouds. However, there are many that have not been identified.

In 1963 one of the previously unidentified "point" radio sources was found to coincide in position with a telescopic star which was known from photographs, but which had never been studied in detail because it did not seem to present any unusual or interesting features. The spectrum of the "star" was obtained, and it turned out not to be a nearby normal star at all. The "red shift" in its spectrum lines (Sec. 31-7) showed that it must be over a billion light-years away; if so, it must be producing as much light and heat energy as many complete galaxies. Yet it looked like a point of light with no detectable breadth.

Since then a number of similar objects have been found—all at very great distances—and they have been christened *quasar*, for "quasi-stellar radio source." We still do not know just what they are; they are much too brilliant for stars, and too small in dimensions for galaxies. We can conjecture that they are the results of tremendous explosions, many times greater than that of a supernova, and that the radio emission comes from an expanding cloud like that of the Crab Nebula, but what might have caused the explosions is a mystery.

31-7   The Expanding Cosmos

In our detective story of the heavens we must take note of the amazing discovery made by Edwin Hubble in 1929: in the spectra of all the distant galaxies the lines are displaced far toward the red end of the spectrum, with a displacement proportional to the estimated distance of the galaxy. The conclusion is that other galaxies are all hurtling away from us with

° The parabolic radio telescope at Jodrell Bank in England is 250 feet in diameter; it can be rotated in two directions so that it can be pointed at any spot in the sky to locate radio sources with precision. There are still larger ones under construction.

speeds proportional to their distances.° At the farthest distance where we can study the spectrum we may look in any direction and we find a speed of about 40,000 miles per second, nearly a quarter of the speed of light.

If galaxies are distributed uniformly all around our own Milky Way, and if they are all flying away from us, it looks at first sight as if we must be at or near the center. This is a completely erroneous conclusion; actually we are no nearer to identifying the "center of the cosmos" than we ever were. Indeed, it is quite possible that "center" is a meaningless term when applied to the cosmos as a whole. It is hard to visualize what is happening, but all we are entitled to conclude from the uniform recession of the distant galaxies is that the cosmos is expanding. Then it does not matter what galaxy we live in; unless there is a limit to the cosmos, and unless we can observe that limit with our telescopes, we can never identify the center; from any point inside we must observe the same effect of uniform distribution and uniform recession.

This is easier to understand if we think of it in one dimension. Imagine a straight strip of elastic, and let it be marked off at 1-inch intervals, labeled ... F, G, H, ... in Fig. 31-4. Let the elastic be stretched by one-half of its original length; every 1-inch interval will be increased to 1½ inches. Now suppose we are sitting at the point F, and suppose also that we cannot see the ends of the strip. When the elastic is stretched, F and G will both move away ½ inch, D and H will move away 1 inch, C and I 1½ inches, and so on. Every inch mark has receded from us by just half of its original distance. Now sit at some other point, say, I; H and J move away ½ inch, G and K 1 inch, F and L 1½ inches, etc. Again, every inch mark has receded from us just one-half of its original distance; the appearance from I is exactly the same as it was from F. We cannot tell from where we

° There have been several attempts to find alternative explanations of the so-called galactic red shift, not involving a general expansion of the cosmos; no such attempts have been successful, and the consensus of astronomers is that the expansion is an inescapable fact.

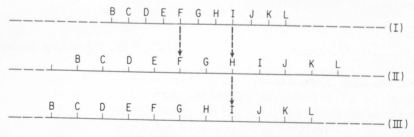

FIG. 31-4

An expanding elastic strip; (II) as seen from the point *F*; (III) as seen from *I*.

sit on the strip where the center is, or whether the strip may not be infinitely long, in which case it has no center. It is just the same for the receding galaxies; we cannot tell from where we live where the center is, or even if there is a center.

The only conclusion we can draw is that the whole cosmos is expanding uniformly, as a mass of gas might expand if the walls of its container were suddenly destroyed. Select any pair of galaxies, anywhere in the cosmos; the distance between them is steadily increasing, as the distance between a pair of molecules in the expanding gas would increase.

31-8   Creation—Catastrophic or Continuous?

Any finite thing known to be changing or developing, continually in the same direction, must have had a beginning, although we may be able to make only a rough estimate of its age. Man himself, in the collective sense of the world society embracing all mankind, has developed—always in the same direction and faster and faster as the centuries pass—from scattered family groups, each around its own campfire, to greater and greater complexity, greater and greater interdependence, greater and greater abundance of manufactured goods, and an ever-increasing totality of knowledge. So man had a beginning; at one time he was not, and at a later time he was, although it is very difficult to fix the beginning, somewhere about 2 million years ago. Life has evolved, and, on the whole, evolution has always been in the direction of more complex organisms, and finally in the direction of brain, intelligence, and consciousness. Life on earth, too, had a beginning, vaguely dated somewhere between 3 and 4 billion years ago. The solar system had a beginning which, as far as the earth is concerned, we have been able to date quite precisely at 4.55 billion years.

Our Milky Way galaxy, along with all the stars in it, is almost certainly aging in one definite direction, although the evidence is less conclusive than it is for the solar system. Because the stars are all describing orbits around the central condensation, those far out in the spiral arms are moving more slowly than those nearer the center. As the distant stars lag behind, the spiral arms slowly wind up tighter and tighter. As new stars are formed the gas and dust is slowly consumed, although there is some replenishment of the gas supply every time a nova appears. It follows that the Milky Way must also have had a beginning; it is estimated to be between 5 and 7 billion years old. It must be older than the sun, but if it were much older the galactic clusters would have been broken up by the gravitational attraction of other stars. The stars would be distributed completely at random, and would be moving in random directions. At the same time the arms would have coiled in upon themselves and lost their identity.

All these things were born, but they originated from something that existed before them. Man evolved from an apelike hominid, and that in turn from a primitive mammal. Life developed from a few giant molecules in the primeval sea and in doing so absorbed a large fraction of the existing carbon atoms. The solar system condensed from a nebula of gas and dust. Even the Milky Way must have originated in the primeval gas, remains of which are known to pervade all space, between the galaxies. In a sense these are all creations, for in each case something now exists which once did not exist. However, we have no reason to think that these creations have involved any new atoms or any violation of the law of conservation of energy—or any other basic physical law. What is new in each case is *organization;* new organization is created every time nature grows a tree or an animal° and every time a man builds himself a house.

If we consider the cosmos as a whole we are inevitably led to a concept of creation on a different level. We saw in Sec. 31-7 that the cosmos is expanding—this suggests that it too had a beginning. There are two competing theories of the expanding cosmos and of its origin. One, the *catastrophic theory,* has been elaborated mainly by George Gamow of the University of Colorado. In this theory it is assumed that the cosmos contains a finite quantity of matter and energy and that in the beginning this was all concentrated in a small sphere, with a density far more fantastic than that of a white dwarf star. Something caused the sphere of matter-energy to start expanding; if the rate of expansion has been constant, it must have begun about 10 billion years ago.

The other theory of the cosmos is the *continuous theory,* which was first suggested by Hermann Bondi and Thomas Gold of Oxford University, and then elaborated by Fred Hoyle, also of Oxford. The theory is based on the one exception to the rule that whatever is evolving continuously must have had a beginning; if the cosmos is infinite in extent, it could also be infinite in time, and so have always existed. According to the continuous theory of cosmology, as the galaxies get farther apart in the universal expansion new galaxies develop between them, so that the picture seen from any one place changes only in detail and not in its essential features. According to this theory, there always have been and always will be galaxies and the *average* distance separating them never changes. No matter how far we travel—in imagination—in any direction, there are always more galaxies beyond and they always seem to be flying away from us. But from any given point—our own Milky Way, for example—we can never see beyond a certain distance or observe more than a definite number of galaxies. At

° In mathematics the whole is equal to the sum of its parts. This is not necessarily true in nature. A man is obviously much more than the sum of the molecules of which his body is composed; he is this sum plus organization. The question posed by natural creation is: What produces the organization?

a distance of about 6 billion light-years the speed of recession would be equal to the velocity of light; the light of galaxies beyond this limit can never reach us; as galaxies pass the limit they vanish from sight.°

Both theories of the cosmos involve features of creation; both involve the concentration of primeval matter into galaxies, followed by the formation of stars from the galactic clouds; both include a theory of the formation of the chemical elements by synthesis in thermonuclear reactions.† In the case of the catastrophic theory the obvious questions are: Where did the small sphere that once contained the whole mass of the cosmos come from? What existed before the expansion started? The theory leaves these questions completely open; the origin could be a collapse of a previous cosmos, followed by a fantastic explosion; it could be a new instantaneous creation.

In the case of the continuous theory the corresponding question is: How do the newly formed galaxies originate? The answer is that they are formed from hydrogen atoms—protons and electrons—that are continually appearing. Where do the hydrogen atoms come from? They are a new creation—from nothing! According to this theory, new creation is going on everywhere all the time. It is a violation of the cherished principle of conservation of mass-energy, but the amount involved is so small that there is no hope of detecting it. It would require only one new hydrogen atom per year in every cubic mile to keep the average density constant as the cosmos expands.

At present there is no sure way of distinguishing between the two theories by experimental observation. According to the catastrophic theory, the composition of the cosmos should be everywhere the same because all the chemical elements would have been synthesized in the first few moments of the expansion, when the density and temperature were high enough for all types of thermonuclear reaction to take place; all galaxies should be approximately the same age—in particular, there should be none appreciably older than our own; galaxies should be uniformly distributed throughout most of the cosmos, but there should be a finite limit to their distance—about 6 billion light-years. Toward the outer limit galaxies should appear to be distributed somewhat more thickly than in our own neighborhood; the most distant galaxies should appear to be younger due to the time required for their light to reach us. Recent observations of very distant galaxies indicate that these two predictions of the theory may be correct.

° There is a common impression that Einstein's theory of relativity does not permit velocities greater than the velocity of light. This is a misconception; relativity does not permit a mass to be *accelerated* by mechanical forces to a velocity greater than that of light (see Sec. 33-11).

† Both theories of thermonuclear synthesis take into account the relative abundance in nature of all the different stable isotopes of the elements, with results in fair agreement with experiment.

According to the continuous theory, the distribution should be uniform everywhere, but everywhere we should see galaxies of many different ages. We do see galaxies of different types (Sec. 30-9) and the differences in appearance could be due to differences in age—some large elliptical galaxies look as if they must be older than the Milky Way. The continuous theory of the synthesis of the chemical elements requires that there be differences in composition in different regions, because the synthesis would have taken place in several steps—the heavy elements inside stars that subsequently exploded. There is some evidence of differences in composition of different stars, seeming to favor this feature of the theory.

For both theories there is observational evidence that seems to support each one, but the observations are difficult to interpret; the problem of the creation and evolution of the cosmos is still far from being resolved.

GLOSSARY

Helium-burning Synthesis of helium into heavier elements by thermonuclear reactions in the stars, accompanied by the production of energy.

Hydrogen-burning Synthesis of hydrogen into helium by thermonuclear reactions in the sun and stars; the principal source of stellar energy, effective during most of the lifetime of a star.

Nova A star that suddenly increases in brightness, and then slowly fades approximately to its former degree of light output; this phenomenon is believed to be caused by an explosion in which as much as 1 per cent of the star's mass may be ejected.

Quasar Quasi-stellar radio source; a distant source of short radio waves, with an intensity comparable to that of a small galaxy, but with dimensions so small that it appears to be a mere point; quasars are apparently the results of enormous explosions, the causes of which are mysterious.

Radio telescope Radio receiver designed for the detection and location of cosmic sources of short radio waves; the most efficient type consists of a large parabolic mirror that can be pointed in different directions, and that concentrates the waves on a small antenna at the focus of the mirror.

Supernova A star that increases to a maximum brightness many times that of a nova; the star does not return to its original condition, and the outburst is believed to be caused by an explosion of the whole star.

EXERCISES

1. What three effects have to balance in the interior of a star so that it may be in equilibrium and shine with a constant brightness?

2. How can the central temperature of a star be estimated?

3. There are relations between the mass, the radius, and the absolute magnitude that hold approximately for all main sequence stars; why should these three quantities be connected?

4. Discuss briefly the source of the energy of the sun and stars. What sources have been suggested in the past, and why are they inadequate? Summarize our modern ideas on the subject.

5. Estimate the maximum possible age of a main sequence star with an absolute magnitude of −5 and a mass equal to 8 suns.

6. Outline briefly what is believed to happen in a nova outburst, and in a supernova explosion.

7. Outline the story of the Crab Nebula and the supernova of A.D. 1054.

8. Why does the temperature increase when a cloud of gas and dust condenses into a star? When and why does the increase stop?

9. Why do astronomers believe that a giant star has a central core composed mainly of helium, surrounded by a vast envelope of diffuse gas?

10. Why does a large star have to lose mass when its internal sources of energy are used up?

11. Explain what is meant by the expansion of the cosmos. Explain why the expansion appears to be the same in all directions.

12. Explain why many large galaxies, including our own, have a spiral structure.

13. Contrast the two theories of the creation of the cosmos, the catastrophic theory and the continuous theory. In each case refer to an observation that seems to support the theory.

REVIEW EXERCISES FOR CHAPTERS 25 THROUGH 31

1. Outline the role that deduction from accepted principles plays in modern science. What type of information is available for deduction concerning: (a) the past history of the earth; (b) the interior of the earth; (c) the properties of individual stars.

2. A popular device for emphasizing the long history of life on earth is to imagine the time scale of evolution to be compressed into one man's lifetime. Imagine that the earth solidified in 1896, and that it is now midnight on December 31, 1966; about when on this scale did the following events take place: (a) the first recognizable traces of life appeared; (b) the trilobite flourished; (c) the first animal whose fossils can be identified moved onto dry land; (d) the earliest possible date at which the star Sirius

might have been born; (e) the great dinosaurs flourished; (f) the Rocky Mountains were thrust up; (g) the first true men appeared; (h) the star that formed the Crab Nebula exploded; (i) the great pyramids of Egypt were built; (j) Columbus landed in America; (k) the first hydroelectric power plant was built at Niagara Falls?

3. Outline the evidence that: (a) Alaska once had a semitropical climate; (b) Alaska and Siberia were joined only a few thousand years ago; (c) Australia was once covered with ice; (d) the Swiss Alps were once under the sea; (e) Antarctica was once covered with luxuriant vegetation.

4. What might be some of the useful scientific and economic results of setting off an atomic explosion underground?

5. Name an important scientific development ascribed to each of the following persons, and give the approximate date: Charles Lyell, Charles Darwin, Mohorovičić, Pierre Laplace, C. F. von Weizsacker, H. C. Urey, Sir James Jeans, Fred Hoyle.

6. What is studied in each of the following scientific specialties: stratigraphy, cosmology, seismology?

7. Describe briefly the principal processes of erosion and transport involved in the wearing down of the mountains and the deposition of sediments.

8. Explain how a change in the climatic pattern of the subarctic regions could lead to another ice age, without a general reduction in the average temperature of the earth. Outline a plausible theory of the climatic change necessary.

9. Write a brief account of the great animal migrations that have taken place during the Cenozoic era.

10. Outline the theories of the origin of the solar system that were accepted by the majority of astronomers in 1930, and in 1965. What development led to the change in the consensus?

11. Discuss briefly the possibility of life on other worlds. Why did the change in accepted theory, referred to in Review Exercise 10, cause also an important change in the consensus concerning life in the cosmos?

12. Outline a plausible theory of the origin of life on earth.

13. Discuss the problem of determining distances in the cosmos, describing briefly methods used for: (a) the moon; (b) the sun; (c) nearby stars; (d) galactic clusters; (e) the limits of the Milky Way galaxy; (f) other relatively close galaxies; (g) the farthest known galaxies.

14. Outline the probable life history of a massive star.

DISCONTINUITY AND UNCERTAINTY

part seven

It is impossible to measure simultaneously, with complete precision, both the position and the velocity of a particle.

—HEISENBERG

the failure of classical physics

In this chapter we shall see why the mechanistic approach to nature has failed to give an adequate description of the facts. By "mechanistic approach" we mean a body of theory and computation based upon Newton's laws of mechanics and the laws of electricity and magnetism. The same is frequently included under the term "classical physics," the physics of the eighteenth and nineteenth centuries, as opposed to the "modern physics" of our own twentieth century.

We have already encountered some of the ideas that underlie twentieth-century physics. Mass and electric charge are *discontinuous quantities;* magnetic and electric fields are *nondelineable;* radioactive transformations involve *probabilities* rather than rigorous causality. But these could—by a little modification of the basic ideas and by a little ingenuity in the application of the laws—be brought within the scheme of mechanistic physics; this was indeed the approach that most physicists attempted to take before 1925. This approach failed; we must see why it failed and why it was necessary to introduce new and—to most people—strange concepts that could not by any stretch of the imagination be included in a mechanistic

543

scheme. There had to be a new scientific revolution, not only involving the introduction of new laws, but leading to a new way of thinking that has only been appreciated by scientists themselves within the last 30 years or so. New scientific discoveries and new laws find practical application sooner or later; we shall find that a number of things we have grown accustomed to in our generation are developments of modern, rather than classical, physics.

32-2   *Mechanistic Laws*

It will be useful at this point to summarize in abbreviated form the most important of the mechanistic laws of classical physics.

MECHANICS

The second law of motion: *Force is proportional to the product of mass times acceleration* (Sec. 4-6).

The law of universal gravitation: *All bodies attract each other with a force proportional to the product of their masses and inversely proportional to the square of the distance between them* (Sec. 6-1).

The law of conservation of energy: *The total energy of any closed system is constant* (Sec. 8-2).

The laws of conservation of momentum and angular momentum: *The vector sum of the momenta of any closed group of bodies is constant; the resultant angular momentum of all rotations and revolutions is constant* (Sec. 8-5).

The general gas law: *For a given mass of any gas the product of pressure times volume is proportional to the absolute temperature* (Sec. 10-4).

Avogadro's law: *Molecular weights of different gases all occupy the same volume at the same temperature and pressure* (Sec. 11-3).

CHEMICAL REACTIONS

The law of conservation of mass: *There is no gain or loss of mass when materials react chemically* (Sec. 9-4).

The law of constant proportions: *A chemical compound always contains the same proportion by mass of its constituent elements* (Sec. 9-6).

ELECTRICITY AND MAGNETISM

Coulomb's law: *Electric charges attract or repel each other with a force that is proportional to the product of the charges and inversely proportional to the square of the distance between them* (Sec. 14-4).

Ampère's law for the magnetic field produced by an electric current, and its converse giving the force exerted by a magnetic field upon a current (Sec. 15-7).

Faraday's law of induction: *The electromotive force induced in a circuit is proportional to the rate of change of the magnetic flux threading the circuit* (Sec. 16-2).

PROPAGATION OF LIGHT

The law of reflection: *Light is reflected from a smooth surface so that the incident and reflected rays make equal angles with the surface* (Sec. 17-3).

The law of refraction: *When light passes from one transparent medium to another the ratio of the sines of the angles of incidence and of refraction is constant* (Sec. 17-5).

The mechanistic laws have certain features in common. They are *continuous.* The entities with which they deal can be present in any amount and in the algebraic expressions of the laws the quantities involved are mathematically continuous.

The laws are all *macroscopic.* They were derived from observations and experiments with quantities of material large enough to see and handle—quantities containing very large numbers of atoms. Some of the laws—particularly the laws of gases and of light—are meaningless on the microscopic scale when single atoms are involved. A "smooth surface" is necessarily very much broader than the diameter of an atom; the very concept of a "gas" is meaningless for a single molecule.

Most important for what follows, the laws are completely *deterministic.* They may have known limitations or be subject to minor corrections, but within their range of validity they permit only that lack of precision which is inherent in the measurements of the quantities involved. In principle, they predict results exactly, with no room, for example, for two or three alternative results. They belong, therefore, to that part of nature wherein causality is rigorous; a cause or a set of causes leads to one unique result.

The mechanistic laws were all well known before the end of the nineteenth century and are still the basis of much of astronomy, of much of chemistry, of geology, and geophysics. Moreover, on the side of practical application, a great deal of our modern technology—including most of the applied science of engineering—is founded upon the classical mechanistic laws.

32-3   Mechanistic Atomic Physics

In the latter half of the nineteenth century attempts were made to take the mechanistic laws, which had been developed on the macroscopic scale, and apply them to the microscopic—to single atoms and molecules. Up to a point these attempts were successful; one outstanding success was the development of a *model* of a gas through the so-called kinetic theory of gases (Sec. 11-4). "Model," in this sense, means merely a description; a mechanistic model is one that might, conceivably, be constructed on an enlarged scale out of actual spheres, wires, batteries, and other pieces of material, although the number of working parts might be so fantastic as to make the construction an impossibility in practice. Such a model can be described in words or depicted in drawings—it is *delineable*.

The classical model of the gas is that in which the molecules are imagined as little hard spheres (or possibly ellipsoids) flying around in all directions, colliding with each other and with the walls of the container. At all times the individual particles are subject to the classical laws of mechanics; that is what we mean by saying that the macroscopic laws have been extended to the microscopic. As we have already seen in Chapter 11, this model accounts very satisfactorily not only for the simple gas law, but also for the known limitations of this law, and for other properties of the gas. When free electrons were identified in the cathode-ray beam, in 1895 (Sec. 21-3), the classical laws—both of mechanics and of electromagnetism —were used successfully to calculate the paths of the electrons.

In the early 1900's most physicists hoped and expected that everything would eventually be explained by means of mechanistic models. Especially, they still thought that nature must be completely deterministic, and that events were uniquely determined by their causes. There was complete acceptance of Laplace's famous statement:

> *If we knew the position and velocity of every particle in the universe, and if we had enough men and adding machines to do the arithmetic, we could predict the whole course of the universe for all time.*

However, this was not to be. By the year 1900 there were already known—but still unexplained—several phenomena destined to revolutionize basic thinking about mechanistic models and about cause and effect. We must now examine three outstanding failures of classical physics—three cases where the mechanistic laws were not only incapable of providing satisfactory models, but where they predicted results in definite disagreement with the observed facts.

32-4 *The Emission of Light*

In 1873 Maxwell had shown that electrical oscillations must produce a wavelike emission of energy, and had suggested that light was the result of such oscillations taking place within the atoms of the light source (Sec. 20-2). In 1895 Thomson identified the electron and showed that it is a constituent part of all matter (Sec. 21-3). A few years later Rutherford demonstrated that atoms consist of a small, heavy, positive nucleus, surrounded by a cloud of electrons (Sec. 22-6). By this time there was much other evidence that Maxwell was right in assuming light to be transmitted by electromagnetic waves, and it was quite clear that the waves must originate in some way in oscillations of the electrons. The problem then arose of trying to conceive a model of an atom which would be mechanically possible, and which would oscillate with the correct frequencies.

The most reasonable mechanistic model was one in which the electrons were assumed to be revolving in orbits around the central nucleus—like the planets around the sun—so that there would be mechanical equilibrium between the electrical attraction of the nucleus and the centripetal force of the orbiting electrons. This would produce electromagnetic waves (that is, light) with a frequency equal to the frequency of revolution of the electron in its orbit. So far so good, but now comes the catch in the theory. As the electron produces radiation it must lose energy; as it loses energy the radius of the orbit must become smaller and the frequency must increase. The electron must, therefore, spiral in toward the nucleus, increasing the frequency of the light emitted as it does so.

The mechanistic model of an atom, based upon orbiting electrons, cannot remain stable for any length of time and cannot produce light of constant frequency. But atoms *are* stable, and when they are in the free state in a gaseous light source they produce a line spectrum (Sec. 19-3) consisting of a number of definite, discrete frequencies. There is something radically wrong with the model; we must try to devise a better model. There were, therefore, many attempts during the early years of the twentieth century to devise mechanistic atomic models, but all of them failed completely in some such way as that described.

The second complete failure of classical, mechanistic physics concerns the continuous spectrum produced by a hot solid or liquid source (Sec. 19-4). In a solid body the atoms have no room to develop their proper characteristic frequencies; when the solid is heated to incandescence all frequencies are possible and the result is a continuous spectrum. In this case we do not have to consider any specific model in order to find a serious discrepancy. Very general arguments°—allied to those that show that the average kinetic energy of gas molecules is independent of the molecular mass and proportional to the absolute temperature—show that in the radiation emitted by a solid the highest possible frequencies are the most likely to be activated. It turns out that it is an unequivocal prediction of classical physics that the energy in the continuous spectrum—at any temperature—should be greatest in the high frequencies or the short wavelengths and should decrease steadily with increasing wavelength. Instead, it takes the form shown in Fig. 19-5, with maximum energy at a wavelength that is inversely proportional to the absolute temperature.

° We shall not give the rather difficult mathematical argument here. In this case—as in many others—the reader will have to trust the mathematician to carry out his task without error.

32-5 *Photoelectricity*

It has been known for a long time that a negatively charged metal plate can be discharged by shining ultraviolet light upon it; when the same plate is positively charged, there is no effect. This can be used as the source of electrons for a cathode-ray tube; thus it is demonstrated that the so-called *photoelectric effect* is an emission of free electrons from the metal surface under the influence of the light. In practice the effect can be most satisfactorily studied in a simple photoelectric cell (Fig. 32-1). In the cell illustrated the light-sensitive surface is a half-cylinder in a vacuum tube with transparent walls. A stiff wire on the axis of the cylinder serves as an electrode to collect the electrons. The cylinder is connected to the negative of a variable voltage source and the central wire to the positive. When light of a suitable frequency is allowed to shine on the tube a current flows in the circuit.

Figure 32-2 shows how the current varies with the potential applied to the tube. For a small voltage in the "wrong" direction (shown as a negative voltage in the graph) a few electrons can cross the tube and produce a current in the opposite direction to the applied voltage. This shows that the electrons are ejected from the metal surface with a certain amount of kinetic energy, which is equal to the work done by an electron in overcoming the small negative voltage AO. For positive voltages the current is constant and measures the total number of electrons ejected.

The empirical laws of the photoelectric effect are as follows:

1. There are no electrons ejected unless the frequency of the light exceeds a certain value, f_0, known as the photoelectric threshold.

2. The energies of the electrons depend only upon the frequency distribution in the spectrum of the light and not upon the light intensity.

3. For light having a given spectrum, the number of electrons ejected—and therefore the current in the circuit—is proportional to the light intensity.

These experimental laws constitute the third complete contradiction of

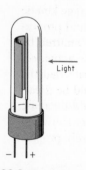
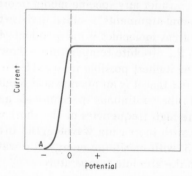

FIG. 32-1

A simple photoelectric cell.

FIG. 32-2

Variation of photocurrent with applied voltage.

the predictions of classical theory. When light of any frequency falls upon the metal surface much of the energy is absorbed since metals are almost completely opaque to light of ordinary frequencies. According to the classical laws which were so successful in the kinetic theory of gases, some of this energy should be shared with the conduction electrons in the metal. The average energy of the electrons ought, therefore, to increase steadily until a few of them acquire enough energy to escape through the metal surface and appear as photoelectrons. The *frequency* of the light ought to have little or nothing to do with it.

It follows from this and similar arguments that there is no classical, mechanistic model of a metal in which the ejection of electrons would take place only under the influence of light with frequency above a certain threshold value; if photoelectric emission takes place at all, it should take place for any frequency that is absorbed by the metal. Moreover, the energy of the electrons should increase with the total amount of energy absorbed; if the intensity of the light is increased, the energy of the ejected electrons should increase as well as their number.

32-6   *The Photoelectric Cell*

It is law 3 of the photoelectric effect which makes the phototube so useful in many modern technological applications, among which the measurement of light intensity is only one. The effect occurs for *any* frequency above the threshold value; it occurs for X rays as well as for light and it can be important in some X-ray techniques. For most metals the threshold, f_0, lies in the ultraviolet and a tube with a cathode of such a metal is useless for visible light. However, the alkali metals have their photoelectric thresholds at lower frequencies; for cesium it is just beyond the red end of the spectrum and this metal is sensitive to all visible frequencies. It is not feasible to make a cathode of solid cesium, because this metal oxidizes with explosive violence when it is exposed to the air. Most commercial phototubes are made with nickel electrodes and a thin coating of cesium is evaporated onto the nickel after the tube has been evacuated.

The application that has probably had the greatest influence on modern living is in the television camera. The scene to be televised is focused on a light-sensitive photoelectric screen. Instead of having a continuous metal surface, this screen consists of several thousand tiny dots of cesium, deposited on a thin layer of insulating material, behind which is the electrode proper. The cesium dots become positively charged, each with a charge proportional to the intensity of the light falling upon it. A fine pencil of cathode rays is deflected by a varying electric field so as to "scan" the screen, that is, to pass over all the dots in succession—420 dots in each horizontal row, 525 rows. When the scanning rays hit a dot that has been charged by photoelectric emission—in a bright area of the picture—the charge is neutralized. This causes a sudden change in the induced charge on the electrode behind the screen and there is a pulse of current in the external circuit. If a dot lies in a dark area of the picture nothing happens when the cathode rays pass over it. The current in the circuit consists of a succession of impulses, each proportional to the amount of light falling on the successive sensitive dots. This can be amplified and transmitted by means of a beam of radio waves, like any other radio signal. In order to give the illusion of a moving picture, the whole process has to be repeated 30 times per second; there are altogether 6,615,000 impulses per second, each of the proper intensity.

In the receiver a cathode-ray beam is made to pass over the fluorescent screen in the picture tube, and is synchronized with the scanning beam in the camera by an auxiliary radio signal. The intensity of the beam that draws the picture is regulated by the current in the impulses as they are picked up in succession by the receiving antenna; thus the picture in the receiver reproduces the tones of light and shade in the scene viewed by the transmitting camera.

GLOSSARY

Deterministic A deterministic law or theory is one according to which a given set of causes is invariably followed by the same, unique results.

Photoelectric effect The emission of free electrons from a metal under the influence of high-frequency electromagnetic radiation.

Photoelectric threshold The limiting frequency below which the photoelectric effect does not occur.

Probability Technically, the probability of an occurrence is defined as the ratio of the number of times the event occurs to the number of attempts, that is, to the number of times the same causes operate so that the event might occur.

EXERCISES

1. "The classical laws are macroscopic, continuous, and deterministic." Explain what is meant by each of these terms, and illustrate your answer with examples drawn from: (a) Newton's laws of mechanics; (b) the gas laws; (c) the laws of electricity and magnetism; (d) the laws of propagation of light.

2. Explain why it is impossible, according to the classical laws, to devise an atomic model in which the electrons revolve in orbits around the nucleus. If this is impossible, why could we not devise a model in which the electrons are normally at rest, and in which they vibrate around their normal positions when the atom emits light?

3. What is actually observed in a simple demonstration of the photoelectric effect? How can it be proved that the effect is due to the absorption of light energy, and the consequent emission of free electrons from the metal?

4. Explain why the empirical laws of the photoelectric effect are in direct contradiction to the predictions of classical theory.

5. Describe how a photoelectric cell is used: (a) in a television camera; (b) in an astronomical telescope; (c) in any other practical device.

quantum theory and relativity

It is rather curious that, of the three outstanding problems discussed in the last chapter, the most difficult was the first to be resolved. In 1900 the German physicist, Max Planck, introduced the concept of light quanta in order to develop a theory of the energy distribution in the continuous spectrum. We will not discuss this theory to explain the quantum principle; instead, we will use the much simpler phenomenon of the photoelectric effect (Sec. 32-5). The fact that the *energy* of the photoelectrons does not depend on the intensity of the light—but only on the frequency —is very simply explained if we assume that all electrons affected receive exactly the same amount of energy (in a light beam of one definite frequency).

In 1906, therefore, Albert Einstein expressed Planck's concept in a more general form than the original and applied it to photoelectricity. In Einstein's form the principle can be expressed as follows:

Whenever light (or any other electromagnetic radiation) is emitted or absorbed the amount of energy exchanged at any one time is a definite "quantum" of exactly h times the frequency, where h is a universal constant.

The quantity h is known as Planck's constant, after the originator of the concept, and its value in MKS units is 6.6257×10^{-34} joule-second. This is very small but it is a definite quantity that can be precisely evaluated by modern experiments. Remember that it has to be multiplied by a frequency and this may be a very large number. For example, a frequency of 6×10^{14} cycles corresponds to a typical yellow-green light; its energy quantum would be approximately 4×10^{-19} joule. A 40-watt bulb produces about 10^{20} quanta per second.

Applied to the photoelectric effect, the Planck-Einstein quantum principle means that, when light of frequency (f) falls upon a metal surface, some of the electrons absorb exactly hf of energy—the rest receive nothing. In order to escape from the metal and produce a photocurrent, the electrons have to do a certain amount of work (W) against the attraction of the positive charges in the metal. If the energy quantum hf is less than W, the electrons cannot escape and the light is simply absorbed by the metal; if hf is greater than W, the electrons can overcome the attraction of the positive charges and photoelectric emission occurs. Therefore the photoelectric threshold frequency is given by

$$hf_0 = W.$$

If f is greater than f_0, the electrons that absorb quanta receive more energy than is necessary for them to escape; some or all of the excess energy appears as kinetic energy of the ejected electrons. Therefore the *maximum* velocity (v) with which the photoelectrons can emerge is given by

$$\tfrac{1}{2}mv^2 = hf - W = h(f - f_0).$$

Electrons that have a certain amount of kinetic energy can do work against an opposing electric field and can produce a current even if there is a small negative voltage applied to the collecting electrode in the phototube. The reverse negative voltage (V) that is necessary to prevent any photocurrent from passing (given by the point A in Fig. 32-2) is found by equating the work done against the electric field to the maximum kinetic energy of the photoelectrons:

$$Ve = \tfrac{1}{2}mv^2 = h(f - f_0),$$

where e is the electronic charge.

When the voltage applied to the collecting electrode is positive—so that electrons are attracted—the number of electrons ejected is equal to the number of quanta absorbed; the photocurrent is proportional to the light intensity. Einstein's quantum theory of the photoelectric effect therefore predicts a photoelectric threshold frequency, current proportional to light intensity, current in the opposite direction to a small reverse voltage, and velocity of the photoelectrons determined solely by the frequency of the light—all in complete agreement with experiment.

The empirical laws of photoelectricity provide the simplest and most convincing proof of the quantum principle for light—invoked in the first place to explain the energy distribution in the continuous spectrum. However, the principle has much wider implications and has been confirmed in many different ways; if it had not, it would not have attained the status that it has today: it is one of the fundamental laws of nature. Obviously, if radiation can only be emitted and absorbed in units of hf, it can only exist in these units—never in fractions of a unit—and so *radiated energy* is discontinuous. We have to add another discontinuity of nature to those we have already discussed.

33-2   *Energy Levels in Atoms*

The next outstanding problem of the early twentieth century was the fact that free atoms in a gaseous light source produce a spectrum consisting of sharp lines with definite frequencies. If this experimental fact is combined with the first quantum principle—that the atom emits its radiant energy in quanta, so that the energy loss from one atom at any one time is a definite quantity—it follows that the energy content of the atom can only take certain definite values. These values are known as the *energy levels* of the atom; they can be determined by an analysis of the line spectrum and can be conveniently displayed on an *energy level diagram.*

Let us take the simplest possible case, that of hydrogen which consists merely of a proton and one electron. Its energy level diagram is shown to scale in Fig. 33-1. Vertical displacement on the diagram represents energy in any convenient unit; it can also represent frequency, because the quanta of energy are proportional to the frequency. Horizontal lines represent the values of energy content that can occur, numbered in order from the normal, nonradiating atom at the bottom.[*] In this simple case the permitted energies (E_n), measured from the top down, are given to a very good approximation by the simple formula

$$E_n = \frac{R}{n^2},$$

where R is a constant and n is an integer.

[*] Horizontal displacement on the diagram has no numerical significance.

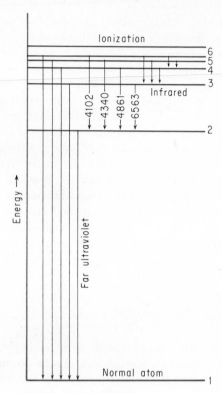

FIG. 33-1

Energy level diagram of hydrogen; the numbered transitions are those that produce the lines of the visible spectrum.

Vertical arrows represent the energy losses when the atom emits radiation. The energy loss must be related to the frequency of the radiation by the quantum principle; therefore the permitted frequencies (f) are given by

$$hf = E_n - E_{n'} = R\left(\frac{1}{n^2} - \frac{1}{n'^2}\right),$$

where h is Planck's constant. Thus each vertical arrow represents a line in the spectrum; those that lie within the visible frequency range are labeled according to their wavelengths in angstrom units. Other lines represented on the diagram are in the far ultraviolet or in the infrared and are not normally seen. However, all lines involving energy levels of small index number (n) have been observed and measured under suitable conditions.

Figure 33-2 is the energy level diagram of sodium; it is typical of all those elements that have one valence electron. This diagram is considerably more complicated than that of hydrogen, but it is simple in comparison with those of elements with several valence electrons, or of elements like iron that have incomplete inner electron shells.° In the case of sodium the

---

° Some elements have hundreds of energy levels and a thousand or more lines in the spectrum. In retrospect it is not surprising that it took the combined efforts of hundreds of physicists more than 50 years to decipher the rules that govern the arrangement of the lines in a complicated spectrum.

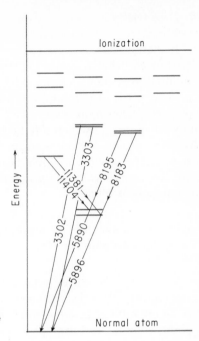

FIG. 33-2

Energy level diagram of sodium, showing the transitions that produce the strongest lines.

energy levels can be classified into groups that are shown in different vertical columns of the diagram. Another characteristic of the "one-electron" spectrum is that the energy levels occur in pairs,° although it is only for the lower levels that the pairs can be separated by means of an ordinary spectrograph.

33-3   The Second Quantum Principle—for Atoms

In 1913 the Danish physicist, Niels Bohr, devised a model of the hydrogen atom that gave the correct energy level diagram and therefore the correct spectrum. He assumed mechanical equilibrium and treated the one elec-tron concerned as a small particle revolving in an orbit around the nucleus. For simplicity, the orbits were assumed to be circular although this sim-plification is not necessary and elliptical orbits were included in a later modification of the theory. To this extent Bohr's model was classical, but next a radical *ad hoc* assumption† had to be made. He assumed that the electron could revolve only in certain selected orbits; when it was in one of these orbits there was no radiation, in spite of the fact that Maxwell's

---

° This is actually the case for hydrogen also; the lines indicated in Fig. 33-1 are very close pairs that can be separated only by refined methods of measurement.

† An *ad hoc* assumption is one designed to attain a specific result. It bears about the same relation to a hypothesis as an empirical law does to a basic principle.

equations of electricity and magnetism require that an orbiting electric charge should radiate energy with a frequency equal to the frequency of revolution. Radiation was assumed to occur when the electron "jumped" from one permitted orbit to another of lower energy. The frequency of the light emitted was then determined by the loss of energy and the quantum principle; it had nothing to do with the frequency of the orbit.

To complete the calculation of the energy levels it was necessary to find a criterion by which to fix the permitted orbits. It turned out that the correct results were obtained if the angular momentum were put equal to $nh/2\pi$, that is, to any integral multiple of $h/2\pi$. This is the first and simplest form of the *second quantum principle*, which may be stated somewhat more generally as follows:

The angular momentum of the electrons in an atom is quantized and can take only specific values. *

Angular momentum, therefore, is discontinuous, the fourth quantity we have found to possess the discontinuous feature. Later this had to be extended to momentum in general, whenever the moving particle is confined to a finite volume. For example, it applies to the conduction electrons in a metal, which are not attached to specific atoms but are confined to the wire.

The permitted orbits of Bohr's model have radii proportional to the squares of the integers, that is, they increase according to the series 1, 4, 9, 16, . . . , as shown in Fig. 33-3. The smallest orbit is that of the normal, unexcited hydrogen atom; its calculated radius agrees with that of the free hydrogen atom estimated in other ways.

The extension of Bohr's theory to elliptical orbits of specific shapes led to the arrangements of electron orbits which one often sees depicted in attempts to draw pictures of heavier atoms. However, Bohr's model is still much too mechanistic; it was a long step in the right direction and provided an essential clue to the eventual solution, but diagrams of electron orbits are liable to be mistaken for something that is actually nondelineable. For lack of a better word, physicists still talk of "electron orbits," but when this term is used we should remember that it is a semiclassical analogy, and that the reality is a diffuse electron cloud with a certain energy and a certain angular momentum.

The mechanical problem of the mutual attractions between three or more particles has never been solved in the general case, and Bohr's semiclassical model is of little use for elements heavier than hydrogen. It has been used to calculate approximately the energy levels of the helium atom

---

* In general the angular momentum is given by an expression of the form $\sqrt{J(J+1)}(h/2\pi)$, where the *quantum number* (J) is either an integer or an integer plus ½.

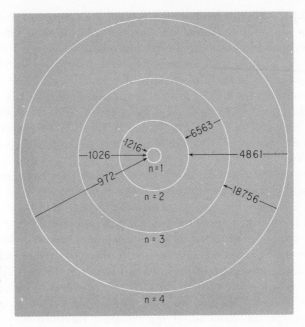

FIG. 33-3

Orbits of the electron in a hydrogen atom, according to the Bohr theory; figures give the wavelengths produced by jumps from one orbit to another.

with a nucleus and two electrons. However, a much more satisfactory solution of the general problem followed a few years later—including a more versatile method of computing energy levels—and the attempt to use Bohr's method for heavy atoms has been abandoned.

33-4   *Quantum Emission of Radiation*

Although in a certain sense one can still say that light originates in electrical oscillations within atoms, we must base our argument on the energy level diagram in order to understand what happens when an atom emits light. In an electrical discharge in a gas at low pressure there are electrons traveling down the tube with velocities determined by the voltage drop through which they have passed. These electrons may collide with atoms of the gas. If the kinetic energy of the electron is less than the energy difference between the first and second levels (Figs. 33-1 and 33-2), the colliding electron simply rebounds. On the other hand, if the electron has enough energy to do so, it can give some up to the atom, and *excite* the latter into the second, third, or higher level. In terms of the semiclassical Bohr model—considered as an analogue of the actual atom—we would say that the orbiting electron is "knocked out" by the collision into a larger orbit (Fig. 33-3), if the colliding electron can provide the necessary energy.

In simple cases like hydrogen or sodium the atom remains in the excited state for about 10^{-8} second on the average.[*] It then falls back into a lower level and loses energy in the process. The energy lost by the atom appears as radiation with frequency determined by the Planck principle; if the frequency is in the proper range it is visible light. The atom may fall from an excited level to its lowest, normal level all in one jump; or it may proceed in a series of steps as if its electron were descending a ladder. Thus it may give one spectrum line or it may give two or more spectrum lines in succession, each of the appropriate frequency determined by the energy loss.

If an electron traveling down the discharge tube has enough energy it can knock a valence electron out of the atom altogether when it collides, leaving a positive ion. Some other electron will then be attracted to the ion, but in combining with the latter it will probably not produce a normal atom at once. Rather it will descend the ladder of energy levels in several jumps, emitting radiation as it does so. If, therefore, the electrical discharge is sufficiently energetic to produce positive ions, there will at any given time be atoms in the tube in the right energy level to radiate any of the permitted frequencies; the tube will produce light comprising all the spectrum lines of the element. If the colliding electrons have only enough energy to cause excitation, without ionization, the discharge tube will produce a part only of the spectrum.

This theory of the excitation process—and therefore of the concept of energy levels—has been confirmed by experiments with gas discharge tubes in which the energy of the electrons is carefully controlled by controlling the voltage through which they pass before they have a chance to collide with any atoms. If the voltage is not sufficient to give the electrons the energy required for the first excitation, the tube remains dark. When the electrons have a little more than this amount of energy, the tube produces radiation with a spectrum consisting of just the one line (or pair of lines) that occurs when the atom falls from the first excited level to the normal level. As the voltage and the electron energy are increased gradually, more lines appear in the spectrum each time the energy passes another energy level of the atom. Finally, when the electrons have enough energy for ionization, the complete spectrum appears.

33-5   Quantum Numbers

If it is misleading to depict the electrons in an atom geometrically as if they were revolving in elliptical orbits, there must be some other way of classifying them. Study of spectra has shown that every energy level—

---

[*] This is estimated by a study of the spectrum from a discharge tube in which the gas is streaming past the electrodes with a known velocity; the atoms travel a certain distance after they are excited before they emit the light.

either of the single electron or of the complete atom to which the electron belongs—can be characterized by a set of four numbers, known as *quantum numbers.*

Let us consider the alkali metals with one valence electron outside closed shells (Sec. 22-7). In sodium, for example, the first two shells are filled and in the normal atom the valence electron is by itself in shell number 3; from there the electron can be excited into any previously unoccupied outer shell, corresponding to a higher energy level. The energy levels are classified as follows:

The first quantum number (n) denotes the shell in which the electron lies; it must be an integer. In the case of hydrogen it is the same as the integer n that determines the orbits and the energy levels in the Bohr model. In other cases n determines roughly the radius of the shell and the energy required to remove an electron from it.

The second number (l) determines the angular momentum of the electron with respect to the nucleus; it takes the integral values $0, 1, \ldots, n - 1$.

The third number (s) gives the intrinsic angular momentum of the electron (known as the *electron spin*); for a single electron s is always ½.

The quantum numbers l and s, which define values of angular momentum, can be treated as vectors; their resultant (j) is the fourth quantum number and defines the resultant angular momentum. For a single electron l and s can be in the same direction, giving $j = l + $ ½, or in opposite directions, giving $j = l - $ ½. In the alkali metals the two possible values of j correspond to slightly different values of the energy; the energy levels therefore occur in close pairs.°

If the atom or the free electron have angular momentum they must also have magnetic moments; in the case of sodium the electron in the free, unexcited atom has $j = $ ½ and the atom must behave as a little magnet. In a magnetic field the sodium atoms have to set themselves so that the component of angular momentum in the field direction is quantized; the atoms must lie with their magnetic moments either parallel to the field or in the opposite direction to the field. It is possible to demonstrate this effect experimentally and to measure the magnetic moments of free atoms, providing direct confirmation of the quantum number system and of the concept of electron spin.† Let sodium vapor be forced through a pair of slits so as to produce a thin stream and let this stream be passed between the poles of a magnet shaped as shown in Fig. 33-4. Atoms whose moments

° For atoms with more than one valence electron, or with incomplete inner shells, the two types of angular momentum of the electrons combine in various ways to produce resultant values for the atom as a whole. Complete shells do not contribute, because the electrons in them are arranged so that the resultant angular momentum is zero. The final quantum number (J) that corresponds to the resultant angular momentum of all the electrons is an integer if the number of electrons involved is even; an integer plus ½ if the number of electrons is odd.

† The method of measurement is known as the Stern-Gerlach experiment after the two men who originated it in 1922.

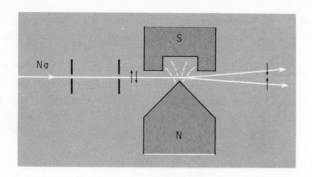

FIG. 33-4

Principle of the Stern-Gerlach experiment, showing how a stream of atoms with $J = \frac{1}{2}$ is divided by a nonuniform magnetic field into two streams with magnetic moment up and magnetic moment down.

lie parallel to the field are attracted into the strongest part of the field and move toward the wedge-shaped pole; atoms whose moments lie in the opposite direction to the field are repelled from the wedge. Therefore the stream is divided in two, each half composed of atoms with their moments lying in a definite direction.

Another important feature of the quantum number system lies in the *selection rules* that govern the *changes* in the quantum number when an atom emits radiation. For example, if an electron in an upper energy level has a choice of several lower levels to which it might jump, it nearly always chooses one such that l increases or decreases by one unit. Strong lines in the spectrum therefore correspond to changes of l by ± 1; other changes of l produce relatively weak lines if they occur at all.

33-6 Photons and the Compton Effect

In all classical and semiclassical thinking light was a wave phenomenon. This was not necessarily contradicted by the discovery of the quantum principle, for a quantum could be considered a bundle of waves having a definite energy content. It was hard to understand how all the energy of such a bundle could be concentrated on a single electron in the photoelectric effect, but a more serious dilemma arose with the discovery of the *Compton effect* by Arthur H. Compton of Washington University, St. Louis, in 1923.

The basic experimental observation was that, when X rays of frequency (f) are diffusely scattered from any material, the scattered radiation may have a frequency less than f. The change of frequency depends on the angle through which the radiation has been deviated but does not depend on the nature of the scattering material. The effect is therefore quite different from the diffuse reflection and scattering of light—where there is no change in frequency—or from fluorescence phenomena in which the scattered frequency is characteristic of the material.

Compton applied quantum theory to the newly discovered effect and succeeded in explaining it—in complete agreement with all the experimental details—as a case of a simple collision between a quantum of the X rays and an electron in the scattering material. When the X ray encounters the electron a small portion of the quantum of energy (hf) is used to set the electron free. Apart from this there is conservation of energy and momentum in the collision (Fig. 33-5), just as in a collision between two gas molecules or between two billiard balls,° and the incident X ray gives up some momentum and energy to the recoiling electron. The scattered X-ray quantum has lost energy, but it must still satisfy the first quantum principle; therefore its frequency is now f', given by

$$hf' = hf - \tfrac{1}{2}mv^2,$$

where v is the velocity of the recoil electron. Compton's theory also predicts the way in which the velocities of the electrons depend on the angle of recoil; this also has been duly confirmed by experiment.

In the Compton effect the quantum of the incident X rays exhibits the characteristics of a material particle; in particular, it possesses the most fundamental property of a particle—it is located at a definite point and follows a definite path. Still the *scattered* X ray behaves as a wave; it shows diffraction and interference effects by means of which its wavelength can be measured and its frequency deduced. The only possible conclusion is that *X rays have both wavelike and particle-like properties;* the same must be true of light and even of radio waves, for these differ from X rays only in the ranges of frequency and wavelength involved. When the particle-like properties of electromagnetic radiation are in evidence, rather than the wavelike properties, it is usual to speak of the quantum as a *photon.*

° Compton had to use the relativistic expressions for the momentum and energy (Sec. 33-11) in order to get the correct results.

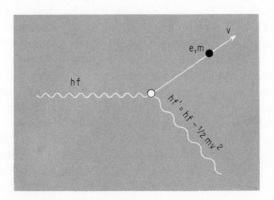

FIG. 33-5

Collision between an X-ray photon and a free electron.

If light waves have certain particle-like properties, perhaps electrons have wavelike properties. This idea occurred to a French physicist, Louis de Broglie, in 1924; when he followed it up he came to the conclusion that, if a cathode-ray electron was to be treated in some respects as a traveling wave, then the orbiting electron in the Bohr model of the atom could be treated as a standing wave. If the electron was assumed to have a wavelength given by

$$\lambda = \frac{h}{mv},$$

where mv is the momentum, then the successive Bohr orbits would contain exactly 1, 2, 3, . . . electron wavelengths in the circumference; the head of one wave would fit precisely onto the tail of the previous wave. De Broglie's assumption did not provide a final answer to the puzzle of the radiation of light energy—or of the electronic structure of atoms—but it was an important step forward. It provided an alternative basis for the *ad hoc* assumptions that Bohr had had to make in order to calculate the energy levels. The assumptions could now be stated as follows: The permitted electron orbits are those in which the electron behaves as a standing wave; standing electron waves do not radiate energy.

We shall see later how de Broglie's idea was followed up in developing the modern theory of the atom (Sec. 35-3). The suggestion had another more direct and more immediate result for it was easy to make a test. According to de Broglie's relation, cathode-ray electrons, produced in a tube with a reasonable voltage, should have wavelengths in the X-ray range. Therefore, if the idea is correct, cathode rays should produce diffraction patterns similar to those produced by X rays. The experiment was promptly tried—by C. J. Davisson and L. H. Germer in the United States, and by James Chadwick in England; Fig. 33-6 shows a typical result. This photograph was obtained by allowing a fine beam of cathode rays to be reflected from a metal film containing a large number of small crystals and then to let it fall on a photographic plate to be recorded. The pattern of rings is exactly the same as that produced by X rays of equivalent wavelength under similar circumstances.

This and similar experiments provide the proof that de Broglie's basic idea is correct and that electrons, which had previously been treated as material particles, do indeed have wavelike properties with a wavelength given by de Broglie's relation. Later it was found that the concept of matter waves had to be extended to protons and neutrons—in fact to any particle of atomic dimensions. At the same time the concept of photons has had to be extended to all kinds of waves. Therefore there is a funda-

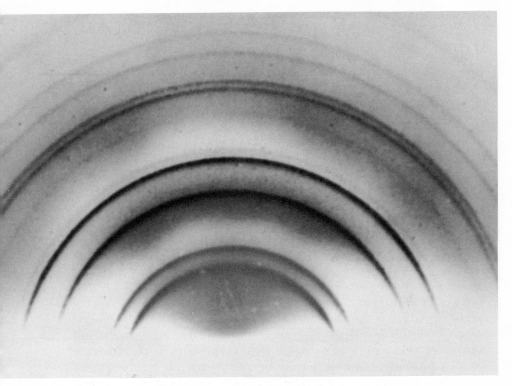

FIG. 33-6

Diffraction pattern produced by electrons reflected from a thin film of aluminum. (Photograph by S. S. Sheinin, University of Alberta.)

mental duality in nature, whereby all those things that appear at first sight to be discontinuous units of *either* mass or energy have *both* wavelike and particle-like properties.

33-8   Masers and Lasers

An ingenious practical application of the principles of quanta and energy levels, with far-reaching possibilities, has added to our vocabulary two new words that are rapidly coming into general use. One of them, *maser*, stands for "Microwave Amplification by Stimulated Emission of Radiation."

Conventional amplifier circuits, using radio tubes or transistors, are "noisy." In an ordinary radio tube, using electrons evaporated from a hot filament by thermionic emission, the electrons are ejected at random intervals with random velocities; the current in the circuit is always subject to

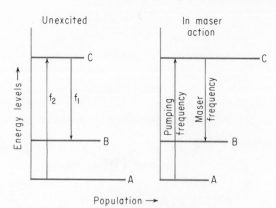

FIG. 33-7

An arrangement of energy levels that can produce amplification by maser action.

minute irregular fluctuations that produce unwanted noise in a receiver. Unless the oscillations produced in the circuit by an incoming signal are greater than the random fluctuations produced by the electrons, the signal can never be distinguished from the noise—no matter how much it is amplified—for the noise is amplified also.

The maser, using an entirely different principle of amplification, is almost completely free from noise; it can therefore be used to detect and amplify minute, high-frequency signals that would be masked by the noise in a conventional receiver. It can also be used in the very high frequency (microwave) range, where conventional circuits are impractical. Suppose we have a material containing atoms or molecules that have three energy levels (a, b, c, Fig. 33-7) separated by frequencies in the microwave range. Normally there will be atoms in all three levels because the populations of the levels are maintained by interchange of excitation energy with the heat content of the material; the number will be greatest in the lowest level, as indicated by the lengths of the lines in the left-hand diagram. Now let radiation of frequency (f_1), corresponding to the transition cb, fall on the material. Atoms in level b will absorb this radiation and be raised to c; at the same time atoms already in c will be stimulated to emit radiation in greater numbers than normal, and will fall back to b in doing so. Normally, because there are more atoms in b than in c, there is a net absorption of the incident radiation.

The secret of the maser is to maintain a population in level c greater than the normal population in b; this is done by exposing the material to radiation of frequency (f_2) corresponding to the transition ac; atoms are "pumped" into level c, producing the relative populations shown in the right-hand diagram. When this is the case the stimulated emission of frequency (f_1) exceeds the absorption and the number of quanta of this frequency is increased; the incoming radiation is amplified.

Maser action was first demonstrated at the Bell Telephone Company laboratories in 1954, using ammonia gas as the active material. However, in ammonia the energy levels involved are fixed properties of the molecule; the maser frequency (f_1) is fixed and the amplifying device cannot be tuned to different frequencies. One of the most useful maser materials is synthetic ruby, in which the separation of three low-lying energy levels is caused by the action of a magnetic field on chromium atoms, and the frequencies can be varied by adjusting the field strength. There is still a little noise in the ouput of a maser, caused by random, spontaneous transitions from c to b. These can be greatly reduced in number by keeping the ruby crystal cold. One possible use for the maser—already being exploited—is the detection of short radio waves coming from galaxies in the outer limits of the observable cosmos, using a ruby crystal cooled by liquid helium.

Theoretically, there is no upper limit to the frequency at which maser action can be effective; it soon occurred to the Bell Telephone scientists that masers might be useful in the infrared frequency range—possibly even for visible light. Thus the idea of the *laser* (Light Amplification by Stimulated Emission of Radiation) was born. The first successful laser was constructed in 1960 and since then laboratories all over the world have been experimenting with them. The almost fantastic possibilities for the use of laser beams arise from the fact that the radiation is *coherent*. In an ordinary light source quanta emitted by different atoms are radiated in different directions and have slightly different frequencies even in the case of a line spectrum; different quanta are completely unrelated and the radiation is said to be *incoherent*. In maser or laser action the stimulated radiation is in exactly the same direction as the incident radiation and the vibrations are in the same phase; all the emitted quanta combine to produce one coherent wave.

In a typical laser source (Fig. 33-8) the light is reflected back and forth between two parallel mirrors, one of which is slightly transparent. From

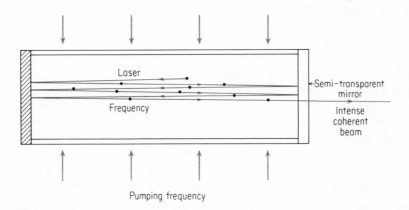

FIG. 33-8

Illustrating the principle of the laser. The laser frequency is amplified each time the beam encounters an excited atom.

time to time an atom in the upper excited level (*c*, Fig. 33-7) makes a natural transition to level *b* and emits a quantum in the direction at right angles to the mirrors. This stimulates more quanta by laser action—also traveling at right angles to the mirrors—and every time the beam is reflected the number of quanta is increased still further. Some of the light escapes through the partially silvered mirror and the device emits a coherent light wave consisting of many quanta, all in phase and all very nearly parallel. Because the wave is coherent it can be projected as a narrow beam to great distances, or all its energy can be focused by a lens onto one tiny spot, producing a concentration of heat that will vaporize any known material almost instantly.

33-9   The Relativity Principle

In 1905 Albert Einstein, then at Zurich,[*] developed the first part of his famous theory of relativity. The basic principle of relativity is quite simple:

All experimenters everywhere—if they make their observations and deductions correctly—should arrive at the same physical laws.

In particular, if two observers study the same set of events while they are moving relative to each other, their measurements of velocity and acceleration, of electrical and other quantities will necessarily yield different numerical values, but the laws connecting the measured quantities must have the same mathematical form.

In order to apply this principle and to develop from it a consistent theory, we imagine a fixed observer—presumably one of us—carrying out experiments in his laboratory (denoted by the coordinate system, *O*, Fig. 33-9), while another observer, located in a system *O′* that is moving past, watches what is going on. For example, we might imagine the laboratory (*O*) to be located beside a railway track, while the moving observer is riding in a train (*O′*) and catches a glimpse of the experiments as he flashes past. The man on the train goes further and attempts to measure things that he sees in the *O* laboratory; obviously he can only do this by means of the light waves emitted by objects in *O*—or possibly by radio signals. More generally, the only possible contact between *O* and *O′* is by means of electromagnetic disturbances traveling with the velocity of light—a fact that is essential to the development of the theory. It is inherent in the

[*] Albert Einstein (1879–1955) was born in Germany but received his higher education in Switzerland and for some years held a succession of appointments in that country. In 1914 he became director of the Kaiser Wilhelm Physical Institute in Berlin, and in 1933 he came to the United States as a member of the Institute for Advanced Studies at Princeton University. He was awarded the 1921 Nobel prize for physics for his theoretical work.

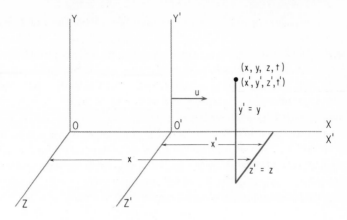

FIG. 33-9

Coordinate systems moving relative to each other with velocity
(u) in the x direction.

relativity principle that neither the man in the laboratory nor the man on
the train has any way of telling which of them is moving and which is at
rest; they know only that they are moving relative to each other. It follows also from the principle that, if an identical experiment is carried out
in a laboratory on the train, the measurements that the man beside the track
makes of things on the train must be identical with those that the man on
the train made of things beside the track.

We now ask the question: What are some of the specific results of the
measurements that the man in O makes when he uses light or radio signals
to study things that are stationary in O' and are therefore moving past? To
answer the question we set up clocks and axes of coordinates in both O'
and in O; we then carry out a *transformation of coordinates* from O' to O.
An event occurs in the O' system at the point (x', y', z') and at the time (t')
as determined by the O' clock; the same event is seen by the observer in O
to happen at the point (x, y, z) at the time (t) as determined by his own
coordinates and clock. The transformation is the mathematical relation
between (x', y', z', t') and (x, y, z, t); by its use we can determine how
events that are happening in O' appear to the observer in O.

We can now put the relativity principle in a more specific form, more
useful for computation:

**If the mathematical expression of a physical law is trans-
formed from one system of coordinates to another system
that is moving relative to the first, the form of the expression
must be unchanged (must be *invariant*). It is a crucial test
of the universal validity of a law that it should satisfy this
condition.**

33-10   *The Special Theory of Relativity*

In the theory published in 1905 Einstein—due to mathematical difficulties —was able to solve the problem only for the special case where the two systems (O and O') are moving relative to each other with a constant velocity in a straight line; this form of the theory is therefore known as the *special* or *restricted relativity theory.*

To simplify the calculation we take the axes of coordinates in the two systems parallel to each other; we take the common x axis in the direction of the relative velocity (u) (Fig. 33-9); we count time in both systems from the instant when the origins of coordinates passed each other. Straightforward geometrical considerations suggest that we should have

$$x' = x - ut, \quad y' = y, \, z' = z;$$

time should be the same in both systems ($t' = t$). If we use this set of relations to transform events from the O' system to the O system, Newton's laws of motion and the law of gravitation retain their algebraic forms, but Maxwell's laws of electricity and magnetism do not. The two sets of laws cannot both be valid; one set or the other must be limited in its range of application.

If the transformation given above is correct, a light signal emitted by a source in O' should appear to the observer in O to have a different velocity in the x direction from that in the y or z directions. However, Michelson and Morley had found that the velocity of light is the same in all directions, regardless of the earth's motion (Sec. 20-3). Einstein therefore took the propagation of light by electromagnetic waves to be an example of a universally valid principle, and assumed:

The velocity of electromagnetic waves in vacuum is a universal constant, the same for all observers and independent of any relative motion of the source with respect to the observer.

If observers in O and O' both measure the velocity of a light or radio signal emitted by a given source, they must get identical results, regardless of the system in which the source is located.

By arguing about the light signals that the observer in O must use in order to study objects in O'—using the principle that *the velocity of light is invariant*—Einstein derived the transformation:

$$\left. \begin{aligned} x' &= \gamma(x - ut), \\ y' &= y, \, z' = z, \\ t' &= \gamma\left(t - \frac{ux}{c^2}\right), \end{aligned} \right\}$$

where $\gamma = \dfrac{1}{\sqrt{1 - u^2/c^2}}$

and c is the velocity of light.

This transformation preserves the form of Maxwell's laws;* therefore these laws are universally valid and Newton's laws require modification, although the errors made by using them for calculations are appreciable only when velocities comparable with the velocity of light are involved.

33-11   Some Deductions from the Special Theory

The important predictions of the special theory of relativity concern bodies moving with high velocities. They are derived by applying the Lorentz transformation to events occurring in the O' system, in order to find out how they will appear to an observer in O. We quote some of the results without proof:

A rod of true length L—as measured by an observer in whose system the rod is at rest—when it is moving past the observer with velocity (u) appears to be contracted and to have a length $L\sqrt{1 - u^2/c^2}$.

An occurrence that requires a *proper time* (T) in its own system appears when it is moving to take an expanded time: $T/\sqrt{1 - u^2/c^2}$. A moving clock therefore appears to run slow.†

A particle whose *rest mass* is m_0—measured in the system where the particle is at rest—appears when it is moving with a speed (u) to have an effective mass $m_0/\sqrt{1 - u^2/c^2}$. This is confirmed by experiments with electrons traveling with very high velocities.

The momentum of the particle is $m_0 u/\sqrt{1 - u^2/c^2}$ and its kinetic energy is $m_0 c^2[(1/\sqrt{1 - u^2/c^2}) - 1]$. This leads to the principle that mass and energy are mutually convertible (Sec. 8-4), and is also abundantly confirmed by experiment. Since the effective mass and the kinetic energy become infinite when $u = c$, it follows that it would require an infinite amount of work to accelerate a mass particle to a velocity equal to that of light.

For photons and neutrinos, which have no rest mass and always travel with velocity (c), the momentum is equal to energy divided by c. This is confirmed by experiments on the Compton effect and on nuclear reactions.

---

* H. A. Lorentz had shown a few years earlier that this transformation preserves the form of Maxwell's equations; the group of relations is therefore known as a *Lorentz transformation*.

† This result is the origin of the famous relativity paradox. A man travels through space with a speed of ⁹⁄₁₀ of the velocity of light for 10 years—as measured by his own clock—and he has aged accordingly. We think he has been away for 22 years and are amazed at his comparatively youthful appearance. However, he must make the same observations of us as we make of him. Who is right about the other person's rate of aging? The catch is that he must have been subject to acceleration when he turned around to come home; therefore special relativity does not apply. The paradox does not arise in the general relativity theory, where accelerations are permitted.

33-12   The General Theory

We shall close this chapter with a brief reference to the *general theory of relativity,* which Einstein published in 1915 and in which he was able to take account of gravitation as well as of systems that are moving relative to each other in any manner whatever. The new theory had features that the scientific world found hard to accept, but the difficulties were greatly exaggerated in the public imagination. Some of the results appear to contradict common sense, but so do a number of other modern scientific findings. The difficulty in the theory arose from the fact that Einstein had to use an unusual mathematical technique for which there had previously been no practical uses and which was familiar only to a very few specialists at the time the relativity theory was published.

In order to see how the relativity principle applies when there is a relative acceleration between the two systems, let us think of a space vehicle orbiting the earth with an astronaut on board; we suppose that he cannot see the earth below him, but he can see the stars and so he can trace his path through the cosmos. From our point of view both the astronaut and the capsule in which he is riding are subject to the gravitational attraction of the earth; they are in a gravitational field in which they are both describing the same elliptical orbit with the same accelerations. From the point of view of the astronaut, he is at rest relative to the walls of his capsule with no tendency to acceleration; he experiences the sensation of weightlessness and is not conscious of any forces acting upon his body. However, because he can see the stars, he is aware that he is traveling a curved path in the cosmos. By transforming to a system in which the axes of coordinates are curved—relative to the cosmos—the gravitational field of the earth has been eliminated.

In the mathematical treatment of the problem it is necessary to use in place of the time (t) the quantity $\sqrt{-1} \cdot ct$ and to use this quantity in the same way as the space coordinates; the four coordinates of *space-time* are treated as if they formed a four-dimensional space.° By a suitable transformation of coordinates a gravitational field can be converted into a curvature of space-time, the degree of curvature depending on the concentration of mass in the vicinity. Newton's law of gravitation is therefore replaced by a law connecting the apparent curvature of space-time with the masses in the neighborhood. However, the result is the same to a very

° Much has been made of the apparent equivalence of the timelike fourth dimension to the three spacelike dimensions. Under certain circumstances two events that are separated in time in one system can appear to be separated in space in a different system, but in general the four-dimensional space-time is a mathematical device. Much has also been made of the curvature of space-time under the supposition that the curves are closed, so that a particle setting out on a journey through the cosmos would eventually return to its starting point. This is still an open question; the cosmos could be finite and contain a finite quantity of matter; it could be infinite (cf. Sec. 31-8).

close approximation; the earth still describes an elliptical orbit in the sun's coordinate system. In most cases computations based on the theory of general relativity agree with those based upon Newton's laws within the limits of accuracy of the observations.

We shall not discuss the theory further, but merely quote three cases where general relativity predicts results that are measurably different from those of classical physics:

For the planet Mercury the relativistic orbit differs slightly from a true ellipse; the result is that the ellipse as a whole appears to rotate around the sun at a rate of 43 seconds of arc per century.

On account of the curvature of space-time, rays of light passing very close to the sun are deviated by about 2 seconds of arc. This can be observed at the time of a total solar eclipse; the image of a star that is very nearly in line with the sun is deflected away from the latter.

In a strong gravitational field clocks should be retarded slightly; where matter is highly concentrated atoms should emit light with a lower frequency than normal. This is observed in the spectra of white dwarf stars; the spectrum lines are shifted toward the red by an amount that cannot be accounted for by the Doppler effect.

GLOSSARY

Ad hoc assumption An assumption that is introduced into a scientific theory in order to attain a particular result.

Coherent radiation A beam of radiation in which all the waves are traveling and oscillating in the same directions, and are all in the same phase.

Compton effect The change of frequency when an X-ray photon is scattered by a collision with a free electron.

Energy level One of the permitted energy values that an atom or molecule can possess.

Energy level diagram Graph on which the permitted energy levels of an atom or molecule are displayed by horizontal lines or points plotted at heights above the base level which are proportional to the energy values.

General relativity Einstein's second relativity theory, in which no restriction is placed on the relative motion of different systems of coordinates, and in which gravitation is taken into account.

Invariant Literally, unchanged; a quantity is said to be invariant if it remains constant in value when the coordinates are transformed to a different system; an invariant law retains its mathematical form under the transformation.

Laser Light amplification by stimulated emission of radiation; a laser can be used to generate intense beams of coherent radiation (Sec. 33-8).

Maser Microwave amplification by stimulated emission of radiation; provides an amplifier of short radio waves that is almost completely free from noise, and so can be used to detect and amplify minute signals.

Planck's constant Universal constant which, when multiplied by the frequency, gives the energy in a quantum of electromagnetic radiation.

Proper time In relativity, time as measured by a clock that is moving with the observer.

Quantum Amount of energy of electromagnetic radiation that is emitted or absorbed in one event at one time, and therefore the discontinuous unit of energy in a beam of radiation; the quantum of energy is proportional to the frequency of the radiation.

Quantum numbers Set of numbers, either integers or integers plus $\frac{1}{2}$, by means of which the energy levels of an atom or molecule are classified; most of the quantum numbers are related to components of the angular momentum (Sec. 33-5).

Relativity Theory based on the proposition that all motion is relative, from which it follows that the motion of a body such as the earth cannot be detected by means of an experiment carried out entirely on the moving body, and that all experimenters should arrive at the same scientific laws, regardless of their state of motion.

Rest mass Mass of a particle as determined by means of an instrument relative to which the particle is at rest.

Selection rules Rules that state the normal changes of quantum number that occur when an atom or molecule emits radiation; hence the rules give the strong lines in the spectrum.

Space-time Four-dimensional coordinate system in which the time of an event is treated on the same basis as the space coordinates that give its location; required for the mathematical formulation of general relativity.

Special relativity Einstein's first relativity theory, in which the relative motion of different systems of coordinates was restricted to constant velocity in a straight line.

Transformation In mathematics, the set of relations connecting the coordinates of two different systems.

1. Explain how the hypothesis that light is emitted and absorbed in discontinuous quanta accounts for the empirical laws of the photoelectric effect.

2. Explain how under some circumstances a photoelectric cell can carry a current in the opposite direction to the applied voltage. What are the limiting circumstances under which this reverse current can exist?

3. Given that the photoelectric threshold of a certain metal is at a wavelength of 8000 Å, calculate: (a) the work done by an electron in escaping from the metal, in joules and in electron-volts; (b) the kinetic energy with which electrons are released under the influence of light of wavelength 5800 Å; (c) the maximum velocity of the electrons in (b); (d) the number of photoelectrons, and the current through the cell if it is receiving 1 watt of this light.

4. Given that the red line in the spectrum of the hydrogen atom has a frequency of 4.553×10^{14}, calculate the frequencies of the three next lines in the visible spectrum.

5. Describe the processes of excitation and of emission of quanta of radiation by atoms.

6. Describe briefly an experiment that provides direct confirmation of the processes referred to in Exercise 5.

7. State the assumptions made by Bohr in his theory of the hydrogen atom. Which of these were of an *ad hoc* nature?

8. Describe an experimental method of measuring the magnetic moments of atoms. What theoretical conclusions are confirmed by experiments of this type?

9. What is the Compton effect, and what does it demonstrate?

10. Calculate the wavelength of electrons that have been accelerated by a potential of 100 volts. Make the same calculation for protons.

11. Describe briefly some of the practical uses of masers.

12. Explain how a laser produces an intense coherent beam of light.

13. State the basic principle of the theory of relativity, and explain how it is applied in the special theory of relativity.

14. Why did Einstein take the propagation of light with a definite velocity in vacuum as the first example of an invariant law?

15. List the important deductions from the special theory of relativity. Which of these deductions have been confirmed by experiment?

16. Calculate the apparent mass that 1 kilogram would have if it were moving past with a velocity of 2.4×10^8 meters per second.

17. Calculate the kinetic energy in joules of the mass in Exercise 16, and compare the result with (a) the apparent increase of mass, (b) the kinetic energy calculated according to the method of Newtonian mechanics.

18. Calculate the apparent length of a meterstick that is moving past with a velocity of 1.8×10^8 meters per second.

CHAPTER **34** **mysterious rays, strange particles, and antimatter**

34-1 Cosmic Rays

In 1908 it was discovered that the earth is continually receiving a very penetrating radiation, which can cause ionization even after passing through several hundred feet of water in a deep lake. The radiation is certainly coming from outside the atmosphere, for its intensity increases upward— on a high mountain top or in a balloon flight. At ground level it seems to be coming indiscriminately from all directions and is a mixture of many things: high-energy gamma-ray photons, neutrons, electrons, and other charged particles, both positive and negative. These produce all together an energy equal to about one-tenth of total starlight. The mixture observed at ground level made it very difficult to decide which of the many things was *primary* and was actually coming from outer space. For a long time, therefore, the true nature and the source of the radiation were mysterious; the rays became known simply as *cosmic radiation*, implying a source somewhere in the cosmos.

574

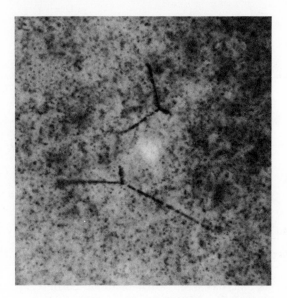

FIG. 34-1

Forked tracks caused by nuclear reactions taking place in a photographic emulsion, enlarged about 2000 times. (Photograph courtesy of L. H. Greenberg, University of Saskatchewan.)

We know a great deal more about it now, thanks largely to methods of studying single high-speed particles;° it is evident that nearly all the particles that reach the ground are produced by nuclear reactions in the atmosphere, and that the primary particles are mostly protons, along with a few nuclei of heavier atoms. When these positively charged particles approach the earth they are deflected by the earth's magnetic field; particles of small energy are deflected completely away from the earth and never reach the lower layers of the atmosphere where they might cause reactions to take place. This effect is greatest at the magnetic equator with the result that the intensity of cosmic radiation varies with magnetic latitude; it is a minimum at the equator and a nearly uniform maximum from 60° to the poles. From the latitude variation it is deduced that 90 per cent of the primary particles have energies greater than 10 billion electron-volts.

Sometimes the reactions produced by a primary particle can multiply as shown in Fig. 34-2 and produce a *shower* of electrons and other particles. The fact that an array of Geiger counters—distributed over an area of 100 square meters—are all discharged simultaneously demonstrates that all the particles in the shower are produced by a single primary. Showers containing over a thousand secondary particles have been observed; the primaries that cause such showers must have energies of at least 10^{16} electron-volts.

° Another method of detection of high-speed charged particles is by means of tracks left in a photographic emulsion. Figure 34-1 is the result of a collision between a high-speed particle and an atom in the film, causing a nuclear reaction. The method is particularly useful for observations of cosmic rays at very great altitudes, for film can be sent up in balloons or rockets.

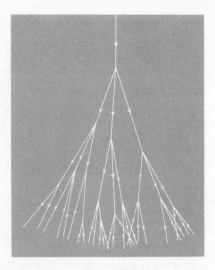

FIG. 34-2

How a cosmic ray shower develops.

With all that has been learned about cosmic rays, there are several mysteries still to be solved. It appears that at least some of the primary particles must come from the sun which is known to eject bursts of ionized gas from time to time—in so-called solar flares—for the flares affect the cosmic-ray intensity a few hours later. However, the particles from the sun cannot have followed a direct path in their journey for they enter the earth's atmosphere from all directions; they must have been deflected by magnetic fields along the way. Did all the cosmic-ray primaries come from the sun originally? Have some of them been wandering around in the solar system for years before hitting the earth? Have some come from other stars in the Galaxy—even from other galaxies? Could they be remnants of a star that destroyed itself in a supernova explosion? Finally—wherever they came from—how did they acquire the tremendous energies that have been observed? Electromagnetic fields in space must have subjected them to a step-by-step acceleration like that in a big particle accelerator; just where and how the acceleration could have occurred is still a mystery. Speculation about the origin of cosmic rays is rife among astronomers and physicists, but nothing is yet certain. However mysterious the source of the rays may be, study of the effects they produce once they enter the atmosphere has led to some basic discoveries in the field of atomic and nuclear physics, as we shall see in succeeding sections of this chapter.

34-2   Mesons

In 1935 a Japanese theoretical physicist, Hideki Yukawa, developed a theory of nuclear forces that required the existence of a previously unknown particle to act as a sort of cement holding the protons and neutrons together in spite of the electrostatic repulsion between the positively charged protons. Yukawa's theoretical particle would have to have a mass about 250 times that of the electron and so he christened it *meson*—middle thing—something between an electron and a proton. Mesons inside a nucleus would not contribute to the mass of the latter, for their mass would be converted into the potential energy of the nuclear forces, but they might—under some circumstances—be ejected from the nucleus.

During the next 2 or 3 years charged particles of intermediate mass began to be found in the mixture produced when cosmic rays pass through a large thickness of matter. Both positive and negative particles were observed, and later measurements gave the mass of both as 206.8 electron masses; the charges are precisely the same as those of the electron and positron. At first it seemed natural to assume that these were the particles predicted by Yukawa and they were assigned the symbol μ for meson; they are now known as μ-mesons or muons. However, it was soon realized that they could not fulfill the role of nuclear cement, for they were highly penetrating and usually passed through large thicknesses of matter without causing any effects other than electrostatic attractions and repulsions. Eventually they decayed spontaneously—after an average lifetime of 2.2×10^{-6} second—the μ^- into an electron and a neutrino, μ^+ into a positron and a neutrino.

Yukawa's particle must be something that reacts strongly with nuclei, causing nuclear reactions and particularly the conversion of a proton into a neutron or vice versa. If it ever exists as a free particle it must have a very short lifetime. Finally in 1947 it was found by a group studying cosmic ray effects in England that the μ-meson is itself the product of the spontaneous decay of a somewhat heavier particle, now known as a π-meson or pion, and Yukawa's particle was found.° Pions can be either positive or negative; they have a mass equal to 273 electrons; they decay with an average life of 2.6×10^{-8} second. There is also a neutral, uncharged pion—denoted by $\pi°$—which is even better fitted to fulfill Yukawa's requirements. It has a mass equal to 268 electrons and lasts in the free state only some 10^{-16} second, decaying either into a pair of gamma-ray photons or into a positron-electron pair.

This by no means ends the story of mesons, for more types are continually being found, and nobody knows whether we yet have them all. There is the rather mysterious group of K's, positive, negative, and two distinct neutral particles, with masses 967 to 974 electrons. They decay into pions and muons and seem—like the pions—to have something to do with nuclear forces and the inducing of nuclear reactions, in a way that is far

---

° This is the third case we have encountered where an elementary particle has been needed to fill a gap in a theory and has later been found actually to exist. We have had Dirac's positron (Sec. 23-9), Pauli's neutrino (Sec. 23-10), and now Yukawa's meson.

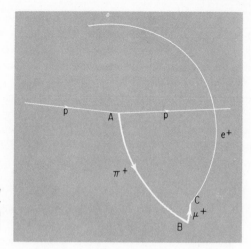

FIG. 34-3

Tracks in a liquid hydrogen bubble chamber, produced by meson reactions. (Drawn from a photograph taken at the Brookhaven National Laboratory.)

from being understood. There are the evanescent η, ρ, and ω, which have masses between that of a K-meson and that of a proton, but which live only some 10^{-23} second. They should probably be considered as excited energy levels of lighter particles, the energy of excitation appearing temporarily as an apparent added mass. There are even some which are heavier than the proton, but which are classed as excited mesons on account of their modes of decay and other properties.

How do we know what we do about the properties of all these particles? Information is, of course, pieced together from many different clues that we cannot discuss in detail, but a great deal of it comes from the study of tracks left in cloud chambers, bubble chambers, and photographic plates. For example, Fig. 34-3 is drawn from a photograph of an event that occurred in the liquid hydrogen bubble chamber at Brookhaven National Laboratory, when the chamber was placed in a strong magnetic field and bombarded with high-energy protons from an accelerator. At A an incoming proton (p) collided with a fixed proton of the liquid hydrogen and one of them was converted into a neutron plus a positive pion (π^+). The meson is identified by the density of bubbles along its track (AB), and its momentum and kinetic energy are determined from the curvature of this track. The neutron passed out of the chamber at the top without doing anything; its presence is inferred from the law of conservation of momentum. At B the pion decayed into a muon (μ^+) and a neutrino. The muon traveled only a very short distance (BC), and so lasted only a very short time, before it decayed in its turn into a positron [which left the long curved track (e), thinly marked in the original photograph] and a neutrino.

The reader will have noticed that the charged single particles (that is, particles which are not clearly composite like heavy nuclei) can occur with either sign of charge. To the electron there corresponds the positron; μ-mesons and charged π- and K-mesons are found with both signs of charge. Very careful measurements of the masses of the positron and of the charged mesons—using the method of magnetic deflections and taking into account the conservation of momentum—have failed to show any difference in mass between the electron and the positron or between positive and negative mesons. In the case of the mesons, the average lifetime seems also to be the same for both positive and negative particles. The conclusion is that all these charged particles exist in complementary pairs—identical except for the sign of their charge and possibly for the direction of spin if they happen to have intrinsic angular momentum. As we express it today, for each particle there is an *antiparticle* of opposite charge.

The question immediately arises: Is this true also for protons? Is there such a thing as an antiproton, identical with the ordinary proton in everything except that it has a negative charge? None had ever been observed in cosmic rays,* but it was well known that positron-electron pairs can be produced by gamma-ray photons of sufficiently high energy. Perhaps a proton-antiproton pair could be produced by a similar conversion of kinetic energy into mass, but the amount of energy required would be very much greater. Not only would it take the energy equivalent of the mass created ($2Mc^2$, where M is the mass of a proton and c is the velocity of light) but the two new particles would have to have a high enough velocity to carry away the momentum of the bombarding particle; about 6 billion electron-volts are required in all.

The first particle accelerator capable of producing energies of this magnitude—the bevatron† at the University of California—went into operation in 1954, and one of the first tasks assigned to it was a search for antiprotons. Chamberlain and Segrè at that laboratory set up an ingenious system to sort out antiprotons from the thousands of other negative particles that are produced in the machine. Their method is illustrated schematically in Fig. 34-4. A beam containing a mixture of all sorts of things is produced by bombarding a target (T) with protons of known energy. A large magnet (M) selects negative particles that have the correct momentum for the

---

* The positron and the antiproton are stable against spontaneous decay, but are instantly annihilated when they collide with their respective antiparticles. It is likely that antiprotons are sometimes formed by cosmic-ray bombardment and that some of the bursts of energy that have been observed in the study of cosmic rays are due to mutual annihilation of an antiproton and a proton, but this has not been proved.

† After Bev, the abbreviation for a billion electron-volts.

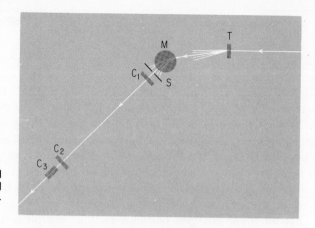

FIG. 34-4

Illustrating the method used by Chamberlain and Segrè to prove the existence of antiprotons.

expected antiprotons and deflects them through a slit (S) onto a counter (C_1). At this stage the beam still consists mainly of negative mesons, but the mesons are traveling with velocities very close to that of light, while the antiprotons would have a velocity of only $0.78c$. To eliminate the mesons a second counter (C_2) was placed about 12 meters away from C_1; mesons would travel the distance C_1C_2 in 40 nanoseconds, while antiprotons would take 51 nanoseconds. It was still possible that one meson might trip C_1 and a different meson trip C_2 just 51 nanoseconds later. To eliminate this a scintillation counter (C_3)—of a special type that responds only to particles whose velocities are close to that of light—was inserted in the path; mesons would trip this counter but antiprotons would not. Thus, if any antiprotons were being produced by the bombarding beam in the bevatron, they would be deflected through the slit, trip C_1, trip C_2 51 nanoseconds later, and *not* trip C_3; the chance of this sequence being produced in any other way was infinitesimal. The result of the experiment was reported in 1955; there were indeed proton-antiproton pairs produced whenever the bombarding particles had sufficient energy, but there were only 2 antiprotons, on the average, in every 100,000 negative particles coming from the accelerator.

When the existence of antiprotons was demonstrated it became evident that for every charged elementary particle there is a complementary antiparticle of the opposite sign. The antiparticle also has the opposite direction of "spin" relative to the direction in which it is traveling. Therefore it is possible to have neutral, uncharged pairs of particles and antiparticles; these have now been identified in most cases where the particles have intrinsic angular momentum. Neutral antiparticles are recognized by their modes of decay or of production and by the angular momentum relations involved in the transformations. For example, neutrons decay into protons and negative electrons; antineutrons decay into antiprotons and positrons, and the result is made evident when the antiproton combines with a positive proton and the pair annihilate each other in a burst of energy. The neutrinos produced when a radioactive nucleus ejects a negative beta-ray electron have angular momentum as if they were spinning counterclockwise around the direction of travel; antineutrinos accompany the ejection of positrons and spin in the opposite direction.°

34-4   Hyperons

Single particles with masses greater than that of a proton are known as *hyperons*, from the Greek word *hyper*, above. The first hyperon known was found in 1947 among the tracks produced by cosmic rays passing through a cloud chamber. What was actually seen was a pair of tracks coming from a single point within the chamber, so that the photograph looked like the Greek letter Λ (Fig. 34-5). These tracks were identified as those of a proton and a negative pion. Both particles were traveling in a generally downward direction and carried a large amount of downward momentum; the horizontal momenta were equal and opposite. It followed that the two particles that had been seen must have been produced by the decay of a neutral particle which had entered the chamber from above, but which had left no track because it was uncharged. From the total momentum carried it was deduced that the invisible particle must have had a mass some 20 per cent greater than that of the proton; it was christened "Λ°-hyperon." It must also have had spin number ½ in order to provide the spin of the proton; the pion has no spin.

The Λ-particles—like mesons and like the host of new particles that soon followed—decay by the conversion of mass into energy or are created by the reverse conversion of energy into mass. Therefore it is convenient to express their masses in energy units; they are nowadays usually expressed

° The neutrinos that were detected experimentally at Los Alamos were actually antineutrinos.

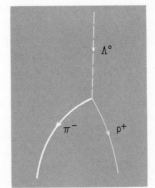

FIG. 34-5

Illustrating the type of track produced in a cloud chamber when a Λ°-hyperon decays into a proton and a pion; the broken line indicates the path of the uncharged Λ° which leaves no visible track.

in million electron-volts. On this scale the proton has a mass-energy equivalent of 937.8, the neutron 939.1 million electron-volts; a precise measurement of the momentum of the Λ-hyperon gave its mass as 1115 million electron-volts.

Since 1950 hardly a year has gone by without the discovery of new hyperons—at first in the cosmic ray mixture and lately as products of bombardment in accelerators that are capable of producing energies of several billion electron-volts. There is an "antilambda" ($\overline{\Lambda}°$) which decays into an antiproton and a positron. There is a group of three "sigmas" (Σ) —positive, neutral, and negative—which belong together because their masses differ among themselves by only 2 to 4 million electron-volts. A recently discovered group of four "deltas" (Δ)—also of nearly equal mass —includes one that carries two units of charge. For most of the known particles the corresponding antiparticles have also been observed and it is confidently expected that any missing antiparticles will soon be found. A list published early in 1964 of the particles known at that time showed 92 in all. These are first of all classified as *leptons* ("light things"), including neutrinos, electrons, and muons; then come the *mesons*, including π, K, etc.; finally the *baryons* ("heavy things"), which include protons, neutrons, and hyperons. The list is probably still incomplete and is not being reproduced here.

34-5   *Four Categories of Interaction between Particles*

We are accustomed to thinking of two types of force: contact force such as that we exert with our hands if we have to push a car that is stuck in the mud, and action at a distance such as the gravitational attraction of the sun for the earth, the force on a falling stone, or the electrostatic attraction between opposite charges. Actually there is no such thing as a contact force. What we feel when we push a car is the electromagnetic repulsion between the electrons belonging to the atoms in our hands and the electrons belonging to the metal of the car. On the microscopic, atomic scale all forces are *actions at a distance;* physicists have recently learned to categorize these into four distinct classes, depending on the order of magnitude of the energy involved.

The two categories with which we have long been familiar are gravitational and electromagnetic forces. (We group electrostatic and magnetic forces together, because the latter are simply the result of electric charges in motion.) Let us compare the gravitational attraction between a pair of protons with the electrostatic repulsion between them—because we are going to consider nuclear binding forces as another category let us assume the two protons to be separated by a distance $r = 10^{-15}$ meter, comparable with the diameter of a compound nucleus. The gravitational attraction is given by GM^2/r^2, where G is the constant of universal gravitation and M is the mass of a proton; this amounts to approximately 2×10^{-34} newton. Similarly, the electrostatic force—by Coulomb's law—is $9 \times 10^9 \cdot e^2/r^2$, where e is the electron charge; this is about 200 newtons. The two types of force vary in the same way with distance—proportional to $1/r^2$—but for charged atomic particles the electromagnetic forces are some 10^{36} times the gravitational forces. Gravitation predominates on the macroscopic scale because, on the whole, matter is electrically neutral and the electromagnetic forces cancel out.

Less familiar are the nuclear binding forces and the forces involved in nuclear reactions. They can be detected—apart from their obvious existence in compound nuclei—by experiments in which a beam of neutrons is passed through hydrogen so that some of the neutrons are deflected by close encounters with protons, but it has not been possible so far to derive a specific law, analogous to Coulomb's law. However, it is clear from this and other experiments that nuclear attractions are not contact forces, but that they also are actions at a distance, although the force decreases very rapidly with increasing distance and is ineffective at distances a little more than the diameter of a nucleus. We cannot calculate the actual force of attraction between the two protons of our example above, to compare it with the electrostatic repulsion, but we can estimate the potential energy of the attractive force. This is roughly the energy equivalent of the mass of a π-meson plus the mass lost by the two protons when they are inside a compound nucleus; it works out to about 30 million electron-volts. In comparison, the potential energy of the electrostatic repulsion is 1.4 million electron-volts. Within their effective range, therefore, nuclear attractions are some 20 times the electromagnetic forces, as they must be in order to produce stable nuclei. They have become known to physicists as the *strong interactions*.

Now, to each of these categories of force there corresponds a type of radiation—or rather a category of quantum transitions or radioactive decay.° To the electromagnetic forces correspond the transitions between the energy levels of an atom or the emission of a gamma ray from an excited nucleus. To the strongly interacting nuclear forces correspond the decays of the very short-lived evanescent mesons and of certain of the heavier hyperons. Excited atoms, about to make an electron transition and emit a spectrum line in the visible range, have a lifetime of about 10^{-8} second; for excited nuclei about to produce gamma rays the average life is much shorter; for the evanescent mesons and hyperons it is about 10^{-23} second. In all these cases the life decreases very rapidly as the strength of interaction increases.

° In this connection emission of electromagnetic radiation and radioactive transformations are classed together. They both represent transitions in which a definite amount of energy is exchanged, and so involve the quantum feature.

Following up this idea has led to the realization that there must be still another category of forces that act at a distance. We know of several types of quantized transition of nuclei and of single particles in which the energetic state has a much longer lifetime than that associated with either nuclear gamma rays or strongly interacting hyperons. For the decay of π- and μ-mesons and of most of the hyperons the average life is 10^{-10} to 10^{-11} second; for the decay of the neutron and for beta-ray emission from a compound nucleus it is much longer—minutes or even days. These transitions are now considered to be associated with what are known as *weak interactions*. We know practically nothing about the forces involved in a weak interaction except that, judging from the lifetime of typical interaction decays, the strength must be roughly 10^{-13} of that of the nuclear attractions.

We can now sum up the four categories of forces between particles. In order of increasing strength of interaction we have, first, *gravitational attraction*, which is very weak, but which acts between macroscopic bodies over a very long range and is then effective because it is always an attraction and the stronger forces have either canceled out or have fallen off to a negligible value. Second are the *weak interactions* whose existence is still essentially a matter of theory. Third come *electromagnetic forces*, which include the forces that bind atoms together and the forces that we usually associate with physical contact, as well as the forces between the nucleus and the electrons within an atom. Fourth and last are the *strong interactions*, the short-range forces that hold the protons and neutrons together in a compound nucleus.

34-6   Systematics and Conservation Rules

There must be some system underlying the list of particles and there must be rules governing their formation and decay. When hyperons began to be discovered there seemed to be no reason for them, and their positions in the scale of mass seemed to be completely random, but as more are found a system is beginning to emerge, just as a system was eventually found for the apparently haphazard arrangement of lines in an optical spectrum. The systematization of the particles is expressed by means of a set of numbers that are reminiscent of the quantum numbers assigned to the electrons in atoms (Sec. 33-5).

We are already familiar with the facts that single particles are found only with *electric charges* of $+e$, 0, $-e$, and (very rarely) $\pm 2e$, that the positive and negative charges are precisely equal, and that *charge is conserved* in any reaction. We have also encountered a number of times the concept of "spin" and spin number (J) and the rule that the total *spin must be conserved*, when the spin numbers are treated as vectors and combined in the same way as vectors.

The first of the new classification numbers is the *baryon number*, which is equal to the mass number (M) when compound nuclei are concerned. This is $+1$ for protons, ordinary neutrons, and hyperons; it is -1 for the corresponding antiparticles; it is 0 for particles lighter than a proton. Then, in any reaction the baryon number must remain constant; that is, *baryons are conserved*. If a proton is created in a nuclear reaction an antiproton must be created with it so that the total baryon number remains zero. Baryons are never converted into lighter particles without leaving behind at least a proton—which is the lightest of the class and the only member which is stable against spontaneous decay. Baryons can be destroyed only by collisions with antibaryons.

Along with the class of baryons there is the corresponding class of *leptons;* it includes the neutrino, the electron, and the μ^--meson as the particles of negative lepton number; the corresponding antiparticles, the antineutrino, the positron, and the μ^+-meson have positive lepton number. *Leptons*, like baryons, *are conserved*, in the sense that the net lepton number must remain constant. Single baryons and leptons both have spin ½ (or sometimes an integer plus ½), and both obey conservation rules. Photons with spin 1, and π- and K-mesons with spin 0 do not have such a rule.

The fact that the particles occur in groups with nearly equal mass has led to the assignment to each group of a number known as the *isotopic spin* (T).* An atomic energy level which has spin (J) splits into a group of $2J + 1$ sublevels, usually separated by only a small energy difference. As a sort of converse of this rule, a group of three particles is assigned isotopic spin $T = 1 (2 \times 1 + 1 = 3)$. Such a group is that of the Σ-hyperons. Particles which occur in pairs with nearly equal mass, protons and neutrons, Ξ-hyperons, are assigned $T = \frac{1}{2}$; lonely particles like the Λ-hyperon have $T = 0$; the group of four Δ-hyperons has $T = \frac{3}{2}$. Isotopic spin is *approximately conserved.* That is, it remains constant in reactions which produce hyperons and in the rapid decay associated with the strong interactions; it can change in decay reactions that have a long lifetime like those associated with the weak interactions.

The next classification number was at first known as *strangeness* (S)—another number that remains constant in the production of hyperons and in strong interaction decays, but can change in the long-lived decays. Its values are assigned on the strength of this approximate conservation rule, but it seems to have no counterpart—or even analogy—in other fields of physics and nobody knows quite what it means, hence the name "strangeness." However, for reasons of symmetry it now seems better to use in place of S a number Y which is equal to S plus the baryon number, and which is known as *hypercharge.* Y obeys the same rules as S, and can take values of 0, ±1, ±2, antiparticles having the opposite value to their corresponding particles.

* "Isotopic" because the group occupies one place in the table of masses but the members of the group differ slightly, like the isotopes of a chemical element.

Finally, there is *parity*. In the field of atomic structure the resultant angular momentum (J) associated with the energy levels of an atom takes integral values if the number of electrons concerned is even; the atom is then said to have even parity. If there are an odd number of electrons involved, the values of J are integers plus ½; the atom has odd parity. A given atom always has the same number of electrons and so all its energy levels have the same type of parity. It follows that whenever an excited level of an atom decays to a lower level—with the emission of a photon—the parity of the atom is unchanged; *parity is conserved* in all reactions associated with electromagnetic forces. Parity, odd or even, can also be assigned to the nuclei by themselves, but an excited nucleus—one that is ready to emit a gamma-ray photon—can have some odd energy levels and some even levels. The gamma-ray transition, by itself, never changes the parity; this requires the presence of a third particle.

In the field of nuclear reactions *conservation of parity* means that a reaction between two like particles (odd or even) must produce a pair of like particles, remembering that the sum of two odds is even; a reaction between an odd and an even must produce an odd and an even. For a long time it was thought that this rule is rigorous; it is always obeyed in reactions associated with the strong interactions as well as in those associated with electromagnetic forces. Now, in the mathematical expression of the quantum theory of atoms states of opposite parity are related to each other as a right hand is to a left—or as an object to its image in a mirror—so that a change of parity would be mathematically equivalent to a mirror reflection. It is easy to see that a reflection can never be changed back into a likeness of the original object—except by another reflection—no matter how much it is moved around, rotated, or turned over. Unless the object is symmetrical like the letter A, mirror reflection changes it into a different object. Conservation of parity therefore seemed to be a logical and very fundamental law. It was a development considered worthy of a Nobel prize when, in 1956, Tsung-Dao Lee and Chen-Ning Yang found that there is a change of parity when a cobalt 60 nucleus decays by the emission of a beta particle. Conservation of parity therefore does not necessarily apply to the weak interactions.

34-7 Symmetry Groups of Particles

We have noticed how mesons and hyperons fall into groups of nearly equal mass, and how this grouping has been used to assign the "isotopic spin" number (I). In 1961 Murray Gell-Mann of the California Institute of Technology and Yaval Ne'eman of Tel Aviv University in Israel independently discussed certain symmetry properties that emerge when the mass-groups are combined into larger groups according to their classification numbers. These larger groups apparently have a real significance because the arrangements can be used to predict the existence of new particles to fill gaps in the groups.

The first larger grouping brings together particles having the same values of Y and I, but different masses and different values of J. In the Gell-Mann system these are treated as "recurrences," or excited states of the same particle; they are denoted by the same Greek letter. For example, the Σ-triplet with $I = 1$, $Y = 0$, $J = \frac{1}{2}$, and average mass 1193 million electron-volts, has a recurrence in the triplet denoted as Σ^*, with $J = \frac{3}{2}$ and average mass 1385 million electron-volts. Similarly to the Ξ-pair with $J = \frac{1}{2}$ and mass 1314 million electron-volts there corresponds a Ξ^*-pair—found in 1962—with $J = \frac{3}{2}$ and mass 1530 million electron-volts.

Another manner of grouping brings together particles having the same value of J and the same parity, but different values of Y and I. It applies to mesons as well as to hyperons and it is clearly significant because the groups exhibit a symmetry of a type well known to mathematicians, analogous to the symmetry found in groups of energy levels when these are arranged according to their quantum numbers. At the same time the masses increase by approximately equal steps within each group.

There are several groups of eight, but perhaps the most interesting is the group of ten, all with $J = \frac{3}{2}$, which was only recognized when the doubly charged Δ^{++} and the Ξ^*-pair were discovered. The symmetrical nature of this group is shown in Table 34-1. When the group was noticed the Ω^--hyperon shown at the apex of the triangle had never been observed. However, the symmetry required that it should exist and that it should have a mass 146 million electron-volts greater than that of the Ξ^*-pair. At the same time the conservation rules indicated that it could be formed through strong interaction when a K^--meson of sufficiently high energy reacted with a proton. A system of magnets was set up at the Brookhaven National Laboratory to select K^--mesons from the mixture of particles produced in the 33 billion electron-volt accelerator and to direct these into a liquid hydrogen bubble chamber. Out of some 50,000 photographs of

TABLE   34-1   **SYMMETRY GROUP OF TEN**
HYPERONS WITH $J = \frac{3}{2}$

Hypercharge Number					Average Mass (Mev)
−2			Ω^-		1675
−1		Ξ^{*-}		Ξ^{*0}	1530
0	Σ^{*-}		Σ^{*0}	Σ^{*+}	1385
+1	Δ^-	Δ^0	Δ^+	Δ^{++}	1238

the bubble tracks taken with this arrangement, 2 showed the brief existence of a heavy negative particle with mass 1675 million electron-volts;
study of the mode of decay showed this to be the predicted Ω^--particle.

34-8   Questions

The classification of the host of newly discovered particles and their
arrangement in symmetry groups is the first step in the clarification of
their meaning, but there are still a number of problems to be solved. Why
is the electric charge always an exact multiple of the quantity e? Is this a
fundamental law, or will it someday be found to depend on a still more
fundamental property of matter or of space? How many distinctly different particles exist? For example, are all the different baryons energy states
of one fundamental entity, the proton being merely the lowest energy
level and the stable state? This seems likely, but if it is so there should be
mathematical equations—based on some fundamental law—that would
allow us to compute the masses of the particles, as we can now compute
the energy levels of an atom. What is the real significance of the new
classification numbers, particularly of the "isotopic spin" and the "hypercharge," and of Gell-Mann's symmetry groups?

These questions may be answered quite soon, perhaps within the decade,
for progress is fast. However, the amount of work still to be done—both
experimental and theoretical—is staggering. It took the combined skill and
labor of a whole laboratory team several months to prove the existence of
the antiproton or to find just two examples of the Ω^--hyperon, using a
billion-electron-volt accelerator as their primary tool.

There is another, most intriguing question, which will not be answered
by laboratory experiments because if an answer exists it lies in the depths
of space. Is there *antimatter?* In the world we know—in the Milky Way
and in other nearby galaxies—stable matter is made of positive protons,
neutrons, and negative electrons. Now, if an antiproton is identical with a
proton except for the sign of its charge and the direction of spin, there
seems to be no reason why atoms could not be made up of negative antiprotons, antineutrons, and positrons. It should then be possible for these
"antiatoms" to combine to form stable antimatter, duplicating all the
properties of the matter we know.

Atoms and antiatoms could not exist together in the same region of
space, for they would immediately annihilate each other, but what determined the fact that our galaxy is built upon protons? Is a stable antiatom
impossible, perhaps because the forces of strong interaction between antiparticles are repulsions instead of attractions? Unless this is the case one
has to suppose that in the very beginning there was an excess of positive
protons in our part of the cosmos, so that any antiprotons which might

have formed were promptly swallowed up. Then, possibly, the reverse could have happened somewhere else in space. We may never know, but the recent discovery of "quasars" (Sec. 31-6) in the vast depths of space, a few billion light-years away, is suggestive. These bodies are pouring out short radio waves on a scale nowhere known in our own more familiar region; they are probably turbulent clouds of gas, the results of explosions many times more intense than a supernova. It has been suggested that quasars, all of which are very old on the cosmic time scale, are pieces left over from the "big bang" that may have produced the known cosmos, but they also might have been the results of collisions between matter and antimatter on an astronomical scale.

GLOSSARY

Action at a distance Force between bodies that are not actually in contact, such as gravitational attraction or electrostatic repulsion.

Antineutron Converse particle to the neutron, distinguished from the latter by the direction of spin and the mode of decay.

Antiparticles Pairs of particles with identical masses, but opposite sign of charge (if charged), opposite direction of spin, and other opposing properties.

Antiproton Negatively charged particle with the same mass as a proton.

Baryons Class of heavy particles that includes the proton, the neutron, various hyperons, and their respective antiparticles. The baryon number is positive for protons, neutrons, and hyperons that decay into protons or neutrons; it is negative for the corresponding antiparticles.

Cosmic-ray shower Cluster of high-speed electrons, mesons, and gamma-ray photons that are produced when a cosmic-ray particle of very high energy enters the atmosphere and causes a series of nuclear reactions; the particles belonging to the shower are identified as such because they are all recorded simultaneously.

Hypercharge One of the numbers used in classifying single particles (Sec. 34-6).

Hyperon Single particle with a mass greater than that of a proton or a neutron.

Isotopic spin number One of the classification numbers used for single particles (Sec. 34-6).

Leptons Class of light particles that includes neutrinos, electrons, muons, and their respective antiparticles; the lepton number is negative for the electron, the negative muon, and the neutrino that accompanies them; it is positive for the positron and the other antiparticles.

Meson Particle of mass intermediate between that of an electron and that of a proton.

Muon, or μ-meson Particle with a positive or negative charge, and a mass equal to 207 electron masses; the lightest particle of the meson class.

Nanosecond One billionth of a second.

Parity Property that can be ascribed to all single particles, atoms, and energy levels of the latter, by which they can be classified as odd or even; mathematically, states of opposite parity are related in a manner analogous to the relation between an object and its image in a mirror.

Pion, or π-meson Particles that can be positively or negatively charged, or neutral, and that have a mass of 268 to 273 electron masses; the second lightest group of the meson class.

Strangeness One of the classification numbers used for single particles; so called because it seems to have no analogy with any other property of atoms or of matter in general.

Strong interactions Forces of the same nature as the binding forces that hold the protons and neutrons together in a compound nucleus.

Weak interactions Hypothetical forces that are assumed to bear a relation to the slow decay by emission of beta particles analogous to the relation between electromagnetic forces and the emission of a photon.

EXERCISES

1. Summarize the evidence that: (a) cosmic rays come from outer space; (b) the primary cosmic rays are positively charged particles most of which have energies of at least 10^{10} electron-volts; (c) a primary cosmic ray of very high energy may produce a shower of a thousand or more particles by reactions in the atmosphere.

2. If π-mesons can be ejected from nuclei in certain types of nuclear reactions, and if they act in a peculiar fashion as the cement holding compound nuclei together, as Yukawa supposed them to do, why is it that they do not add to the mass of the compound nucleus?

3. (a) Find the minimum value of the kinetic energy of the two particles when a pion disintegrates into a positron-electron pair; (b) find the corresponding velocity of the particles; (c) find the wavelength of the gamma rays if the pion disintegrates into a pair of photons.

4. Outline the principles involved in the identification of the particles when a nuclear reaction is observed in a cloud chamber.

5. Outline the steps that were necessary in order to prove that antiprotons were being produced in the bevatron.

6. Summarize the properties of an antineutron.

7. Why is the force of which we are conscious when we exert a push or a lift actually an action at a distance?

8. Summarize the four categories of action at a distance. Give the relative order of magnitude of the forces involved; state where and under what conditions the forces are observed; give the evidence for the existence of the weak interactions.

9. Explain briefly, without going into detail, how the many single particles that have been identified recently are being classified. With what previous development in physics is this classification analogous?

10. What is meant by the conservation of parity? Why was it considered a discovery of major importance when it was found that parity is not always conserved?

11. Speculate on the possibility of antimatter; what is it, and is there any evidence of its existence?

CHAPTER 35 **the new scientific revolution**

35-1   *The Danger of Extrapolation*

Ever since science came into its own in the sixteenth and seventeenth centuries the average working scientist has professed skepticism about the finality of the laws of nature, but in practice he has been conservative in his ideas. He has said that no law of nature is necessarily absolute, that there may always be limitations, and that any law may have to be modified or abandoned in the light of new knowledge. However, when it comes to his daily work, he has assumed that the laws he already knows are valid in any new situation and he has been very reluctant to abandon any principle that seems to be well established. The failures of the classical laws and the success of the quantum theory have forcibly demonstrated that we do not know everything and that our cherished laws are not necessarily valid under all circumstances. In spite of the great advances that have been made in such subjects as astronomy by assuming that the laws of nature are the same throughout the cosmos and that they can be used to deduce facts about the stars, we know now that we may have to proceed with caution.

592

One situation where caution has been especially necessary is in extrapolation, that is, in applying knowledge that has been gained on one scale of size or of time to a different scale. As already pointed out (Sec. 32-2), the classical, mechanistic laws are macroscopic. They were derived from experiments and observations on' bodies ranging in size from tangible objects in the laboratory to planets revolving around the sun. It ought not to have caused surprise when it was discovered that some of the laws did not apply on the microscopic scale—to single atoms and electrons or to single quanta of energy.

In this concluding chapter we must see how the realization that things are not always what they seem and that extrapolation to the microscopic is not always possible has led not only to new laws, but to fundamental changes in scientific thinking. In their way these changes are just as radical as the transition from the scholastic philosophy of the Middle Ages to the scientific manner of thought based upon Galileo and Newton and their successors. That transition—the first scientific revolution—has long ago permeated the whole of society, so that the average man on the street thinks about the world in the same way as did Newton. The new thinking is aptly referred to as the twentieth-century scientific revolution. Although its manifestations are evident everywhere—in applied atomic physics and in worry about nuclear warfare—the manner of thought has only permeated scientific society within the last 30 or 40 years and it is still only beginning to percolate through to the informed layman.

35-2   Science Abandons the Mechanistic Model

The desire for a picture—the desire for a description in words—dies hard among scientists as well as among laymen. The "model" that would satisfy this desire is necessarily mechanistic, for all our descriptive words are based upon mental images of actual objects. It is hard to accept the fact that there are things in nature that are nondelineable and cannot be depicted or described. For a long time after the basic discontinuity of nature became known and the two quantum principles were well established there were still attempts at descriptive and pictorial models. Useful as it was in establishing the second quantum principle and in pointing the way to the eventual solution of the problem of atomic spectra, Bohr's model of the hydrogen atom was such an attempt. So was de Broglie's idea of standing electron waves corresponding to the Bohr orbits. Even after the fundamental duality of the wave and particle aspects of an electron or a light quantum was realized, attempts to reconcile the two aspects continued with concepts such as that of "wave packets."

Today one rarely sees in the serious scientific literature attempts at mechanistic models or descriptions of things like atoms that cannot be so displayed. At best, the descriptions were only analogies and analogies can be misleading, just as extrapolation may be misleading. Gradually atomic physicists have had to learn to dispense with the mechanistic model, to use laws that can only be expressed in the form of mathematical equations, and to use a new kind of "model" (the word is still used), one that is also expressed as a mathematical equation rather than as a picture.

One still has to use words for the nondelineable concepts, words like "field of force," "quantum," "photon," still more abstruse concepts like "hypercharge," and others which have not been discussed in this book, such as "wave function" and "eigenvalue." Some of the terms used in modern physics had their origin in attempts to devise descriptive models and may have a mechanistic connotation, like "spin," or "matter wave." However, it now has to be realized that all these words are mere names and that the concepts have to be defined operationally by what the things do, rather than descriptively.

One must not think that, because the new concepts cannot be delineated, they are in any way unreal or imaginary. A field and a photon are real things, because they can produce observable, measurable effects. One simply has to accept the fact that on the microscopic, atomic scale nature works in a different way than on the macroscopic scale. Further, one must not think that in abandoning the mechanistic model science has lost. On the contrary, freedom from the fetters of mechanistic thinking has resulted in powerful methods of computing measurable results, and has made possible the great advances in atomic physics and chemistry of the last 30 years or so.

35-3   *Quantum Mechanics*

It is impossible in a book of this nature to develop the mathematics upon which much of the new scientific thinking is based. It is unfortunate in one way that the trend toward abstruse mathematical equations has had to take place, for it means that much of modern physics is incomprehensible to one who has not been trained in modern mathematical methods and that there is a wider gap than ever between the physical scientist and the intelligent layman. We must, however, attempt to explain some of the basic ideas.

In 1926 Erwin Schrödinger at Zurich, Switzerland, followed up the clue suggested by de Broglie and considered in a general mathematical manner, first, how the electron waves would be propagated and, second, the conditions under which they would *not* be propagated but would be represented by stationary waves; these would presumably be associated with the energy levels of an atom. In the latter case Schrödinger's equation for a single electron reduces to[*]

$$\frac{d^2\psi}{dx^2} + \frac{d^2\psi}{dy^2} + \frac{d^2\psi}{dz^2} + \frac{8\pi^2 m}{h^2} (E - V)\psi = 0.$$

In this ψ is the *wave function* which has to be evaluated by solving the equation. It is a function of the coordinates (x, y, z) and represents in some nondelineable way the amplitude of the electron wave at the point (x, y, z). E is the (constant) total energy of the electron and V is the potential energy it would have if it were located at (x, y, z), so that $E - V$ represents kinetic energy; m is the electron mass and h is Planck's constant.

Schrödinger's equation has the peculiarity that in general the solutions for the function ψ can take a whole gamut of different values at a particular point (x, y, z). However, for certain specific numerical values of E this is not the case and there is only one solution to the equation. Now a physical quantity—whether or not it represents something delineable—cannot have two different values at the same place at the same time. Therefore only the single-valued solutions are physically meaningful; the values of E for which the solutions are single-valued must be the energy levels. If the potential energy V is taken to be that of an electron in the neighborhood of a singly charged positive nucleus, the energy levels derived from the equation are precisely those of the hydrogen atom.

The more complete theory, which is not confined to stationary energy levels, but in which the wave function is allowed to vary with the time, indicates how radiation must occur when the electron makes a transition from one energy level to another and shows that the frequency of the radiation must be given by the first quantum principle. It is possible to extend the method to atoms containing several electrons, much more readily than was the case with Bohr's semiclassical model, and many things that were previously unexplained can be brought into the scheme of *quantum mechanics*.[†] However, the mechanistic model has completely disappeared. In answer to the question: "What does an atom look like?" all one can do is write down Schrödinger's equation or Heisenberg's even more abstruse equivalent.

35-4   *Probability and Predictability*

We have already discussed an example of another feature of the new scientific thought, in the law of radioactive decay (Sec. 23-3). Funda-

[*] Schrödinger's equation is quoted here because in the modern thinking it, or something similar, is the only legitimate "model" of an atom. In the same year as Schrödinger did his work, Werner Heisenberg at Göttingen arrived at the same final result, starting from quite a different basis. Later developments showed that either of the two methods can be derived mathematically from the other; therefore both are valid ways of attacking the problem.

[†] For example, the behavior of the conduction electrons in a metal.

mentally, this is a probability law and states that there is a certain probability that a particular atomic nucleus will disintegrate—and convert into the next element of the series—in the next second. There is, however, no way of predicting just when the atom will disintegrate. It follows that if we have a large number of atoms there will be a definite rate of conversion. That is, a definite number per second will disintegrate, but there is no way of knowing which atoms these will be.

The probability feature is present also in the quantum theory of the emission of light by atoms. When an atom is excited to an upper energy level (Sec. 33-4) and is in a position to lose energy and produce light radiation, there are in general several different ways in which it can descend the ladder of energy levels. For example, a hydrogen atom in level number 3 (Fig. 33-1) can return directly to normal and emit a spectrum line in the extreme ultraviolet; or it can first drop to level number 2, emitting the well-known red line of the visible spectrum of hydrogen, and then a little later drop to normal and emit a different ultraviolet line. The same atom cannot do both and there is a definite probability that it will follow either of the possible routes; these probabilities can be calculated with the aid of Schrödinger's equation. If a light source contains a large number of atoms, we can calculate the number that will make any particular quantum transition; since the intensity of a spectrum line must be proportional to the number of atoms that produce the line, we can predict the relative intensities of the different lines in the spectrum and can confirm the prediction by measurement. But there is no way of predicting which atoms will give which spectrum lines, or when.

The probability feature in the new physics is very general on the microscopic scale and it upsets another cherished idea of the classical physicist—the belief in precise predictability. The classical laws summarized in Sec. 32-2 are all definite and permit no "choice"* on the part of the inanimate objects with which they deal. In principle, they can be used for exact prediction of future events, within the known limitations of the different laws; they represent a completely deterministic view of nature. But in the microscopic world of single atoms—the world of quantum theory, of radioactivity and nuclear reactions, of the strange new particles—this is no longer the case.

It has been said that, along with the disappearance of complete predictability, causality—the relation between cause and effect—has disappeared from modern physics. This is only partly true. Rigorous causality or complete determinism would demand that a given cause or set of causes should produce one unique effect. However, we now find that on the microscopic scale a cause can produce any of several different effects, or that the effect follows after an indeterminate time. There is still a cause

---

* The word "choice," in quotation marks, is not meant to imply that an atom has any kind of mentality which would give it the power to make its own choice.

and an effect; but the relation between them is less definite and less rigorous than we used to think or than a mechanistically-minded person would
like. Some writers, very reluctant to give up the idea of rigorous causality
and precise predictability, have suggested that there must be some still
unknown law that would determine just when the radioactive nucleus will
disintegrate, or which spectrum lines the excited atom will produce. However, the consensus today is that probability and limited causality are
inherent in nature on the atomic scale and that no such law will ever be
found.

When very large numbers of atoms are involved, the probability of a
certain course of events gives the proportion that will follow that course;
the larger the number of atoms, the more precise the relative proportion.
Therefore on the macroscopic scale causality and predictability are still
valid, but with a minute margin of error which is inherent in the situation.
The classical laws are, in general,° macroscopic laws, derived from observations involving very large numbers of atoms. Strictly speaking, they
state what will happen on the macroscopic scale; on this scale they are still
useful for more or less exact predictions.

35-5   The Uncertainty Principle

One more feature of the modern thinking about the microscopic scale
remains to be discussed: how is the duality of wave and particle, which
applies both to light radiation and to electrons, to be reconciled? The
answer is closely connected with quantum mechanics and with the idea
that the atomic laws yield probabilities rather than a rigorous connection
between cause and effect.

In 1927 Heisenberg pointed out that we cannot make any observation
or measurement without there being a change of some kind in the thing
we are trying to observe. *Observation causes a reaction on the thing
observed.* In measuring a length or in weighing a tangible body, the reaction is infinitesimal. So it is in making observations of the stars, although
in this case it is easy to see that the reaction does exist. We observe the
stars by means of the light they produce; every time a star emits as much
as a single quantum of light there is a change somewhere in its constitution and it loses a tiny amount of mass. Or one might prefer to say that
the thing we observe is the light rather than the star. We use the light
energy to expose a photographic plate or to affect the retina of the eye;
the thing we have observed is actually destroyed by the process of observation. Heisenberg examined in the light of this thought several imaginary
experiments that might be used to determine the position and the momen-

° The laws of conservation of energy and of momentum seem to be universal and to be valid
on the microscopic scale as well.

tum of atomic particles and photons. He came to the conclusion that any experiment that yields position necessarily alters the momentum; conversely, any experiment designed to measure the momentum makes the position impossible to find.

A few examples may help the reader to understand the idea. A standard method of determining the momentum, and therefore the velocity, of a charged particle is to measure the radius of the circular path it describes in a magnetic field. But this causes the particle to deviate from its original path, and it will no longer strike the point at which it was aimed.

Conceivably, we could determine the positions of the electrons in a piece of material by photographing them in the light of an X-ray beam. But to do this the X rays would have to be scattered by the electrons, just as in photographing a landscape the light we actually receive is that which has been scattered by the trees and buildings. In scattering the X rays, Compton effect would cause the electrons to recoil (Sec. 33-6) and they would acquire momentum. Again thinking of Compton effect, the X-ray photon strikes a particular electron so that its position is determined. But the scattered photon may recoil in any direction and is changed in frequency, which means a change in energy and momentum so that its subsequent motion is unknown.

One more example: in order to determine the frequency of light, and so the energy and momentum of the photons, we usually perform an interference experiment (Sec. 18-7). But interference effects cannot occur unless the wave is spread over a large area, so that the photons have no definite position.

Heisenberg's conclusion was that there is no way of determining simultaneously, with ideal precision, both the position and the momentum of any particle. The precise determination of position makes the subsequent momentum completely indefinite, and vice versa. More generally, if the position is determined within a limit of error that we may call Δx,[*] then the act of measurement renders the momentum uncertain by an amount Δp, where the product

$$\Delta x \cdot \Delta p > h,$$

where h is Planck's constant. The same applies to time and energy; one cannot know with ideal precision both the time when an event happened and the amount of energy exchanged.

This is Heisenberg's *uncertainty principle*,[†] which appears to be a very fundamental law of physics on the microscopic scale. It clearly limits predictability and so is closely related to the mathematics of the quantum theory, which yields only probabilities and not rigorous determinism.

[*] This does not mean "Δ times x," but is the standard mathematical notation for a small change in x.

[†] It must be emphasized that this uncertainty is inherent in the nature of things. It has nothing to do with that uncertainty of measurement which depends on the limitations of the measuring instruments and which is always present as well.

35-6   The Duality of Wave and Particle

We may now examine the wave-particle duality in the light of the uncertainty principle, and we shall see that this, too, is inherent in the nature of things; it is not to be reconciled by trying to invent a mechanistic model of something that could be sometimes a wave and sometimes a particle. To begin with, the term "wave" is meaningless unless the entity occupies a space of dimensions much larger than the wavelength, and so position is indeterminate. On the other hand, the word "particle" implies an object of minute dimensions.

An experiment that demonstrates wavelike properties is essentially an interference experiment and could be used to measure the wavelength. But the wavelength is related to the momentum—directly by de Broglie's relation (Sec. 33-7) in the case of electrons and other subatomic mass particles—indirectly through the frequency and the quantum principle in the case of photons. Thus the performance of an interference experiment, with either light or electrons, is related to a determination of momentum and precludes any simultaneous determination of position.

Experiments that display the particle-like properties are studies of cathode rays and nuclear collisions in the field of subatomic particles, or of photoelectricity and Compton effect in the case of electromagnetic radiation. These are essentially determinations of position; according to the uncertainty principle simultaneous determination of momentum is impossible. In these experiments the particle or photon is at a certain point at a certain time; it cannot spread out to produce interference effects and demonstrate its wavelike properties.

An entity on the microscopic scale can appear to be either a particle or a wave, but not both at once, except to the extent that the product of the uncertainties satisfies Heisenberg's principle. Whichever is observed, particles or waves, depends on the method of observation. In the end, all we can say about the wave-particle duality is that *we get what we look for.* If we design an experiment to demonstrate waves, we get waves; if we look for particles we get particles.

35-7   What of the Future?

About 1890 it was suggested that there was nothing left for scientists to do except to repeat standard experiments on different materials, with improved accuracy. Many people thought that all the basic discoveries had been made—in the classical, mechanistic laws, and in the atomic theory as expanded in the kinetic theory of gases. Then came the electron, radioactivity, X rays, and the quantum principles as expressed in the early quantum theory of Planck, Einstein, and Bohr. The whole basis of scientific thinking was revolutionized within three or four decades, with the development of quantum mechanics, with the new importance of discontinuity, with probability laws and the uncertainty principle replacing rigorous determinism on the atomic scale, and with the disappearance of the mechanistic model.

Along with the revolution in basic physics, whole new fields of scientific study have been opened up. The study of nuclear reactions has fulfilled the ancient dream of the alchemists—of converting one element into another—but in a manner and with results that they never dreamed about. Just as the atom of Dalton's hypothesis and of the kinetic theory seemed to be a tiny hard sphere, but later proved to have a structure, so now the discovery of things like electron spin and rapidly decaying strange particles has shown that protons and electrons must have some kind of structure, although it may be nondelineable and impossible to describe except in mathematical terms.

A better understanding of the atom and of the structure of gross matter has led to unimagined advances in chemistry. In biochemistry and biophysics we are well on the way to an understanding of the machinery of inheritance and of evolution. We talk intelligently and with confidence about the interior of the earth and about its age, about the constitution and mechanism of the stars, and even about galaxies so remote that it takes their light billions of years to reach us.

Where is physics heading today? It is doubtful that any physicist would be so bold as to make a remark similar to that of the 1890's and to suggest that the only thing left to do is to apply twentieth-century principles— essentially the principles of quantum mechanics—to more and more specific situations, until everything in the cosmos is explained. On the other hand, will the new principles stand or are they likely to be abandoned in favor of something still newer, as the early forms of the quantum theory have been superseded? Here physicists would almost all agree that present-day methods, such as that of the Schrödinger equation, will always be useful within their proper range of validity, just as Newton's laws and the laws of electricity are still useful within their proper range—the range of the macroscopic. After all, what we mean when we say that a physical law is "true" is that it is useful within certain limitations and that it gives results in agreement with observation when it is used as a basis of computation.

That the present laws apply to all possible situations and that there are no new basic laws to be discovered would be a very bold assumption. At the time of writing there are at least two very fundamental problems that have only been partially solved. One concerns the strange particles and the weak interactions that apparently control the decay of most of them. Another concerns the structure of atomic nuclei and the forces which hold them together. There has been significant progress toward the solution of the latter problem through the application of the methods of quantum mechanics, but it is possible that there is still some important principle missing. Finally, there is the whole problem of action at a distance, for it seems that there ought to be some consistent method of treating all four categories of interaction between particles. Einstein tried to bring gravitation and electromagnetism together in his "unified field" theory, but with only partial success, and now the problem is further complicated by the discovery of the weak and strong interactions.

In the end, all we can say about any account of the laws of nature is: This is the picture this year; who knows what the picture will be 100 years from now!

GLOSSARY

Extrapolation The extension of a physical law or mathematical equation from the scale of size or of time where it is known to be valid to a larger or smaller scale.

Quantum mechanics Mathematical theory based upon the quantum principles, including the uncertainty principle; developed primarily for discussion of the properties of electrons and atoms, but applicable in principle to matter generally.

Uncertainty principle Principle that it is impossible to measure simultaneously, with absolute precision, both the momentum and the position of a particle, or both the energy and the time of an event.

Wave function Mathematical function that describes, in a nondelineable manner, the distribution of the wave associated with an electron or other particle; from the wave function can be derived the observable properties of the electron.

EXERCISES

1. Quote cases where extrapolation from the macroscopic to the microscopic has led to error.

2. Describe briefly three attempts to devise mechanistic models of things that can only be treated mathematically by the methods of quantum theory.

3. To what extent has causality disappeared from modern physics?

4. Which of the macroscopic, mechanistic laws of physics appear to be valid on the microscopic scale?

5. Give examples to illustrate the hypothesis that the act of making an observation always reacts on the thing observed, even though the effect of the reaction may be minute: (a) in classical mechanics; (b) in chemistry; (c) in optics; (d) in astronomy; (e) in biology; (f) in psychology; (g) in sociology.

6. State and explain Heisenberg's uncertainty principle.

REVIEW EXERCISES FOR
CHAPTERS 32 THROUGH 35

1. Discuss three cases where the laws of classical physics have proved insufficient to describe behavior on the microscopic scale.

2. Discuss briefly the effect on twentieth-century science of the idea that it ought to be possible to explain everything in nature in mechanistic terms.

3. Name an important development, with the approximate date, that is attributed to each of the following scientists: Max Planck, Niels Bohr, A. H. Compton, Louis de Broglie, Erwin Schrödinger, Werner Heisenberg.

4. Name four physical quantities that have proved to be discontinuous. Who (in modern times) first suggested that these things might be discontinuous? Why did he make the suggestion, and when? How and when was the discontinuity proved experimentally?

5. Name two phenomena in which one can predict only the probability of an occurrence, rather than the precise effect of a given cause. Explain how the probability feature is involved in each case.

6. Describe experiments that demonstrate (a) that electromagnetic radiation consists of particles; (b) that electrons are waves. To be strictly logical, one should not have said here: "electrons *are* waves." What should one have said?

7. Collect the references to Einstein's theory of relativity that have appeared in the earlier chapters of this book.

8. Discuss briefly four cases in which a new particle has either been predicted theoretically, or has been assumed in order to fill a gap in a theory, and the particle has later been discovered actually to exist.

9. Which were the first four single particles to be identified, and through what type of experiment were they found? About how many different single particles are now known? An important problem in contemporary physics is the classification of the known single particles; summarize the progress that has been made in this classification.

10. Which of the following particles are stable, and if they are not stable, what happens to them: electron; positron; proton; alpha particle; neutron; photon?

11. "The manner of thinking of the scientific revolution of the seventeenth and eighteenth centuries has long ago permeated society, so that the average citizen in the Western nations thinks about nature in essentially the same way as a nineteenth-century scientist, but the manner of thought of twentieth-century physical science is still strange." Discuss and criticize this statement, giving examples of the way people thought about nature at different stages of history.

12. "Such and such a physical law is true." Precisely what is meant by a statement of this kind?

Appendices

Appendix A   *Some Numerical Values*

Conversion Factors

1 meter = 39.37 inches (by definition of the inch)
1 mile = 1609.35 meters
1 light-year = 5.8803×10^{12} miles = 9.4637×10^{15} meters
1 year = 3.15569×10^7 seconds
1 mile per hour = 0.447041 meters per second
1 kilogram = 2.2046223 pounds-mass
1 ton = 907.185 kilograms
1 pound-weight = 4.4482 newtons
1 newton per square meter = 1.4504×10^{-4} pound per square inch
1 standard atmosphere = 101,325 newtons per square meter = 14.696 pounds per square inch = 76 centimeters of mercury (by definition)
1 foot-pound = 1.35582 joules
1 kilowatt-hour = 3,600,000 joules
1 calorie = 4.186 joules
1 electron-volt = 1.6020×10^{-19} joule
1 horsepower = 745.7 watts
$t°C = (1.8t + 32)°F = (t + 273.16)°K$

Physical Constants

Velocity of light, $c = 2.99796 \times 10^8$ meters per second
Constant of gravitation, $G = 6.668 \times 10^{-11}$ MKS units
Mass of the earth, 5.977×10^{24} kilograms
Mean radius of the earth, 6,371,229 meters
Mean distance of the moon, 384,400 kilometers
Mass of the sun, 1.991×10^{30} kilograms
Mean distance of the sun (astronomical unit), 1.4960×10^8 kilometers
Standard value of the acceleration due to gravity, $g = 9.80621$ meters per second^2
Volume of a mole of ideal gas at 0°C and 1 atmosphere pressure, 22,416 cubic centimeters

Gas constant for an ideal gas, $R = 8.31436$ joules per mole per degree

Faraday constant, $F = 96,488$ coulombs per mole

Electron charge, $e = 1.6020 \times 10^{-19}$ coulomb

Avogadro's number, $N_0 = 6.0234 \times 10^{23}$ molecules per mole

Ratio of charge to mass for electrons, $e/m = 1.7592 \times 10^8$ coulombs per gram

Mass of the electron, 9.107×10^{-28} gram

Mass of the hydrogen atom, 1.6733×10^{-24} gram

Ratio of the mass of the proton to that of the electron, 1836.6

Planck constant, $h = 6.6257 \times 10^{-34}$ joule-second

Appendix B   Bibliography of Supplementary Reading

General

Arons, A. B. and A. M. Bork, *Science and Ideas.* Englewood Cliffs, N.J.: Prentice-Hall, Inc., 1964.

Ashford, T. A., *From Atoms to Stars.* New York: Holt, Rinehart & Winston, Inc., 1960.

Christiansen, G. S. and P. H. Garrett, *Structure and Change.* San Francisco: W. H. Freeman & Co., 1960.

Gamow, G., *Matter, Earth and Sky* (2nd ed.). Englewood Cliffs, N.J.: Prentice-Hall, Inc., 1965.

Hutchings, E., *Frontiers in Science.* New York: Basic Books, Inc., 1958.

Pyke, M., *The Boundaries of Science.* London: George G. Harrap & Company, Limited, 1961.

Basic Physics

A list of available texts on general physics and chemistry would be too extensive. The following works do not require sophisticated mathematics.

Beiser, A., *Basic Concepts of Physics.* Reading, Mass.: Addison-Wesley Publishing Co., Inc., 1961.

Beyer, R. T. and A. O. Williams, Jr., *College Physics.* Englewood Cliffs, N.J.: Prentice-Hall, Inc., 1957.

Gamow, G. and J. M. Cleveland, *Physics: Foundations and Frontiers.* Englewood Cliffs, N.J.: Prentice-Hall, Inc., 1960.

Basic Chemistry

Johnsen, R. H. and E. Grunwald, *Atoms, Molecules and Chemical Change* (2nd ed.). Englewood Cliffs, N.J.: Prentice-Hall, Inc., 1965.

Nathans, M. W., *Elementary Chemistry.* Englewood Cliffs, N.J.: Prentice-Hall, Inc., 1963.

Quagliano, J. V., *Chemistry* (2nd ed.). Englewood Cliffs, N.J.: Prentice-Hall, Inc., 1963.

Astronomy

Baker, R. H., *Introduction to Astronomy* (6th ed.). New York: D. Van Nostrand Co., Inc., 1961.

Gamow, G., *A Planet Called Earth.* New York: The Viking Press, 1963.

Hoyle, F., *Frontiers of Astronomy.* London: William Heinemann, Limited, 1961.

Inglis, S. J., *Planets, Stars and Galaxies.* New York: John Wiley & Sons, Inc., 1960.

Mehlin, T. C., *Astronomy.* New York: John Wiley & Sons, Inc., 1959.

Page, T. (ed.), *Stars and Galaxies: Birth, Aging and Death.* Englewood Cliffs, N.J.: Prentice-Hall, Inc., 1962.

Simak, C. D., *The Solar System.* New York: St. Martin's Press, Inc., 1962.

Geology and Geophysics

Harland, W. B., *The Earth.* New York: Franklin Watts, Inc., 1960.

Hodgson, J. H., *Earthquakes and Earth Structure.* Englewood Cliffs, N.J.: Prentice-Hall, Inc., 1964.

Moore, R. C., *Introduction to Historical Geology.* New York: McGraw-Hill Book Company, 1958.

Stokes, W. L., *Essentials of Earth History.* Englewood Cliffs, N.J.: Prentice-Hall, Inc., 1960.

Sullivan, W., *The Assault on the Unknown.* New York: McGraw-Hill Book Company, 1961.

White, J. F. (ed.), *Study of the Earth: Readings in Geological Science.* Englewood Cliffs, N.J.: Prentice-Hall, Inc., 1962.

Wilson, J. T., *IGY, the Year of the New Moons.* Toronto: Longmans, Green & Co., Inc., 1961.

History of Science

Anderson, D. L., *The Discovery of the Electron.* Princeton, N.J.: D. Van Nostrand Co., Inc., 1964.

Gamow, G., *Biography of Physics.* New York: Harper & Row, Publishers, 1961.

Hall, A. R., *Scientific Revolution*. London: Longmans, Green & Co., Inc., 1962.

Jordan, P., *Science and the Course of History*. New Haven, Conn.: Yale University Press, 1955.

Mason, S. F., *A History of the Sciences*. New York: Collier Books, 1962.

Philosophy of Science

Bohr, N. H. D., *Atomic Physics and Human Knowledge*. New York: John Wiley & Sons, Inc., 1958.

Bridgman, P. W., *The Logic of Modern Physics*. New York: The Macmillan Company, 1960.

————, *The Way Things Are*. Cambridge, Mass.: Harvard University Press, 1959.

Kemeny, J. G., *A Philosopher Looks at Science*. Princeton, N.J.: D. Van Nostrand Co., Inc., 1959.

Smith, Huston, "The Revolution in Western Thought," in *Adventures of the Mind* (2nd series). New York: Alfred A. Knopf, Inc., 1961.

Von Weizsacker, C. H., *The World View of Physics*. London: Routledge & Kegan Paul, Ltd., 1952.

Whitehead, A. N., *The Interpretation of Science*. Indianapolis: The Bobbs-Merrill Company, Inc., 1961.

Science, Religion, and the Nature of Man

Berrill, N. J., *Man's Emerging Mind*. New York: Dodd, Mead & Co., 1955.

Boschke, F. L., *Creation Still Goes On* (trans. by L. Parks). New York: McGraw-Hill Book Company, 1964.

de Chardin, P. T., *The Phenomenon of Man* (trans. by B. Wall). New York: Harper & Row, Publishers, 1959.

Pollard, W. G., *Chance and Providence*. New York: Charles Scribner's Sons, 1958.

Schrödinger, E., *Mind and Matter*. London: Cambridge University Press, 1958.

Biography

Brodetsky, S., *Sir Isaac Newton*. London: Methuen & Co., Ltd., 1927.

Fermi, L., *Atoms in the Family*. Chicago: University of Chicago Press, 1954.

Kesten, H., *Copernicus and his World*. New York: Roy Publishers, Inc., 1945.

MacDonald, D. K. C., *Faraday, Maxwell and Kelvin*. New York: Doubleday & Company, Inc., 1964.

Science and Society

Clareson, T. D., *Science and Society*. New York: Harper & Row, Publishers, 1961.

Conant, J. B., *Modern Science and Modern Man*. New York: Doubleday & Company, Inc., 1952.

Hoyt, J. B., *Man and the Earth*. Englewood Cliffs, N.J.: Prentice-Hall, Inc., 1962.

Oppenheimer, R., *Science and the Common Understanding*. New York: Simon & Schuster, Inc., 1954.

Russell, Bertrand, *The Impact of Science on Society*. London: George Allen & Unwin, 1952.

Thomson, G. P., *The Foreseeable Future*. London: Cambridge University Press, 1960.

Atomic and Nuclear Physics

Andrade, E. N. da C., *An Approach to Modern Physics*. London: G. Bell & Sons, Ltd., 1962.

Gamow, G., *The Atom and Its Nucleus*. Englewood Cliffs, N.J.: Prentice-Hall, Inc., 1961.

Goldschmidt, B., *The Atomic Adventure*. New York: The Macmillan Company, 1964.

Harvey, B. G., *Introduction to Nuclear Physics and Chemistry*. Englewood Cliffs, N.J.: Prentice-Hall, Inc., 1962.

Energy Sources and Nuclear Energy

Allibone, T. E., *The Release and Use of Atomic Energy*. London: Chapman & Hall, Ltd., 1961.

Emmerich, Werner *et al.*, *Energy Does Matter*. New York: Walker & Company, 1964.

Jungk, R., *Brighter Than a Thousand Suns*. New York: Harcourt, Brace & World, Inc., 1958.

Thirring, H., *Energy for Man*. Bloomington, Ind.: Indiana University Press, 1958.

Biophysics

Butler, J. A. V., *Inside the Living Cell*. New York: Basic Books, Inc., Publishers, 1959.

Shapley, H., *Of Stars and Men*. Boston: Beacon Press, Inc., 1962.

Meteorology

Blair, T. A. and R. C. Fite, *Weather Elements* (5th ed.). Englewood Cliffs, N.J.: Prentice-Hall, Inc., 1965.

Pilkington, R., *The Ways of the Air*. London: Routledge & Kegan Paul, Ltd., 1961.

Sutton, O. G., *The Challenge of the Atmosphere*. New York: Harper & Row, Publishers, 1963.

Satellites and Space Travel

Berkner, L. V. and H. Odishaw, *Science in Space*. New York: McGraw-Hill Book Company, 1961.

Ley, W., *Harnessing Space*. New York: The Macmillan Company, 1963.

Page, Thornton and L. W. Page (eds.), *Wanderers in the Sky*. New York: The Macmillan Company, 1965.

index

(References in bold type are to formal definitions or to the glossaries.)

Aberration of lens, 279
Absolute humidity, 182, **194**
  magnitude, 505, **519**
  temperature, **106**, 173, 307
  zero, 104, **106**, 159
Absorption, **282**
  of light, 274
  spectrum, 309, **314**
Acceleration, **51**, **60**
  due to gravity, 52
  uniform, 51
Accelerator, for particles, 380, **389**
Acetic acid, 202
Achromatic lens, 280, **282**
Acid, 144, **149**
  organic, 202, **211**
Action and reaction, 58, 115
  at a distance, 582, **589**
Activity of radioactive elements, 373, 376
Ad hoc assumption, 555, **571**
Adrenaline, 206

Aftershock, 460, **471**
Age of the earth, 429, 432
  solar system, 433, 489
Alaska earthquake, 457, 460
Alchemist, 132, 138, **149**
Alcohol, 202, **210**
Aleutian Islands, 457
Alexandria, 14
Algae, fossil, 434, **451**
Algol, 510
Alkali metals, 145, 365
Alkaline earth metals, 146, 365
Alnico, 239, **249**
Alpha particle, 361, 373, 385
Alpha ray, 356, **370**
Alps of Switzerland, 418
Alternating current, 255, **264**
Alternating-current generator, 257
Altimeter, 157, **164**
Aluminum, production of, 257
Amino acid, 205, **210**

Ammonia in solar system, 495
Ampère, André Marie, 247
Ampere, unit of current, 228, **231**
Ampère's law, 247, 544
Amphibian, 441, **451**
Amplifier, 349, **352**
Amplitude of oscillation, **125**
Ancient chemistry, 131
Anderson, C. D., 387
Andromeda galaxy, 514, 517
Angstrom unit, 304, **314**
Angular momentum, **115, 125**
  conservation of, 115, 467, 490
  discontinuity of, 556
  of solar system, 490
Animal electricity, 224
Animal migration, 483
Antenna, 323, **333**
Anticyclone, 190, **194**
Antimatter, 588
Antineutron, 580, **589**
Antiparticle, 579, **589**
Antiproton, 579, **589**
Aperture of lens, 280, **283**
Aphelion, 39, **45**
Apogee, **45**
Appalachian Mountains, 477
  revolution, 443
Applied science, 350
Approximate conservation, 585
A priori assumption, 4, **6**
Aquinas, St. Thomas, 21
Arabian science, 20, 132
Arbitrary units, 68, **71**, 269
Archeopteryx, 447
Archeozoic era, 428, 433, **451**
Arctic Ocean, 484
Aristarchus, 14
Aristotle, 16, 48, 138, 414
Armature, **264**
Artificial radioactivity, 386, **389,** 394
Artificial satellite, 82
Asteroids, 38, **45**
Aston, F. W., 368
Astrology, 13
Astronomical unit, **45**
Astronomy, beginnings of, 11
  deductive, 415
  Greek, 14
Atlantic Ocean, 469
Atmosphere, composition of, 181
  evolution of, 495
  sources of information, 179
  standard, 157
  structure of, 183
Atmospheres of the planets, 492
Atmospheric pressure, 155
  refraction, 276

Atom, **149,** 167
Atom smasher, 380, **389**
Atomic bomb, 396
  hypothesis, 169, 176
Atomic number, 364, **370**
  pile, 398, **406**
  spectrum, 307, **314**
  weight, **140, 149**
Aurora borealis, 181, **195**
Australia, wandering of, 470
Available energy, **125**
Avogadro, Amadeo, 170, 176
Avogadro's law, 170, 544
  number, 171, 176, **177,** 347
Azoic era, 428, 433, **451**

Babylonia, 13
Bacon, Sir Francis, 4, 470
Badlands, 443, **451**
Band spectrum, 309, **314**
Bar magnet, 241
Barometer, 156, **164**
Barren Grounds, 484
Baryon number, 585
Baryons, 582, **589**
Basalt, 422, **424**
Base, 144, **149**
Battery, electric, **232**
Bay of Fundy, 81
Becquerel, Henri, 354
Beginning of evolving entity, 533
Beginnings of astronomy, 11
Bell Telephone Company laboratory, 564
Benzene ring, 201, **210**
Bering Strait, 485
Bessel, F. W., 26
Beta particle, 374, 385
Beta rays, 356, 370
Bevatron, 579
Big bang theory, *see* Catastrophic theory
Big Horn Mountains, 475
Binary stars, 508, **519**
Biological effects of radiation, 404
  origin, rock of, 419
Birds, origin of, 445
Blackbody, 269, **282,** 307
Block fault mountain, 475, **486**
Blue sky, 274
Bøggild, J. K., 360
Bohr, Niels, 396, 555
Bohr's model of hydrogen atom, 555, 593
Boiling point, 161
Bondi, Hermann, 534
Bow River Valley, 477
Boyle, Robert, 157
Boyle's law of gas pressure, 104, 157
Brahe, Tycho, 41, 526

Brain, development of, 449
Bridgman, P. W., 243
Brontosaurus, 445
Bronze, 131
Brookhaven National Laboratory, 382, 578 587
Brown, Robert, 174
Brownian movement, 174, **177**
Bruno, Giordano, 22
Brushes, on electrical machines, 255, **264**
Bubble chamber, 361, **370,** 578
Buffon, Georges, 470
Butane, 201

Calcareous shells, **451**
Calcining, **149**
Calcium carbonate, 420
Calder Hall, 403
Caloric, 100, **106,** 136
Calorie, **100,** 105, 106
Calorimeter, **232**
Calx, 136, **150**
Cambrian period, 433, **451**
Canadian Shield, 414, 421, **424,** 434
glaciation of, 483
Canals of Mars, 34
Candlepower, 269, **282**
Carbohydrate, 202, **210**
Carbon, cycle in nature, 204, 439
dioxide, change of state, 163
in metabolism, 203
Carbon, oxides of, 140
peculiar properties of, 200, 367, 435
Carbonates, 203
Carbon 14 dating, 431
Carbon-nitrogen cycle, 524
Catastrophic theory of cosmos, 534
Catastrophism, 414, 423, **424**
Cathode, hot, 345, **352**
Cathode glow, 340
Cathode rays, 399, **352**
diffraction of, 562
Cathode-ray tube, 345
Causality, 596
Cavendish Laboratory, 343
Cell, voltaic, 224
Cellulose, 202, 205, **210**
Celsius scale, 101, **106**
Cenozoic era, 429, 448, **452**
Centigrade temperature, *see* Celsius scale
Central orbit, 76, **88**
Central plain of North America, 418
Central temperature of sun, 523
Centrifugal force, **88**
Centripetal acceleration and force, 74, **88**
Cepheid variable, 513, **519**
Ceres, 38

CERN accelerator, 382
Cesium, photoelectric effect in, 549
CGS units, 56
Chadwick, James, 382, 562
Chain reaction, 395, **406**
controlled, 397
Chalk, 420, **425**
Chalk River laboratory, 396
Chamberlain, O., 579
Change of state, liquid to gas, 161
solid to liquid, 159
Charge, electric, 217, 223
sign of, 222
Charge number, ionic, **150**
Charles, J. A. C., 158
Charles' law of gases, 158
Chemical equation, 142, **150**
formula, 141, **150**
potential energy, 110, **125**
symbols, 140, **150**
Chemistry, ancient, 131
organic, 203, **211**
China, 120, 132, 236
Chinese supernova, 527
Chinook wind, 193, **195**
Chitin, **452**
Chlorophyll, 203, **210,** 328
Chordate, 441, **452**
Chromatic aberration, 280, **282**
Chromosome, 207, **210**
Chubb Crater, 37
Circuit, electric, 226, 229
Circumference of the earth, 15
Classical physics, 320, **333,** 542
Cloud chamber, 359, **370,** 379
Clouds, formation of, 191
Coal, 118, 420
Coast Ranges, 477, 480
Cobalt 60, 386
Code of inheritance, 209
Coherent radiation, 565, **571**
Cohesion, **164,** 173
Coin and feather experiment, 49
Collision, of masses, 59
photon-electron, 561
Colloidal suspension, 174, **177**
Columbia Icefield, 480
Columbia River, 480
Columbus, Christopher, 15
Combustion, 142, 395
Comets, 39
Committee on Units and Nomenclature, 58
Commutator, 257, **264**
Compass, magnetic, 236
Compound, chemical, 138, **150**
Compounds in sun, 311
Compton, A. H., 560
Compton effect, 560, **571,** 598

Concave diffraction grating, 305
Concave mirror, 272
Condenser, electrical, **333**
Conduction electrons, 366, **371**
Conductor, electrical, 219
Conglomerate, 420, **425**
Conjunction, **26**
Conservation, approximate, 585
 of angular momentum, 115, 467, 490
 of baryons, 585
 of charge, 584
 of energy, 111, 254, 544
 laws, 113, **125**
 of leptons, 585
 of mass, 113, 136, 544
 of mass-energy, 114
 of momentum, 115, 185, 544
 of parity, 586
 of spin, 584
Constant combining weights, law of, 139
Constant proportions, law of, 139, 544
Constellations of stars, 13, 511, **519**
Contact force, 582
Continental block, 467, 470
 drift, 470, **471**, 476, 484
 shelf, 467, **471**
Continuous quantity, 168, **177**, 544
 spectrum, 307, **314**, 547
 theory of cosmos, 534
Contraction, relativistic, 569
Controlled chain reaction, 397
Convection, **195**, 467
 in atmosphere, 184
Converging lens, 277, **282**
Copper, electron structure of, 365
 implements, 131
Core of earth, 464
Corona, solar, 30, **45**, 84
Corpuscular theory of light, 297, **300**
Cosmic radio source, 531
Cosmic rays, 387, **389**, 436, 574
Cosmology, 414, **425**
Cosmos, 14, **26**
 center of, 23, 532
 expansion of, 532
Coulomb, Charles, 223
Coulomb, unit of charge, 228, **231**
Coulomb's law, 223, 231, 241, 544, 583
Covalent bonding, 199, **210**, 366
Cowan, Clyde, 389
Crab Nebula, 494, 526
Craters, lunar, 36
Creation in the cosmos, 534
Critical mass for nuclear explosion, 396, **406**
Critical temperature of liquid, 163, **164**, 174
Crookes radiometer, 109
Crossopterygian, 441, **452**
Crust of earth, 463

Crust of earth (*cont.*)
 changing, 416
 thickness of, 466
Crystals, 159, 198, 331
Cumulus cloud, 192, **195**
Curie, Marie Sklodowska, 354
Curie, Pierre, 354
Curie-Joliot, Irène and Frédéric, 382
Current, electric, 222, 224
Current balance, 231
Current energy supply, 118, 124
Current-voltage relations, 229, 259
Curvature of space-time, 570
Cycle, **264**
Cycles per second, 259, 289
Cyclone, 189, **195**
Cyclotron, 381, **389**

Dalton, John, 140, 169, 176
Darwin, Charles, 415, 424
Davisson, C. J., 562
Decay of mesons, 578
 of radioactive elements, 376
Declination, magnetic, 244, **250**
Deduction in science, 415
Deferent, 19, **26**
De Forest, Lee, 349
Delineable model, 546
Delta of river, 416, **425**, 480
Democritus, 167
Dempster, A. J., 368
Derived units, **71**
Deterministic laws, 545, **550**
 view of nature, 596
Deuterium, 370, 384
Deviation of light ray by sun, 571
Dew point, 183, **195**
Dialogue of Galileo, 22
Diesel engine, 123
Diffraction, 296, **300**
 of cathode rays, 562
 grating, 305, **315**
 of X rays, 331
Diffuse reflection, 273
Diffusion, 169, **177**
Dimorphodon, flying reptile, 447
Dinosaurs, 427, 443
Diode tube, 349, **352**
Dip needle, 244
Dipper, constellation of, 512
Dirac, Paul, 387
Direct current, **264**
Direct-current generator, 256
Discharge tube, 340, **352**
Discontinuity in nature, 167, 542
 of angular momentum, 556
 of charge, 340
 of radiant energy, 553

Dissociation, 143, **150**
Diverging lens, 278, **282**
DNA, 207, 436
Doldrums, 186, **195**
Domains, magnetic, 239, **250**
Donn, W. L., 484
Doppler, Johann, 313
Doppler effect, 313, **315**, 509
Double bond, 199
Double stars, 509
Drumlin, 482, **486**
Dry cell, 226
Dry ice, 163
Duality, wave-particle, 563, 597, 599
Dynamo, *see* Generator

Earth, age of, 429, 432
    circumference of, 15
    interior of, 455
    magnetic field of, 243, 456, 467
    mass of, 76
    as a planet, 29
    rotation of, 15, 29, 67, 185, 189
    structure of, 463
Earthquake, 456
    focus of, 459, 462
    waves, 459
    zones, 457, 475
Ebonite, 219
Eccentricity, **45**
Eccentric orbit, 19
Eclipse of moon, 86
    of sun, 84
Eclipsing binary, 510, **519**
Ecliptic, 13, **26**
Ectoconus, early mammal, 449
Edison, Thomas, 263, 344
Effective current, 259, **264**
Efficiency of machine, 113, **125**
Egyptian science, 13, 131
Einstein, Albert, 87, 396, 551, 566
Elastic energy, 110, **125**
Electrical conductor, 219
    energy, 110
    power system, 260
    resistance, 229, **232**
    units, **230**
Electric charge, 217, **218**, 223
    circuit, 226, 229
    clock, 66
    current, 222, 224
        magnetic field of, 245
    fluid, 221, 348
    generator, 122, 227, 255
    light, 263
    motor, 262
    potential, 228, **232**

Electricity, frictional, 218
Electrode, **352**
Electrolysis, 143, **150**, 227, 232, 257
    law of, 339
Electrolyte, **233**
Electromagnet, 249
Electromagnetic forces, 583
    induction, 252, 254, **264**
    spectrum, 324
    waves, 319, 321, **333**
Electromotive force, 228, 233
Electron, 222, **233**, 340, 344, 357
    charge on, 346
    manifestations of, 348
    mass of, 347
    orbits, 555
    shells, 364, **371**
    spin, 559
    wavelike properties of, 562
    waves, standing, 593
Electronics, 349
Electron-volt, 376, **389**
Electroscope, 219, **233**, 354
Electrostatics, 217, **233**, 237
Element, **137, 150**, 169
Elements of Chemistry, 137
Ellipse, **45**
e/m, 342
Emission of radiation, 557, 596
Empirical laws, 52, **60**, 277
Emulsion tracks, 575
Energy, **96**
    conservation of, 111, 254, 544
    consumption of, 111
    conversion of, 112
    forms of, 109
    levels, 553, 571
        of hydrogen, 553, 595
    molecular, 173
    radiant, 267
    sink, 111, **125**
    of sun and stars, 116, 523
    supply, 118, 124, 402
    use of, 119, 123
    of voltaic cell, 226
Enriched uranium, 404, **406**
Enzyme, 206, **211**
Epicycle, 19, **26**
Equilibrium, 54, **60**
    chemical, 143
    in sun, 522
Equinoxes, 13, **26**
Era of earth's history, 427
Eratosthenes, 15
Eros, minor planet, 39, 44
Erosion, 478
Erratic boulders, 482, **487**
Escape of gas from planets, 493

Escape velocity, 46, 493
Eskers, 482, **487**
Ester, 202
Ethane molecule, 367
Ether, electromagnetic, 240, **249**
Europe, medieval, 120
European Council for Nuclear Research, 382
Eurypterid, 438, **452**
Evaporation, 161
Evidence of geological change, 416
Evolution, 413, 533
    biological, 424
    of earth's atmosphere, 495
Ewing, Maurice, 484
Excitation process, 558
Expansion of the cosmos, 532
Experimentation, importance of, 5
Explosion, of star, 530
    waves in atmosphere, 180
    waves in earth, 463
Extrapolation, 593, **601**
Extrusive rock, **425**

Fahrenheit, G. D., 101
Fahrenheit scale, 101, **106**
Fallout, radioactive, 401, 405, **407**
Families, chemical, 145
Faraday, Michael, 221, 240, 252, 319, 339
Faraday constant, 339, 347, **352**
Fault, geological, 456, **471**
Fermi, Enrico, 396
Fermi, Laura, 396
Ferromagnetic materials, 239, **249**
Feughelman, M., 208
Field, concept of, 241
    magnetic, 241, **250**
    strength of, 241, **249**
First law of motion, 53
Fissionable materials, 406
Fission of nucleus, 394
    products, 394, **406**
Flares, solar, 31, **46**, 576
Fleming, J. A., 349
Floodplain, 416, **425**, 480
Fluorescence, 329, **333**, 358
Fluorescent lighting, 329
Fluoroscope, 329, **333**
Flux, magnetic, 248, **250**, 254, 260
    luminous, see Lumen
Focal length, 278
Focus, principal, 278, **282**
Folded strata, 420, 475
Fold mountains, 475, **487**
Footcandle, 270, **283**
Foot-pound, **96**, **106**
Force, **53**
    units of, 56, 58

Formula, chemical, 141, **150**
    structural, 200, **211**
Fossil, 422
    fuels, 118, 123, **125**
    magnetism, 468, **471**
    population, 424
Four-dimensional space-time, 570
FPS units, 58, 153
Franklin, Benjamin, 222
Fraser River, 480
Freon, **371**
Frequency, 289, **300**
Fresnel, A. J., 299
Friction, 97, **106**
Frictional electricity, 218
Front, atmospheric, 188, 194, **195**
Frontal low, 194
Fundamental units, 68, **71**
Fusion reaction, 401, **406**

Galactic cluster, 512, **519**
Galaxies, recession of, 531
    types of, 518
Galaxy, external, distance of, 513
    local, 513
    mass of, 517
    structure of, 516
Galileo Galilei, 2, 22, 49, 51, 66
Galvani, A., 224
Galvanometer, **264**
Gamma rays, 356, 359, **371**, 404
Gamow, George, 534
Gas, definitive property of, 157
Gas law, general, 159, 171, 544
Gas pressure, theory of, 172
Gay-Lussac, J. L., 158
Geiger, H., 358
Geiger counter, 358, **371**, 384
Gell-Mann, Murray, 586
General theory of relativity, 87, 570, **571**
Generator, electric, 122, 227, 255
Genes, 207, **211**
Geocentric system, 23, **26**
Geological era, 427
    record, 422, 429
Geometrical optics, **283**
Geophysics, 416, **425**
Germer, L. H., 562
Giant star, 507, **519**
    structure of, 529
Gilbert, William, 244
Glacial till, 481, **487**
Glaciation, 482
Glaciers, mountain, 480
Globular cluster, 513, **519**
Gold, the noble metal, 131, 133
Gold, Thomas, 534

Gold-leaf electroscope, 219, **233**
Gram-molecular weight, 170
Grand Canyon, 423, 468, 480
Granite, 421, **425**
Graphite deposits, 434
Gravitation, constant of, 76, **89**
　law of, 73, 87, 223, 543
Gravitational attraction, 52, 570, 582
　energy, 98, 492, 523
Gravity, acceleration due to, 52
Greek philosophy, 16, 138, 167
　science, 14, 218
Greenland current, 486
　ice cap, 483
Grenville Mountains, 434
Grid of electron tube, 345, **352**
Gulf Stream, 486

Hahn, Otto, 393
Half-life of radioactive element, 377, **390**
Halley's comet, 40
Halogens, 146, 365
Heat energy, 99
　in electric circuit, 227
　exchanger, 402, **406**
　sink, **125**
Heavy hydrogen, 370
　water, 384, 398, **406**
Heisenberg, Werner, 595, 597
Heliocentric system, 21, 23, **26**
Helium, change of state of, 163
　ion, 356
Helium-burning in stars, 525, **536**
Hemoglobin, 204, **211**
Henry, Joseph, 252
Heredity, mechanism of, 207
Hertz, Heinrich, 321
High-pressure area, 190
Himalaya mountains, 413
Hipparchus, 502
Historical geology, 416
Hominids, **452**
Homopolar bonding, 199
Homo sapiens, 449
Hormones, 206, **211**
Horse, primitive, 449
Horse latitudes, 187, **195**
Horsepower, **96, 106**
Hoyle, Fred, 534
Hubble, Edwin, 531
Humidity, 182
Huygens, Christian, 297
Hydrocarbons, **150,** 200
Hydroelectric power, 122, 263
Hydrogen, 149
　bomb, 401
　burning in stars, 524, **536**

Hydrogen (*cont.*)
　chloride, 143, 171
　energy level diagram of, 553
　ions, 144
　isotopes of, 370
　molecule, 366
　in solar system, 495
Hydrostatic paradox, 154, **164**
　pressure, 154, **164**
Hydrostatics, **164**
Hydroxyl ions, 144
Hypercharge, 585, **589**
Hyperons, 581, **589**
Hypothesis, **6**

Ice age, Permian, 442
　recent, 467, 481
　theory of, 484
Iceland Ridge, 486
Ice-pail experiment, 221
Ice point, 101, **107**
Ichthyosaur, 449, **452**
Ideal gas, 104, **107,** 159, 173
Idealization, 53
Igneous rock, 419, 421, **425**
Illumination, 269, **283**
Image, optical, 271
Impulse, 59, **60**
Incandescent electric light, 263
Inclination, magnetic, 244, **250**
Index of refraction, 275
India, 132
Induced current, 253, **264**
　EMF, 254
　magnetization, 237, 240, 248, **249**
Induction, law of, 254, 319
　motor, 262, **264**
Industrial Revolution, 121
Inert gases, 146, 365
Inertia, **55, 60**
Infrared photography, 327
　radiation, 304, **315,** 327
Insulator, 219
Insulin, 206
Intensity of light source, 269, **283**
Interference in light, 299
　of waves, 294, **300**
　of X rays, 331
Internal combustion engine, 112, 123
International Atomic Energy Commission, 403
　Bureau of Weights and Measures, 56, 65,
　　69, 231, 269
　kilogram, 56
　meter, 64
　standard of atomic weight, 141
Intrusive rock, **425,** 475
Invariance of velocity of light, 568

Invariant, 567, **571**
Invasion of the land, 440
Iodosulfate of quinine, 317
Ionic bonding, 198, **211**, 365
  compounds, 145, **150**
Ionization potential, 376, **390**
Ionosphere, 184, **195**
Ions, 143, **150**
  in gas, 339
Iron, abundance of, 311, 465
  deposits of, 434
  magnetization of, 239
  use of, 131
Isobar, 189, **195**
Isomer, 201, **211**
Isostatic equilibrium, 466, **471**
Isotopes, 137, 141, **150**, 368, 385
  radioactive, 386
  separation of, 369
Isotopic spin, 585, **589**

Jeans, Sir James, 524
Jodrell Bank telescope, 531
Joule, J. P., 95, 105, 172
Joule, unit of work and energy, **95, 107**, 230
Jupiter, 29, 35, 492
  atmosphere of, 495
  moons of, 22

Kelvin scale, 104, **107**
Kepler, Johannes, 41, 526
Kepler's laws, 41, 75, 82, 116
Kilocycle, 289
Kilogram, International, 56
Kilowatt-hour, 96, **107**
Kinetic energy, 99, **107**
  of molecules, 173
  relativistic, 569
Kinetic theory of gases, 172, 176, **177**, 546

Labrador iron deposits, 434
Land, invasion by life, 440
Land bridges, 483
Laplace, Pierre, 489, 545
Laser, 565, **572**
Latent heat, **164**
Laurentian Mountains, 477
Lava, 422, **425**
Lavoisier, Antoine, 113, 137
Law, physical or scientific, 2, **6**, 414
Law of electromagnetic induction, 254, 545
Law of gravitation, 73, 87, 544
Lawrence, E. O., 381
Laws of motion, 52

Lead isotopes, 432
Lee, Tsung-Dao, 586
Left-hand rule, 247, 342
Legislate nature, attempts to, 3
Leibnitz, G. W., 88
Length, measurement of, 64
Lenses, 277
Lepton number, 585
Leptons, 582, **589**
Libration of moon, **46**
Life, conditions for, 497
  origin of, 435
  on other worlds, 496
Life history of a star, 528
Light, electromagnetic theory of, 320
  energy, 109, 267
  flux, 269
  intensity, 269
  quanta, 551
  velocity of, 280, 321, 566
  waves, 297
Lightning, 222
Light-year, 504, **519**
Limestone, 420, **425**, 434
Linear accelerator, 382, **390**
Lines of force, 240, **249**
Line spectrum, 306, **315**, 553
Liquid, definitive property of, 153
Liter, 67
Lobe-finned fish, 441, **452**
Lodestone, 236, 244, **250**
Long Island, 481
Longitudinal wave, 288, **300**
Lorentz, H. A., 569
Los Alamos, 389, 396
Love (L) wave, 459, **472**
Low-pressure area, 188
Lumen, 269, **283**
Lunar, *see* Moon
Lune, **89**
Lungfish, 442
Lyell, Charles, 415, 423

Macroscopic laws, 545, 593
  object, 168, **177**
Magellan, Ferdinand, 517
Magellanic clouds, 517
Magma, **425**, 464
Magnet, 236, 241
Magnetic deflection of particles, 343, 356,
    368, 575
  field, 241, **250**
    of a current, 245
    of the earth, 243, 467
  flux, **248, 250**, 254, 260
  materials, 238

Magnetic deflection of particles (*cont.*)
  north pole, 244, **250**, 468
  pole, 238, 248
  storm, **46**
Magnetism, 237
Magnetite, 236, 468
Magnetization, 238
Magnitude, absolute, 505
  of a star, 502, **519**
Main sequence stars, 506, **519**
Mammals, origin of, 448
Man, primitive, 450
Manhattan Project, 396
Mantle of earth, 463, **472**
Marble, **425**
Marconi, Guglielmo, 324
Mariner space probes, 33, 79, 499
Mars, 18, 29, 33, 493
  life on, 499
Marsupial, 448, **452**
Maser, 563, **572**
Mass, conservation of, 113, 136, 543
  definition of, **55**
  measurement of, 67
  number, 369, **371**
  relativistic increase of, 569
  spectrograph, 368, **371**
Mass-energy, conservation of, 114
  relation, 114, 117, 376, 524
Massif, **472**
Mathematical model of atom, 594
Mathematics, role of, 87
Matter waves, 562
Maximum vapor pressure, 161, **164**
Maxwell, J. C., 172, 241, 319, 546
Maxwellian stresses, 241, 320
Maxwell's laws, 319, 569
Mayan civilization, 11
Meandering river, 479, **487**
Mean solar day, 66
Measurement, importance of, 63
  precision of, 70
Mechanical equivalent of heat, 105, **107**
Mechanical wave, 287, **300**
Mechanistic atomic physics, 545
  laws, 544
  model, 593
Mediterranean civilization, 131
Megacycle, 289
Megaton, 401, **406**
Meitner, Lise, 393
Melting point, 161
Mendeleev, Dimitri, 146
Mercury, orbit of, 571
  planet, 29, 33, 87, 493, 498
Mercury, element, spectrum of, 329
  vapor lamp, 306

Mesabi Range, 434
Mesons, 577, 582, **590**
Mesopotamia, 131
Mesozoic era, 427, 429, 443, **452**
Metabolism, 204, 206, **211**
Metamorphic rock, 419, 422, **425**
Metaphysical hypothesis, 4, 48
Meteor, 40, **46**, 181
Meteor Crater, 37
Meteorite, 41, **46**, 465
  age of, 433
Meter, 64
Methane, 200
  combustion of, 142
  in solar system, 495
Metric system, 64
Michelson, A. A., 281, 321
Michelson-Morley experiment, 321, 568
Mid-Atlantic Ridge, 469
Migration of animals, 483
Milky Way, 514, 533, *see also* Galaxy
Millikan, R. A., 345
Mississippi River, 416, 479
Mixture, 138
MKS units, 56, **60**, 95, 153, 230
Model, 546
  mathematical, 594
Moderator of neutrons, 384, **390**, 398
Mohorovičić, A., 463
Mohorovičić discontinuity (moho), 463, **472**
Mole, 170, **177**
Molecular spectrum, **315**
  weight, 140, **150**
Molecule, **150**, 169
Momentum, **56**, 59, **60**
  of atomic particle, 599
  conservation of, 115, 185, 544
  relativistic, 569
Monsoon, 187, **195**
Montgolfier brothers, 179
Moon, 36, 74, 79
  distance of, 43
  eclipse of, 86
  life on, 498
  mass of, 79
  statistics, 29
Moraine, glacial, 481, **487**
Morley, E. W., 321
Mountain building, 418, 428, 456, 474
  range, age of, 478
Mount Palomar Observatory, 518
Mount Rainier, 477
Mount Rundle, 192
Mount San Antonio, 281
Mount Wilson Observatory, 281, 311
Multiple proportions, law of, 140
Mu-meson or muon, 577, **590**

Muscular energy, 110
Mutation, 404, 436

Nanosecond, **590**
Natural gas, 118
Natural science, 1
Neap tide, 82, **89**
Nebular cloud, 490, **500**
  theory, 489, **500**
Ne'eman, Yaval, 586
Neon, isotopes of, 368
  sign, 306, 340
Neptune, 29
Neutralizing reaction, 144
Neutrino, 388, **390**
Neutrons, 383, **390**, 404
  discovery of, 383
  from reactor, 399
Newcomen, Thomas, 121
Newton, Sir Isaac, 2, 52, 73, 88, 297, 415
Newton, unit of force, 56, **60**, 230
Newton's laws, 53, 320, 568
  rings, 298
Niagara Falls, 122, 263
Niagara Gorge, 417
Nile River, 416, 480
Nitrogen molecule, 367
Noble metals, 131, 146
Nondelineable concept, 243, **250**, 321, 543, 593
North Pole, 484
Nova, 525, 530, **536**
Nuclear atom, 361
  energy, 111, 124, **125**, 386, 393
  explosion, 396
  fission, 394, **407**
    energy of, 397
  forces, 385, 583
  fuel, 398, **407**
  power, 402
  reaction, 117, 374, **390**
    energy of, 375
    induced, 378, **390**
  reactions in stars, 524
  reactor, 386, 398
  structure, 384
  submarine, 403
Nucleic acids, 207, **211**
Nucleus, size of, 363

Oak Ridge, 370
Observation, reaction of, 597
Occultation of star, 493, **500**
Ocean tides, 79
  waves, 286
Oersted, H. C., 245
Ohm, Georg, 229

Ohm, unit of resistance, 229, **231**
Ohm's law, 229, 259
Oil-drop experiment, 345, **352**
Olduvai Gorge, 450
Operational definition, 218, **233**, 594
Order in nature, 4
Organic acids, 202, **211**
  chemistry, 203, **211**
Organization, creation of, 534
Origin of life, 435
Orogenesis, 474, **487**
Orogenic forces, 476
Osiander, 21
Otto, Nicholas, 123
Oxbow lakes, 479
Oxidation, 134, **150**
Oxides, 134, 136, 145, **151**
Oxygen, absorption spectrum of, 329
  in atmosphere, 182, 495
  cycle, 204, 439
  discovery of, 136
  in metabolism, 204
Ozone, 180, 182, 328

Paleozoic era, 429, 437, 452
  glaciation, 442, 484
Paracelsus, 134
Paraffin, 200, **211**
Parallax, **26**
  of moon, 43
  of star, 24, 503
  of sun, 44
Parallel beam, 278, **283**, 292
Parity, 586, **590**
Particle accelerator, 380
  atomic, detection of, 357, 575
  fundamental property of, 561
Particles, systematization of, 584
Pauli, Wolfgang, 389
Penumbra, 85
Peptide chain, 205, **211**
Perigee, **46**
Perihelion, 39, **46**
Periodic table, 145, **151**, 364
Permafrost, 484, **487**
Permanent magnet, 238
Permian period 442, **452**
Perturbations of planets, **46**
Petroleum oil, 118, 120
Phases of Venus, 24
Philosophy, Greek, 16, 138, 167
  of Middle Ages, 22, 593
Phlogiston, 136, **151**
Photochemical reaction, 328, **333**
Photoelectric cell, 267, 548, 549
  effect, 548, **550**
    theory of, 552

Photoelectric cell (*cont.*)
  threshold, 549, **550**
Photographic film, 267, 328
Photons, 359, **390**, 561
Photosphere, 30, **46**
Photosynthesis, 117, **125**, 203, 328
Physical law, 2
  truth of, 600
Pi-meson or pion, 577, **590**
Pitchblende, 355
Pitch of musical note, 290, **300**
Pith-ball experiment, 219
Pixii, 255
Planck, Max, 551
Planck's constant, 552, **572**, 598
Plane mirror, 271
  wave, 292, **300**
Planets, 13, 32, 492
  atmospheres of, 492
  growth of, 491
  masses of, 78
  motion of, 17, 41
  statistics, 29
Pleiades, 512
Pleistocene glaciation, 482
  period, **487**
Pluto, planet, 29
Plutonic rock, 432, **452**, 466
Plutonium, 394, 399, 404
Polar easterlies, 187
  front, 188, **195**
Polarization of light, 317, **333**
Polaroid, 317, **334**
Polyatomic ions, 143
Porpoise, 449
Position, determination of, 599
Positive and negative charge, 222
Positrons, 387, **390**, 579
Potassium-argon reaction, 431
Potential difference, **228**, **232**
  energy, 98, **107**
    barrier, 135, **151**
Pound, **58**
Pound-mass, 67
Power, **96**
Power-of-10 notation, 69
Power plant, 258
  nuclear, 402
Power system, electrical, 260
Precambrian times, 433, **452**
Precision of measurement, 70
Predictability, 596
Pressure, 153, **165**
  atmospheric, 155, 188
  hydrostatic, 154
  measurement of, 155
Prevailing westerlies, 187
Priestley, Joseph, 136

Primary coil, 253
Primary (P) wave of earthquake, 459, 463, **472**
Primates, 450, **452**
Prime mover, 121, **126**
Primeval crust, 422, **425**, 432
Principia of Newton, 52
Principle of relativity, 566, 572
  of uniformity, 413
Prism spectrograph, 304
Probability in nature, 378, 542, **550**, 596
Probable error, **71**
Proconsul, 450
Prominences, solar, 31, **46**, 84
Propagation of light, 268, 277
Proper motion of star, 504, **519**
Proper time, 569, **572**
Protein, 205, **211**
Proterozoic era, 428, 434, **452**
Protons, 222, **233**, 369
  ejection from nucleus, 379
Protoplanet, 491, **500**
Proust, J. L., 139
Proxima Centauri, 504
Ptolemaic system, 16
Ptolemy, Claudius, 16
Pulsating star, 513, 529
Pure substance, 138
Pyramids of Egypt, 119

Quantum, **572**
  emission of radiation, 557
  mechanics, 595, **601**
  number, 556, 559, **572**
  principle for atoms, 556
    for light, 551
Quartz spectrograph, 304
Quasars, 531, **536**, 589

Radiant energy, 267, 553
Radiation, 267, **283**
  damage due to, 404
Radical, chemical, 143, **151**
Radioactive dating, 430
  decay, 376, **390**, 595
  disintegration, 373
  elements, 149, 374
  fallout, 401, 405, **407**
  isotopes, 386
  series, 374, **390**
  tracer, 386, **391**
  waste, disposal of, 405
Radioactivity, 151, 355
  artificial, 386, **389**, 394
  in atmosphere, 405
Radio-iodine, 386
Radiometer, 109, **126**

Radiophosphorus, 386
Radio receiver, 292
  source, cosmic, 531
  telescope, 531, **536**
  transmission around earth, 181
Radiosonde, 180, **195**
Radio waves, 323, 325
  in cosmos, 527
Radium, discovery of, 355
Radon, 377
Rain, causes of, 191
Rain forest, 188, 193
Range of alpha particles, 361, **371**
Rare earths, 149
Rate of change, 51
Ravine, mountainous, 416
Ray, of light, 268, 292
Reactor, nuclear, 386, **390**, 398
  source of neutrons, 399
Real image, 271, **283**
Reality, 3, 243, 594
Reciprocating motion, **126**
Rectifier, 349, **352**
Rectilinear propagation, law of, 268
Red shift, relativistic, 571
Reducing agent, 136, **151**
Reduction, 136, **151**
Reflection, law of, 270, 545
  of waves, 292
Refraction, 274, **283**
  of earthquake wave, 459
  law of, 275, 545
Refractive index, 275, **283**, 303
Reines, Frederick, 389
Relative humidity, 182, **196**
Relative motion, 23, 567
Relativity, general theory of, 87, 570, **571**
  paradox, 569
  principle, 566, **572**
  special theory of, 114, 535, 568
Reptiles, dominance of, 443
  flying, 445
Resistance, electrical, 229, **232**
  thermometer, 230
Resonance, 291, **301**, 309
Rest mass, 569, **572**
Restricted relativity theory, 568
Resultant, 54, **60**
Retina, 267, 326
Revolution, biological, 427, **453**
  mechanical, 15, **27**
  scientific, 543, 593
Right-hand rule, 247
Rigidity, 159, **165**
Rings of Saturn, 35, 489
Ripple photographs, 297
River meanders, 479
Rivers, history of, 478

RNA, 207, 436
Rock, types of, 419
Rockets, 59
Rocky Mountain revolution, 427, 448
Rocky Mountains, age of, 476
Roentgen, Wilhelm, 330
Roentgen rays, 330, **334**
Roman Empire, 120
Roosevelt, President Franklin, 396
Root mean square value, 260, **264**
Rotation, 15, **27**
Rotor, 259, **264**
Rumford, Count, 105
Russell, H. N., 506
Russell diagram, 506, **519**, 529
Rutherford, Lord Ernest, 355, 361, 368, 379, 546

Salts, chemical, 144, **151**
Sandstone, 418, 419, **425**, 443
Saskatchewan River, 480
Satellite, **46**
  artificial, 82
  weather, 59, 83, 180
Satellites of the planets, 38
Saturation, **165**
  magnetic, 240
  pressure, 161
Saturn, 29, 35, 489
Scalar quantity, 50, **60**
Scattering of radiation, 274, **283**, 327
  of X rays, 560
Scheele, Carl, 136
Schiaparelli, G. V., 34
Scholastic philosophy, 22, 413, 593
Schrödinger, Erwin, 594
Schrödinger's equation, 594
Scientific law, 2, **6**
  method, 4, 350
  revolution, first, 593
    new, 543, 593
Scintillation, alpha-particle, 358, **371**
  counter, 358, **371**
S Doradus, 505
Second, definition of, 66, 69
Secondary coil, 253
Secondary standard, 65, 231
Secondary (S) wave of earthquake, 459, 464, **472**
Second law of motion, 55, 97, 544
Sedimentary rock, 419, **426**
Segrè, E., 579
Seismic, *see* Earthquake
Seismograph, 460, **472**
Seismology, **472**
Selection rules for radiation, 560, **572**
Self-induction, **264**
Self-reproducing molecule, 207, 435
Self-sustaining reaction, 395

Shale, 419, **426**
Shooting star, 40, 181
Shower, cosmic-ray, 575, **589**
Significant figures, 70, **71**
Silicon, abundance of, 465
Silt, **426**
Silver, standard of current, 232
Sirius, 502, 505, 525
  companion of, 508
Sliprings, 255, **265**
Slow neutrons, 384, **391**, 398
Slug, unit of mass, 58, **60**
Smelting of metals, 132
Smith, William, 415, 423
Snell, Willebrord, 275
Soddy, Frederick, 368
Sodium atom, 309
  chloride, 143, 198, 365
  energy level diagram of, 554
Soft iron, 239, **250**
Solar constant, 116, **126**
Solar flares, 31, **46**, 576
Solar system, age of, 433, 489
  description of, 23, 29, 489
  origin of, 489
  structure of, 490
Solar wind, **46**
Solenoid, 247, **250**, 253
Solid, definitive property of, 159
Solstices, 13, 16, **27**
Solution, 138
Sound energy, 109
  velocity of, 290
  waves, 289, 295
Sounding balloon, 179
Space flight, 82
Space-time, 570, **572**
Special relativity, 114, 535, 568, **572**
Specific charge, **352**
Spectrograph, 304, **315**
Spectroscope, **315**
Spectroscopic binary, 509, **520**
Spectrum, 303, **315**
  absorption, 309
  atomic, 307
  band, 315
  continuous, 307
  electromagnetic, 324
  line, 307
  molecular, 315
  solar, 310
  stellar, 312
Speed, **50**
Spherical aberration, 280, **283**
Spin, conservation of, 584
  of atomic particle, 348, 387, 389, **391**, 580
  of electron, 559
Spiral galaxy, **520**

Spring tide, 82, **89**
Sputnik, 82
Standard atmosphere, 157
  of atomic weight, 141
  kilogram, 56
  of measurement, 64
  meter, 65
  temperatures, 101
  yard, 65
Standing wave, 291, **301**
Stanford University, 382
Star, diameter of, 506
  distance of, 503
  evolution of, 528
  lifetime of, 525
  mass of, 509
  spectrum of, 312
  temperature of, 506, 522
Starch, 202
Star clusters, 512
Stars, classification of, 507
  typical, 505
Stator, 259, **265**
Steady state theory, *see* Continuous theory
Steam engine, 121
Steam point, **102**, **107**
Stefan's law, 307, 311, 506
Stern-Gerlach experiment, 559
Step-by-step acceleration of particles, 381, 576
Stone Age peoples, 132
Stonehenge, 12
Stoney, G. J., 340
Strangeness, 585, **590**
Strassmann, Fritz, 393
Stratigraphy, 424, **426**
Stratosphere, 184, **196**
Stratum, **426**
Strong interactions, 583, **590**
Strontium 90, 405
Structural formula, 200, **211**
Styracosaurus, 446
Sublimation, 163, **165**
Sugars, chemical nature of, 202
Sulfuric acid cell, 225
Sun, atmosphere of, 311
  composition of, 525
  distance of, 44
  eclipse of, 84
  energy of, 116, 522
  mass of, 78
  nature of, 28, 311
  rotation of, 32
  spectrum of, 310
  temperature of, 30, 311
Sunspots, 32
Supercooling, 101, **107**
Supergiant stars, 507, **520**
Supernova, 526, 536

Syene, 15
Symbols, chemical, 140, **150**
Symmetry groups of particles, 587
Synthesis of hydrogen into helium, 524
Systematics of atomic particles, 584

Tagged atoms, 386, **391**
Tar sands, 123
Technology, 350
Television camera, 549
  receiver, 346, 550
Temperature, **100, 173**
  inside earth, 456, 465
  of sun and stars, 311, 506, 522
Terrestrial, *see* Earth
Thermionic emission, 345, **352**
Thermoelectricity, 125, **126**
Thermometer, 102
  resistance, 230
Thermonuclear reactions, 126, 401, **407**, 524
Third law of motion, 58, 115
Thompson, Benjamin, Count Rumford, 105
Thomson, Sir J. J., 343, 368, 546
Thorium, 355
Thyroid gland, 206
Tides, ocean, 79
Till, glacial, 481
Time, measurement of, 66
Tiros satellite, 59, 83
Topographic cloud, 192, **196**
Tornado, 194
Torricelli, E., 156
Torsion balance, 223, **233**
Tracer, radioactive, 386, **391**
Tracks in photographic film, 575
Trade winds, 187, **196**
Transformation of coordinates, 567, **572**
Transformer, 260
Transmutation of elements, 133, 379
Transverse wave, 288, **301**
Travel time tables, 462, **472**
Tremor, 472
Trigger action, 135
Trilobite, 437, **453**
Triode tube, 349, **352**
Troposphere, 183, **196**
Truth of law, 600
Tundra, 484, **487**
Tuning fork, 289
Tyrannosaurus rex, 446

Uintathere, early mammal, 449
Ultraviolet light, 304, **315**, 328
Umbra, 85, **89**
Uncertainty principle, 598, **601**

Uniformity, principle of, 413, 423, **426**
United States Atomic Energy Commission, 382
Units, electrical, 230
  fundamental, 68, **71**
  metric, 60, 64, 230
  MKS, 56, 60, 95, 153, 230
  revision of, 69
  systems of, 68
Universal constant, **89**
  gravitation, law of, 73
  motor, 262, **265**
Universe, *see* Cosmos
University of California, 579
University of Chicago, 398
Unstable elements, 149
Uranium, activity of, 355
  half-life of, 377
  nuclear fuel, 398
  in rocks, 430
  source of energy, 124, 402
  235, 370, 394
Uranus, 29
Urey, H. C., 495
Ursa Major, 512
U.S.S.R., 82, 403

Vacuum pump, 351
  Torricellian, 156
Vacuum ultraviolet, 329
Valence, 199
  electrons, 365, **371**
Van de Graaff accelerator, 381, **391**
Vapor, **165**
  pressure, 161
Vector, 50, 53, **60**
Velocity, 50, **60**
  of light, 280, 321, 566
    invariance of, 568
  of sound, 290
  of wave, 289
Venus, 17, 24, 29, 32, 493
  life on, 499
Vertebrates, 440, **453**
Virtual image, 271, **283**
Viscosity, **165**
Viscous liquid, 154
Visual binary, 508, **520**
Vitamins, 207, **212**
Volcanoes, 475, 477
Volt, unit of potential, 228, **231**
Volta, Alessandro, 224
Voltage, 229, **233**
Voltaic cell, 224, **233**
Von Jolly's experiment, 77
Von Weizsacker, C. F., 491
Vulcan, 86

Water, importance in chemistry, 144
Watt, James, 96, 121, 261
Watt, unit of power, 96, **107**, 230
Wave function, 595, **601**
Wavelength, 289, **301**
  of light, 299
  of sound, 291
Wavelike properties of electrons, 562
Wave motion, 286
Wave-particle duality, 563, 597, 599
Waves from oscillating circuit, 321
  interference and diffraction of, 294
Wave theory of light, 297
Wave velocity, 289
Weak interactions, 584, **590**
Weather map, 191
Wegener, A. L., 470
Weight, **54**, 57
Wells, H. G., 496
Weston mercury-cadmium cell, 232
White dwarf stars, 507, 508, **520**, 530
Wien's law, 308, 310
Wilson, C. T. R., 359
Wind, causes of, 184, 194

Wind (*cont.*)
  zones, 186
Wireless, 324
Work, **95**, 97
World circulation of wind, 184
  energy problem, 123, 402

X-ray crystal analysis, 332
  photography, 332
  spectrum, 331
X rays, 330
  interference of, 331
  scattered, 560

Yang, Chen-Ning, 586
Yard, standard, **65**
Young, Thomas, 298
Yukawa, Hideki, 576

Zinc, electrode of cell, 224
Zodiac, 32, **46**